No Direction Home

THE UNIVERSITY OF NORTH CAROLINA PRESS
CHAPEL HILL

Natasha Zaretsky

No Direction Home

The

American

Family

and the

Fear of

National

Decline,

1968

–

1980

© 2007 The University of North Carolina Press
All rights reserved
Manufactured in the United States of America
Designed and typeset in Electra and Franklin Gothic
Extra Condensed by Eric M. Brooks

The paper in this book meets the guidelines for permanence
and durability of the Committee on Production Guidelines for
Book Longevity of the Council on Library Resources.

A portion of chapter 2 appeared previously as "In the Name
of Austerity: Gender, the Middle Class Family, and the OPEC
Oil Embargo of 1973–74," in *The World the Sixties Made: Culture
and Politics in Recent America,* edited by Van Gosse and Richard
Moser (Philadelphia: Temple University Press, 2003).

Library of Congress Cataloging-in-Publication Data
Zaretsky, Natasha, 1970–
No direction home: the American family and the fear of
national decline, 1968–1980 / Natasha Zaretsky.
     p. cm.
Includes bibliographical references and index.
ISBN-13: 978-0-8078-3094-9 (cloth: alk. paper)
ISBN-13: 978-0-8078-5797-7 (pbk.: alk. paper)
1. Middle class—United States—Economic conditions.
2. Middle class—United States—Political activity. 3. Middle
class—United States—History. 4. United States—Social
conditions—1960–1980. 5. United States—Politics and
government. I. Title.
HT690.U6Z37   2007
305.5'50973—dc22   2006027688

cloth   11 10 09 08 07   5 4 3 2 1
paper   11 10 09 08 07   5 4 3 2 1

For my parents

and in memory of Judi

Terrific dangers and troubles
that we once called "foreign"
now constantly live among us.
LYNDON BAINES JOHNSON,
Inaugural Address,
20 January 1965

I was born in San Francisco in 1970, and my parents were activists in the New Left, antiwar, and feminist movements of the era. Their activism provides the backdrop for my earliest childhood memories: playing with toys in the back office of the bookstore where my father helped edit a radical journal; holding my mother's hand at protest rallies where people spoke passionately about things that I could not understand; reading feminist fairy tales that celebrated princesses for their independence and smarts; and enjoying the excited bustle within our home, where my parents' friends lavished me with affection as they talked politics. Because I was so young at the time, the people in my parents' community seemed very old to me, but now that I am past their age, I can recognize them for who they were: young men and women who had come to California hoping to start a new life, not only for themselves but for the whole society. Many years later, walking down the street on a sunny San Francisco hillside, an old friend of my mother's turned to me and said from out of the blue: "You have to understand. When your parents and I first came here, we thought that a revolution was coming very soon, within a few years."

By the time I was an adolescent, the world had both changed and not changed in the wake of my parents' generation's activism. On the one hand, the girls at my high school worried about their appearance and their popularity with boys, but on the other hand, they excelled at organic chemistry and physics, won trophies in competitive sports, and excitedly planned to attend the best universities where they went on to embark on illustrious careers. Gay teenagers who once would have hidden their sexuality came out to their classmates and were accepted by them. The students at my school formed organizations committed to nuclear disarmament and volunteered for Amnesty International. Yet when I shifted my gaze beyond the San Francisco Bay Area, the picture became more complicated. By the mid-1980s, Wall Street power brokers and air force fighter pilots were celebrated icons, Reagan was at the height of his popularity, and his administration was presiding over the dismantling of social welfare programs and a redistribution of wealth that hurt poor and working-class people. As my friends and I walked through San Francisco's beautiful streets, we noticed homeless people begging for money, food, and shelter. Every time we passed a hospital, we knew that inside were gay men dying. The society had indeed changed, but not in the way my parents had in mind.

This book emerges out of my attempts—first personal and later scholarly—to explain the contradictions that shaped my own upbringing: the contradiction between how much my parents' activism had transformed American culture and how little it had altered American politics; the gulf between my native San Francisco, where most people embraced the transformations unleashed by the 1960s, and other parts of the country, where those transformations remained contested; the contradiction between the warmth and affection that I associated with the radical activists of my childhood and my dim awareness that there were people who were very angry at them; and, finally, the contradiction between my earliest childhood memories, populated by people who believed that history was on their side, and my adolescence, when the same people watched the Reagan Revolution with confusion and sorrow.

I have finished this book, but many of the questions that compelled me to write it remain open. I do not know all of the reasons why San Francisco moved in one direction after 1968, while so many other cities, towns, and communities moved in another. I do not fully understand the rupture that occurred during these years in the lives of people like my parents. Nor have I determined how the activists of my childhood could have achieved so much yet fallen so short. No single book can possibly answer all of these questions. This book simply offers one place to begin the search: the early years of the 1970s, when nation and family collided, broke apart, and came back together in ways that helped create the political world we now inhabit.

No Direction Home

Introduction

Between 1968 and 1980, a succession of upheavals challenged a confident assumption of the previous two decades: that the United States possessed the political, military, economic, and moral resources to prevail in world affairs and provide for domestic prosperity. By 1968 the war in Vietnam had deeply wounded the moral authority of the United States. By 1973 American troops had withdrawn. By 1975 it was evident that the United States had failed to reach its political and strategic objectives there. The gradual recognition of military defeat was accompanied by other disruptions and revelations. In October 1973 the Organization of Petroleum Exporting Countries (OPEC) declared an oil embargo against the United States, revealing how dependent the nation had become on oil imports from the Middle East. At the same time, an economic recession challenged an earlier Keynesian order that had prevented inflation and unemployment from rising simultaneously. Meanwhile, Japan and West Germany threatened American dominance over the world economy. In August 1974, President Richard Nixon resigned from office amid the Watergate scandal. The resignation undermined the institution of the presidency, the very embodiment of national authority, and contributed to the sense that the country had lost its direction. Journalists, politicians, and policymakers began warning that the United States was going the way of imperial Rome, that what Henry Luce famously called the "American Century" was coming to a premature and ignoble end, and that the nation had entered an era of decline.

1

This was certainly not the first time that fears about American decline had come to the fore, even during the post–World War II period. In the late 1940s, policymakers insisted that the Communist threat could only be contained through extraordinary vigilance and the commitment of tremendous resources. In the late 1950s, after the Soviets launched Sputnik, the Eisenhower administration's Gaither Commission warned that the United States was falling behind the Soviet Union in the realms of science, military, and technology.[1] But what set the late 1960s and early 1970s apart was the sheer number of crises that beset the country simultaneously: the failure of a costly military effort in Vietnam and the worldwide protests unleashed by the war; rising rates of inflation and unemployment and growing foreign competition; the revelation that the United States could no longer count on crucial commodities, especially oil; and the shock that even an institution as sacred as the presidency could be strained to the breaking point. Taken together, these developments not only undermined the postwar order. They also challenged the exceptionalism at the center of American identity—the idea that the United States did not lose wars, its natural resources were boundless, its leaders wise and secure, and its economy capable of infinite expansion.

As policymakers contemplated the nation's future, a second series of alarms was sounded, this time over the nuclear family. This alarm emerged out of the cultural and social ferment of the 1960s. In the latter part of the decade, new social movements surfaced that challenged the nuclear family ideal that had shaped postwar American culture. The women's liberation movement contended that the family was a site of patriarchy and women's subordination. Meanwhile, men and women in an increasingly visible gay liberation movement began elaborating models of love, sexuality, and kinship that could not be contained within the normative heterosexual family.[2] Policymakers and social scientists claimed that the institution of the family was under unprecedented strain, and editorials began appearing in newspapers and magazines that asked whether the traditional family was permanently out of favor. In this context, the family became a lightning rod in American politics. After the 1973 *Roe v. Wade* decision, a profamily movement arose that perceived the family to be under attack by organized feminism, abortion rights, and gay liberation; its activists would soon become an influential force in the Republican Party.

Noting these various upheavals, historians have argued that the early 1970s was a time of profound economic, social, and cultural dislocation, when anxieties about both national decline and family decline came to the fore. But historical accounts of the 1970s have tended to treat these two sets of anxieties as analytically distinct, with the theme of national decline falling under the provenance of diplomatic, military, political, and economic history and the theme of family decline falling under the provenance of cultural, social, and gender history. Thus historical surveys devote separate chapters to themes such as the Vietnam War, on the one hand, and to family upheaval, on the other; rarely do they ask about the relationship between them. Yet a substantial body of twentieth-century thought has called such boundaries into question, productively blurring the lines between the public and the private, the foreign and the domestic, and the war front and the home front. Taking its cues from this thought, this book shows that, contrary to being distinct, the debates over national decline and family decline that came to the fore in the 1970s emerged in tandem and profoundly shaped one another. These debates did not simply rehash standard tropes of national weakness and fragile families. Rather, they had both a ubiquity and specificity to them that reveal in hindsight that the United States was entering a new era in its history.

We can understand the intertwinement of debates about national and family decline between 1968 and 1980 if we begin with the actors who tried to make sense of the events as they unfolded. Thus the relatives of men serving in Vietnam struggled to understand why the United States seemed incapable of winning the war, while the architects of American foreign policy searched for the proper lessons to be taken from their failed military intervention. Similarly, during the oil crisis of 1973–74, the Nixon administration, Congress, the large oil companies, and private citizens clashed over whether the United States should accept or confront OPEC's new assertiveness on the world stage. As foreign automobiles and other goods became more popular within the domestic market, assembly-line workers attributed the decreased competitiveness of American products to harsh managerial rules and speed-up, while corporate executives argued that an older work ethic had gone into decline. As diverse groups puzzled over why the United States no longer seemed able to control its own fate, their efforts fell into two broad camps. Some understood the crises of the time to be a result of imperial hubris and called for a more modest and cooperative international policy and for social reform at home. Others argued that the crises revealed weakness, and that only a thoroughgoing renewal of American power and authority could resolve them.

Whatever their differences, however, these diverse interpretations shared a common feature: a preoccupation with the family. Over and over again, and in remarkably varied and contradictory ways, the family stood at the center of the major debates about national decline that surfaced in the early 1970s. The family's role in these debates was paradoxical. On the one hand, policymakers and economic leaders portrayed the family as a culprit, arguing that it had produced young men unwilling to fight wars, workers unable to produce competitive goods, women no longer willing to mother, and consumers incapable of exercising appropriate restraint. But at the same time the family assumed the status of a victim, the primary locus of the nation's confusion and suffering. What made the Vietnam War and the oil embargo so dire, one news account after another agreed, was that these events caused psychological and economic pain within the private realm. As both perpetrator and victim, as the site where the origins of national decline could be discovered and where the damages wrought by it could be assessed, the family served as a symbol for the nation itself. As such, it profoundly shaped debates about America's future in the 1970s in ways that have reverberated into our own time.

To understand how, we need to recall the critical role the family has played at other turning points in the past. At any given point in American history there is a common fund of ideas and images clustering around the idea of the family and intrinsic to a sense of national identity. It includes such themes as masculinity and femininity, domesticity, childhood, old age, marriage, kinship, and community. This loose fund operates at the level of assumptions rather than assertions, and values rather than descriptions. Normally, it is both flexible enough to respond to social and cultural change and precise enough to help constitute a national community. In nineteenth-century America, for example, the dominant family ideology celebrated the white, middle-class home as a refuge from the ravages of industrial capitalism. Of course, there were families that did not conform to this ideal: Native Americans who lived in tribes, African Americans who lived under slavery, and Slavic, Italian, and Chinese immigrants who lived in all-male ethnic communities. But as the dominant social class, the middle class embodied what can be described as a national family ideal.[3]

During periods of large-scale social transformation, however, this fund of familial values invariably has undergone revision. Thus the American Revolution was accompanied by a shift from the colonial "goodwife" to Republican motherhood. The Civil War was fought to preserve the union and abolish slavery but also for American Victorianism: the dual sphere family, the full-time mother in the home, a protected childhood, and a rational-moderate rather than chivalric ideal of masculinity. Progressivism witnessed the birth of companionate marriage, the entry of women into public life, and a renewed "crisis of masculinity." This book contends that the late 1960s and the 1970s represented another historical turning point when both America's national identity—its political alignments, welfare institutions, and international policies—and its family ideal were transformed as part of a single process.

The Family and the American Century, 1941–1968

The starting point for this transformation had emerged three decades earlier when in February 1941, ten months before the United States entered World War II, *Life* magazine editor Henry Luce called on the nation to embrace "the opportunities of leadership in the world." America had acquired enormous power over the previous four decades, he asserted, but so far it had failed to assume the mantle of world leadership. This leadership would comprise four related projects: the promotion of free enterprise; the sharing of American technical and artistic expertise; the elimination of world hunger and destitution; and the spread of American ideals—"a love of freedom, a feeling for the equality of opportunity, a tradition of self-reliance and independence and also of co-operation." Taken together, this was Luce's influential vision of the American Century.[4]

More than any other institution, the American family crystallized Luce's aspirations. For Luce, the family was not just any family, but rather an idealized model: a white, middle-class family made up of a male breadwinner, a full-time wife and homemaker, and children. Nowhere was this family more celebrated than in the pages of Luce's own *Life* magazine. Week after week, with an estimated readership of twenty million people, the magazine circulated images of American family life that fused collective ideals of middle-class consumption with Cold War imperatives. Mothers, fathers, and children smiled cheerfully in detached suburban homes; toddlers played in family gardens; contented wives prepared dinner in shiny, appliance-filled kitchens; and excited families embarked on cross-country vacations. Reproduced over and over, these images served as unassailable proof of the moral, political, and economic legitimacy of the American Century. They implied that more and more people were entering the ranks of the middle class and fulfilling the American Dream, that new household commodities and technologies were creating unprecedented leisure, and that the sacredness of the domestic realm made the Cold War worth fighting.[5]

As in the nineteenth century, countless families never conformed to this ideal. The Mexican American family in wartime Los Angeles, the African American family in the Jim Crow South, the Chinese American family in Northern California, the white coal mining family in Appalachia, the Barbadian immigrant family in Brooklyn: these families rarely appeared in the pages of *Life*.[6] In these families, extended kinship networks often flourished, men encountered discrimination that barred them from well-paying jobs, and women worked outside the home. But despite the gulf between fantasy and reality, the image of the white, middle-class, nuclear family expressed an ideal that had meaning for Americans of all races and classes: the ideal of the family wage. With its origins in industrial capitalism and especially in the New Deal, that ideal maintained that a male head of household—whether middle or working class—should garner enough earnings to support a wife, who would maintain the household and take care of children. Aiming to ensure that the ravages of the Great Depression would never be suffered again, that ideal contained a promise of security that had universal meaning for all families, even those who had in fact been excluded from its fulfillment.[7]

The white, middle-class family ideal embodied the aspirations of the American Century, but it was also an object of sustained criticism and anxiety. Thus, when Luce first elaborated his vision of the American Century, he did not present it as a fait accompli. On the contrary, even as he drew on earlier notions of American exceptionalism, he questioned whether the nation possessed the moral and psychological reserves to fulfill his vision. Surveying war-torn Europe, Luce remarked that the British were "calm in spirit" precisely because they were "fighting for their lives." Americans, by contrast, were the most fortunate people in the world, but, according to Luce, they were also unhappy, nervous, gloomy, and apathetic. The American Century was not a birthright, he suggested. Instead it was something that would have to be fought for and earned.[8]

Luce's essay anticipated a question that would appear repeatedly in American social and cultural criticism after World War II: did the nation possess the moral character, military virtues, and psychological reserves required for world leadership? When, in 1949, Arthur M. Schlesinger Jr. defined the era as an "age of anxiety," he was not alone in appropriating the language of psychology for a bleak diagnosis of the national mood.[9] As the Cold War intensified in the late 1940s and early 1950s, critics worried that the nation was losing its bearings. These worries stemmed from the same consumer society showcased each week on the pages of *Life*. Greater participation in the worlds of mass consumption and leisure, the explosive growth in home and car ownership, the spread of suburbia: these were all cited as evidence of the superiority of Western capitalism over Soviet communism. But they also raised troubling questions about whether the United States was becoming soft and conformist, thus losing the spirit of individuality that had supposedly shaped the American character from its inception.[10] This dilemma was at the heart of the American Century. On the one hand, affluence lent credence to the belief that it was the nation's destiny to play a global leadership role, but on the other it begged the question of whether or not the nation possessed the internal resources the role demanded.

Within this dilemma, a troubling portrait of the white, middle-class family slowly took shape. It was shaped in part by developments in the fields of psychiatry, psychoanalysis, and sociology. During World War II, the Office of Strategic Services and the Office of War Information had commissioned national character studies that attempted to explain why the nation's enemies had fallen prey to fascism and belligerence. In their research, scholars argued that the roots of German and Japanese aggression could be traced back to overprotective mothers, punitive fathers, or both. Although some arguments that emerged from these studies were later rejected, all social scientists, researchers, and clinicians shared the premise that the family was the key mediator between the individual and the society. Within psychoanalysis, the rise of ego psychology stressed the mother's role in the psychosexual development of children. Within sociology, Talcott Parsons argued that the nuclear family was the site at which boys and girls internalized their proper societal roles. Taken together, these disciplines identified the family as the main conduit of the politics, culture, and society of the nation. In the context of the American Century, the family thus shouldered enormous national responsibilities. It had to prepare children for the duties of liberal citizenship and democratic participation, it had to instill a healthy work ethic and a sense of military honor into boys, and it had to socialize girls for the demands that would one day be required of them as wives, mothers, and homemakers.[11]

These responsibilities created certain contradictions. Because men were out in the workplace as breadwinners, mothers were assigned the primary task of childrearing and inculcating societal norms into their children. But how could duties and values historically associated with men—military service, the work ethic, political citizenship—be transmitted effectively from one generation of men to the next? In 1942, social critic Philip Wylie famously warned in *Generation of Vipers* that America's democratic ideals were under threat by mothers who wielded too much power within the home. Wylie's white, middle-class mom smothered her sons, emasculated her husband, and chose crass material gain over civic commitment. As he saw it, so long as these mothers remained at the helm of middle-class family life, the nation was at risk of being destroyed by what he called "Momism." While the acerbic tone of Wylie's best-selling book stood out, *Generation of Vipers* was by no means unique in placing a dominating mother figure at the center of national anxieties. In an ironic twist, the very attributes that made the normative middle-class family such a compelling symbol also raised doubts about its viability as a repository for democratic citizenship. In an age of mass consumption, suburban sprawl, and overpowering moms, could the family create citizens, public servants, and soldiers with the moral and psychological fiber worthy of the American Century?[12]

Anxiety surrounding the psychological health and moral fitness of the family also contained a racial subtext. As historian Ruth Feldstein has shown, beginning in the 1930s, the growing commitment to racial liberalism moved the subject of racial identity out of the realm of biology and into the realms of culture and psychology. One consequence was that the themes of gender, sex roles, and family assumed a new centrality in discourses of racial difference. Many sociologists, anthropologists, and psychoanalysts trained in the interdisciplinary field of "culture and personality" studies argued that slavery had left a disturbing mark on the black family in the form of gender inversion. According to this theory, African American men had emerged from slavery unable to fulfill their obligations as breadwinners and were, as a result, almost in a state of arrested development—feminine and childlike. African American women, meanwhile, were dominating matriarchs who wielded an inappropriate amount of economic and emotional power within the home. These arguments were often premised on an implicit contrast between a pathological model of black family life and a normative white ideal. But the postwar discourse of Momism betrayed a profound anxiety that white and black families actually had more in common than at first appeared.[13] Thus if photo essays in *Life* portrayed the white, middle-class family as harmonious, protected, and secure, postwar critics and researchers expressed fears about this family that would reappear in the 1970s as debates about gender, family, race, and national decline came together.

With the social and cultural upheavals of the 1960s, these earlier critiques of Luce's family ideal were reworked and deepened in significant ways. The two dominant political issues of the 1960s—civil rights and the Vietnam War—did not revolve explicitly around contested definitions of family life. But the young men and women who became activists during this period rejected the cultural logic of postwar America and challenged the domestic ideal that had emerged in tandem with a mass consumption economy in the 1950s. In large numbers, young people deserted "the system," critiqued the affluent society for its failure to provide their lives with real meaning, and argued that the spread of middle-class suburban prosperity had been predicated on violence and deprivation in other places: the rural South, the inner city, Vietnam. Sexuality emerged as a profoundly disturbing and liberating force. Countercultural critiques of American society and the quest for authenticity often went hand in hand with visible redefinitions of masculinity and femininity. Youth was posed against age, protest against obedience, authenticity against conformity, and freedom against authority.

The Transformation of the American Family in the 1970s

By the late 1960s, the starting point of this book, military, political, and economic dislocations were further challenging Luce's American Century and the family ideal contained within it. The growing revelation that the United States was failing to meet its military objectives in Vietnam undermined the Cold War foreign policy of containment, which its architects had insisted was vital for the protection of American families and their way of life. The crisis of global security was accompanied by an economic recession. Throughout the postwar years, Keynesian fiscal policies had balanced inflation and unemployment, thereby ensuring that the national economy did not suffer high levels of both simultaneously. But beginning in the early 1970s, Keynesianism began to fall apart as a recession led to both high unemployment and soaring inflation. This lethal combination suggested that the steady economic growth and rising standard of living that had continued unabated throughout the postwar years was coming to an end.[14] Fears about the economy were exacerbated during the oil embargo of 1973–74, when OPEC's decision to block oil to the United States challenged a long-standing assumption that had taken on new meaning since World War II: that natural resources like oil were boundless. Within a remarkably short period of time, a string of interrelated events threw into crisis the norms that had infused the nation's optimistic self-image since 1945. In this context, the earlier place of the family in debates about American national identity began to undergo dramatic revision. Anxieties about the family that had been present all along exploded just as the cultural idealizations that had surrounded the family began to come apart. The consequence was a heightened level of fear about the future of the American family.

This fear was expressed in diverse ways and in multiple settings. Between 1970 and 1975, a range of political, educational, and cultural institutions devoted considerable resources to assessing the new demands bearing down on men, women, and children. In September 1973, the Senate Subcommittee on Children and Youth held a three-day hearing in which it listened to testimony from demographers, psychologists, anthropologists, economists, and members of the clergy attesting to the unprecedented pressures on families in the United States. Organizations like the Carnegie Corporation commissioned studies on children, childhood, and the family, and social historians wrote books about the history of the family, asking where the institution was headed. In 1973, the television documentary "An American Family" premiered on PBS and portrayed the dissolution of one white, middle-class family. Newspapers published editorials in which opinion makers questioned the fate of the family, and legislators attempted to figure out which governmental programs helped or hurt them. All of these hearings, conferences, commissions, and studies revolved around a host of themes: the new economic pressures confronting families in an era of inflation, the ways in which outside institutions (such as schools) and cultural forces (such as the mass media) were transforming the meanings of both childhood and parenthood, and the proper relationship between the family and the state.[15]

Often these discussions came down to one question: was the family disappearing? That question had been prompted by census data that demonstrated how much the structure and composition of families in the United States had changed over the past two decades. In one hearing and commission meeting after another, social scientists and policymakers cited statistics that showed that the family was in the throes of several transformations. One of the most dramatic involved the growing role of women in the labor force, and in particular the rising number of married women and mothers with young children who were now working outside the home. In 1950, less than one-fourth of married women were in the labor force, and among women with children under the age of six, the number was 12 percent. By 1972, however, 40 percent of all married women worked outside the home, and the figure for mothers with children under the age of six was up to 30 percent.[16] By 1976, for the first time, the number of married women with school-age children in the labor force exceeded 50 percent. It was clear that even the presence of very young children was no longer considered a bar to women's employment, the Department of Labor reported in 1973.[17] As the Carnegie Council on Children observed in 1977, "We have passed a genuine watershed: this is the first time in our history that the typical school age child has a mother who works outside the home."[18]

The growing participation of mothers in the labor force was correlated with a change in the structure of the family—a dramatic increase in the number of female-headed households in which the father was absent. By the autumn of 1973, the national divorce rate was approaching 50 percent, and the rising percentage indicated that four out of every ten American children would spend at least part of their childhoods in a family headed by a single parent, usually the mother. No less significant, this rise in female-headed households appeared to be gaining momentum: the number of these households had grown twice as fast in the 1960s as it had in the 1950s, and the numerical increase between 1970 and 1973 was the same as it had been during the previous ten years.[19] The consequence was that more and more children were growing up in homes without fathers. By March 1973, the Department of Labor noted that approximately 855,000 preschoolers were living in fatherless families.[20] By the early 1970s, one out of every six children was living in a family where the father was either absent, unemployed, or out of the labor force.[21] The increase in numbers of women who were having their first babies outside of wedlock—from 5 percent in the late 1950s to 11 percent in 1971—suggested that the trend would continue. Taken together, the data painted a picture of the United States as a country in which the nuclear family once featured on the pages of *Life* was becoming less and less common at the same time that new family forms—families shaped by divorce and separation, single parenthood, and dual wage earning—were becoming more visible.

Although the full implications of these census figures were not clear in the early years of the 1970s, with the benefit of hindsight we can see that these changes reflected a global transformation in the structure of the economy.[22] Within advanced capitalist countries, this transformation meant that the great industrial megaliths of the twentieth century—automobiles, steel, and oil—would be relocated, restructured, disintegrated, and dispersed both within and beyond the territorial boundaries of the nation. In the United States, the consequence was the contraction of the industrial sector and the expansion of information and service-based economies that would employ a workforce that was more multiracial, more international, and composed increasingly of women. News stories often interpreted the rising numbers of both women in the labor force and unemployed men as symptoms of a cyclical (and therefore temporary) recession, implying that older family arrangements could be restored once the economic downturn passed. In retrospect, we can see that the census data that so preoccupied policymakers, social scientists, and legislators reflected a structural transformation that would not be reversed: the birth of what sociologist Daniel Bell in 1976 called a "post-industrial" society.[23] This society was transforming the older, nuclear family model, which defined its security largely in terms of the family wage, into one in which both men and women would need to enter the labor market in order to sustain a household. Although this had in fact always been the case for most working-class families in the United States, and although the transition occurred over many decades, in the early 1970s the two-earner family emerged as a norm for the American middle class.

As this norm became visible, it became a source of anxiety. Between 1970 and 1980, many observers interpreted the rising numbers of working mothers and single-parent households and father absence as a cultural, social, and moral crisis emanating from the institution of the family itself. Building on earlier fears, they argued that the crisis revolved around questions of parental authority, in particular the diminished role of the father. In hearings and commission meetings, social scientists and policymakers insisted that the erosion of parental authority was the single biggest threat confronting families. Parents now had to compete with a range of external forces when it came to the socialization of their children: schools and childcare centers, federally funded after-school programs, youth culture and peer groups, expert advice literature on parenting, and television and mass media. These forces supposedly undermined the capacity of the family to provide for itself and became all the more powerful within families where both parents worked outside the home or where one parent, usually the father, was not living in the household.

Observers pointed out that although this erosion of parental authority was most acute for poor and working-class families, even affluent families were vulnerable. "In a sense, our families, or at least our children, are being victimized by prosperity, are they not?" asked Minnesota senator Walter Mondale, who was chairing the hearing of the Senate Subcommittee on Children in September 1973. When the question was posed to psychologist Urie Bronfenbrenner, he answered affirmatively. The cocktail hour, Bronfenbrenner explained, had replaced the children's hour. As a result, the nation's children were paying the price for what psychologist William James had described in 1906 as the "bitch-goddess Success." Bronfenbrenner went on to describe an experiment in which babies born into middle-class families had a microphone affixed to their clothing during the first year of life. Researchers heard the father's voice on average less than forty seconds a day.[24] The shocking finding suggested that a literal crisis of father absence within poor and working-class families was being mirrored by a figurative crisis of father absence within middle- and upper-class homes. Even men who resided under the same roof as their children were in effect missing. In a 1977 article in the *Washington Post*, Bronfenbrenner spoke of "The Calamitous Decline of the American Family." Middle-class families, he contended, were "now approaching the social disintegration of lower class families a decade ago."[25]

This anxiety that middle- and upper-class families were coming to resemble their poorer counterparts was accompanied by the related fear that the ostensibly stable divide between white and black families was breaking down. Demographers and statisticians pointed out that virtually all of the changes transforming the family were far more visible among black Americans, where rates of female-headed and single parent households had always been substantially higher than in the nation as a whole.[26] Changes in the family were not only moving up the class ladder from the poor to the affluent, observers argued, but also traversing racial boundaries from black to white. Over the prior three decades, critics like Wylie had challenged the racial integrity of the white, middle-class family by implicitly establishing an affinity between black and white families, since both bore the stamps of maternal domination and crippled male authority. In the debate over the family that coalesced between 1970 and 1975, postwar anxieties came to the surface as academics and legislators cited census data as proof that cultural traits once confined to African American families were infiltrating the white middle class. As historian Christopher Lasch explained, the middle-class family had become nothing more than "a pale copy of the ghetto['s]."[27]

By the early 1970s, the fear that the family was becoming a site of racial dissolution took on a new sense of urgency in the midst of what some legislators saw as a growing welfare crisis. Between 1961 and 1971, enrollment in the Aid to Families with Dependent Children (AFDC) program had increased from 3.5 million to 11 million women and children. At the same time, the racial demographics of AFDC underwent revision, as more

African American women asserted an entitlement to social provisions that had been denied them in the past.[28] The expansion of welfare in the 1960s had been due to heightened political mobilization, but the program's critics insisted that its growth was symptomatic of a cultural and psychological disorder within African American families. In 1965 Daniel Moynihan wrote "The Negro Family: A Case for National Action," a controversial policy paper that provoked strong reactions from both defenders and critics. Assistant secretary of labor under Lyndon Johnson, Moynihan argued that slavery had turned familial relations of gender and power upside down, with women wielding too much authority and men wielding too little, resulting in the failure of black men to fulfill their responsibilities as economic providers. The result was a matriarchal family form, what Moynihan called a "tangle of pathology." Arguing that the cycle of welfare dependency could only be broken by a massive commitment to job creation for black men aimed at reinstating male authority within the family, the Moynihan Report intensified anxieties over gender inversion and racial merging.[29] As reformers sought to identify the causes, symptoms, and cures of what they called the national "welfare mess," new census data suggested that the problem of diminished male authority could no longer be attributed to African American families alone.

At the same moment that these anxieties were coming to the fore, the family was assuming a new centrality within the social and cultural movements of the era. By early 1973, American forces were pulling out of Vietnam, and with the troop withdrawal, the New Left lost the single issue that had unified it. As the war in Vietnam moved from center stage, the New Left fractured and came apart, and in its wake new movements emerged that placed heightened emphasis on the family. After the Stonewall uprising in June 1969, gay men and lesbians became more visible in the public sphere, and in the process, they challenged the view that the heterosexual, nuclear family was the only space in which sexuality could find legitimate expression.[30] Building on the countercultural experiments of the 1960s, men and women formed communes and devised other alternative living arrangements, while advocates of the sexual revolution encouraged couples to explore nonmonogamy, cohabitation without matrimony, and open relationships in ways that undermined traditional conceptions of marriage. In the 1970s, gay and lesbian liberation, the counterculture, and shifting sexual mores all offered new ways of thinking about the meaning of family life.

But it was the feminist movement of the 1970s that precipitated the deepest anxieties surrounding the family. In the second half of the 1960s, women began engaging in various forms of mobilization designed to promote gender equality and eradicate discrimination against women. Some women became involved in groups like the National Organization for Women (NOW, founded in 1966) that used legal means to eliminate sexism in the workplace, the schools, and the justice system. Other women who had been active in civil rights and the New Left grew frustrated with the sexism they perceived within those movements and began forming their own groups in which they could address the issue of women's oppression on its own terms. As historians have shown, the feminist movement that emerged in the late 1960s was internally differentiated. Feminists were divided along axes of race, class, sexuality, and region, and they were scarcely in agreement in defining organizational goals, tactics, and strategies.[31] But in part because the movement was so diverse, feminism's effects on American culture and society were profound. Between 1970 and 1980, feminists agitated for laws to protect women in the workplace from job discrimination and sexual harassment. They worked successfully to see that abortion became a constitutionally guaranteed right (the *Roe v. Wade* ruling was in 1973), and they fought to ensure that all women had access to medical care that would protect their reproductive freedom. They contributed to the 1972 passage of Title IX, which mandated equal gender access for sports funding in all federally financed schools. They also built a wide array of institutions throughout the 1970s, launching feminist bookstores, publishing houses, women's health clinics, battered women's shelters, daycare centers, and educational programs. Meanwhile, they organized demonstrations that called attention to the more subtle but no less damaging ways that women's oppression had shaped the dominant culture: through the promulgation of unrealistic standards of female beauty, through cultural practices like pageants that they believed degraded women, and through the use of everyday language and speech that was sexist.

A critical reappraisal of the nuclear family was central to the feminist project of the 1970s. Throughout their writings, feminists often identified the family as the primary site of women's oppression, although their understanding of what that meant and their remedies for addressing it were not always the same. Some feminists believed that sexism within the family would automatically be overcome by addressing the legal and institutional barriers to women's full participation in public life. Others critiqued the nuclear family as a place where women had been burdened with the responsibilities of housework and childrearing to the detriment of their own development as autonomous human beings.[32] Others contended that sexual relations between a man and a woman within the family were inherently exploitive and argued that women could only be freed from sexism by leaving heterosexual families behind and forming communities and partnerships with other women.[33] Still others emphasized the ways in which dominant cultural expectations surrounding motherhood had impeded women from discovering their own hopes, dreams, and aspirations in the wider world.[34]

Feminist critiques of the family were quite varied in substance, but they were unified by one element: their questioning of the traditional liberal distinction between public and private spheres. The feminist interrogation of the public-private split was captured by the movement's best-known slogan, "the personal is political." By challenging the ostensible divide between the public world of politics, economy, and society and the private world of family, sexuality, and motherhood, feminists were demanding nothing short of a total reappraisal of the meaning of private life. Activities and interactions that had once seemed sequestered from the political realm—from mopping the kitchen floor to a fight between husband and wife—were now recognized as deeply implicated in relationships of power, authority, and control. To be sure, some feminist issues like reproductive freedom appealed to traditional notions of privacy by insisting that women's bodies belonged to them and should be protected from outside state intervention and regulation. But the overall thrust of feminism challenged the distinction between public and private life by suggesting that relations within the family that had once seemed natural, benign, and preordained were in fact socially determined and thus open to political negotiation and cultural contestation.

The relationship between the flowering of feminism and the debate over the future of the family was complex. Some contended that the women's liberation movement was to blame for the recent transformations in American family life, but they were confusing cause and effect, since the census data left no doubt that the most dramatic changes taking place within the family—rising numbers of working women and female-headed households—were well under way before the resurgence of feminism. As sociologist Judith Stacey has argued, feminism did not produce these changes. Rather, the movement emerged, at least in part, out of the contradiction between women's growing participation in an emerging postindustrial labor force and the persistence of sexism.[35] Ironically, feminists shared many legislators' and academicians' concerns about the fate of the family. Like the statisticians who analyzed census data, they feared that the rise in female-headed households rendered women and children more vulnerable to poverty. And many feminists would surely have agreed with Bronfenbrenner that there was something alarming about the finding that middle-class fathers spent less than forty seconds a day with their babies. But while Bronfenbrenner drew on this data to show that the problem of father absence was encroaching into the middle-class home, feminists would have argued that it demonstrated the extent to which men were not assuming their fair share of responsibility for childrearing. The place of feminism in the debate about the family, in other words, was complicated by points of agreement as well as tensions.

But over the course of the 1970s these subtleties fell from view, and feminism gradually became identified as both a cause and a symptom of family decline itself, especially as grassroots organizers began mobilizing against the Equal Rights Amendment (the ERA, which began moving through the states for ratification in 1972) and abortion rights. Many feminists had called for men's greater participation in fathering and childrearing, but those who opposed the movement associated feminism with the diminished authority and presence of men within the home.[36] Feminists had interrogated the public-private distinction, but that interrogation became identified with the invasion of the family by hostile external forces that were undermining parental autonomy. For many, the family had come under attack by a dangerous new collaboration between feminists, the courts, and an overly interventionist state. Thus in 1980 Nevada Republican senator Paul Laxalt explained why more and more men and women had come to champion the cause of the "traditional family": "The family is now facing social and political threats of such magnitude as to compel a political defense."[37]

By the 1970s, then, the family ideal that Henry Luce had placed at the center of the American Century was in deep crisis. As older assumptions crumbled, new social movements on both the Left and the Right took up the symbol of the family and made it central to their mobilization. A great internal process of political fragmentation was under way at the same moment that a series of national crises—defeat in Vietnam, détente, the oil crisis, and the transition to a postindustrial society—was unfolding. This book argues that this historical confluence had two interrelated effects: fears about the fate of the family shaped debates about American national decline, and fears about the nation's future were mediated through the family.

An Aggrieved American Nationalism
and the Family-under-Siege

By exploring the mutually constitutive relationship between debates about national and family decline, this book shows that the years between 1968 and 1980 marked a significant moment in the history of American nationalism in the twentieth century. American nationalism, scholars agree, has been characterized by two conflicting impulses: a civic nationalism defined by a universal set of democratic and individualist beliefs and principles that unify diverse groups, and an ethno-racial, exclusionary nationalism that conceives of Americans in terms of common blood, ancestry, and skin color.[38] Recently, Anatol Lieven has argued that this second, ethno-chauvinist strain of American nationalism often includes a sense of "righteous victimhood," rooted in the belief that the nation has been wounded and that the wound must be avenged. This "wounded" American nationalism, Lieven argues, tends to become more visible at moments of acute social crisis and can be seen in the nativist sentiments of early white Anglo-Saxon and Scots-Irish settlers, in the Jacksonian frontier of the 1830s, in the deep ressentiment that surfaced in the American South after the Civil War, and, most recently, in the wake of the terrorist attacks of 11 September 2001.[39] This book argues that the years immediately following the Vietnam War were another moment when this aggrieved American nationalism exploded to the surface, that 1970s debates about national decline were a crucial arena where this strain of nationalism found expression, and that the family—precisely because of its associations with blood, kinship, honor, and loyalty—was at the center of those debates. Military defeat, I contend, gave rise to a wounded American nationalism that constructed the nation as an endangered family.

The link in the 1970s between a wounded national community and family peril had deep and enduring roots in American political and literary culture. Indeed, Senator Laxalt's contention that the family was under attack invoked a symbol that went back to the captivity narratives that were widespread in the colonial landscape of the late seventeenth century: the symbol of a family under siege.[40] Often featuring a white female captured by Indian savages and torn away from her community, these first-person accounts generally opened with violent scenes of family disruption, dissolution, and death. Although they declined in popularity as a literary genre over the course of the eighteenth century, the defining tropes of captivity narratives—those of bondage and family disruption—have resurfaced at moments of national upheaval, ranging from the American Revolutionary War to the Iranian hostage crisis of 1979.[41] At such moments, captivity narratives work by analogizing the nation to the family in ways that idealize both institutions at the same time. The entire nation is transformed into a family-under-siege, the private sphere becomes a locus of unjust injury inflicted from the outside, and the enemy's violent act of separating captive from kin is cited as proof of national righteousness. The power of the captivity narrative resides in its construction of the nation as an imperiled family. As Melani McAlister has argued, the classic move of the narrative is to identify the captive "with the feminized space of the family and sexuality" as a way of conferring innocence, purity, and goodness on the nation.[42]

The symbol of a family-under-siege was certainly at the center of debates about welfare, feminism, childhood, and parenthood in the 1970s. But, as we shall see, it was also central to concerns about the nation's world position as Americans struggled to understand defeat in Vietnam or the OPEC oil embargo. With its connotations of family suffering and trauma, the symbol conveyed the pain and the gravity of what it meant for the United States to lose: to lose a war, to lose control over oil, to lose command over the economy, to lose an indisputable lead in the arms race, to lose the allegiance of a former ally like Iran. What made events like Vietnam and the oil embargo so dire, the symbol implied, was that geopolitical disputes that had once seemed very far away had made their way into the most intimate space of all: the protected realm of the family. Thus the symbol of a family-under-siege established an affinity between foreign threats (such as the North Vietnamese, the Arab oil producers, and the Russians) and domestic ones (such as the welfare state, the federal government, feminism, and gay liberation). Even if all of these external forces were different from one another, they had something crucial in common: they were all invading the family.

The symbol also crystallized a growing anxiety in the 1970s about a long-standing distinction at the heart of modern warfare: the distinction between the soldier and the civilian. The horrors of World War II, the Holocaust, and the bombings of Hiroshima and Nagasaki had revealed how unstable that distinction had become in an age of total war. But two things happened in the 1970s that deepened earlier fears. First, by the late 1970s, the threat of nuclear annihilation gained renewed attention as peace groups that had focused on the Vietnam War returned to the theme of nuclear disarmament. At the same time, there was growing attention to the problem of international terrorism, a form of political violence whose sine qua non was the targeting of civilians. In the first half of the decade, extensive news coverage of spectacular terrorist acts, such as the hostage-taking and massacre of Israeli athletes at the Munich Olympics of 1972 and the hijacking of an Air France airplane from Tel Aviv to Entebbe, Uganda, in 1976, created the impression that the problem of terrorism was confined to the Arab-Israeli conflict. But by decade's end, the media's obsessive coverage of the Iranian hostage crisis suggested that the terrorist threat had moved still closer to home.[43] The threat of nuclear annihilation originated in the Cold War age, while international terrorism anticipated the emergence of a post–Cold War order. But both threats obliterated the distinction between soldiers and civilians, thus drawing families into the orbit of political violence and war.

Of course, the family was not only constructed as a site of national danger. The family was also viewed as a locus of problems, as an institution in need of reform, or, alternatively, as a source of national renewal. Nevertheless, the image of a wounded family, with its absent members—often, but not always, male—runs throughout the period discussed in this book, a period that stretches from 1968, the year that the Nixon administration prepared a campaign to call public attention to American prisoners of war and their families, to 1980, the year that Ronald Reagan's campaign for the presidency unfolded in tandem with the Iranian hostage crisis.

Each chapter of this book probes the place of the family in debates about American decline during what one historian has called "the long 1970s."[44] Chapters 1, 2, and 3 look at three crises that were interpreted at the time as evidence of American national decline: military defeat in Vietnam, the OPEC oil embargo, and the productivity slowdown. The book begins with the Vietnam War because more than any other single event, the gradual realization that the nation had lost the war threatened earlier presumptions of American power. The first chapter analyzes the 1968–73 campaign to publicize the plight of American POWs and their families, showing that it combined the themes of military failure abroad and male absenteeism within the home in a particularly pronounced way by featuring ubiquitous images of families without fathers. Over time, these images, originally meant to sanctify the national cause, took on new meanings as POW wives— influenced by the rise of feminism—assumed more independence in their husbands' absences and were unwilling to relinquish it upon repatriation. After POWs returned in 1973, the theme of male absenteeism—now focused on MIAs—translated into a critique of a supposedly weak and corrupt federal government, a government that had "left men behind."

Chapter 2 turns to the OPEC oil embargo of 1973–74. While chapter 1 explores the link between male absenteeism in the home and national military defeat abroad, chapter 2 looks at the ways in which the nation's compromised position during the embargo was attributed to the consuming excesses of the postwar middle-class family. OPEC instituted the oil embargo, which lasted from October 1973 to March 1974, in retaliation for American support of Israel in the October War, a support governed by what Henry Kissinger termed a "new realism" in American foreign policy after Vietnam. Although the effects of the embargo varied from region to region, its psychological impact was profound. During the winter of 1973, corporate advertisers, oil company executives, and conservation advocates defined the embargo as a crisis of dependency that could be traced back to the family's appetite for high-energy appliances and goods. Drawing on earlier traditions of social criticism that cast consumer culture as a threat to the traditional family, commentators claimed that the oil crisis was a deserved punishment for the profligacy of the consuming family and predicted that it could inaugurate a return to austerity for the American middle class. Thus, the oil embargo was not interpreted as a symptom of national decline alone; it was also seen as an occasion for the moral rearmament of the middle-class family in an era of diminishing resources.

Chapter 3 turns to another trope of national decline throughout the decade—what economists called "productivity lag." While chapter 2 explores the critiques of middle-class consumption that emerged during the embargo, this chapter looks at the flip side of this critique: cultural anxieties about the nation's productive capacity that surfaced at the same time. During the postwar years, productivity rates had risen steadily, but by the late 1960s economists began noting that productivity was slowing down in the steel and automobile industries. To explain the lag, industrial psychologists, corporate managers, and labor leaders contended that postwar fathers had failed to socialize a generation of male breadwinners. The consequence, they argued, was a "new breed" of worker no longer responsive to the economic incentives that had compelled an earlier generation of men to work. In response, business leaders implemented quality of work life programs that borrowed the psychological language of self-fulfillment in the service of heightened efficiency. Arguing that work could become meaningful if workers could affirm their commitment to quality goods, corporations romanticized the figure of the male artisan and craftsman. Chapter 3 argues that this revival of a "producerist ethic" emerged in response to deindustrialization, the expansion of the service sector, and the end of the family wage.

Chapter 4 also explores this producerist ethic, but in a different context. It analyzes the Bicentennial of 1976 as an attempt to redress the intertwined anxieties about national and family decline that had come to the fore by mid-decade. Drawing on the records of the American Revolution Bicentennial Administration (ARBA), the federal commission devoted to commemorative planning, the chapter traces the ways in which planners crafted a national celebration with Vietnam, Watergate, and economic recession very much on their minds. To meet these challenges, they adopted a counterintuitive strategy that decentralized the celebration, distanced it from the federal government, and honored the family, the ethnic tribe, and the local community in lieu of the nation. As part of this refashioning, household producerism became a standard feature of the celebration, from museum recreations of colonial kitchens to folk festivals showcasing tribal art and craftsmanship. The Bicentennial was thus transformed into a celebration of a pure American family—economically self-reliant and ostensibly freed from the corrupting influences of modern state intervention and mass consumption. In an ironic twist, the federally orchestrated Bicentennial articulated a widening public sentiment against the government over the course of the 1970s. Chapter 4 concludes by looking at another effort to overcome the challenges of the recent past that revolved around the nation's world position after Vietnam. If the Bicentennial celebration was legitimated by one variety of nationalism, what I call "diversity nationalism," this group, led by neoconservatives, articulated a second nationalist strain: the revival of patriotism and military order. Here, too, the family played a constitutive role.

Chapter 5 turns to the intellectual debate about American decline at decade's end centered on the claim made by historian Christopher Lasch that the nation had degenerated into a "culture of narcissism." According to Lasch, this culture resulted from the decline of paternal authority within the family, as the sphere of personal life was gradually eroded by the welfare state, the mass media, peer groups, and cults of expertise. In his best-selling book, *The Culture of Narcissism: American Life in an Age of Diminishing Expectations* (1978), Lasch argued that the decline of paternal authority—so pronounced within the African American family—had spread to the middle class and had left a devastating and potentially irreversible mark on American society and culture. The chapter traces this debate over "narcissism" and describes the way the concept was incorporated into President Carter's famous "Crisis of Confidence" speech in July 1979. Carter, like Lasch, believed that the 1970s drama of decline and regeneration called for a new level of introspection and self-understanding. Ironically, this belief was one factor that destroyed his presidency.

In the book's conclusion, I explore the political realignment of the 1970s by looking at Ronald Reagan's 1980 presidential campaign. In assessing the place of the family in the campaign, scholars have emphasized Reagan's opposition to the ERA and abortion rights. But I focus instead on the ways that the campaign effectively invoked the family as a site of national injury and vulnerability after Vietnam. This invocation, rather than any crude appeal to the traditional family, was one secret to Reagan's victory in 1980, and it helps to explain the inroads he made with historically Democratic constituencies. It was the social movements of the Left—women's liberation, black liberation, gay liberation—that had initiated the "politics of the family." But in 1980, it was Reagan who was able to capitalize on this politics by linking it to a narrative of American rebirth and regeneration. By recuperating all of the perceived crises of the 1970s—the captured POWs and MIAs, diminishing natural resources, a faltering work ethic, eroding patriotism, and the Iranian hostage crisis—Reagan was able to launch a new hegemonic synthesis that combined an attack on the New Deal welfare state with the restoration of American military authority after Vietnam.

Homeward Unbound

Prisoners of War, National Defeat, and the Crisis of Male Authority

On 6 March 1970, the House of Representatives Committee on Armed Services gathered to hear the testimony of a small group of military wives whose husbands had disappeared over the jungles and waters of Southeast Asia.[1] The purpose of the hearing was to call attention to the failure of the North Vietnamese to comply with the guidelines for prisoners of war laid out in the 1949 Geneva Accords. The accords, which the North Vietnamese had signed in 1957, required that the names of all captured prisoners of war be released, that all prisoners receive adequate medical care and food, that camps be inspected by a neutral third party, and that captives and their families be allowed to exchange mail. The United States accused North Vietnam of flagrantly violating these requirements, but the North Vietnamese countered that because the United States had never formally declared war against North Vietnam, the 1949 Geneva Accords did not apply. In their estimation, the men being held captive were not prisoners of war but were war criminals.[2]

The women who appeared before the House committee hoped to remind the public that these captured men, regardless of their official, wartime status, were also husbands, fathers, and sons. What made the North

Vietnamese violation of the Geneva Accords so egregious, both the wives and the committee members agreed, was that by failing to release vital information about the condition of the prisoners, the North Vietnamese were drawing innocent women and children into the fold of war. According to the chairman of the House committee, the North Vietnamese were "a bunch of heathens" and were guilty of "toying with these ladies' tender feelings."[3] In a phrase that would be repeated over and over again, these women wanted to learn whether they were "wives or widows," and they needed to be able to tell their children, many of whom had "never seen their fathers," the truth.[4] By depriving them of information, angry committee members charged, the North Vietnamese were engaging in a form of sadistic psychological warfare that blurred the boundaries between public and private, soldier and civilian, war front and home front. For their part, these women, most of them newcomers to political mobilization, recognized that the only weapon at their disposal was public opinion. As one POW wife told the committee, "I am a wife and a mother. I have no accoutrements of modern warfare at my disposal, no rifle, no ammunition. The only weapon which I have is opinion—public opinion here in this country, and throughout the world."[5]

The mounting public anxiety surrounding the status, treatment, and eventual repatriation of American prisoners of war in Southeast Asia brought together a number of international and domestic themes that had come to the fore in American cultural and political life by the early 1970s. The first and most obvious theme was the specter of American military defeat in Vietnam. By the late 1960s, public revelations that American fighting men were being tortured and placed in solitary confinement by their Vietnamese captors emblematized the growing perception that U.S. military intervention in Southeast Asia was failing—and failing badly. This is not to say that POWs were identified solely with failure or powerlessness; on the contrary, as this chapter will show, the POW was often portrayed as the lone hero in a war devoid of heroism. But there is no question that as the war dragged on, the American prisoner of war, reportedly tortured at the hands of his Vietnamese aggressor, became a powerful metaphor for the growing intractability and futility of the war itself.

The anxiety over the POWs also reflected the widespread fear that the private realm of the family was being absorbed by the public world of war and politics. This fear had surfaced first in 1968, when the Nixon administration prepared to launch a full-blown campaign to call attention to Hanoi's alleged refusal to comply with the rules for prisoners of war laid out in the 1949 Geneva Conventions. At the heart of the campaign was the specter of an innocent family drawn into a war over which it had no control. Between 1968 and 1973, a range of sentimental images designed to elicit both rage at the North Vietnamese and sympathy for the relatives of POWs bombarded the American public: bewildered children growing up without fathers, frightened wives living in a state of quasi-widowhood, and mothers and fathers desperate for any information about their captured sons. With little information available about the captives, prisoners themselves were conspicuously absent from the campaign. Instead, the campaign focused on the prisoners' families, precipitating a host of questions: When and how could the stories of POWs and their families be "made public"? What was the connection between private suffering and war? What was the relationship between the POW's identity as a husband, brother, father, or son and his status as a fighter pilot?

Understanding the POW campaign in this way adds a new layer to the history of the Vietnam War. Noting the ubiquity of the POW in post-Vietnam literature, film, and television, Elliot Gruner and Susan Jeffords have suggested that the POW embodied the rebirth of heroism out of defeat, a rebirth tied to the project of national remilitarization in the 1980s. What defined the POW, they have argued, was hyper-masculinity: the complete and successful exclusion of any traits traditionally identified with the feminine, including weakness, passivity, vulnerability, or loss. According to Gruner, the POW represents a nation "whose most recent heroes are over muscled male bodies bristling with an array of lethal weaponry."[6] According to Jeffords, POW narratives conform to standard American war narratives. Their defining feature is that they are "a 'man's story' from which women are excluded."[7] The story of the POWs, like that of American war in general, Jeffords concludes, was shaped by what it repressed—the feminine realm.

I take issue with this contention and argue in this chapter that the original campaign to publicize the POW issue proceeded from a radically different logic. Far from stressing masculinity, it consistently identified the captured soldier with those realms traditionally linked to femininity and womanhood: domesticity, sentimentality, the private sphere, and the affective ties of the family.[8] By linking captured men to their families and transforming the POW story into a domestic drama, the campaign simultaneously vilified the North Vietnamese and portrayed America as victim rather than aggressor. In this way, the campaign constructed the private world of the family as a wounded and violable space of national injury, one under threat from a foreign adversary.

But the POW publicity campaign also changed over time in ways that disturbed any simple identification of the family with national victimization. By the early 1970s, journalistic and psychological accounts of the POW family were still preoccupied with the impact of male absenteeism on women and children left behind, but the picture was becoming more complicated. Significantly, what differentiated POWs in Vietnam from their historical antecedents was not the number of men held in captivity (the number of Vietnam War POWs was considerably smaller than the number of men captured during the Korean War and World War II), but rather the duration of captivity.[9] The longest-held POW in North Vietnam was captured in 1964 and was not released until 1973, and many POWs lived in captivity for five years or longer. Thus, as the military prepared for their repatriation in February 1973, the media portrayed these returning men as "Rip Van Winkles" whose homecoming constituted a form of time travel. News accounts were quick to point out that the years that the POWs had spent in captivity were ones of profound social upheaval, and they cited the women's liberation movement and the sexual revolution as the most shocking evidence of just how much had changed in American society. These broader cultural discussions were mirrored by individual portraits of POW families, in which wives frequently described their own transformation from deferential, loyal dependents into assertive, self-sufficient women during their husbands' captivities, and in which children had not only survived but had thrived in the fathers' absences. Coming at the time that the women's liberation movement was gaining public attention, these stories raised the question of whether male authority within the family had been rendered obsolete in ways that made a true homecoming impossible.

This book begins with the POW publicity campaign for several reasons. More than any other single event of the late 1960s and early 1970s, the Vietnam War challenged earlier conceptions of American power, morality, and authority. Many who supported the war effort believed that the failure of U.S. military forces to meet their declared objectives in Southeast Asia had its roots in neither political, tactical, nor strategic errors, but rather in a collective collapse of national will, determination, and resolve on the part of the American people. As we will see, all of the debates about national decline that followed in the wake of the war—from the OPEC oil embargo to lagging productivity to détente—were filtered through the lens of national military defeat abroad. I begin with the POW/MIA story because it captured how intimately this sense of national defeat was bound up with anxieties about the state of the American family, and it sets the stage for a number of this book's recurring themes. Perhaps more than any other perceived threat, observers of the family feared an "epidemic of fatherlessness" during these years, and the POW controversy captured that fear in a particularly acute way. POW families seemed to confirm what many feared—that a failure of national leadership had dire implications for leadership within the family, and vice versa. An epidemic of fatherlessness, so pronounced within the black community, was now extending its reach into the sanctified realm of the white, middle-class domestic sphere. This epidemic was further exacerbated by the women's liberation movement, which was characterized throughout the POW controversy as a destructive domestic force with the power to further demoralize an already-demoralized nation. Finally, as the POW controversy gave way to the MIA controversy after 1973—and families shifted their blame from Hanoi to the U.S. government—the story of national military defeat abroad became entangled with a renegotiation of the relationship between the family and the state. Although accusations against the State and Defense Departments ranged from charges of incompetence and bureaucratic bungling to theories of deception and outright conspiracy, MIA activists were in agreement on one critical point: the U.S. government had abandoned its military men in order to bring false closure to a contentious war. The charge of abandonment not only proceeded from the premise that the U.S. government had failed in its execution of the war, but it also constructed the federal government as an impediment to the reunited, intact, male-headed household.[10] The allegation that the U.S. government had abandoned men in Southeast Asia advanced another argument that would reappear in debates about American national decline after Vietnam: the state itself, rather than any foreign adversary, was exacerbating an epidemic of male absenteeism with dire consequences for family and nation alike.

Mothers in a Fatherless World:
The Go-Public Campaign, 1966–1972

Although U.S. personnel were captured and taken prisoner of war in Southeast Asia as early as 1961,[11] the dramatic story of POWs and their families did not receive public attention until 1966. Prior to that time, the government pursued what it called a policy of "quiet diplomacy," later dubbed the "keep quiet policy" by one disillusioned POW wife.[12] Premised on the assumption that publicizing information about POWs might jeopardize their safety and derail ongoing negotiations with the North Vietnamese, this policy advised the families of captured and missing men to stay out of the public eye, refrain from contacting the press, and keep their private concerns about their men precisely that—private.

Beginning in 1966, a number of international and domestic forces converged to undermine this policy. As the government began to receive reports of prisoner mistreatment, the Johnson administration became more proactive on the POW issue, establishing a Committee on Prisoner Matters within the State Department in April of 1966. Around the same time, both the Central Intelligence Agency and the Defense Intelligence Agency became heavily involved in POW information gathering. Two months later, the matter assumed greater public urgency when the North Vietnamese, in what U.S. intelligence forces interpreted as a misguided attempt to garner international sympathy, released film footage showing manacled American prisoners being marched at gunpoint through the streets of Hanoi, surrounded by hostile crowds.[13] Less than a year later, in April 1967, *Life* magazine featured a full-page photograph of captured naval officer Richard Stratton at a Hanoi press conference, apparently bowing in submission. It was, according to one sympathetic POW chronicler, an arresting image of "a big, husky pilot" now looking "like an automaton, like someone who had been made into a puppet." A haunting reminder of the speculations about brainwashing and collaboration that had surrounded the experience of Korean War POWs, Stratton's "Pavlovian performance" alarmed his family, government officials, and the American public.[14]

However disturbing these images, the "go-public" campaign did not take off in earnest until late 1968, when the mounting demands of POW families converged with the political interests of Richard Nixon's presidential campaign. By the late 1960s, many relatives of POWs had grown angry and frustrated, not only by the dearth of information coming out of Vietnam, but also by the policy of quiet diplomacy, which they had come to see as an excuse for government inaction. Sybil Stockdale, a mother of four whose husband, naval commander James Stockdale, had been captured in 1965, had met on numerous occasions with officials in the Naval and State Departments and had come to the disheartening conclusion that "official silence and secrecy can cover up incompetence and just plain inertia."[15] On 27 October 1968, she defied the government's policy and went public with her husband's story in the *San Diego Union Tribune*. Stockdale was not acting alone but was part of an informal network of POW wives, parents, and siblings who were taking matters into their own hands and engaging in grassroots organizing, many for the first time in their lives. They launched letter-writing campaigns to members of Congress and the White House, appealed to the press, attempted to establish direct contact with Hanoi in the hope of gathering information, and sent POW wives to Washington, D.C., and to the Paris peace talks to demand North Vietnamese compliance with the terms of the Geneva Convention. In 1970, this informal network of family lobbyists became the National League of Families of American Prisoners and Missing in Southeast Asia, still in operation today.[16]

By 1969, the Nixon administration had its own reasons for wanting to publicize the POW issue. With opposition to the war growing, the new president recognized that Hanoi's refusal to disclose information about missing and captive men could prove to be a public relations boon, one that could deflect attention away from disturbing reports coming out of Vietnam—about the My Lai massacre, the indiscriminate killing of Vietnamese civilians, the free-fire zones, napalm, and defoliation. Indeed, it was only within this context of widening scrutiny of American war conduct that the interests of POW families, the Nixon White House, and Congress converged, however provisionally. On 19 May 1969, Defense secretary Melvin Laird ended the policy of quiet diplomacy, publicly charging Hanoi with prisoner mistreatment and demanding that if the Vietnamese did not release the prisoners, they at least had a humanitarian obligation to disclose vital information about their conditions.[17]

Initially, the explicit aim of the go-public campaign was relatively narrow: to bring international pressure to bear on the North Vietnamese by calling attention to Hanoi's ostensible refusal to comply with the Geneva Convention's rules for prisoners of war. When viewed historically, however, it is clear that the campaign was actually much wider, and it advanced a vision of American victimization that would shape Vietnam War discourse for years to come: whatever physical wounds the United States military had inflicted on Vietnam, the psychological wounds inflicted by the Vietnamese on the United States were ultimately more dire. The claim that, through defying the Geneva Convention, Hanoi had extended its reach into the most intimate sphere of the family became a constitutive part of the process of recasting the United States as psychological casualty, rather than military aggressor.

Taking the plight of prisoners of war and their families to the public between 1968 until 1973 required a range of interrelated rhetorical strategies. First, the military role of the POW was downplayed as government officials and family members consistently foregrounded his civilian, and specifically his familial, identity. The vast majority of captured men were, in fact, an elite group. On the whole, they were "glamorous aviators" and commissioned officers whose planes had been shot down during Operation Rolling Thunder, the planned bombing raids over North Vietnam between 1965 and 1968.[18] But the critical role that these men had played in the war's execution quickly slipped from view as the public was instructed to consider the POW problem through the eyes of a child. "Pretend you're 12 years old and your father's a Prisoner of War in Southeast Asia," instructed the National Advertising Council's 1971–72 POW advertising campaign. A twelve-year-old child would not understand the "maneuvers of the bargaining table," the advertisement conjectured, but would only want someone believable to tell him that his father was safe. Calling on Hanoi to allow neutral observers into the prison camps, the advertisement claimed to speak for "all the boys and girls, wives and parents whose fathers, husbands, and sons are being held in secret captivity."[19]

Members of the antiwar movement challenged this obfuscation of the POW's military identity. In March 1972, activist and writer Grace Paley reminded *New York Times* readers that "the man in the sky is a killer," an unsavory fact willfully overlooked because, in Paley's estimation, politicians and newsmen spoke of the POWs "as though these pilots had been kidnapped from a farm in Iowa." Paley's fiery editorial provoked letters of both rage and respect, with one admiring Vietnam veteran applauding her courage, writing that he had "no sympathy for the plight of the downed jet jockies who flew and strafed and bombed because it was fun."[20] To be sure, reminders of the POW's military role were morally compelling. But they overlooked precisely what had made the strategy of obscuring the POW's military identity so effective in the first place. Recasting the POWs as fathers, husbands, and sons was not simply a process of concealing the havoc that these fighter pilots had wrought from the air in North Vietnam. It was also about producing a new constellation of victims within the domestic space of the United States: namely, the wives, children, parents, sisters, and brothers of the POWs themselves.

Over the next four years, these domestic victims assumed center stage as the public was bombarded with images and stories of the loyal wives, grief-stricken parents, and uncomprehending children of American prisoners of war. Editorials in both the military and the mainstream press blamed the North Vietnamese for transforming the home front into a "fatherless world," one of hapless sons and daughters who, according to one editorial in the *Armed Forces Journal*, had "a right to know if their fathers [were] dead or alive."[21] In December 1970, *Life* and *Look* magazines featured photo essays documenting POW children growing up without their fathers, contrasting early family photographs of cheerful, intact families with more recent, somber photographs in which the father was conspicuously absent.[22] Meanwhile, the POW wife was left with the nearly impossible task of explaining her husband's disappearance to a child with no understanding of war. As Frank Sieverts, the State Department's top official on POW/MIA matters, reported during the same period: "The telephone rings all the time. In the holiday season, it is especially bad. Wives call up asking me what to say to their children, how to explain that they don't know where their husbands are, whether they are dead or alive, when all the other kids have their fathers."[23] Through its policy of silence and secrecy, according to these accounts, Hanoi had placed innocent women and children in a cruel state of suspension, alienating them from the rest of society and generating enormous confusion and uncertainty within the family. "It's a very lonely existence," revealed one POW wife whose husband had been shot down in 1967. "You're married but you're not married. You're not single. You're not divorced or widowed. Where does that put you in society? That puts you in your own world."[24]

By accusing Hanoi of drawing women and children into the fold of war, the go-public campaign mined two dominant discourses: one, a racial discourse that assigned Asian captors a unique capacity for psychological cruelty, and the other, a Cold War discourse that constructed Communism as transgressive of the division between public and private spheres, a division crucial to conceptions of Western liberal democracy. The POW publicity campaign combined these two discourses, conjuring up a profile of the Vietnamese captor who was at once a psychological sadist and a violator of the boundaries between battleground and prison camp, and by extension, war front and home.

The racial dimension of this profile hinged on the claim that for American prisoners of war, the experience of Asian captivity was demonstrably worse than the experience of captivity in the West. With little concrete information at their disposal, military psychologists drew on prior historical examples in order to speculate about what might be occurring in Southeast Asian prison camps and how POWs might fare down the road. Military studies contrasted the earlier repatriation of POWs from Germany to those from Japan and Korea, concluding that being captured by "Oriental forces" entailed a higher degree of physical stress and deterioration, and

What does "Missing in Action" mean in the middle of the night?

ANY woman can understand the prisoner-of-war question very easily.

All she has to do is imagine for a moment how another woman feels as the night hours drag slowly on and she wonders.

Wonders where and how her husband is. Wonders whether he's alive or dead. Whether...

Any woman, any human being, can understand that there is a human side as well as a political side to the prisoner-of-war issue.

This message is concerned with the human side.

Of course, we all want the war to end and the prisoners to be released as soon as possible.

But meantime there is no need for Hanoi and its allies to delay even a day in answering this plea.

Open the prison camps in North Vietnam, South Vietnam, Cambodia and Laos to official neutral observers.

Through these neutral observers, tell the wives and families of American prisoners where they are and how they are.

Is that too much for a wife to ask? Is that too much for Hanoi to give? Is that too much for the conscience of the world to demand?

SUPPORT OUR PLEA TO HANOI AND ITS ALLIES:

Clear away the doubts —
Open your prison camps to neutral observers...
now!

We ask no more than we give. All American and South Vietnamese prison camps are inspected regularly by official neutral observers — The International Committee of the Red Cross.

✚ American Red Cross

Advertising contributed for the public good

National League of Families of American Prisoners and Missing in Southeast Asia.
1608 "K" Street, N.W., Washington, D.C. 20006

How do you tell a 6-year-old you don't know where his daddy is?

A YOUNG boy whose father is missing can't understand when he hears people saying things like...

"the prisoner-of-war question is a political issue"

"this is not a war so how can there be prisoners of war?"

All he knows is that his father is "missing in action" and that nobody can tell him where his father is and how his father is.

This message to Hanoi — this message to the people of the world — is in behalf of the children, the wives, the fathers and mothers of Americans being held in secret captivity in North Vietnam, South Vietnam, Laos and Cambodia.

Of course, we all want the war to end and the prisoners to be released as soon as possible.

But meanwhile there is no need for Hanoi and its allies to delay even a day in answering this plea.

Let official neutral observers into the prison camps to see who the prisoners are, how they are, where they are and whether or not they are being humanely treated according to the standards of civilized nations.

It is so human for little boys to ask.

It would be so humane for Hanoi to answer.

SUPPORT OUR PLEA TO HANOI AND ITS ALLIES:

Clear away the doubts —
Open your prison camps to neutral observers...
now!

We ask no more than we give. All American and South Vietnamese prison camps are inspected regularly by official neutral observers — The International Committee of the Red Cross.

✚ American Red Cross

Advertising contributed for the public good

National League of Families of American Prisoners and Missing in Southeast Asia.
1608 "K" Street, N.W., Washington, D.C. 20006

Advertisements from the National Advertising Council's campaign to publicize the plight of POWs and their families, 1972. Courtesy of the University of Illinois/Advertising Council Archives.

HOMEWARD UNBOUND

that on the whole, prisoners returning from "Oriental captivity" were more prone to auto accidents, mental breakdowns, divorces, and suicides.[25] In an attempt to offer a political explanation for this purported difference, Dr. Charles Stenger, a clinical psychologist for the Veterans Administration POW Program, attributed "Asian cruelty" to the excesses of Western imperialism, speculating that Asian captors seized the opportunity to vent their rage at Western arrogance. Referring specifically to the Japanese treatment of American prisoners during World War II, Stenger speculated that "they had to humiliate them and show them that they weren't king. So there was a purposeful humiliation and degradation in Oriental POW situations."[26]

Both throughout the go-public campaign and in the years after repatriation, condemnations of Hanoi's silence surrounding the POWs implicitly appealed to this notion that Asians possessed a unique propensity for psychological cruelty and were inherently more secretive than their Western counterparts.[27] According to one congressman speaking at the Committee on Armed Services Hearing in 1970, North Vietnam had adopted a "barbaric policy" that was using the prisoners as "pawns" in an attempt to "wage psychological warfare against the United States."[28] The Communists of both Hanoi and Korea were "master psychologists," according to another representative speaking on the House floor a year earlier.[29] These charges of psychological manipulation had obvious racial overtones, but they also targeted a Communist political system that refused to honor the sanctity of the private sphere. Within the context of the Vietnam War, the accusation suggested that it was the relatives of POWs who were the latest victims of Communist aggression, even though they remained within the territorial boundaries of the United States. According to one 1969 editorial on the plight of POW wives, these women, no less than their husbands, were "captives of fear as the Communists play cat and mouse with their emotions."[30] This was the linchpin of the go-public campaign: through extending its reach into the sanctified sphere of the family, Hanoi was violating not only the rules of warfare but also the norms of Western liberal humanism. At the precise moment that a burgeoning antiwar movement was accusing the American military of indiscriminately bombing Vietnamese schools, hospitals, and homes, the go-public campaign deftly redirected the accusation: it was Communist Hanoi that had drawn innocent civilians into the hellish world of war, not the U.S. government.

Throughout the campaign, government officials and POW family members insisted that Hanoi's silence constituted a humanitarian crime rather than a political or military one. This was another crucial component of the publicity campaign: to define the POW issue as strictly humanitarian in nature. Despite its ties to the Republican Party, the League formally positioned itself as "politically neutral," and military officials advised POW wives to adopt an explicitly humanitarian approach when talking to the press, one that shied away from partisan politics and emphasized the anxieties they were forced to endure as a result of Hanoi's refusal to release information about their husbands' welfare.[31] Although the North Vietnamese insisted that the prisoner of war issue was deeply political, in that it spoke to the illegality of U.S. military intervention in Southeast Asia, American government officials countered that compliance with the Geneva Accords was a "basic, simple humanitarian question."[32] Anyone who doubted this need only look at the photographs of POW wives and children featured in the Ad Council's 1971–72 campaign, which called on Hanoi to allow neutral official observers into the prison camps in order to assure the world that they were treating the prisoners "according to humane standards long practiced by civilized nations." "That's the issue," the advertisement declared. "It's that simple. It's that non-political. It's that human." Through complying with the Geneva Accords, Hanoi would not only "earn the gratitude of millions of Americans," the campaign predicted, but it would "find new stature in the eyes of the world."[33] As the international community expressed mounting horror at the war's deadly toll among Vietnamese civilians, the go-public campaign attempted to shift the humanitarian burden to the North Vietnamese, contending that the central question of the war revolved not around the U.S. military's war conduct, but rather around the treatment of captured American soldiers: would Hanoi act in compliance with the universally accepted norms laid out in the Geneva Convention, or would it continue to violate them?

By defining the POW issue in this way, the go-public campaign also insisted that this theme could unite all Americans regardless of their broader political positions about the war. "We Americans have certainly debated endlessly about the war," Sybil Stockdale told the readers of *Good Housekeeping* in 1970, "but a simple issue such as cruelty and inhumane treatment of helpless men is easy for anyone to understand. On that all Americans and most of the world are united."[34] One implication of this claim was that, although certain forms of war dissent might be acceptable, the failure to sympathize with the plight of POWs and their families was traitorous, inhumane, and uncivilized. But this claim also assigned a unique cultural capacity to the POW, one that would gain increasing urgency in the months leading up to homecoming: the power to somehow bring hawks and doves together and to heal the domestic divisions wrought by the war.

In the early 1980s, former secretary of state Henry Kissinger remembered the Vietnam War as a mutual conflict between two aggressors who had wielded very different kinds of weapons. "Hanoi and Washington," he wrote, "had inflicted grievous wounds on each other, theirs were physical, ours psychological and thus perhaps harder to heal."[35] During the late 1960s and early 1970s, government officials, some members of Congress, and the relatives of captured and missing men crafted a public relations campaign

"My husband, Alexander, is a Lt. Commander in the Navy. Four years ago he was reported missing in action. There's a chance he was taken prisoner and is still alive. But I don't know. And I can't find out. Hanoi won't tell our government. Hanoi won't tell me."

One side of the POW question is not complicated. That's the human side.

ALTHOUGH the prisoner-of-war question is often complex and even confusing, one side of it should be very simple. That's the part that deals with the treatment of prisoners of war. That's not a political issue, but a human issue.

Of course, we all want the war to end and the prisoners of war to be released as soon as possible.

But meanwhile there is no need for Hanoi and its allies to delay even a day in answering this plea:

Let your POW camps in North Vietnam, South Vietnam, Cambodia and Laos be visited by neutral observers.

Let the world know the names of the men you have held so long in secret captivity.

Assure the world through unbiased official observers that you are treating American Prisoners according to humane standards long practiced by civilized nations.

That's the issue.
It's that simple.
It's that non-political.
It's that human.

Hanoi can open its prison camps to neutral observers without bargaining, even without consultation.

By doing so now, Hanoi would earn the gratitude of millions of Americans and find new stature in the eyes of the world.

✚ American Red Cross

Advertising contributed for the public good Ⓐ

National League of Families of American Prisoners and Missing in Southeast Asia.
1608 "K" Street, N.W., Washington, D.C. 20006

Advertisement from the National Advertising Council's campaign to publicize the plight of POWs and their families, 1972. Courtesy of the University of Illinois/ Advertising Council Archives.

that laid the cultural groundwork for Kissinger's retrospective claim. The campaign argued that the North Vietnamese were agents of psychological violence and that through their defiance of the Geneva Convention, they had infiltrated the domestic space of the United States and had brought the war home. Indeed, this notion of the war "coming home" became a standard feature of both scholarly and popular treatments of the Vietnam War and is usually used to connote the profound domestic divisions engendered by it.[36] But to those who were championing the cause of the POWs between 1968 and 1973, the war had come home in a more literal sense. According to the campaign, Hanoi had wrought emotional havoc on the private sphere by creating a fatherless world in which loyal women did not know whether they were wives or widows and innocent children did not know whether they had fathers or were semi-orphaned. These sentimentalized images of women and children produced a resilient narrative about the war itself, one that linked the condition of fatherlessness to the emergence of the United States as the war's primary psychic and spiritual casualty.

The "Ultimate Weeper": Operation Homecoming and the Struggle for Reentry

On 12 February 1973, one month after the signing of the cease-fire agreement in Paris, the first returning prisoners of war arrived at Clark Air Base in the Philippines on their way to the United States.[37] The next day, the front page of the New York Times featured a photograph that captured the returning POW's vexed status as both hero and victim. It showed an air force captain being carried from a jet plane on a stretcher. Yet he was still smiling jubilantly, with his arms outstretched above his head in a victorious gesture.[38] Over the next six weeks, a total of 587 prisoners of war returned home, where they were greeted by throngs of euphoric crowds. Indeed, Operation Homecoming, the military's official name for the repatriation of the prisoners, quickly exploded into a full-blown media event.[39] Described by Newsweek as the "ultimate weeper," homecoming was indeed a sentimental spectacle: crowds carrying signs reading "Welcome Home Daddy!" and "Happiness Is a Dad," husbands and wives racing across the tarmac and collapsing into each other's arms, fathers knocked off their feet as their children engulfed them with hugs and kisses, and returning men proudly saluting their military superiors, appearing every bit as patriotic as the day they had left for Vietnam.[40]

These evocative images, omnipresent in the national and local press

FIFTY CENTS   FEBRUARY 19, 1973

TIME

THE PRISONERS RETURN

"The Prisoners Return," cover of Time magazine, 19 February 1973.
Courtesy of TIME Magazine, © 1973 Time Inc.; reprinted with permission.

throughout the early months of 1973, reveal the extent to which the POW had become the object of emotional and ideological investment. At one level, during the years of the go-public campaign, captivity came to symbolize the wider failure of American foreign policy in Vietnam. Expressions of frustration over the POW issue often went hand in hand with bafflement and confusion over the larger question of why the United States

Released prisoner of war Lt. Col. Robert L. Stirm reunites with his family at Travis Air Force Base in Fairfield, California, 17 March 1973. Courtesy of AP Photo.

was failing to win the war. "How could the most powerful military in the world be unable to overwhelm that small backward strip of territory?" Sybil Stockdale asked in her memoir, incredulous about both the government's execution of the war and its failure to obtain information about her captured husband.[41] And although the POWs themselves did not exactly blame their captivity on the U.S. government, their memoirs suggest that many did feel that they had been asked to fight the war by half measures. Years later, Arizona senator and former prisoner of war John McCain recalled that his fellow pilots believed that their civilian commanders did not "have the least notion of what it took to win the war," and he remembered being dumbfounded by the "haphazard, uncertain prosecution of the war, with its utterly illogical restraints on the use of American power."[42] By the early 1970s, the fact that American fighting men had been in prison camps year after year contributed to the growing conviction within the military that the United States, due largely to its own lack of resolve, had become unwitting hostage to the war in Southeast Asia.

But if captivity connoted failure and entrapment, the prisoner of war himself emerged as a symbol of heroism and sacrifice. The POW's courage, according to one 1973 account in *U.S. News and World Report*, was literally "the only good thing" to have come out of the conflict in Southeast Asia.[43] News stories on Operation Homecoming repeatedly commented on the fact that, although the war had bred disillusionment at home, the POW's commitment had never faltered. "How can you say it's a war without heroes when you look into their faces?" one POW wife reportedly asked.[44] Just as the go-public campaign had insisted that the POW issue could provisionally unite hawks and doves, the return of the men was seen as an occasion in which everyone, regardless of their wider views of the war, could come together "in a surge of admiration."[45] Defenders and critics of the war alike were permitted—indeed expected—to feel unabashedly patriotic as they observed repatriation, and POWs, having learned of the antiwar movement while in captivity, expressed relief and joyful surprise at the warm reception. At a crucial moment, Operation Homecoming attempted to reconfigure the meaning of patriotism by distancing it from the actual war and aligning it instead with a far more inclusive commitment to the process of national healing and reconciliation.

But if the POW was cast as both hero and healer, he was also constructed as one of the most highly visible victims of the conflict, albeit one who appeared to be coming home in better physical and psychological condition than anyone had predicted.[46] As we have seen, although the go-public campaign had called attention to the plight of the POWs through publicizing reports of prisoner mistreatment, it had strategically foregrounded the suffering of the POW's immediate family members: those civilians who had been psychologically and emotionally drawn into the conflict through no fault of their own. But as soon as all of the 587 prisoners had been repatriated to the United States, the concrete experience of captivity came into clearer view, as returnees began providing testimony that confirmed earlier reports of interrogation, indoctrination, torture, illness, untreated wounds, and malnutrition.[47] The frequent characterization of the North Vietnamese captor as an agent of "diabolical psychological torture" was now complemented by a more disturbing picture of the captive, who at times resembled a victim of the Nazi Holocaust.[48]

Historian Peter Novick has argued that the Holocaust became a defining feature of American political culture in the late 1960s and 1970s, especially in the aftermath of the Arab-Israeli wars of 1967 and 1973. What Novick and others have overlooked is how powerfully a growing Holocaust consciousness also converged with Vietnam War discourse during this period.[49] Both go-public campaigners and POWs themselves made multiple references to the Holocaust in their discussions of captivity. These references again figured the POW as a victim rather than an aggressor of the war. Thus in 1969, as House members debated a resolution condemning the North Vietnamese for prisoner mistreatment, one congressman declared that the tales of brutality and deprivation coming out of the prison camps were enough to "shock a generation of Americans already inured to the horror stories of Nazi Germany." The horror being perpetrated by the captors, according to another representative, was "like a story out of the barbaric days" of the Nazi past.[50] Throughout the publicity campaign, these references to Nazism served a straightforward purpose consistent with Cold War dictates: they were meant to suggest that Communism and fascism were cut from the same totalitarian cloth. At the same time, prisoners themselves drew on Holocaust iconography during captivity as a way to narrate the ordeal to themselves and to one another. According to several memoirs, POWs sometimes compared sick and emaciated captives to concentration camp inmates in order to convey the severity of their condition, a guerrilla camp was dubbed "Auschwitz" by its prisoners, and one guard with a particularly bad reputation was nicknamed "Little Hitler."[51] After homecoming, these references would appear throughout POW memoirs. But even earlier, prisoners of war collectively mobilized the Holocaust as a kind of framing device for their own experiences.

Military personnel also drew on the Holocaust as they prepared for POW repatriation. In order to develop a psychological profile of the returning POW, navy medical staff did not consult former prisoners of war, as one might expect, but instead interviewed concentration camp survivors, thus locating the prisoner of war and the Holocaust survivor along the same psychological and experiential continuum. Drawing on these interviews, military psychologists predicted that as a result of years in confinement, the returnees would display symptoms of what was known as "concentration camp syndrome," including pervasive anxiety, depression, and insomnia.[52] By treating the experience of the Holocaust survivor as paradigmatic, military psychologists were eliding crucial historical and political distinctions, including the difference that had been blurred so consistently throughout the go-public campaign: that between military and civilian captives.

All of these political, psychological, and impressionistic references to the Holocaust advanced the idea that the POW, like the concentration camp inmate, was unambiguously the victim of a cruel and merciless captor. According to this logic, captivity in a North Vietnamese prison was no less morally and politically cut-and-dried than captivity in Auschwitz or Dachau. Within the context of the war, a growing Holocaust consciousness made available an instantly recognizable vocabulary of evil, one that located evil in the obliteration of the public-private distinction and thus proved instrumental in identifying the prisoner of war—and, by extension, the American nation—as an innocent victim of the conflict.

This is not to suggest that the POW was identified exclusively with victimization. On the contrary, the role of the POW was riddled with contradictions. The returning prisoner of war was at once a courageous hero, an unwavering patriot, a healer of national wounds, a powerless captive, an unrepentant killer, and an innocent victim. This confusion surrounding the status of the returning POW reflected the domestic divisiveness and bitterness engendered by the war: the contention that the United States had lost its moral compass in its waging of the war, the claim that an obstructionist bureaucracy had prevented the military from doing its job, the gradual realization that the United States had lost the war, the sense that the nation had somehow sustained a psychological trauma that would be impossible to heal, and the dire need to invest the failed war with some sense of purpose. Because the repatriation of the POW would somehow have to address all of these national fears and needs simultaneously, the cultural stakes of Operation Homecoming were enormously high.

The stakes of homecoming were also high because this was a familial drama as much as it was a national one. The media coverage of Operation Homecoming tied the return of the POW as a national hero to his instantaneous and painless reintegration into the family, as husband, father, and son. As we saw, jubilant family reunions were a defining part of a "hero's welcome," as the endless stream of photographs and film footage of overcome husbands, wives, and children made clear. These widely reproduced images conveyed the sense that, after years of disruption, order was finally being restored within the domestic spheres of both nation and family. After years of deferral, the public was finally being presented with a familiar and reassuring version of homecoming, one that resonated with earlier homecomings from less divisive wars. After years of uncertainty, the widely publicized plight of POW wives, parents, and children appeared to be over, as fragmented families could now be made whole again.

But despite the sentimentalized family reunions orchestrated by Operation Homecoming, reintegration turned out to be a far more emotionally and psychologically fraught affair. The prisoner of war's reentry into the family was complicated by three transformations that had occurred during his captivity: the POW wife's growing claims to autonomy, the family's adaptation to life without a male head of household, and the culture shock of the women's liberation movement. These shifts challenged the meaning of repatriation and suggested that the prisoner of war was now at risk of being victimized twice: first within the North Vietnamese prison camp, and second within the private sphere of his own family. These changes revised and challenged the meaning of homecoming. As one returning POW would later write in his memoir about readjustment to life after captivity, "Whether I even wanted to 'adjust,' I didn't know."[53]

Here one could see the extent to which the POW story converged with broader cultural anxieties about declining male authority within the family and the fear that fathers and husbands had somehow become emotionally obsolete. As we will see in later chapters, this anxiety was pervasive and informed debates about everything from household energy waste to narcissistic personality disorder. The go-public campaign had proceeded from the premise that the condition of fatherlessness had constituted a true domestic emergency, but the picture that emerged after repatriation suggested the opposite: that POW families had actually coped surprisingly well in the absence of male authority, and that fathers were returning to their homes as strangers, intruders, and interlopers. At the center of this reversal was the shifting role of the POW wife. Although the loyal wife of the early go-public campaign had not disappeared by the early 1970s, she was now joined by a host of competing images that positioned her as a political and emotional traitor: the wife who had defied her husband by embracing antiwar activism, the wife who had betrayed her husband by divorcing him while he was in captivity, and, finally, the wife who had been forced by the exigencies of war to assume more autonomy and who discovered, upon her husband's repatriation, that she had no desire to relinquish it.

In order to understand the cultural significance of these competing images, it is important to take a closer look at the women-turned-activists who had initially spearheaded the go-public campaign in the late 1960s. The wives of POWs and MIAs who were instrumental in forming the National League of Families defy easy political categorization, in part because they themselves insisted that their cause was strictly humanitarian, apolitical, and nonpartisan. Although they condemned the government's policy of "quiet diplomacy," they repeatedly expressed discomfort at having to take an antagonistic stance toward the state.[54] After all, many of these women had spent their entire lives in military communities. They strongly supported the war in Southeast Asia and explicitly distanced themselves from protest movements. To be sure, they were engaging in women's grassroots organizing, but, politically, they were worlds apart from the feminist activists of the period, not least in their divergent views of motherhood. In contrast to feminists who identified motherhood and marriage as primary sites of women's oppression, these military wives were mobilizing a maternalist discourse, one that appealed to essentialist ideals of motherhood in order to make political demands on the state. But while maternalism has historically been aligned with pacifism, these women were unapologetic hawks who were foregrounding their roles as wives and mothers in order to condemn the North Vietnamese and demand more American military intervention, not less.[55] Thus the political profile of the wife-turned-activist is complex: loyal to the government but also increasingly antagonistic and distrustful of it; maternalist in rhetoric but in the service of militarism; hoping for her husband's safe return while simultaneously wanting him to wage and win the war. What is not ambiguous, however, is that the original POW wife believed that she was acting in her husband's interest and doing what he would have wanted her to do. During the early years of the publicity campaign, she served as his loyal lieutenant, the champion of his cause, and a heroine who had worked tirelessly to remind the nation of its "forgotten men."

By the early 1970s, this portrait began to change as more and more POW wives, sisters, and mothers became active in the antiwar movement. In May 1971, several relatives who had originally been involved in the League formed a splinter group called POW-MIA Families for Immediate Release, which urged the League to adopt an overtly political position by demanding the immediate withdrawal of U.S. troops. By July of that year, approximately three hundred POW relatives had joined the group, claiming that the Nixon administration was now using the prisoners as a justification for prolonging the war and insisting that the president negotiate the prisoners' release without regard to the political fate of South Vietnam. As one member of the group graphically exclaimed, "They cannot use my husband to spread the blood of 45 young men a week on Viet Nam." Rejecting the ostensible political neutrality of the League, these relatives insisted that their missing men had by this point become the political hostages of both Hanoi and the Nixon administration.[56] While some of them aligned themselves with the antiwar movement primarily for pragmatic reasons (believing that ending the war would be the quickest way to get the prisoners home), others had come to believe that American military involvement in Vietnam was morally wrong, above and beyond the POW issue.

This growing antiwar activism challenged the earlier image of the ever-loyal POW wife. Now it appeared that some wives had defied their husbands by allying themselves with the antiwar movement. By the late 1960s, reports of the burgeoning antiwar movement in the United States had traveled widely throughout the prison camps, and POWs later recalled feeling demoralized and deeply troubled by the news.[57] The revelation that some women within their own families had adopted an antiwar stance added insult to injury. Revealingly, memoirs suggest the extent to which POWs not only felt uniquely wounded by women's opposition to the war, but also associated antiwar activism with women, regardless of the movement's actual gender composition. Highly visible figures like Joan Baez and Jane Fonda who opposed the war were angrily labeled "traitorous bitches," women's antiwar organizations like Women Strike for Peace were singled out for condemnation, and POWs expressed a singular sense of shock that American women could turn on them through their wartime opposition.[58] One POW recalled his captors forcing him and other prisoners to listen to an audiotape of women demonstrating outside an army base at Fort Dix, New Jersey, singing a song entitled "Fuck the Army!": "We sat there in shock, trying to adjust to the harsh realization that these were our own American women! We couldn't believe that they would involve themselves in such filth to show their dissension and encourage our soldiers to desert!"[59]

Within the context of Operation Homecoming, this turn to antiwar activism among some POW families begged the question of how returning men would respond when they learned that their wives, sisters, and mothers had spoken out publicly against the war. Only days before the first returning POWs arrived at Clark Air Base, the sister of Lieutenant Commander Everett Alvarez, the longest-held prisoner in North Vietnam, predicted that her brother would "face a shock" when he learned that his family had embraced antiwar activism during his absence. According to Delia Alvarez, her family's political reorientation was part of a larger societal transformation that would surely come as an unwelcome surprise to her brother, whose fighter plane had been shot down almost a decade earlier. Her family's new views reflected the shift from an unquestioning faith in the government to profound cynicism.[60] And in the months and years after repatriation, as it became clear that many POW marriages would not survive, returnees cited women's antiwar activism as a primary reason for the disproportionately high rates of divorce among former POWs.[61] The political breach, according to one psychological study conducted after Operation Homecoming, "appeared to be one of the most difficult to heal."[62] John McCain explained in an interview in December 1973: "In cases I know of personally, while a man was being tortured for refusing to make a propaganda statement, his wife had gone along with the antiwar movement back home, because she thought it was in her husband's interests. But this created a wound that in many cases could not be healed."[63] There are two aspects of McCain's statement that are particularly revealing, in part because they are contradictory: first, his implicit rejection of the possibility that the POW wife might have allied herself with the antiwar movement for political and moral reasons (as opposed to personal and pragmatic ones), and second, the disturbing parallel that McCain draws between torture within the prison camp and women's defiance at home.

The continuity between prison torture abroad and feminine betrayal at home was critical to the construction of the POW as a victim, and nowhere was this more apparent than in discussions of divorce. Even before repatriation it was clear that several POW marriages would not survive the ordeal. Despite the image of the loyal wife mobilized throughout the go-public campaign, the reality was more complicated. Several men had been married for only a few months or even weeks at the time of their capture, and as the years passed, some wives, not surprisingly, fell out of love with their absent husbands and pursued relationships with other men. The longevity of the war was particularly hard on the wives of those men who were missing in action—women who literally had no idea whether their husbands were dead or alive. Although the League presented a united front to the public, the organization was internally divided when it came to the question of official status changes for these missing men. In several cases, an MIA wife, convinced that her husband was dead, wanted the military to change his status to KIA (killed in action), so that she could remarry and move on with her life. But the parents of the same man, committed to the possibility, however remote, that their son might still be alive, insisted that his status as an MIA remain unchanged until the military acquired irrefutable evidence of his death.[64] Cases like these did not simply create divisions between the wives and parents of individual MIAs. They also implicitly advanced the notion that the MIA wife who asserted her autonomy by demanding a status change for her husband was conspiring with the American government in attempting to resolve the MIA issue as expediently as possible, a charge that would become more significant as the controversy surrounding MIAS assumed center stage in the years after repatriation.

But what emerged early on in the accounts of former POWs is the extent to which divorce, much like antiwar activism, could dramatically transform the POW wife from a loyal advocate into an enemy collaborator. Although some POWs only learned that their wives had divorced them upon their return to the United States, others had been told the news while still in captivity. In either case, POWs recalled, the revelation was often emotionally and physically devastating. One POW could not remember crying "through all the years of beatings and persecution" until repatriation, when he was informed at the military's processing center that his wife had left him, at which point he broke down.[65] For those who learned about the divorce while still in prison, the outcome could be even more dire. "When I received the news . . . that my wife had divorced me and remarried," wrote former POW Larry Chesley, "the emotional shock brought on some serious physical developments." For weeks after receiving the letter, Chesley later remembered, he felt as though he had "been kicked in the stomach."[66] If the North Vietnamese captor was assigned a unique capacity for psychological torture, then the POW wife was also assigned a singular power that could go in one of two opposing directions: she could either sustain her captured husband through her loyalty, or she could betray him, severely undermining his already diminished morale and, in the process, become an unwitting collaborator of the North Vietnamese.

The story of naval officer Everett Alvarez Jr. brought together these themes of psychological torture, divorce, and war opposition. Because Alvarez was the longest-held prisoner of war in North Vietnam (he was imprisoned from 1964 to 1973), he returned to the United States as one of the most highly visible and celebrated heroes of the conflict. But Alvarez was also distinguished by the family dramas surrounding antiwar activism and divorce that had played out during his absence. During the nine years of his captivity, his wife, Tangee, had divorced him and remarried, his parents' marriage had disintegrated, and his mother and sister had become activists in both the antiwar and United Farm Worker movements, the latter of which was centered in Salinas Valley, California, where Alvarez had grown up. Unlike those returnees who only received news about their families at the time of repatriation, Alvarez had learned about both his wife's divorce and his sister's opposition to the war while still in prison. As he later wrote in his memoirs, "My jailors had gleefully and immediately passed along the letter from my mother that informed me that my wife had left me, as well as the accounts of my sister Delia's prominent role in the peace movement."[67] According to one POW chronicler, the news of Tangee's divorce left Alvarez feeling that he was "back in torture," and Alvarez himself later recalled feeling "stranded and bewildered in a godforsaken land far from home" when he received the letter.[68] Like McCain, Alvarez perceived a link between prison torture and womanly betrayal, but even more striking is Alvarez's description of the jailors "gleefully" relaying the news to him. Here Alvarez echoed the contention, so central to the publicity campaign, that the North Vietnamese captor displayed a proclivity for psychological sadism. But while the campaign had proceeded from the premise that women at home were the innocent victims of this sadism, Alvarez's account suggested the opposite: it was women who, through either political betrayal or emotional desertion, provided captors with potent weapons for demoralizing and humiliating prisoners.

If divorce and antiwar activism were the two most visible ways that POW wives could defy their husbands, both actions spoke to a broader change that almost all returning men would have to confront in one form or another: their wives' growing claims to independence. Although POW wives had appealed to traditional ideals of marriage and motherhood throughout the go-public campaign, political mobilization turned out to be a deeply transformative experience for many women. News accounts of repatriation noted the irony, pointing out that many wives who had become active in the League on their husband's behalf were now unwilling to "return to the role of a docile homebody whose highest achievement is a casserole," "to change back into major's sweet wife," or to "revert to their passive 'yes, dear' roles."[69] Many POW wives described themselves in similar terms, as having undergone an irrevocable and ultimately positive change. One wife remarked that she had "become pretty aggressive" in her husband's absence and another stated simply, "I'm not a honey anymore."[70] Originally, the POW wife might have been compelled by war to assume more autonomy, but now that homecoming appeared imminent, she wondered how this newfound independence would be reconciled with her returning husband's reintegration into the family.

The role of the POW wife during the early years of the go-public campaign had been unambiguous: she was her husband's loyal champion and an innocent victim of North Vietnamese aggression. However, by the time of repatriation in 1973, some wives had become active in the antiwar movement, some had chosen to divorce their captured husbands without their consent, and some were making broader claims to independence in a world without their husbands. These transformations challenged the image of an imperiled family central to the earlier go-public campaign. If the POW wife was once identified exclusively as a victim, she was now also seen as an independent agent who had the power to inflict psychological harm on her husband. In an ironic twist, the POW wife was now located along the same axis as the North Vietnamese captor. When returning prisoners described the prison camp and the home front as contiguous, they were highlighting their status as victims of the war while also suggesting that certain expressions of female autonomy could thwart the fragile processes of homecoming and family reintegration, thus perpetuating their victim status after their return. This shifting position of the POW wife—from healer to traitor—reveals the extent to which the discourse surrounding POWs cannot only be analyzed in relation to the Vietnam War, but must also be viewed within the context of women's increased self-assertion with the rise of feminism. The return of the prisoners of war in early 1973 provided an opportunity for the public to reflect on two interrelated cultural transformations not normally associated with military conflict abroad but central to the politics of women's liberation: first, women's growing claims to public and private power, and second, the related perception of declining male authority within the white, middle-class family, the subject to which we now turn.

The Stranger in Charge: The Obsolescence of Male Authority in the POW Family

As we have seen, the go-public campaign brought together two apparently unrelated preoccupations: military defeat in Southeast Asia and fatherlessness within the family. By fusing these themes, go-public activists sought to implicate the North Vietnamese for transgressing the intimate, private world of the family. In the process, they hoped to shift the humanitarian burden of the war away from the United States and back to Hanoi. Underlying the publicity campaign was the premise that fatherlessness constituted a true domestic crisis that had thrust POW families into a state of peril. Revealing the hidden plight of fatherless families was at the heart of the campaign: from photo essays featuring pictures of children growing up without fathers to somber advertisements of POW wives pleading for information from Hanoi, from news editorials decrying the suffering of women to congressmen attacking the North Vietnamese on the grounds that many young children could not even remember what their fathers looked like. These strategies were all intended to offer the American public a glimpse into what was widely taken to be a nightmarish scenario: a presumably stable, loving family needlessly deprived of vital information about a husband, a father, or a son.

As repatriation approached, however, the earlier image of father absence was revised in complex ways. To be sure, there was still a great deal of discussion about the damaging psychological effects of father absence on the POW family. But by homecoming in 1973, many POW wives had functioned as heads of their family for years, and some predicted that their husband's return would prove more traumatic than his disappearance. For their part, many returning POWs expressed surprise and even anger at how well their families had coped in their absence, and they feared that they were returning as outsiders or intruders. The publicity campaign had mobilized arresting images of fatherlessness to garner public sympathy for POW families, but with repatriation, father absence was approached from a very different direction. Now, in a move that reflected the deep connection between the military and psychology, military psychologists recognized that they had a unique opportunity to assess the impact of incarceration on military men and their families. They poured money and resources into the study of POW family reintegration in the hope of gaining deeper insight into a condition that had implications far beyond the 587 military families under investigation: the psychic world of the modern family in the absence of male authority.[71]

This psychological appraisal took place at a moment when the theme of declining male authority within the family was being addressed from a number of different directions. The women's liberation movement identified the nuclear family as a locus of patriarchal power. Frequent statistical reports showed rising divorce rates and a dramatic increase in single-parent families. Governmental studies like the Moynihan Report attributed expanding welfare rolls to the proliferation of female-headed households. And, as we will see in chapter 5, American scholars influenced by Frankfurt School critical theory contended that paternal authority within the modern family had essentially collapsed, with devastating cultural results.[72] The close, in-depth study of POW families provided a unique opportunity to probe themes addressed in these wider debates: the impact of father absence on children's emotional development, the psychosexual dynamics between mothers and children that played out when men disappeared, and, perhaps most significantly, the question of whether male authority could be effectively reinstated after so many years of absence. As one Operation Homecoming study predicted, successful reunion would hinge "on realigning power and authority within the family in light of the husband's return."[73]

Although the study of the POW family reflected these broader debates, it was also exceptional in its focus on the emotional and psychological repercussions of reentry. Much of the discussion of declining paternal authority had revolved around the husband's role as economic provider. Historically, the most overtly debilitating impact of male absenteeism on the family had been economic because the death of or desertion by a family's (typically male) primary wage earner could propel it into a downward spiral toward poverty. The case of the POW family was different, however, because military policy dictated that the POW wife continue to receive at least a significant portion of her husband's salary during the duration of his captivity. For this reason, within psychological studies of the POW family, the economic effects of male absenteeism largely (although not entirely) receded and the psychic fallout of fatherlessness came into fuller view.

Ultimately, though, the study of the POW family starkly linked family reintegration to national recovery in the wake of the war. Debates about waning male authority were intimately tied to anxieties about national decline, and discussions of POW family reintegration clearly reveal this connection. The images of family reunion endlessly reproduced in February 1973 desperately fused the seamless reintegration of the POW family to the project of national reconciliation in the aftermath of one of the most contentious wars in American history. But these images notwithstanding, the question of whether or not family reintegration could be achieved remained open. Questions about the future of the POW family begged the larger question of whether or not the nation would ever truly recover from the trauma of the war.

Conducted both during and after repatriation, the military's psychological studies of POW families simultaneously reflected and complicated many of the central motifs of the earlier publicity campaign. On the one hand, military psychologists found much evidence that male absenteeism had indeed wrought considerable havoc on family members left behind, particularly on young boys. On the other hand, this havoc did not mean that the return of the father would be an uncomplicated or even happy affair. On the contrary, because the family had been compelled to make a range of psychological adjustments during the war, it was not at all clear that these adjustments would be undone or reversed in the wake of homecoming. Wives had gone from positions of dependency to independence, and once young, deferential children had grown into full-blown, often rebellious, adolescents.

What is so striking about the psychological appraisals of POW families both during and after repatriation, particularly in contrast to the earlier publicity campaign, is their repeated concern that paternal authority within these families had somehow become superfluous. One clinician speculated in 1974 that after years of captivity, former POWs were now experiencing the amorphous problem of "role panic," and this speculation seemed to be borne out in descriptions of the returnee. He was a "stranger-father," an "interloper," a "familiar stranger," an "intruder," and, in one formulation, "the stranger in charge."[74] According to one returnee's wife, her husband's renewed presence within the home after many years was not a cause for celebration but rather a violation. In her words, it was "as if an outsider had come in and begun ordering them about."[75] For their part, returning POWs reported feeling that they were now extraneous within their own families, and, according to one study, many POWs were stunned "to see their family getting along so well without them."[76] As one wife described it, "He seems to resent the fact that I was self-sufficient, that I was able to cope with everything, while there he sat in his unchanging world."[77] If the go-public campaign had constructed fatherlessness as a family crisis, psychological accounts of reintegration offered a different spin: fatherlessness was indeed a crisis, but not because families had fallen apart. On the contrary, it was because they had stayed together and managed, at least on the surface, to function so well.

This is not to say that father absence did not exact a heavy emotional toll on POW families. POW wives frequently expressed concern that their children were growing up without male authority figures, and several studies found that particularly for young boys the psychological consequences of this absence could be devastating.[78] According to one study, children of POWs and MIAs suffered from a range of anxiety symptoms, including frequent crying, nightmares, rebelliousness, shyness, and nail biting.[79] A twelve-year-old son of an MIA described a haunting dream that had persisted for years: "I dreamed my father returned but he was in two parts, one half was alive and the other half was dead."[80] In one 1973 *Newsweek* story, a POW wife described her seven-year-old son's difficulties conjuring up any image of his father, who had been captured six years before. When asked to draw a picture of his father coming home (an event that was in fact two weeks away), the boy had left the page completely blank. The child had expressed a deep desire for his father's return but had absolutely no sense of what such a return might look like.[81]

Emotional problems among POW and MIA children were reportedly exacerbated by domestic divisions engendered by the war. The fatherless military family suffered from a double stigma, explained one 1975 study. According to three specialists affiliated with the military's Center for Prisoner of War Studies, the POW family was treated "as a social deviant in the military system and an enigma to a civilian community struggling to reconcile the appropriateness of the military conflict that left this family fatherless."[82] Interviews with children found that they "suffered a painful inferiority to children with intact families . . . feelings [that were] apparently fostered by the public's questionable attitude towards the war," and one fourteen-year-old daughter of an MIA told the story of a close friend who, in a moment of anger, had proclaimed that her father had deserved his fate.[83] Here again, political opposition to the war emerged as a force that could inflict psychological harm on the military family, this time on its most innocent members: its children. Simultaneously, the plight of these children pointed to a larger social and psychological phenomenon: the experience of children growing up in families that were viewed by society as somehow deviant, incomplete, fractured, or inferior.

Descriptions of children's anxiety symptoms and social stigmatization were certainly troubling. But even more disturbing were revelations about the pathological psychosexual dynamics between mothers and children (and sons in particular) that played out in the absence of the father. According to a number of studies, many POW wives, desperate and alone, had grown excessively dependent on their children's love and as a result had resorted to blatant forms of emotional exploitation and manipulation in order to control them. Such manipulations, in turn, derailed children's healthy individuation. POW wives reported using somatic symptoms and emotional outbursts to exert control over their children's behavior, and some even admitted to exhibiting physical symptoms as "weapons to prevent their sons from dating seriously." When asked to account for their behavior, they explained that such manipulations allowed them to get their way with their children without ever having to explicitly assert parental authority.[84]

These descriptions of covert maternal selfishness and exploitation were not unique to the POW family. Indeed, the smothering and manipulative mother who thwarted her child's development had emerged decades earlier as a staple of postwar psychoanalytic theory and social criticism, and, as we will see in chapter 5, this mother would reappear in debates about cultural narcissism that played out toward the end of the decade.[85] But what was remarkable about the POW family was that it made literal a more pervasive metaphorical state: a condition of fatherlessness in which mothers wielded more psychological authority within the emotive world of the family as fathers receded further from view. POW families were distinguished by the fact that they had to deal with the *physical* disappearance of a husband and father, but as a psychic condition, fatherlessness was becoming endemic.

Because mothers had treated their sons as surrogates for their missing husbands, some young men reported feeling threatened and displaced by their returning fathers. As one study explained, because "many sons (especially the oldest sons) were repeatedly reminded that they were the 'man of the house now and must take care of mother,'" it was understandable "that many viewed their stranger-fathers as interlopers upon their return."[86] One POW wife described the challenge in strikingly candid terms: "My son loves the feeling of being my No. 1 boyfriend, but when Spank comes home I'm going to say, 'Go find your own girl, Mike.' It won't be easy for any of us."[87] Again, these tales of out-of-control Oedipal romance were nothing new. Freud's theory of the Oedipus complex was the most well known of psychoanalytic concepts. But these descriptions were notable for the fact that they had become formulaic. As the centerpiece of the publicity campaign, the plight of the reintegrating POW family was depicted as dramatic and extraordinary. But as an object of inquiry, the POW family was valuable precisely because it provided a window into pathologies and dynamics that were increasingly common.

Psychologists claimed that tensions between POW fathers and sons were compounded by the acrimony engendered by the war and the rise of the counterculture, a contention that revealed yet again the extent to which the domestic politics of the war was never far from view. Many sons had been young children when their fathers had left for Vietnam and were well into adolescence at the time of homecoming. POWs expressed shock when they first saw photographs of their "long-haired," "shaggy" teenage sons, some of whom had publicly supported George McGovern's antiwar platform when he campaigned for the presidency in 1972.[88] Just as the POW wife's turn to antiwar activism had made for a gripping news story, so too did these portraits of POW families who, physically reunited, remained deeply divided when it came to the war itself. One apocryphal story told of a POW wife who had a barber on hand during the first few weeks of homecoming, just in case her returning husband decided that his son's long hair could not be tolerated.[89] Another story told of a navy flier who, after seeing his long-haired, marijuana-smoking son for the first time in six years, was said to have proclaimed: "The hippies have won!"[90] Such light-hearted anecdotes notwithstanding, more than one POW wife expressed real concern that attitudes about the war would divide fathers from children. Sybil Stockdale later commended her eldest son for having walked "a fine line between the influences of his antiwar peer group and loyalty to his military father," and in the early months of 1973, according to the *New York Times*, "more than one POW wife dreaded the moment when . . . her children tell their father that they feel the war was a big waste."[91] Memoirs later penned by POWs suggest that on the whole returnees eventually accepted their family members' antiwar sentiments with aplomb, tolerance, and even compassion (many respectfully "agreed to disagree" with those family members who had opposed the war). But in the early months of 1973, these antiwar sentiments were seen as divisive to the POW family, hurtful to the returnee, and damaging to the fragile process of national and familial reintegration. As Everett Alvarez later recalled in his memoir, he had returned to America after almost a decade "to find the bleeding wounds of divisiveness in my country and in my own family."[92]

For their part, many POW wives worried that returning husbands would see their sons' long hair and antiwar sympathies as evidence of their own failures as disciplinarians during the war, a worry that was part of the larger question of whether returnees would support the choices that women had made in their absence. Psychologists described the typical POW wife as approaching homecoming not only with relief and excitement but also with guilt, trepidation, and resentment. As several studies pointed out, wives had gone from positions of complete dependence to having sole power over family decisions. They had learned how to manage the family income through buying and selling houses and cars, financial transactions that were entirely new to many of them. Some had taken jobs or pursued professional degrees. They had weathered family emergencies and had made crucial judgment calls about their children's health and education. Some had gone through dramatic changes in appearance and lifestyle. Many had become politically engaged for the first time in their lives and had been compelled to draw their own conclusions about the war. Thus, on the eve of homecoming, psychologists described these women in ways that diverged significantly from the stream of photographs and film footage of jubilant family reunions. According to them, the wives of returning men were deeply ambivalent about their husband's return, subsequently guilty for harboring negative feelings about what was supposed to be a joyous event, and "beset with apprehensions" as to whether these men would approve of the jobs they had done as the temporary heads of their families.[93]

On the other hand, some POW wives appeared more than happy to relinquish their provisional authority within the family. Certain accounts of reintegration were consistent with the celebratory, upbeat tone of Operation Homecoming and its rendition of painless marital reunion. Almost a year after repatriation, one former POW explained that readjustment had in fact been easy because he had a "staunch and loyal wife," and according to the memoir of former POW Richard Stratton, his wife, Alice, had told him that she was prepared to "turn command" of the family over to him as soon as he was ready.[94] As one POW wife explained to readers of *Time* one week before homecoming, "I'm ready to turn it over. The boss is coming home. I don't like having to make all the decisions."[95] When an activist in the League learned that her husband was finally returning, she even concocted a makeshift ritual to mark her abandonment of what she self-deprecatingly dismissed as her "amateur efforts" to secure his release. With the help of her sons, she gathered together her political papers and burned them in a bonfire in her backyard, a celebration of what she called "the end of Mom's public life."[96] On the surface, these recollections suggest that some women, understandably relieved that they would no longer be the lone decisionmakers within their families, were pleased as homecoming approached. But, more revealingly, the language of "turning command" back over to a "boss," coupled with the potent image of a woman destroying all evidence of her own political activism, suggests that these wives saw the distribution of power within their families as a zero-sum game. They anticipated (and apparently accepted) that the return of their husbands would require relinquishing their own newly acquired power.

On the opposite end of the spectrum were those marriages that did not survive repatriation. As we have seen, some POW marriages had fallen apart before prisoners of war were released, and this trend only accelerated after Operation Homecoming. A number of the marriages joyously showcased on television and in newspapers in February and March of 1973 would be over within the year. One POW wife remembered a poignant detail of a Nixon White House dinner honoring the POWs in May of 1973 that illustrated the high marriage casualty rate: men were afraid to greet a fellow

POW's companion for the evening by his wife's name, because so many marriages had collapsed within a few months.[97] Indeed, during the first twelve months after repatriation, a full 30 percent of POW marriages dissolved, a figure that, while consistent with overall divorce rates within the civilian population, was disproportionately high for ranking military officers.[98] Although military psychologists attributed this epidemic of divorce to a range of factors, they cited the reluctance of wives to give up their independence after their husbands' returns as a primary cause. The problem was not that independence had led women to reject their returning husbands outright, but rather that they now saw marriage as a more flexible and fluid institution. "Marriages were now seen by some wives as renegotiable," explained one naval study, "with demands that consideration and recognition be given to their independence, acquired abilities, and new skills." Drawing on research from World War II that indicated that women who had managed particularly well during separation were more likely to have rocky reunions with their returning soldier-husbands, the study predicted that a number of POW marriages would be terminated in light of wives' new claims to independence.[99] What is significant about these accounts is just how much the success or failure of family reintegration hinged on the woman's relationship to her own expanded autonomy. Would she relinquish her power so that the family could return to its prewar structure, or would she insist that her marriage be redefined on entirely new terms? For military psychologists, as well as for many returning POWs, this appeared to be the crux of the matter.

One POW wife addressed this question in her diary, excerpted and reprinted in *McCall's* magazine in February 1974. The wife of Michael Christian, a naval lieutenant, and the mother of three young daughters, Charlotte Christian first learned that her husband was captured in April 1967, when his plane was shot down during a bombing mission over North Vietnam. Over the next six years, Charlotte had become active in the League and had eventually voted for George McGovern, believing that the Nixon administration cared more about protecting the Thieu government than securing her husband's release. The diary excerpts published in *McCall's* were intended to shed light on Charlotte's efforts to "reconstruct her marriage" in the first six months after repatriation.

Charlotte's diary tells a story of initial joy, mounting frustration, and eventual resolution. It recounts her excitement at hearing her husband's voice on the phone after six years and at their first dinner alone. She recalls her children sharing scrapbooks, picture albums, and records with their father as they tried to bring him up to speed on their young lives. But within two weeks, according to her diary, Charlotte had become frustrated: Mike was deeply upset with her for having voted for McGovern, and they had "bitter arguments" about the war. Mike wanted to immediately buy a house but Charlotte wanted to wait. Charlotte felt that she was "competing with [her] three daughters for Mike's affection," and she was stung by Mike's criticisms of her childrearing. By the end of March, she wrote that she was "on the verge of tears all the time" and "ready to can the whole thing."

The moment that Charlotte cited as the "turning point" in their marriage was telling. Mike found a house he loved, and although Charlotte believed that they could not actually afford the new home, she decided to comply with his wishes and let him be the one to worry about meeting the mortgage. "I think that more than anything this made me realize that I was no longer the head of the family," she wrote of the decision. "It was a role I wanted to give up, but for reasons I still can't explain I fought to hold on to it. Once I let go of the reins I became more relaxed." By August, according to Charlotte, "the dazed look" had left Mike's eyes, he had "taken over" the checkbook, and he had even given their youngest daughter a spanking for "talking smart." It had taken six months, but they had eventually resumed life as, in her words, "a normal American family."[100]

What can we really learn from Charlotte Christian's account? Despite the tone of intimacy and self-disclosure, it is impossible to imagine all of the fragile renegotiations and painful confrontations that must have taken place. And it is certainly easy to poke fun at Charlotte's formulaic and clichéd reinscription of traditional gender arrangements, as she "handed over the reins" to her husband and he reasserted himself as both money-manager and disciplinarian. But her story and others—crafted, compiled, and circulated by psychologists, journalists, POWs, and their relatives—are significant not for what they actually tell us about the complex inner workings of these families, but rather because of their preoccupation with the crisis of male absenteeism. These stories return over and over again to the same questions: What were the psychological implications of fatherlessness on children? How would women's heightened responsibilities and tasks be reconciled with the reintegration of returning men? Could male authority be effectively reinstated within these families, and, if so, what form might reinstatement take? These questions were never answered definitively, but they reflected a wider cultural preoccupation with the multiple meanings of fatherlessness in a time of war—and as we will see, in peacetime. In the case of POW families, paternal absence emerged as a crisis in two senses that were in some ways paradoxical. At one level, the family of the prisoner of war was seen as the embodiment of a more pervasive psychological and cultural problem, that of declining paternal authority within the domestic sphere. But at the same time, the returning POW's status—however contested—as a "war hero" meant that his successful reintegration into the family would signify reconciliation after a bitter and highly contested war. The returnee's ability to effectively "take the reins" would prove that after years of disruption order was finally being restored both domestically and nationally.

The Rip Van Winkle Effect:
Gender Subversion at Home and Abroad

The lingering question about whether returning men could be reincorporated into the intimate sphere of the family was mirrored by a related question: had the politics of feminism and sexual liberation unleashed an unacceptable level of gender and sexual confusion within the United States? As we have seen, the women's liberation movement was never far from view as military psychologists studied the POW family and contemplated its future in an age of women's growing claims to autonomy. But the connections between the plight of the POW and the politics of feminism were elaborated further within discussions of the returnee's reentry. On the eve of homecoming, the military and mainstream press portrayed the returning prisoners as modern-day "Rip Van Winkles" who would be shocked and disoriented when they first encountered signs of gender upheaval, such as boys with long hair and women in "unisex" pants. Here, the POW was assigned yet another crucial role—that of a barometer of cultural and social change vis-à-vis gender and sexual politics. Because some POWs had been imprisoned for almost a decade, returnees could presumably offer a unique perspective on transformations in American society and culture. But more important, predictions of rocky reentry and culture shock suggested that the returning POW now ran the risk of being victimized yet again by the women's liberation movement itself. The implication was that feminism and sexual liberation were violent social forces that—not unlike Hanoi's purported silence about American prisoners—had somehow eroded the distinction between wartime and peacetime, home front and prison camp.

This fear was fueled by portraits of the POW prison camp as a locus of sexual perversion and gender inversion, specifically among the Vietnamese. Running throughout POW testimonials and memoirs were accounts of interrogators who masturbated during questioning, guards who were "limp-wristed and girlish," Vietnamese men who were sickly and emasculated, and Vietnamese women who were overly masculine and "more likely to do the real work."[101] According to one air force lieutenant who provided testimony immediately after homecoming, there were "lots of queers" in Vietnamese society and, in a claim that resonated with stereotypes of Asian sadism, "[m]any of these people enjoyed their job and did it more thoroughly than necessary."[102] Indeed, it is striking just how often returning POWs equated captivity with homosexuality. Writing years later, James Stockdale remembered the first thing he saw after his plane had been shot down in North Vietnam and he regained consciousness: two Vietnamese men at his feet holding hands. "What are they, queers?" he asked himself, literally inaugurating his experience of captivity.[103]

It is tempting to analyze these bald characterizations of the North Vietnamese in terms of what could be called "homosexual panic," that is, to see them as deflections of POWs' own anxieties about the specters of homosexuality and emasculation while in captivity. There is certainly validity to this interpretation, particularly in light of scattered reports of homosexuality among captured men that surfaced in the wake of homecoming.[104] But even as POWs distanced themselves from the sexual deviance that they ascribed to their Vietnamese captors, they spoke with remarkable candor about the prison camp as a rare space of male intimacy, a closeness that was key to their survival and was unlike anything they had experienced before. Toward the end of the war, one POW computed the number of hours he had spent with his cellmate and found that each of them had spent more time with each other than either had spent with their respective wives.[105] Recalling his relationship with Bob Craner, a captured air force major who was in an adjacent cell in the Hanoi Hilton, John McCain wrote: "For two years, I was closer to him than I had ever been to another human being." Craner, speaking only a few months after release, reflected that, although he and McCain had been separated by eighteen inches of brick, they "got to know each other more intimately, I'm sure, than I will ever know my wife."[106] What emerges here are two contrasting versions of the largely male homosocial world of the prison camp divided along axes of race and nation: one of Vietnamese perversion, deviance, and sadism, and another of American endurance, mutual sustenance, and martial virtue. Depending on whether they were describing their captors or themselves, returnees described the male-dominated world of the camp as a space of sexual pathology and degeneracy or, alternatively, as a space of redemptive intimacy among men.

Presumably, both aspects of this prison world would be left behind with repatriation. As the ubiquitous images of family reunion suggested, homecoming was meant to mark the prisoner's successful reentry not simply into the family unit, but also into the normative heterosocial world of men and women, boys and girls. But just as the process of family reintegration was fragile and tentative, so too was the prisoner's reentry into a society newly transformed by women's liberation and the sexual revolution, transformations that implied a certain continuity between gender deviance abroad and gender defiance at home. Even before they had left prison, older POWs were reportedly being briefed by new arrivals about what they could expect to encounter upon their return to the United States: "long-haired boys, mini-skirted women, X-rated movies, Detroit's newest automotive wonders, pro-football's superbowl, and the moon landing."[107] Although the military had provided the returnee with reference materials meant to bring him up to speed on his years in captivity (including summaries of the news, dictionaries of recent slang, and film footage of sports), nothing could adequately prepare him for the culture shock he would inevitably experience.[108] Commentators predicted that the returnee would be bombarded with disturbing images that he had never witnessed before, including girls in long pants, women's liberation banners, Andy Warhol films, an explosion of pornography, and a burgeoning drug culture. Many accounts pinpointed fashion as the most visible manifestation of gender subversion, noting that returnees would encounter for the first time unisex clothes on women and "men in high heels." As one playful profile of the "new Rip Van Winkle" in *Time* depicted it, the returnee who peered into the window of a "unisex shop" would have to "[hold] fast to the corner of a building to maintain his balance."[109] The fictionalized portrait was one in which the fragile returnee was reentering a world in which gender norms had been subverted in ways that were strangely akin to the Vietnamese prison camp.

These graphic accounts of culture shock were predicated on the psychological claim that the returnee was at risk of sensory overload after years in confinement. As one military study put it, "The liberated POW cannot readily tolerate . . . the sensory input of a normal environment, with its rapid pace, confusion, and demands for decision making."[110] According to Charles Stenger, the planning coordinator of the Veteran Administration POW program, the typical risks of culture shock were exacerbated by the fact that the POW had internalized the innate passivity of his Asian captors.

Drawing on stereotypes of Asian obsequiousness and servility, Stenger explained that "the P.O.W. has become partly acclimated to Vietnamese culture, which is much more inner, self-oriented, and passive than ours."[111] In other words, the problem was not simply that American culture had been transformed during the war, but rather that the POW himself had absorbed an essential "Asianness" that threatened to derail his successful reentry. As this chapter has shown, much of the POW discourse appealed to racial difference, but here the implication was that certain racial attributes—such as passivity—were fluid, transferable, and infectious. Stenger's account of the POW's psychological recovery advanced the notion that the POW had somehow "gone native," and that this transmutation would have to be reversed in order for him to reenter American society with his masculinity intact.

In his 1976 memoir, former POW Jeremiah Denton remembered homecoming as a time of disillusionment as well as joy. "In the first weeks," he wrote, "unhappily, I began to note some dark corners in America. I saw the evidence of the new permissiveness, group sex, massage parlors, X-rated movies, the drug culture, that represented to me an alien element."[112] For Denton, homecoming did not signal a swift return to safety, but rather had taken him from one "dark" environment to another. What Denton called "the new permissiveness" blurred the distinction between the alien and the familiar and the foreign and the domestic. Like so many accounts of homecoming, Denton's memoir suggested that POWs had not simply returned to the intimate and safe comforts of home but had simultaneously reentered a world fractured by the disorienting and divisive politics of feminism and sexual revolution. If POW repatriation was meant to somehow redeem the Vietnam War and feminism was seen as a social force that threatened to derail the process of redemption, then feminism emerged as an obstacle not just to reentry, but to the larger project of national recovery.

While historians of the war have recognized Operation Homecoming as a carefully crafted effort on the part of the military and the Nixon administration to endow an unpopular war with heroism, they have said little about the centrality of gender to such an attempt.[113] And while historians of feminism have traced the relationship between the Vietnam War and women's liberation, they have tended to focus on one aspect of this relationship: the ways in which their marginalization in the antiwar movement compelled women to begin organizing on their own behalf.[114] But the story of the repatriation of the POWs in 1973 suggests that the connections between the Vietnam War and feminism in fact went deeper. Above all, Operation Homecoming represented a desperate attempt to remake the Vietnam War into something both instantly familiar and ultimately recuperable—to create a version of the war that had connotations of heroism, sacrifice, and bravery rather than of decline, upheaval, and transgression. As this chapter has argued, this attempt to craft a redemptive war narrative was premised largely on a normative ideal of middle-class family life, one made up of loyal wives and deferential children, and one in which paternal authority was essential, vital, and easily reconstituted. But over and over again, women's liberation was cast as a threat to repatriation: through calling into question the assumption that women would remain loyal, both personally and politically, to returning men; through critiquing the role of paternal authority within the family at the moment this authority seemed precarious and unstable; through dramatizing just how much had changed in American society and culture during the war; and through the creation of new norms of gender and sexuality that resonated with POWs' accounts of gender subversion in the prison camps. In the immediate wake of military defeat abroad, feminism was constructed as a subversive force that imperiled the returnee by remaking the home front itself into a realm of war.

The State as the New Enemy:
MIAs after Homecoming

Operation Homecoming did not bring an end to the controversy surrounding POWs and MIAs. On the contrary, the controversy not only intensified in the years after 1973 but changed direction in important ways, as bereaved family members gradually came to blame the U.S. government, no less than Hanoi, for their continuing pain and suffering.[115] The earlier go-public campaign had identified North Vietnamese Communism as the clear, unambiguous enemy of the POW/MIA family. After 1973, however, the League turned its attention to the unresolved question of MIAs, those men who remained missing in action in Southeast Asia.[116] Increasingly frustrated by the lack of information about these men and angered by what they perceived as governmental indifference to their plight, the League shifted the blame from Vietnam to the U.S. government. In an ironic twist, MIA relatives accused the State and Defense Departments of many of the same traits earlier accorded the North Vietnamese: coldness, indifference, heartlessness, and deception. One MIA wife expressed her own transferring of blame in December of 1974: "It is an awful thing to say, but I have come to the point where I feel my own Government is my enemy almost as much as the North Vietnamese Communists in Hanoi."[117]

A thorough examination of the ongoing MIA controversy is beyond the scope of this chapter, although, as historian H. Bruce Franklin has shown, it constitutes a defining theme in the history of the Vietnam War's cultural legacy.[118] But even a cursory look at the evolution of this controversy after 1973 illuminates yet again the centrality of the family to debates about the Vietnam War. Coinciding, as we shall see, with the global structural trans-formations of post-Keynesianism, post-Fordism, and the breakup of the New Deal coalition, the MIA controversy fueled a growing perception that an overly bureaucratic and ineffectual state had become the enemy of the sanctified, intact, male-headed household. By the mid-1970s, the charge that the state had abandoned the MIAs for the sake of political expediency not only was shaping Vietnam War discourse but was contributing to the widening sentiment that the federal government was hurting rather than helping American families.

In certain respects, this placing of blame on the U.S. government after 1973 was not surprising. The relationship between the relatives of POWs and MIAs and the government had always been characterized by antagonism and distrust. After all, family members had initially formed the League in order to compel the government to revise a policy of "quiet diplomacy" that they saw as both callous and ineffective. The wives, mothers, and fathers of POWs and MIAs became politically mobilized not only because they wanted to condemn Hanoi but also because they feared that, without public pressure, the American government might abandon its fighting men in Vietnam. Indeed, the rhetoric of abandonment—usually assumed to have come much later—was already in use by the late 1960s, long before the war was even over. During the go-public campaign, the interests of the Nixon administration and the League did momentarily converge, but this alliance was always tentative and fragile. Throughout the entire campaign, the administration sought to control and monitor the actions of the League, and family members never stopped expressing skepticism about whether the administration was doing everything it could to bring their men home.

However, this skepticism and antagonism became more acute after re-patriation. The Nixon administration contended that all living American prisoners had come home during Operation Homecoming, but some family members refused to accept this claim and insisted that the League had to keep fighting to obtain a "full accounting" of missing men. This was the crux of the matter: the State and Defense Departments firmly believed that there were no living American soldiers remaining in Southeast Asia, while some relatives of MIAs would not accept this conclusion in the absence of definitive proof.[119] This post-homecoming breach between the League and the administration only widened after Gerald Ford assumed the presidency in August 1974, largely as a result of two steps taken by the new administration. First, Ford announced in September a plan to grant amnesty to men who had dodged the draft during the war. Second and even more significant, he proposed that after a twelve-month waiting period the Defense Department could automatically change the status of missing men from MIA to PFOD, the acronym for "presumed-finding-of-death."

The League reacted to both of these proposals with anger, shock, and disillusionment. According to press releases issued before and after the announcement of Ford's amnesty plan, League members were "bewildered and disillusioned with the commander-in-chief," who in their estimation prioritized the amnesty of "draft dodgers and deserters" over the plight of the MIAs, those heroes and patriots who had selflessly fought for their country. "The 1,300 unaccounted-for men have earned their reentry," a press release explained, "whether they arrive alive and walking or in a casket. Mr. President, please get your priorities in order."[120] For many, the granting of amnesty before a full accounting of MIAs constituted a profound betrayal. As Gladys Brooks, the mother of an MIA and the state coordinator of the League's New York chapter, asked Deputy National Security Advisor Brent Scowcroft in a 1975 letter, "With amnesty taking priority over our young men who were willing to lay down their lives to ensure freedom for strangers in a far away land, what lesson will our young people learn from this injustice?" Convinced that President Ford had washed his hands of the MIA issue in order to declare the war over once and for all, Brooks ended the letter by describing the erosion of her own faith in the government: "I firmly believed that my government would not, could not turn its back on our sons, I am deeply shaken! Such a betrayal!" She signed the letter "Another duped mother."[121]

As enraged as some family members were by the amnesty plan, a far more serious rift between the administration and the League hinged on the proposed change in reclassification procedures within the Defense Department. According to a modified set of guidelines, the army, navy, and air force would have a new option for changing the official status of a missing soldier. If after one year, the military had obtained no new information about an MIA, his status could automatically be changed to either "presumed-finding-of-death" or "killed-in-action, body not recovered." The proposed change was premised on the conclusion that there were no living American soldiers in Southeast Asia, and that even the recovery of soldiers' bodies would be extraordinarily difficult. The chaotic nature of the military conflict, the dense jungle terrain, the duration of time that had lapsed, and the fact that many MIAs had been shot down over water all combined to make the recovery of bodies nearly impossible. Much to the dismay and disgust of some League families, the House Subcommittee on Missing Persons in Southeast Asia (a committee that the League had actually fought to create) came to the same conclusion in December 1976, finding that "no Americans [were] still being held alive as prisoners in Indochina" and urging the armed services to initiate reclassification efforts as soon as possible.[122]

More than anything else, this attempt to modify procedures for status changes and accelerate the reclassification process convinced some—although not all—MIA relatives that the administration had written off the soldiers for the sake of political expediency, in an effort to turn public attention from what had turned out to be an unpopular and ultimately unwinnable war. The option of "forgetting" about the war was simply unavailable to them, MIA relatives told President Ford over and over again in letters during these years.[123] Although their accusations against the government varied, relatives agreed that the powers-that-be had heartlessly turned their backs on the MIA and, in the process, were guilty of Hanoi's earlier crime: leaving the MIA family in a cruel and needless state of suspension.[124] As a lawyer for the families explained it, their growing distrust stemmed from the harsh realization that "those who used and merchandised us and then lied to us now are seeking to abandon us and our MIAs."[125] This portrayal of the government as cold, indifferent, and abandoning was captured by one father's account of an MIA family march held in front of the White House on 11 November 1974. Marchers had brought thirteen hundred red carnations, one for every missing man. "As [the father of an MIA] read the first name," the man recalled, "a wife or mother dropped the carnation over the cold iron fence onto the White House lawn." A simultaneous display of womanly devotion and a critique of the callous indifference of the administration, the ritual was "the saddest sight" he had ever seen.[126]

Throughout, the images of endangered family life that had been so pervasive during the earlier publicity campaign were still in play: captured men without families, innocent children without fathers, loyal wives without husbands, and bereaved parents without sons. But while the earlier publicity campaign had mobilized these images in order to condemn North Vietnamese Communism, the MIA campaign mobilized these images to indict the U.S. government. In the years after 1973, MIA relatives claimed that they had suffered not one, but two wrenching losses as a result of the war, one personal, the other political: the loss of a loved one and the loss of their faith in government. This second loss assumed centrality after 1973. One Texas congressman described the mood in a 1975 letter to the White House: "Everywhere I go, I find that the wives of men missing in action do not trust our government to do what it should have done to find out about those men."[127] Of course, there was a causal relationship between these two losses, in that the personal trauma set the stage for political disillusion-ment. But one could argue that, on a deeper level, the MIA controversy was only partly about the ultimate fate of the MIA himself. Its content also had to do with the collapse of faith in the national government and the strong need among military families to somehow have this faith restored. As the brother of one MIA reflected almost twenty years after homecoming: "I am involved in the cause not because I believe that my brother is alive, but be-cause I lost confidence in the men he fought with, and in the Government that he gave his life for."[128]

In the years after 1973, MIA activists not only voiced their disillusionment over and over again, but they repeatedly expressed discomfort with their unfamiliar role as antagonists of the state. Ann Griffith, the sister of an MIA and a prominent activist in the League, explained her feelings in a letter to Richard Lawson, military assistant to President Ford and a liaison between League families and the administration: "I can honestly say that never in my lifetime did I think I would see my parents picketing anywhere for any reason," she wrote; "yet they do—out of frustration and desperation." The administration needed to do whatever it could to obtain new information about MIAs, she continued. "But even above that, we urgently need to have our faith in our own government restored." Griffith concluded her letter on a note of personal disclosure: "I personally want to believe in people the way I have been raised to do, but General Lawson, the experiences in the past few years have been shattering to me. I feel terribly let down and dis-appointed."[129] Griffith's letter captured many sentiments expressed by MIA relatives during these years: the claim that their antagonistic stance toward the state felt unnatural and wrong, the sense that their shattered trust in the government had been almost as emotionally traumatic as the disappear-ance of their loved one, and the contention, expressed with remarkable candor by Griffith, that the acquisition of new information about MIAs was in fact secondary to the task of the government somehow convincing these families that they had not been abandoned after all.

In May 1975, a young boy from Colorado sent President Ford a letter: "Dear Mr. President, How have you been? I have been fine. Has the war in Vietnam stopped completely? I want to know because my dad is still M.I.A. I hope he comes home soon."[130] In a sense, the young boy answered his own question: the war had not "stopped completely" because he was still waiting for his missing father. His simple question strikes at the heart of MIA politics after 1973. Indeed, as MIA relatives painfully portrayed it in their letters to the Ford administration, the war was far from over for them. The rest of the country could move on, but they could not. They still remained Hanoi's victims of "mental torture," but now their victimization was being reenacted over and over again by adversarial forces within the nation: by a general public that was urgently trying to forget the war, by a libertine culture that favored draft dodgers, resisters, and deserters, and above all by a once-trusted government that had "written off" missing men and their families in the name of political expediency. This construction of the abandoned MIA family would leave its mark on the cultural representations of the war that began to emerge in the late 1970s.[131] But this construction also had serious, long-term foreign policy ramifications. At the very least, as diplomatic historian T. Christopher Jespersen has shown, the ongoing political mobilization of these families over the next twenty years contributed greatly to the derailment of joint efforts to normalize relations between the United States and Vietnam.[132]

The young boy's letter also captured how much the perceived crisis of fatherlessness within the family remained a constitutive feature of the MIA controversy. The crucial difference was that now the American government was to blame. "What can I tell my kids?" asked one MIA wife who was profiled on 60 Minutes in 1974. "You know, how can I instill a love of their country? . . . How can I say don't look at what's happened to your dad? Don't look at the fact that your country just doesn't . . . do anything?"[133] The earlier preoccupation remained, but it was now coupled with the emergence of the state as the new enemy. Both the continuities and the discontinuities from the earlier publicity campaign suggest that the MIA story performed not one but two distinct kinds of cultural work after Vietnam. On the one hand, MIA activists continued to use arresting images of fatherlessness to perpetuate the notion that America had been the Vietnam War's innocent victim rather than its knowing aggressor. On the other hand, the dramatic shift in blame after 1973 from an external enemy to an internal one contributed to a widening antigovernment sentiment that arose out of the politics of the war but extended beyond it. This sentiment proceeded from the premise that an obstructionist state was somehow exacerbating rather than ameliorating the decline of the American family. To be sure, this public sentiment was internally differentiated, riddled with contradictions, and directed at diverse sectors of the state. For example, the attacks on welfare that coincided with the unfolding of the POW/MIA controversy advanced the claim that a bloated and overly indulgent federal welfare program had attempted to do too *much* to aid needy families and in the process had bred dependency in its applicants. Obviously, this was a very different accusation from the one being leveled by MIA families: namely, that the State and Defense Departments had done too *little* to determine the fates of missing men and had failed them through neglect and inaction. But the consequences were the same: men without families, and families without men. The war had left in its wake a world without fathers.

2

Getting the House in Order

The Oil Embargo, Consumption, and the Limits of American Power

Realism, Restraint, and the October War

On 29 March 1973 President Nixon appeared on national television and announced that the Vietnam War was over. For the first time in twelve years, there were no American forces in Vietnam, and the POWs were on their way home. The time had come for Americans to "put aside those honest differences about war which divide us" and look ahead to national revitalization in an era of peace. The United States was a great nation built on extraordinary military might and economic power, he reminded the public, but its greatness was also rooted in a less tangible but more significant third element: national character. Now that the war had come to an end, Nixon warned, Americans could not be complacent. They would need to marshal their resources in order to avoid the fate that had befallen other great nations in the past. "The pages of history are strewn with the wreckage of nations which fell by the wayside at the height of their strength and wealth because their people became weak, soft, and self-indulgent, and lost the character and the spirit which had led to their greatness," he explained.[1] Less than seven months later, this warning would take on new meaning and the illusion of tranquility would be shattered when another crisis emerged, this one centered on a region that would become increasingly important in American foreign policy after Vietnam: the Middle East. The crisis was the oil embargo, declared on 18 October 1973 by the major Arab oil-producing nations in retaliation for American support of Israel during the October War. The embargo lasted throughout the winter of 1973–74 and was lifted on 18 March 1974.

The oil embargo came at a peculiar moment in the history of the Vietnam War. It began only nine months after the signing of the cease-fire agreement in Paris but eighteen months before Americans were to watch the dramatic scene on television news that confirmed that its military intervention had failed: the frantic and disorganized helicopter evacuation from the roof of the U.S. embassy in Saigon on 30 April 1975. This occurred the same day that Duong Van Minh, the president of South Vietnam, announced the unconditional surrender of the country to the Vietcong. Thus, at the time of the embargo, there was a certain ambiguity about whether the nation had in fact lost the war. For those who had mobilized against it, the failure of American intervention in the region had long been apparent, but the official story was different. As Nixon presented it in his speech in March 1973, the United States had succeeded in its aim of preventing the establishment of a Communist government by force in the South, and Vietnamization, the plan to provide support to the South Vietnamese government as American forces withdrew, was working. "The 17 million people of South Vietnam have the right to choose their own Government without outside interference," he explained. "And because of our program of Vietnamization, they have the strength to defend that right."[2] By 1973, the fact that the Vietnam War had been intractable, lengthy, divisive, and costly was beyond dispute. But its status as a "lost war" was still contested, and the oil embargo took place in the midst of this contestation.

Long before the evacuation of the American embassy in Saigon, however, government officials and policymakers recognized that the Vietnam experience raised crucial questions about the future of American foreign policy, not only in Southeast Asia but in other parts of the globe as well. Beginning in the early 1970s, a debate took shape within foreign policy circles that revolved around whether the United States should pursue its earlier policy of Cold War containment with the same vigor it had shown in the past or instead develop a more restrained approach to world affairs. This approach would affirm the superpower status of the United States while recognizing that the nation had military, economic, and political limitations that would need to be taken into account.[3] Of course, many on the Left had been calling for less American military intervention for decades on moral grounds, but this was a different argument, one that identified restraint with the national interest. By the time of the oil embargo in 1973, Nixon's foreign policy team, under the leadership of Henry Kissinger, was attempting to define and pursue just such a foreign policy, one that acknowledged the nation's unique position in the world while recognizing the new geopolitical reality revealed by the Vietnam War: the United States, like other nations, had limitations that could no longer be denied. Over the five-month embargo, the middle-class home emerged as one crucial site where the meanings of American restraint and limitations could be assessed.

By the autumn of 1973, Henry Kissinger had become one of the most influential figures in American foreign policy. A native of Germany who fled the Nazis and came to the United States in 1938, he was educated at Harvard University, where he later taught in the Department of Government and at the Center for International Affairs. In 1969, he left academia for the White House, serving first as President Nixon's national security advisor and later as his secretary of state, a post he assumed less than one month before the embargo began. During his early years in public office, Kissinger emerged as one of the most powerful and controversial members of Nixon's cabinet. Many of those who had opposed American military intervention in Vietnam considered him a war criminal, and in the years ahead he would be attacked from the right for his pursuit of détente. But in the early 1970s, Kissinger was attempting to develop a post-Vietnam foreign policy, one that would signal that the nation had reached a new state of maturity. He later recalled in his memoirs: "In the life of nations, as of human beings, a point is often reached when the seemingly limitless possibilities of youth suddenly narrow and one must come to grips with the fact that not every option is open any longer. This insight can inspire a new creative impetus, less innocent perhaps than the naïve exuberance of earlier years, but more complex and ultimately more permanent. The process of coming to grips with one's limits is never easy."[4]

For Kissinger, this movement toward national maturity required a renewed commitment to what he called realism, or "realpolitik," in the foreign policy realm. As a scholar, he had studied the history of balance-of-power politics, and one of his heroes was Klemens von Metternich, the Austrian statesman who had built a stable alliance system after the defeat of Napoleon. Metternich's genius, according to Kissinger, was that he had eschewed power politics, ideology, and moralism, crafting instead a diplomacy based on the rational pursuit of shared interests and a collective desire for stability. The Metternich system, Kissinger believed, offered the United States valuable lessons, not only about what had gone wrong in Vietnam but about how to chart a path toward the future.

One of the lessons was that moral pursuits and national interests needed to be carefully differentiated. For those who had mobilized against the war, Vietnam represented a moral nadir in the nation's history. But for Kissinger, Vietnam captured the opposite problem: a misguided commitment to morality on the part of the United States in world affairs. Because the war had not been rooted in the national interest, he explained, it had "set the country adrift on a sea of undifferentiated moralism."[5] A second lesson for Kissinger was that the nation had limitations; here, he and his adversaries were in agreement, however divided they were about the morality of Vietnam. As Kissinger later remembered, the war exposed a painful truth: "We were becoming like other nations in the need to recognize that our power, while vast, had limits. Our resources were no longer infinite in relation to our problems; instead we had to set priorities both intellectual and material."[6] For Kissinger, priority setting demanded a return to national interest as the overarching criterion in the crafting of foreign policy. This renewed emphasis on national interest would replace the pursuit of legal principles, moral claims, and ideological loyalties with concrete causes and objectives.[7] As Nixon explained in his 1970 annual report on foreign policy, "Our interests must shape our commitments, rather than the other way around."[8] The aim of this approach was to stake out a middle ground between isolation and overextension, and it proceeded from the premise that the United States could neither dominate nor reject the wider world; rather, it would have to "manage" it. Management would require, in Kissinger's view, a foreign policy purged of "all sentimentality."[9]

The new awareness of limits, together with a sharpened conception of interest, underwrote several significant foreign policy decisions made by the administration in the late 1960s and early 1970s. Both tendencies informed what came to be called the Nixon Doctrine, a plan first introduced in November of 1969. That doctrine extended the logic of Vietnamization to the rest of the Third World and stated that, in the future, American interests would be protected by regional proxies and allied forces rather than by direct U.S. military intervention, a move that seemed to ensure, in the words of historian Robert Collins, that "there would be no more Vietnams."[10] The new attention to national interest also guided the gradual normalization of relations with China, a move based not on affinity for the Beijing government but rather on a desire to create a triangular relationship between Russia, the United States, and China that would maximize the administration's leverage in its dealings with both countries. In addition, both considerations were key to the pursuit of détente, which Kissinger understood less in terms of friendship or a softening of tensions between the United States and the Soviet Union and more within the logic of realpolitik. Détente was a strategy for a "relationship between adversaries," he argued, that hopefully could provide a stabilizing framework in which both countries could pursue their own national interests.[11] Finally, the administration's awareness of limits was reflected most literally in the military budget, where defense spending was reduced by 32 percent between 1969 and 1975, the largest reduction in almost two decades.[12]

The October War, which triggered the oil embargo, represented a moment of crisis in which Kissinger was able to assess both the strengths and the limits of his foreign policy approach. The war began on 6 October 1973 when Egypt and Syria launched a surprise attack against Israel in an attempt to reclaim territories lost in the 1967 war. The attacks came on Yom Kippur, the holiest day of the year for religious Jews and an Israeli national holiday, and the country was caught completely unaware. Abba Eban, who was Israel's minister of foreign affairs at the time, conveyed the sense of shock this way: "Historians who read the Israeli newspapers published in the first days of October will be startled to find that there was no hint of any crisis, let alone of imminent war."[13] The first days of the war were marked by a string of Arab military successes and significant losses for the Israeli military. The Egyptian armies crossed the Suez Canal and made inroads into the Sinai Peninsula at the same time that Syrian forces moved into the Golan Heights. By the end of the third day of the war, the Israeli military had sustained major damage. It had lost 1,000 soldiers, 49 planes, and one-third of its tank force, and its army was running out of ammunition.[14] Israel had been blindsided by both the suddenness and the initial success of the attacks.

The Nixon administration was also caught off guard by the Arab offensive, falsely convinced that Israel's vast military superiority made such an attack impossible.[15] Kissinger recalled being stunned to realize the precariousness of the balance of power in the Middle East, despite substantial military deliveries to Israel over the prior three years.[16] But in the days that followed, the administration moved quickly to craft a response that took into account several U.S. interests in the Middle East, some of which were in conflict with each other (a point that captured one of the challenges inherent in the application of realpolitik): support for the state of Israel, the need for an uninterrupted oil supply from the Gulf monarchies, containment of Soviet expansion in the region, and the pursuit of détente. Many of these interests had shaped American foreign policy in the Middle East since World War II, but in the early 1970s these interests deepened as Britain completed its historic withdrawal of military forces from the area, the Soviet Union intensified its presence in Syria, Iraq, and Algeria, and Anwar Sadat expelled all Soviet military advisors and technicians from Egypt. These changes convinced Kissinger that the region was assuming a new centrality in the Cold War.[17] The war, then, was a turning point, not only for the Arabs and Israelis, but also for the United States as it attempted to stake out its position in a Middle East in transition while heeding the call for "maturity" and "limits."

In this context, Nixon made a number of decisions. After three days of Egyptian and Syrian gains and heavy Israeli damage, he ordered his defense secretary, James Schlesinger, to begin airlifting arms, declaring that "the Israelis must not be allowed to lose."[18] Soon, the United States was sending the Israeli military a thousand tons of war materiel a day, including artillery, guns, small arms, tanks, and electronic equipment. On 14 October, Nixon responded to a request by Israeli prime minister Golda Meir for more assistance by instructing the Pentagon to "send everything that will fly."[19] Over the next month, the U.S. Air Force flew close to seven hundred sorties and delivered eleven thousand tons of military hardware to the Israelis. By the time it ended on 15 November, the operation had surpassed the Berlin airlift of 1948–49. The assistance helped the Israeli military to regain the upper hand, while also sending a message to the Soviets, who were airlifting supplies to Syria and Egypt: it was the United States, rather than the Soviet Union, that would determine the final outcome of the war.[20]

Even as the administration displayed its commitment to Israel, it pursued the politics of détente. Throughout the war, Kissinger remained in daily contact with the Kremlin, and as the war entered its third week, he traveled to Moscow, where the two superpowers drafted a cease-fire that was soon endorsed by the United Nations Security Council and accepted by the warring parties on 22 October. Still the crisis was not yet over. At the time of the cease-fire, Israeli forces had encircled the powerful Egyptian Third Army along the Suez. On 23 October, the Soviets contacted Kissinger to tell him that the Israeli military had broken the cease-fire, and that night Brezhnev sent a message indicating that if the cease-fire were not enforced, the Soviet Union would consider taking military action. In response, the Nixon administration put all American conventional and nuclear forces on worldwide military alert. Meanwhile, behind the scenes, Kissinger warned the Israelis that the United States would not allow Egypt's Third Army Corp to be destroyed. Later that afternoon, the United Nations Security Council passed a second cease-fire resolution, bringing an end to the war.[21]

The war had revealed many truths to Kissinger: Israel was more vulnerable than he had imagined, the Egyptian and Syrian armies had fought harder than he had predicted, the Soviets were more aggressive than he would have liked, and the worldwide military alert was a crisis point that he had hoped to avoid. Nevertheless, the war convinced Kissinger that a policy based on limits and restraint could work. The administration provided crucial support to an ally, but without the direct use of military force, an achievement that proved that the Nixon Doctrine was effective. At the same time, détente enabled the Soviet Union and the United States to calm the situation and resolve the crisis, while encouraging the Soviet Union to show moderation. "The war was contained," he recalled, "and the United States maneuvered successfully to reduce the Soviet role in the Middle East."[22] As we will see, in the years to come, Kissinger's critics would offer a very different interpretation of the war, but in the autumn of 1973, it was Kissinger's interpretation that carried the day. That interpretation lent support to his vision of a new foreign policy of maturity that would restore the nation's world position after Vietnam.

"Having Another Fix": The Oil Embargo as a Crisis of National Dependency

There was one American interest in the Middle East, however, that could not be contained within a policy of restraints, limits, and maturity, and that was oil. The major Arab oil producers responded to the October War by taking several decisive political and economic steps that would reverberate within the United States.[23] In retaliation for the American airlift to Israel, they announced that they would begin cutting back on oil production until Israel withdrew from the territories it had taken during the 1967 war. Three days later, the producers instituted a complete oil embargo against the United States, followed by an embargo against the Netherlands, the country that had expressed the most support for American policy. At the same time, the six Persian Gulf members of OPEC increased the price of oil by 70 percent in an attempt to recoup profit losses caused by the devaluation of the dollar in 1971. As Kissinger later conceded, the embargo was largely a symbolic gesture, since other producers could make up the difference. But the combination of the embargo, production cutbacks, and OPEC price hikes set off a wave of panic buying that strained the economies of the United States, Europe, and Japan throughout the winter of 1973–74. From May 1973 to June 1974, the retail price of gasoline in the United States rose from 38.5 cents to 55.1 cents per gallon. In a televised address on 7 November 1973, President Nixon asked for a lowering of household thermostats to sixty-eight degrees, a reduction of air travel by 10 percent, increased carpooling efforts, and a lowering of highway speed limits. He warned Americans that the country was heading toward the most acute shortage of energy since World War II.[24]

News stories stressed the surprise of the embargo, but it had not come from nowhere. Between 1968 and 1973, the rules dictating oil supply and demand had undergone dramatic revision. Throughout much of the 1960s, most policymakers had not viewed OPEC as a serious cartel, and an earlier attempt to embargo oil during the 1967 war had failed.[25] But by the early 1970s, OPEC had become effective and well coordinated. Between 1971 and 1973, the cartel had successfully nationalized some oil-producing facilities, orchestrated a series of price increases, and set production ceilings. More important, the demand for oil within the United States had grown exponentially. Between 1950 and 1974, the nation's consumption of oil had doubled and oil imports went from 8 percent to 38 percent, with much of this oil coming from the Persian Gulf and North Africa. Until the early 1970s, the United States had produced oil far below full capacity, enabling the country to maintain control over both production rates and price. But in 1972, the Texas Railroad Commission authorized full production in response to growing demand, a decision that in Kissinger's view "signaled the end of America's ability to set the world oil price."[26] All of these changes meant that well before the October War, oil policy experts realized that the era of cheap and plentiful oil was drawing to a close, and already by the winter of 1972 the rising costs and restricted availability of energy resources were receiving sustained public attention. But it was the oil embargo that formally inaugurated the energy crisis of the 1970s. In the words of one historian, "America's energy crisis began symbolically in the third week of October 1973."[27]

In the days and weeks that followed the announcement of the embargo, news accounts portrayed a sense of shock and anger among middle-class men and women as they tried to adapt to the domestic inconveniences and price increases that were now unfolding in tandem with events in the Middle East. Regardless of the earlier history of growing concern with energy shortages, the association of the embargo with "shock" (indeed, the two terms would come to be used synonymously) implicitly referred back to the October War, creating a powerful identification between Americans and Israelis as two peoples in very different parts of the world who had nonetheless both been caught unaware in a conflict with Arab adversaries. News accounts also stressed that the ability of the Arab oil producers to brandish the "oil weapon" revealed something disturbing about the nation's world position. At a time when the reality of American military defeat in Vietnam was setting in, the embargo pointed to another alarming problem: the nation had moved from a state of independence into a condition of dependency on Middle Eastern oil. This condition undermined an important feature of American exceptionalism, namely, the belief that the nation had been founded on independence and that this independence had been sustained throughout the country's history. As one *Reader's Digest* editorial explained it, "Independence was America's birthright" and "we don't sell that birthright for a barrel of oil."[28]

As the oil crisis unfolded, a discussion ensued among newspaper editorialists, politicians, public intellectuals, and laypeople about the meaning of this new condition of national dependency. Central to this discussion was an attempt to differentiate oil from other commodities in order to convey a sense of urgency about the extent to which access to cheap and plentiful petroleum had underwritten postwar economic growth. From highway construction to home building, from the spread of the suburbs to the expansion of the steel and automobile industries, U.S. economic development had not only required cheap oil, it had been premised on the assumption that the oil would always be there for the taking. The psychological power of the embargo lay in the fact that it threw that premise into question. As a result, oil emerged not simply as a vital commodity, but as *the* commodity that fueled the economy, what one commentator described as the "life's blood of American civilization." Since oil was identified as the blood that ran through the national body, OPEC was accused of having cut off "the oil artery to the industrialized West." The association of oil with blood was meant to capture the dire nature of the crisis. But comparing the nation to a human body reflected a deep sense of wounded outrage: after all, how could the Arab oil producers deprive the human body of its own blood?[29]

Oil was equated with blood, but it was also identified as an addictive drug that had brought the nation to its knees. The identification of oil as a narcotic led to a second accusation against the Arab oil producers. That the producers were depriving the nation of its blood was replaced by the no-less-disturbing idea that they had foisted a drug upon Americans, only to cruelly withhold it from them now. In editorial cartoons, oil suppliers from the Middle East were depicted as heroine pushers, replete with intravenous needles, feeding tubes, and syringes. One cartoon showed a haggard Uncle Sam, outstretching a bare pockmarked arm to an Arab sheik who reassured him: "We're gonna let you have another fix."[30] Another showed a sheik forcing a flask of oil down the throat of a prostrate man and taunting him with the words "Say Uncle."[31] Still another cartoon was set in a casbah where the bottle labels read "raw crude" and "diesel." As he pours a drink for a dejected Western businessman, the Arab bartender observes, "That's a terrible habit you've got there."[32] This portrayal of the oil producers as drug pushers associated the OPEC cartel with racialized crime, a move that combined domestic and international images of racial transgression. But it also resonated with the earlier discussions that surrounded POWs and their captors: the sense that a foreign enemy had inappropriately gained the upper hand and was wielding power against the United States in ways that were not simply unfair, but immoral and sadistic.

But if Arab oil producers were drug pushers, then the United States occupied the ultimate abject position: that of junkie. Psychiatrist Thomas Szasz explained in a *New York Times* editorial in March 1974: "Having betrayed our commitment to dignity and liberty we now whimper and whine, a whole nation in the grips of auto petroleum withdrawal pains."[33] The image of the nation as junkie conveyed a deep sense of shame about the newly compromised position of the United States and, more specifically, about the out-of-control nature of American oil consumption. It also raised questions about the parental fitness of Americans. As one engineer stated, the nation had gotten hooked on the "worst kind of narcotic," cheap energy, and Americans wanted "their supply of dope" to continue "for the balance of their lives even if their children and their children's children have

'We're gonna let you have another fix'

"We're gonna let you have another fix." Houston Post *cartoon, 22 April 1974.*
© 1974 Houston Post; *reprinted with permission; all rights reserved.*

to pay for their greediness."[34] This was the most unanticipated aspect of the
public debate that took shape during the embargo. That the embargo unleashed feelings of anger toward the Arab oil producers was not surprising.
What was surprising was that politicians, policymakers, and commentators
shifted the blame away from OPEC and toward energy consumers within
the United States. It was the nation itself, rather than any foreign enemy,
they argued, that had produced the conditions for its own decline through
an unhealthy and reckless addiction to oil. Like the junkie forced to go
cold turkey, the nation now found itself in a state of withdrawal that, while
painful, was somehow deserved.

This accusation was tied to a troubling statistic cited over and over again
in speeches and editorials in the winter of 1973–74: the United States made
up only 6 percent of the world's population but it was consuming one-third
of the world's available energy sources.[35] By the time of the oil crisis, environmentalists and ecologists had been calling attention to this imbalance
for years, and they saw in the embargo the same opportunity that Kissinger
discerned in the Vietnam debacle: the chance for the United States to
enter a new era of maturity rooted in an appreciation of limits. As one ecol-
ogist portrayed it in the magazine *Natural History*, the oil crisis marked a

turning point for Americans that bore a striking resemblance to Kissinger's understanding of the place of Vietnam in the life cycle of the nation: "The time has come, in a sense, for America to grow up. For some two centuries we have lived luxuriously off the energy-rich land, like a spoiled child off wealthy parents. Now, crises are forcing us into a period of maturity, to an awareness of the consequences of high energy consumption. The development of this maturity could bring a style and richness of life that Americans have never known."[36]

Editorials like these brought a new level of public awareness to environmental concerns, and in particular to the problem of diminishing natural resources. But the environmental movement's most profound insight was buried in the mainstream debate over the embargo. Throughout their activism, ecologists and environmentalists had urged Americans to consider their use of natural resources within spatial frameworks both wider and smaller than the modern nation-state. For ecologists, the operative frameworks were ecosystems and local habitats. For environmentalists, the operative framework was planetary: the earth. Throughout the embargo, however, the fact that Americans were consuming one-third of the world's available energy emerged as a distinctly *national* problem. In late November 1973, President Nixon insisted that the oft-quoted statistic about energy consumption should inspire pride rather than shame, explaining that because Americans were "the richest, strongest people in the world" with "the highest standard of living," the nation's extraordinary consumption of energy was justified.[37] But his assurances rang hollow and seemed strangely out of place. It was Arizona congressman Morris K. Udall who better captured the sentiment at the time. "We have been on an energy binge," he warned readers in the *New Republic*, "and the hangover could be protracted and painful."[38]

The claim that the country had been on an energy binge contained an implicit question that would appear in different guises in debates about national decline in the years to come: did the American people possess the will and discipline required to kick the oil habit and restore the nation's world position? This question had first surfaced in debates about the Vietnam War. For those who supported the war, the withdrawal of U.S. troops from Vietnam had amounted to a profound failure of nerve that raised troubling questions about the nation's capacity to meet its commitments. Their doubts did not concern weapons, hardware, or manpower, but instead revolved around the question of national character that Nixon had raised several months before the embargo: did the country possess the moral and psychological resources necessary to function as a superpower? Richard Armitage, who fought in Vietnam and later became a prominent member of the defense community, remembered the U.S. withdrawal: "I found it very akin to getting a lady pregnant and leaving town. It's not a pretty image, but I thought we were a runaway dad."[39] The metaphor implied that the failure of the military intervention in Vietnam had not been rooted in strategic miscalculations or misinterpretations but rather in the abdication of responsibility. The oil embargo revived and revised the same question. William C. Westmoreland, the former commanding general of U.S. forces in Vietnam, summed up the connection in December 1973. "We have become literally and figuratively fat," he explained. "Perhaps the crisis will bring us back to some of the virtues that made this country great, like thrift and the belief that waste is sinful."[40] With the war over and the troops home, Westmoreland implied, the question of national will needed to be taken up on the domestic front.

Throughout the winter of 1973–74, as editorialists weighed in on the meaning of the nation's dependency on Middle Eastern oil, the middle-class home emerged as a crucial site at which both the causes and effects of the embargo could be assessed in the most directly personal and heartfelt ways. Much like discussions of the nation as a whole, discussions of the middle-class home contained a paradox: the private sphere of the home was both a locus of injury from the outside and a site where the condition of national dependency had been perpetuated, rendering the country strategically vulnerable. On the one hand, news accounts of middle-class families struggling throughout the embargo conveyed the same message that had been sent during the POW publicity campaign: conflicts in distant, foreign places were encroaching on the private sphere in ways that had not been seen since World War II. But while the POW publicity campaign had portrayed the private sphere as a locus of psychological violence, news coverage of the oil embargo identified that sphere with material deprivation and sacrifice. At the same time, however, the middle-class home emerged as a source of deviance, a place where the nation's "energy binge" and "oil addiction" had been encouraged, enabled, and indulged.

Soon after the embargo was announced, reporters began going into local communities, cities, and suburbs to see how the rising costs and limited availability of heating oil and auto fuel were affecting the lives of average Americans. In the weeks and months that followed, there emerged a frightening if embellished picture of imperiled middle-class domesticity that suggested that the material comforts of American life were under direct attack. This picture was a composite of certain stock images reproduced over and over again between October 1973 and March 1974: two-hour lines at gas stations, car owners hoarding and stockpiling gasoline, families freezing in cold living rooms, women and men trapped in their homes because they did not want to squander auto petroleum, irate drivers fighting with each other as they waited to fill their gas tanks. Empirical research suggested that the economic consequences of the oil embargo were both less severe and more uneven than such images suggested, but their cumulative effect was nonetheless dramatic.[41] The middle-class family was under siege, they seemed to say, and suddenly average American consumers were in the throes of what Daniel Yergin later called a "commodity panic," one that led them to consider oil in entirely new ways.[42] One New York suburbanite explained the changed mentality: "You have to think all the time about gas, the use of gas, having enough gas left for emergencies and where you're going to get the next tankful." It was, he concluded, "a silly way to live."[43]

Images of domestic peril revolved around two economic indicators that affected family income in intimate ways: inflation and unemployment. The embargo had caused neither of these trends. To begin with, the cost of food staples such as meat and wheat had shot up in the early 1970s, so much so that by March 1973 news stories began to point to the "high cost of eating."[44] But the soaring costs of heating oil and auto petroleum crystallized the effects of inflation on people's daily lives, and the embargo provided a framework for contemplating the hurdles that average Americans were now confronting. Suddenly, it seemed that middle-class consumers had been thrown back to an earlier historical period of austerity. "Well, it looks like your 'good old days' are finally back," read one caption to a cartoon in the *New Yorker*.[45] The accompanying illustration showed a married couple perched in matching chairs in a comfortable living room with drapes and a landscape painting hanging on the back wall. All appeared normal except for the fact that they were sitting in candlelight and were decked out from head to toe in winter clothes, details that suggested that regardless of the superficial accoutrements of the middle-class home, this space was no longer what it seemed. Such cartoons captured the heightened sense of vulnerability that accompanied the embargo, the sense that the comforts of home could no longer be taken for granted.

Some accounts of material privation among the middle class contrasted the inflationary spiral within the United States to the accumulation of pet-

"Well, it looks like your 'good old days' are finally back."

"Well, it looks like your 'good old days' are finally back."
New Yorker *cartoon, 18 February 1974.* © The New Yorker *Collection,*
1974, Robert Weber, from cartoonbank.com.; all rights reserved.

rodollars within oil-rich countries in the Arab world, suggesting that a zero-sum game was taking place. One article in *Time* described the challenges facing a typical American living under the disorienting and confusing conditions of the embargo. Driving along the freeway, he learned that the speed limit had been lowered to fifty miles per hour. At the gas station, he discovered that a gallon of gas cost two cents more than it had the day before. At the office, he felt a chill because the thermostat was set at sixty-eight degrees. On his way home from work, he noticed that his town's outdoor advertising lights were extinguished. And upon arriving home, he learned that his children's school would be closed for a month due to oil shortages. Meanwhile, the article described Saudi Arabia as a "backward but wakening desert kingdom." "Building cranes stuck their necks up everywhere in the few cities," the article continued. "Ferraris and Mercedes glistened in the showrooms, and the market bulged with imported consumer goods."[46]

This portrait bordered on caricature, but it was not unique in establishing a causal link between the curtailment of middle-class consumption within the United States and the new ability of countries like Saudi Arabia to amass wealth and create their own dream worlds of conspicuous consumption.

The looming problem of unemployment also figured prominently throughout the embargo. In the winter of 1973–74, workers in the automotive, construction, airlines, petrochemical, aerospace, and tourist industries suffered both temporary and permanent layoffs. Although oil shortages exacerbated the trend in some regions of the country, the embargo was not the root cause of unemployment. Instead, rising unemployment was a symptom of deindustrialization, a process under way by 1973 that was part of a broader transition from a Fordist economy based on the mass production of industrial and consumer goods to an economy based on the production of information, services, and new technologies.[47] The full dimensions of this transition were only dimly understood at the time, but two of its consequences were already becoming a cause of public concern: the growing visibility of out-of-work men and the rise of the two-earner family. The embargo provided a dramatic window onto both. On 8 March 1974, ABC News told the story of the Wallace family of Anderson, Indiana. Because of the oil crisis, the reporter explained, Dick Wallace, the family breadwinner, had recently been fired from the local automotive plant along with almost three thousand other workers. As a result, economic and emotional chaos had been unleashed within this family of five. "Dick Wallace is the family's chief cook, babysitter and homemaker," explained the reporter. "Linda Wallace helps out, of course, but she's away from home whenever she can find temporary employment." Filmed at his kitchen table with his three children, Wallace recalled how his eldest son had recently shoveled a neighbor's walkway for fifty cents and given him the earnings: "He comes in and says 'Here Dad, here's fifty cents. You probably need this money since you don't have a job.' . . . it makes you want to go into the other room and cry, you know, but then, too, you want to grab him and hug him."[48] By attributing the father's job loss to the oil crisis, the story linked the family's reversals of power and authority with those supposedly occurring between the Arab oil-producing nations and the consuming countries of the industrialized West. The crisis, then, had produced humiliating role inversions within the Wallace home that troubled not only gender distinctions but generational ones as well.

Here, too, one could see the extent to which the concern with paternal authority that had come to the fore during the POW publicity campaign

endured throughout the oil embargo. While the earlier campaign had focused on the psychological and emotional dimensions of waning paternal
authority, the embargo focused on the inability of men like Dick Wallace
to fulfill their roles as family breadwinners. As the ABC news story made
clear, this had profound psychological consequences within the family,
as men assumed the roles of women, women assumed the roles of men,
and children assumed the roles of parents. In both the POW campaign and
the oil embargo, a crisis of male authority within the home was linked to
the nation's compromised world position, in the first case to the specter of
national military defeat and in the second to the nation's dependency on
foreign oil. Research conducted at the time suggested that women workers
were actually more vulnerable to shortage-related layoffs than men, but
it was the problem of male unemployment that loomed throughout the
embargo.[49] As one member of the Nixon administration explained, the new
world of scarce energy was a scary one indeed, a world of "men without
jobs, homes without heat, children without schools."[50] In other words, it
was a world that, much like the interior world of the Wallace family, had
been turned upside down.

The attention to inflation and unemployment during the oil embargo
established the middle-class home as a site of national suffering where the
wounds inflicted by what the media called "the oil weapon" were made
visible. At a time when both inflation and unemployment were producing painful effects in people's everyday lives, the embargo provided a vivid
if inaccurate explanation for the economic downturn. But as the months
passed, a more damning portrait of the family emerged, one that, like the
problem of oil addiction, revolved around the problem of dependency.
This portrait focused less on individuals and more on a range of energy intensive commodities and appliances associated with middle-class domestic
life: cars, vacuum cleaners, dishwashers, air conditioners, and refrigerators.
In the 1940s and 1950s, these commodities had been associated with the
spread of middle-class affluence. Now they became symptomatic of the
nation's insatiable need for foreign oil.

This was a striking, although temporary, reversal. Throughout the postwar period, household goods had functioned as affirmative symbols of
Luce's American Century. Underwriting Luce's vision was the belief that
more and more Americans would be able to share in the fruits of material
abundance by purchasing affordable, mass-produced consumer goods. In

the 1950s, Luce's own *Life* magazine reported that supermarket shoppers could choose from "thousands of items on the high-piled shelves . . . until their carts became cornucopias filled with an abundance that no other country in the world has ever known"; and in the famous "kitchen debate" of 1959, Richard Nixon presented consumer appliances to Soviet premier Nikita Khrushchev as evidence of the superiority of American capitalism over Soviet communism.[51] The shining kitchen appliances on display at the Moscow trade show were, according to the *New York Times*, a "lavish testimonial to abundance."[52] Throughout the postwar years, this domestic world of middle-class consumption legitimated the nation's political, economic, and cultural dominance in the Cold War order. Even foreign policy experts like Henry Kissinger grasped this fact. As he later recalled, "The picture-perfect families gracing the television screens of the 1950s had been the cultural support group of the moral high-mindedness of Dulles and the soaring idealism of Kennedy."[53] Now the symbolic meaning of consumer goods was turned on its head.

To be sure, the association of consumerism with national decline was not new. A range of social critics throughout the postwar years had worried about the damaging effects of mass consumption on the national character, described by historian Daniel Horowitz as "the anxieties of affluence." Historian Howard Brick has pointed out that the ubiquity of the term "abundance" in the late 1950s reflected "a criticism of conventional thought and practice" rather than an endorsement of it.[54] But with the embargo, these earlier critiques of consumer culture became linked to economic upheaval and transformation. Only fourteen years after the kitchen debate, the consumption practices of the middle class no longer embodied strength but instead were endemic of a binge, a disease, and an orgy.[55] As one historian described it at the time, the oil embargo revealed that the nation was in the grips of a "prosperity psychosis."[56] Such a damning characterization advanced a different picture from the stories about the suffering unleashed by inflation and unemployment. No longer a victim but a culprit, the middle-class family was reaping what it had sown, and the oil embargo, contrary to being a sadistic act by the OPEC cartel, was a deserved punishment for decades of energy excess. One clergyman explained: "We are being punished for our past sins of conspicuous consumption and planned obsolescence."[57]

Nowhere was this reversal more pronounced than in the case of the automobile. More than any other commodity, the car was the symbol of postwar mobility: literal mobility across geographical space, social mobility across class and racial divisions, and psychological mobility as it freed the individual from the limits of space and time. Indeed, the automobile had functioned as a metonym for affluence: the Fordist compromise, which claimed to enable workers to buy the same goods that they had produced; the spread of the suburbs; a widening sphere of leisure that would enable Americans to hit the open road; the freedom and pleasure of premarital sexuality. With the embargo, however, the roomy family automobile was deemed by an angry *New York Times* reader to be a "gas gulper, pandering to the gross tastes of a depraved consuming public."[58] The major car companies responded to the changed sentiment by tailoring their advertising campaigns around the new awareness that petroleum was neither as cheap or as available as it had been. A savvy advertisement by Volkswagen declared that "this country has the biggest drinking problem in the world." The proposed cure? The fuel efficient Beetle, a superior alternative to the hulking gas-guzzlers produced in Detroit.[59]

Although the car was the most prominent commodity associated with the oil crisis, household appliances were also linked to energy excess. According to an article in *Foreign Affairs*, the crisis had its origins in the fact that "millions and millions of energy gobbling products," including "profligately trivial household gadgets," had flooded the market.[60] Newspapers and magazines assumed a pedagogical role as they enlightened readers about the ways in which seemingly benign household commodities were burning up energy. "What's Your Energy IQ?" queried one writer, who proceeded to administer a true/false test on thermostat settings, insulation, and indoor lighting.[61] "Where Does All the Energy Go?" read another headline for an article that divulged the silent but voracious energy appetites of the space heater, the air conditioner, and the refrigerator.[62] Appearing in periodicals such as *Better Homes and Gardens, Good Housekeeping*, and *House Beautiful*, these how-to guides for household conservation were directed at women, who were seen as bearing responsibility for household energy waste.[63] One editorial even suggested that in addition to making the public more aware of conservation, the crisis could bring families closer together. By cutting back on the use of fuel-consuming appliances such as dishwashers, it argued, individual family members would be able to communicate better since "normal conversation is hard against background noise exceeding 55 decibels."[64]

Ironically, at a time when the two-earner family was becoming the norm, the association of blenders, dishwashers, and refrigerators with energy waste sometimes spilled over into a wider critique of "convenience,"

Cars line up on Sunday, 23 December 1973, at a New York City gas station.
Despite Nixon's plea for stations to close on Sundays, this station remained open.
Courtesy of AP Photo.

a web of goods and practices designed to help families meet basic needs quickly and efficiently. The most obvious and elemental example was food. Not surprisingly, the use of convenience and frozen foods grew dramatically in the postwar period, and the trend accelerated in the 1970s as women entered wage labor in greater numbers.[65] Advertisements depicted the challenges that accompanied the transition to the two-earner family, often featuring images of the harried, over-worked wife and mother and promoting frozen foods as commodities that could ease her burden.[66] During the embargo, however, frozen foods symbolized a domestic realm in which older forms of care, nurturance, and provision had become obsolete in a new era of convenience, speed, and energy waste. Thus the same editorial that celebrated the energy crisis for its potential to cure family alienation also condemned "TV dinners" for destroying the tradition of the home-cooked meal.[67] "Housewives, especially younger ones, are either too lazy, too busy, or don't know how to cook," declared one food retailer.[68] One study by the Federal Energy Administration contrasted energy consumption patterns in the United States with those of Europe and Japan and concluded that the high rate of energy use in American households had its origins in a string of practices that had replaced "Old World" tradition with convenience. American households relied on frozen and convenience foods, while European and Japanese households were more likely to use fresh foods. American households shopped at large, dispersed shopping facilities, while European and Japanese households relied on small grocery stores and local neighborhood specialty shops. Large refrigerators meant that American families made weekly shopping trips, while European and Japanese families shopped daily for perishables.[69] The study did not condemn the rise of convenience, nor did it recommend that Americans return to older practices. But in arguing that a preference for convenience over tradition explained the extraordinary rates of energy consumption in the United States, it extended Kissinger's search for "limits" and "restraint" to the domestic realm.

Anthropologist Margaret Mead remarked at the time that the national discussion provoked by the oil embargo demonstrated that the basic problem was "the way our everyday life is organized, the way each family lives."[70] When an article or pamphlet encouraged families to adopt conservation measures, it helped individuals to situate their everyday, private practices in a wider framework. But the emphasis on household conservation throughout the oil crisis was also distorting. Research showed that the oil crisis had only a marginal effect on household energy consumption and that once the embargo was lifted, rates of energy use within the home continued to climb. These findings support historian David Nye's claim that energy consumption actually increased in the United States throughout the 1970s.[71] The attention to conservation also presented the crisis as one that afflicted middle-class families alone because they had the power and means to consume, thus obscuring the impact of the crisis on families living below the poverty line. For them, the central drama of the crisis did not revolve around energy waste but instead around the choice between food and heat.[72] But above all, the emphasis on conservation assigned disproportionate blame to the middle-class family, suggesting that energy reform could best be achieved through private retrenchment rather than structural change. In truth, domestic households consumed a small percentage of the nation's energy resources compared to large corporations.

Indeed, discussions of household conservation were moral, not economic. Much like the revelation that the country as a whole was consuming one-third of the world's available energy sources, the recognition that the home was a site of waste was gradually transformed into a moral indictment, one that went well beyond thermostat settings, speed limits, and gasoline prices. With its lexicon of dependency, excess, and waste, the conservationist discourse converged with a fear that would figure more and more prominently over the course of the decade: the fear that the white, middle-class family had failed as a source of moral authority and national character. In the case of the oil embargo, this failing hinged on the belief that the spread of mass consumption had led to profligacy within the home and had undermined the family's ability to transmit the traits that had been essential to its survival under industrial capitalism: discipline, abstinence, and character.

Like the critique of consumerism, anxiety concerning generational transmission had its origins in the early years of industrial capitalism, when a strong father figure presumably had ensured that fiscal discipline was maintained within the bourgeois middle-class home.[73] But with the explosive growth of mass consumption and the growing popularity of credit, debt, and installment planning in the mid-twentieth century, fathers were robbed of their perceived role as economic regulators and a crucial source of paternal authority collapsed. The feared consequence was a middle-class family in which earlier ethics of thrift and self-discipline would be displaced by the new traits dictated by a mass consumption economy: hedonism, entitlement, and the pursuit of immediate gratification. These were the same traits that Henry Kissinger was attempting to temper in the foreign policy realm. Thus the claim that the nation's dependency on foreign oil represented a moral lapse, much as substance abuse represented moral weakness, synergized anxieties in both the domestic and international spheres.

The clergy brought out the underlying concern with traditional authority most forcefully. "I truly believe America is shot full of waste," proclaimed Robert Schuller, the pastor of the nation's largest drive-in church in Orange County, California.[74] "We're an undisciplined and profligate people," he continued, wasting "gas, money, and time."[75] Accusations of energy waste often slipped into indictments of other forms of excess, particularly in the realm of sexuality. As the Catholic journal *America* explained, the oil crisis revealed a contradiction at the heart of affluence: "Although we are the richest people in the world, we are probably the least sane and the least happy." Out of a sense of despair, Americans "turn to drugs, trade wives and patronize pornographic films. Our young people are hopeless and alienated, and our cities rot."[76] This portrait of a culturally degenerate American society stood in dramatic contrast to contemporaneous accounts that extolled the Arab ability to balance rapid economic modernization with moral rectitude and religious tradition.[77]

The slippage between energy excess and moral excess was also apparent in news accounts that suggested that shortages were compelling Americans to reaffirm familial and communitarian ties. There was no empirical evidence to support this claim, but as the months of the embargo passed, its ostensibly redemptive features began to gain attention. According to several reports, the crisis was strengthening families, deepening religious commitments, and inspiring neighborhood loyalties. The gas shortage was "the greatest thing for Christianity since World War II," exulted one minister, who claimed that church attendance was on the rise thanks to the embargo's dampening of Sunday driving trips.[78] A sociologist predicted that the crisis would lead to a rediscovery of friends and families "because it will be harder to run away."[79] Shortages were forcing people to stay at home and become more oriented toward their neighbors, according to an article that celebrated the resurrection of the neighborhood block party.[80] One Connecticut housewife expressed frustration at an overloaded schedule that had her chauffeuring her children from school to ballet classes to birthday parties and concluded that less driving would deepen her family relationships.[81] A *Newsweek* editorial imagined that some day "Americans may look back nostalgically at this cold comfort winter as a time when tightly knit families triumphed over adversity." Reflectively, the editorial wondered if the "energy crisis may even end up like the other crises, wars and upheavals in American history—as the setting for a warmhearted TV series."[82]

As news stories portrayed it, the embargo had precipitated a widespread reexamination of consumption and national identity. NBC anchorman John Chancellor observed on 10 January 1974 that "people sit in their kitchens surrounded by refrigerators, freezers, toasters, blenders, and other useful appliances, talking about the beauty of the old days, when people weren't dependent on gadgetry." But there were still Americans who had not succumbed to the lure of gadgetry, Chancellor reminded viewers. They were the Amish, who, in his words, heard "the rhythms of an earlier time." For the next three minutes, viewers watched the Amish riding in horse-drawn buggies, tending their horses, and raising barns. The Amish did not "totally reject modern convenience," an off-screen reporter comforted viewers; "they simply feel the less of it, the better." The Amish were seen but not heard until late in the segment, when an old man, walking alone through the woods, explained: "Change feeds on change. And if we advance too fast things will get out of control."[83] Normally, the Amish were depicted as a curious cultural anomaly, but in the context of the embargo, they appeared to have a distinct advantage over middle-class Americans because of their commitment to moderation and restraint.

Finally, the embargo linked the family to survivalism. A forty-three-year-old divorced mother of five children from Portland, Oregon, who got up before dawn each day to get gasoline before coming home to cook breakfast for her children, described herself as "a hunter who has gone out and gotten his supplies for the week."[84] A married couple conducted what they called a "no energy weekend experiment." "Edie looked like a true pioneer heating the soup over the open fire," the husband recalled in the May 1974 *House Beautiful*. "Later, [we] sat together in the den. Warm candlelight flickered off our faces. It had been a good day. We had found a source of new energy within ourselves that was not dependent on oil, gas, or coal."[85] In contrast to news reports that emphasized the suffering unleashed by the embargo within the middle-class home, these images suggested that the embargo could endow the private sphere with enhanced psychological and spiritual meaning by compelling people to fall back on their own resources.

Such appeals to familial survival and self-sufficiency emerged out of the revelation that there was a causal link between the American consumer's dependency on energy-intensive commodities and the nation's dependency on Middle Eastern oil. But these appeals must also be analyzed in relation to a second crisis of family dependency that was preoccupying policymakers in the early 1970s: a deepening welfare crisis.[86] In 1973, writing at the precise moment that the term "energy crisis" was entering the popular lexicon, Daniel Moynihan drew a distinction between poverty and dependency, arguing that welfare was a crisis of the latter category. "To be poor is an objective condition," he wrote; "to be dependent a subjective one as well." Dependency, Moynihan continued, was "an incomplete state in life: normal in the child, abnormal in the adult. In a world where completed men and women stand on their own two feet, persons who are dependent—as the buried imagery of the word denotes—hang."[87] The belief that welfare programs like Aid to Families with Dependent Children (AFDC) perpetuated dependency in their recipients fueled a demand for reform. By 1971, news reports were describing welfare in exactly the same terms that they would soon use to describe domestic energy consumption—as out of control.[88] Indeed, in his 1971 State of the Union address, President Nixon anticipated the rhetoric of the oil crisis when he decried the welfare system as a "monstrous, consuming outrage—an outrage against the community, against the taxpayer, and particularly against the children it is supposed to help."[89]

These growing calls for welfare reform had a racial subtext. Poor families, often overgeneralized as African American, had supposedly grown too dependent on the welfare state. Burdens of the state rather than contributors to society, they were allegedly guilty of receiving assets that they had not earned. This stereotype resonated with a belief, voiced throughout the embargo, that the Arab oil sheik's acquisition of wealth was undeserved because it reflected neither industry nor hard work, but instead was a lucky accident of geography, what one reporter described at the time as "the caprice of geology."[90] Both stereotypes—of the lazy black welfare chiseler and the Arab oil sheik—cited dependency as a condition that had come about because certain hallmarks of maturity (self-discipline, resourcefulness, a commitment to the work ethic) were lacking. Thus both the oil embargo and the welfare crisis drew on racialized notions of dependency.

At the same time, the oil embargo suggested that dependency was becoming a pervasive condition. Debates about welfare proceeded from an implicit contrast between a pathological model of black family life and a normative ideal of the white, middle-class family. But the oil embargo revealed that even this ideal family type suffered from dependency, this time on cars, household electrical appliances, gadgetry, and convenience. There were significant differences in these two discourses, not least in the fact that the stigmatization of African American families was far more enduring. But the similarities were also revealing. During the embargo, it appeared that the white, middle-class private sphere, not unlike the ostensibly dysfunctional space of the African American home, had failed as a repository of national character in ways that were now hurting the country, domestically, morally, and strategically. Meanwhile, the attack on programs like AFDC would be the opening salvo in a full-scale assault on the welfare state itself.

Occurring less than one year after the withdrawal of troops from Vietnam but before the full reality of American military defeat had set in, the oil crisis posed the same question being asked by those who had supported American military intervention in Southeast Asia but who were trying to understand what had gone wrong: did the American people have the internal will and moral reserves to protect the nation's world position? As one commentator portrayed it in the spring of 1974, the oil crisis pinpointed the three different kinds of resources Americans needed—"natural resources, human resources, and if you will, moral resources."[91] Like the POW publicity campaign, the debate surrounding the oil embargo portrayed the family both as a victim and as an institution that—through a series of moral lapses—had rendered the United States newly vulnerable on the world stage. The images of material privation that emerged during the oil embargo extended the logic of the earlier campaign, suggesting that the family was a victim of outside injury and that newly intimate forms of violence were no longer emanating from Southeast Asia alone, but also from the region at the center of Kissinger's post-Vietnam vision: the Middle East.

At a time when the nation was undergoing a foreign policy shift from idealism to realism, the family served as a metaphor, a crucible, and a mirror of national identity. The confusion surrounding the family's status during the embargo (victim or culprit?) reflected confusion about the global position of the United States; should it, for example, accept or reject OPEC's new power? Simultaneously, a postwar emphasis on immediate gratification associated with late Fordist mass consumption gave way to a new respect for moderation and self-control, as national virtues such as independence, simplicity, and community were rediscovered and celebrated. The family itself—an object of critique throughout the late 1960s and early 1970s—thus emerged as the site of multiple meanings inextricably tied to the nation. These diverse meanings intersected, collided, and gave way to one another in ways that augmented the family's power as a national symbol. In the years after the embargo, it would become clear that the political force that captured control of this symbol would gain a terrific resource in its efforts to achieve power.

The End of the Embargo and the
Birth of a Corporate Counteroffensive

There had been no consensus about the significance of the oil crisis throughout the winter of 1973–74. But after OPEC lifted the embargo on 18 March 1974, policymakers continued to debate its meaning and implications as they developed proposals for protecting the United States from future shortages. By the time the embargo ended, larger quantities of oil were flowing back into the international market, the effects of OPEC's production cutbacks were diminishing, and some Arab leaders who initially supported the embargo felt that it had lost its utility.[92] The Nixon administration also played a role in the embargo's resolution through two foreign policy initiatives. The first was to maintain a diplomatic presence in the Middle East in the wake of the October War. Throughout the winter of

1973–74, Kissinger engaged in "shuttle diplomacy," traveling to the region several times and facilitating a disengagement agreement between Egypt and Israel. The second aim, especially germane to the problem of dependency, was to create a sense of solidarity among the industrialized nations that relied on oil imports from the OPEC producers and had been hurt by the embargo.

For Kissinger, this was the single most decisive if challenging dimension of the administration's post-embargo foreign policy: to establish a common goal for the United States, its European allies, and Japan. As he would later write of the embargo, "The industrial democracies could not permit themselves to be turned into panicked, paralyzed bystanders while the oil producers played fast and loose with the internal cohesion of their societies."[93] According to Kissinger, the only way that OPEC's power could be contained was through a coordinated response by the West (Japan was assigned honorary membership) that demonstrated in no uncertain terms the political and economic cohesion of the industrial democracies and their collective refusal to be intimidated. Kissinger faced considerable obstacles, however, when it came to coordinating such a response. Some European governments were critical of the Nixon administration's display of support for Israel and wanted to distance themselves from it. Furthermore, France, England, and Japan were far more dependent on the Gulf monarchies for their oil supply than was the United States, and their economies were incurring heavier damage as a result of the price spiral. In light of this, their governments sought to avoid adversarial relations with the Arab oil producers.

These challenges did not deter the Nixon administration. From Kissinger's point of view, a consumer coalition was the key not only to ending the embargo but also to protecting the West from future oil disruptions. According to him, the United States should lead such a coalition, since it was less dependent on foreign oil imports and thus better equipped to withstand external pressure. In February 1974, an international energy conference was held in Washington at which representatives from twelve nations formed an Energy Coordinating Group (later the International Energy Agency) to develop a program for consumer solidarity designed to keep OPEC in check.[94] The formation of the group complicates the assumption that the embargo was a symptom of American decline alone. The embargo may have revealed that the United States occupied a compromised position of oil dependency vis-à-vis the Middle East, but it also offered a strategic opportunity for the United States to reassert its moral and political credibility and its role as a leader within the West in the immediate wake of Vietnam. In keeping with the logic of realpolitik, Kissinger rejected the idea of a military response to the oil embargo, not on moral grounds, but rather because he believed that the embargo was a moment in which the United States could demonstrate its maturity and realism. The way to do this was not through military intervention but through reasserting the nation's rightful leadership role for the presumptive benefit of all.[95]

The Nixon administration's response to the oil embargo also contained a domestic dimension: the launching of a national energy program that would help the United States to regain its footing in the wake of the "oil shocks." On 7 November 1973, three weeks after the embargo had been declared, President Nixon announced the creation of Project Independence, an ambitious and indeed utterly unrealistic program to make the United States free of all reliance on foreign energy by 1980. The program demanded a new commitment to both conservation and the development of alternative energy sources, and the president identified the private sphere of the home as a crucial site of the national project. The impending fight for energy independence would be waged, he claimed, not "just here in Washington but in every home, in every community across the country."[96]

As we have seen, Nixon was not alone in his call for household conservation. This call emanated from a number of different directions in the early 1970s: from household guides in newspapers and magazines, from environmentalists and ecologists, from editorialists and pundits, and from official government pronouncements. But the conservation message also came from another significant source: the major oil and gas companies. In the immediate wake of the embargo, these companies had found themselves in the midst of a public relations crisis of considerable proportions. They too had been caught off guard by events in the autumn of 1973. What blindsided them, however, was not the embargo itself but the public response to it. Opinion polling in the winter of 1973–74 suggested that there was widespread public skepticism about the nature, the origins, the severity, and even the existence of the oil crisis. This skepticism had its origins in the Vietnam War. Over the course of the war, the American public had grown suspicious of official accounts of the overseas conflict, leading to what came to be called a credibility gap. This gap deepened during the oil embargo, since the crisis was unfolding at the same time that the scope of the Watergate scandal was being revealed. In a climate of suspicion and fear of conspiracy, many people believed that the oil crisis had been contrived or, alternatively, that its severity was greatly exaggerated. According to one Gallup poll taken in March 1974, even those who believed there was an oil crisis were far more likely to blame the major oil companies or the Nixon administration rather than OPEC.[97] In a 1974 congressional hearing, the major oil companies were accused of having concocted the crisis in order to drive independent gas stations out of business. Critics charged the Nixon administration with having colluded with the oil companies in order to abet corporate profiteering, or in a less conspiratorial vein, with having created the conditions for the crisis through mismanagement.[98] Others wondered if President Nixon had orchestrated the crisis in order to deflect attention away from the Watergate debacle.[99] The cumulative result was pervasive public doubt about whether the oil crisis was real. As William Simon, the head of the Federal Energy Administration, complained, "The American public wants us to dipstick every tank in the country."[100]

In this setting, the major oil companies moved quickly to launch a public relations counteroffensive. One advertiser at the J. Walter Thompson Company, a leading international advertising firm, said that the crisis was "going to have to be advertised and promoted and sold to the public."[101] This project of "selling the oil crisis" would have to accomplish several goals simultaneously: dispel widespread skepticism about the causes and severity of the crisis, offer an explanation as to why the companies were accruing enormous profits at a time when the Nixon administration was calling on citizens to make personal sacrifices, and convince oil and gas consumers that they needed to adopt a more restrained approach to energy consumption. The situation required, in the words of company president Henry Shachte, "a very delicate communication."[102] One 1974 in-house advertising publication summarized the thinking: "What we say and what we do will come under the closest scrutiny."[103]

The first and perhaps most urgent task was to convince the public that the crisis was not what one congressman called "the [oil] industry's latest gimmick."[104] An advertisement from Exxon in the autumn of 1973 confronted the accusation head on. "There's talk around that the energy shortage is contrived," the text of the advertisement read. "It's not. It's real."[105] Another 1974 Mobil advertisement poked fun at the idea of a conspiracy by claiming that the only thing the industry had "conspired" to do was to keep Americans warm through the winter.[106] But a more common tactic was to address the accusation circuitously by urging consumers to use less rather than more fuel. The president of Standard Oil Company of Indiana conceded that this reversal was a shock to the oil industry, observing that the switch to a conservation message was "quite a change for us after training our people to go out there and sell. Suddenly, we are saying: 'Please don't come in and ask for so much.'"[107] Another Mobil advertisement called attention to the irony of asking its customers to show restraint in their consumption of gasoline: "That may seem funny to you, coming from an oil company; but we simply think it's the right thing to do in the circumstances."[108] These advertisements mobilized the rhetoric of conservation to counter the charge that the major oil companies had either orchestrated or exaggerated the shortages in order to serve their own interests. They posed a rhetorical question that placed the companies beyond suspicion: after all, what possible motive would companies like Exxon and Mobil have for encouraging consumers to curb their fuel consumption in the absence of actual shortages?

These corporate calls for consumer restraint were not without historical precedent, since advertising had been used before to promote both wartime rationing and moderation during postwar economic reconversion.[109] But the considerable public skepticism about the crisis lent the campaign for restraint a unique sense of urgency. "It won't be an easy task to educate our citizenry about how to behave during the energy crisis," reflected Dan Seymour, chairman of the J. Walter Thompson Company in December 1973; "nor will they be easily persuaded to its true significance without a well-thought-out and sustained communications campaign."[110] In lieu of selling products, advertisers must now "move more and more toward communicating ideas" and toward conveying "what we want people to believe and to do."[111]

To that end, advertisers cast the middle-class home as a place where energy could be conserved rather than consumed. "Discover More Gas for America. Right in Your Own Home," declared a 1973 American Gas Association advertisement that provided a long list of household conservation measures.[112] Get your "energy house in order," recommended another.[113] Such reminders were often accompanied by placidly reassuring domestic images of interior spaces, quite different from the alarming portraits of consumer chaos and commodity panic that had appeared earlier. One series of advertisements for the American Gas Association, for example, featured photographs of sterile, clean, and empty living rooms, accompanied by instructions urging the lowering of thermostats and the use of adequate insulation. The emphasis on conservation was useful in helping consumers think about the relationship between personal behavior and national energy consumption. But it also cast the oil and gas companies as moral agents while implying that the war against energy excess could best be waged through private efforts rather than institutional reform. This transfer of responsibility from corporate to individual agency did not go unnoticed at the time. Thus writer Hendrik Hertzberg asked what sacrifices the oil companies were making at a time when private citizens were called on to observe limits.[114]

The casting of the oil companies as moral agents was deepened by a second feature of the corporate response: an unprecedented attempt to educate the public about the inner workings of the oil companies themselves. Mobil Oil was on the vanguard of this new approach, launching an aggressive public relations campaign in the early 1970s that blurred the line between advertising and editorializing by eschewing the advertising industry's typical use of bold graphics and illustrations and developing instead a series of dense, text-based print advertisements that described the intricate and costly operations of the oil industry. In 1971, the corporation purchased weekly advertising space in the *New York Times*, a decision that effectively made Mobil, in the words of business historian David Vogel, "a regular Times columnist."[115] Over the course of the decade, Mobil's advertisements countered accusations of corporate manipulation and profiteering by detailing the vast costs of research and development, the need for continued offshore drilling, the nature of corporate investment, and the enormous capital required to locate, drill, refine, and transport oil. These advertisements suggested that the record profits of the oil industry only appeared excessive. In truth, they were modest when considered in relationship to overhead. As one 1974 Mobil advertisement asked: "Are oil profits big? Right. Big enough? Wrong."[116] Thus the oil companies established an identification between themselves and consumers; both were involved in creating the new "limits" and "restraint" appropriate to America's refurbished global role.

But the most significant feature of Mobil's advertising campaign was to make the case that the industry functioned best without outside—that is, government—interference. As we have seen, the identification of oil as a unique commodity was essential to the foreign policy reorientation to the Middle East. But the unique status of oil was also central to a growing debate about whether the federal government should play a greater regulatory role in the oil industry. During the embargo, the Federal Energy Administration had asserted more control over the pricing and distribution of oil, and some policymakers believed that more aggressive regulation was essential to minimizing the possibility of future shortages. As one congressional subcommittee concluded in spring 1975, "In a democracy, important questions of policy with respect to a vital commodity like oil, the lifeblood of an industrial society, cannot be left to private companies acting in accord with private interests."[117] The need for more government oversight was a consistent theme in the congressional hearings about the oil crisis, and some members of the Senate advocated the creation of a federal oil and gas corporation that would compete with private companies in order to increase the nation's oil supply and help control prices.[118]

The threat of governmental regulation contributed to what one executive described at the time as a "siege mentality" within the corporate community.[119] Corporations responded by warning consumers that government regulations would only exacerbate the problems they promised to ameliorate. One Mobil advertisement reminded readers of what happened after the postal service was federalized: the cost of a penny postcard had risen eightfold. In another, the company acknowledged that the government had a role to play in the energy industry, that of creating a "healthy climate for investment." However, the ad explained, "government should *not* try to perform economic functions that the marketplace performs more efficiently and more equitably."[120] Of course, government regulation, especially of energy, had been a prominent theme in American politics since the Progressive Era. But the new identification between private organizations and private individuals, sparked by the oil crisis and mediated by the image of an endangered family, now tipped the balance against a supposedly intrusive state.

In fact, the corporate counteroffensive launched by the oil industry went through the same shift that had shaped the POW campaign: away from the perception of a foreign, external enemy and toward the perception of an overly bureaucratic state. At first, during the five-month oil embargo, the media had painted a dramatic portrait of money-hungry Arab oil producers invading the domestic space of the middle-class home. But in the years that followed, the oil industry established a different picture of what had gone wrong. In their interpretation, excessive government regulations had not only caused the shortages but were creating the conditions for future shocks. The relatives of MIAs had charged the state with abandonment and neglect of missing men and their families. The oil industry made a different accusation but one that also revolved around a perceived threat to privacy: an overly regulatory bureaucratic state was eroding the nation's strategic position by invading the world of private fortune. The accusation established an affinity between the two spheres that figured so prominently in corporate advertising campaigns—the middle-class home and the corporation. By stressing the virtues of both personal restraint and private enter-prise, these campaigns did more than simply insist that the oil companies could be trusted to provide oil to American families. They implied that companies were essentially like families, in that both entities could resolve the crisis through their own initiative and without outside interference. Taken as a whole, the POW campaign followed by the oil crisis created the sense that the gravest threat to the nation—both to its world position and to the freedoms accorded its private citizens—emanated not from the Middle East but from the state itself.

The oil crisis was a historic turning point in ways that could not have been anticipated at the time. Ironically, the problems that received sus-tained attention, national dependence on foreign oil and American rates of energy consumption, changed the least in its wake. On the contrary, these problems only deepened after 1974 as rates of domestic energy consump-tion continued to climb and the nation's reliance on foreign oil grew.[121] In addition, while the critique of dependence on household appliances and automobiles that surfaced during the embargo compelled consumers to pay more attention to conservation when making purchasing decisions, it neither curbed consumer spending nor overturned the enduring equation of mass consumption with national strength. But the embargo was a signifi-cant watershed in American foreign policy, culture, and domestic politics in several ways that would shape debates about the family and national decline in the years that followed.

First, coming on the heels of the troop withdrawal but before the col-lapse of the South Vietnamese regime, the embargo deepened the con-cerns over national will and character that had been raised by supporters of the war in Vietnam. At the same time, the embargo moved the drama from Southeast Asia to the Middle East. Advancing a vision of Arab aggres-sion that would prove enduring, one of political actors wielding power in ways that breached the boundary between the foreign and the domestic, the embargo evoked the earlier POW publicity campaign's portrayal of the Communist enemy while anticipating the role that the international ter-rorist threat would soon come to play. The supposed danger of national decline and foreign incursion, then, with its profound resonance in the private realm, would continue.

Second, the oil industry's public relations campaign was part of a wider corporate counteroffensive that successfully redirected public suspicion and hostility away from big business and toward the regulatory state. Many intellectuals and academics reinforced this suspicion. The new political realignment that emerged—consumers and corporations versus the state—gave shape to subsequent debates over national decline. Indeed, the oil companies would not be caught unaware again. When the next major oil panic occurred in 1979, it was the Carter administration rather than big business that bore the brunt of public resentment.

Third, the images of middle-class domestic peril reproduced in news stories in the winter of 1973–74 were distorted and embellished, but they contained an element of historical truth. After 1973 the relative prosperity of the 1950s and 1960s would not return, and the "new austerity" that generated so much commentary would become a permanent feature of the economic landscape. Some historians have lamented the oil crisis as a moment of lost opportunity when Americans were made aware of the need for conservation and sacrifice, only to forget the lesson. The problem with this interpretation is not that it is incorrect but rather that it assumes the crisis was about energy alone. The vivid if overdrawn narratives of deprivation that emerged during the embargo capture a new sense of precariousness among the American middle class at a moment when the older rules of Keynesian economic orthodoxy began to come apart, and when a postindustrial order made up of two-earner families (and with an earner often holding down more than one job) took its place.

The oil embargo would have one final consequence. As we have seen, the entire period that stretched from the October War through the oil crisis was permeated by the call for limits, restraint, and maturity. But maturity can have many meanings. In the years after 1973, a growing body of intellectuals and policymakers would come to reject Kissinger's articulation of a post-Vietnam foreign policy based on a healthy respect for limits. These members of the foreign policy and defense communities would form organizations, publish position papers, and write articles in which they would cite the oil embargo as a decisive event that revealed Kissinger's foreign policy approach for what they believed it was: a sign of American weakness, passivity, and defeatism in the wake of a war that had been lost because the American people had lacked the resolve to see it through. Between 1976 and 1980, this group would put forth a very different vision of the nation's appropriate role in the world after Vietnam. As we will see, in this vision, too, the family would reappear.

3

Productivity Lag and the End of the Family Wage

"The Great Male Cop-Out"

On 3 March 1972 autoworkers in Lordstown, Ohio, shut down the plant that General Motors had predicted would set a new standard for productivity and competitiveness within the American automobile industry. Hailed in the business press as the "plant of the future" when it opened in 1966, Lordstown was stocked with the most sophisticated machinery and time-saving devices. When operating at full capacity, its automated assembly line could produce over one hundred Chevy Vegas per hour, a speed that made it one of the most productive plants on earth. GM believed that both this production speed and the subcompact Vega were essential in an era of mounting foreign competition in the domestic car market. At the same time, the company recognized that the extraordinary speed of the line would require young workers with the physical stamina to keep up the pace. Thus GM decided to build the plant in a cornfield outside of Warren, Ohio, in the Mahoning Valley. By the late 1960s, there was a critical mass of young men in the region who needed employment and hoped to benefit from GM's relatively high wages and generous fringe benefits. Some of these men had grown up in the area and were the children of industrial workers who had been employed for decades in the local steel mills and rubber factories. Others had come up north from the disappearing coal-mining communities of Virginia and Kentucky. GM came to northeastern Ohio in pursuit of these men, who typically ranged in age from twenty-three to twenty-eight, were in the physical primes of their lives, and often had wives and children to support. GM was also drawn to Ohio for another reason: the company was repelled by the labor agitation and racial strife that plagued the city of Detroit, and its managers presumed that workers at Lordstown would be less predisposed to militancy.

This presumption proved false. In October 1971, the Lordstown plant came under the management of the General Motors Assembly Division (GMAD). Prior to that time, the plant had been divided into two separate units, Fisher Body and Chevrolet Assembly. Each unit had its own management and work rules. But in the fall of 1968, GM decided to combine Fisher and Chevy operations throughout the country with the aim of increasing efficiency. At a time when imported cars were gaining in popularity among American consumers, GM assumed that workers, fearing the threat of job loss, would be willing to comply with managerial imperatives. But three years later, when GMAD took over operations at Lordstown, managers did not find the compliant workers they had imagined. Upon assuming control of the plant, GMAD outraged the autoworkers by reducing the workforce. From there, it implemented a new work standard that reduced the number of workers per job. When workers resisted these speed-up efforts by working at a normal pace, management responded by issuing an unprecedented number of disciplinary lay-offs.[1]

The autoworkers fought back against the new management. Members of the United Autoworkers (UAW) Local 1112 indicted GMAD on the pages of its monthly newsletter. They tinkered with the GMAD acronym—"Get Mean and Destroy" and "Gotta Make Another Dollar."[2] They accused the new management of treating workers as though they were nothing more than robots, profit-making machinery, and "thousands and thousands of surplus parts."[3] The war of words was coupled with reports of industrial sabotage. Press accounts warned that the Vega was plagued by slit upholstery, scratched paint, dented bodies, cut ignition wires, and loose or missing bolts.[4] According to a story that circulated among the plant's workers, one engine had moved down the line with a perfectly positioned shell covering a sea of unassembled parts.[5] Finally, on 3 March 1972, after only five contentious months under GMAD management, Lordstown workers shut down the plant, initiating a strike that lasted for twenty-two days.

There was nothing unprecedented about either GM's efforts to increase efficiency or worker resistance at places like Lordstown. GMAD's new work rules reflected the enduring logic of a Taylorist model of scientific management aimed at extracting more and more labor from the individual, while the autoworkers were drawing on a long adversarial tradition that challenged this model through slowing down the line, walking off the job, going on strike, and even industrial sabotage. But the enduring contest between capitalist and worker took on new meaning in the early 1970s. The imperative of GM to respond to rising foreign competition depended on whether a new generation of workers would comply with efforts to increase efficiency and streamline production. This question about worker compliance was at the center of a third debate about national decline in the early 1970s that also revolved around the family, a debate over what economists called "productivity lag."

This debate began in the mid-1960s. Defined as the amount of goods or services that the average worker creates in one hour on the job, the productivity index provided economists with a crucial (if imprecise) measurement for gauging the nation's economic vigor. During the postwar years, economists had tied both the nation's rising standard of living and its dominance over global finance and trade to a steady increase in the output of the average American worker. But by the end of the 1960s, articles in *Fortune* and *Business Week* began painting a gloomier picture of the global economy that raised troubling questions about the nation's future productivity. The rates of productivity in both Japan and West Germany were climbing as American productivity was slowing down. Meanwhile, American exports were shrinking as foreign goods flooded domestic showrooms.[6] By the early 1970s, fear of declining productivity had migrated from the business press to mainstream publications. Thus an April 1972 *Newsweek* cover story, "World Trade: Can the U.S. Compete?" pictured a winded Uncle Sam jumping over a series of hurdles labeled "tariffs," "labor costs," "inflation," and "productivity gap." Trailing behind him were a Japanese sprinter and a burly Bavarian, carrying an effete Frenchman and a British dandy on his shoulders. Bringing up the rear were a Russian bear and a goose-stepping Maoist. While Uncle Sam trumped his competitors in stature, they appeared to be gaining on him in speed.[7] Appearing at the same moment that oil shortages were gaining public attention, stories like this implied that ex-

Workers assemble a Chevy Vega at the General Motors plant in Lordstown, Ohio, 25 January 1972. Courtesy of Special Collections, Cleveland State University Library.

cessive consumption was accompanied by declining production. Like the oil crisis, "productivity lag" seemed to suggest that the nation had entered an era of enervation, weakness, and fatigue.

Although news stories interpreted waning productivity in the steel and automobile industries as a sign of decline, the claim that these industries were falling behind foreign competitors needs to be situated in two related contexts, one narrower and the other wider than the framework of the nation. First, the debate over productivity lag took shape at a moment of acute economic, political, and cultural crisis for big business within the United States. Large American firms that had seen profits peak in the mid-1960s watched profit margins narrow in the early 1970s, a trend that suggested that it was actually a crisis of profitability (rather than of productivity) that preoccupied companies like GM during these years. Throughout the same period, both large and small businesses confronted intensified levels of governmental regulation, largely set in motion by the protest movements of the 1960s. Between the mid-1960s and the early 1970s, federal regulatory agencies like the Occupational Safety and Health Administration and the Environmental Protection Agency had been established, and Congress passed extensive environmental and consumer protection legislation such as the Clean Air Act. Although a public interest movement committed to protecting consumers and the environment from business had historical antecedents, the movement changed character in the wake of the 1960s. Antiwar activists had implicated corporations like Dow Chemical in the nation's alleged crimes in Vietnam, consumer advocates like Ralph Nader contended that large companies routinely prioritized profits over safety, and a new generation of investigative reporters, empowered by the media's influential coverage of both the civil rights movement and the war in Southeast Asia, wrote critical and rigorous exposés of corporate wrongdoing. The cumulative effect was a considerable public relations crisis for big business. On the surface, productivity lag appeared to contribute to this crisis, but at the same time, like the attention to oil shortages, it afforded corporations an opportunity to communicate with the public about the inner workings of their operations and to elaborate on the challenges they faced in an era of heightened foreign competition. The productivity lag would thus contribute to the growing animus against government.[8]

Second, the debate about productivity lag took place in a transnational context, another feature that linked it to the oil embargo. By the late 1960s, the capitalist economy was undergoing a structural transformation that was global in scope. Within advanced capitalist countries like the United States, this transformation entailed the restructuring, disintegration, and dispersal of heavy industries such as automobiles and steel that had fueled the American economy since the 1920s. Large companies began moving plants abroad in search of lower wages and relying more heavily on outsourcing (the purchase of partially completed products and parts from independent companies) in order to reduce expenditures. The terms that scholars would later use to describe this transformation—"post-Fordism" and "globalization"—were not yet in wide use. But intellectuals like Daniel Bell were already heralding the arrival of a postindustrial society in which information and services would eclipse heavy industry, while writers like Richard Barnet were detailing the "global reach" of multinational corporations once territorially bound to the nation-state.[9] Although these transnational dimensions were often obscured in the debate over productivity lag, the debate played out against this wider global framework and implicitly raised concerns about the future of industrial production in the United States. Much as they did with the oil embargo, journalists filtered the productivity crisis through the lens of national decline. Only with the benefit of hindsight can we see that both crises revolved around the future of American power in a new era of globalization, one in which earlier conceptions of national sovereignty would undergo revision.[10]

Just as the family figured prominently in debates about Vietnam and the oil embargo, it also shaped the debate about productivity lag. No sooner had economists issued warnings about America's declining rates of productivity than social scientists, industrial psychologists, and pollsters began to explain the slump by probing the psychology of what they called a "new breed" of worker. Observing workplace resistance at assembly plants like Lordstown, they argued that a new generation of white, male, blue-collar workers was no longer willing to engage in alienating and stultifying work for a decent wage. The new breed's apparent refusal to assume his breadwinning duties suggested that the industrial father of the postwar era had failed to transmit the work ethic to his son, revealing another aspect of the same crisis of male authority and familial regulation that had surfaced during the POW campaign and the oil embargo. The consequence of this failure, according to productivity experts, was a generation of men who expected too much from work. Indeed, it seemed as if young men were in danger of repudiating their breadwinning role in exchange for a 1960s-style commitment to self-realization. *Business Week* described this collective act of repudiation in 1977 as the "great male cop-out from the work ethic."[11] By mid-decade, large corporations were responding to the challenge posed by this new breed of worker by launching job enrichment programs and advertising campaigns that drew on the language of personal self-fulfillment, authenticity, and teamwork in the service of heightened efficiency. By the end of the 1970s, however, psychocultural discussions of the new breed gave way to concern over male unemployment, corporate restructuring, and deindustrialization. The hippie-worker was replaced by an older image: the unemployed male breadwinner. This shift brought into full relief the broader transformation simmering below the surface of the productivity debate from the beginning: the dissolution of an industrial economy made up of a majority white, predominantly male, unionized workforce, the end of the family wage ideal, and the rise of the two-earner family. The productivity crisis would pass, but this transformation was permanent.

The Counterculture Comes to the Assembly Line:
Dr. Spock, Paternal Failure, and the New Breed

Initially, the debate about productivity lag that emerged in the second half of the 1960s was confined to economists, who were preoccupied with its causes. They attributed the lag to several factors: the comparatively high wage rates of American labor, corporate inattention to research and development, a lack of capital investment in new technology and equipment, and a rise in federal environmental and safety regulations. Another significant factor in the declining productivity rates, they argued, was the overall expansion of the service sector. This factor raised a question that went beyond causality: was a measurement like the productivity index still viable in an economy increasingly defined by service and information? Economists conceded that their methods for gauging productivity in the service industry were primitive at best, explaining the challenge to the layperson with a rhetorical question: "If a fiddler fiddles faster is that more output?"[12] For economists, the problem was not so much that workers were failing to produce more goods at increasing rates, but that the production of services was eclipsing the production of tangible goods, thus rendering traditional economic logic problematic.

This question about service work touched on a second theme that animated the debate about productivity: the changing demographics of the workforce. In an argument that reflected the implicit centrality of the rise of the two-earner family to the productivity debate, economists and other observers contended that the recent influx of women (especially married women) into the labor force was undermining American rates of productivity. Not only were these inexperienced and unskilled workers slowing down productivity within manufacturing and industry, they argued, but they were also disproportionately represented within the service and clerical sectors, where productivity was most difficult to measure.[13] By identifying them as newcomers to the workforce, this argument effaced the long and complex histories of women's waged work. Although couched in the ostensibly neutral language of social science, the argument betrayed a deeper cultural anxiety that an expanding world of service work made up of an increasingly feminized workforce was eroding the nation's economic strength.

But if what the business press soon dubbed the "new workforce" was distinguished by its changing gender composition, it also reflected a psychological reorientation among white, male industrial workers, a group that historically had been accorded the decisive role in the economic well-being of the nation. By the late 1960s, the debate over productivity moved beyond the domain of economics as industrial psychologists, motivational experts, corporate managers, and social scientists began to weigh in. These groups contended that the motivations that had once compelled blue-collar industrial workers to fulfill their responsibilities as wage earners were no longer firmly in place. Both the economic growth of the 1960s and rising rates of retirement among men who had entered the workforce after World War I meant that a new generation of young workers had been entering industrial plants in unprecedented numbers.[14] The result, they argued, was a different kind of worker reared in affluence and unfamiliar with scarcity. A desire for self-fulfillment set this worker apart from his father, who, traumatized by the Depression, required no other motivation to work than the fear of unemployment. In 1974, pollster Daniel Yankelovich described this young male worker as a "new breed," and the term became ubiquitous in debates over the productivity crisis.[15]

The new breed represented a break with the male industrial worker of the 1940s and 1950s. The economic expansion of the postwar period had been fueled largely by the steel and automobile industries, and the male industrial worker was both symbol and agent of American dominance.[16] Although the number of white-collar and service jobs had surpassed the number of blue-collar ones by the mid-1950s, both business and union leaders celebrated the industrial worker for his contribution to national strength.[17] This worker was also accorded a critical cultural role, since his entrance into the middle class was seen as the fulfillment of the American dream. Assembly-line work was monotonous and grueling, but employment at a company such as GM provided the worker with a range of compensations secured by collective bargaining: rising wages, a solid pension, health care, and unemployment insurance. The result, as sociologist Ruth Milkman has described it, was the creation of "a private welfare state" that transformed autoworkers into the "blue collar aristocrats of the age."[18] At the heart of this transformation was the ability of the autoworker to provide for his family in a range of ways: garnering a living wage to support a wife and children; securing health insurance, retirement benefits, and a pension that inoculated the family from financial and medical risks; working an eight-hour day that afforded him leisure time for family relations; and bringing home a disposable income that could be used for the consumption of the same goods he produced on the factory floor. The industrial worker's ability to provide for his family made him a powerful symbol of the American Century, and the notion that a new breed might deviate from this earlier quid pro quo was disturbing.

Most troubling about the new breed was his conscious and deliberate renunciation of the world of work. Citing rising incidences of absenteeism, high job-turnover rates, and shoddy workmanship, both corporate managers and labor leaders attributed the nation's ebbing productivity to a new generation of men unwilling to assume its breadwinning duties. Other newcomers to the workforce undermined productivity because they lacked training and experience, but the challenge posed by the new breed was psychological in origin and thus more elusive. Shortly before his death, UAW president Walter Reuther attempted to explain the problem of absenteeism through probing the psyche of this new worker. According to Reuther, the young worker gets three or four days' pay and figures "I can live on that. I'm not really interested in those material things anyhow. I'm interested in a sense of fulfillment as a human being. The prospect of tightening up bolts every two minutes for eight hours for thirty years doesn't lift the human spirit."[19] Two years later, Ken Bannon, the vice president of the UAW, explored the new ethos in a 1972 *Business Week* article about "the spreading Lordstown syndrome." "New and younger workers will be less attracted to repetitive and uninteresting and physically arduous routine tasks," Bannon explained, implying that workers of a bygone era had engaged in boring and monotonous work because they were attracted to it. Bannon went on to argue that this resistance to assembly-line monotony reflected a waning work ethic among the young, contending that "the traditional concept that hard work is a virtue and a duty, which older workers have adhered to, is not applicable to younger workers."[20] Taken together, both Reuther's and Bannon's characterizations encapsulated a number of attitudes attributed to the new breed of worker throughout the 1970s: a rejection of materialism, a repudiation of an older, duty-bound work ethic, a new commitment to self-fulfillment, and an unwillingness to engage in mind-numbing, repetitive tasks.

In order to understand the new breed, industrial psychologists and social scientists turned their attention to the early years of socialization. They attributed the young worker's attitude not only to permissive childrearing, but also to the idea that the affluent society itself had eroded parental authority and dulled the acquisitive drive. For productivity experts, the new breed's problems could be traced back to the father's failure to transmit the work ethic to his son. Ironically, by insulating his child from the deprivations that had framed his own Depression-era experiences, it now turned out that the father had done his son a disservice by failing to ready him for the discipline and rigor of work. The new worker's already compromised attention to breadwinning was further imperiled by a narcissistic culture that prized self-fulfillment over familial obligation.[21]

Corporate managers were also drawn to the notion of a new breed of worker. Supposedly spoiled by parental overindulgence and postwar affluence, the new breed was to blame for the nation's lagging productivity rates. One industrial psychologist who worked for GM recalled the answers offered by the company's general managers in 1970 when asked to explain declining customer satisfaction and unmet production schedules: "There's a different kind of worker out there now. The Doctor Spock and his lousy child-rearing practices has started a whole new generation of hippies, malcontents, nincanpoops [sic]."[22] News stories about the new breed often referred to Dr. Benjamin Spock's *The Common Sense Book of Baby and Childcare* (1946), suggesting that young workers' resistance to hard work and discipline could be traced back to the parental permissiveness supposedly advocated by the country's most famous pediatrician. A 1972 article in *Time* magazine entitled "Is the Work Ethic Going Out of Style?" asked whether "the nation's 22.5 million workers under 30, nursed on television and still showing their Spock marks, may in fact be too educated, too expectant and too anti-authoritarian" for the nation's jobs.[23] Even those who sympathized with younger workers described them as "the Spock generation growing up."[24]

Social scientists, managers, and labor leaders argued that parental permissiveness was responsible for a host of ills now pervading the contemporary workplace. First, it had produced a generation of young workers resistant to workplace discipline. "The young workers won't accept the same old kind of discipline their fathers did," UAW vice president Douglas A. Fraser explained to readers of *Fortune* magazine in 1970.[25] Because of his permissive upbringing, the factory floor was often the first place where a young man encountered any discipline at all. Managers complained that workers often responded by ignoring directives and even walking off the job. An older steelworker contrasted his own deference to the attitude of a new generation: "These kids . . . don't even know how to take the crap we took."[26] It was not only that the family had failed to discipline the young worker, but that it had actively encouraged him to challenge authority, to "question why [he] must do things," and to "talk back."[27] Many of these disciplinary problems stemmed not only from a permissive model of family life but also from rising opportunities for education. Presumably, a better-educated workforce would benefit the nation's economy; but productivity experts came to the opposite conclusion in the early 1970s, arguing that, in addition to making workers more defiant, higher levels of education had raised their expectations and fueled their discontent. Newcomers to work discipline had been taught to question the very necessity for authoritarian relations and were thus unprepared for the exigencies of the assembly line.[28]

A second problem confronting managers was that, because they had never experienced economic adversity, workers displayed insufficient gratitude for their jobs. Prosperity, it appeared, had eroded productivity. Citing rising absenteeism and high turnover rates, managers worried that young workers were "unfamiliar with the harsh economic facts of earlier years" and would skip a day's work on a whim.[29] Apocryphal stories about the typical Lordstown worker became popular fare among corporate managers. One story quoted a young Lordstown worker who, when asked why he routinely came to work only four days a week, answered, "Because I can't live on what I make in three." According to GM's vice president of personnel, "It was time for young workers to show more appreciation for what they had."[30]

By dulling their acquisitive drive, postwar affluence had unleashed a host of extraeconomic expectations that young workers were bringing to the workplace. Literature suggested that the new breed felt a sense of entitlement, an "increased selfishness, even as the national economy falters."[31] According to a 1970 *Fortune* article, corporations like GM had for too long assumed that "economic man was served if the pay was okay."[32] But in an era of affluence, the man who defined himself solely in economic terms was hard to find. Reared to expect rather than be grateful for a decent wage, the young worker was no longer motivated by monetary incentives alone. Managers had to recognize that the worker who once placed a premium on material reward now expected work to be a "fulfilling, personally rewarding experience," thus requiring new managerial approaches that would appeal to nonmaterialistic values. A product of the 1960s, the new breed of worker looked to his job not only as a source of income, but also as a place to cultivate self-esteem, recognition, and satisfaction.[33]

The pursuit of self-fulfillment had consequences for the family. Supposedly, postwar parents had overindulged their children, but the male worker who chose self-realization in lieu of breadwinning was guilty of the opposite crime: he threatened to abdicate his commitment to family life altogether. "In the new breed," reported Daniel Yankelovich, "we see the beginnings of an ethic built around the concept of duty to oneself, in glaring contrast to the traditional ethic of obligation to others."[34] Tied to this new emphasis on the self was the fear that the widening sphere of leisure might woo men away from work and family permanently. Within an older value system, according to these accounts, a paid job had been the classic road to self-respect. Success had been rooted in "a new car, an achieving child, a job promotion."[35] But now, the younger worker was turning inward and focusing on his own needs and desires and relinquishing his obligations to family life. According to one analyst looking back on waning productivity rates throughout the 1970s, this new emphasis on the self had had a deleterious impact on the nation's economic strength. "The 'Looking Out for No. 1' philosophy eschews self-denial in favor of self-indulgence," James O'Toole wrote in 1981. "This may produce prodigious consumers, but it makes for lousy workers. The new narcissism . . . stresses entitlements without concomitant responsibilities."[36]

For some, this rejection of family life explained the new breed's resistance to workplace discipline. One older Ford autoworker celebrated the new generation of autoworkers in Studs Terkel's *Working*, observing that what enabled them to fight back was that they "had nothing to lose." They were not only young, but "they ain't got no wife, so they don't worry about it."[37] A utility man at an auto plant explained his plant's increased absenteeism in the same terms: "We got this younger generation in here. Lot of 'em single. . . . They're not settled yet and they live from day to day." He went on to predict that the problem of absenteeism would solve itself once younger male workers succumbed to the demands of family life: "When they settle down, they do like myself. They have a routine."[38] Business owners echoed these observations as they complained about the dearth of responsible young workers. An Associated Press article contrasted the earlier crews of "Lithuanians, Latvians, Russians," who had taken pride in their work, to a new generation of young men, defined not by their ethnicity, but by being single. One owner observed: "It isn't like being 25 and married with a baby and a house payment and a car payment. They just don't have any responsibilities."[39] These observations advanced the notion that it was the family that made men into breadwinners. The economic demands of family life would discipline young male workers in the end.

These descriptions also suggested that the racial and gender identities of the industrial worker were more fluid than they had been in the past. African American men had long been stigmatized for lacking a commitment to the work ethic. As we have seen, by the mid-1960s, policymakers were arguing that the defining symptom of African American cultural pathology was the failure of black men to assume their breadwinning duties. This argument was premised on an implicit contrast to white men, who presumably displayed no such resistance to wage labor. But accounts of the new breed undermined this distinction by implying that a new generation of white men resembled their black counterparts. Simultaneously, the emphasis on personal self-fulfillment established an affinity between young working-class men and women, particularly those drawn to the politics of feminism. As we will see in chapter 5, the language of personal self-fulfillment and gratification that shaped discussions of the new breed echoed almost verbatim the rhetoric associated with the women's liberation movement, suggesting that young men were asking some of the same questions that young women were asking by the early 1970s.

But the most crucial question about the new breed's identity hinged on the newly permeable relationship between the counterculture and the assembly line. By the late 1960s, industrial psychologists were drawing a correlation between campus unrest and workplace insubordination, suggesting that mounting feelings of frustration and disaffection among young workers might make them more susceptible to the student movement. In 1969, a group of psychologists based in New York City urged executives to attend "The New Face of the Labor Force," a one-day seminar that would help business leaders understand "what makes the new work force tick." The seminar's promotional leaflet featured two lists, presented side by side, charting recent upheavals within both society and the workplace. Outside your company, the leaflet explained to the executive, you can witness campus riots, racial tension, teenage "turning on and dropping out," alienation and unrest, the challenging of authority, and antisocial behavior. Inside your company, it continued, you encounter low productivity, high personnel turnover, recruiting difficulty, disloyalty, sabotage, and a "don't give a damn attitude." Featuring sessions on themes like the generation gap, the seminar promised to help executives develop motivational techniques for spurring these new workers on and immunizing their companies against corrupting outside elements.[40]

By the early 1970s, it appeared that youth rebellion had infiltrated the assembly line so completely that worker discontent eclipsed student upheavals, at least in the news stories of the day. In 1974, Daniel Yankelovich drew a series of contrasts between the late 1960s and the early 1970s, arguing that the campus rebellions had become moribund and that it was working-class youth who exhibited the orientations once associated with college youth: freer sexual morality, a waning work ethic, skepticism toward authority, and feelings of discontent and dissatisfaction.[41] Young blue-collar workers revealed their new orientations by adopting a hippie style of dress, by listening to rock music like Led Zeppelin and the Rolling Stones, and by smoking dope and dropping acid.[42] News articles described Lordstown as an industrial Woodstock and noted the long hair, ponytails, and bell-bottoms of the assembly-line workers. Corporate managers substantiated these portraits, observing that young workers often sported long hair, sandals, and beads, symbolic displays of their identification with the counterculture.[43]

The counterculture's arrival on the assembly line was also taken up in popular culture. The blue-collar archetype of the period, Archie Bunker, of the CBS hit sitcom *All in the Family,* was known for his contempt for the counterculture; but the 1970 film *Joe,* often cited in literature on the blue-collar worker, offered a more complicated portrait. In an early scene, steelworker Joe spouts off to no one in particular about the black welfare recipients who only "make money through making babies." But he reserves his real hatred for the counterculture, contending that its repudiation of hard work has unleashed both wanton sexuality and a voracious appetite for consumer goods: "The kids, the white kids, they are worse than the niggers. Money don't mean nothing to them. Motorcycles, marijuana, five-dollar records. The money ain't worth shit. The white kids, the rich kids, the worst. . . . The cars, the best colleges, vacations, orgies, Christmas, Easter. They go some place like a fancy resort and have orgies. Easter orgies! The day Christ rose they're all screwing one another. And the poor kids, the middle class kids, they're all copying the rich kids. They're all going down the same goddamn screw-America way! Hippies!"[44]

In this salvo, Joe expresses his fear that the decadent mores of the rich are trickling down to his own class, but Joe himself is not as impervious to countercultural influences as this diatribe would have viewers believe. Although Joe never abandons his bigotry, by the end of the film he has penetrated the hippie milieu of Greenwich Village, smoked marijuana, and indulged in an orgy. His frustration with his own eroding social position moves him in two opposing directions at once, fostering his allegiance to reactionary, authoritarian politics and compelling him to mine the counterculture as a means of escape. While Joe's firm belief in the unassailability of racial differences enables him to define himself squarely against the black welfare recipient, his relationship to the counterculture is more slippery. Although the film presents Joe as a stereotype, its real concern is with the precariousness of his blue-collar identity and the ease with which he can be seduced by a world he claims to despise.

Job applicants at the Ford Motor Company plant in Brook Park, Ohio, 10 March 1976. Courtesy of Special Collections, Cleveland State University Library.

This ambiguity surrounding blue-collar identity extended to the blue-collar vote. Since the 1930s, unionized workers had made up a core constituency of Roosevelt's New Deal coalition; but by the late 1960s there were signs that their political allegiance was up for grabs. In the presidential race of 1968, unionized workers voted for segregationist third-party candidate George Wallace in surprisingly high numbers, and Richard Nixon's campaign appealed to the blue-collar worker as the "forgotten man" who supported law and order at home and anticommunism abroad. Throughout the race, Nixon argued that the upheavals of the 1960s had eclipsed the struggles of this silent majority, one made up of white working-class men and women, often residing in the nation's violence-ridden cities, working hard for their meager earnings, and dutifully paying their taxes.[45] By the early 1970s, academics and journalists had seized on the theme of the "blue-collar blues," arguing that feelings of frustration among manual laborers stemmed as much from their eroding social status as from the precariousness of their class position. In an era of heightened automation and technology, "the laborer feels that he's a low man," a stonemason told Studs Terkel in 1972.[46] In this vein, Nixon believed that the political wooing of the blue-collar worker required the bolstering of morale as much as economic relief. Thus a 1970 report to the president entitled "The Problem of the

119

Blue Collar Worker" suggested that skilled trades be honored with national awards and commemorative postage stamps in an attempt to ameliorate the blue-collar worker's sense that his work has "no 'status' in the eyes of society, the media, or even his own children."[47] Nixon's appeal to "the silent majority" was premised on the assumption that the blue-collar worker felt alienated and disgusted by the counterculture. But the new breed worker undermined this premise; he, in fact, was an amalgam of the two social types that Nixon hoped to pit against one another: the blue-collar worker and the countercultural rebel.

Further blurring the distinction between these two social types was younger workers' shifting attitudes toward Vietnam. These workers were disproportionately represented in the fighting, often arriving at the plant after having served in Vietnam, and almost always having friends and family members fighting overseas. Thus they were prone to support the war. But by the early 1970s many had become outspoken in their opposition. Nevertheless, journalists highlighted the role played by middle-class college students in the antiwar movement, alienating even blue-collar workers who were against the war. Nixon sought to profit from the ostensible divide between workers and activists, a strategy bolstered by dramatic news stories of violent confrontations between antiwar protesters and hard hats.[48] Still, between 1970 and 1973, unionized blue-collar workers became more mobilized against the war.[49] Here again, the allegiance of industrial workers appeared to be moving in two directions at once: to the right vis-à-vis the Republican Party and to the left vis-à-vis their opposition to the Vietnam War.

Following defeat in Vietnam and the oil crisis, then, the productivity lag was taken as a third symptom of national decline in the early 1970s, and the family was again at its center. Popular accounts of the new breed portrayed labor struggles as family disputes, thus making stories about the assembly line accessible to a public more familiar with the generation gap than with speed-up and grievance procedures. In the process, labor conflict was recast in terms of blood and kinship relations. The story became one of parental failure rather than corporate exploitation, lack of early discipline rather than draconian work rules. At the heart of the story were struggles between different generations of men: managers and workers, older male workers and younger male workers, fathers and sons. The omnipresence of the generational motif captures the ways in which a range of actors transformed a complex story about economic change into a sentimentalized family drama in which women were often absent. But lest we conclude that the father-son theme was imposed on the new breed by an older generation, it is important to recognize that young workers drew on the familial motif themselves. Thus, according to Gary Bryner, president of Lordstown's union local, the older generation had demonstrated its manliness by being able to "work hard and have big strong muscles," but young men asserted their manliness by standing up to their supervisors. While the father felt indebted to the man who had given him a job, "the young guy believes that he has something to say about what he does." "The almighty dollar is not the only thing," he added. "There's more to it—how I'm treated. . . . I can concentrate on the social aspects, my rights."[50] Older workers also had more complicated attitudes. Mike LeFevre, a Chicago steelworker, told Studs Terkel that he resented his younger, college-educated supervisor but nonetheless hoped that his own son would grow up to be an "effete snob" who could "quote Walt Whitman." "I want my kid to look at me," LeFevre added, "and say 'Dad, you're a nice guy, but you're a fuckin' dummy.' Hell yes, I want my kid to tell me that he's not gonna be like me."[51]

The fact is that many new-breed workers would soon be subject to the same constraints that had afflicted their parents. Thus Ben Hamper, a Flint, Michigan, autoworker, described his family as a long line of "shoprats" who responded to GM's call for workers with almost "Pavlovian compliance."[52] Factory servitude felt as though it was "something so predestined within [his] genes" that Hamper even imagined himself in utero practicing assembly maneuvers, as his mother called out to her husband, "Bernard, I can feel the baby kicking. No wait—he's RIVETING!"[53] Similarly, a GM worker, who also served as the president of a UAW local, remarked in 1970: "Every single unskilled man in my plant wants out. . . . The whole generation has been taught by their fathers to avoid the production line, to go to college to escape, and now some of them are trapped."[54] Such accounts, infused as they are with pain, ambivalence, bitterness, and raw humor, reveal the extent to which the notion of the new breed was predicated on a series of false premises: that fathers always wanted to create sons in their own images, that a family legacy was inherently positive, that workplace discontent and resistance were rooted in filial relations gone awry, and that working-class men could always "opt out" of the world of wage labor. Nonetheless, much as it had throughout the oil embargo, the family emerged as cause, symptom, and solution for the problem of productivity lag. Ironically, as we will see, in the years after 1973 the path to the coming austerity would proceed through the new breed.

Self-Realization and the
Revival of a Producerist Ethic

The initial debate about productivity lag postulated an inherent conflict between the new breed's quest for self-fulfillment and corporate interests. But by the early 1970s, the debate changed direction as corporate managers and business leaders drew on the language of self-realization to convince younger workers that the modern corporation could be a locus of personal meaning, a place committed to the production of high-quality goods. Increasingly, the more affirmative term "quality" replaced the loaded one "productivity." Above all, new job enrichment programs contended that the productivity crisis required that workers and managers abandon the adversarial relations of the past and initiate a new era of teamwork. The metaphor of the team was not the same as that of the family, but it worked in a similar way by suggesting that conflicts over power and authority within the workplace could best be resolved without outside interference. In this way, the team concept constructed the assembly line and the industrial plant as quasi-familial spaces in which struggles and disputes could be overcome from within. If at first corporate managers and business leaders blamed workplace discontent on declining paternal authority, after 1973 they began attempting to remake the corporation in the image of a nonpatriarchal family.

In his 1970 best seller *The Greening of America*, Charles Reich had challenged the perception that the younger generation exhibited an aversion to work. In his book, Reich argued for the (distinctly non-Marxist) revolutionary potential of the counterculture, insisting that it was not work that young people were rebelling against but the specific forms of work engendered by what he called the corporate state. "Most work available in our society is meaningless, degrading and inconsistent with self-realization," wrote Reich. By repudiating such work, the young person was paving the way for the development of "[his] true potential as a human being." According to Reich, this constituted one of the "greatest and most vital forms of liberation."[55] For Reich, revolution would be achieved not through class struggle, but through the recuperation of an authentic self that had been stymied by the unrelenting and driven nature of industrialized work.

At first glance, it is hard to imagine that business executives would have paid attention to Reich's predictions. As we have already seen, the business community had more dire concerns: growing public skepticism toward big business, distress over mounting regulations, the oil embargo, economic

forecasts about the nation's declining productivity, and reports of heightened foreign competition.[56] Nevertheless, business leaders and corporate
managers seized on the theme of self-realization. Adopting the language of
humanistic psychology, they seemed to agree with Reich that workers deserved jobs that were meaningful, challenging, and fulfilling. Indeed, they
portrayed the problem of job dissatisfaction as inseparable from the larger
problems besetting American industry. Corporations like GM and unions
like the UAW came together to develop quality of work life (QWL) programs
that would simultaneously address the twin challenges of job dissatisfaction and waning productivity rates. If the worker could find fulfillment on
the job through a renewed commitment to the production of high-quality
goods, he would at once restore his sense of self-worth and the nation's
leadership in global trade.[57]

This was not the first time that industrial firms had searched for solutions
to the problem of worker alienation. In the wake of the labor upheavals of
World War I, managers in manufacturing centers like Chicago had created
personnel and industrial relations departments and encouraged foremen to
adopt less paternalistic attitudes toward workers.[58] During the same period,
Harvard Business School's Elton Mayo conducted his famous experiments
at Chicago's Western Electric Company, concluding that worker productivity was more contingent on personal feelings of recognition than classic
labor-struggle demands.[59] But this was the first time that job enrichment
was directly linked to a transformation in family life and was identified so
explicitly as a solution to the problem of national decline.

The renewed corporate attention to job enrichment was also notable
because it took place at a pivotal moment in the history of big business.
As historian David Vogel has shown, the early 1970s business community
launched a powerful political counteroffensive that gained momentum
after 1976. Emerging in response to the various crises confronting big business, this counteroffensive was multidimensional and included grassroots
lobbying, the creation of corporate political action committees that raised
and distributed campaign funds, the establishment of trade associations
and public affairs offices, the reinvigoration of the Chamber of Commerce,
the formation of corporate foundations, the launching of think tanks and
research institutes, and the funding of professorships committed to "free
enterprise" at American universities. The scope and ambition of the counteroffensive was reflected in the formation in 1973 of the Business Roundtable, a group of corporate executive officers who met with members of
Congress to plan legislation.[60] The job enrichment and QWL programs

launched after 1973 were one front in this counteroffensive, capturing the extent to which productivity lag, like the oil embargo, proved to be both a crisis and an opportunity for corporations.

As they developed these programs, key corporations in the older Fordist auto and steel industries began to present themselves as organizations that welcomed rather than lamented the new breed. "The last thing our country needs is dull, unquestioning conformity on the part of our young people," contended Stewart S. Cort, the chairman of Bethlehem Steel, in a 1974 advertisement. Rejecting the "revolutionary" and "violent" tactics of the recent past, young people today retained their commitment to creativity, originality, and social progress. Accordingly, there was now a "quiet revolution" going on in corporate corridors, Cort continued, as firms searched for the employee "who wonders, who doubts, who questions, and who tries hard to find new and better answers to the old, nagging problems." Cort ended with a direct address to the new worker: "So I urge you, whatever your ideology, to join the established institutions and 'do your own thing.' If you want to promote higher standards of moral conduct, if you want to humanize working conditions, if you want to make institutions more democratic, if you want to make them more responsive to the people they serve, you can do it best from the inside." If some blamed the new breed for waning productivity, here Cort identified him as part of the solution.[61]

The transformation of the new breed from corporate antagonist into ally required responding to his therapeutic need for "self-realization." Through the development and implementation of QWL programs, managers hoped to endow work with personal meaning and satisfaction, thereby neutralizing the dissatisfaction and ingratitude nurtured by the counterculture and now pervading the assembly line. The factory could be transformed into a site of self-fulfillment where workers affirmed their commitment to the production of high-quality goods. According to proponents of QWL programs, this commitment to quality would benefit both workers and their companies. It not only would enrich jobs but also would serve the needs of American corporations in an era of increased foreign competition. By appealing to an earlier producerist ethic that romanticized the figure of the white male artisan and craftsman, corporate managers and motivational experts appropriated the language of self-fulfillment in the service of heightened efficiency.

The producerist ethic was rooted in ideals of early American republicanism that stressed the economic independence of rights-bearing men as the prerequisite of political citizenship.[62] Historically, these ideals had

Imagine a steelmaker wanting a student's radical ideas.

Great inventions have always been the product of radical ideas. Consider the "horseless carriage" or the "aeroplane."

For the past five years Armco's Student Design Programs have encouraged that kind of radical thinking. Industrial design classes of leading colleges are given a challenging, topical subject. They probe, ponder and create. Then present their design ideas to top government and industry people. They talk. We listen.

Subjects have covered the home, transportation, agriculture, the sea, and leisure. Ideas have ranged from a furniture system to an underwater bike to electronic shrimp harvesters to a Heartmobile that is already saving lives in Columbus, Ohio.

The ideas come. In the process we all learn more about where we're going and about the talented young people who will get us there.

Strange role for a steelmaker? Not for Armco, because Armco is different.

Armco Steel Corporation, Middletown, Ohio 45042.

Imagine Armco

Armco Steel reaches out to the new worker in this 1970 advertisement.
Courtesy of AK Steel Corporation; advertisement provided by J. Walter Thompson Company Archives.

been undermined by the realities of slavery, patriarchy, and indentured servitude, and in the nineteenth century they were displaced by the spread of wage labor. But the status of the white, male property owner as an independent economic producer persisted as a normative ideal that reappeared in American culture at moments of economic upheaval. This ideal highlighted pride in workmanship, appealed to romantic images of the artisan and craftsman, and was always linked to family, as in the later ideal of the family wage. In the context of the productivity crisis, it was being redefined again, this time in relation to a therapeutic ethic.

Corporate appeals to the producerist ideal converged surprisingly easily with discussions of the new breed. Most importantly, these appeals assumed that workers' economic demands had been largely superseded by psychological ones. The demand for a decent wage, once the touchstone of labor politics, would now be accompanied by the quest for personal gratification in the workplace. One UAW local president explained that while the union knew that its primary task remained the improvement of the worker's economic life, union leadership also needed to recognize that "times had changed" and that the union now "had a broader obligation . . . to help [workers] improve the whole quality of life at work beyond the paycheck."[63] Proponents of QWL programs often cited humanistic psychologist Abraham Maslow's hierarchy of needs to support the claim that once workers' economic demands were met, demands for self-fulfillment on the job would gradually assume greater importance. A mainstay in QWL literature, Maslow's hierarchy suggested that as primary needs for food and shelter are satisfied, subtler needs for self-esteem and self-actualization (defined as being able to realize one's potential to the full) come to the surface. Observers of the new workforce asserted that this was precisely what had happened by the late 1960s. According to *Work in America*, a report commissioned by the Department of Health, Education, and Welfare in 1971, "The very success of industry and organized labor in meeting the basic needs of workers has unintentionally spurred demands for esteemable and fulfilling jobs."[64] With the problem of "basic needs" presumably out of the way, business managers and union leaders would need to identify the features that would make the workplace a locus of self-fulfillment for a new generation of workers.

Making jobs personally fulfilling required a number of workplace reforms. First, QWL proponents argued that the new workforce called for less paternalistic, more participatory styles of management. According to the *Work in America* report, the workplace would have to lose its "authoritarian aura" in order to become the setting for "satisfying and self-actualizing activity."[65] The hard and abrasive foreman of the 1920s and 1930s—the model of the stern father—needed to be replaced by a benevolent supervisor who recognized that his workers were his "greatest resource," a slogan increasingly adopted by companies.[66] Consultants for QWL programs routinely found that a universal complaint among workers was that they were infantilized by supervisors. Workers at Southwestern Bell Telephone Company told one such consultant that they resented being in a "day care center" where they were required to raise their hands in order to go to the restroom, timed by supervisors with stopwatches, and threatened with punishment the way one would treat a seven-year-old. According to the consultant, there was absolutely no excuse for this kind of treatment of mature adults on the part of any level of management.[67] Such methods were needlessly cruel, and, perhaps more important, they were archaic and ineffectual. According to one prediction, if managers continued to rely on antiquated methods in their supervision of the new workforce, they would only be exacerbating a contradiction between an increasingly democratic society and the authoritarian sphere of work. If workers were asked to lead a "double life—flexibility in the community and rigidity in the workplace," employers would ultimately pay the price in the form of compromised job performance.[68] In order to keep pace with the changing times, companies needed to encourage workers to play a participatory role in the workplace. QWL programs routinely advocated more open lines of communication between supervisors and workers, encouraging the implementation of quality circles, in which workers and managers could meet voluntarily in order to solve shop-oriented production-quality problems together.[69] According to one article in *Psychology Today*, workers needed to be recognized as "grown-up human beings with useful contributions to make on how to do their jobs, and even how to run the company."[70]

New levels of worker participation required that a "new spirit of cooperation" replace the traditionally adversarial relationship between labor and management. That QWL programs were jointly sponsored by employers and labor unions distinguished them from earlier job enrichment efforts of the 1950s and 1960s, orchestrated exclusively by companies. If nothing else, QWL claimed to inaugurate a new era in labor-management relations, one necessitated by the dual challenges of worker disaffection and the specter of national decline. Assuming a unified front in the face of mounting foreign competition would require labor and management to improve communication, cultivate trust, and pursue informal methods of conflict resolution.

This theme pervaded discussions of lagging productivity. According to a 1974 U.S. Steel advertisement, "Labor and business can no longer continue their adversary relationship. . . . All of us are inseparably linked in the productivity quest."[71] This spirit of cooperation would require a quid pro quo, in which management acknowledged labor's "important know-how, imagination and ingenuity" and labor accepted its share of responsibility for improving productivity.[72] Historically, the aims of workers and management were seen as mutually exclusive. Now, the specter of national economic decline meant that workers and managers needed to unite. Productivity experts and QWL advocates insisted that job dissatisfaction and productivity lag were two sides of the same coin. An operating principle of QWL was that "what proves effective in human terms will ultimately improve the effectiveness of employees, the Company and the Union."[73] The QWL banner would allow the corporation to become "both a better place to work *and* a more efficient competitor."[74]

General Motors, the preeminent corporation of the Fordist era, led the way in the development of QWL programs. The company's interest was tentative at first. But in 1971, after it surveyed five thousand of its workers and found that they craved greater levels of participation in management decisions, GM divided its personnel department between labor relations and personnel. The latter focused on working conditions outside of the parameters of collective bargaining, such as orientation programs for incoming workers, leadership training sessions for first-line supervisors, and the allocation of tasks (such as inspections) to workers that previously had been under the supervisor's control.[75] Two years later, the UAW joined with the company in sponsoring these efforts, in part because plants that had implemented workplace reforms were showing a stronger performance.[76] In 1973, GM and the UAW issued their first collaborative statement on job enrichment that introduced the phrase "quality of work life." Over the next five years, GM began holding annual conferences on QWL, surveying employees every year about their attitudes toward work, and sponsoring annual training programs for supervisors and managers. Increasingly, into the 1980s, the term "quality of work life" appeared in literature on productivity, referring to greater levels of worker participation, less paternalistic modes of supervision, the company's solicitation of workers' ideas about the production process, and the implementation of a team concept that organized workers into smaller groups that rotated assignments and encouraged collective or "team-based" problem solving.

Calls for "team spirit" often cited Japan as the paradigmatic example of a nation whose economic success was rooted in harmonious relations between workers, employers, and unions. In the business press, countless reports marveled at the Japanese corporation's ability to instill in its workers a degree of loyalty and devotion reserved in the West for family ties. According to articles in *Fortune* and *Business Week*, the distinctions between nation, family, and corporation, so stark in the United States, were largely meaningless in Japan. "All Japanese work first and foremost for the 'national family'—the Rising Sun family," wrote *U.S. News and World Report* as it enviously described the national "team spirit" that overrode dividing lines among Japanese government, business, and labor.[77] The typical industrial Japanese company was "an extension of the family, where worker and boss are both on the same team."[78] The Japanese worker valued his company even more than his home life, making it "a hard mistress to beat."[79] In exchange for his loyalty, the worker was rewarded with lifetime employment, annual bonuses, and generous benefits. According to one *Reader's Digest* article, "Most employers are as reluctant to fire [a worker] as they are to turn a son out of the family. . . . The father and son loyalty is a major factor in the high quality of Japanese goods."[80] An article in *Science News* took the familial metaphor a step further, tracing the worker's devotion to his company back to the unique bond between Japanese mother and child: "The sustained dependence of the [Japanese] child upon the mother . . . results in a lifelong search for belonging, a primary identification as a member of a group rather than as an independent person."[81] Marveling at how Japan was able to transform its once devastated, war-torn economy into a formidable competitor, these media accounts were often contradictory, alternatively insisting that the "Japanese model" could be successfully imported to the United States *and* claiming that this same model was ultimately rooted in the particular and enigmatic psychology of the Japanese people, whose "swift passage out of feudalism . . . [had] not completely erased the stoic acceptance of a fixed hierarchical order."[82]

As corporate managers looked with envy at this Japanese workplace model, they recognized the need to instill this same sort of company pride into a new generation of American workers. As the Japanese model made clear, economic success would not only hinge on more congenial relations between labor and management; it also required instilling in the worker devotion to the firm and its products. This emphasis on product quality became the touchstone of both QWL and productivity campaigns. Through encouraging pride in workmanship and appealing to romantic images of the artisan and craftsman, these campaigns hoped to dispel the perception that American goods were shoddy and second-rate while simultaneously depicting the assembly line as a place where the male breadwinner could find personal meaning and self-fulfillment. This emphasis on pride in workmanship reveals the extent to which fears of national economic decline and anxieties about the status of the male breadwinner became enmeshed. By appealing to a producerist ethic rooted in early republicanism, these campaigns harkened back to an imaginary "golden age," in which the productive capacity of both the nation and its men had been beyond dispute.[83]

This producerist motif was perhaps most visible in corporate and government advertising. By emphasizing craftsmanship in its advertising, a corporation like GM was obviously affirming its commitment to the production of high-quality goods. But it was also depicting the assembly line as a place where men could still be craftsmen despite the imperatives of mass production. A 1973 GM advertisement featured Frank Mason Jr., a middle-aged African American man and an assembly-line worker whose task it was to discover imperfections on cars before they were painted and polished. "Frank Mason, Jr. can run his hands over the raw metal of an automobile hood and feel imperfections the human eye can't see," the advertisement began in bold letters, asserting that there was no machine that could do the work that he did. "In Europe, they call a man who does that kind of work an artisan," continued the advertisement. "For some reason, Americans say he's just a man who works on an assembly line. Maybe Americans are shy. Or else, maybe we think that because cars are mass produced, there's no craft involved." If the reader still had any doubt about the "consummate skill" that Frank Mason's job entailed, they were invited to give it a shot themselves: "Try it yourself on a piece of unpainted metal. Then try doing it quickly. Then imagine doing it on hundreds of cars, maintaining your concentration, keeping in mind the sleekness and beauty of the metal after it's painted, the pleasure someone will get when they buy it." There was only one difference between Frank Mason and the "Old World craftsmen," the advertisement concluded: "Frank Mason works in Flint, Michigan, USA at the leading edge of the 20th century."[84]

The emphasis on craftsmanship in this advertisement is revealing in a number of ways. First, the finished product itself—the GM automobile—is absent from the advertisement. Here, GM is not primarily selling cars (although they are certainly doing that), but selling first and foremost a specific kind of worker and experience of assembly-line work. Second, the emphasis on language and naming is key. GM speculates about why the same man is called an artisan in Europe and an assembly-line worker in America, concluding that the problem is ultimately one of misrecognition and lack of respect. Americans have simply failed to acknowledge the craft involved in mass production. If they only understood what Frank Mason's job entailed, they would see that there was nothing uniquely "Old World" about "Old World" craftsmanship; on the contrary, it was alive and well in modern Flint, Michigan. Finally, despite the overall aim of the advertisement, the essentially routinized and repetitive nature of Mason's job unwittingly slips back into view when readers are encouraged to simulate the job themselves, "doing it quickly" and "doing it on hundreds of cars" without losing their concentration. Simply calling Mason an "artisan" instead of an "assembly-line worker" cannot magically purge the work of its routinization, despite what GM might have us believe.

This emphasis on craftsmanship was also central to the Advertising Council's productivity campaign entitled "America. It Only Works as Well as We Do." The campaign was initiated by the National Commission on Productivity, established in 1970 to enlist labor, management, and state and local governments in the quest for productivity growth. Featuring print, television, and radio advertising, the campaign implored American workers to "sign their work" and "do the kind of work you'd be proud to put your name on," a message that, according to the Advertising Council, applied as much to the short-order cook as it did to the family farmer or skilled craftsman. "America needs more work that's good enough to sign," announced one advertisement that featured a re-creation of the signing of the Declaration of Independence, romantically harkening back to a colonial period in which a white masculine producerism had fostered national independence and strength. Not unlike the GM advertisement, this campaign proceeded from the premise that the malaise afflicting American workers could be remedied not primarily through job redesign or redistribution, but rather through restoring status to degraded forms of work. But by advancing the notion that a fast-food hot dog was somehow as worthy of a signature as a piece of handcrafted art, the campaign suggested that even the most seemingly banal work could become meaningful if only the worker could take pride in the goods he produced.

The Advertising Council developed the "sign your work" theme only after realizing that the concept of "increased productivity" would prove exceedingly difficult to sell to the general public. Workshop sessions and focus groups conducted during the campaign's developmental research found that "productivity" was a term that provoked either indifference or anger among participants. Focus group members either had no idea what productivity meant, or they associated it with speed-up, corporate exploitation, and job elimination.[85] Even those who recognized that increased productivity was in the best interest of the nation's economy still could not identify with the problem. According to McCann-Erickson, the advertising agency commissioned to develop the campaign, "While the public is in general agreement with the overall aim of increasing productivity, they offer stiff resistance when it comes to personal application of the principle."[86]

The challenges of public ignorance, apathy, and skepticism, coupled with workshop participants' tendency to blame the productivity problem on someone else, meant that the campaign had to be motivational and upbeat rather than accusatory or negative. Thus the initial proposal for a campaign theme, "America didn't get great by goofing off," was ultimately rejected as too punitive and wrist-slapping in tone.[87] The campaign would need to use a "positive approach" rather than one based on fear, threats, or accusations.[88] According to McCann-Erickson, such an approach would require that the term "increased productivity" be purged from the campaign altogether. Ironically, the most effective way for the Advertising Council to "sell productivity" would be by making no reference to it at all. A 1973 strategy paper advised the commission to "consider the development of an alternate or substitute phrase for the term 'increased productivity' that would not have the same degree of negative attitudinal predispositions."[89] In order for the campaign to succeed, it would need to attack the productivity issue indirectly, "through a problem which the average individual is very much concerned with and concerned about; that is, the *quality* of goods and services. If people can be motivated to real concern about the *quality* of work they and the people around them do, the end result will almost certainly be increased productivity."[90]

The substitution of "quality" for the more contentious term "productivity" alleviated a number of the challenges facing the campaign. Perhaps most obviously, it offset the negative association between productivity and speed-up harbored by the general public. Quality, unlike productivity, was a concept "behind which corporations can place their efforts without fearing charges of exploitation."[91] More important, the quality theme allowed individuals to identify with the campaign as both workers *and* consumers. According to the strategy paper, because the worker was also the consumer of goods and services, "he provides his own motivation and incentive to take pride in his job."[92] Greater pride in workmanship would not only improve worker morale; it would also benefit the consumer who wanted to purchase high-quality, affordable goods made in America.[93] Despite the campaign's romantic appeal to an earlier golden age of producerism, its success finally hinged on its ability to appeal to the consumer.

Through asserting that it was "just human nature to want to sign your work," the Advertising Council campaign located all forms of work—from teacher to short-order cook, from steamfitter to city manager—along the same continuum, suggesting that even the most seemingly miserable work would be enhanced if the worker could only fancy himself an artisan, his signature—even if only imaginary—illuminating the deep pride he felt for his product or service. Essentially, the campaign implied that improving workplace morale ultimately depended on the workers' powers of imagination; it was up to the worker to retrieve the romantic elements of his task, no matter what they entailed. Like the GM advertisement, the productivity campaign sought to reconfigure the modern workplace—regardless of its actual content—as a site of personal fulfillment and gratification. Young men who might be wooed away from the world of work in pursuit of "self-realization" were now being told that they could find it on the job. In the process, the campaign also assured consumers that American goods were neither shoddy nor second-rate.

This strategy of "selling productivity" through an emphasis on quality was not unique to advertising. Indeed, the very phrase "quality of work life" was meant to reassure workers that QWL was "*not* a productivity gimmick," in the words of Howard Carlson, GM's director of QWL Research and Development.[94] In their efforts to forge the first jointly sponsored QWL agreement in 1973, both Howard Carlson and Irving Bluestone, the head of UAW's GM department, agreed that the more traditional "organizational development" should be replaced by "quality of work life," a term that "aroused less suspicion among union people."[95] Like the Advertising Council campaign, the success of QWL programs would require a ban on the term "productivity," a strategy supported by both GM and the UAW. Irving Bluestone warned that "if the first emphasis by any manager in the introduction and acceptance of a QWL program is 'How do I reduce labor costs? How do I get more out of the workers?' there will be no QWL program."[96] GM's vice president of personnel, Stephen Fuller, took this caveat seriously, explaining that educating GM managers about QWL was a lesson in lexical maneuvering as much as anything else: "I tell my people not to talk about improving efficiency, productivity, or profits when they are talking about QWL. Those may be interesting byproducts, but they are not the main point. The union wouldn't accept QWL if we said they were. Besides, I sincerely believe that QWL is not a means to an end, it's an end in itself. It is morally right to involve people in the decision-making process, and it would be right even if it didn't lead to improved productivity, profits and costs."[97]

What is significant here is not only the prohibitions that Fuller set on the terms "efficiency," "productivity," and "profits," but also his own ambiguity about whether these guidelines reflected a cynical corporate strategy or an authentic moral commitment on the part of GM. Fuller cannot quite figure out whether he is urging a ban on words like "productivity" in order to persuade unions to jump on the QWL bandwagon, or because improving the QWL is, in his words, "an end in itself." Either way, GM managers would now be urged to keep the aim of increased productivity to themselves, voicing instead their commitment to making GM a place where "the higher order intrinsic needs of individuals" could be satisfied.[98]

Thus far, we have traced the ways in which corporate, labor, and political leaders addressed the problems of lagging productivity and worker malaise through mobilizing the category of "quality" in reference to both products and the experience of work itself. This emphasis on quality allowed business executives to address the nation's productivity woes without incurring the charges of corporate exploitation associated with speed-up and job elimination. At the same time, through appealing to ideals of artistry and craftsmanship, corporate advertising and job enrichment programs appropriated the language of self-realization, constructing work as a sphere where the new breed of worker could satisfy his psychological needs for self-fulfillment and personal meaning. Through encouraging "pride in craftsmanship," advertising campaigns implicitly challenged the perception that American goods were inferior in quality to their European and Japanese counterparts.

These corporate appeals to quality did not go uncontested, however. Just as workers challenged the dominant portrait of the new breed, they also undermined corporate efforts to retain control of the term "quality" by casting themselves as its true guardians in a corporate environment increasingly prone to speed-up, job elimination, and downsizing. This rhetorical strategy was evident on the pages of Lordstown's union newsletter, "See Here," in the early 1970s. In letters and editorials, members of Local 1112 challenged GM by questioning its commitment to the production of a high-quality automobile, insisting that, despite its rhetorical pledge to quality, the corporation cared only about the bottom line. In October 1971, Ray

Lewis, an 1112 committee member, explained that GM's failure to ensure a fair and normal work pace for Lordstown workers resulted in a "cold, hard product with no soul (quality) or that attraction that draws the consumer's attention over other like products." Speed-up and fear of job loss had effectively coerced the worker into repudiating product quality, forcing him to care only about quantity and the "cold dollar."[99] According to another worker in the Vega paint department, the implementation of GMAD was systematically destroying "the working man, his pride in his work, his dignity." By imposing work rules that destroyed the connection between the worker and the goods he produced, Local 1112 members argued, GM was violating its own purported commitment to quality. "If GMAD wants to do away with jobs and build an inferior product, we cannot force them not to," advised the worker. "But we can and should make certain that our family, friends, neighbors and the general public know that if they buy an All American Vega just how little quality they may be buying."[100]

Throughout "See Here," Lordstown workers appealed to ideals of craftsmanship not unlike those advanced by GM's own advertising campaign. But their political aims could not have been more different. Their appeals to craftsmanship served to indict GM for betraying both the autoworker, who found himself vulnerable to speed-up and job elimination, and the consumer, who would ultimately be shortchanged by an inferior product. As workers challenged GM's appeals to "quality" and "craftsmanship," the company recognized that, in order to safeguard its public reputation, it would need to maintain rhetorical control over the concept of quality. But workers at Lordstown were not willing to cede this control without a fight.[101]

This battle over the rhetoric of "quality" was unique neither to Lordstown nor to the early 1970s. Corporate public relations had emphasized high-quality goods since its inception, while industrial workers had a long history of appealing to a producerist ideal.[102] But such appeals—from both business elites and industrial workers—took on a new salience during this period. Corporate elites, beset by foreign competition, appealed to an earlier producerist ideal in order to dispel the perception that American goods were shoddy and inferior. Workers, in turn, appealed to the ideal as a way to counter corporate hypocrisy. Through invoking an earlier national identity rooted in producerism, both sides reconfigured the workplace as a site of self-realization for a new breed of worker, defined as much by his psychological desire for personal fulfillment as his material need for a paycheck. Both industrial workers and corporate capitalists, ostensibly opposed on the question of "quality," drew on a common reservoir of familial images and meanings.

At the same time, industrial workers, particularly those in the steel and automobile industries, were responding to a unique set of pressures when they appealed to a producerist ideal: growing fears of job loss and corporate downsizing, frustration over what they saw as the steadily eroding status of manual labor, the prediction that automation would render the assembly-line worker obsolete, and the perception that a national economy once driven by industrial work was giving way to one increasingly propelled by a growing service sector. When they appealed to earlier ideals of producerism and craftsmanship, industrial workers were both illuminating the numbing, alienating effects of assembly-line work (as they had done historically) and raising a new host of questions about its potential obsolescence.

Mike LeFevre's testimony in Studs Terkel's *Working* about his experience in a steel mill captures this tension perfectly. The work of moving steel day after day exacts a horrible physical and psychic toll on LeFevre, but he nonetheless laments his own status as a "dying breed."[103] He oscillates back and forth between describing his work as brutally debilitating and identifying himself as part of a noble tradition going all the way back to the ancient Egyptians who built the pyramids. LeFevre loathes his work in the steel mill, but he nonetheless yearns for its recognition. "Picasso can point to a painting. What can I point to?" he asks Terkel. "A writer can point to a book. Everybody should have something to point to."[104] Not unlike the Advertising Council campaign, LeFevre is obsessed with somehow restoring the guild craftsman's signature. But his means for doing so are quite different from those prescribed by the National Commission on Productivity: "Sometimes, out of pure meanness, when I make something, I put a little dent in it. I like to do something to make it really unique. Hit it with a hammer. I deliberately fuck it up to see if it'll get by, just so I can say I did it. It could be anything. . . . I'd like to make my imprint. . . . A mistake, *mine*."[105]

Sabotage becomes the only way for LeFevre to lay claim to his own labor, to "sign his work," as the Advertising Council admonishes him to do. In spite of the material and psychological damages that he has incurred as a result of a lifetime in the steel mill, LeFevre is still compelled to invest this same work with meaning. Even though what he wants more than anything else is for his sons to escape the steel mill and go to college, he nonetheless expresses grief about the decline of "strict muscle work." LeFevre's appeals to producerism are of course rooted in the historical experience of industrial workers and their own yearnings for humane and meaningful work. But LeFevre also displays a certain prescience about the future when he describes himself as a "dying breed," raising the question of whether mass production will survive at all.

The Return of Austerity

That question came increasingly to the fore over the course of the 1970s, as discussions of worker malaise were gradually eclipsed by discussions of growing unemployment. It was not so much that the theme of workplace discontent had disappeared by decade's end, but rather that it was effectively ensconced in QWL programs, where corporate and labor elites could define its parameters. Meanwhile, the fear that a generation of wayward men would somehow abdicate breadwinning was replaced by the specter of widespread male unemployment. After the serious recession of 1974–75, the figure of the freewheeling, antiauthoritarian new worker gave way to that of the fallen male breadwinner, emasculated by plant closings and corporate downsizing. By the late 1970s and early 1980s, men's self-fulfillment would no longer hinge on the content of work—it would simply come down to having any job at all.[106]

Like earlier social-scientific accounts of the new breed, male unemployment was identified as a symptom of decline. But there were significant differences between accounts of the new breed and the unemployed male breadwinner. Characterizations of the new breed were premised on the notion that postwar affluence had produced a permissive and overindulgent model of middle-class family life, and that the explosive growth of the mass media, leisure, and consumer culture had eroded parental authority. Widespread affluence, according to productivity experts, had eroded the nation's productivity. But after the recession, observers of the workforce began talking less about affluence and more about austerity. The new austerity also undermined the integrity of the male breadwinner, but through the threat of unemployment rather than the seductions of affluence and leisure. The shift from economics to psychology that had animated accounts of the new breed, in other words, would prove to be short-lived.

This new attention to austerity coincided with the rising prevalence of the two-earner family and the changes in gender roles unleashed by it. Organizations like NOW, for example, insisted that economic reforms made in the name of austerity were actually inflicting unfair penalties on women.[107] But media accounts of the economic recession focused on the deleterious effects of downsizing and plant closings on the nation's male industrial workers who resided in the once-thriving rust belt. Reminiscent of the Great Depression, accounts of the decline of the industrial worker in Detroit's and Pennsylvania's steel towns were filled with pathos meant to arouse a sympathy in readers that simply did not extend to women workers.[108] "Lack of work, especially for a male, puts him in a psychological no-man's land," explained psychologist Hannah Levin to the readers of *Today's Health*.[109] "The lack of work reflects a sense of dependency," she continued. "If a man cannot fulfill his social role as a worker and wage earner, he loses respect for himself because he cannot meet the expectations and responsibilities of his family, friends and community."[110] Studies on the psychological and physical impact of plant closings on newly unemployed men found that they disproportionately suffered from increased rates of alcoholism, mental illness, suicide, heart disease, ulcers, and sexual impotence. These problems, in turn, wrought havoc on family life, leading to higher incidences of child and spousal abuse, marital discord, the erosion of parental authority, and divorce.[111]

At first glance, the figure of the fallen male industrial worker seems to offer a paradigmatic example of masculinity in crisis. Accounts of the unemployed man portrayed him as rudderless and emasculated, his family torn apart by a sudden and unexpected economic vulnerability that not only robbed him of his livelihood but added insult to injury by forcing his wife out of the home and into the workforce. But when we consider these accounts in relationship to the new breed, we can begin to see the extent to which they in fact harkened back to a more traditional gender order. The perception that men might be lost to the sphere of work in their pursuit of self-realization was now replaced by the insight that job loss, above all else, threatened a man's sense of identity and selfhood.[112] News accounts of plant closings and corporate downsizing offered alarming descriptions of a defeated masculinity, descriptions that celebrated the figure of the male breadwinner even as they mourned him. However scary the specter of widespread male unemployment, it was oddly familiar when contrasted with the more anomalous threat posed by the enigmatic new breed. As the decade progressed, the possibilities, however quixotic, of a gender revolution were gradually replaced by a much more prosaic gender crisis.[113] Thus when the cover of the August 1980 UAW national newsletter featured a photograph of a little girl holding up a sign that read "Give Back

My Daddy's Job!" it simultaneously pointed to the autoworker's heightened economic vulnerability and naturalized his status as his family's primary breadwinner, even as, in all likelihood, his wife was earning an increasing share of the family income.[114]

Nevertheless, the corporate turn to quality had not been without significance. Almost serendipitously, two different processes had converged. On the one hand, corporate work had seemed to lose its meaning for many young people in the 1960s, who were influenced by the widespread demand for authentic experience and larger purpose. These workers needed to be remotivated. On the other hand, corporations had needed to reorganize themselves along more decentralized, flexible, and consumerist lines. By the mid-1970s, the moment had passed and the traditional priority of economics reasserted itself. By that time, business leaders recognized that the prospect of national economic decline, however daunting, could play an ameliorative role: it could restore acquisitive drives and reinvigorate the work ethic. One personnel executive deemed the recession a "blessing in disguise," making the real world more quickly apparent to the young worker and compelling him to appreciate the job he had.[115] One corporate president noted that young workers had now "gotten the '60s out of their system," and the vice president of U.S. Steel Corporation apparently agreed, observing that workers in 1976, in contrast to those from the late 1960s, "are anxious to get to work."[116]

Like the oil embargo, the productivity lag was significant for reasons that could not have been fully appreciated at the time. Following the upheavals of the 1960s, defeat in Vietnam, and the oil embargo, the debate about productivity came at a time when big business had lost political, economic, and cultural ground in the United States. At one level, the productivity lag reflected the challenge of foreign competition emanating from Japan and West Germany. But at another level, it was less a symptom of business crisis and more an aspect of the highly coordinated business counteroffensive that gained momentum after 1973. As they had during the oil embargo, corporations mobilized the rhetoric of national decline throughout the productivity debate to criticize government controls and deepen their identification with the public.

As with the POW campaign and the oil embargo, no ideal was more important than the family when it came to working through anxieties about productivity lag. Thus when social scientists and industrial psychologists attempted to explain why the new breed of worker was undisciplined and lazy, they turned to the family, arguing that postwar fathers had failed to successfully transmit the work ethic to their sons. The notion of the new breed proceeded from the premise that the growing spheres of affluence and leisure had eroded patriarchal authority. To be sure, mothers were assigned some of the blame for the productivity crisis; but the crisis was ultimately interpreted as a sign of paternal—rather than maternal—failure. Like military defeat in Southeast Asia, productivity lag was not only cited as evidence of national decline during these years; significantly, it was also linked to the diminishment of male authority within the private sphere of the home.

Just as the anxieties that underlay the productivity crisis referred back to the family, so the proposed solutions also hinged on conceptions of family life. Just as the oil embargo had inspired fantasies that the contemporary family could somehow refashion itself along the lines of the survivalist and the pioneer, the productivity debates sparked a related return to producerism, this time on the assembly line. Managers insisted that the nation's productivity woes and the dissatisfaction of young workers could be redressed simultaneously by remaking the modern workplace into a sphere in which a new synthesis between a producerist and a therapeutic ethic could find expression. In the process, the workplace was reconstructed in quasi-familial terms, free from outside interference. As we will see, this valorization of the artisan and the "old time" producer would also become a key component to the nation's search for moral fortitude during the Bicentennial of 1976.

Ultimately, the most profound significance of the productivity debate revolved around the end of the family wage. While the early coverage of the new breed had stressed avoiding work as a choice, the deeper structural transformations taking place were limiting the options available to industrial workers and narrowing the world they inhabited. The contraction of the manufacturing sector and the disintegration and dispersal of industrial megaliths like automobiles and steel, the shedding of jobs within the United States and the relocation of assembly-line plants abroad, the declining power of industrial unions, and the rise of a service and information-based economy in which women and men of all races and nationalities would now be competing for the same jobs, all pointed to the hollowness of the older producerist ethic, as well as to its distant echoes among the new breed. For male workers within the steel and automobile industries, the most immediate effects of these transformations occurred within the family, where, from now on, it would take two wage earners to bring home the living wage that had been garnered by the industrial male breadwinner of the 1950s and 1960s. By the late 1970s, as the symbol of the new breed gave way to the figure of the out-of-work man, the dimensions of this transformation were coming into fuller view, and one could see the productivity debate for what it had been all along: a lament for the loss of the independent, male producer on the eve of a new postindustrial order.

4

The Bicentennial and Cold War Revivalism

The Spirit of '76

Writing in the journal *Public Interest* in the fall of 1975, as the country prepared for its upcoming Bicentennial celebration, Daniel Patrick Moynihan reflected on America's Centennial one hundred years earlier. Like the commemoration that was fast approaching, the Centennial, Moynihan recalled, had also taken place during a time of great national upheaval. When the 1876 World's Fair opened in Philadelphia, the country was in the throes of an industrial depression, labor agitation was growing, the Indian wars were being waged on the Great Plains, and Reconstruction was coming to an end, raising troubling questions about the place of emancipated slaves in the post–Civil War nation. But for Moynihan there was a crucial difference between the two commemorations. However divided the nation had been in 1876, what he called the "symbols of the republic" had remained intact. The World's Fair had displayed the scientific and technological wonders of the age, he continued, but the real sensation of the fair had been A. M. Willard's 1875 painting *The Spirit of '76*. It would be absurd, Moynihan speculated, "to suppose that any such response could be evoked by a patriotic painting today." "In no one thing has the American civic culture declined more in recent decades," he lamented, "than in the symbols of love of country, and of manly or womanly pride in the nation."[1]

Moynihan's remarks encapsulate a central thesis of this book. Unlike the Centennial, the Bicentennial took place in the context of a perceived national decline in which the key unifying symbols of family and nation were subject to profoundly diverging, even opposing, interpretations. 1976 proved to be a turning point in this history. During that year, there were two major attempts to redress the anxieties about national decline that had surfaced over the previous five years. The first was the Bicentennial celebration itself. In the years leading up to 1976, commemorative planners were very aware of the dilemma alluded to by Moynihan: the task of crafting a celebration of the country's two hundredth birthday at a moment when key patriotic symbols were no longer easily available to them. After all, planning for the Bicentennial occurred not only in the wake of Vietnam and Watergate and in the midst of recession, but at a time when the social and cultural movements that emerged out of the 1960s were challenging the nation. The planners' solution, the articulation of what I call "diversity" or "pluralist" nationalism, was one that sought to create a sense of national unity precisely through a carefully coordinated showcasing of difference.

The second attempt took place within the foreign policy establishment and revolved around America's world position after the failed military intervention in Vietnam. What lessons should be taken from the experience? Some members of this establishment came to question the relevance of Cold War containment and the application of American military force, while others called for a renewed commitment to Cold War militarism. The result was a second strain of nationalism that found expression in 1976: a Cold War nationalism grounded in an effort to recommit the nation's resources to unrivaled military superiority over the Soviet Union.

These two nationalistic strains—diversity nationalism on the one hand and Cold War nationalism on the other—were very different. Diversity nationalism revolved primarily (although not exclusively) around a set of domestic questions about the relationship between American national identity and subnational or transnational axes of identity, including race, gender, ethnicity, culture, and region. Cold War nationalism revolved primarily (although also not exclusively) around a set of global questions about the world position of the United States after Vietnam. Diversity nationalism had its origins in the cultural and social movements that had emerged out of the civil rights movement and the New Left in the 1960s, while Cold War nationalism had its origins in a newly mobilized conservative counteroffensive that had emerged in reaction to those movements.

But both nationalist strains emerged in response to a broadly shared (if also contested) perception of national decline.

That these two responses found expression during the country's two hundredth birthday was no coincidence, since, as historian Arthur Herman has argued, the idea of decline is "a theory about the nature and meaning of time."[2] The standard vision of national decline is premised on the belief that the effects of time on the nation are the same as its effects on the human body: decay, degeneration, and eventual collapse. This analogizing of the nation to the body places reproduction at the center of the problem of decline, since healthy reproduction is associated with the antithesis of the decaying body: birth and rebirth, fertility, continuity, new life, and regeneration. In contrast to Herman's view, the problem of American national decline in the 1970s was never posed as a problem of senescence, decay, and death—on the contrary, as we saw in chapter 2, it was experienced as a crisis of coming-of-age. Nevertheless, it *was* experienced as a crisis of reproduction: reproduction of national authority, reproduction of collective sentiments of patriotism, reproduction of postwar affluence, and reproduction of U.S. world dominance. Decline was also cast as a crisis of generational reproduction, since critics contended that the nation had been weakened because the white middle class had repudiated its commitment to parenthood and progeny, a repudiation supposedly demonstrated by the growing acceptance of homosexuality, feminism, and the youth revolt.

Emerging in reaction to these various crises of reproduction, both diversity nationalism and Cold War nationalism relied on the family for legitimation—the subject of this chapter. In the first case, the family functioned as a simultaneous (and thus indispensable) symbol of difference and unity—difference because every group had its own cultural paraphernalia adhering to the family, unity because each group's attachment to family-related themes (roots, tradition, culture) linked one group to another. In the second case, foreign policy experts turned to the family as a site of moral and psychological reserves, a place that could either buttress or erode the nation's defenses. The centrality of the family to these different articulations of American nationalism captured the symbol's multivalence and potency. There was now no debate over the nation's fate that was not simultaneously a debate over the family.

Getting the State out of the National Celebration: Commemorative Planning in the Midst of Upheaval

The early 1970s was a terrible time to be planning for a national commemoration. As we have seen, between 1970 and 1975 several traumas
strained an international order that had fostered American political, economic, and military dominance. Within the United States, these traumas
undermined the sense of national unity that commemorations ostensibly
require. Most prominent among them was the war in Vietnam, a war that
in contrast to earlier military conflicts left the country deeply divided and
thus, as historian Gary Gerstle has argued, "could not be turned to nation-
building purposes."[3] Any sense that domestic order would be easily restored
had been shattered by the OPEC oil embargo in the winter of 1973–74,
which occurred in tandem with both spiraling inflation and high unemployment, and the August 1974 resignation of President Nixon, a blow to a
presidential institution already shaken by assassination (John F. Kennedy
in 1963 and Robert Kennedy in 1968).[4] This history was very much on the
minds of the planners as they prepared for the Bicentennial. As a final report on the commemoration later recalled, "We entered the Bicentennial
year having survived some of the bitterest times in our brief history. We
cried out for something to draw us together again."[5]

The task of planning was made still more difficult by the challenge from
the social movements of the period. By the early 1970s, a new cultural nationalist model of political organization and affiliation had come to dominate the field of social activism. This model was complex and internally
differentiated but was associated with a reinvigorated sense of racial pride, a
rejection of assimilation into the dominant society, the creation of autonomous social, political, and cultural institutions, and a quest for identity as a
means of fostering forms of collective self-respect that had been damaged
by structural racism. This cultural nationalist model had its origins in the
black power movement that had emerged after 1964, but by the early 1970s,
it had been adopted by other social movements as well, including the Chicano movement, the Asian American movement, and women's liberation.
History—both as a disciplinary field and as a tool of political empower-
ment and psychological amelioration—assumed a central role within the
cultural nationalist paradigm. Movement leaders stressed that knowledge
of the past—"knowing where you came from"—was essential for the recuperation of group self-esteem and self-love. Many activists had entered the
academy, transforming the discipline of American history by expanding the

fields of social history, women's history, and black history. In the process of restoring women, slaves, and other subaltern groups to the historical record, these activists-turned-scholars also challenged a hegemonic premise of American history that had underwritten earlier commemorations—that the driving forces of the nation's history, those of growing democratization, ever-expanding freedom, and social progress, made for national unity.[6]

This cultural nationalist turn raised daunting questions for Bicentennial planners. How would the country come together to honor the nation's past, they wondered, when American history was being reinterpreted in terms of violence, oppression, and exploitation? What would a Bicentennial mean when the very concept of a singular "national history" was being challenged by black and Chicano activists, who posited alternative conceptions of national and transnational identity, by the American Indian Movement, which contended that the country's history was one of genocidal invasion, and by feminists, who claimed that traditional approaches to American history had failed to account for women's experiences?[7] Thus questions of who would be represented, how they would be represented, and how the nation's entire history would be represented loomed large over the planning.

In addition, by the early 1970s, many white ethnic groups such as Italian Americans and Irish Americans were making their own demands for greater recognition, thus adding yet another dimension to the debate.[8] These demands were premised on the assumption that, like African Americans, white ethnic groups had been the victims of both institutional discrimination and cultural misunderstanding, and that, unlike wealthy liberals, they bore the brunt of policies designed to redress racial inequality, such as busing and affirmative action. In this setting, white ethnic groups saw the Bicentennial as an opportunity to highlight the role that their ancestors had played in the nation's independence. By the early 1970s, ethnic organizations were demanding recognition for unsung military heroes and statesmen of Jewish, Italian, Hungarian, Polish, and Slovak descent.[9] Such demands posed yet another challenge to planners as they attempted to craft a celebration that could address the needs of an ever-multiplying number of groups.

Finally, the American Revolution Bicentennial Commission (ARBC) was itself mired in controversy. Created by the Johnson administration in 1966, the bipartisan commission was designed to bring together political, corporate, and academic leaders who would determine the parameters of the Bicentennial celebration. Revamped into the American Revolution Bicentennial Administration (ARBA) in 1973, the commission produced promotional literature, issued commemorative coins and stamps, and developed programs to showcase the American Revolution. By the early 1970s, the news media and members of Congress were portraying the commission as ineffective and hampered by red tape. Echoing more serious charges then surfacing in relation to Watergate, critics accused Nixon of appointing only political loyalists and corporate CEOs to a commission that was supposed to be bipartisan and inclusive. Meanwhile, in a claim that resonated with broader anxieties about the quality of American goods, commentators argued that the Revolution's true meaning was being lost in a sea of kitschy, cheap commemorative trinkets, including Bicentennial beer cans, sanitary napkin bags, condoms, and toilet paper. Because the word "bicentennial" was in the public domain, the commission had no control over the production of these goods, but they nonetheless contributed to the sense that the upcoming commemoration was going to be a tawdry affair, what reporters dubbed a "Buycentennial."[10]

Within this context, Bicentennial planners realized that celebrating the nation as a unified community simply would not work.[11] Instead, they would need to downplay the category of the nation, foregrounding instead the local, the tribal, and the familial. Rather than attempting to reinstate a singular American national identity, planners would need to do the opposite: refashion the Bicentennial to highlight the federal government's commitment to localism, cultural pluralism, diversity, and difference.[12]

This refashioning of the celebration required a range of strategies. First, planners made the conscious decision to decentralize the commemoration.[13] In the 1960s, the city of Philadelphia had campaigned to host the nation's upcoming birthday, proposing an elaborate and costly plan for an international exposition. But by May 1972, the proposal had been rejected for several reasons. Some city residents resented the idea of spending large sums of money on the event in the midst of a recession (one estimate was as high as one billion dollars), and a local petition drive against the proposal garnered 20,000 signatures.[14] But planners also recognized that international expositions and world fairs had become riskier enterprises than they had been in the past. During the New York World's Fair of 1964–65, hundreds of demonstrators had participated in sit-ins and shouted down President Johnson as he dedicated the U.S. pavilion.[15] Planners worried that another world's fair or international exposition could become a site of protest. In 1971, activist Jeremy Rifkin formed the People's Bicentennial Commission, an organization that condemned corporate dominance of

ARBA and insisted that a true commemoration required mobilizing against both the Nixon administration and large corporations.[16] In December 1973, as the OPEC oil embargo entered its third month, the group staged a demonstration at a reenactment of the Boston Tea Party.[17] By decentralizing the celebration, planners realized that they would also be decentralizing (and therefore defusing the impact of) social protest.

But the original idea of an international exposition was also discarded because it entailed financial risks that the federal government could not afford by the mid-1970s. The New York World's Fair had been under attended, leaving organizers with a twenty-million-dollar deficit.[18] By jettisoning the idea of an international exposition and transforming the Bicentennial into a dispersed event, the fiscal burden of the celebration could be shifted away from the federal government and to individuals and local communities. As ARBA's final report later recalled with pride, every federal dollar spent on the commemoration "was matched by almost four dollars from either state, local, or private funds."[19]

Once the idea of an international exposition in Philadelphia had been rejected, a more decentralized and diffuse vision began to emerge. Planners such as ARBA administrator John Warner (who was then secretary of the navy and would become a senator of Virginia) began describing the commemoration as a "grassroots Bicentennial" and as "a hometown affair" animated by a "do-it-yourself" and "can-do" spirit.[20] This refashioning of the Bicentennial went hand in hand with a conscious effort on the part of planners to sever all ties between the celebration and the federal government. In the fall of 1974, Warner contended that the commission's initial difficulties were being remedied by a turn away from Washington and toward the local. There was now "enormous momentum in the States and communities," he observed favorably, "and direction of the Bicentennial is where it should be—in the hands of the people, not the bureaucrats."[21] As Warner later recalled, the Bicentennial had gradually been transformed into "the most massive volunteer movement in peacetime history."[22] The commemoration would be more meaningful, one White House planner added, if it lacked "a 'made in Washington' label."[23] Even President Nixon apparently understood that the success of the celebration hinged on distancing it from the federal government. In a March 1974 radio address, he told Americans, "The bicentennial is not going to be invented in Washington, printed in triplicate by the Government Printing Office, mailed to you by the U.S. postal service, and filed away in your public library."[24]

Decentralization entailed refashioning the commemoration into a celebration of what planners called "cultural pluralism."[25] The term itself had been invented in the 1920s to signify the autonomy and endurance of ethno-racial groups. As historian David Hollinger has argued, the influence of the concept had waned during the civil rights era, but the late 1960s witnessed the reconsideration of integrationist goals on the part of African American leaders, a backlash against affirmative action on the part of white ethnic groups, and the dramatic increase in immigration from Asian and Latin American countries in the wake of the Immigration Act of 1965, which lifted national origins quotas put in place four decades earlier.[26] By the early 1970s, a revived emphasis on cultural pluralism was once again challenging the "melting pot" image, according to which ethno-racial groups arrived in the United States, quickly shed their customs and rituals, adopted a homogeneous and uniform American cultural identity, and became "Americanized."

Accordingly, ARBA members realized that the Bicentennial needed to showcase rather than downplay cultural pluralism. This was a realization that they arrived at gradually as they encountered criticism from minority groups. One of the most potent challenges the ARBA confronted came from Native American tribes and organizations. Native Americans wrote the commission often, regularly condemning the upcoming celebration as a sham that would address neither America's history of violence nor the persistence of inequality.[27] Some tribes threatened to boycott the celebration altogether. "Who would want to participate in the 200th year of the rip-off of our country?" asked one Native American woman. "If the Government would say 'okay, we'll honor all your old treaties . . . and we'll give back land that was stolen,' that would give the Indians something to celebrate," she added.[28] Native Americans also offered damning reinterpretations of the standard tropes of American history. For example, the director of an Indian program in Portland, Oregon, refused to join a Bicentennial wagon train that celebrated westward expansion, reflecting that "the invitation was like the Germans inviting the Jews to celebrate Hitler's rise to power."[29]

Similar challenges came from the African American community. Local NAACP leaders wrote the ARBA asking how the celebration could possibly account for two hundred years of racial discrimination.[30] Frederick Douglass's famous 1852 speech in which he posed the question, "What to the Slave is the Fourth of July?" was frequently reprinted in the African American press. A spirited debate about whether African Americans should participate in the Bicentennial played out in the pages of *Ebony* in August 1975, as the magazine's senior editor, Lerone Bennett Jr., urged his readers to reject the Bicentennial as a charade that the nation had been perpetuating for two hundred years, what he called "the game of freedom." "Why," he asked, "do Americans make a practice of unfreedom and a profession of praising freedom?" Vernon Jordan, then the executive director of the National Urban League, answered that black people understood the meanings of freedom, liberation, and equality better than whites. These concepts "cannot be taken for granted," he explained, "by a people who just got the right to fair housing seven years ago, the vote ten years ago, the right to work eleven years ago, and the right to quality integrated schools barely twenty years ago." Precisely because these rights were still "honored more in the breach than in observance," he argued, it was imperative that black Americans use the Bicentennial to "press our uncompleted revolution."[31]

Bicentennial planners paid close attention to these debates. As early as 1971, an ARBA program officer called for the aggressive recruitment of prominent black leaders, predicting that a failure to enlist their support could hurt commemorative planning.[32] The call was extended to other racial minorities and women, as well. But if the wooing of minority leaders and women began as a preemptive tactic, it also conformed to the constitutive themes of diversity and cultural pluralism. In January 1973, ARBA organized a three-day conference in Tucson, Arizona, to address the issue of Native American participation in the celebration, and in July of the following year, ARBA opened a Native American Programs Office in Denver, Colorado. In response to demands for greater women's participation in the Bicentennial, ARBA invited national women's organizations to a Washington, D.C., meeting in December 1973 to discuss the ways that women could be honored throughout the celebration. In June 1974, ARBA sponsored another meeting in the capital at which ethnic and racial groups gathered to discuss Bicentennial programming. The meeting, which was cochaired by Father Geno Baroni (the president of the National Center for Urban Ethnic Affairs and a prominent white ethnic leader), called for the formation of a nonpartisan council called the Bicentennial Ethnic Racial Council (BERC) that would focus exclusively on the role of ethnic and racial communities in the celebration.[33] As the report from the meeting noted, this was "the first time that a federal agency had sought the consultation of such a diverse ethnic and racial group."[34] The constitutive focus on race, ethnicity, and gender was also reflected in the formation of a new White House Bicentennial Advisory Council in January 1975 that included figures like Maya Angelou, Alex Haley, Betty Shabazz, and Richard Gambino, an Italian American writer associated with the white ethnic revival.

By 1976, all of these efforts had transformed the Bicentennial into an occasion to showcase cultural pluralism. As John Warner explained, "We are a nation of nations, proud of the richness and diversity of our cultures; the Bicentennial marks the end of any thought of being a melting pot."[35] In meetings and correspondence, ARBA planners proposed numerous alternative metaphors to describe the American nation, including those of a patchwork quilt, a mosaic, and a tapestry.[36] Ironically, while these metaphors did break with that of the melting pot, they simultaneously reinforced its ideals of inclusion, unity, and harmony, replacing a model based on sameness with one based on infinite difference and variety. Conflating slavery, immigration, and gender conflict in ways that occluded the specificity of each history, the ARBA decided to jettison the more contentious term "minority," choosing instead terms like "ethnic and racial heritage," "ethnic community," and "pluralism." As one ARBA staff member put it, "We are all minorities."[37] Geno Baroni recalled one Native American participant at the first BERC gathering as exclaiming, "We didn't know that white people had so many tribes."[38]

The planners turned to cultural pluralism primarily to defuse the racial politics surrounding the commemoration, but the paradigm was also essential to the projection of a benign vision of America's global role. Such a vision was vital, not only in the wake of the Vietnam War, but at a time when corporations were becoming more and more multinational, thereby expanding the reach of American dominance. By highlighting cultural pluralism, the Bicentennial advanced a claim about the unique nature of American power: because the nation had been constituted by diverse ethnic and racial groups from every region of the world, its culture was already global. In Bicentennial literature, the United States was repeatedly described as "a laboratory for the world" and "a world in miniature."[39] This idea of the nation-as-world-microcosm suggested that American domination was more the result of natural affinities than something imposed from the outside. Thus the highlighting of cultural pluralism demonstrated the nation's commitment to diversity at the same time that it projected a benevolent image of post-Vietnam American power.

By early 1976, planners felt that they had devised a successful approach to the upcoming Bicentennial. John Warner reported happily that commemorative planning was gaining momentum in states, cities, towns, and tribes and that the people themselves were in charge of the event. The transformation of the celebration into a "hometown affair" would democratize it while minimizing the effects of protest and the risks of financial

Photo montage celebrating diversity from the ARBA *Final Report.*

loss. By making the theme of cultural pluralism a centerpiece, planners believed that they were inviting Americans of all races and ethnicities to be part of a new national "mosaic." But planners could not completely protect the commemoration from violence. In June 1976, with the holiday only one month away, *Ebony* published an editorial, entitled "The Bicentennial Blues," that featured a photograph taken two months earlier showing two white men beating a black man with an American flag in the midst of an antibusing demonstration outside of Boston's City Hall. Did the people of Boston "understand and believe in the Declaration of Independence?" the editorial wondered. "And if they don't believe in and understand the Declaration and the great dream it symbolizes," it continued, "what, in God's name, are they celebrating?"[40] Despite planners' efforts, these questions haunted the celebration.

The Colonial Household and the Immigrant Home: The Domestic Sphere in Commemorative Programming

The centrality of "the family" and "the domestic" throughout the Bicentennial reflected both the underlying logic and the inherent instability of ARBA's strategy. As planners sought to distance the celebration from the federal government and relocate it to the state and local arenas, the family emerged as a vital site. Planners urged Americans to celebrate the commemoration within their own families and through the affirmation of kinship and blood ties. At the same time, Bicentennial museum exhibits and literature portrayed a range of domestic spaces as sites of both the original fight for national independence and the contemporary struggle for national renewal in the wake of Vietnam and in the midst of recession. All of these efforts established a powerful analogy between the family and the nation that actually revealed the fragility of the consensus that planners had forged about the meaning of the celebration. As political scientist Roger Smith has written, "Precisely because political communities are at once so indispensable and yet such potent sources of exploitation and inhumanity, it is difficult to decide what moral status to assign them, and the quest for analogy to focus moral thinking is a sensible one." Among the most serviceable of these analogies is the family, he points out, because of its associations with the natural and the benign.[41] In both form and content, then, planners drew on the family to meet the challenges they confronted.

At the most literal level, the family, like the hometown and the local community, emerged as a crucial locus for the celebration. Analogizing the nation to the family, planners described the commemoration as a "family reunion," while the Smithsonian Institution urged citizens to observe the Bicentennial "family style," by holding their own family reunions, writing family histories, making home movies, and conducting oral history interviews with older relatives.[42] Meanwhile, reflecting a growing popular interest in genealogy, individuals submitted their own family histories to ARBA, hoping that they might be incorporated into commemorative planning.[43] Planners believed that the emphasis on genealogy and family history gave individuals a stake in the commemoration they would otherwise lack. According to a Smithsonian press release, family history provided Americans with "a personal approach to understanding the evolution of the republic."[44] Genealogical research, wrote Wilton S. Dillon, director of the Smithsonian Office of Symposia and Seminars, gave "novices a sense of the craft and art of historiography" as well as "a personalized understanding of the processes of nationhood."[45] Amateur family history made the celebration more inclusive while also democratizing the discipline of history, giving laypersons a chance to "make their own history." Moreover, genealogy was an essential tool at a time of national introspection. "There's a recognition that we've reached a turning point in our national history," observed Dillon in 1976. "It's a good time to discover who we are and where we are going."[46]

Like the return of cultural pluralism, the popularity of genealogy created a new level of mediation between the individual and the nation. During the Vietnam War, the oil embargo, and the productivity crisis, the family had provided an emotive language through which national trauma could be experienced; with the Bicentennial, the family was now tied to national rebirth. The ability to claim a concrete identity, whether that of one's own family, race, ethnicity, or tribe (as opposed to the broader history of the nation), was crucial to the resurgence of nationalism anticipated by the Bicentennial. As the head of the Chicago Genealogical Society explained, people were no longer coming to him only to learn their ancestors' dates of birth and death; they wanted to know about the actual lives of these people. They were searching for information that would "give people identity and that's what they want now."[47]

The popularity of family genealogy during the Bicentennial was closely related to another mass cultural event of the mid-1970s: the publication of Alex Haley's *Roots*, which was dedicated to the nation on its two hundredth birthday.[48] Although the book was not published until July 1976 and the television miniseries based on it did not premiere until January 1977, the story of Haley's painstaking reconstruction of his own family tree generated considerable interest in the years leading up to the book's phenomenal publishing debut. A feature article about Haley appeared in the *New York Times Magazine* in July 1972, a condensed version of the book was published in *Reader's Digest* in May and June 1974, and Haley, already made famous by his collaboration with Malcolm X in the writing of his autobiography, was the subject of countless interviews. Planners followed Haley's story with great interest, and it confirmed their decision to emphasize the themes of family and kinship in commemorative programming. Even before the book was published, news accounts were linking *Roots* to both the "new ethnicity" and the "genealogy craze" as well as to the upcoming Bicentennial celebration.[49]

News stories stressed the universal dimensions of Haley's search for his roots. After many years of difficult research, Haley had traced his family history back through slavery to Kunta Kinte, the man whom his grandmother and aunts had referred to as "the African," who was captured by slave traders in the Gambia and transported by slave ship to Annapolis, Maryland, in 1767. Within the African American community, Haley's remarkable recovery of his family history took on two distinct meanings. First, it stressed the continuity, endurance, and survival of the black family, earlier assumed to have been ravaged and broken by the slave system. Second, by beginning in the Gambia, the book resonated powerfully with a Black Nationalist politics that encouraged African Americans to deepen their ties to the continent of Africa and consider their own racial identities in a transnational frame. Nevertheless, within the context of the Bicentennial, these meanings were eclipsed as *Roots* was celebrated for its ability to speak for all Americans. As the book's subtitle made clear, *Roots* was "the saga of an American family" rather than an African American one alone. Haley himself emphasized the synthesizing, even transcendent, dimensions of his story in *Reader's Digest*: "In all of us—black, brown, white, yellow—there is a desire to make this symbolic journey back to the touchstone of our family."[50] The ostensible universality of *Roots* made it a significant resource for Bicentennial planners, who appointed Alex Haley to the White House Bicentennial Advisory Council and selected David Wolper (the executive producer of the *Roots* television miniseries) to serve as the council chair. Haley's story convinced planners that "the family" was a universal category that could foster a sense of connection among diverse Americans and thus overcome the challenge posed by cultural nationalism. An article in *Time* quoted Haley in January 1977: "When you start talking about family, about lineage, and ancestry, you are talking about every person on earth. We all have it. It's a great equalizer."[51]

As planners seized on the family as a crucial locus for the celebration, they also accorded a significant role to the home throughout commemorative programming. During the Bicentennial, historical reenactments were common as a means of recalling the watershed events associated with the nation's founding: the Boston Tea Party, the battles of the Revolutionary War, and the drafting of the Declaration of Independence.[52] A subtle form of reenactment featured the colonial household as a locus of economic production. Museum exhibits re-created colonial interiors and displayed everyday objects and utensils of the pre-Revolutionary period. In fairs and festivals, women dressed in colonial garb demonstrated the activities of the colonial household: churning butter, making candles and soap, baking bread.[53] These demonstrations stressed the vital role that women had played in the colonial and Revolutionary economies, as commemorative pamphlets, educational literature, and news stories recalled the colonial goodwives who helped defeat the British by producing homespun cloth and spearheading nonimportation campaigns.

Celebrations of the early American home as a site of economic production and of women as economic agents reflected the widening influence of both the women's liberation movement and the growing field of women's history. By the mid-1970s, many of the social movements of the 1960s were in disarray, but organized feminism was gaining momentum institutionally, culturally, and politically. At the heart of the feminist project was the examination of the division between private and public spheres, and in particular of the historical construction of the home as an exclusive space of emotion, intimacy, and leisure. Out of this interrogation emerged a key feminist argument: in the past, women had engaged in multiple forms of unremunerated labor within the home that had been neglected in traditional accounts of American history, including cooking, cleaning, childrearing, and housework. The Bicentennial provided an occasion to address this neglect by honoring the economic contributions of colonial and Revolutionary women to the nation. One major Bicentennial museum exhibit sponsored by the Pilgrim Society was entitled "Remember the Ladies" (after Abigail Adams's famous 1776 admonition to her husband). As the accompanying press kit explained, colonial women had engaged in endless tasks of economic production: cooking, cleaning, spinning, sewing, quilting, mending, candle making, soap making, and gardening; the everyday objects featured throughout the exhibit were meant to illustrate the point. The traveling exhibit, which began in Plymouth, Massachusetts, and traveled to five major cities in 1976 and 1977, left little doubt that women had played a vital role in the colonial economy, one that helped set the stage for national independence.

These tributes to women's economic role within the colonial household reflected feminist influence as well as the new salience of women's full-time waged and salaried labor, but they also took on a paradoxical meaning in light of the inflationary spiral of the 1970s. This was most evident in the many commemorative cookbooks and recipes that celebrated the resourceful colonial goodwife who provided her family with hearty meals made from produce gathered from the kitchen garden.[54] Reminiscent of advice that had appeared throughout the oil embargo, these cookbooks suggested that the contemporary homemaker could best combat inflationary prices through adopting the same ethic of resourcefulness that had characterized colonial settlers. "Inflation has forced some of us to run out [of supplies], too," explained one advertising cookbook issued in honor of the Bicentennial. What was the solution? Housewives would need to borrow some ingenuity from the "frugal housewives" of the past by substituting cheaper ingredients for costlier ones. "Mindful even then of the cost of living," the colonial woman baked from scratch, making nearly every ingredient herself, the book reminded readers.[55] By transposing an anachronistic term like "the cost of living" onto the colonial period, the cookbook drew a false analogy between the hardships of colonial settlement and those of the 1970s, ironically assigning women responsibility in the fight against inflation.

There was a second feminist claim taken up throughout the commemoration, the idea that the colonial period constituted a "golden age" for American women. Indeed many women's historians had argued that the Industrial Revolution eroded women's status by moving economic production out of the home and into the factory.[56] This argument reflected a key historiographical intervention of women's history: what did an ostensible moment of progress look like when women were placed at the center of the story?[57] In the case of industrialization, women's economic powers had actually diminished; a stark division between home and work emerged, the home was constructed as a refuge, and women were reduced to their wifely and maternal duties. In the years ahead, the characterization of the colonial era as a "golden age" for women would be complicated as scholars drew careful distinctions between colonial women's economic responsibilities (which were many), their economic opportunities (which were few), and their economic power (which was limited). But in the mid-1970s, the "golden age" thesis exerted great influence.

This thesis lent Bicentennial representations of the colonial household a nostalgic cast. Linda Grant de Pauw, a women's historian and the main historical consultant for the "Remember the Ladies" exhibit, was a proponent of the "golden age" thesis. Colonial women were "more liberated than at any time since," she claimed, a state that "changed when the Industrial Revolution came along." "The affluence that occurred turned them into dependent women." After the Industrial Revolution, women turned "towards more ornamental pursuits," so their power diminished.[58] To museumgoers unfamiliar with the field of American women's history, the idea that women might have had more power before the Industrial Revolution than after was profound, but by asserting a causal relationship between affluence and dependency, de Pauw's arguments echoed the sentiments that had surfaced during the oil embargo. In line with these sentiments, Bicentennial classroom guides advised elementary schoolteachers to get their students to churn butter in an old-fashioned churn and bake bread and urged students to observe "colonial night" at home, an exercise that was similar to the "no energy weekend experiment" proposed three years earlier. "[Try] to use what you think the early settlers had in their homes," the handbook suggested. "Avoid as many modern conveniences as you can. For example, eat by candlelight and heat the bath water."[59]

Like the oil crisis, then, the Bicentennial tapped into long-standing American anxieties about the meaning of dependency, which were exacerbated by new fears of decline. The early founders had viewed private property ownership and household independence as the prerequisites for republican self-governance, a view that contributed to the fierce individualism of the American character. With the rise of wage labor, anxiety surrounding the conjoined meanings of independence and dependence deepened as ostensibly independent wage laborers defined themselves against a body of stigmatized dependents, including women, paupers, and slaves. In the nineteenth century, dependency gradually came to be defined as a moral, psychological, racial, and gendered pathology.[60] This stigmatization of dependency, ever changing, proved remarkably resilient and gave shape to debates about both national decline and family decline in the twentieth century, and particularly in the 1970s. The colonial revivalism that accompanied the Bicentennial reflected these anxieties about the place of dependency within a nation that ascribed unprecedented significance to individualism. Repeated over and over again in a range of commemorative settings, images of colonial women churning butter, spinning cloth, and baking bread lent credence to the enduring belief that domestic self-sufficiency was a prerequisite for national strength. Ironically, the same commemorative programming that honored women's labors in the past contained within it an implicit critique of dependency that indicted women in the present.

If the colonial household was the domestic space most commonly featured throughout the Bicentennial, there was a second one that assumed nearly as much significance: the turn-of-the-century immigrant home. With cultural pluralism a constitutive feature of the Bicentennial, planners turned their attention beyond the colonial era to another crucial moment in the history of the nation: the decades between 1880 and 1920 when unprecedented numbers of Eastern and Southern Europeans had emigrated to the United States. For many white ethnic groups, these were the decades during which their stories intersected with the story of the American nation. Thus the immigrant home emerged as a crucial space that revealed the complex nature of this intersection, one shaped by both survival and loss.

Like celebrations of the colonial household, commemorative tributes to the immigrant home focused on the themes of thrift and industry. "Do you remember when washday meant scrubbing by hand in a wooden tub?" asked one Bicentennial pamphlet, recalling how Finnish American women had spun yarn from wool, sewn bedsheets from flour sacks, and made soap from leftover cooking grease. Although many of these domestic tasks had disappeared with the introduction of mass-produced goods, the pamphlet continued, the immigrant woman had maintained her commitment to frugality by "getting along with what could be obtained at the least cost."[61] These tributes picked up where the colonial revival left off, but because they moved forward in time, they also turned to the rise of mass consumption that had supposedly placed an older ethnic resourcefulness at risk. "Conspicuous consumption . . . was a sure sign of moral madness," intoned Richard Gambino, who served on the White House Bicentennial Advisory Council. Italian Americans, by contrast, "tend to live below their financial means. . . . Their homes, clothes, and cars often represent less than they might afford."[62] Conceding that their supposed repudiation of luxury had made Italian Americans the objects of misunderstanding and even ridicule, Gambino also contended that it gave them the moral high ground. Other champions of the new ethnicity agreed. "In the old days, mothers and grandmothers were economically indispensable. They canned food, they baked; they made clothes," reminisced Michael Novak in *The Rise of the Unmeltable Ethnics* (1971), the most famous book associated with the ethnic revival. In order to inoculate ethnic identity against the deadening effects of mass consumption, he went on, these tasks needed to be returned to the neighborhood and the home. "Why *can't* people of talent organize for their own needs, providing for them locally?" Novak asked, echoing Bicentennial planners.[63]

This portrait of the immigrant-home-under-siege played a critical role in "A Nation of Nations," the main commemorative exhibition at the Smithsonian Institution's National Museum of History and Technology and the largest single exhibit mounted at the museum up until that time. Approximately 35,000 square feet in size and including over 3,000 tools, fabrics, and eating utensils culled from the material culture of everyday life, "A Nation of Nations" opened in early 1976, perhaps the closest thing to a centralized exposition in the Bicentennial.[64] As its title made clear, the exhibit aimed to foreground the distinctiveness of the United States by illuminating the ways that various groups had arrived in the nation, forged a new life, and become American, while simultaneously retaining their ethnic heritage. At the same time, the exhibit celebrated what the country had contributed abroad by looking at the many globally circulating American goods, services, and ideas. As one description put it, "The ultimate unit of social life is not the nation but the world community."[65]

As visitors moved through the chronologically organized exhibit, they encountered a scene both familiar and distant when they arrived at the section devoted to the early twentieth century: a cut-away balloon frame structure of an immigrant home, circa 1910–20. As planners conceptualized it, the structure would demonstrate the tension between ethnic identity and mass consumption. The home included mass-produced wallpaper and floor coverings, standardized plumbing and lighting, and household goods, including a sewing machine, a phonograph, and a parlor piano, but it also held survivals from the old country: crucifixes, family portraits, keepsakes, and a foreign language newspaper. The combined effect, however, suggested that ethnic relics were no match for cheap, mass-produced commodities. What Americanizing, homogenizing forces did the first or second or third generation encounter? asked historian Peter Marzio, the author of the book that accompanied the exhibit. "Of course, they were innumerable, but among the most important were those in his own home!"[66] Within that ostensibly intimate space, Marzio continued, the immigrant confronted "machine-produced uniformity and drabness," making "each home less special to the point where a sense of uniqueness could hardly be created." "Lost in the aggressive pursuit of the 'middle class new' was much of the individuality each immigrant possessed."[67]

Why did curators place such a high value on ethnic survivalism and loss?[68] In the context of the Bicentennial, they were transforming a nationalist challenge emanating from African Americans and Native Americans—who insisted on the historical specificity of race—into a cultural pluralist solution that brought white ethnic groups into the fold of national diversity. Thus "the domestic" emerged as a powerful tool for transforming what historian Gordon Wood has called a "hard multiculturalism" based on a rejection of assimilation into a "soft multiculturalism" that reconciled an appreciation of diversity with loyalty to the nation.[69] Much as they seized on the family as a universal trope, planners saw in "the ethnic-domestic" a means of containing the thorny racial politics that surrounded the commemoration.

The interplay of domesticity and soft multiculturalism had been apparent from the start. In 1973, Chermayeff and Geismar Associates, the firm commissioned to design the exhibit, proposed the inclusion of a reconstruction of a slave ship that would bring the experience of the Middle Passage back "to life in all its horror."[70] C. Malcolm Watkins, the National Museum of History and Technology's senior curator, rejected the proposal, arguing that the "rather horrendous life-like scene" was better suited to a wax museum. The reconstruction would undermine the aim of the exhibit, Watkins asserted, what he called the "shock effect" would "go beyond what is the purpose of the Nation of Nations to do. It would seem to me that black people as well as white people would be turned off by such an explicit retailing of horror."[71] Insisting that this was not a "racist cop-out," Watkins affirmed his commitment to honoring the contributions black Americans had made to the nation.[72] But he believed that such a disturbing display would strike the wrong chord with visitors expecting to come away from a commemorative exhibit uplifted rather than depressed. At a time when the nation was racked by internal division, the atmosphere of the exhibit would need to be, in his words, "eloquent, strong, but low-keyed."[73]

In the years that followed, the exhibit's planners determined that the best way to create such an atmosphere would be to highlight the institutions that had shaped the immigrant's acculturation: the workplace, the school, the spheres of leisure and entertainment, and the home.[74] Discrimination and prejudice would not be ignored, they decided, but the emphasis would be on the affirmative ways that ethnic and racial groups had adapted. The re-creation of the immigrant home reflected this approach. Evocatively interrogating the relationship between ethnicity and mass consumption, the display was predicated on what it displaced: a slave ship. The ostensibly benign presence of a house in the exhibit worked to establish that the immigrant experience, rather than the trauma of slavery, would be paradigmatic throughout "A Nation of Nations," and the association of the home with intimacy and warmth accorded this paradigm a cultural common sense it would have otherwise lacked. In the home, planners saw a place where the effects of mass consumption on ethnic identity might be revealed. But more than that, they saw within it a place where the racial violence that haunted the commemoration could be contained and where a conciliatory vision of cultural pluralism appropriate to the Bicentennial could find expression.

But even as the "ethnic-domestic" served to suppress race, it simultaneously reintroduced the disturbing specter that figured so prominently in discourses of national decline after Vietnam: that of a family-under-siege. This time, however, it was neither Asian Communists, Arab oil producers, or Japanese exporters but the American state itself that was intruding on the family. While commemorative literature had described the immigrant home as the victim of mass consumption, the image of an "ethnic-home-under-siege" took on new political meaning as white ethnic groups mobilized against court-mandated busing and affirmative action. "The value deepest in the psyche of southern and eastern Europeans . . . is an instinct for family," wrote Michael Novak. "When agents of the state were in the village, it could only mean some form of death was on its way."[75] Arguing that hostile external forces were encroaching upon the private realm, this emphasis on the white ethnic family's independence stood in contrast to stigmatizations of black family dependency.

Ironically, this heightened demarcation between white ethnic and African American identity emerged at a time when white ethnic leaders were taking many of their linguistic and tactical cues from black nationalists.[76] In the early 1970s, Black Nationalism offered white ethnic leaders what Gary Gerstle has described as a "a new imaginative landscape on which to build their individual and group identities."[77] Caught in a tension between their attraction to Black Nationalist strategy and their antipathy toward black culture, white ethnic leaders stressed that they made demands on the state in violation of their own instincts and only because such demands were a "necessary evil" in a political culture dictated by group rights. As

Mario Albi, the chairman of the National Coordinating Committee of American Italian Organizations, explained to President Ford in 1976, "We didn't make those rules, but we will have to play by them." "It is not in the nature of Americans of Italian Heritage to look to government for either their material or physical well-being. . . . We are fiercely individualistic . . . and we are more accustomed to giving than receiving."[78] As Albi vacillated between asking for state assistance on the one hand and affirming Italian American individualism on the other, the racial subtext became clear: asking for state assistance came naturally to African Americans, but for Italian Americans, it represented a violation of principles deeply rooted in the family. Emerging throughout the Bicentennial as a repository of both ethnic survival and loss, the immigrant home endorsed this white revivalist vision of the ethnic family and thus became implicated in the hostile relations between African Americans and white ethnic groups in the mid-1970s. These were hostilities that could be obscured, but never fully suppressed, by the creation of a national mosaic.

The Tribal Village and the Indian Artisan: Race and Folk Culture in the Bicentennial

The role of the "ethnic-domestic" in minimizing racial conflict was complemented by one of the most popular genres within Bicentennial programming: the folk festival. In the summer of 1976, cities throughout the nation hosted local and regional folk festivals, folk music groups and dance companies toured throughout the country, and the Smithsonian Institution, the National Park Service, and the ARBA cosponsored the Festival of American Folklife, a twelve-week outdoor event on the Washington Mall. Frequently defined as traditional, expressive, oral, informal, community-oriented, and nonprofessional, folklife or "vernacular culture" had garnered growing attention from scholars, archivists, and curators.[79] Bicentennial planners recognized that celebrations of folklife could play a vital role in programming. As one ARBA feasibility study calling for the formation of the American Folklore Performing Company explained it, "'folk' or 'traditional' expressions may unify and give focus to the forthcoming national celebration."[80]

The folk theme was reflected in commemorative programming. Planners placed all activities under one of three headings: Heritage 76, which was devoted to the nation's history and included reenactments of the signing of the Declaration of Independence and tributes to the Founding Fathers; Horizons 76, which focused on the future and oversaw local community improvement projects like tree planting and housing development; and Festival USA, designed to highlight the nation's fine art and folk craft traditions. It was under the heading of "Festival USA" that the commemoration's many folk festivals and performances were listed. Intuiting an affinity between folk culture and the domestic realm, ARBA planners described the festival as "an invitation to dust off the family heirlooms, spruce up the family homestead—and celebrate."[81] Meanwhile, the Smithsonian's 1976 Festival of American Folklife featured a site devoted to family folklore, including souvenirs, quilts, ribbons, and picture albums.

A key dimension that linked folk culture to the domestic realm was its presumptive status as something that existed outside the cash nexus. As planners stressed, what made folk culture such a valuable resource for the commemoration was its "authenticity." Not only did it lack any commercial component, it had not been completely annihilated by what one planner derisively called "show business." Taking their cues from contemporary scholarship, planners claimed that folk culture was "a-commercial" or "non-commercial." The fact that folk festivals such as the Smithsonian's were sponsored by corporations like American Airlines and General Foods did not faze the planners.[82] "Although there are exceptions," one feasibility study wrote, "most folk performers perform for the sheer joy and love of the medium rather than for the money involved."[83] The fragile integrity of folk culture was constantly at risk, planners continued, and the worst possible thing would be for the Bicentennial to exacerbate the problem by creating "ersatz folk art," thus facilitating a "Hollywood-like impresario type of situation." In fact, according to one member of ARBA's performing arts panel, folk art would become worthless if its authenticity were diluted in any way.[84] By establishing such a sharp distinction between folk culture and commerce, planners hoped to prop up the Bicentennial's claims to authenticity at a time when ARBA was itself fending off charges of crassness and subservience to corporate interests.

If folk culture was defined against commercialism, on the one hand, it was defined against the federal government and the world of politics, on the other. In contrast to commemorative activities that focused on the birth of the nation-state, folk festivals were meant to affirm those traditions that had survived the onslaught of the modern age, such as tribal rituals, storytelling, and handcrafted goods. Planners hoped that contact with forgotten traditions could revive a depressed, cynical, and anxious nation on the eve of its two hundredth birthday and "help Americans get in touch with

Photo montage of the Smithsonian Institution's 1976 Festival of American Folklife from the ARBA *Final Report.*

themselves again."[85] Folk festivals could even facilitate acceptance of the national government, so long as it remained frail and toothless. As folklorist Alan Lomax explained, "We realize how beautiful we are. Black is beautiful and Appalachia is beautiful and even old tired Washington sometimes is beautiful when American people gather to sing and fall in love with each other again."[86] Folk culture's supposed detachment from centralized authority made it an invaluable resource for planners who sought to disassociate the commemoration from the federal government.

Commemorative folk festivals and performances referenced a third domestic space that assumed a significant role during the commemoration: the tribal village. Throughout 1976, Indian powwows were held throughout the country, folk dances were performed in over sixty cities and thirty states, and re-creations of an African house and a Caribbean marketplace were featured in the Smithsonian's 1976 Festival of American Folklife. Demonstrations of Native American basket weaving, moccasin making, and beading proliferated. The tribal village was not a literal home or house, but as scholar Laura Wexler has pointed out, an image can be domestic without necessarily representing "a so-called separate sphere of family life." "What matters," Wexler writes, "is the use of the image to signify the domestic realm."[87] Bicentennial references to the tribal village worked in this way. They accorded a sense of the familiar and intimate to racial scenes that might have otherwise seemed foreign to white visitors who had little real contact with African Americans or Native Americans within a racially segregated society. Much as the immigrant home worked to contain the racial violence that haunted "A Nation of Nations," the tribal village worked as an imaginary domestic space in which racial difference could be transformed into something festive rather than threatening.

The relationship of the folk festival and the tribal village to race was complex.[88] On the one hand, there is no doubt that planners genuinely sought to honor racial groups for their contributions to the nation. Folk festivals, they believed, would transport the celebration beyond the walls of the museum and into the open air. They could create what the Smithsonian called "a living museum," where spectators could get a firsthand view of what Alan Lomax described as "the art that people had made out of their own experience."[89] At the same time, by celebrating racial groups primarily as the repositories of folk culture and tradition, these festivals had the effect of situating these groups if not exactly outside of history, then outside of the modern history of their country.[90] The trifurcated organization of Bicentennial programming contributed to this. Unlike the other two program areas,

Festival USA was not chronologically defined—it was linked to neither the nation's past nor its future. Instead, Festival USA featured performances that were by their very nature both timeless and ephemeral. The idealized nature of the folk festival thus left unanswered the crucial question that fueled the skepticism surrounding the commemoration: how could African Americans, Native Americans, and other subaltern groups be integrated into a narrative of national history? By honoring these groups for their connection to tradition rather than for their struggles against oppression, Bicentennial folk festivals elided the same theme suppressed in "A Nation of Nations": the trauma of racial violence.

Similarly, ARBA planners turned to the tribal village as a place where racial antagonism could give way to reconciliation. That was the aim of an ARBA-produced public service announcement entitled "Indian Village." Set in a re-created Cherokee village in northeastern Oklahoma, the short film included close-up shots of tribal members working with their hands— an older woman tanning an animal hide, a young woman weaving a basket, men doing handiwork. The voice-over elaborated: "This is the way it was some two hundred years ago. A life close to nature, a life of dignity with pride in work well-done, nourished by tradition, centered on the family and the tribe. This is the wellspring of the inner strength which has enabled the Cherokees to endure great injustice, yet to shun bitterness and to rise like a Phoenix from the ashes, to rebuild and go forward, to take their rightful place in America. The American Bicentennial: a time for Americans to appreciate one another."[91]

Perhaps the most striking feature of this voice-over was its claim that the Cherokee had shunned bitterness, a bold assertion in light of the fact that Native American activists were among the commemoration's most vociferous critics. Even more telling was what the Cherokee shared with the colonial household and the immigrant home: their "pride in work well-done," "nourished by tradition" and "centered on the family." Here, however, these skills were also cited as sources of racial healing that enabled the Cherokee to eschew bitterness and assume their proper place within the nation. The film portrayed the Cherokee as a purveyor of valuable lessons—pride in handiwork, the inherent value of tradition, and the rewards of a life centered on the ties of kinship and clan, but it also associated these values with the collective gesture required of the Cherokee: the act of forgiveness for past injustice.

ARBA's short film captured the complicated role of the tribal village throughout the commemoration. On the one hand, planners invoked it

Film stills from Indian Village. *Courtesy of the Motion Picture, Sound, and Video Holdings of the National Archives and Records Administration.*

to defuse the racial tensions surrounding the commemoration. On the other hand, the village, like the colonial household and the immigrant home, was defined as a domestic space of economic production. The Native American, the colonial goodwife, and the immigrant craftsman all had skills threatened by mass production. As the Smithsonian explained, the festivals documented "traditions which are constantly being eroded and may soon vanish."[92] Observing a woman dressed in colonial garb churning butter or an Indian weaving a basket provided a powerful antidote to the accusations of commercial crassness leveled against ARBA and counteracted the proliferation of kitschy, cheap commemorative goods that had sullied the celebration. In this way, the tribal village worked to protect the Bicentennial against charges of irreparable harm at the hands of government bureaucrats and commercial schemers. Even more, against the background of oil dependency and a declining global economic position, handmade baskets, moccasins, and beadwork helped redeem American nationhood by testifying to the productive capacities of the family and the tribe.

In the days and weeks following 4 July 1976, reporters and commentators deemed the Bicentennial celebration a success, in no small measure because of its decentralized, culturally pluralist, artisan-centered form.[93] There was no question that federal planners had faced a series of formidable challenges. In the wake of military defeat, the oil embargo, and Watergate, they had to convince Americans that there remained much to celebrate. In the midst of an economic recession that combined lagging productivity, unemployment, and inflation, they had to persuade states and local communities to commit resources to the celebration. As cultural nationalists and feminists began reinterpreting the nation's history from a subaltern point of view, planners had to make the case that the American Revolution remained worthy of collective remembrance. As white ethnic groups demanded representation, they had to draw an ever-multiplying number of groups and organizations into the fold of the commemoration. And all the while, planners fended off the charges of corruption, commercialism, racism, and incompetence leveled against them.

Planners seized on the family and domesticity in an effort to meet all of these challenges. By analogizing the family to the nation, they aimed to make the celebration inclusive and participatory. At the same time, they saw the family as a linchpin that gave citizens a personal stake in the celebration. By mobilizing the family as a universal category, they transformed a cultural nationalist challenge into a cultural pluralist solution predicated on the idea that every American had a distinct ethnic identity rooted in the family that made him or her a legitimate member of the national mosaic. The centrality of the family and the domestic throughout the Bicentennial also reflected the political, social, and cultural upheavals of its own historical moment. The showcasing of the colonial household responded to feminist demands, and the celebrations of the immigrant home dovetailed with the white ethnic revival. The immigrant home displaced the history of racial violence that loomed over the commemoration and reasserted the primacy of the immigrant experience over slavery as a historical paradigm at a moment when it was being challenged. Planners' multiple efforts to mobilize the family and the domestic were a testament both to how much they hoped to exorcise upheaval from the commemoration and to the ultimate impossibility of the task. For, as we have seen, both "the family" and "the domestic" unwittingly conjured up the very violence they were meant to suppress.

Finally, the themes of family and domesticity were intimately related to the decentralized and localized form of the commemoration and helped solve the greatest problem the planners faced: the unpopularity of the federal government in 1976. It was above all through mobilizing symbols of the domestic sphere that planners achieved this end. In an ironic twist, the Bicentennial—in both form and content—enhanced the antigovernment sentiment that was fueling the rise of the Right, which would soon find expression in Ronald Reagan's campaign for the presidency. Rather than celebrating national citizenship, the commemoration brilliantly redefined it by highlighting the affective ties historically defined against it: blood, kinship, and clan. By taking the "state" out of the national celebration, planners honored the local, the familial, and the tribal for their independence and productive capacities, thereby confirming that the federal government was the problem and not the solution.

Beyond Containment:
America's World Position after Vietnam

Throughout the Bicentennial, the family had proven to be a persistent if fragile symbol of unity. But the same conflicts over the content of American national identity that pervaded the commemoration also erupted in the foreign policy realm, where another nationalist strain emerged at mid-decade that also invoked the family: Cold War nationalism. The Cold War revival occurred at a moment when two interrelated shifts were taking place in American political culture: society was becoming more polarized, and the family was becoming a lightening rod. By the mid-1970s, the challenges to the postwar family ideal that had surfaced in nascent form in the counter-culture and New Left of the 1960s had flowered into a series of full-blown struggles over women's liberation, homosexuality, abortion rights, and the Equal Rights Amendment. As Americans became more divided over these issues, disparate groups within the foreign policy community were putting forth different conceptions of the relationship between the family and the nation. One of the most revealing debates of the period pitted those historian Jerry Sanders has termed the foreign policy managerialists (many of whom had positions in the incoming Carter administration) against what Daniel Yergin has called the "arms coalition." The debate helped to launch the neoconservative movement.[94]

Vietnam, refracted through the lens of the nation's two hundredth birthday, precipitated the debate. Vietnam forced a rethinking of the United States' basic struggle against the Soviet Union—a struggle that had roots in 1917, had swung into high gear around the time of Luce's self-proclaimed American Century, had defined American national identity for much of the twentieth century, and had culminated in the failures of Vietnam. Did the struggle arise out of the nation's true identity, a country dedicated to freedom, or was it merely contingent, a matter of limited goals and clear statements of interest? Had the defeat occurred, accordingly, because the policy had been misguided? Or because the nation had lacked the resolve to carry it out? These questions were at the center of the debate over national decline in the 1970s, one that inevitably addressed the country's future.

The Bicentennial provided a forum for the debate. Many policy journals seized on the country's birthday as an opportunity to reflect on the state of the nation. Among them was *Foreign Policy*, founded in 1970 to deal with the questions raised by the failure of American policy during the Vietnam War. In commemorative symposia, contributors often mentioned the same conundrum that was on the minds of the ARBA planners: the Bicentennial was taking place at a moment when the meaning of national identity was in disarray. As the editors of *Foreign Policy* observed, "Our bicentennial coincides with a by-now nearly universal awareness that our role in the world has changed."[95] The failed war demanded a new framework for understanding the place of American power, leadership, and military force in the wider world. For some, the tradition of American exceptionalism was in question.

While it is impossible to fully summarize a series of debates that were so far ranging, one can discern two broad positions. The managerialists, associated with the Carter administration, had deep roots in the pragmatic experimentation of the New Deal, the engineering and managerial ideologies of the Progressive Era, earlier traditions of "Yankee" realism, and even in Puritan ideals of "stewardship." In the foreign policy world of the 1970s, the best expression of the managerial point of view was one we have already seen: Henry Kissinger's emphasis on "limits," "realism," and "national interest," as expressed throughout the October War and the oil embargo. Within that broad framework, there was room for much disagreement. Among the figures arguing for "realism" in 1976 were several key members of Carter's State Department: Richard Holbrooke, assistant secretary of state for East Asian and Pacific Affairs; Leslie Gelb, director of political military affairs; Anthony Lake, head of policy planning; Paul Warnke, Carter's chief arms-control negotiator; and Cyrus Vance, Carter's secretary of state.

The managerialists can be understood as the diplomatic counterpart to the ARBA bureaucrats who "managed" the Bicentennial. Like the Bicentennial managers, they were involved in revising and adapting what they regarded as a basically sound conception of national identity. Like the ARBA, their main concern was to avoid conflict, this time on a global scale. They opposed "fanaticism," ideology, and extremism, whether in domestic politics, Palestinian nationalism, or Communism. With strong ties to an increasingly liberal or left-liberal academic community, they were skeptical of unitary notions of national identity, including that of the United States, which they sought to revise in light of a new awareness of diversity.

A remark of Kissinger's already cited will give us the key to the managerial position: "In the life of nations, as of human beings, a point is often reached when the seemingly limitless possibilities of youth suddenly narrow and one must come to grips with the fact that not every option is open any longer. This insight can inspire a new creative impetus, less innocent perhaps than the naïve exuberance of earlier years, but more complex and ultimately more permanent."[96] Almost lovingly, then, the managerialists sought to restrain the excesses that they associated with the nation's youth and immaturity, that is, with its vast, open frontier and its explosive burst into mass consumption. Like benign parents, they urged a prudent policy that took account of the nation's limitations. In essence, they counseled three self-corrections in American identity, each associated with the transition from adolescence to maturity: less reliance on force and more on reason; cautious, thoughtful husbanding of resources that had previously been mindlessly squandered; and greater responsibility for others, not out of a sense of charity, but out of a deeper conception of self-interest.

At the heart of the managerialist project was a reassessment of the place of military force within American foreign policy after Vietnam. One of the principal lessons of the previous decade, Paul Warnke and Leslie Gelb had written in the 1970 inaugural issue of *Foreign Policy*, was that "military force is a singularly inept instrument of foreign policy" that should be used only if the nation's security was under direct military threat.[97] As the Vietnam War demonstrated, unleashing military strength did not always or necessarily produce the desired outcome. There was no question that the United States remained the most powerful nation in the world militarily, Richard Holbrooke explained in 1976, but measuring national power by military capacity was "outmoded." There were other forms of power assuming new importance: "economic power, resource and energy power, food power."[98] The limits of military superiority were particularly striking in regard to nuclear weaponry, which in an era of "mutually assured destruction" had become politically and operationally meaningless. The managerial reorientation away from force was reflected in the pursuit of détente, the French word for "thawing" or "softening." The Strategic Arms Limitation Talks (SALT) began in November 1969, and SALT I was signed in May 1972. The managerialists sought to build on the logic of détente. Like the ARBA managers, they equated the outbreak of force with failure.

The oil embargo sparked a second managerial insight: as control over resources such as oil became more critical, divisions between the Northern and Southern Hemispheres would eclipse those between East and West. The oil embargo pointed toward several aspects of what managerialists saw as a nascent new world order: the unprecedented centrality of vital resources in global politics, the emergence of different kinds of players in the political realm, the new assertiveness of Third World actors, and the growing importance of the "developing world."[99] The fact that the embargo had been declared by a transnational economic organization (OPEC) rather than a nation-state further compromised the effectiveness of military force. Commenting on the force option in a hypothetical future oil crisis, Henry Kissinger remarked, "We should have learned from Vietnam that it is easier to get into a war than to get out of it."[100] The managerialist critique of force was linked to the rejection of the Manichean confrontation of the Cold War. Like the ARBA planners, the managerialists were deeply aware of national and cultural diversity, this time on a global scale.

The insight that limited resources required careful management was linked to domestic policies such as conservation, but it was also linked to a new conception of America's global role. When Paul Warnke was asked, "Do you think it's important that we remain No. 1?" he answered no.[101] In place of supremacy, the managerialists argued that if the world was moving inexorably toward greater interdependence, if natural resources were diminishing, and if the United States was becoming more reliant on other regions for raw materials and vital commodities like oil, American foreign policy should aim at building an international order hospitable to its interests. Such a policy would emphasize world trade over militarism, would try to resolve local and regional political conflicts in the name of international economic balance, would attempt to induce rather than coerce other economic players to act in the "enlightened self-interest" of all, and would rely more heavily on rationalized institutions that would promote financial cooperation across national borders.[102] Other nations had to see their own interests as aligned with those of the United States. The underdeveloped countries of the Southern Hemisphere needed the monetary aid, the technological expertise, and the markets of the Northern Hemisphere. Meanwhile, the industrialized countries of the Northern Hemisphere needed the raw materials, natural resources, and export markets of the Southern Hemisphere.[103] The idea was to create an economic quid pro quo between the Northern and Southern Hemispheres. Just as the ARBA had managed to coordinate Native American, African American, white ethnic, and feminist and other self-oriented entities into a reasonable semblance of cooperation and interdependence, so the United States should try to coordinate a global interdependence that would make the world, in the words of political scientist Joseph Pescheck, "more manageable and less troubling."[104]

The opposition to the managerialist worldview also had deep roots in American history, in the idea of the United States as a "chosen people," in Jacksonian nationalism and Anglophobia, in Southern chauvinism and military culture, and, above all, in the long history of anticommunism that had so much come to define the United States. The opposition was made up of long-standing Cold War figures like Paul Nitze, author of NSC-68, the widely circulated National Security Council blueprint for the nation's Cold War policy; Eugene Rostow, Lyndon Johnson's undersecretary of state; Democratic senator Henry "Scoop" Jackson, the powerful chair of the Armed Services Committee; Richard Perle, a recent graduate student in political science at Princeton University who headed Jackson's staff; Donald Rumsfeld, Ford's White House chief of staff and later his secretary of defense; and Richard Cheney, who had served first as Rumsfeld's deputy and later replaced him as White House chief of staff.[105] But what made this group something more than a bureaucratic faction was its connection to a new group of intellectuals, the neoconservatives, who were able to provide a rationale capable of resuscitating the anticommunism discredited by Vietnam. These included Norman Podhoretz (the editor of *Commentary*), Nathan Glazer (the editor of *Public Policy*), and academics like Daniel Bell and Seymour Martin Lipset. Often coming out of an American Marxist tradition, the neoconservatives had grown alienated from the Democratic Party, partly because of their anticommunism and partly because of what they perceived to be the failures of the welfare state.

Like the managerialists, the neoconservatives believed that Vietnam had been a turning point in American history. But their analysis of this turning point was entirely different. Whereas the managerialists viewed Vietnam as a sign that the United States had not yet achieved maturity, the neoconservatives saw it as a trauma that had replaced clarity with confusion, strength with weakness, and confidence with self-doubt. As *Commentary* editor Norman Podhoretz wrote, "To the casualties in blood of the Vietnam War was added another casualty—the loss of clarity which had marked the policy of the United States for twenty years through Democratic and Republican Administrations alike."[106] In a 1975 *Commentary* symposium entitled "America Now: A Failure of Nerve?" Midge Decter commented: "We appear to be in a state of retreat from our own power quite beyond the natural call of even so massive and costly a failure as we have experienced in Vietnam."[107] If the managerialists appeared as benign, if somewhat distant and abstracted, fathers, the neoconservatives came across as overprotective, neo-Victorian scolds.

A return to the supposedly clear anticommunism of the pre-Vietnam era, along with a simple affirmation of American national identity was at the heart of the neoconservative vision. Many of them Jewish, the neoconservatives found their best analogy to America's recent "retreat" in the appeasement policy that had preceded Germany's rise to power before both world wars. As Eugene Rostow recalled, the historical similarities had first struck him during the "final bitter phases of the Vietnam War," as he watched the government react with "the same fear, passivity, and inadequacy which characterized British and American policy so fatally in the Thirties, and British policy before 1914."[108] Walter Laqueur supplied the core theory: appeasement always originated in trauma. The British and French appeasement of Hitler had emerged out of the earlier trauma of

World War I, while the American tendency to appease the Soviet Union emerged from the trauma of Vietnam. The First World War had ended in apparent British and French victories, while the Vietnam War had ended in American defeat, but the psychological consequences were the same: "the rationalization of weakness," a proclivity for "wishful thinking," "moral flaccidity," a loss of instinct for "national self-preservation," and a descent into masochism. Quoting Yugoslav dissident Milovan Djilas, Podhoretz elaborated: "The West has inflicted certain psychological wounds on itself which have no parallel in the Soviet Union."[109] The managerialists believed the United States was in the throes of a kind of adolescent identity crisis, but the neoconservatives believed it had suffered a grievous blow.

This interpretation led the neoconservatives to reject all three aspects of the managerialist outlook. First, they refuted the idea that military force was becoming less relevant as an instrument of policy. Perceiving themselves as the beleaguered champions of an authentic détente, one based not on a weak admission of parity but on an unassailable position of strength, they attacked both détente and SALT. "Do we lack the power?" Norman Podhoretz asked of the ability of the United States to contain the Soviet threat. "Certainly not in terms of economic, technological, and military capacity," he argued. "The issue boils down in the end then to the question of will. Have we lost the will to defend the free world against the spread of Communism?"[110] Self-correction was necessary—but self-correction from the turn the country had taken in the 1960s, not self-correction from the nation's core identity. It would need to be on the basis of an affirmation rather than rejection of American exceptionalism, and on the basis of a return to the Cold War, not its end. The nation had to recognize that "the principal threat to our nation, to world peace, and to the cause of human freedom is the Soviet drive for dominance based upon an unparalleled military build up."[111]

The neoconservatives also rejected the managerial reorientation toward resource control and toward the Southern Hemisphere with its many new and diverse players. Far from declining in importance, the East-West confrontation was becoming more important, because it was there that the line between freedom and dictatorship was being drawn. For the managerialists, the October War had revealed that there were conflicts that could not be reduced to superpower rivalry. But for the neoconservatives, the Syrian and Egyptian offensives proved that the Cold War was only intensifying. The weak U.S. response to those offensives had opened the way for the oil embargo, the event that, even more than Vietnam, had convinced them that the United States was suffering from "a failure of nerve." What the realists called "a new maturity," they wrote, actually demonstrated the "loss of political will."[112] Fifteen years ago, the editors of *Commentary* hypothesized in 1975, the United States would have responded to OPEC's actions with either the threat or use of military force. The refusal of the United States to take military action against OPEC, Norman Podhoretz commented, "marked the beginning of a period in which militarily powerless parties were able [to act] without fear of retaliation."[113] As a direct result, another *Commentary* contributor declared, "the world is presently living quite at the mercy of the Arabs and the Russians."[114]

The oil embargo had also supplied the neoconservatives with an alternative to the managerialists' fanciful delusions of an identity-politics–inspired "new world order." The Middle East, they believed, and especially the Persian Gulf, was a site where the United States could expunge the experience of military defeat in Vietnam—with the dense and heavily populated jungle terrain of Southeast Asia replaced by a barren and empty Arabian Desert, American technology and military superiority would certainly prevail. With the embargo's images of commodity panic and domestic peril still fresh in memories, and with the problems of rising inflation and unemployment showing no signs of abating, it was taken for granted that American citizens would instantly see why such a military operation was vital to the national interest. Only the willingness to use force was still lacking. Here again, the October War was instructive. The surprising nature of the Arab offensives during that war—the fact that neither "the United States nor Israel could bring itself to conclude that Egypt and Syria would make war"—resembled "Stalin's refusal to believe that Hitler would attack him." Would the October War be remembered as the "unequivocal Pearl Harbor" that it was, Eugene Rostow wondered, or would it be dismissed as "a minor episode, as Britain dismissed the occupation of the Rhineland nearly forty years ago?"[115]

The answer to this question hinged on a deeper understanding of the wrong turn taken in the 1960s. At root, Norman Podhoretz argued, the 1960s had been a turn away from the family—that is, away from parental, especially paternal, responsibility—the source of values that lead a nation to protect itself and to esteem its own members above all other human beings. Like Laqueur, Podhoretz analogized 1970s America to Britain between the two world wars. In both cases, one witnessed a disdain for patriotism conjoined with a "generalized contempt" toward middle-class life and the sense that a married person was "an utterly dreary middle class bore." Such sentiments, Podhoretz continued, would be recognizable to anyone familiar with "homosexual apologetics in America today," citing the writings of Allen Ginsberg, James Baldwin, and Gore Vidal. At stake was much more than some benighted homophobia or gender inequity, but rather "hostility to one's own country" and "derision of the idea that it stands for anything worth defending." Words like "soldier" and "fighting" became distasteful, and works like *The Iliad* "could no longer be comfortably read," Podhoretz recalled of Britain after World War I. A posttraumatic culture, wounded by world war, had refused "fatherhood and all that fatherhood entailed: responsibility for a family and therefore an inescapable implication in the destiny of society as a whole."[116] By casting off the role of the father, British men had repudiated "their birthright as successors to their own fathers in assuming a direct responsibility for the fate of the country."[117] That was the root of British appeasement, and that was what had been unleashed in the United States in the wake of the 1960s.

Podhoretz's portrait of what he called "a culture of appeasement" explicitly linked America's retreat to the same danger that had appeared during the POW publicity campaign, the oil embargo, and the productivity debate: the loss of the father. But even when they were not made explicit, fears about the family—both as a victim of foreign aggression and as a failed repository of moral authority—consistently fueled neoconservative arguments. When neoconservatives expressed astonishment at the nation's presumably tepid response to the oil embargo, they were predicating their arguments on the images of middle-class domestic peril that had circulated in the winter of 1973–74. Their anger that the Nixon administration had not taken military action against OPEC was premised on the underlying logic of those images: that the embargo had been tantamount to a declaration of economic war against the American middle class. Arguing that the nation had lost its resolve in the wake of Vietnam, they implied that the defining problems of American foreign policy were neither strategic nor tactical, but rather psychological and moral in origin, thus invoking the family as a locus of failed moral, psychological, and spiritual resources. All of these arguments established a causal relationship between the fates of the nation and the family that cut both ways. On the one hand, if the United States recoiled from its own power and responsibility, the nation's adversaries would be emboldened in ways that would unleash untold injury within the private world of the family. At the same time, if the family failed as a repository of moral authority and American men refused to assume their paternal responsibilities, the nation's future would be endangered. At mid-decade, as the debate about the nation's compromised world position after Vietnam intensified, the family emerged as both highest stake and most damning symptom.

In the mid-1970s, two different groups addressed the doubts, ambiguities, and anxieties about American identity that had surfaced over the previous five years. The first group, the men and women who planned the Bicentennial, were preoccupied with the problem of social dissent within the nation and turned to diversity nationalism for resolution. The second group, the arms coalition and the neoconservatives, were concerned with the damaged world position of the United States after Vietnam and sought to revive Cold War nationalism. Both groups took it as a given that the nation had endured a traumatic series of setbacks over the previous five years, and both believed that American citizens needed a renewed sense of national purpose and self-confidence. Bicentennial planners sought to reinstill this confidence through a carefully coordinated celebration of difference that appealed to Americans not as citizens within a national political community but on the basis of their ethnic, racial, familial, tribal, and local affiliations. The neoconservatives sought to restore a sense of national purpose by calling attention to the Soviet threat. Both attempts at restoration—the Bicentennial and the Cold War revival—drew heavily on the family in ways that revealed its symbolic versatility: a unifying metaphor for the nation in one moment, a locus of personal (as opposed to national) identity in the next; a source of national regeneration and renewal in one setting, and a site of moral flaccidity and appeasement in another; in one instance, an innocent victim of foreign aggression, and in the next, a failed institution that had placed the nation in jeopardy. Not surprisingly, the same paradoxes that had shaped the family's place in debates about national decline over the previous five years were also at work in the attempts at mid-decade to overcome it.

On the surface, diversity nationalism and Cold War nationalism could not have been more different. Diversity nationalism revolved around relationships between various constituencies within the nation, while Cold War nationalism revolved around the position of the United States in the wider world. The tone of diversity nationalism was upbeat, hopeful, and celebratory, while the tone of Cold War nationalism was ominous and alarmist. Diversity nationalism had its origins in the social movements of the 1960s and the transformations in race and gender relations unleashed by them, while Cold War nationalism had its origins in a new alliance within the foreign policy community made up of older Cold War warriors and newly mobilized opponents of détente.

But when we examine diversity nationalism and Cold War nationalism together, we can see that they often worked with, rather than against, one another. A constitutive part of the antigovernment sentiment that shaped the Bicentennial, diversity nationalism was premised on the same argument that had surfaced in different forms during both the POW publicity campaign and the OPEC oil embargo: an overly bureaucratic and regulatory state was a cause of national enervation. Cold War nationalism focused on an external threat, awakening the anxiety originally captured by the symbol of a family-under-siege. This seemed to be enough to tip the balance to the right, at least in the short run, as California's governor, Ronald Reagan, prepared to run for president on a Republican platform that combined an unprecedented attack on the New Deal welfare state with a renewed commitment to Cold War militarism. At mid-decade, the outcome of Reagan's ultimate quest for the presidency could not yet have been predicted. But in the two spirits of '76, one could already make out the contours of the Reagan Revolution that was just around the corner.

5

Narcissism, "Malaise," and the Middle-Class Family

The World as a Mirror

In March 1977, the Academy of Motion Picture Arts and Sciences held its fiftieth annual awards ceremony, at which the film *Network* was among the most honored films of 1976. The film told the story of Howard Beale, a veteran news anchorman, who, upon learning that he is going to be fired due to poor ratings, announces on live television that he has decided to kill himself. His executives are at first mortified by what they call the "grotesque incident," but they soon discover that Beale's very public meltdown and transformation into a "mad prophet of the airwaves" may in fact amount to a ratings bonanza. The newly hired vice president of programming, Diana Christensen (played by Faye Dunaway, who received an Oscar for the role), first recognizes Beale's commercial potential. Viewers want shows that articulate "popular rage" and Howard Beale is just the man to do it, Diana explains to her boss. Manically pleading for creative control, ignoring the distinction between dramatic programming and news broadcasting, Diana predicts that she can make a newly refashioned "Beale show" into the highest-rated news program on the air. "TV is show business," she declares, "and even the TV news has to have a little showmanship."[1]

Diana Christensen is beautiful, shrewd, and wildly ambitious. She pulls no punches with her underlings and fearlessly pushes her agenda with her superiors. Divorced, childless, and completely consumed by her career, she declares herself "inept at everything" except her work. About to embark on an affair with Max Schumacher, the married, middle-aged, soon-to-be-fired head of the network's news division, Diana exhibits pseudo-self-awareness as she offhandedly relays reports about her inadequacies as a lover. "I can't tell you how many men have told me what a lousy lay I am," she tells Max. "I apparently have a masculine temperament. I arouse quickly, consummate prematurely, and can't wait to get my clothes back on and get out of that bedroom." This caveat in no way deters Max, but when the two become romantically involved, her self-assessment is born out. During a weekend getaway, Diana talks incessantly about the network, breathlessly discussing ratings, shares, and programming as she and Max walk along the beach, sit in front of the fire, and have sex.

As *Network* unfolds, viewers are increasingly led to see Diana through the eyes of Max, who, although deeply infatuated, regards her with considerable wariness. Max's wariness stems not primarily from a gender war, but from a generational chasm. A television pioneer and self-described maverick during the industry's "great early years," Max exudes gravitas, while Diana, reared on television, embodies the emotional hollowness and degraded nature of the medium itself. When Max reveals his affair to his shattered wife, she asks him if Diana loves him. He replies: "I'm not sure she's capable of any real feeling. She's television generation. She learned life from Bugs Bunny. The only reality she knows comes to her over the tv set." It is not so much that Diana is psychically numb or emotionally cold; rather, television has rendered her incapable of distinguishing between spectacle and reality, a distinction that Max desperately tries to clarify as their affair unravels. "This is not a script, Diana. There's some real, actual life going on here. . . . I'm real. You can't switch to another station," he explains in a last ditch effort to elicit some emotion from her. When Max prepares to leave Diana and return to his wife, he comes up with the most damning indictment he can muster: You are "television incarnate," he tells Diana. "Indifferent to suffering, insensitive to joy. . . . You even shatter the sensations of time and space into split seconds and instant replays."

More than simple unchecked ambition or careerism, Diana's fundamental crime is that she flouts distinctions between fiction and nonfiction, between drama and news, between politics and entertainment, and between spectacle and reality. But if she perpetrates epistemological confusions, she is also a victim of them. At the network, it is Diana rather than Max who wields professional power. Max embodies television's moribund past, while Diana represents its future, degenerate though it may be. But in the private, interior world of "pleasure and pain and love," it is Diana who desperately needs Max, not the other way around. As Max perceives it, his love for Diana is the only thing that separates her from "the shrinking nothingness [she lives] the rest of the day," an assessment that Diana implicitly confirms when she feebly asks him not to leave her. He is, he tells her, "her last contact with human reality."

Diana's character symbolized the emergence of a new psychological type that received sustained attention from both psychoanalysts and social critics throughout the 1970s. This type was known as the narcissist, and Diana appeared to be a textbook case: in her inability to feel empathy and forge authentic emotional ties, in her command over the language of psychology without any true self-knowledge, and in her impoverished personal life (falsely compensated for by a succession of heady but ultimately empty professional triumphs). To be sure, when *Network* was first released in 1976, Diana was also meant to serve as a disturbing caricature of the contemporary feminist—a professional powerhouse who abdicates her commitment to family life. But, revealingly, Diana also provided a case study in narcissism, widely recognized by the 1970s as *the* personality disorder of late twentieth-century America and seen as a symptom of the political decline and cultural malaise that Podhoretz deplored.

This chapter traces the transformation of narcissism from a psychiatric into a cultural condition between 1975 and 1980. By the time Christopher Lasch published his best-selling book, *The Culture of Narcissism: American Life in an Age of Diminishing Expectations,* in 1978, the term had moved beyond the psychoanalytic community and had become a topic of debate among journalists, scholars, and social critics. Proceeding from the unverifiable premise that narcissism had emerged as a rampant personality disorder among middle-class Americans after World War II, commentators sought to identify its causes, symptoms, and cures. But as the decade drew to a close, narcissism became more than a simple clinical condition. It emerged as a cultural condition as well, one that appeared to provide a partial explanation for the political and economic turmoil of the recent past. Now there were not simply narcissistic personalities, but narcissistic generations, decades, and trends. An endlessly protean and at times hopelessly vague concept, "narcissism," once a narrow psychoanalytic category, came to serve as the diagnosis for a diseased national culture by the end of the 1970s.

At the center of the discussion of narcissism was the same threat that had appeared in other guises in the midst of Vietnam, the oil embargo, and the Bicentennial: the threat of a family under attack from hostile outside forces. Tracing the origins of narcissism to the white, middle-class family of the postwar years, psychoanalysts argued that the double blow of smothering yet cold mothers and absent fathers had set the stage for the narcissistic personality disorders that clinicians were now encountering with growing frequency among their adult clients. Meanwhile, social critics and scholars attempted to historicize this shift in symptomatology, arguing that narcissism could be traced back to the decline of paternal authority within the family, as the sphere of personal life was gradually narrowed by the welfare state, the mass media, the peer group, and the cult of expertise. Narcissism, in other words, was linked to the perceived erosion of family life. Incapable of reflecting on the past or the future, severed from the ties that historically had linked one generation to the next, the adult narcissist threatened to abdicate his or her commitment to both marriage and biological reproduction. This abdication located the narcissist along the same continuum as both the new breed of worker and the pacifist/appeaser supposedly responsible for defeat in Vietnam.

But if the family was central to discussions of narcissistic personality disorder, so too was feminism. As the film *Network* illustrated, the emergence of feminism and the pathology of narcissism were linked in popular culture. This was not primarily because narcissism was defined as a distinctly feminine disorder or that mothers received the lion's share of the blame for its prevalence.[2] Rather, it was because the theory of narcissism provided social critics with a potent language for indicting feminism for its purported crimes: its blurring of the distinction between public and private, its rhetoric of what Christopher Lasch called "pseudo-liberation," and its ostensible retreat from "real" politics. Above all, social critics cited both narcissism and feminism as evidence of the same phenomenon that Podhoretz had observed in his account of a culture of appeasement: a spreading antinatalism and rejection of reproduction among the American middle class. Indeed, critics from both the Left and the Right turned to narcissism—as both individual psychopathology and cultural condition—in order to construct feminism as a disaster for the middle class, and, by extension, for the nation. In the early 1970s, the POW publicity campaign had suggested that the women's liberation movement threatened to derail homecoming by transforming loyal wives into independent women. At the end of the decade, the narcissism debate again constructed feminism as a social force that threatened the integrity of the nation precisely through its incursion into the private realm of the family.

But the debate over narcissism did more. As we have seen, anxieties about the future of the middle-class family shaped debates about international politics—the war in Vietnam, national dependency on Middle Eastern oil, and the threat of mounting foreign competition in the steel and automobile industries. The claim that the nation had descended into narcissism gave an open-ended, psychological thrust to these discussions. It brought together the recurring anxieties about both the state of the family and the state of the nation that had come to the fore over the previous decade: the claim that declining paternal authority within the family had wrought psychological and cultural havoc; the contention that mass consumption and the decline of a producerist ideal had paved the way for a feminized (and inherently degraded) national culture; the assertion that the modern family had grown excessively dependent on outside state intervention; the charge that feminism was a social force that was not simply destroying American families, but sapping national strength; and, finally, the growing sense that the middle-class family of the postwar years had failed to adequately socialize its own children and that the nation's current economic and political woes could be traced back, at least in part, to this parental failure. Indeed, even as the debate was unfolding, journalists and social critics used the term to describe the national mood and characterize the 1970s. This characterization set the stage for a historical contention about the decade that would endure for years to come: that the 1970s were essentially shaped by political retreat, a turn to personal preoccupations, and narcissistic self-indulgence.

"A Disguised Cry for Help": Defining Narcissism as a Clinical Condition

When Sigmund Freud first wrote "On Narcissism" in 1914, he was identifying neither a personality disorder nor a cultural condition. Among other things, he was attempting to chart two distinct paths of psychosexual development for boys and girls. In his famous essay, he drew a distinction between two kinds of object choice: anaclitic object choice (love for an object that one is dependent on for primary needs) and narcissistic object choice (love for the self or someone who resembles the self). Since the early care of infants was almost exclusively performed by women, Freud contended that the psychosexual growth of boys and girls proceeded along two very different axes: boys had an infantile precedent for anaclitic object choice (since they were different from their mothers), whereas girls had no such precedent, making narcissistic object choice fundamental to their later attachments. Freud's essay was deeply influential, in no small measure because it represented one of his first attempts (however partial and flawed) to address the "woman question" within psychoanalytic theory.[3]

Although the essay was read among Freud's followers, the concept of narcissism actually received relatively little attention in wider psychoanalytic and psychiatric circles in the years prior to World War II. After the war, however, psychiatrists began to note a shift in symptomatology among their patients that prompted them to revisit Freud's original concept. The patient who only a few decades earlier may have suffered from physical paralysis, obsessive hand washing, or sexual repression—all classical symptoms of hysteria—was now more likely to complain of vague feelings of emptiness and ennui. By the 1950s and 1960s, psychoanalysts reported that hysteria, the neurosis par excellence of bourgeois Victorianism, had been largely displaced by a new cluster of what psychiatrists called "character disorders." These disorders were characterized less by specific neurotic symptoms and more by elusive feelings of dis-ease and chronic dissatisfaction.[4] Narcissistic personality disorder was an umbrella term for these new character disorders.

Although the clinical description of narcissism had evolved since Freud's 1914 definition, the disorder was marked by a number of essential features. Most significantly, the narcissist suffered from delusions of grandeur and self-importance. Believing that he was special, the narcissist felt entitled to fame, success, and power, even in the absence of real achievements. He had contempt for "despicable, worthless mediocrity" (what one might normally perceive as "average") and saw himself as uniquely gifted.[5] But while the narcissist often appeared excessively pretentious, his self-esteem was extremely fragile. Thus, he required constant praise from the outside world and experienced criticism as catastrophic. As a result of his voracious need for external admiration, the narcissist's interpersonal relations were often parasitic and exploitative. Because the narcissist did not recognize where others left off and he began, he lacked empathy and failed to recognize that other people possessed emotional needs distinct from his own. In the words of psychoanalyst Otto Kernberg, to the narcissist, other people were nothing more than "lifeless shadows or marionettes." When he felt wronged or rejected, the narcissist could respond with rage and contempt. Under a charming and engaging veneer, he could be cold and ruthless. At the same time, in contrast to those suffering from more overtly debilitating character disorders (such as borderline personality disorder), the narcissist could be highly functional, socially adept, and professionally successful. But if one scratched below the surface, the narcissist's emotional life was revealed as shallow and severely compromised by chronic feelings of restlessness and boredom, feelings that could only be momentarily relieved through external rewards.[6]

In the 1950s and 1960s, the rise of character disorders, narcissism among them, had been intimately linked to larger debates about motherhood and maternal failure.[7] In a somewhat circular argument, postwar American psychoanalysts attributed the rise of character disorders to mothers who were themselves narcissistic. Thus, according to psychoanalytic literature, the narcissistic mother not only failed to differentiate between herself and her children—she also exhibited an odd combination of smothering overprotectiveness and lack of affect. One 1961 article, entitled "The Disguised Cry for Help: Narcissistic Mothers and Their Children," described the growing number of mothers who brought their presumably "troubled" children in for psychiatric treatment without recognizing that they were actually pleading for help for themselves. According to the authors, the narcissistic mother could only recognize her child as a mirror of her own unresolved childhood disturbances. She would be withholding in the face of her child's dependence, but also punitive when confronted with her child's developing autonomy. In response to confusing maternal signals, the child was forced to erect his own narcissistic defenses, thus perpetuating the pathology of narcissism within the family.[8]

This disturbing combination of maternal coldness and overprotection had implications far beyond the psychiatrist's office. As early as 1942, Philip Wylie had appropriated the language of psychoanalysis to blame parasitic, smothering mothers for emasculating the nation's men and undermining American civic traditions. *Generation of Vipers* had located the figure of the narcissistic mother—and the epidemic of "Momism" she was meant to embody—at the center of broader cultural debates about a nation whose future was imperiled by materialism, enervation, and overconsumption. Despite her deceptively innocuous trappings, Wylie charged, the white, middle-class, suburban mom endangered the healthy psychological development of a generation of American boys and thus constituted a threat to national security. Almost single-handedly, Wylie transformed the narcissistic mother from a psychoanalytic type into a staple of social criticism.[9]

The supposed spread of narcissism as a clinical condition in the 1970s built on this World War II discourse. If white, middle-class adults were exhibiting narcissistic tendencies in the 1970s, it was presumably because the psychogenic seeds of the disorder had been planted several decades earlier. Indeed, clinical accounts of narcissism in the 1970s strongly resonated with Wylie's book. Prominent psychoanalysts and psychiatrists such as Otto Kernberg and Herbert Hendin, both of whom specialized in the disorder, agreed with their predecessors that maternal coldness had gradually transformed narcissism from a normal infantile condition (what psychoanalysts called primary narcissism) into an increasingly common adult pathology.[10] In particular, a thwarted maternal relationship was at the heart of Kernberg's influential account of narcissistic personality disorder.

A key player in debates about narcissism in the 1970s, Kernberg was a classically trained psychoanalyst who had fled Nazi-occupied Europe as a young boy, come of age and received his training in Chile, and later emigrated to the United States. Throughout his work, Kernberg claimed that narcissism was a psychopathology that contained no retrievable elements, a claim that directly refuted the position of his theoretical adversary Heinz Kohut. In *Borderline Conditions and Pathological Narcissism* (1975), Kernberg argued that the main etiological element within narcissism was "the predominance of [a] chronically cold, narcissistic, and at the same time overprotective mother figure." This mother figure, according to Kernberg, functioned well on the surface of a "superficially well-organized home." But underneath the veneer, she exhibited "callousness, indifference, and nonverbalized, spiteful aggression" toward her children. In his influential study, Kernberg presented a lucid and disturbing picture of how narcissism was transmitted from one generation to the next. The narcissistic mother might appear to be caring, loving, and responsible. But, in fact, she was "chronically cold," "extremely envious," and "intensely aggressive" toward her children. As a defense against this covert maternal hostility, her children were forced to seek refuge in grandiose illusions of uniqueness and special gifts, illusions that they carried with them into adulthood.[11]

Herbert Hendin took Kernberg's insights a step further by exploring narcissism as a generational phenomenon. A psychiatrist at Columbia University who would later become a renowned expert on suicide, Hendin published *The Age of Sensation* in 1975. In his influential study, Hendin attempted what he called "an open-ended psychoanalytic study" of college youth in America. After conducting interviews with hundreds of students, Hendin painted a bleak picture of a "disengaged, detached, fragmented, and emotionally numb" generation. Much like *Network*'s Diana, the young people of Hendin's study avoided emotional intimacy at all costs and cultivated a "cool, detached, uncaring resignation." Hendin argued that this "flight from emotion" was symptomatic of narcissism's pervasiveness and could be seen in everything from recreational drug use to growing sexual antagonism, from the prominence of male homosexuality to rising rates of student suicide. Significantly, Hendin contended that this generational flight from emotion eroded the once-stable racial boundary between black and white. What so alarmed him was that the psychological divide between "blacks in the ghetto" and white, middle-class college students appeared to be narrowing. According to Hendin, the hopelessness and despair of ghetto life had compelled blacks to pursue "sensory escape," to "live in the moment," and to opt for "immediate gratification" over enduring commitments. But now the epidemic of narcissism meant that the white middle class was mimicking this "ghetto mentality": they too increasingly saw life as a trap and aimed to attain whatever pleasure they could in the present moment.[12]

The cold yet smothering mother appeared frequently throughout Hendin's study. Young women who failed to forge intimate emotional bonds with men had been the victims of "devouring mothers" who enlisted their daughters as confidantes, coconspirators, and accomplices (often against an emotionally distant husband). One woman described the phenomenon with what Hendin termed "devastating simplicity," portraying her mother as "overprotective without any real warmth." Similarly, the young men in Hendin's study frequently described their relations with their mothers as characterized by "coolness, estrangement, frustration, and loss." One young male homosexual told Hendin that his mother possessed "an Arctic mentality." Like the mother figure described by Kernberg, she was "an efficient machine with no heart or warmth" who had "more feeling for her cocker spaniel than for anyone else." Hendin detected in his interviewees a consistent maternal pattern that produced devastating results: the mother initially exhibited coldness toward her infant, and then, once the child reached a certain age, she enlisted her child as loyal ally and fawning admirer—essentially as nothing more than a provider of narcissistic supplies to the mother herself. Having reached adulthood, the children of affluence were now suffering from what Hendin called "profound emotional impoverishment."[13]

Accounts like Hendin's and Kernberg's must be seen within the context of a specific postwar psychiatric discourse in the United States, one that blamed mothers for everything from bed wetting and nail biting to communism and racial bigotry. But these accounts of narcissism's etiology must also be seen as specific to the 1970s. This book has argued that debates about national decline often took aim at the postwar middle-class family, and the narcissism debate was no exception. In Hendin's words, the emotionally impoverished lives of his subjects had "exploded" the popular myth of fifties togetherness. By the mid-1970s, the affluent middle-class family of the 1950s had been exposed as a breeding ground for narcissism; the frightening repercussions of Wylie's "Momism" were coming into full view.[14]

Having Only One Life:
Narcissism as a Cultural Condition

If discussions of narcissism had remained confined to psychoanalytic circles, its growing prominence as a clinical diagnosis alone would have revealed much about cultural attitudes toward mothering and family life. But, in fact, social critics appropriated the term "narcissism" and transposed it onto a national culture during this period.[15] Not only did this appropriation reveal the by-now-compulsive journalistic tendency to label decades with catchy clichés (even in the midst of them), but it was also suggestive of the enormous influence of psychoanalytic thought in twentieth-century American culture.[16] As narcissism emerged as the popular diagnosis of a presumably sick nation, commentators located under its rubric a range of phenomena and entities that had little in common. Endlessly protean, narcissism's meanings and connotations grew increasingly amorphous as the term entered popular discourse. At the same time, very disparate accounts of cultural narcissism shared a common feature: they all expressed the same fear that narcissism exposed a disturbing antinatalism among the American middle class. A culture of narcissism was one in which young men and women, reared in postwar affluence, were bartering their futures in exchange for the empty pursuit of self-realization. And perhaps more than any other movement of the age, the narcissism debate suggested, it was modern feminism that reflected this growing ambivalence about biological reproduction.

One of the most popular renderings of narcissism came from writer and social critic Tom Wolfe, who famously defined the 1970s as the "me" decade.[17] A member of the East Coast literary elite, Wolfe was also a proponent of New Journalism, a form of reportage that relied on fictional devices in order to get beyond what Wolfe described as the "pale beige tone" of news reporting.[18] He achieved that goal with "The Me Decade" essay, which appeared in *New York Magazine* in August 1976. Wolfe began his essay by reflecting on a slogan made famous by an advertising campaign for Clairol hair dye fifteen years earlier: "If I've only one life, let me live it as a blonde!" According to Wolfe, this seemingly banal advertising slogan in fact captured a profound cultural shift that had reached its apex by the mid-1970s. An earlier conception of selfhood rooted in generational affiliation had given way to a new cult that revolved around remaking, elevating, and polishing a self that had no connection to either past or future generations. "Most people, historically, have *not* lived their lives as if thinking 'I have only one life to live,'" Wolfe explained. Instead, they had identified strongly with the lives of both their ancestors and their offspring. The husband and wife who sacrificed their own material comfort for their children's future, the soldier who risked his life in battle, the man who devoted himself to a goal that could not possibly be realized during his lifetime, the pregnant woman: all of these people, according to Wolfe, conceived of themselves as "part of a great biological stream" or as "inseparable from the great tide of chromosomes." But now, the article concluded, this age-old conception of the self was on the wane as white, middle-class Americans abdicated their commitment to future generations, pursuing instead "personal transformation" and "self-actualization."[19]

With a tone of derision, Wolfe cited a range of contemporary cultural and social trends to describe what he dubbed "the third great awakening": the success of encounter groups such as Esalen and EST, the rise of psychedelic and New Left communes, an obsession with authenticity and a quest for what Wolfe called the "Real Me," a heightened interest in Eastern religions and mysticism, the conversion of 1960s political radicals into spiritual devotees, the revival of charismatic Christianity, the women's liberation movement, a surging divorce rate, the sexual revolution, and the growing popularity of group therapy and marriage counseling. All of these trends, according to Wolfe, reflected the desire among their predominantly white, middle-class practitioners to pursue personal transformation in order to endow their own lives with special meaning.

What was the historical explanation for this "delicious look inward," to borrow Wolfe's expression? Like psychoanalysts attempting to locate the etiology of narcissistic personality disorder, Wolfe traced the origins of the "me decade" back to the spread of wealth and leisure among the American middle class in the years after World War II. Social theorists from Karl Marx to Émile Durkheim to José Ortega y Gasset had bleakly characterized the modern man as "helpless, bewildered, and dispirited," Wolfe explained, but they had failed to anticipate the full cultural impact of unbridled economic growth on "the mass man." "Once the dreary little bastards started getting money in the 1940s, they did an astonishing thing—they took their money and ran," concluded Wolfe. "They did something only aristocrats (and intellectuals and artists) were supposed to do—they discovered and started doting on Me! They've created the greatest age of individualism in American history!"[20] Just as dominating mothers had bred narcissism in their children, so widespread affluence had unleashed individualism among the middle class. And in an ironic twist, now that the pursuit of individualism (historically seen as so essential to the American character) had been democratized, it had devolved into something pathological and even absurd. In a claim that would be made repeatedly by cultural critics between 1976 and 1980, Wolfe contended that it was not simply the psychiatric patient but the entire American middle class that bore the stamp of narcissism.

Wolfe's famous essay captured the ways in which the meaning of "narcissism" changed as the concept morphed from psychiatric into cultural diagnosis. First, its exact definition became increasingly difficult to pin down. Much of the psychoanalytic discussion of narcissism was aimed at defining its precise parameters, not only by identifying the specific constellation of symptoms that constituted it but also by differentiating it from other clinical conditions—such as borderline and histrionic personality disorders—that shared some of its common elements.[21] But once narcissism became a cultural signifier, all attempts at precision went out the window. Now, everything from jogging to feminist encounter groups to Buddhist meditation was defined (and derided) as a narcissistic indulgence. This movement from precision to vagueness, while an inevitable part of narcissism's emergence as a popular buzzword, meant that crucial distinctions between political movements (such as feminism), demographic shifts (such as rising divorce rates), and cultural trends (such as EST) would be obscured. When a critic like Wolfe defined all of these as constitutive features of the "me decade," he implied that the deadly serious and the downright silly were cut from the same degenerate cultural cloth.

There was also a significant shift in tone as "narcissism" traveled beyond psychoanalytic circles. While it was clear that the classical narcissist could be both insufferably self-aggrandizing and shamelessly exploitive in his relations with others, psychoanalysts were clear that narcissism was in fact an extremely painful clinical condition and that patients who suffered from it deserved compassion and care. As clinicians frequently reiterated, narcissism could not be equated with self-interest, individualism, or selfishness. On the contrary, narcissism was the result of the failure of healthy individuation during infancy and early childhood. But as narcissism became a buzzword, the subtle psychoanalytic distinctions between narcissism, selfishness, and individualism dropped out of view. Not only did social critics equate narcissism with selfishness, but they also drew on the term to argue that healthy individualism had been displaced by something unhealthy and grotesque.[22]

But despite their differences in content and tone, psychoanalytic and journalistic discussions were both concerned with the subjectivity of the American middle class. For their part, psychoanalysts like Kernberg and Hendin argued that when placed under close clinical scrutiny, the seemingly "ideal" white, middle-class family (with its detrimental disjuncture between maternal competency and maternal aggression) was a breeding ground for the personality disorders that were now more and more prevalent. Journalists like Wolfe traced narcissism to the prosperity that had unleashed individualist aspirations on a massive scale, leading to a shocking degree of self-absorption among the American middle class. As both psychological condition and cultural disorder, narcissism was identified with the excesses and the hypocrisies of the affluent society. At the same time, it would be wrong to assume that critics appropriated the category only to indict the middle class for selfishness. Journalistic accounts of narcissism often shuttled back and forth between attacking middle-class excess and expressing fears about the future in an era of inflation, rising divorce rates, ecological disaster, and shifting sexual politics.

This oscillation often occurred within the same account. For example, in his 1976 book *The Awareness Trap: Self-Absorption Instead of Social Change*, writer Edwin Schur attacked the awareness movements of the 1970s as "the new opiate of the people," making them "politically innocuous and socially complacent." Attacking middle-class Americans for turning inward and abdicating their commitment to social change, Schur put forth a familiar litany of arguments. Meditation and encounter groups were nothing more than Madison Avenue innovations. Such cultural trends diverted attention away from persistent forms of social injustice. Followers of the new movements were guilty of both rampant narcissism and political naïveté. "The average ghetto-dwelling addict . . . needs decent housing and jobs more than rapping and meditation," Schur didactically explained to his imaginary reader (presumably a deluded encounter group participant). Drawing a stark distinction between material and psychological needs, Schur dismissed the new emphasis on self-realization as fundamentally diversionary and indicted the middle class for turning its back on poverty, racism, and environmental decay.[23]

But, simultaneously, Schur offered a gloomier and in some ways more sympathetic interpretation of what he called "the awareness trap." Drawing on Marxist scholar Russell Jacoby's influential *Social Amnesia* (1975), he suggested that the new awareness movements also reflected the internalization of a "survivalist mentality" among a middle class that saw its own position as increasingly precarious. "The compulsive effort at happiness invariably tends to belie itself," contended Schur. "The smile buttons seek to chase from mind the daily carnage and drudgery; one smiles because the living are sad. . . . The whole program, in brief, is grin and bear it." Thus Schur argued that the new awareness movements revealed psychic exhaustion and resignation among the middle class. In contrast to Wolfe, who had linked the "me decade" exclusively to the postwar expansion of wealth, Schur suggested that, even while steeped in class bias, the turn to self-realization was rooted in a spreading sense of psychological scarcity.[24]

In this second interpretation, the new attention to self-awareness emerged as a symptom of desperation rather than luxury among the middle class. As Peter Marin portrayed it in a 1975 *Harper's* essay, entitled "The New Narcissism," encounter group practitioners were a beleaguered bunch. Initially, Marin had planned on writing an essay on the California-based encounter group Esalen that showed "the ways in which selfishness and moral blindness now assert themselves . . . as enlightenment and psychic health." But Marin's criticism of selfishness became a meditation on the middle class's desperation in what he called "an age of catastrophe." The turn to new therapies like EST and Esalen was narcissistic, he argued, but such expressions of narcissism were ultimately "grief stricken." The new cult of psychic health reflected a "broken faith with the world." Recalling an Esalen conference in San Francisco that he had attended in the fall of 1973, Marin noted that it was not the hope for world peace but rather the threat of the OPEC oil embargo that loomed over the proceedings. To the audience, he speculated, the "future must have seemed frightening. . . . One could feel in the air and see on their faces the early signs of a collective paranoia, as if they were haunted by the world's possible vengeance." Far from being celebratory, the mood of the crowd was "restless, impatient, volatile; one could feel rising from it a palpable sense of hunger, as if these people had somehow been failed by both the world and their therapies." The message of Marin's essay was clear: the new narcissists could run from the outside world, but they could not, in the end, hide from it. He concluded his essay with a kind of homespun curse that fused sexual politics and geopolitics: "The shadows of those neglected others—dying in Asia, hungry in Africa, impoverished in our own country—fall upon every one of our private acts, darken the household and marriage bed for each of us."[25]

What emerges from these discussions of cultural narcissism is a bleaker picture of middle-class consciousness than one might at first expect. To be sure, critics like Wolfe did tend to equate narcissism with selfishness, and they refashioned narcissism into a cultural category in order to condemn and poke fun at what they viewed as the excesses of middle-class self-absorption. But the category of narcissism also offered social critics a way into the more subterranean dimensions of middle-class subjectivity during this period, including fears of declining status in an age of economic recession, depleting natural resources, and disintegrating marriages. A culture of narcissism, then, was meant to reflect both middle-class privilege *and* middle-class instability, both cultural folly *and* psychological dis-ease. Like its clinical counterpart, cultural narcissism was not, despite appearances to the contrary, much fun.

Fears of family decline were critical to this dual conception of narcissism. Like the new breed of worker, one of the narcissist's defining features was that he abdicated his commitment to family life and biological reproduction. When Wolfe fretted about Clairol's advertising campaign, he was in fact expressing a broader concern that members of the "me generation" were fetishizing the present and bartering away the future through their deferral or outright rejection of family pursuits. The vigorous demands of self-actualization would now outweigh the historical demands of reproduction and cross-generational affiliation, he suggested. According to popular accounts of narcissism, rising divorce rates, growing sexual antagonism, and declining birthrates all suggested that both men and women of the middle class were rejecting the traditional ties of biological kinship in favor of a new emphasis on the untapped potential of the self. Narcissism was a cause for alarm because it raised frightening questions about the capacity of the middle class to reproduce itself. As a clinical condition, it punctured the normative ideal of the postwar family by reducing the mother's "superficial competence" to "chronic coldness." As a cultural phenomenon of the 1970s, it was no less frightening: it appeared to constitute a form of "class suicide" on the part of its white, relatively affluent, and well-educated converts.[26] As we saw in chapter 4, Norman Podhoretz had identified the appeaser with a national crisis of reproduction. In the growing debate about narcissism, it was the feminist above all who threatened the cross-generational, reproductive responsibilities of the American nation.

The identification of the feminist with antinatalism emerged in part out of the politics of the women's liberation movement in the 1970s. During this period, feminists engaged in passionate debates about the meaning of motherhood, and some activists identified mothering as a primary source of women's oppression. The feminist critique of motherhood was complex and encompassed several related but distinct themes: the idea that historically women had been assigned disproportionate responsibility for childrearing and child care; the related claim that men and the society as a whole needed to assume more responsibility for this vital work; the contention that the burden of motherhood had handicapped women in the worlds of paid employment, culture, intellectual life, and politics; the belief that motherhood had been sentimentalized and its status as labor overlooked; the argument that mothering had been presented to women as their destiny rather than their choice; and the assertion that in the past women had not been permitted to express their ambivalence about the maternal role, to the detriment of women and children alike.[27] Not all feminists were in agreement on all of these points, but most agreed that traditional conceptions of motherhood needed to be revised in order for women's emancipation to be achieved.

This feminist critique of motherhood, and in particular its emphasis on maternal ambivalence, took on a specific set of meanings in the context of the debate about narcissism. Since psychoanalysts traced narcissistic disorders to mothers who expressed hostility toward their children and journalists identified a rejection of reproduction as the hallmark of cultural narcissism, the feminist who exhibited resistance to mothering emerged as the narcissist par excellence. At the same moment that the women's liberation movement was attempting to redefine motherhood as a freely chosen path rather than as a preordained destiny, the narcissism debate figured maternal ambivalence as pathological cause and childlessness as pathological symptom. As a result, discussions of narcissism often contained within them an implicit critique of feminism, even if the word was never mentioned. For example, in a 1981 essay on narcissism, Russell Jacoby reflected on the recent emergence of childlessness among young, relatively wealthy, professional couples—a demographic profile that would become iconic in the 1980s with the "yuppie" phenomenon. These child-less couples, according to Jacoby, were simply unwilling to expend "the psychic energy, affection, and attention" required of childrearing. As the psychic household of the individual was remodeled into a financial coun-seling service, "children receive a poor rating; they are high risks, requiring too much initial investment and too few guaranteed returns."[28] Jacoby con-tinued: "Exchange value has not simply knocked at the door but migrated into bedroom, nursery, and sickroom. This means that the family casts off unequal relationships. All relationships are appraised with an eye on the psychic bank account; spending must balance earnings. Consequently, the family contracts, eliminating the old and other kin. Requiring more care and attention than they can return, they are herded off to the state agencies and institutions. Psychic bankruptcy is avoided by retrenching, cutting off losing investments: the old, the children, the sick, and so on."[29]

The emergence of what Jacoby called a "childless society" complicated any easy definition of narcissism as hedonistic and excessive. Despite the trappings of hedonism, Jacoby contended, a narcissistic culture was, in the end, dictated by parsimony and endless calculation of a sort once confined to the marketplace. Jacoby cited the affluent, childless couple as damning evidence that the logic of market exchange had invaded even the most intimate spheres of life and was annihilating rather than revivifying the bourgeoisie: "The exchange principle, capitalism's own weapon, is used by the bourgeoisie to prune its own family. Hedonism devours itself."[30]

Jacoby made no mention of contemporary feminism in his essay, but, in some ways, he did not have to. Given the centrality of critiques of the nuclear family and motherhood to feminist politics, the implications were clear. Jacoby's argument proceeded from the premise that the choice not to have a child—a choice viewed by feminists as potentially liberating for women—was, in the end, no choice at all. If an upwardly mobile woman chose not to become a mother, she was not emancipating herself, but in-stead engaging in stingy, psychic economizing. And if narcissism was hope-lessly embroiled in the logic of commodity exchange, so, too, surely was feminism. Of course, Jacoby's critique of the "language of the commodity" reflected more rarified intellectual debates about narcissism that did not make their way into the popular press. But they did nonetheless have an impact on feminism's larger reception. Even as Jacoby complicated the equation of narcissism with simple self-gratification, his arguments lent credence to the popular perception that the decision not to have a child (a decision at once narcissistic and feminist) was calculated and selfish.

Childlessness, according to Jacoby, may have been a symptom of parsimony rather than indulgence, but it was, after all, a symptom.

Society without the Father:
Christopher Lasch and The Culture of Narcissism

This new conception of cultural narcissism received its most sustained and nuanced treatment at the end of the decade. In 1978, historian Christopher Lasch deepened the debate with the publication of *The Culture of Narcissism: American Life in an Age of Diminishing Expectations*. Described by one reviewer as a "civilized hellfire sermon," the book contributed more to the popularization of the term than any other publication of the 1970s.[31] *The Culture of Narcissism* surprised everyone, not least its author, by becoming a national best seller, temporarily bridging an ever-widening divide between scholarly and popular writing, and more than fulfilling Lasch's aim to address a readership beyond the academy. Capitalizing on its initial success, the publisher of the paperback edition promoted *The Culture of Narcissism* as one of the "greatest books on society's changing values," along with Alvin Toffler's *Future Shock*, Charles Reich's *The Greening of America*, Gail Sheehy's *Passages*, and Nancy Friday's *My Mother Myself*. A critic of these other works, Lasch would later malign this promotional campaign as "ill-conceived" and express frustration that his book had been widely misinterpreted as, in the words of one reviewer, the "latest addition to the 'what's wrong with us' bibliography."[32]

The story of how Lasch came to write a best-selling book on narcissism is essential not only to tracing the history of the term but also to understanding the centrality of the family to debates about national decline as the 1970s drew to a close. What led Lasch to write a book about narcissism? His intellectual biography had followed a distinctive but not unfamiliar trajectory. A cultural historian at the University of Rochester, he was a native Midwesterner and the son of a political journalist. Reared in what he described as an "intellectual atmosphere of positivistic liberalism" and "Middle Western progressivism," Lasch had grown increasingly disillusioned with liberalism during the late 1950s and 1960s because of what he called the "the follies and crimes" of American Cold War foreign policy. It was also during this time that he received his first introduction to psychoanalytic thought through the politicized interpretations of Norman O. Brown and Herbert Marcuse, an introduction that he would recall as having "opened another world to me, as exotic to an American positivist as

Christopher Lasch.
Courtesy of W. W. Norton
and Company; photograph
by Ken Hawkins.

China to Marco Polo." Like so many other intellectuals of the Left during the 1960s, Lasch's attempts to understand the social roots of economic and military domination—reflected so clearly in the disaster of Vietnam—led him to the writings of Marx and Freud and to works like Marcuse's *Eros and Civilization* that attempted to synthesize them.[33]

Lasch had grown disenchanted with the positivistic liberalism of his upbringing, and it would not be long before he became disillusioned with the New Left. According to Lasch, the New Left suffered from a number of serious deficiencies: a profound theoretical poverty and anti-intellectualism; a weakness in critical thinking and an attraction to Marxism in its most mechanistic and orthodox form; a failure to adequately address the roles of religion and tradition in the lives of working-class people; an ignorance of conservative traditions of opposition to modern industrial society; and an infatuation with spectacle and theatricality. By the mid-1970s, Lasch's growing sense of estrangement from the New Left was cemented by the advent of the women's liberation movement. In his autobiographical introduction to *The True and Only Heaven: Progress and Its Critics* (1991), Lasch wrote with remarkable candor about the connection between feminism's growing influence and his own waning commitment to the New Left during these years. "My own faith in the explanatory power of the old ideologies began to waver in the mid-seventies," he wrote, "when my study of the family led me to question the left's program of sexual liberation, careers for women, and professional childcare."[34]

Lasch's estrangement from traditional liberalism, the New Left, and the women's liberation movement was compounded by his sense that he was out of step with contemporary life. He explained the feeling in a letter to a colleague: "To tell the truth, I feel remote not only from radicalism but from the modern world in general—the same way I always felt, only more so."[35] But if Lasch felt remote from the modern world, his scholarship during this period was very much in keeping with the contemporary zeitgeist. Despite his ambivalence toward the women's liberation movement, Lasch, like so many feminists at the time, recognized that the institution of the family was critical to any true understanding of "the woman question." Indeed, for several years, Lasch had been struggling to produce a book-length manuscript on women and women's liberation before realizing that his real subject was not women per se, but rather the history of the family. "My study of the family will deal with the burning question of women and women's liberation only in connection with the family," he explained to his editor. "I am now convinced that this is the best if not the only way to deal with it."[36]

Although Lasch's interests suggested an affinity with feminism, his investigation into the history of the family led him in a very different direction. Feminist scholars sought to interrogate the boundary between public and private spheres, but Lasch worried that this boundary had already been destroyed. In *Haven in a Heartless World: The Family Besieged* (1977), he described the history of the modern family in ways that were akin to how one might describe the history of a colonized nation—that is, as fundamentally marred by invasion, plunder, and expropriation. Just as production had been removed from the household and transferred to the factory during the early stages of the industrial revolution, Lasch contended, so parental functions once confined to the private sphere had been appropriated by agents of a burgeoning welfare state, including doctors, psychiatrists, social workers, teachers, and child guidance experts. Contrary to aiding the family, these members of the purported "helping professions" were in fact shoring up their own newly acquired authority and undermining the family's capacity to provide for its own needs. This expropriation of parental authority had been initiated in the nineteenth century, and it had rapidly accelerated with the advent of progressive reform (much of it spearheaded by middle-class women) between 1900 and 1930. As a result, the twentieth-century family had been disabled from the start. "With the rise of the 'helping professions' . . . society in the guise of a 'nurturing mother' invaded the family," Lasch charged.[37]

What so alarmed Lasch about this self-perpetuating cycle was not simply that it fostered the family's dependency on outside experts, but that, in doing so, it undermined parental authority, eroding the roles of both mothers and fathers. Historically, Lasch argued, the family had provided the last stronghold of precapitalist thought and feeling. But once contaminated by instrumental rationality, the family could no longer function as a refuge from a hostile world. As the forces of rationalization invaded the private sphere, motherhood was proletarianized and the once-sanctified relations between mother and child were eviscerated. "[The] coldness that prevails in the marketplace also pervades the family," Lasch observed grimly. As the mother became more and more reliant on the knowledge of outside experts, her desperate need for professional assistance was matched by a frightening lack of real affection toward her children. Bearing the stamp of both Philip Wylie and Herbert Hendin, Lasch's mother figure was at once dominating, calculating, smothering, devoted, and cold. In a portrait that would have resonated with readers of both *Generation of Vipers* and *The Age of Sensation*, Lasch depicted a world in which the American mother had imposed "her madness on everybody else"—a world of middle-class families devoid of spontaneous feeling in which children had become the "objects of intense, suffocating devotion."[38]

But it was the erosion of the father's role within the modern family that most alarmed Lasch. If the "helping professions" had robbed mothers of their maternal instincts by turning them into an army of professionals, the consequences for fathers were no less devastating. Fathers appeared to be missing in action, according to Lasch. Drawing a clear line of descent from the patriarchal family of bourgeois Victorianism to the "fatherless" family of the late twentieth century, Lasch claimed that the history of the modern family was essentially a history of declining paternal authority. Whatever its shortcomings, Lasch contended, the Victorian bourgeois family had provided young boys with the single, essential ingredient they needed for healthy ego development, namely strong father figures. Lasch claimed that it was the son's Oedipal struggle against a powerful patriarch—and its eventual resolution—that had once assured strong character growth. But as the family's traditional functions were expropriated to outside agencies, the father was stripped of his rightful authority and the son's individuation was thwarted. As social workers, guidance counselors, and psychiatrists wielded more and more authority within the private sphere, contended Lasch, the father's role was whittled away to nothing more than that of breadwinner. Although still a physical presence in the family, he concluded, the father had literally fallen off the map of psychosexual development, with dire political and psychic consequences.[39]

Here, one could see the extent to which Lasch was attempting to build on the insights of the Frankfurt School and the notion of a fatherless society. In the years that he was working on *Haven in a Heartless World*, Lasch read and reread the writings of Wilhelm Reich, Erich Fromm, Herbert Marcuse, Theodor Adorno, and Max Horkheimer, always with an eye to their shifting position on the family. This position, Lasch would write to friend and interlocutor Russell Jacoby, continued to puzzle him.[40] The Frankfurt School theorists had drawn on psychology, sociology, and Marxian analysis in order to link the origins of European fascism to alterations in personality that were rooted in the changing structure of the family. But Lasch noted a discrepancy between the Frankfurt School's initial hypothesis and its eventual findings. These theorists started out, he surmised, from a Reichian position that indicted the bourgeois family for "perpetuating authoritarian personality structures." But the findings of *The Authoritarian Personality* (1950) seemed to Lasch to point in exactly the opposite direction: It was not that the German father wielded too much power, but that he wielded too little. It was the erosion of familial authority that provided the psychological underpinnings of despotism, setting the stage for political passivity. In a private correspondence, Lasch cited German psychoanalyst Alexander Mitscherlich's *Society without the Father* as one of the works that had most influenced him, revealing not only the centrality of the notion of a fatherless society to his thinking, but also the extent to which Lasch, like his Frankfurt School progenitors, tended to accept the German case as paradigmatic.[41]

Published only two years after *Haven in a Heartless World*, *The Culture of Narcissism* represented Lasch's attempt to come to terms with the psychic repercussions of this decline in paternal authority. Here, Lasch drew on the psychoanalytic insights of Otto Kernberg and Melanie Klein in order to put forth an argument that was both counterintuitive and highly original. Rejecting the commonsensical inference that a decline in paternal authority had led to the decline of the superego,[42] Lasch came to precisely the opposite conclusion: in the absence of the father, the superego had instead become more harsh, more archaic, and more punitive: "The changing conditions of family life do not produce a decline in the superego but rather an alteration of its contents."[43] What made the father's withdrawal into the world of work so damaging, Lasch had argued in *Haven in a Heartless World*, was not simply that it had deprived the child of a necessary role model, but rather that the child's infantile fantasies of an "omnipotent, wrathful, and punitive father" had been left largely undisturbed. As the modern father grew more and more remote and inaccessible, the child's earliest archaic impressions of him would no longer be tested and revised against everyday experience.[44]

This insight was at the heart of Lasch's *Culture of Narcissism*. It was no longer the authoritarian personality, Lasch claimed, but rather the narcissist who embodied the pathology of the times. Despite the trappings of hedonism, Lasch was quick to point out, narcissism represented a form of brute survivalism in a psychic universe dictated by archaic fantasies and infantile drives. Accepting the clinical claim that narcissism had emerged as a rampant disorder among adult psychiatric patients, Lasch agreed with psychoanalysts like Kernberg and Hendin that narcissism's etiology could be traced back to a thwarted maternal relationship. The narcissist, asserted Lasch, was the victim of an immature mother who was herself narcissistic—a mother "who [had lavished] suffocating yet emotionally distant attentions on her offspring." Entangled in the web of the mother's own neuroses, the child lacked the emotional equipment needed to differentiate between "the self and the world of objects."[45]

His account of narcissism's etiology resonated with those of contemporary psychoanalysts, and so too did Lasch's profile of the adult narcissist. The classical narcissist, according to Lasch, could be an entertaining dinner party guest but would turn out to be your own worst nightmare: "Facile at managing the impressions he gives to others, ravenous for admiration but contemptuous of those he manipulates into providing it; unappeasably hungry for emotional experiences with which to fill an inner void." Reflecting Kernberg's view that the narcissist was so difficult to treat but that the effort was necessary because of the pain he suffered as he aged, Lasch described the narcissist as "terrified of aging and death." To this list, Lasch added what he called "the secondary characteristics" of narcissism, including "pseudo self-insight," "calculating seductiveness," and "nervous, self-deprecatory humor."[46] Convinced that the narcissist had emerged as the definitive psychological type of the age, Lasch confidently predicted that readers would recognize these telltale personality traits instantly.

With his psychoanalytically informed account of narcissism's etiology and symptomatology, Lasch hoped to clarify a debate that he felt had become increasingly muddled and confused. Assessing the growing literature on the "me decade," Lasch observed that the concept of narcissism had strayed too far from its psychoanalytic origins. Too often, Lasch contended, critics like Tom Wolfe and Edwin Schur had treated narcissism simplistically as a synonym for selfishness and had failed to grapple with its deeper psychological and social implications. In *The Minimal Self* (1980), Lasch would later describe narcissism as "a difficult idea that looks easy—a good recipe for confusion," and with *The Culture of Narcissism*, Lasch sought to walk a fine line between capitalizing on narcissism's crossover into the popular lexicon and critiquing the oversimplifications that had accompanied it.[47]

But above all, Lasch wanted to link the emergence of the narcissistic personality type to the historical claims about the family that he had put forth in *Haven in a Heartless World*. The cold, yet smothering mother—the primary culprit in narcissism's proliferation—was inevitable in a world where motherhood had been revamped into a professional career. The intervention of the "helping professions" into the private sphere had deprived mothers of their capacity for authentic affection, replacing their maternal instincts with expert advice. Intimately tied to the narcissistic mother was the emotional retreat of the father, whose once formative role within the family had been reduced to a purely economic one. A provider and nothing more, the father would symbolically stand outside of the home and watch powerlessly as children came of age in the absence of paternal authority. Narcissistic personality disorder, Lasch forcefully contended, was endemic to a world without fathers.

Having traced its familial, psychological, and social origins, Lasch argued that narcissism had wrought cultural havoc as well. Lasch described a range of cultural degradations in depressingly vivid detail: the vapid obsession with celebrity and spectacle, the denigration of competitiveness and sport, the rise of a consumer culture that created what Lasch called "a world of mirrors," and the erosion of relations between men and women.[48] At the heart of Lasch's bleak cultural portrait was what he described as "a waning of the sense of historical time." One of the most disturbing tendencies of the classical narcissist, Lasch contended, was the fetishization of the present. Despite its emancipatory trappings, Lasch contended, the ethic of "living in the moment" betrayed a profound psychological pessimism. Fearful of old age and death, the narcissist could neither "create a store of loving memories with which to face the latter part of his life" nor contemplate the world beyond his own death. Now, Lasch extrapolated, the clinical narcissist's fetishization of immediacy reflected the cultural logic of the American middle class. Drawing a parallel between ontogenetic and national memory, Lasch concluded that the devaluation of the past mirrored the "poverty of the narcissist's inner life." "To live for the moment is the prevailing passion—to live for yourself, not for your predecessors or posterity," Lasch noted in an observation that echoed Wolfe's ruminations on the great biological stream and resonated with Podhoretz's vision of a culture of weakness and decline. "We are fast losing the sense of historical continuity, the sense of belonging to a succession of generations originating in the past and stretching into the future." The devaluation of the ties between the living and the dead, the old and the young, the life-giving and the unborn, was the constitutive feature of Lasch's fatherless, narcissistic society. So central were these temporal, generational, and historical motifs to his overarching project that, before settling on "The Culture of Narcissism," Lasch had tentatively entitled his manuscript "Life without a Future." Despite the "gloomy outlook" suggested by this alarmist-sounding choice, the book would be "full of laughs," he wryly reassured a friend.[49]

This breakdown of a collective sense of generational and historical continuity had dire implications, Lasch contended. The seemingly upbeat psychological advice that urged people to "live for today" in fact reflected the extent to which an ethos of barren survivalism had spread from the poor to the privileged. A popular self-help book like Gail Sheehy's *Passages* was, in truth, nothing more than a rote survivalist manual, albeit one cloaked in the language of personal growth. According to Lasch, Sheehy's "no panic" approach to aging proceeded from the premise that life was nothing more than a psychic endurance test. Betraying his penchant for martial language, Lasch observed that, in an era of pseudo-liberation, personal relationships had increasingly taken on "the character of combat" as society became "a war of all against all." Elaborating on Peter Marin's more tentative speculations, Lasch confirmed that, although seemingly hedonistic, the new awareness movements exposed profound disquietude among their practitioners. As Lasch's suggestive subtitle made clear, the age of narcissism was ultimately one of diminishing—rather than excessive—expectations.[50]

Lasch's observation that middle-class society had become increasingly warlike hinged on the idea that class and race distinctions were being eroded. Echoing Hendin's observation that the young people of his study were internalizing a "ghetto mentality" in their rejection of enduring emotional commitments, Lasch observed that middle-class society had now "become a pale copy of the ghetto." The poor had always been compelled by exigency to live from one day to the next, Lasch noted, "but now a desperate concern for personal survival, sometimes disguised as hedonism, engulfs the middle class as well." A defender of the Moynihan Report, Lasch claimed that Daniel Moynihan's sole mistake was not that he had gone too far with his claims, but rather that he had not gone far enough. By confining his discussion of the twin disasters of male absenteeism and maternal domination to the black family, Moynihan had actually exaggerated "the distance between the ghetto and the rest of American culture." Contending that these conjoined family pathologies were in fact far more pervasive than Moynihan recognized, Lasch made his position plain: middle-class "Momism" was simply a muted version of black "matriarchy."[51]

For Lasch, then, the increasingly "warlike conditions" of American middle-class life constituted what was simultaneously a class, race, and gender crisis. Unlike critics who took aim at middle-class privilege, Lasch mobilized the notion of a narcissistic society in order to portray the American middle class as essentially coming apart at the seams, or, as he put it to his editor, "the bourgeoisie at the end of its tether."[52] Despite the facile charge that psychoanalysis—as both a practice and a body of thought—was hopelessly limited to the sequestered worldview of white, highly educated elites (who also, according to stereotype, tended to be Jewish Manhattanites), Lasch developed the psychoanalytically grounded concept of a narcissistic society in order to portray a social world in which the once-stalwart psychological boundaries between rich and poor, black and white, ghetto and suburb, and "Mom" and "matriarch" had dissolved.

Even love, the rosy center of the middle-class family, had gone into decline. At one level, Americans appeared to be investing personal relations with "undiminished emotional importance" as the sexual revolution and the spread of birth control held out the promise of a new level of emotional and erotic intimacy between men and women. But Lasch argued that in fact the opposite had occurred: "The cult of intimacy conceals a growing despair of finding it. Personal relations crumble under the emotional weight with which they are burdened."[53] According to Lasch, this new cult of intimacy—largely spearheaded by women—had upped the ante too much. Modern feminism had placed undue pressure on heterosexual relationships by raising what was originally a "healthy" sexual antagonism to the level of all-out warfare. In addition, by critiquing the nuclear family as a locus of women's oppression, modern feminists were historically out of step; they were taking aim at an institution that in Lasch's view had already been decimated by the state and the helping professions. In an era of ersatz sexual liberation, Lasch observed (again drawing on Hendin's study), men and women approached interpersonal relationships with suspicion and trepidation, and the realm of personal life could no longer provide comfort. The contemporary sexual scene, marred by rampant divorce, sexual promiscuity, and open marriages, did not reflect a new age of freedom but rather "a wary avoidance of emotional commitments."[54] Lasch's sense of the erosion of heterosexual relations was more than a theoretical abstraction. His fear that marriage and the nuclear family were becoming obsolete was rooted not only in his interpretation of family history but also in his cultural milieu, where Lasch watched as both marriages and long-standing friendships fell apart, sometimes over the "woman question." Letters from friends and colleagues throughout the 1970s are filled with news of disintegrating marriages, frayed friendships, rocky breakups, and nasty divorces. Indeed, in a 1972 letter to writer and former Harvard roommate John Updike, Lasch jokingly revealed that since almost everyone he knew "has been divorced at least once," he had taken to calling his own marriage "the last marriage."[55]

Ultimately for Lasch, then, the crisis of cultural narcissism amounted to a crisis in the reproductive capacity of the white middle class—both its literal capacity to reproduce itself through marriage and childrearing and its capacity to securely reproduce its own values and norms. At every turn, Lasch's study betrayed profound anxiety about the reproductive future of middle-class society—from his historical claims about the socialization of reproduction to his bleak view that contemporary heterosexual relations had become combative and warlike; from his Wylie-inspired fears of a devouring mother to his claim that fathers had been reduced to mere breadwinners; from his spirited defense of the Moynihan Report to his "trickle up" theory of ghetto culture; from his contention that the adult narcissist fetishized the present to his broader claim that Americans had collectively lost interest in the future. So deep were Lasch's fears surrounding antinatalism that toward the end of *The Culture of Narcissism*, he took aim at the one social movement that most literally embodied it: the movement for zero population growth. Rather than reflecting environmentalist concerns about the earth's natural resources, this movement, in Lasch's estimation, testified to "a pervasive uneasiness about reproduction—to widespread doubts, indeed, about whether our society should reproduce itself at all."[56] In an era of diminishing psychic and material resources, Lasch grimly predicted, survivalism and not posterity defined the psychological world of the middle class.

"The Civilized Hellfire Sermon":
Making Sense of the Book's Reception

Lasch had written *The Culture of Narcissism* for a number of different reasons. Intellectually, he hoped to work through the psychological implications of the shifts in family structure that he had charted in *Haven in a Heartless World*. On a more practical level, Lasch hoped to publish a book that, unlike most academic titles, might actually achieve some commercial success. With four children coming of age in the 1970s, Lasch, the primary breadwinner, regularly complained in letters to friends about the challenge of supporting a large family on a professor's modest salary.[57] But Lasch's aim to reach an audience outside of the academy was not simply mercenary. It also reflected his identification with a specific tradition of what he called "connected" social criticism, which transcended rarified academic debate and addressed a wider public. As someone who had "wanted to be a writer before [he] wanted to be a historian," Lasch loathed academic jargon and took his stylistic inspiration from journalists and fiction writers rather than from other academics. With *The Culture of Narcissism*, he aimed to participate in a broader public debate about American society and culture.[58]

But when *The Culture of Narcissism* exceeded all expectations by becoming a national best seller, Lasch found himself with divided feelings. Obviously, he had more than fulfilled his aim of reaching a readership beyond the narrow confines of the academy, and he watched with surprise as the hardback book remained on the best seller list for seven straight weeks. But Lasch was disturbed by the book's popular reception and his own sudden status as a celebrity. Reviewers tended to characterize the book as a jeremiad and as yet another diagnosis of "our national maladies"—characterizations that Lasch wholeheartedly rejected.[59] With *The Culture of Narcissism*, Lasch insisted, he had hoped to make a contribution to social theory, "not to the literature of moral indignation." Thus he watched with disgust as reviewers treated his book as what he contemptuously called one of "those pseudo-critical confections, neither honest journalism nor honest sociology, which the publishing industry likes to pass off as profound social commentary."[60] Resentful that his publisher had done little to promote the book until it became a best seller, Lasch made no secret of his contempt for the media.[61] When asked by one friend whether he liked being a celebrity, he answered: "You ask how I like it. I don't. To my publisher's unbounded annoyance, I've turned down interviews with CBS, Barbara Walters, and many others."[62] At every opportunity, Lasch sought to clarify the central aims of his intellectual project. He had not written *The Culture of Narcissism* in order to indict Americans for selfishness, he insisted, but rather to speculate about the shifts in personality structure engendered by late capitalism, with the family as the primary mediator between the individual and society. Now that the book had been widely hailed as the "latest addition to the 'what's wrong with us' bibliography," Lasch lamented, the subtleties of his argument had dropped completely out of view.[63]

Lasch's sense of frustration was exacerbated by the book's reception among the New Left. Already alienated from so much of contemporary politics, Lasch felt unfairly maligned by what he called "self-styled 'critical theorists'" who rejected the book once it had been praised on the pages of *Time* and *Newsweek*. But it was the feminist response to the book that most rankled him. Feminists had critiqued both *Haven in a Heartless World* and *The Culture of Narcissism* on psychological, historical, and political grounds. First, they argued that Lasch's definition of narcissism was premised on a distinctly masculine theory of psychosexual development, one that inherently pathologized femininity. Second, they argued that by constructing a clear narrative of family decline from Victorianism to modernism, Lasch displayed a troubling nostalgia for the bourgeois patriarchal family and an utter failure to confront women's oppression within it. Finally, feminists situated Lasch's work within the larger context of antifeminist backlash during the latter part of the 1970s. At a time when the traditional family appeared to be back in favor, Lasch seemed to have contempt for a feminist movement attempting to move forward in the face of conservative retrenchment. According to feminist writer Vivian Gornick, *The Culture of Narcissism* exposed nothing more than Lasch's own temperamental inclinations "that reveal a fatal lack of sympathy for the time in which he finds himself." Contrary to being an "age of diminishing expectations," Gornick contended, feminist America was a vibrant world of "weeds pushing through the concrete." All that an unsympathetic Lasch could see, in her estimation, was "the breaking concrete."[64]

Lasch was enraged by these feminist criticisms, which he took deeply personally. Canceling a speaking engagement at Berea College in early 1979, he reported that he no longer found lecture tours enjoyable, since feminists regarded him as "Public Enemy No. 1."[65] Later that year, at a time when Lasch might have been enjoying the success of *The Culture of*

Narcissism, he painted a rather bleak picture of the current state of affairs in a letter to friends who were living overseas. He was lecturing at a furious pace in order to keep up with inflation, and, meanwhile, his contempt for both the media and the American Left was only growing. But he saved his harshest rebuke for "the feminists," whose "hysterical reactions" to his two recent books evinced "a seemingly endless capacity for misrepresentation, slander, vilification, and character assassination."[66] If *Haven in a Heartless World* had made clear his disaffiliation from feminism, then *The Culture of Narcissism* finalized an acrimonious divorce. Misapprehended by the media, wrongfully attacked by feminists, increasingly alienated from the Left, Lasch saw himself as an intellectual-under-siege. It was becoming more and more difficult to talk about the problems of modern society, he bitterly complained to friends, without having to counter charges of "sentimentality, nostalgia, and elitism."[67]

Despite the fact that Lasch felt personally attacked, the breach between him and his feminist critics reflected an even deeper intellectual impasse than either party realized. For feminists, women's liberation was a heroic movement for human freedom. But in the 1970s, Lasch was trying to understand feminism as one dimension of a broader historical transformation in the structure of the family. Feminists saw women's liberation as a legitimate response to the family's patriarchal structure, but Lasch was more concerned with the overall dissolution of the family, understood as the linchpin of generational continuity and trust. Feminists saw the advent of the movement as a hopeful sign of progress, but Lasch believed that by the time the women's liberation movement of the 1970s had arrived, the institution that feminists identified as the source of women's oppression — the nuclear family — had already been eviscerated by market forces and the state. There was truth to both positions in the debate, but no synthesis was ever achieved.

At the same time that Lasch was angered by his work's reception among feminists, he was heartened by letters from readers praising him for "speaking the truth" and reporting that they had recognized themselves in the narcissistic personality type that he had rendered so vividly. The book "came into our lives at an opportune time," wrote Judith Goldrich, a clinical psychologist from New York, "since it expresses with great clarity many of the reasons behind a sense of dissatisfaction with the quality of life in this country that we have not been able to shake over the past decade." Confirming Lasch's depiction of a beleaguered middle class surrounded by chaos, she went on: "Personally and professionally our lives are rewarding, yet there is a recurrent feeling of living on a hard-won little island of sanity in a sea of insanity." Other readers were less self-referential, but equally moved. "I have been to San Francisco," wrote one sympathetic reader of *Haven in a Heartless World*, who clearly viewed the city as a latter-day Sodom. "I can sense the hostility between the sexes and I can see the fatherless sons." Still other readers thanked Lasch for empowering them as parents in an age of declining authority. "Inspired by your book," proclaimed a mother from Savannah, Georgia, "I really cracked down on my four year old daughter to help clean up. Then we had an unusually nice evening—really companionable; it also was without my usual tiredness." Reflecting on the improvement, she speculated about the possible benefits of "cracking down" and her desire to keep at it. "Can it be discipline releases energy and sociability rather than stifling them? I'm determined to try again." In sympathy with Lasch's hatred of outside experts, she assured him that, thanks to "mother instinct," she had never read a parent-child "shrink" book.[68]

Letters from critical readers could also be amusing. Offended by his cavalier dismissal of everything from welfare reform to humanistic psychology, one reader accused Lasch of being hopelessly out of touch with real relationships and urged him to "read Karen Horney or maybe some poetry or scriptures and gain a more integrated, more sane, perspective." In a similar vein, another reader, presumably a devotee of the new awareness movements, urged Lasch to pursue his own self-transformation by learning more about bioenergetics, primal therapy, the writings of Abraham Maslow, and Zen Buddhism. Lasch's wholesale attack on the new consciousness movement, the letter writer concluded, was simply not justified. As easy as it was to poke fun at the idea of Christopher Lasch in a primal therapy session, what is striking about such letters is their earnestness. These disappointed readers of *The Culture of Narcissism* honestly felt that, by locating everything from Eastern mysticism to humanistic psychology under the misleading rubric of "pseudo-liberation," Lasch was ignoring their redemptive features.[69]

Ultimately, both admiring and disgruntled readers posed the same question to Lasch over and over again: what was to be done? Here Lasch's speculations were far more tentative. At times he suggested that coming up with an adequate answer to this question was simply beyond his purview. "I have more confidence in my ability to analyze our society than to change it," he told one inquiring reader. To another he insisted that the task of radical intellectuals was not "so much to incite change, much less set themselves up as a revolutionary vanguard, but to interpret it." At other times, however, he ventured some provisional suggestions, all of which hinged on ending the epidemic of dependency through the restoration of local control. Gesturing toward the communitarianism that would inform his later work, Lasch's vague remedies included a return to decentralized planning and grassroots organizing.[70] Socialism was definitely not the answer, he told one reader. "I guess at this point I'd lean more to a politics based on ecological concerns, localism, grassroots democracy," he suggested in somewhat broad strokes. Like so many social critics, Lasch vacillated between refusing to be programmatic (on the grounds that this was not the task of the intellectual) and trying to provide his questioning readers with some political orientation.[71]

"The Ennui of Affluence": Narcissism and Carter's "Crisis of Confidence" Speech

Lasch's book had made a powerful impression on the American intellectual community and on countless readers. Serving as a lightning rod for broader debates about national decline, feminism, heterosexual relations, and the modern family, the book remains central to any intellectual history of the period. But the book is also significant because it made its way into the echelons of high politics, eventually reaching the Carter White House.[72] In the summer of 1979, Jimmy Carter turned to Lasch's work and attempted to integrate some of his ideas into a speech on energy policy that he hoped would revive his ailing presidency. The Carter administration's engagement with Lasch's book reflected just how far the concept of narcissism had traveled from Freud's original definition of narcissism in 1914 — from European psychoanalysis to American psychiatry, emerging finally as a diagnosis of the disease that plagued the national body politic at the end of the 1970s.

The Culture of Narcissism made its initial impression in the White House on a young pollster named Patrick Caddell. Described as the "resident intellectual of the Carter White House," Caddell had spent the spring of 1979 trying to make sense of an apparent paradox in his research findings.[73] Comparing the attitudes of Americans toward the end of the decade to the tumultuous years of 1973–74, Caddell was disturbed to discover that although economic conditions had shown some signs of recovery since the upheavals of the early 1970s, Americans appeared to have grown more pessimistic. There were two dimensions of this pessimism that Caddell found particularly alarming. First, he noted that feelings of despair had extended to the elites—"the young, the college educated, and the higher income groups"—precisely those groups that should have been most hopeful about the future. Second, and even more significantly, Americans not only were pessimistic about the future of the country but also were increasingly despairing about their own personal futures. According to Caddell, Americans had weathered the political and economic upheavals of the late 1960s and early 1970s through retaining confidence in their own lives. But by the late 1970s, an unprecedented 30 percent of survey respondents expressed a pessimism that, according to Caddell, not only threatened the stability of the country but also amounted to a "psychological crisis of the first order."[74]

It was this psychological crisis more than any material one that President Carter would have to somehow defuse in order to secure his reelection, Caddell warned. But rather than attributing this growing sense of insecurity to mounting economic pressures and rapid inflation, Caddell made the opposite claim. Taking his cues from humanistic psychologist Abraham Maslow, Caddell contended that the growing sense of pessimism throughout the country was rooted in a "post-survivalist society" or what one editorialist called "the ennui of affluence." Now that basic material needs had been satisfied, Caddell surmised, a growing sense of psychological unease had come to the fore. This was "a crisis of confidence marked by a dwindling faith in the future," Caddell wrote, pitching a phrase that would become immortalized three months later in Carter's ill-fated speech of the same name. Not unlike the symptomatic shift from classical hysteria to narcissistic personality disorder, the problems now besetting the country could not be located in any of the usual places, Caddell explained. There were no violent marches or street demonstrations. Instead, he contended, the late 1970s were characterized by subterranean and indecipherable feelings of malaise. In explaining why pessimism had grown rather than diminished since the traumas of the late 1960s and early 1970s, Caddell showed the extent to which he conceived of the body politic as a psychotherapy patient. "Psychologists I have consulted feel that this is not unusual given the course of normal neurosis," he wrote by way of explanation for the apparent delayed reaction. "Unhealed damage to value and attitude structure results in a period of anomie shrouded in deceptive calm that finally leads to further decline and breakdown."[75]

So what were the symptoms of this "crisis of confidence"? Caddell cited a range of indicators, including a precipitous decline in voting, an explosion of consumer spending and debt, falling productivity rates, and a weakening of governmental institutions. But he also identified the advent

Jimmy Carter and Patrick Caddell at the White House.
Courtesy of the Jimmy Carter Presidential Library.

of the "me generation" as a significant cultural symptom of the psychological crisis now gripping the nation. Although Lasch had tried to distance his own intellectual position from the "me generation" cliché, Caddell praised Lasch's "depressing, important best seller" for explaining how and why personal gratification and selfishness had "replaced national involvement everywhere." Indeed, the "crisis of confidence" portrayed by Caddell bore a striking resemblance to the narcissistic society portrayed by Lasch. This national spiritual crisis, not unlike the crisis of paternal authority, was characterized by pervasive pessimism about the future, despair and resignation among elites, the explosion of consumer culture, and the erosion of political participation. There was no question that Caddell's reading of

The Culture of Narcissism had helped him to interpret and give shape to his survey data.[76]

In the late spring and summer of 1979, Caddell's findings became all the more significant when President Carter faced his lowest approval ratings since taking office. With the price of oil soaring and long lines at the gas station, the energy crisis was again front-page news, and opinion polls showed not only mounting frustration about rising energy costs but a growing perception that the Carter administration lacked the authority to deal with the crisis. Having campaigned as a Washington outsider, Carter found himself on the receiving end of growing public cynicism toward the federal government and toward the institution of the presidency in particular. Taking his cues from Caddell (along with other staff members), he decided to enlist the help of intellectuals in order to revive his presidency. Thus, on the evening of 30 May 1979, Christopher Lasch found himself dining on lamb chops and asparagus at the White House.[77]

Lasch was not the only public intellectual invited to attend that evening. Harvard sociologist Daniel Bell, whose *Cultural Contradictions of Capitalism* had also made a strong impression on Caddell, was there as well. Also in attendance were President Carter, First Lady Rosalyn Carter, Jesse Jackson, Bill Moyers, John Gardner (of *Common Cause*), Press Secretary Jody Powell, two Washington reporters, and Caddell. With Caddell's research findings furnishing the basis of discussion, the group spent the evening contemplating the meaning and origins of the nation's "crisis of confidence." Although Lasch would later describe his own contributions to the discussion as meager and clumsy, he did recall making two points over the course of the evening. First, he insisted that an erosion of public confidence in the government and the future, rather than reflecting some amorphous spiritual or psychological condition, had "a basis in reality" and reflected "real and legitimate fears." Lasch's second contribution concerned the energy crisis, and here he made a point that he would later reiterate when asked to account for the possible connections between *The Culture of Narcissism* and Carter's forthcoming "Crisis of Confidence" speech. It made little sense, he warned the president, to ask people to make personal sacrifices (such as turning down the heat in their homes) when sacrifice itself was so unevenly distributed throughout the society. In response, Carter asked Lasch point-blank what he would do to solve both the energy crisis and the more elusive "crisis of confidence." Lasch replied that he had no idea. It was at this point, he would later recall, "that I realized that my career as a presidential adviser was destined to be a short one."[78]

Whatever Lasch's deficits as an advisor, his best-selling book continued to inform White House discussions throughout the summer of 1979.
With the president's approval ratings plummeting, Carter's staff members
spent several weeks working on an energy speech that would somehow
differ from the four forgettable and ineffectual speeches on energy policy
that had preceded it. The speech would not only have to be specific in its
prescriptions for dealing with energy shortages, Carter's advisors insisted,
but it would have to rehabilitate Carter's badly bruised public image and
restore faith in his authority. For his part, Caddell continued to urge the
president to address the deeper spiritual and psychological issues at stake.
"Consuming doesn't fill emptiness of lives," his proposed speech outline
read. "Rather than a generation that builds for the future, we have become
the 'me generation'—'me first, me last and me always.' We have come to
believe we *deserve* an easy life."[79]

After ten days of conferencing at Camp David, President Carter finally
delivered his "Crisis of Confidence" speech on the evening of 15 July 1979.
Although the speech initially buoyed Carter's standing in the polls, it was
savaged in the press and ultimately contributed to his defeat in the election of 1980.[80] Part psychospiritual evaluation and part policy prescription,
the thirty-three-minute speech proceeded from the premise that the energy
crisis was at once material, psychological, and spiritual in origin. Gasoline lines, energy shortages, inflation, and recession were only the outward
symptoms of a deeper psychological and spiritual condition, Carter contended. It was an internal "crisis in confidence," rather than any external
military or economic challenge, that now constituted the biggest threat to
American democracy. Historically, it had been confidence in the future
that "served as a link between generations"—Americans had "always had a
faith that the days of our children would be better than our own." But now
Americans were fast losing faith in the future, Carter claimed, and had
turned to consumption as a form of false compensation. Drawing directly
from Caddell's proposals, Carter continued: "Too many of us now tend to
worship self indulgence and consumption. Human identity is no longer
defined by what one does, but by what one owns. But we have discovered
that owning things and consuming things does not satisfy our longing for
meaning. We have learned that piling up material goods cannot fill the
emptiness of lives which have no confidence or purpose."

The average American's penchant for material goods not only had de-
pleted the nation's energy resources, Carter claimed, but had led to a pervasive sense of personal despair and emptiness. For this reason, he contended

that the energy crisis, while a "clear and present danger," simultaneously held the key to national spiritual recovery. This was the same argument that had been made many times throughout the oil embargo of 1973–74. Being forced to make material sacrifices and adopt a conservationist ethic would enable people "to take control over [their] own lives," to "conquer the crisis of the spirit in our country," and to "rekindle our sense of unity." The remedy for both the psychological crisis and the material one, it now turned out, would be one and the same.[81]

Although Carter never mentioned the word "narcissism" in his speech, there was a connection, however attenuated, between Lasch's "fatherless society" and Carter's "crisis of confidence." No smothering mothers or emotionally emasculated fathers appeared in what would later be dubbed the "national malaise" speech in the press (the word "malaise" was never actually used in the speech itself). Nor were there any damning psychological profiles of the narcissistic personality type. But the cultural parallels were still there in Carter's critique of consumption as an illusory source of personal meaning, and even more significantly, in his claim that a nation in psychological crisis was in essence a nation that had lost faith in the future. Just as Lasch had traced the emptiness of the narcissist's inner life to his inability to locate himself along a historical axis, now Carter linked the nation's spiritual malaise to a fractured sense of generational continuity.

Typically, Lasch had mixed feelings about the speech. On the one hand, he praised Carter's efforts to link cultural and economic issues, and he even suggested years later that the speech had shown courage and imagination. But Lasch rejected the notion that *The Culture of Narcissism* had played a key role in the speech's conceptualization. The speech, in his words, "owed as much to *The Culture of Narcissism* as it owed to *The Communist Manifesto*." In a letter to a former student, Lasch conceded that although he recognized some of his own phrases in the speech, his ideas had been "torn out of context and came across as a moral denunciation of selfishness." By equating narcissism with selfishness, Carter had made the same interpretive mistakes that had dogged the book since its publication. The speech confirmed what Lasch had already suspected: the president had misread his book. During the White House dinner, Carter had assured Lasch that he had read his book, but in the same conversation had touted the merits of speed-reading. "All I can say is that subsequent events confirmed my own prejudice *against* speed-reading," Lasch would later write.[82]

Carter's misappropriation of *The Culture of Narcissism* compelled Lasch to modify some of his earlier positions and return to a more strictly materialist analysis, if only for the sake of political argument. If Americans had lost faith in the future, Lasch now contended, it was with good reason. The American loss of faith was rooted not in some mysterious "malaise" or erosion of national confidence, but rather in the economic recession. This recession had made Americans doubt whether the next generation would improve upon the last. Because it lacked any true political context, Carter's speech was doomed, in Lasch's words, to "come across as a rather petulant attack on the American people, designed to shift the blame . . . to the ordinary American's passion for 'things.'" If his book had influenced Carter's thinking, Lasch concluded, it was almost certainly for the worse. "In a way, the book played right into Carter's hands," he later wrote, making it possible for him "to shift the blame to a nation of 'narcissists' and away from the failure of political leadership."[83]

With *The Culture of Narcissism*, Lasch had wanted to clarify a term whose meaning had become muddled and confused. But the story of the book's popular and political reception was ultimately a story about the author's loss of control over his own intellectual project. As reviewers, readers, and pollsters cited the book as evidence of the selfish tendencies of the "me generation," Lasch returned again and again to his contention that narcissism needed to be recognized as something distinct from self-indulgence. When Carter attributed the nation's "crisis of confidence" to a waning faith in the future, Lasch moved away from his original position that despair about the future constituted a narcissistic symptom and insisted that this lapse in faith was justified in an era of rapid inflation and diminishing resources. Feeling that his book had been widely misinterpreted as a wrathful jeremiad, Lasch did his best at damage control.

But Lasch's own protests notwithstanding, was it really any wonder that Carter had drawn on *The Culture of Narcissism* in order to link national psychospiritual recovery to the repudiation of consumption? As Lasch himself pointed out, the book had played right into his hands. It had presented readers with a deeply disturbing vision of middle-class family life in which the domestic sphere had been invaded by outside experts, feminist reformers, and commodity culture. It was this invasion, Lasch asserted, that had perpetuated narcissistic patterns of infantile dependency, thus eroding the bonds of political citizenship and creating a world of clients and consumers. Taking their cues from Lasch's diatribe against consumption, Caddell and Carter came to a peculiar conclusion in light of the economic hardships facing more and more Americans during this period. Rather than rooted in inflation or recession, the nation's "crisis of confidence" was, in essence, a crisis of overaccumulation. Americans had simply accumulated too many "things" and were now suffering the economic, psychic, and spiritual consequences. Carter's message was clear: the restoration of faith in the national future would hinge on neither government policy nor intervention but instead on a deeply personal process of material and psychological retrenchment.

Although there were no direct references to dominating mothers or absent fathers in his "Crisis of Confidence" speech, Carter's ill-fated address to the nation proved to be the culmination of the discourse on narcissism and, indeed, the closing moment in the discussion of national decline in the 1970s. With the help of Caddell, Carter had transposed the symptomatology of the narcissist onto the body politic. Not unlike the narcissistic patient portrayed by Lasch, a nation in psychospiritual crisis was a nation that had somehow become historically and temporally disoriented. It was a nation that, like the narcissist, had lost its sense of the future. And just as the individual narcissist looked to commodity culture for the momentary gratification of infantile cravings, so an entire nation of narcissists, suggested Carter, had become deluded by what Lasch had called "a world of mirrors." Through consuming less and conserving more, Carter's speech suggested, Americans could find their way out of this distorted, kaleidoscopic world. And through extricating the family from the trap of overaccumulation, a degraded nation of clients and consumers could be remade, once again, into one of public servants and citizens.

Conclusion

The Familial Roots of Republican Domination

In recent years, historians and social theorists have revised their understanding of American national identity. It had long been assumed that American political culture was dominated by a civic nationalism, often referred to as the American Creed, that defines the United States as a multicultural and universalistic society made up of diverse groups united by democratic and individualist principles. Scholars have shown that, at certain moments, this civic nationalism has been subverted or supplanted by a second, more intense nationalist impulse: an ethnoreligious, chauvinistic nationalism that draws the boundaries of the national community on the exclusionary basis of shared race, blood, and ancestry.[1] Nonetheless, it was assumed that this more ominous nationalist strain represented an episodic, aberrational, and shadowy exception to the American Creed rather than a defining feature of American nationalism itself.

The American response to the terrorist attacks of 11 September 2001 complicated this picture by suggesting that this second, ethnoreligious strain of American nationalism was more powerful than scholars had acknowledged. Equally significant, the attacks revealed that this nationalist strain was fueled by a collective sense of injury and violation. In the wake of the terrorist attacks, an aggrieved nationalism exploded to the surface, driven by the belief that the nation had been wounded and that the wound must be avenged. This wounded American nationalism was not without precedent. It had been seen before in the nativism of the eighteenth century, in the Jacksonian frontier of the 1830s, and especially in the American South after the Civil War. A notable departure from the postnational orientation of contemporary Europe, this strain of nationalism is shaped above all by what scholar Anatol Lieven calls a sense of "righteous victimhood."[2]

This book shows that this post-9/11 reversion to an aggrieved nationalism had profound roots in the 1970s. In the years immediately after the Vietnam War, military defeat combined with oil shortages and economic recession to convince many that the nation had sustained injuries from which it might never recover. At that moment, too, a collective sense of righteous victimhood came to the surface, and within this context, the family emerged as a site of national injury. Of course, the early captivity narratives suggest that there had always been a powerful affinity in American culture between community endangerment and family peril. But in the 1970s, this affinity deepened as the nation was cast as a family that had lost some of its members to a hostile enemy or was in danger of being invaded and overwhelmed by an alien force.

This affinity between national danger and family injury was at the center of the three key concerns of the 1970s: the future of American foreign policy after Vietnam, the need for continued access to natural resources like oil, and the nation's place in a globalizing economy. In each case, the family was constructed as an innocent victim of foreign aggression, and the home emerged as a place of unjust injury inflicted from the outside. A sense of intimate danger rooted in primal experiences of dependency and vulnerability became linked to national precariousness, and the nation itself was cast as the pristine and protective womb of domesticity. At the same time, changes occurring within the family suggested that it might not only be a national victim but a potential culprit as well. The decline of the family wage and the attendant rise of the two-earner family in particular called into question traditional elements of paternal authority: the father as leader and protector, regulator of consumption, and transmitter of skills. In each case, the threat of male absenteeism—both literal and figurative—implied that the family was not only a site of suffering but also a failed repository of moral resources. Its paradoxical role as both victim and perpetrator placed the family at the center of debates over national decline.

By situating these debates about national decline within a longer history of American nationalism, this book rejects the view that the early 1970s ushered in a period of American decline. It is beyond dispute that there was a jarring series of disruptions and upheavals and that they produced profound and lasting effects. But there was no consensus about the meaning of the diplomatic and foreign policy crises of the early 1970s. There *was* a collective sense that earlier modes of American power were no longer effective, but there was no agreement about how the nation should proceed. Thus the Vietnam War's supporters saw the defeat as the result of a collapse of American national will, while the war's opponents saw it as evidence that the United States had overreached and that a small Asian country could defeat a world power. Some described the OPEC oil embargo as a humiliation for the United States, while others saw it as an occasion for the nation to adopt a conservation ethic, and still others saw it as a chance for the United States to reclaim its leadership vis-à-vis the energy-consuming nations of Europe after Vietnam. The story of national decline in the early 1970s, in other words, is not a story about how or why the nation declined. Instead, it is about a struggle over interpretation—about the conflicting meanings assigned to these events and why the interpretation of decline won out at some moments and not at others.

The 1970s, then, did not mark the end of Henry Luce's American Century so much as the realignment of American power and authority in a new era of globalization. Indeed, many of the crises of the 1970s were not uniquely American. Historian Eric Hobsbawm has described 1973 as the beginning of "the crisis decades," when the tremendous economic expansion of the postwar years drew to a close, inaugurating a new era of disruption throughout advanced capitalist states. David Harvey has cited 1973 as the year when the old Fordist regime came to an end, initiating a new phase of global economic instability and decomposition that he has located under the rubrics of both "post-Fordism" and "postmodernism."[3] In the early 1970s, most of these terms were not yet widely used, and many people engaged in debates about American decline took the nation for granted as their frame of reference. However, there were attempts to understand what was happening in a framework that transcended the nation-state. Over a decade before the collapse of the Soviet Union, some members of the foreign policy community argued that the defeat in Vietnam signified the emergence of a multipolar world order in which Cold War antagonisms would exert less influence over world affairs. During the oil embargo, environmentalists saw the crisis as the beginning of a new era of global interdependence with respect to natural resources. Finally, some politicians and intellectuals in the early 1970s linked the changes in the American economy to the increasing power of multinational corporations no longer bound by the nation-state and its interests. All of these arguments reflected an unfolding struggle between those who interpreted recent upheavals through a nationalist lens, and those who were already coming to grips with a nascent post–Cold War transnational order.

The family was at the center of this interpretive struggle. As a national symbol, the family worked against these alternative narratives that sought to explain what was happening in a wider framework than the one provided by the modern nation-state. As political scientist Roger Smith has argued, there has always been a temptation to use the family as an analogy for the nation. The analogy is tempting, he argues, for two reasons. First, the association of the family with nature endows the modern nation with an essential character that it otherwise might lack. Second, the association of the family with the benign obscures the violence that accompanies the formation of political communities.[4] As an analogy for the nation, the family functioned in both of these ways between 1968 and 1980. But this book has also shown that the national symbol of a family-under-siege did a specific kind of work in this new era of globalization. The construction of the nation as a family under attack from external threats worked to establish clear lines of demarcation between the inside and the outside and between the foreign and the domestic at a time when political, military, and economic upheavals were calling those boundaries into question. The symbol of a family-under-siege was powerful not only because it conferred a sense of innocence and injury upon the American nation but also because it worked to reassert the boundaries of the nation itself at a moment when a transnational order was coming into being.

This insight about the family's symbolic role sheds new light on the "politics of the family" in the 1970s. Scholars describe a struggle during this period between those who championed women's and gay liberation and those who mobilized against these groups in the name of traditional family values; between activists who sought to legitimate diverse family forms, and profamily activists who contended that the only healthy family was the heterosexual, nuclear one. There is obviously truth to this interpretation, but it alone cannot explain the role of the family in the political realignment that occurred over the decade. Rather, one must look beyond explicitly "profamily" advocates and turn to the various constituencies on the Right that participated in the debate about national decline during the 1970s. Members of the defense community, corporate and business leaders, neoconservative intellectuals, and military men and women drew on the family as a national symbol in ways that were enormously versatile, intricate, and contradictory, and it was this versatility that ultimately made its political counteroffensive so effective.

Ronald Reagan, the Iranian Hostage Crisis, and the 1980 Republican National Convention

This final point brings us to this book's culminating event: the 1980 Republican National Convention, at which Ronald Reagan accepted his party's nomination for the presidency, inaugurating a long era of Republican hegemony. I end with an extended discussion of this event because, as I wrote in the preface, it was Reagan's 1980 victory that prompted the original questions that eventually led me to write this book. As we have seen, during the Bicentennial year there had been several efforts to redress the fears surrounding national decline that had surfaced over the previous eight years. As far-reaching tendencies toward racial, ethnic, gender, and political fragmentation called the project of a single national celebration into question, commemorative planners responded by celebrating the family in lieu of the nation as a source of both personal identity and social renewal. At the same time, foreign policy managerialists called for a new acceptance of limits in an attempt to restore American power and complete the national transition from childhood to maturity described by Henry Kissinger.

But both attempts to "manage" upheaval proved fragile and tentative. Indeed, after 1976, the nation became ever more polarized as a newly mobilized group of conservatives identified the restoring of traditional familial values, and in particular responsibility for future generations, as the cure for national decline. Meanwhile, the Carter administration called for a new acceptance of limits in the three spheres explored in this book: defense (détente and managerialism), energy (conservation and restraint), and economic life (savings and thrift). But, as we have seen, Carter's limits-based reconceptualization of American identity met resistance. It was not until 1980 that Ronald Reagan elaborated a vision of American nationalism that actually took hold, one that brilliantly drew on some strains of these earlier efforts (the Bicentennial's antigovernment sentiment and its mobilization of the family as a unifying symbol) while scornfully rejecting others (the managerialist call for limits). The result was a version of American nationalism that succeeded where these earlier versions had failed, thus solidifying the Right's political power for decades to come.

At the heart of Reagan's nationalism was the symbol that had figured so prominently in debates about national decline over the previous decade: a family-under-siege. As we have seen, the capture of American fighter pilots in Vietnam had brought to light the intimate, internal dimensions of what appeared to be an external military affair. Looming over Reagan's political ascent was a second foreign policy crisis that again linked captivity, national peril, and family suffering: the Iranian hostage crisis of 1980. That crisis reflected the reorientation toward the Middle East that followed defeat in Vietnam, but it was also the result of long-standing American decisions in the spheres of foreign policy (anticommunism), energy policy (cheap oil), and economic policy (mass consumption and unrestrained growth).

In the case of Iran, U.S. policy had been formulated during the Roosevelt administration and was intrinsic to Luce's 1941 vision of the American Century. It included American support of the undemocratic and often deluded Shah against several democratic or leftist alternatives, including the popularly elected Mohammed Mossadegh in 1953. American presidents had long heralded the Shah as a leader who was bringing stability and modernization to the Middle East, but the relationship between the Shah and the United States deepened after the creation of the Nixon Doctrine in 1969. As we have seen, that doctrine extended the logic of Vietnamization to other parts of the globe. Stating that the United States would depend on local surrogates rather than using its own military, the doctrine urged the United States, in the words of historian Thomas McCormick, to supply "guns and money, but little manpower," to regional clients. In the Middle East, three regional clients emerged: Israel, Saudi Arabia, and the Shah of Iran.[5]

Between 1972 and 1979, the Shah and successive American administrations worked closely together. For the United States, Iran promised to offset the power of neighboring Baathist Iraq, contain Soviet expansion, and police the Persian Gulf.[6] The Shah promised the United States access to Iran's lucrative oil fields, a guarantee that became vital after the OPEC oil embargo of 1973. In return, the U.S. Army and the CIA developed what McCormick describes as a "close, symbiotic relationship" with the Iranian military and SAVAK, Iran's secret police. The United States also sold the Shah a staggering amount of U.S. weaponry, with estimated totals ranging from $9 billion to $20 billion.[7] Throughout the decade, as American leaders championed the Shah's commitment to modernization, many Iranians mobilized against a regime they associated with class inequality and political repression. By the late 1970s, a diverse coalition began to demand the Shah's removal from power, and in January 1979 he fled the country. Radical students seized the embassy the following November, hoping to foment a break between the new regime and the United States. Sixty-five Americans, most of them State Department officials, were taken hostage. Thirteen were freed within weeks, but fifty-two remained in captivity until 21 January 1981.[8] The POW captivity story had repeated itself.

For his conservative opponents, the hostage crisis highlighted all that was wrong not simply with Jimmy Carter but with the managerialist approach to foreign policy. Even before the seizure of the embassy, they argued, the Shah's overthrow revealed the flaws of the Nixon Doctrine. In the future, local surrogates alone would not be enough to protect American interests in the Middle East. Those interests would need to be protected by military force. More disturbing still, Carter's failure to get the hostages home pointed to a dangerous paradox at the heart of U.S. foreign policy after Vietnam: the United States was the most powerful nation in the world, but it could be paralyzed by a handful of students. The resolution of this paradox depended on the willingness to use overwhelming force. Because he had not threatened such force immediately, conservatives argued, Carter had effectively "deprived himself of any serious leverage."[9] His two attempts to apply pressure—the halting of oil imports from Iran and the freezing of Iranian assets within the United States—had failed to bring the hostages home. In an astonishing twist of political fate, the president of the United States had been left with "relatively few weapons at his disposal."[10]

This growing sense of powerlessness became more urgent on 24 April 1980. As the crisis approached the six-month mark, a military attempt to rescue the hostages ended in disaster when a helicopter and a transport plane crashed during a refueling mission in the Iranian desert. The crash left eight military personnel dead and five others injured. The dramatic spectacle of an aborted rescue mission brought back memories of the April 1975 helicopter evacuation of the American embassy in South Vietnam and the same theme of abandonment that animated the MIA controversy.[11] It also underscored the sense that Carter was an impotent leader who could protect neither the hostages nor the servicemen who had tried to rescue them.[12]

Predictably, Carter's failure to resolve the crisis became a critical factor in the presidential race. Early in the campaign, Reagan had promised to say little about the crisis, claiming that he did not want to second-guess the president or do anything that might hurt efforts to secure the release of the hostages. But as weeks turned into months, Reagan began to invoke it as both a consequence of his opponent's softness and a national disgrace. By January 1980, he was posing a rhetorical question on the campaign trail:

"How did we come to the point that a rag-tag revolutionary mob can invade an embassy of ours, seize our people, and now be holding them into the third month, and we seem unable to do anything about it?"[13] Throughout the spring, he accused the administration of "dillydallying" and argued that it was a foreign policy "bordering on appeasement" that had emboldened the students to seize the U.S. embassy in the first place.[14] Although he refused to offer a specific plan for securing the return of the hostages, he assured audiences that, in implicit contrast to his opponent, he "wouldn't just stand there and do nothing."[15]

By the summer of 1980, the hostages had been in captivity for over six months and the Reagan campaign was gaining momentum. On 17 July 1980, one year after President Carter delivered his ill-fated "Crisis of Confidence" speech, the candidate stood before an audience of delegates in Detroit's Joe Louis Arena and accepted his party's nomination for the presidency. Describing the scene at the convention a month later in the *National Review*, conservative columnist Robert Novak contrasted its tone to that of the 1964 Republican National Convention, where Barry Goldwater had accepted the nomination and gone on to suffer a crushing defeat against Democratic incumbent Lyndon Johnson. All of the anger that had been on display in 1964 was gone now, Novak noted approvingly, replaced by a new spirit of congeniality and conciliation that boded well for the prospect of a Republican victory in November.[16]

Reagan came to Detroit that summer calling for national unity. "More than anything else," he asserted, "I want . . . to unify the country." But the convention itself was sharply divided from the city that surrounded it. It was headquartered at Detroit's upscale Renaissance Center, a hotel and office project financed by the Ford administration with the aim of reviving the city's devastated downtown economy. But its fortress-like design undercut the promise of revitalization. A thirty-foot concrete wall surrounded the center, and black business owners complained that the convention's overwhelmingly white delegates were too afraid to patronize downtown stores. Urban labor unrest also separated the Republicans from the city outside. By 1980, Detroit's unemployment rate was almost 20 percent.[17] Reagan had at first disapproved of the city as the convention host because of its traditional identity as a unionized, blue-collar Democratic stronghold.[18] But by July, Detroit had emerged as the perfect choice in light of what Reagan and his campaigners had come to understand: that winning the election would require wooing blue-collar, unionized, traditionally Democratic workers who were wavering in response to the global economic changes of the 1970s.[19] But at this point, the blue-collar vote was undecided. Shortly before the convention, nine thousand municipal workers had walked off the job, leaving piles of garbage on city streets and threatening to create a public relations disaster for convention planners. The strike lasted six days and was settled only sixty hours before the convention began.[20]

At the same time that the convention reflected deep divisions of race and class, the Republican Party withdrew support for women's rights, which had widespread public backing. Even as economic forces were making the two-earner family inevitable, the Republican Party adopted one of the most socially conservative platforms in its history.[21] The platform opposed ratification of the Equal Rights Amendment, overturning forty years of Republican support for the amendment. It expressed support for a constitutional ban on abortion and included a plank, condemned by one moderate Republican senator as "the most outrageous plank" he had ever seen in a party platform, that called for the appointment of judges who "respect the traditional family values and the sanctity of innocent human life."[22] As delegates adopted this platform inside the arena, twelve thousand protesters gathered in the streets of downtown Detroit to express their support for the ERA.[23] The following November, NOW president Eleanor Smeal described Reagan's election as a "catastrophic defeat" for the women's movement, while anti-ERA activist Phyllis Schlafly proclaimed herself "on top of the world."[24]

How can the Reagan victory be explained? How did the Republicans win a majority on the basis of ostensibly minority views? Certainly, what would come to be called the "culture wars" played a role in securing Reagan the nomination. Reagan's supporters included profamily voters, who opposed abortion rights, the ERA, and gay liberation.[25] But these positions alone did not bring together constituencies as diverse as unionized blue-collar workers, disillusioned Democrats, white inner-city dwellers, Southern Baptists, religious Protestants, Roman Catholics from the urban Northeast, Jewish Americans concerned about the future of Israel, and upwardly mobile young business entrepreneurs. As New Right strategists such as Paul Weyrich and Howard Phillips had grasped, the perception that the family was under siege from destructive outside forces had played a crucial role during the perceived decline of the 1970s. A politician who evoked that image, they believed, could bridge traditional divisions of class, culture, religion, and geography, thus linking the political universe of the secular conservative businessman opposed to government to the evangelical mother incensed by the content of her child's school curriculum to the patriotic black single mother concerned about her son in the army. By the summer of 1980, Weyrich had predicted in the *Conservative Digest* that the family could be to the New Right what Vietnam had been to the New Left—"the means by which the movement came to political maturity."[26]

The fear that the family was under threat was so primal and cut so deep that it precipitated unanticipated and even counterintuitive shifts in political allegiances. That was exactly what the Republicans needed. Thus, as Reagan traveled throughout the country in the spring of 1980, he linked his well-known antipathy to big government to the perception that the family was in peril. Echoing Christopher Lasch's *Haven in a Heartless World*, he contended that the modern state had invaded private life, leaving bureaucrats with the false sense that they knew more about childrearing than parents did. "I would like to take government back from being—or attempting to be—parent, teacher, and clergyman," he told journalist Robert Scheer.[27] By July 1980, Reagan's staff recognized that when he accepted his party's nomination, the candidate would need to appeal to voters not as profamily ideologues but as human beings whose ties to their families were the deepest and most enduring in their lives. In order to make this appeal, staff members took their inspiration from the intricate symbolic meanings that had been assigned to the family over the previous decade. Invoking the family as a unifying trope and as a symbol of national vulnerability, as a site of economic and psychological injury and as a source of national renewal, they wrote a speech that established a powerful link between the nation's domestic suffering and its compromised world position. As Republican writer John Saloma recalled in 1984, conservatives had successfully "appropriated powerful words and symbols—freedom, family, work, religion—in a way that has caught the liberals unaware."[28] Reagan's acceptance speech, entitled "Time to Recapture Our Destiny," was a key moment in that appropriation.

The speech began by mobilizing the family symbol as an expression of profound national unity. Using rhetoric with deep roots in American history, but one that had taken on new import in the 1970s, Reagan began by addressing the American people not as voters, workers, or citizens, but as members of families. During his campaign, Reagan had traveled to the regions of the country most devastated by the decline in manufacturing that had been featured in accounts of the new breed, including steel towns along the Ohio River, industrial cities like Cleveland and Pittsburgh, and once-thriving company towns in the upper Midwest. In those towns, he had developed the concept of a "community of shared values" made up of people of different classes and ethnicities united by a constellation of values that revolved around family, work, school, and country. According to campaign communications director Peter Hannaford, it was this idea that Reagan wanted incorporated into his nomination acceptance speech.[29] "I want to carry our message to every American," Reagan began, "regardless of party affiliation, who is a member of this community of shared values."[30]

At the same time, Reagan condemned the Democrats by linking family suffering to what he called the "three grave threats to our very existence": "a disintegrating economy, a weakened defense, and an energy policy based on the sharing of scarcity." Rejecting all of the introspective baggage associated with the "malaise" discourse, Reagan accused the Carter administration of crippling American families by failing to control unemployment and inflation. He charged the administration with having cooked up "a new and altogether indigestible economic stew, one part inflation, one part high unemployment, one part recession, one part deficit spending, and seasoned by an energy crisis." This economic stew had "turned the national stomach."[31] Echoing a theme he had rehearsed throughout the campaign, he distinguished abstraction from real-life consequences: "Ours are not problems of abstract economic theory. These are problems of flesh and blood; problems that cause pain and destroy the moral fiber of real people."[32]

Reagan's critique extended to Carter's energy policy: "Those who preside over the worst energy shortage in our history tell us to use less," he complained. But conservation, he insisted, with its liturgy of self-recrimination, was not the answer. The restoration of self-confidence, rooted in voluntarism, localism, and family values, was. Aligning himself with suffering families and Carter with cold indifference, he assailed the elitist insensitivity that supposedly underlay the "Crisis of Confidence" speech. "Americans aren't losing their confidence," he had declared in April, "they are losing their shirts."[33] And on the night he accepted the nomination, he angrily complained that the victims of government-created unemployment and inflation were suffering the further indignity of being told that it was "all somehow their fault." "We do not have inflation," he concluded, "because—as Mr. Carter says—we have lived too well." Rather, he continued, we have inflation because "our federal government is overgrown and overweight." The government, not the people, need "to go on a diet."[34]

How was a vocal opponent of labor unions and a visible corporate ally able to portray himself as a champion of working families? Certainly Reagan's uncanny understanding of the still relatively new medium of television played a role. Press secretary Lyn Nofziger explained: "The most effective thing we can do is put him on television wherever we can."[35] But Reagan's staff also realized that the candidate could appeal to working-class voters as members of families. "We don't approach the worker as a union man," a Teamsters official who was also a Reagan advisor explained in September, "but as a man trying to raise a family while his paycheck shrinks, as a man who might be out of a job, or as the son of aging parents who are trying to scrape by on a fixed pension."[36] Taking his cues from profamily activists who insisted that inflation was to blame for rising numbers of working mothers, Reagan insisted that the economic convulsions of the 1970s had blurred the traditional distinction between public and private issues. "Political experts used to tell us there were social issues and economic issues," he explained in April 1980, but "the economic disaster confronting the U.S. hurts family values, destroys savings, and eats away at the very heart of family hopes and dreams."[37]

But it was in the realm of defense policy that the ideal of the family proved most crucial. In the months leading up to the convention, Reagan had attacked Carter for pursuing a foreign policy based on what he described as "vacillation, appeasement, and aimlessness."[38] Reagan saw signs of danger everywhere: the Soviets were on the march in Algeria and Southern Africa, they had launched a surprise invasion of Afghanistan in December 1979, and they were vastly outspending the United States on both strategic and conventional arms.[39] Echoing the arguments of Norman Podhoretz, he described the compromised position of the United States as a problem of national will and capacity rather than a problem posed by an external enemy. This failure was now evident in multiple locations throughout the globe. Along with Afghanistan, it could be seen in Cuba, where a Soviet combat brigade was training only ninety miles from American shores, in Europe, where allies had turned to America "for leadership and failed to find it," and, most pressingly, in Iran, where fifty-two American men and women were being held hostage.[40]

On the night that he accepted his party's nomination, Reagan referred to the hostage crisis only twice. The first reference came at the end of a list of Carter's foreign policy failures that focused on the nation's inability to contain the Soviet threat. But in a move that anticipated the growing centrality of terrorism in American foreign policy in the 1980s, he ended by turning to the hostage crisis. "And, incredibly, more than fifty of our fellow Americans have been held captive for over eight months by a dictatorial foreign power that holds us up to ridicule before the world."[41] The second reference came at the end of the speech when he celebrated the American nation as a refuge for "all those people in the world who yearn to breathe free: Jews and Christians enduring persecution behind the Iron Curtain, the boat people of Southeast Asia, of Cuba and Haiti, the victims of drought and famine in Africa, the freedom fighters of Afghanistan and our own countrymen held in savage captivity."[42] Taken together, the two references embodied the dual nationalist sentiments that had been unleashed by the hostage crisis. As a symbol of the nation's compromised world position after Vietnam, the crisis evoked feelings of incredulity, outrage, and humiliation. But Reagan's speech also revealed the way the crisis affirmed American exceptionalism: in contrast to other countries whose histories were marred by bondage and persecution, the United States was a space of freedom, a refuge.

The hostage crisis referred back to events in the recent past, combining constitutive features of both the POW publicity campaign and the OPEC oil embargo. Like the oil embargo, it was interpreted as a moment in which the United States had been blindsided by a group of Middle Eastern actors who were audaciously wielding a new political weapon in ways that were out of proportion to their actual geopolitical power but that were nonetheless inflicting deep harm within the domestic space of the United States. Like the POW campaign, the hostage crisis cited the violent separation of captive from kin as incontrovertible evidence of American victimization. Indeed, media accounts of the crisis resonated with the POW campaign. Relatives of the hostages described the crisis as a "cruel form of mental torture" and as "psychological warfare," photo essays featured the family members left behind, and the children of the hostages were again quoted as asking the one question that left no doubt as to the brutality of the captors: "Where's daddy?"[43] The scene of the drama had shifted from Southeast Asia to the Middle East, and the North Vietnamese communist adversary had been replaced by Iranian militants, but the crime was the same: the enemy had managed to wound America in its most vital, and most vulnerable, secret space.

Thus, the hostage crisis, like the POW campaign, extended the status of captive from the hostages themselves to their family members, and, finally, to the nation. As Melani McAlister has demonstrated, news accounts portrayed the hostages not in their official capacities as military personnel or state department employees, but rather as individuals whose affective ties to their families were under imminent threat. The relatives of the hostages emerged as key players in the crisis, and their well-documented suffering became a synecdoche for what the nation as a whole was supposedly enduring.[44] Indeed, many of the same psychologists who had studied POW families during the Vietnam War now turned their attention to the hostage families and asserted that they, even more than the hostages themselves, were the true victims of the crisis. As Charles Figley, a psychiatrist assigned to work with hostage families for the State Department, explained, "The family is a system like a spider web—when you pluck one strand, the entire web is affected. . . . The families of the hostages are suffering a great deal more than the hostages themselves." Figley went even further, offering a diagnosis of the state of the country: "All of us are survivors of this. We've been traumatized as a nation."[45]

But if the Iranian hostage crisis resonated with the earlier POW campaign, there was also a crucial difference: it succeeded where the early campaign had failed. The POW publicity campaign had represented a manic and defensive attempt on the part of the Nixon administration to deflect attention away from revelations about American war conduct in Southeast Asia and to recast the nation in the image of an imperiled family in the midst of a deeply divisive war. But, ultimately, the campaign did not work. It could neither halt growing international and domestic opposition to the war nor obscure the disastrous nature of a conflict that had compromised the United States militarily, politically, economically, and, above all, morally. It was precisely because of the *failure* of the publicity campaign that, after Vietnam, the figure of the prisoner of war had been resurrected over and over again by those who hoped to remake the war into, in Ronald Reagan's words, a "noble cause."[46]

The hostage crisis was different. With little public understanding of the historical origins of the U.S embassy seizure, the identification of the nation as a wounded family seemed more plausible and compelling this time around. The moral questions about American war conduct that had haunted the earlier POW publicity campaign were gone now, and the identities of the victims and the perpetrators on the surface appeared far more stable and unambiguous. The result was what Norman Podhoretz gleefully described at the time as the unleashing of a "new nationalism," one rooted in a collective sense of injury and violation. Indeed, the nationalist rituals and symbols that had seemed out of reach to Bicentennial planners in 1976 now appeared throughout the country. People donned yellow ribbons to display their support of the hostages (and, implicitly, their identification with one another), and American flags flew everywhere. When the hostages returned on 21 January 1981, ticker-tape parades were held in cities

Freed hostages arriving at Rhein-Main U.S. Air Force base in Frankfurt,
West Germany, from Algeria, 21 January 1981. A sign on the plane door reads,
"Welcome back to freedom." Courtesy of AP Photo.

and towns, the torch on the Statue of Liberty was fully lit, the lights on the
national Christmas tree were turned on after two years of darkness, and the
Empire State Building glowed red, white, and blue.[47] After many years of
discord, the crisis had succeeded where the Bicentennial had failed: it had
provisionally united the country, albeit around a shared sense of anger and
bewilderment.

237

Buses carry former hostages and their family members down Pennsylvania Avenue to the White House, 27 January 1981. Courtesy of AP Photo.

21 January 1981 was also the day that Ronald Reagan was sworn in as president of the United States. On inauguration day, two stories—one about the hostages and their families, the other about the nation's world position—again came together, but in a new way. The anticipation of the imminent return of the hostages combined with the expectation of a new era in foreign policy in which vacillation would be replaced by vigilance. At the start of a new decade, a wave of joyful family reunions marshaled in a return to American militarization that combined the long-standing fear of Soviet expansion with the concern that would come to dominate the post–Cold War landscape: the terrorist threat.

Scholars have long recognized that fears surrounding American national decline in the wake of Vietnam were critical to Reagan's political success in 1980. They have demonstrated that Reagan had a unique ability to allay those fears and assure Americans that there was a way to move beyond them. This book has shown that the family was at the center of the articulation of those fears between 1968 and 1980. By the time that he took to the podium in Detroit, Reagan was armed with a symbolic vocabulary that tied nation and family together in several powerful ways. When he invited all voters to join him in a community of shared values, he was promising the restoration of the family as a source of moral authority, something that many Americans believed was necessary after Vietnam. When he portrayed the family as a site of national injury, he was implicitly recalling all of the images that had been elaborated over the previous twelve years: the family suffering that had been the linchpin of the POW publicity campaign, the commodity panic among middle-class consumers described by news reporters during the oil embargo, the dislocations within the family that were occurring with the end of the family wage, and the family peril that structured accounts of the Iranian hostage crisis. To be sure, Reagan did oppose the Equal Rights Amendment and abortion rights, and this had real meaning for some of his supporters. But in the end, his political success was rooted in neither a crude antifeminism nor a mean-spirited attempt to differentiate healthy families from defective ones. Rather, Reagan was able to tap into the psychic fears and needs surrounding family life that had exploded over the 1970s. The historical irony is that while Reagan's rhetoric in 1980 assuaged those fears, the policies he went on to enact only exacerbated them.

In trying to explain the recent conservative ascendancy in American politics, scholars and writers have often interpreted the Right's appropriation of the family as a method of deflection. That is, they have described it as a means by which politicians have appealed to voters on the basis of morality and cultural values, while obscuring the deeper economic inequities that deprive so many of these same voters of health insurance, a living wage, decent public education, and financial security. Thomas Frank has recently offered a troubling portrait of the rise of the Conservative Right in his native Kansas, showing how working-class voters there have bartered their economic interests for cultural ones by electing candidates who claim to embrace traditional family values while they enact legislation that destroys the infrastructures that enable real families to survive.[48] In one election after another, Frank shows, conservative candidates in Kansas have won victories by capitalizing on wedge issues like abortion and homosexuality while implementing economic policies that destroy working families. Frank's portrait reveals much about both the cynical strategies and the devastating consequences of the conservative realignment in his home state.

But it misses what Reagan's speechwriters grasped back in 1980: that as a political symbol, the family was never just about culture, society, morality, or sexual politics. Nor was it just about the economy, foreign policy, or the nation's world position. After Vietnam, they realized, the family was the place where it could all come together.

"National Decline" after 1980

Although Reagan's 1980 victory represented an extraordinary political, cultural, and symbolic achievement for the Republicans, it did not bring an end to the fears of national decline that had surfaced in the 1970s. During Reagan's first two years in office, the economic recession deepened, exacerbating unemployment in the industrial rust belt of the Northeast and Midwest, the regions that had delivered him his November victory. By 1982, an economic recovery did take hold, bringing under control the spiral of unemployment and inflation that had proven so politically fatal to the Ford and Carter administrations. Economists disagreed over the roots of the recovery, however. Adherents of supply-side economics contended that the tax and budget programs enacted by the new administration had fulfilled the promise of producing high investment and economic growth. Traditional Keynesian economists, on the other hand, argued that the nation was experiencing a cyclical (and therefore predictable) recovery after a steep recession, one stimulated by consumer spending, high deficits, and easy money.[49]

The recovery did not alleviate anxieties about the nation's economic health. The productivity of the United States continued to lag behind that of other advanced capitalist states, diminishing the nation's share of world manufacturing output. Many American industries, from textiles and steel to computers and cars, were not able to keep pace with foreign competitors, particularly from Japan. Referring to the ubiquity of Japanese electronic goods in the United States by 1990, one college president described the threat of foreign competition as "a slow-motion Sputnik. It's there beeping at you every time you turn on your VCR or load your camera or turn on your fax machine."[50]

Furthermore, between 1982 and 1986, the value of assets owned by foreigners within the United States roughly doubled, a phenomenon that unleashed new sentiments of economic nationalism. Even more alarming was the growing national debt. Between 1981 and 1987 the United States was transformed from a principal creditor nation to the world's largest debtor. In 1981, the United States had had a net credit of $141 billion, but by 1987, it had a net debt of $400 billion.[51] In 1989, a real estate developer erected a national debt clock in New York City's Times Square. It was an electronic billboard with an odometer display that tracked the mounting debt, sometimes rising as fast as $13,000 per second. The billboard even included a display entitled "Your Family's Share" that soared alongside the national figure.[52] For critics of Reagan's economic policies, the explosive debt suggested that the recovery was superficial.

Much as it had in the 1970s, the fate of the middle-class family figured prominently in the debate about the national economy. Over the course of the 1980s, the size of the American middle class contracted, and families found that they now needed two full-time wage earners in order to maintain the same standard of living that had been attainable with one breadwinner a few decades earlier. On the whole, the average weekly earnings of American workers declined over the course of the 1980s, in part because most new job creation occurred in the low-wage service and manufacturing sectors. Because many new jobs were temporary or part time, workers found themselves taking two or three jobs in order to garner the same wages that in the past had come from one. According to economist Wallace Peterson, by 1990 "the real weekly income of a worker" was actually 19.1 percent below the level reached in 1973, a statistic that convinced him that the country was in the throes of "a silent depression." Over the same twenty-year period, average family incomes in the United States went up slightly, but the tiny increase was due to larger numbers of mothers and wives entering the labor force. Ironically, the large-scale entrance of women into the workforce had the effect of concealing the loss of real family income. Even after 1982, as the recession lifted, there was no true return to the prosperity of the postwar years. This point was born out in the realm of popular culture. The defining symbol of national affluence would no longer be the middle-class family, as it had been throughout the 1950s. Instead, there would be a new set of cultural icons that would better reflect the spirit of the age: the freewheeling entrepreneur, the Wall Street power broker, and the yuppie.[53]

The end of the family wage meant that "the family" would become a site of even greater political and cultural contestation after 1980. In the 1970s, much of the public debate around the family had revolved around whether the institution was becoming obsolete. But underlying this debate was a deeper question that came to the fore in the 1980s and 1990s: what, in the end, makes a family? Sociologist James Davis Hunter has argued that, throughout the culture wars, the family emerged as perhaps "the most conspicuous field of conflict," one in which the question of whether the institution is surviving or deteriorating was less significant than the "contest over *what constitutes the family* in the first place."[54] Violent conflicts over abortion, feminism, and homosexuality were never about the family alone, but contested definitions of family life were always in play in those struggles.[55] If men and women both earn wages and work outside the home, how should authority within the family be delegated? In an era of legalized abortion, is a woman's primary obligation to herself or to her offspring? How can traditional conceptions of motherhood be retained as new reproductive technologies revise notions of procreative sex and pregnancy? What does it mean that gay men and lesbians are creating their own "chosen families" in the absence of ties of biology, blood, and procreative sexuality? All of these questions surfaced at a time when the economic underpinnings of the family wage model were fast disappearing, and they revealed just how up for grabs definitions of family and kinship had become in this altered socioeconomic setting.[56]

Just as anxiety over the economy did not disappear after 1980, fears about the nation's eroding world position persisted. Once inaugurated into office, Reagan pursued an aggressive, ambitious, and costly foreign policy agenda. Relying on tactics that would ensure that the United States would not become embroiled in another war like Vietnam, his policies included the waging of proxy wars in Afghanistan, Cambodia, Nicaragua, and Angola, weapons sales and military assistance in El Salvador, the invasion of Grenada, military aid to both sides in the Iran-Iraq war, and direct military interventions in Libya and Lebanon.[57] These endeavors reflected the administration's commitment to a new era of military assertiveness. But they also captured the extent to which, even before the collapse of the Soviet Union, Reagan's foreign policy team was straddling the Cold War and post–Cold War worlds, pursuing military objectives that combined a renewed attempt to contain the Soviet Union with attention to the threat that had assumed center stage during the Iranian hostage crisis: international terrorism.

Nor did anxieties about the nation's world position disappear after the fall of the Soviet Union. It is often assumed that the end of the Cold War marked a moment of triumph for American foreign policymakers, but the truth is more complicated. To be sure, those who had opposed détente in the 1970s now insisted that the collapse of the Soviet Union proved what they had been arguing all along: that a strong military posture was the key to ending the Cold War and maintaining global stability. But the end of the Cold War also raised a number of troubling questions about the place of the United States in the larger world. By the late 1980s, Congress, newspaper editorialists, and the General Accounting Office began to speak again (as they had at the end of the Vietnam War) of the coming "peace dividend," the money that would be freed up by the end of the Cold War that could now be redirected to long-neglected domestic programs.[58] According to one economist, the public schools were filled with young children who could "hardly read, write, or count" and the nation's physical infrastructure lay "in ruin."[59] Some members of Congress even suggested that the military budget could be cut in half.[60]

In 1987, Yale historian Paul Kennedy came at the same themes from a different direction when he published *The Rise and Fall of the Great Powers*. Like Christopher Lasch's *The Culture of Narcissism* a decade earlier, Kennedy's book came at a fortuitous moment. In his best seller, Kennedy observed that the United States was unrivaled both militarily and strategically, but that it was at risk of what he called "imperial overreach." Using a comparative approach, Kennedy argued that like Imperial Spain in 1600 and the British Empire of the late nineteenth century, the United States "was the inheritor of a vast array of strategical commitments which had been made decades earlier, when the nation's political, economic, and military capacity to influence world affairs seemed so much more assured."[61] These commitments, he continued, were eroding the nation's domestic economy and would eventually propel the United States, like imperial nations before it, into a period of decline.

In the midst of a soaring budget deficit and the winding down of the Cold War, Kennedy's influential book raised the same question that was on the minds of many policymakers: why was the United States continuing to devote so much of its resources to the military? The question did not go unanswered. By the early 1990s, President George H. W. Bush and his foreign policy advisors were painting a frightening picture of a post–Cold War world in which the earlier Soviet threat had been replaced by a new constellation of dangers: the spread of nuclear, chemical, and biological weapons, terrorism and hostage taking, and renegade regimes led by erratic rulers. As they developed a blueprint for a new American foreign policy, those who had once opposed détente borrowed many of the same arguments that managerialists had put forth in the mid-1970s: the East-West divide would become less significant, the growth of regional powers (rather than the threat of a rival superpower) would need to be monitored carefully, and control of resources such as oil would become more vital in the determination of national interests.[62]

After the 1992 election of Bill Clinton, this frightening picture did not disappear from view. But it did fade into the background—not because the defense budget diminished or because foreign policy became less militarized (neither of which was the case),[63] but because Clinton and his advisors emphasized in their rhetoric the same questions that managerialists had raised, albeit in nascent form, in the 1970s: How could the United States best protect and pursue its interests in an era of economic globalization? What modes of engagement and diplomacy would most effectively convince other nations to see their own interests and those of the United States as aligned? These questions proceeded from the premise that, for the vast majority of Americans, the post–Cold War world was filled with potential risks and losses, but not with imminent dangers.

All of that changed on 11 September 2001, when an earlier, more ominous vision of the post–Cold War world returned with a vengeance. In the days that followed the attacks on the Pentagon and the World Trade Center, the symbol that had been so prominent between 1968 and 1980—that of a family-under-siege—also returned. Americans and many other people around the world watched their television sets in horror as frantic family members held up pictures of the missing, and they listened to the heartbreaking recordings of final phone calls that victims had made to their loved ones in the hours and minutes before they died. Without question, the nation had suffered a cataclysm, and so the families of the victims became the objects of public compassion and sympathy. But the devastating sounds and images of family pain had the cumulative effect of producing not simply a vision of a wounded nation—but a vision of a nation-in-constant-danger. By the time that the nineteen members of Al Qaeda hijacked the four airplanes, the defense budget of the United States was greater than the combined defense budgets of the next-largest twenty-five nations.[64] But in the months that followed, the attacks had a kaleidoscopic effect, transforming the reality of America's astounding military might into a collective fantasy of national vulnerability. The psychic rupture caused by the attacks created the illusion that this was a new era: that history had started from scratch on the eleventh of September.[65] But in reality, this collective fantasy was three decades in the making. Underwriting it was the same symbol unveiled during the POW publicity campaign almost thirty-five years earlier: a family under violent attack from a foreign enemy.

Following in a long tradition of keen European observers of the United States, British journalist and historian Godfrey Hodgson has noted a peculiar oscillation that has characterized American nationalism since the Vietnam War. In a world of frenetic media accounts that collapse distinctions between belief, opinion, and fact and political campaigns that have become more and more vitriolic, public perceptions of the nation's world position since Vietnam have swung back and forth like a pendulum, moving from "alarmism to complacency," from delusions of invulnerability to fears of an imminent deadly threat, and from fantasies of "impotence to omnipotence and back again." Propelling the pendulum is not only the fear of foreign danger, but the question that was asked throughout the 1970s: did the United States possess the will required to protect its national interests? "After Vietnam," Hodgson writes, "it was not the resources that were in question, but the will to use them, and the purposes for which they would be used."[66] From 1968 to 1980, the family gave shape to those debates about the nation that surfaced in the wake of military defeat. Emerging at the same time as a site of national injury and as a repository of national will, the family was assigned the paradoxical role of both victim and perpetrator in a nationalist discourse that swung back and forth between two poles. In one moment, the nation was omnipotent and fortresslike; in the next, vulnerable and endangered. This earlier history has cast a long shadow over the present, and, as of this writing, the pendulum has not stopped moving. As we continue to watch it swing back and forth, the family will always be there.

Abbreviations

ACC	Advertising Council Collection
CAC	Competitive Advertisements Collection
CLP	Christopher Lasch Papers, University of Rochester, Special Collections, Rochester, New York
CWAC	Communications Workers of America Collection, Robert F. Wagner Labor Archives, New York University, New York, New York
GRFL	Gerald R. Ford Library, Ann Arbor, Michigan
HC	John W. Hartman Center for Sales, Advertising, and Marketing History, Duke University Rare Book, Manuscript, and Special Collections Library, Durham, North Carolina
JCPL	Jimmy Carter Presidential Library, Atlanta, Georgia
JWT	J. Walter Thompson
JWTA	J. Walter Thompson Company Archives, John W. Hartman Center for Sales, Advertising, and Marketing History, Duke University Rare Book, Manuscript, and Special Collections Library, Durham, North Carolina
NARA II	National Archives and Records Administration II, College Park, Maryland
RG	Record Group
SIA	Smithsonian Institution Archives, Washington, D.C.
UAWRDC	United Autoworkers Research Department Collection, Wayne State University Archives of Labor and Urban Affairs, Detroit
UIUC	University Archives, University of Illinois, Urbana-Champaign
VTNA	Vanderbilt Television News Archive, Vanderbilt University, Nashville, Tennessee

Introduction

1 For a useful overview of the theme of national decline in recent American history, see Huntington, "The U.S.—Decline or Renewal?"

2 On alternative models of family life within gay and lesbian communities, see Weston, *Families We Choose.*

3 Coontz, *Way We Never Were.*

4 Luce, "American Century."

5 On depictions of the family in *Life,* see Kozol, *Life's America.* On the role of the middle-class family ideal in Cold War culture, see May, *Homeward Bound.*

6 On the relationship between the ideal and the reality of postwar family life in the United States, see Coontz, *Way We Never Were.* Historical and literary works that portray the diversity of family life in the United States during and

after World War II include Sanchez, *Becoming Mexican American*; Moody, *Coming of Age in Mississippi*; Kingston, *Woman Warrior*; and Marshall, *Chosen Place, Timeless People*.

7 As scholars of the modern welfare state have demonstrated, the family wage ideal produced effects that were sexist, racist, and classist. It created gender-based wage differentials that hurt women in the workplace, it remained out of reach for many minority men who confronted job discrimination, and by privileging male breadwinning, it contributed to the stigmatization of the poor and the needy. At the same time, the ideal of the family wage contained within it a promise that took on new content with the rise of New Deal liberalism in the 1930s: the promise of family security. For a discussion of the role of the family wage in the formation of the modern welfare state, see L. Gordon, *Women, the State, and Welfare*. On the centrality of security to Roosevelt's conception of the New Deal, see Lichtenstein, *State of the Union*.

8 Luce, "American Century."

9 Schlesinger, *Vital Center*, 1. On the tendency to apply psychological categories to the nation after 1945, see Buhle, *Feminism and Its Discontents*; Feldstein, *Motherhood in Black and White*; and E. Herman, *Romance of American Psychology*.

10 Wilson, *Man in the Gray Flannel Suit*; Riesman, *Lonely Crowd*; Galbraith, *Affluent Society*.

11 On the role assigned to the family within the fields of psychology and sociology, see Buhle, *Feminism and Its Discontents*, 125–64; and E. Herman, *Romance of American Psychology*.

12 Wylie, *Generation of Vipers*.

13 Feldstein, *Motherhood in Black and White*.

14 By the end of 1974, the United States had experienced its worst inflationary spiral in five decades and the unemployment rate had soared to 7.2 percent. This combination of high inflation and rising unemployment joined with falling productivity to create "stagflation," a new economic condition that would persist in some form until the early 1980s. Collins, *More*, 123, 155–57.

15 Senate Subcommittee on Children and Youth of the Committee on Labor and Public Welfare, *American Families: Trends and Pressures, 1973*; Keniston, *All Our Children*. For academic discussions, see Bane, *Here to Stay*; M. Gordon, *American Family in Social-Historical Perspective*; Shorter, *Making of the Modern Family*; and Lasch, *Haven in a Heartless World*.

16 Senate Subcommittee on Children and Youth of the Committee on Labor and Public Welfare, *American Families: Trends and Pressures, 1973*, 8.

17 Ibid., 19.

18 Keniston, *All Our Children*, 4. The growing presence of married women and mothers in the workforce was accompanied by a declining birthrate that showed no signs of abating. A study conducted by the census bureau found that 26 percent of young wives had expected to have four children or more in 1967; the number was down to 9 percent by 1972, and the average family now had only 2.3 children (as opposed to 2.9 in 1967). Senate Subcommittee on

Children and Youth of the Committee on Labor and Public Welfare, *American Families: Trends and Pressures, 1973,* 22.

19 On divorce, see Keniston, *All Our Children,* 134–36, 148–50. On the rise in the number of female-headed households during this period, see Senate Subcommittee on Children and Youth of the Committee on Labor and Public Welfare, *American Families: Trends and Pressures, 1973,* 4.

20 Senate Subcommittee on Children and Youth of the Committee on Labor and Public Welfare, *American Families: Trends and Pressures, 1973,* 27.

21 Ibid., 21.

22 Harvey, *Condition of Postmodernity,* 145; Hobsbawm, *Age of Extremes,* 403–32; Jameson, *Postmodernism.*

23 Bell, *Coming of Post-Industrial Society.*

24 Senate Subcommittee on Children and Youth of the Committee on Labor and Public Welfare, *American Families: Trends and Pressures, 1973,* 136.

25 Urie Bronfenbrenner, "The Calamitous Decline of the American Family," *Washington Post,* 2 January 1977, C1.

26 Senate Subcommittee on Children and Youth of the Committee on Labor and Public Welfare, *American Families: Trends and Pressures, 1973,* 4, 19.

27 Lasch, *Culture of Narcissism,* 67–68.

28 The welfare rights movement began at the local level in 1963, and the National Welfare Rights Organization (NWRO) was formed in 1966. In this setting, a number of Supreme Court rulings asserted federal authority over state programs in order to ensure that all eligible women and children received benefits. As political scientist Gwendolyn Mink has shown, there were many pressures to "democratize, regularize, and nationalize access to welfare benefits." Mink, *Welfare's End,* 49.

29 Rainwater and Yancey, *Moynihan Report and the Politics of Controversy.*

30 Duberman, *Stonewall.*

31 On the history of feminism in the late 1960s and early 1970s, see Echols, *Daring to Be Bad;* Evans, *Personal Politics;* and Rosen, *World Split Open.*

32 See, for example, Friedan, *Feminine Mystique.*

33 Echols, *Daring to Be Bad,* 139–203.

34 On motherhood, see Rich, *Of Woman Born.* For a useful historical overview of feminist debates about motherhood, see Umansky, *Motherhood Reconceived.*

35 Stacey, "Feminism as Midwife to Post-Industrial Society."

36 For histories of the New Right during this period, see Crawford, *Thunder on the Right;* Diamond, *Roads to Dominion;* Miles, *Odyssey of the American Right;* and Saloma, *Ominous Politics.* For the New Right's position on the family during the 1970s, see Abbott, *Family and the New Right;* and Gordon and Hunter, "Sex, Family, and the New Right."

37 "'Pro-Family' Push: Political Mine Field," *Washington Post,* 25 July 1980, 1.

38 Gerstle, *American Crucible.*

39 Lieven, *America Right or Wrong,* 1–18.

40 On the cultural history of the captivity narrative, see Slotkin, *Regeneration through Violence,* 94–145. Useful literary histories include Pearce, "The Signifi-

cances of the Captivity Narrative"; and Fitzpatrick, "The Figure of Captivity." On the relationship between captivity narratives and sentimentalism, see Burnham, *Captivity and Sentiment*. For a study that traces the endurance of captivity narratives into the twentieth century, see Castiglia, *Bound and Determined*.

41 On the ways colonists mobilized captivity metaphors during the American Revolution to portray themselves as victims of British bondage and servitude, see Sieminski, "The Puritan Captivity Narrative." On the centrality of tropes of captivity and bondage during the Iranian hostage crisis of 1979, see McAlister, *Epic Encounters*, 198–234. Writing specifically about moments of racial upheaval, Castiglia notes that "captivity narratives flourish in moments of racial 'crisis' in America: the colonial confrontation with Native America, the Civil War, the civil rights movement" (*Bound and Determined*, 14).

42 McAlister, *Epic Encounters*, 209.

43 Ibid., 155–235.

44 Schulman, *The Seventies*. Schulman's "long 1970s" actually runs from 1968 to 1984.

Chapter One

1 House of Representatives Committee on Armed Services, *Hearing on Problems of Prisoners of War*.

2 On the Geneva Convention rules for prisoners of war in the Vietnam context, see House of Representatives Committee on Armed Services, *Hearing on Problems of Prisoners of War*, 5995; Veith, *Code-Name Bright Light*, 37; and Rochester and Kiley, *Honor Bound*, 188–91. The North Vietnamese POW policy varied over the duration of the war and was complex. Although they considered captured soldiers to be war criminals and not POWs, they abandoned the idea of war crime tribunals after 1966. Contrary to the accusations waged against them, the North Vietnamese did release information about and correspondence from POWs, but only to liaison groups that opposed the war.

3 The committee's chairman was L. Mendel Rivers, a Democratic representative from South Carolina. House of Representatives Committee on Armed Services, *Hearing on Problems of Prisoners of War*, 5999.

4 Ibid., 5995–97.

5 Ibid., 6019.

6 Gruner, *Prisoners of Culture*, 171.

7 Jeffords, *Remasculinization of America*, 49.

8 For the ways a similar logic was at work during the Iranian hostage crisis, see McAlister, *Epic Encounters*, 198–234.

9 For a useful comparison of the numbers of American prisoners of war in major U.S. interventions since World War I, see Rochester and Kiley, *Honor Bound*, 597. During the Vietnam War, there were 771 soldiers captured and interned, in contrast to 7,140 during the Korean War, 130,201 during World War II, and 4,120 during World War I.

10 On the ways this shift in blame informed cultural representations of the war, see Jeffords, *Remasculinization of America*, 144–67.

11 Rochester and Kiley, *Honor Bound*, 600.

12 On this policy of "quiet diplomacy," see Veith, *Code-Name Bright Light*, 243; Rochester and Kiley, *Honor Bound*, 201; and Stockdale and Stockdale, *In Love and War*, 307.

13 On the Hanoi March and its impact on the Johnson administration's POW policy, see Rochester and Kiley, *Honor Bound*, 188–207.

14 On the Richard Stratton case, see Hubbell, *P.O.W.*, 264; and Parks et al., *Code of Conduct*. On the ways the experience of POWs in Korea informed the Vietnam POW discourse, see Gruner, *Prisoners of Culture*, 10; "A Celebration of Man Redeemed," *Time*, 19 February 1973, 17; and McCain, *Faith of My Fathers*, 239.

15 "At Least I Know Jim's Alive," *Good Housekeeping*, February 1970, 78–79, 215–22.

16 On the history of the National League of Families of American Prisoners and Missing in Southeast Asia (hereafter referred to as the League), see Jespersen, "The Politics and Culture of Nonrecognition." For the perspective of one of its founders, see Stockdale and Stockdale, *In Love and War*.

17 On the history of the go-public campaign, see Franklin, *M.I.A. or Mythmaking in America*, 49–60; and Jespersen, "The Bitter End and the Lost Chance in Vietnam." On the connection between the go-public campaign and revelations about American war atrocities, see Gruner, *Prisoners of Culture*, 19; and "Dear President Nixon . . . ," *New York Times Magazine*, 3 October 1971.

18 On who was likely to be a POW, see "Healthier Adjustment for Vietnam POWs," *Science News*, 17 September 1977, 182. Rochester and Kiley describe the POWs as "glamorous aviators" in *Honor Bound*, ix–x. The elite status of these POWs explains why they were overwhelmingly white, a fact that reflected the stratified nature of the military. Although the war was fought by men of color in numbers that were disproportionate to the general population, most POWs were white fliers in the navy and air force (although all branches of the military were represented). Out of the 586 returning POWs who were repatriated during Operation Homecoming, only 16 were African American. In contrast, an estimated 550,000 black servicemen were actively involved in Vietnam between 1963 and 1973. At the height of the conflict in 1967–68, African Americans represented 27 percent of the number of U.S. servicemen in Vietnam. On the subject of African American POWs, see "Black Prisoners of War Return," *Ebony*, June 1973, 96–100. Although this book focuses on POWs who were held captive in the North, there were also American POWs held in the South, albeit in smaller numbers.

19 File: National League of Families of American Prisoners and Missing in Southeast Asia, 1971–72, Box 6, ACC, HC. Despite the relatively small number of African American POWs, a few advertisements from the Ad Council campaign featured African American families. I was not able to determine why advertisers made this choice. On the whole, both print and visual materials generated during the POW publicity campaign portrayed white military families.

20 Grace Paley, "The Man in the Sky Is a Killer," *New York Times*, 23 March 1972, 43; "Letters," *New York Times*, 12 April 1972, 44.

21 "A National Disgrace," *Armed Forces Journal*, 27 September 1969. Reprinted in Appendix A of the House of Representatives Committee on Armed Services, *Hearing on Problems of Prisoners of War*, 6048.

22 "Memories of Divided Families," *Life*, 4 December 1970; "What Is Christmas to the P.O.W. Wives?" *Look*, 15 December 1970.

23 "Living with Uncertainty: The Families Who Wait Back Home," *Time*, 7 December 1970, 20.

24 Ibid., 19.

25 Segal, "Therapeutic Considerations in Planning the Return of American POWs to Continental United States"; "Psychological Hangups of Returning Prisoners of War," *Science Digest*, October 1973; "Re-entry Problems," *Newsweek*, 31 July 1972, 23.

26 "Psychological Hangups of Returning Prisoners of War."

27 On the history of these stereotypes within American popular culture, see Lee, *Orientals*.

28 House of Representatives Committee on Armed Services, *Hearing on Problems of Prisoners of War*, 6000–6001.

29 House, *Treatment of American Prisoners by the North Vietnamese*, 8024.

30 "Fighting Women," *San Diego Union*, 29 November 1969. Reprinted in Appendix 1 of House of Representatives Committee on Armed Services, *Hearing on Problems of Prisoners of War*, 6034.

31 On the connections between the League and the Republican Party, see "Politics and POWs," *New Republic*, 3 June 1972. On the ways in which POW relatives were advised on how to handle the media, see "The P.O.W. Families," *New York Times Magazine*, 3 October 1971, 56.

32 House of Representatives Committee on Armed Services, *Hearing on Problems of Prisoners of War*, 5994.

33 Box 6, File: National League of Families of American Prisoners and Missing in Southeast Asia, 1971–72, ACC, HC. The Ad Council POW-MIA Campaign was initiated on behalf of the American Red Cross and the League in 1971.

34 "At Least I Know Jim's Alive," *Good Housekeeping*, February 1970, 78–79, 215–22.

35 Kissinger, *Years of Upheaval*, 42.

36 The film *Coming Home* is the most obvious example of this tendency within popular culture. James Miller describes domestic antiwar activism as "bringing the war home," in *Democracy Is in the Streets*, 290. This notion of the war "coming home" is in no way unique to scholarship on the Vietnam War. See, for example, D. Cohen, *War Come Home*.

37 On the cease-fire agreement, see Herring, *America's Longest War*, 255–56; and Young, *Vietnam Wars*, 285–90. All returning POWs spent three to five days at Clark Air Force Base, where they were debriefed and underwent medical evaluation and could place calls to family members before being cleared for the journey home. On the military's repatriation procedures, see Rochester and Kiley, *Honor Bound*, 581.

38 "First Prisoner Release Completed," *New York Times*, 13 February 1973, 1.

39 The military's original name for the repatriation operation was "Operation Egress-Recap," a name that lacked associations with family and home and thus had less popular appeal.

40 "The Ultimate Weeper," *Newsweek*, 26 February 1973; "Home at Last!," *Newsweek*, 26 February 1973; "Home at Last! The POWs Return," *Reader's Digest*, May 1973; "The Prisoners Return," *Time*, 19 February 1973.

41 Stockdale and Stockdale, *In Love and War*, 216.

42 McCain, *Faith of My Fathers*, 186, 262.

43 "For the POWs, 'Happy Holidays in Many Ways,'" *U.S. News and World Report*, 31 December 1973, 45–48.

44 "The POWs Show Pride and Gratitude," *New York Times*, 18 February 1973, 1.

45 "Home at Last!," 16, 19–24.

46 According to several military accounts, this was due to the fact that prison conditions improved dramatically in the later years of the war, particularly after the fall of 1969. See Rochester and Kiley, *Honor Bound*, 479–96.

47 The whole question of torture was one of the more controversial dimensions of the POW story, with some antiwar activists insisting that POWs were exaggerating or lying about torture within the prison camps. Testimony provided by returnees after repatriation suggests that although there were incidences of torture, prisoners also received food and medical care that were equal to North Vietnamese standards. See "The Horrors of Captivity," *New York Times*, 1 April 1973, 4:4.

48 House, *Treatment of American Prisoners by the North Vietnamese*, 8051.

49 Novick, *Holocaust in American Life*.

50 House, *Treatment of American Prisoners by the North Vietnamese*, 8031, 8034.

51 Rochester and Kiley, *Honor Bound*, 219, 245, 460, 467, 486; Risner, *Passing of the Night*, 200.

52 On concentration camp syndrome, see McCubbin, Hunter, and Metres, "Adaptation of the Family to the PW/MIA Experience"; "Re-entry Problems," *Newsweek*, 31 July 1972, 23; and "The Rough Road Back for POWs," *New York Times*, 11 February 1973, 38.

53 Chesley, *Seven Years in Hanoi*, 153.

54 See Letter from Ann Griffiths to General Richard Lawson, 15 November 1974, Box 16, File: Missing in Action/National League of Families, GRFL, Theodore C. Marrs Files.

55 On the connection between maternalism and pacifism, see Higonnet, Jenson, Michel, and Weitz, *Behind the Lines*; and Elshtain, *Women and War*. On the role of maternalism within the antiwar movement, see Jeffreys-Jones, *Peace Now!*, 156. For an account of women's shifting roles in Britain after World War I that follows a similar trajectory, see Kent, *Making Peace*.

56 On the formation of POW-MIA Families for Immediate Release, see "POWs: Speaking Out," *Time*, 11 October 1971, 21; "The Families Are Frantic," *Time*, 26 July 1971, 17–18; "Politics and POWs," *New Republic*, 3 June 1972, 17–19; "Prisoners of War: They Also Serve," *Newsweek*, 27 December 1971, 17–18; "POW Wife," *Life*, 29 September 1972, 32–42; and "POW Politics," *New York Times*

Magazine, 3 October 1971, 56. Part of this turn to the antiwar movement was practical, since it was antiwar groups who were serving as liaisons between POWs and their families.

57 On the spread of the news throughout the prison camps, see Rochester and Kiley, *Honor Bound*, 412; and McCain, *Faith of My Fathers*, 217.

58 On the role of women in the antiwar movement, see Jeffreys-Jones, *Peace Now!*, 142–77. For examples of POW anger toward highly visible women and those women's organizations that opposed the war, see Hubbell, *P.O.W.*, 336–37; and Guarino, *P.O.W.'s Story*, 157.

59 Guarino, *P.O.W.'s Story*, 322.

60 "Sister of POW Thinks He Will Face a 'Shock,'" *New York Times*, 8 February 1973, 16. On the Alvarez story, see Alvarez and Pitch, *Chained Eagle*; and Alvarez, *Code of Conduct*.

61 POW divorce rates were about 30 percent, a rate that, although roughly proportional to divorce rates within the general population, was significantly higher than rates of divorce within military communities. See Hunter, "Combat Casualties Who Remain at Home."

62 Andersen, "Operation Homecoming: Psychological Observations of Repatriated Vietnam Prisoners of War."

63 "One POW's Fresh Appraisal of U.S.," Interview with Cdr. John S. McCain III, *U.S. News and World Report*, 31 December 1973, 47–48.

64 On possible conflicts between MIA wives and parents, see Spolyar, "The Grieving Process in MIA Wives," 77–84.

65 Rochester and Kiley, *Honor Bound*, 587.

66 Chesley, *Seven Years in Hanoi*, 48, 124; "How POW Marriages Were Saved," *Ladies' Home Journal*, January 1974, 112.

67 Alvarez, *Code of Conduct*, 2. For a similar account, see Risner, *Passing of the Night*, 228. Risner writes: "To give me the letter telling me of Mother's death was standard operating procedure with the Vietnamese." For a closer look at the Alvarez family story, see N. Zaretsky, "Private Suffering and Public Strife."

68 Hubbell, *P.O.W.*, 589; Alvarez and Pitch, *Chained Eagle*, 217–18, 242.

69 "They Are Different Men Now," *New York Times*, 11 February 1973, 4:2; "When Johnny Comes Marching Home Again—or Doesn't," *Life*, 10 November 1972, 32–39; "POW Wives Await Peace with Joy and Dread," *New York Times*, 6 December 1972, 1.

70 "When Johnny Comes Marching Home Again—or Doesn't"; "An Emotional, Exuberant Welcome Home," *Time*, 26 February 1973, 12–17.

71 These military studies were conducted at the Center of Prisoner of War Studies, which was established in April 1972 as a special facility of the Navy Medical Neuropsychiatric Research Unit, in San Diego, California (which became the Naval Health Research Center in September 1974). According to the center's director, the American POW experience in Vietnam "represented an unusually unique situation for gaining a better understanding of the long-term effects of stress upon both the incarcerated military member and the members of his

family." The center's policy and programs reflected these concerns. See Mc-Cubbin et al., *Family Separation and Reunion*, xix–xi.

72 For one of the most salient examples of this intellectual scholarship, see Lasch, *Culture of Narcissism*, discussed at length in chapter 5.

73 McCubbin, Dahl, Lester, and Ross, "The Returned Prisoner of War: Factors in Family Reintegration."

74 On role panic and the return of the POW as an interloper, see "The Rough Road Back for POWs," *New York Times*, 11 February 1973, 38; Hunter, "Combat Casualties Who Remain at Home," 32; Philpott and McCain, *Glory Denied*, 298; McCubbin et al., *Family Separation and Reunion*, 139, 152; and McDaniel, *After the Hero's Welcome*, 95–98.

75 Hall and Malone, "Psychiatric Effects of Prolonged Asian Captivity: A Two Year Follow Up."

76 "Psychological Hangups of Returning Prisoners of War," *Science Digest*, October 1973, 10–15.

77 "POWs a Year Later: Most Adapt Well," *New York Times*, 10 February 1974, 1.

78 Hall and Simmons, "The POW Wife: A Psychiatric Appraisal."

79 McCubbin, Hunter, and Dahl, "Residuals of War: Families of Prisoners of War and Servicemen Missing in Action."

80 McCubbin, Hunter, and Metres, "Children in Limbo," 71.

81 "When the POWs Come Home Again," *Newsweek*, 29 January 1973, 19.

82 McCubbin, Hunter, and Dahl, "Residuals of War: Families of Prisoners of War and Servicemen Missing in Action."

83 McCubbin, Hunter, and Metres, "Children in Limbo," 71.

84 Hall and Simmons, "The POW Wife: A Psychiatric Appraisal"; McCubbin, Hunter, and Metres, "Adaptation of the Family to the PW/MIA Experience," 43; McCubbin, Hunter, and Metres, "Children in Limbo," 73.

85 See Wylie, *Generation of Vipers*, 184–205. On postwar discourses of white maternal failure, see Buhle, *Feminism and Its Discontents*, 125–64; and Feldstein, *Motherhood in Black and White*, 40–61.

86 Hunter, "Combat Casualties Who Remain at Home," 32. For more on this dynamic, see Hall and Simmons, "The POW Wife: A Psychiatric Appraisal."

87 "When Johnny Comes Marching Home Again—or Doesn't," *Life*, 10 November 1972, 32–39.

88 On long-haired sons, see McDaniel, *After the Hero's Welcome*, 80; Powers, "National League of Families and the Development of Family Services," 10; "A Good Reason to Celebrate," *House Beautiful*, November 1973, 16; and Stratton, *Code of Conduct*, 274. On support for McGovern within POW families, see "Voting Splits a POW's Family," *New York Times*, 10 September 1972, 49; and Risner, *Passing of the Night*, 257.

89 "A Celebration of Man Redeemed," *Time*, 19 February 1973, 17.

90 "POWs a Year Later: Most Adapt Well," *New York Times*, 10 February 1974, 1.

91 Stockdale and Stockdale, *In Love and War*, 414; "They Are Different Men Now," *New York Times*, 11 February 1973, 4:2.

92 Alvarez, *Code of Conduct*, xii.

93 Hunter, "Combat Casualties Who Remain at Home"; Hall and Simmons, "The POW Wife: A Psychiatric Appraisal"; "Living with Uncertainty: The Families Who Wait Back Home," *Time*, 7 December 1970, 20; Powers, "National League of Families and the Development of Family Services," 10; McCubbin, Hunter, and Metres, "Adaptation of the Family to the POW/MIA Experience," 36.

94 "For the POWs, 'Happy Holidays in Many Ways,'" *U.S. News and World Report*, 31 December 1973, 45–47; Stratton, *Code of Conduct*, 323, 349.

95 "Some of the Bravest People," *Time*, 5 February 1973, 18.

96 McDaniel, *After the Hero's Welcome*, 87.

97 "Michael Christian Comes Home," *McCall's*, February 1974, 144.

98 Hunter, "Combat Casualties Who Remain at Home," 32.

99 McCubbin, Hunter, and Metres, "Adaptation of the Family to the PW/MIA Experience," 41.

100 "Michael Christian Comes Home," 132–35.

101 Hubbell, *P.O.W.*, 353, 488–89; Guarino, *P.O.W.'s Story*, 160.

102 "Former POWs Charge Torture by North Vietnamese," *New York Times*, 30 March 1973, 1, 18.

103 Stockdale and Stockdale, *In Love and War*, 103.

104 Rochester and Kiley, *Honor Bound*, 424.

105 "How POW Marriages Were Saved," *Ladies' Home Journal*, January 1974, 112.

106 McCain, *Faith of My Fathers*, 229–30. For more on these relationships, see Andersen, "Operation Homecoming: Psychological Observations of Repatriated Vietnam Prisoners of War," 68–69.

107 Hubbell, *P.O.W.*, 585.

108 Segal, "Therapeutic Considerations in Planning the Return of American POWs to Continental United States"; Rochester and Kiley, *Honor Bound*, 542–43; "How POW Marriages Were Saved," *Ladies' Home Journal*, January 1974, 12, 16, 112; "When the POWs Come Home Again," 19.

109 "The Returned: A New Rip Van Winkle," *Time*, 19 February 1973, 32.

110 Segal, "Therapeutic Considerations in Planning the Return of American POWs to Continental United States."

111 "The Psychology of Homecoming," *Time*, 19 February 1973, 18.

112 Denton, *When Hell Was in Session*, 238.

113 See, for example, Herring, *America's Longest War*, 257.

114 On the role of women in the antiwar movement, see Jeffreys-Jones, *Peace Now!*, 142–77. On the ways in which women's marginalization within the New Left contributed to the emergence of the women's liberation movement, see Evans, *Personal Politics*; and Robin Morgan, "Goodbye to All That," in Bloom and Breines, *Takin' It to the Streets*, 499–503.

115 Susan Jeffords traces this shifting of blame in Hollywood action films of the 1980s. See Jeffords, *Remasculinization of America*, 146.

116 The League and the Ford administration were in disagreement when it came to the number of men who remained missing in Southeast Asia. By 1976, the League placed the number somewhere between 1,300 and 2,500 men, while the Ford administration, drawing on classifications provided by the State and

Defense Departments, argued that the number was closer to 800. See Jespersen, "The Bitter End and the Lost Chance in Vietnam," 289.

117 "'Missing in Action' . . . How Agony of Vietnam Lingers," *U.S. News and World Report*, 30 December 1974, in Box 17, File: MIA—Public Mail (5), GRFL, Theodore C. Marrs Files.

118 See Franklin, *M.I.A. or Mythmaking in America*.

119 Not all relatives of MIAs felt this way. Their letters to the Ford administration suggest that some MIA family members desperately wanted status changes to proceed as quickly as possible. These relatives felt that it was cruel to maintain MIA status for men who could not have survived the war and that it only prolonged the agony of those family members left behind. The picture that emerges, then, is not one of consensus but rather of MIA relatives internally divided on the issue of reclassification.

120 National League of Families Press Releases, 5 September 1974 and 17 September 1974, 1974–76, Box 16, File: Missing in Action, National League of Families, GRFL, Theodore C. Marrs Files.

121 Letter from Gladys Brooks to General Brent Scowcroft, 4 May 1975, Box 17, File: MIA—National League of Families (4), GRFL, Theodore C. Marrs Files.

122 House Select Committee on Missing Persons in Southeast Asia, *Hearings on Missing Persons in Southeast Asia*, 23 September 1975. For a discussion of the committee's findings and recommendations, see Jespersen, "The Bitter End and the Lost Chance in Vietnam," 290.

123 For letters to the Ford administration from MIA activists during the mid-1970s, see Boxes 1 and 2, GRFL, Milt Mitler Files; and Box 17, File: MIA Public Mail, GRFL, Theodore C. Marrs Files.

124 For one account of the MIA story that portrays the government as conspiratorial and deceptive, see Jenson-Stevenson and Stevenson, *Kiss the Boys Goodbye*.

125 Memorandum from Dermot G. Foley to Martin Hoffman, 30 May 1974, 2, Box 61, File: MIA-POW, 6 July–8 August 1974, GRFL, John O. Marsh Files.

126 "March of the MIA Families," Box 1, File: MIA/POW October–December 1974, GRFL, Milt Mitler Files.

127 Letter from Olin E. Teague to John O. Marsh, 30 June 1975, Box 16, File: POW-MIA (1), GRFL, John O. Marsh Files.

128 Senate, *Hearings before the Select Committee on POW/MIA Affairs*, 339.

129 Letter from Ann Griffiths to General Lawson, 15 November 1974, Box 16, File: Missing in Action/National League of Families, GRFL, Theodore C. Marrs Files.

130 Letter from Russell (last name unidentifiable) to President Ford, 19 May 1975, Box 18, File: MIA Public Mail (7), GRFL, Theodore C. Marrs Files.

131 See Franklin, *M.I.A. or Mythmaking in America*; Jeffords, *Remasculinization of America*; and Lembke, *Spitting Image*.

132 Jespersen, "The Politics and Culture of Nonrecognition."

133 Transcript of *60 Minutes* piece on reclassification procedures, 28 July 1974, Box 61, File: MIA-POW, 6 July–8 August 1974, GRFL, John O. Marsh Files.

1 For a reprint of the speech, see "As Nixon Shifts His Guns to Domestic Targets," *U.S. News and World Report*, 9 April 1973, 86–88.

2 Ibid.

3 On this foreign policy debate, see Sanders, *Peddlers of Crisis*.

4 Kissinger, *White House Years*, 55–56.

5 For Kissinger's views on Klemens von Mitternich, see Kissinger, *Diplomacy*. Quote is from ibid., 658.

6 Kissinger, *White House Years*, 57.

7 Kissinger, *Diplomacy*, 711.

8 Ibid.

9 Ibid., 704, 742; Kissinger, *White House Years*, 191.

10 Collins, *More*, 106. For a useful overview of the Nixon Doctrine, see McCormick, *America's Half Century*, 176, 187.

11 For Kissinger's views of the Nixon administration's China policy, see Kissinger, *Diplomacy*, 721–24; and Kissinger, *White House Years*, 191. For his views on détente, see Kissinger, *Diplomacy*, 714; and Kissinger, *Years of Upheaval*, 600.

12 On the defense reductions, see Collins, *More*, 105. The 32 percent figure is measured in constant dollars.

13 Quoted in Kissinger, *Years of Upheaval*, 459. On the history of the October War and the American response, see Lenzcowski, *American Presidents*, 116–40; and Little, *American Orientalism*. Kissinger's account of the war appears in *Years of Upheaval*, 450–613.

14 These figures are taken directly from Lenzcowski, *American Presidents*, 129.

15 Kissinger, *Diplomacy*, 739.

16 Kissinger, *White House Years*, 565.

17 On the British withdrawal from the region, see Lenzcowski, *American Presidents*, 117; and Little, *American Orientalism*. On the growing Soviet presence in the Middle East during the same period, see Kissinger, *White House Years*, 346. Although by this time the Middle East was already a site of considerable American political, economic, and symbolic investment, the presence of the U.S. military in the area lacked the scope it would later assume. For example, the Persian Gulf in the 1970s was, according to journalist James Mann, "almost off the map in the Pentagon's worldwide military planning." At the time of the October War, there was no American military command for the Gulf, a fact that, as Mann points out, seems startling in light of the country's later military presence in the region. Mann, *Rise of the Vulcans*, 82–83.

18 Quoted in Kissinger, *Years of Upheaval*, 495.

19 Quoted in Little, *American Orientalism*, 106.

20 On the American airlift, see Lenzcowski, *American Presidents*, 129–30; Little, *American Orientalism*, 106; and Quandt, *Decade of Decisions*, 183–87. For Kissinger's account of the airlift, see Kissinger, *Years of Upheaval*, 492–96.

21 On the final stage of the conflict, see Lenzcowski, *American Presidents*, 131; and Quandt, *Decade of Decisions*, 187–206. On his contact with the Soviet Union during this period, see Kissinger, *Diplomacy*, 740.

22 Kissinger, *Years of Upheaval*, 507.

23 The founding members of OPEC from the Middle East were Saudi Arabia, United Arab Emirates, Qatar, Libya, Kuwait, Iraq, Iran, and Algeria. Notably, Iran did not participate in the oil embargo.

24 For useful overviews of the 1973–74 oil embargo, see Lenzcowski, *American Presidents*, 131–36; Little, *American Orientalism*, 60–65; Vietor, *Energy Policy*, 193–271; and Yergin, *Prize*, 588–652. For Kissinger's account of the embargo, see *Years of Upheaval*, 854–95; and *Years of Renewal*, 665–71. For the oil embargo's domestic impact and the Nixon administration's response, see Matusow, *Nixon's Economy*, 241–75; and Vietor, *Energy Policy*, 193–271.

25 Kissinger, *Years of Upheaval*, 855.

26 Kissinger, *Years of Renewal*, 665.

27 Vietor, *Energy Policy*, 193. For overviews of American oil policy during the postwar period, see Odell, *Oil and World Power*, 30; and Stobaugh and Yergin, *Energy Future*, 3–55. On the relationship between business and government in energy policy after World War II, see Vietor, *Energy Policy*, 91–145; and Yergin, *Prize*, 409–49. For a history of oil focusing on the period from 1941 through 1954, see Painter, *Oil and the American Century*. On changes in oil supply and demand, see Little, *American Orientalism*, 60–65. For one of the most widely read policy predictions of future oil shortages at the time, see Akins, "The Oil Crisis."

28 Walter J. Hickel, "The Energy War II: What We Must Do at Home," *Reader's Digest*, February 1974, 102.

29 For the equating of oil with blood, see *ABC Nightly News*, 22 February 1974, VTNA; Energy Policy Project of the Ford Foundation, *Time to Choose*, 1; and "Energy Crisis: Paradox of Shortage Amid Plenty," *New York Times*, 17 April 1973, 26. The "oil artery" quote comes from "Public Releases on a Time to Choose, the Final Report of the Energy Policy Project, 1974," ConEd History, Box 9, File: Energy Policy, 4-82 (insert only), Duke University, Special Collections, Louis H. Roddis Papers. For an illuminating account of the embargo that also focuses on U.S. notions of entitlement to Arab oil, see McAlister, *Epic Encounters*, 136–39.

30 Baylor University Editorial Cartoon Collection, Box 57, File 1589.

31 Ibid.

32 Ibid., File 1588.

33 Thomas S. Szasz, "When History Comes Home to Roost," *New York Times*, 6 March 1974, 37.

34 Speech by Chalmer G. Kirkbride, "American Ingenuity: Will It Survive the Energy Crisis?" Energy Policy, Box 10, File 4-167, "Energy Crisis," a collection of various materials, vol. 3, 1975–76, Duke University, Special Collections, Louis H. Roddis Papers.

35 Comments on this statistic include Morris K. Udall, "Ending the Energy Binge," *New Republic*, 16 June 1973, 13; Ford Foundation, *Time to Choose*, 6; "Talk of the Town," *New Yorker*, 10 December 1973, 37; Margaret Mead, "The Energy Crisis—Why Our World Will Never Be the Same Again," *Red-*

book, April 1974, 54; and "An Age of Scarcity," *New York Times*, 7 April 1974, 16.

36 Kenneth E. F. Watt, "The End of an Energy Orgy," *Natural History*, February 1974, 16–22.

37 "Remarks at the Seafarer's International Union Biennial Convention," Office of the Federal Register, *Public Papers of the Presidents: Richard Nixon, 1973*, 980. For a commentary on this speech, see "Talk of the Town," *New Yorker*, 10 December 1973, 37.

38 Udall, "Ending the Energy Binge," 13–14.

39 Quoted in Mann, *Rise of the Vulcans*, 47.

40 "Cold Comfort for a Long, Hard Winter," *Time*, 10 December 1973, 34.

41 On the ways in which the embargo's effects varied regionally, as well as the ways in which the embargo inspired regionalism, see James Reston, "Even Texas Is Running Short," *New York Times*, 14 November 1973, 45; "U.S. Energy Crisis Stirs Self Interest of Regions," *New York Times*, 20 December 1973, 1; "On Fuel Shortages and Damages to Regions," *New York Times*, 2 February 1974, 29; and "Oil Is a National Problem, but Seriousness Varies," *New York Times*, 3 February 1974, 4:2.

42 Yergin, *Prize*, 617.

43 "Fuel Crisis Is Hobbling Suburbs," *New York Times*, 25 February 1974, 1, 15.

44 "The High Cost of Eating," *Newsweek*, 5 March 1973, 52.

45 *New Yorker*, 18 February 1974, 37.

46 "The Arabs New Oil Squeeze: Dimouts, Slowdowns, Chills," *Time*, 19 November 1973, 88.

47 For the impact of deindustrialization on these industries, see Bluestone and Harrison, *Deindustrialization of America*, 140–90. For media discussions of the impact of the oil crisis on employment, see "Job Rolls Show Energy Crisis Toll," *New York Times*, 7 February 1974, 26; "Energy and Jobs," *New York Times*, 29 December 1973, 25; "Energy Crunch: Who'll Get Hurt," *U.S. News and World Report*, 26 November 1973, 17; and "Winter's Grim Impact on Homes, Industries," *U.S. News and World Report*, 22 January 1973, 49. For the impact of unemployment on families during the energy crisis, see Perlman and Warren, *Families in the Energy Crisis*, 90. For government publications on this theme, see Senate Committee on Labor and Human Resources, *Hearing on Unemployment and the Energy Crisis*; and Senate Subcommittee on Labor of the Committee on Labor and Public Welfare, *Hearing on the Effects of the Energy Crisis on Employment Dislocation*.

48 *ABC Nightly News*, 8 March 1974, VTNA.

49 Testimony of Joelle Juillard, NOW, Senate Committee on Labor and Human Resources, *Hearing on Unemployment and the Energy Crisis*, 117.

50 "Winter Forecast: Cold Comfort for a Long Hard Winter," *Newsweek*, 8 October 1973, 79.

51 Quoted in Lasch, "The Culture of Consumption," 1381. On the kitchen debate, see May, *Homeward Bound*, 16–20.

52 Quoted in Patterson, *Grand Expectations*, 317.

53 Kissinger, *Diplomacy*, 700–701.

54 Horowitz, *Anxieties of Affluence*; Brick, *Age of Contradiction*, 2.

55 Udall, "Ending the Energy Binge," 12; Edward Teller, "The Energy Disease," *Harper's*, March 1975, 16; Watt, "The End of an Energy Orgy"; Herbert Meredith Orrell, "More Does Not Always Mean Better," *America*, 2 March 1974, 148.

56 Eric F. Goldman, "What We Have Here Is a Prosperity Psychosis," *New York Times*, 11 January 1974, 31.

57 Letter from Rev. Dennis G. Ruby, *New York Times*, 18 December 1973, 40.

58 Letters to the Editor, "Energy: A Crisis of Negligence," *New York Times*, 15 November 1973, 44.

59 Box 23, File 13, Volkswagen Advertisement, CAC 1973, JWTA.

60 Amuzegar, "The Oil Story."

61 James A. Cox, "What's Your Energy IQ?" *Reader's Digest*, November 1974, 157–59.

62 "Your Home: Where Does All the Energy Go?" *American Home*, February 1974, 18.

63 Other examples include "Coping: How Women across the Country Solve the Energy Problem," *Vogue*, February 1974, 166; "Eight Steps You Can Take to Conserve Household Energy," *House & Garden*, January 1974, 24; "50 Ways to Save Fuel and Keep Warm," *McCall's*, February 1974, 36; "46 Ways to Conserve Energy in Your Home," *Better Homes and Gardens*, November 1973, 36; "How to Heat and Cool Your Home with Less Fuel," *Good Housekeeping*, March 1974, 139; and "What Every Family Should Know—And Do—to Solve the Energy Crisis," *Parents* 49, 1974, 22.

64 Ralph Keyes, "Learning to Love the Energy Crisis," *Newsweek*, 3 December 1973, 17. In the kitchen debates, household appliances were identified with liberation, and new labor-saving devices were seen, whether accurately or not, as having the power to free individuals within the family to pursue leisure, pleasure, and intimacy. Here, they became associated with two very different trends: national dependency on foreign oil on the one hand and growing alienation within the home on the other. For historical analyses that challenge the association of technological innovation with liberation, see Cowan, *More Work for Mother*; and Strasser, *Never Done*.

65 On the history of frozen foods, see Levenstein, *Paradox of Plenty*; Levenstein, *Revolution at the Table*, 207–8; and McIntosh, *American Food Habits*, 119–20.

66 See, for example, an advertisement for Mrs. Paul's Onion Rings from *Good Housekeeping*, November 1972, from Box 16, File 23: Misc. Frozen Foods, CAC 1972, JWTA; as well as one from Stouffer's in the same file. For an in-depth look at how the JWT Company was assessing the impact of women's changing roles on advertising during this period, see "The Moving Target," Box 15, File: The Moving Target, JWT Publications, JWTA.

67 Keyes, "Learning to Love the Energy Crisis," 17.

68 *Information Center Flash*, JWT Chicago, 6 January 1970, Newsletter Collec-

tion, Domestic Series, Chicago Office, Box 2, File: 1970, 6 January–10 August, Information Center Flash, JWTA.

69 Federal Energy Administration, "Per Capita Energy Consumption and Per Capita Income: A Comparison of the United States with Other Wealthy Western Countries," Energy Conservation, Box 14, File 9-72, Conservation, vol. 1, 1973–74, Duke University, Special Collections, Louis H. Roddis Papers.

70 Mead, "The Energy Crisis—Why Our World Will Never Again Be the Same," 54, 58.

71 See Nye, *Consuming Power*, 217–46. For studies that trace the effect of oil shortages on household energy consumption, see Chateau and Lapillone, "Energy Consumption in the Residential Sector since 1973"; and Perlman and Warren, *Families in the Energy Crisis*, 79–116. See also "Will Energy Plan Work? Recent Study of Family Attitude Hints at Rough Going," *New York Times*, 10 October 1974, 56.

72 On the heightened vulnerability of the poor to energy shortages, see Perlman and Warren, *Families in the Energy Crisis*, 117–42. For the effects of the energy crisis on African Americans, see "Crisis Said to Hurt Blacks the Most," *New York Times*, 22 February 1974, 12; and "The Energy Crisis: For Blacks, A Disproportionate Burden," *New York Times*, 9 February 1974, 29. On the impact of the crisis on the elderly, see *Energy Crisis Impact on Low-Income and Elderly*, Senate Select Committee on Nutrition and Human Needs, 22–23 January 1974.

73 In truth, women in the family wage economy exerted a great deal of managerial control over the household budget, partly because they were responsible for providing food to the family. See Tilly and Scott, *Women, Work, and Family*, 136–39.

74 For the history of grassroots conservatism in Orange County, California, see McGirr, *Suburban Warriors*.

75 "Energy Crisis: Bleakness or Blessing?" *Christianity Today*, 21 December 1973, 33–34.

76 Orell, "More Does Not Always Mean Better," 14.

77 See, for example, Edward R. F. Sheehan, "Unradical Sheiks Who Shake the World," *New York Times Magazine*, 24 March 1974, 14.

78 "The Coldest Winter?" *Newsweek*, 31 December 1973, 8.

79 "Cold Comfort for a Long, Hard Winter," 34.

80 "Energy: How Bad Now? Painful Changes in Life Styles," *U.S. News and World Report*, 11 February 1974, 19.

81 "The Coldest Winter?" 8.

82 Ibid.

83 *NBC Nightly News*, 10 January 1974, VTNA.

84 "Gasoline Shortages Are Forcing Exurbanites to Readjust Their Life-Style," *New York Times*, 7 February 1974, 29.

85 William Hoffer, "No Energy Weekend Experiment," *House Beautiful*, May 1974, 16.

86 For a useful historical overview of welfare policy during this period, see Abramowitz, *Regulating the Lives of Women*, 349–81. For the ways Nixon's

quest for a guaranteed income ultimately undermined federal welfare policy, see O'Connor, "False Dawn of Poor Law Reform." On the political consequences of women's economic dependency, see Lister, "Women, Economic Dependency and Citizenship"; and Nelson, "Women's Poverty and Women's Citizenship." On the black family, see Moynihan, "Negro Family."

87 Moynihan, *Politics of a Guaranteed Income*, 17.

88 "Welfare Out of Control—Story of Financial Crisis Cities Face," *U.S. News and World Report*, 8 February 1971, 32.

89 State of the Union Address, 22 January 1971, Office of the Federal Register, *Public Papers of the Presidents: Richard Nixon*, 1973, 51.

90 I borrow the term "caprice of geology" from Sheehan, "Unradical Sheiks Who Shake the World," *New York Times Magazine*, 24 March 1974, 53. This theme is also explored in McAlister, *Epic Encounters*, 136–39.

91 "A Global Challenge to Communicators: Protecting Resources and Environment, Protecting Our Moral Resources," Speech delivered by Don Johnston in May 1974 at the International Advertising Association 24th World Congress in Tehran, Iran, Box 15, File: 1974, Spring, May, June, July, JWT World Highlights: New York Office, Newsletter Collection, Domestic Series, JWTA.

92 Yergin, *Prize*, 631. Yergin points out that both Libya and Syria dissented from the decision to lift the embargo.

93 Kissinger, *Years of Renewal*, 668.

94 On the energy conference, see Yergin, *Prize*, 629.

95 Ibid., 884. See also Kissinger, *Years of Renewal*, 677. This is not to say that such a response was not considered. In a press conference on 21 November 1973, Kissinger warned OPEC that if the embargo continued indefinitely, the United States would have no choice but to "consider what countermeasures it would have to take." "We would do this with enormous reluctance," he continued, "and we are still hopeful that matters will not reach this point." During the month of November, Kissinger backed up his vague warning by ordering a number of contingency studies to explore what he later called "countermeasures against Arab members of OPEC." Throughout the five-month embargo, however, Kissinger emphasized the need for a diplomatic response to the crisis rather than a military one. Any authentic resolution to the embargo would require that the industrial democracies recapture what he called "control over their own destinies." Kissinger, *Years of Upheaval*, 880.

96 "Address to the Nation about Policies to Deal with the Energy Shortages," 7 November 1973, Office of the Federal Register, *Public Papers of the Presidents: Richard Nixon*, 1973, 53.

97 *Gallup Opinion Index*, February 1974, Report Number 104, 4–5.

98 See "Energy Crisis: Second Look," *Nation*, 19 February 1973, 229–30; "No Shortage of Skepticism," *Time*, 28 January 1974, 30; "The Gas Shortage—How Real Is It?" *U.S. News and World Report*, 25 June 1973, 34; and "Energy: Many Skeptical on Reasons for Crisis," *New York Times*, 23 December 1973, 18.

99 Yergin, *Prize*, 618.

100 Quoted in Rand, *Making Democracy Safe for Oil*, 332.

101 Speech delivered by Thornton Lockwood, "Energy and the Consumer: Is This the End of the Big Car?" Society of Automotive Security Analysts, Cleveland, Ohio, 7 June 1977, Box 24, File L-Misc 1930, 1960s–1970s, Writings and Speeches Collection, JWTA.

102 Speech delivered by Henry Schachte, president, JWT Company, "Communication with the Consumer in Today's Gas Climate," Southern Gas Executive Management Conference, Ponte Vedra, Florida, 20 November 1972, Box 31, File: Henry M. Schachte, 1968–1977, Writings and Speeches Collection, JWTA.

103 Box 15, File: One Advertiser's Response to Pollution, Inflation, Shortages, and Whatever's Next, 1975, Publications Collection, JWTA.

104 Quoted by Representative Les Aspin in "Big Oil's Latest Gimmick," *Nation*, 3 June 1973, 75.

105 Box 24, File 26, Exxon, CAC 1973, JWTA.

106 Box 25, File 15, CAC 1974, JWTA.

107 "We Can Squeak By, If—," *U.S. News and World Report*, 4 June 1973, 26.

108 Box 25, File 5: Mobil Gas and Mobil Oil, CAC 1973, JWTA.

109 Yergin, *Prize*, 409–10.

110 Speech delivered by Dan Seymour, "An Advertising Outlook," New York Society of Security Analysts/Advertising Age Seminar, New York, 11 December 1973, Box 33, File: Dan Seymour, 1973, Writings and Speeches Collection, JWTA.

111 Box 4, File: American Gas Association Minutes, 1973, Review Board Records, JWTA. This emphasis on consumer behavior meant that advertisements could at times adopt tones of didacticism and prohibition. For example, in its 1974 national conservation campaign, the Advertising Council admonished energy consumers with the slogan "Don't Be Fuelish." Although the Federal Energy Administration worried that the play-on-words might be too negative, the Advertising Council felt confident that it would successfully convey the conservation message. "We wanted a clear, penetrating idea," explained Carl W. Nichols, the chairman of Cunningham & Walsh, the agency commissioned for the project. The slogan fulfilled all of the requisites. "People instantly understood it and grasped its serious implications," Nichols said. "They remembered it, too." The "Don't Be Fuelish" campaign demonstrated the ways advertising firms accommodated themselves to the anomalous circumstances of the oil crisis. For the Federal Energy Administration debate about the campaign, see "Don't Be Fuelish" Campaign, Conference Report, Federal Energy Administration Energy Conservation Program, 28 February 1975, 3, ACC, UIUC. "They remembered it too" is from File: Energy Conservation, 1974–75, Advertising Council, "Don't Be Fuelish" Campaign, in *Public Service News: How Do You Urge Americans to Save Energy?* "Advertising Council Volunteer Agency Cunningham & Walsh Meets the Challenge," 2, ACC, HC.

112 Box 22, File 17, American Gas Association, CAC 1973, JWTA.

113 Box 15, File: One Advertiser's Response to Pollution, Inflation, Shortages, and Whatever's Next, 1975, Publications Collection, JWTA.

114 The government official was Connecticut attorney general Robert Killian, who was quoted in "The Gas Shortage—How Real Is It?" 34. Hertzberg quoted in "Cold Comfort for a Long, Hard Winter," 33.

115 See Vogel, *Fluctuating Fortunes*, 217.

116 Box 25, File 13, CAC 1974, JWTA.

117 Quoted in Little, *American Orientalism*, 72.

118 "Trying to Control the Pampered Oil Industry," *New York Times*, 3 March 1974.

119 Quoted in Saloma, *Ominous Politics*, 66. According to a *New York Times* article in March 1974, an unprecedented level of public scrutiny and regulatory oversight was creating a climate of "extraordinary trauma" in the oil industry in particular.

120 Box 25, File 14, CAC 1974, JWTA. These advertisements were notable for their tone of rational accommodation. In other settings, spokespersons for the oil industry could sound shrill and alarmist. For example, the president of the American division of Gulf Oil warned in a 1974 editorial that unlimited expansion of the government could one day "transform the United States into a complete socialist state." Z. D. Bonner, "Protecting Free Enterprise," *New York Times*, 6 May 1974. But Mobil's public relations approach was more tempered and cautious as the company systematically refashioned itself into a patient, cogent, and trustworthy educator of a wary and confused public.

121 See Nye, *Consuming Power*; and Stobaugh and Yergin, *Energy Future*.

Chapter Three

1 On events at Lordstown in the early 1970s, see Thompson, "Autoworkers, Dissent and the UAW"; and Aronowitz, *False Promises*, 21–50. On race, labor politics, and the Detroit auto industry, see Sugrue, *Origins of the Urban Crisis*, 89–152; and Georgakas, *Detroit, I Do Mind Dying*.

2 "Get Mean and Destroy" is from "See Here," December 1971, Box 1, Folder: "See Here" 1971, Wayne State University Archives of Labor and Urban Affairs, Detroit, UAW Local 1112 Collection; "Gotta Make Another Dollar" is from Terkel, *Working*, 190.

3 "See Here," May 1971, November 1978, May 1974, Box 1, Folders: "See Here" 1971, "See Here" 1978, and "See Here" 1974, Wayne State University Archives of Labor and Urban Affairs, Detroit, UAW Local 1112 Collection.

4 "Sabotage at Lordstown?" *Time*, 7 February 1972, 99.

5 Aronowitz, *False Promises*, 49.

6 See Chafe, *Unfinished Journey*, 446–47; and Vogel, *Fluctuating Fortunes*, 229.

7 "World Trade: Can the U.S. Compete?" *Newsweek*, 24 April 1972. For other articles on lagging productivity, see "Spotlight on Productivity—Why It's a Key to U.S. Problems," *U.S. News and World Report*, 4 October 1971, 25–28; "The ABC's of Productivity—Its Meaning to You," *U.S. News and World Report*, 17 August 1970, 54–55; "The New Inefficiency," *Business Week*, 20 September 1969, 45; "Lower Productivity Threatens Growth," *Business Week*, 1 January 1972, 36–37; "Why U.S. Workers Are Producing Less," *U.S. News and World*

Report, 1 May 1978, 95–96; "Productivity: Seeking That Old Magic," *Time*, 2 August 1971, 56–59; "Vanishing Vigor," *Time*, 26 June 1978, 51; and "Perils of the Productivity Sag," *Time*, 5 February 1979, 126–27.

8 On declining profit margins during this period, see Lichtenstein, *State of the Union*, 213; and Useem, *Inner Circle*, 151–52. On the broader crisis confronting big business during this time, see Vogel, *Fluctuating Fortunes*, 55–59, 112.

9 Bell, *Coming of Post-Industrial Society*; Barnet, *Global Reach*.

10 See Harvey, *Condition of Postmodernity*, 145; and Hobsbawm, *Age of Extremes*, 403–32.

11 "The Great Male Cop Out from the Work Ethic," *Business Week*, 14 November 1977, 156.

12 See, for example, "Lower Productivity Threatens Growth," 36–37; "Service Economy Grows—But Does It?" *Business Week*, 15 February 1969, 126; and "Is the Shift to Services Really a Drag?" *Business Week*, 9 September 1972, 84–87.

13 For arguments that tied lagging productivity to the entrance of women and minorities into the workforce, see Kendrick, "Recent Productivity Trends in the U.S.: Causal Forces, Impacts and Prospects," *Vital Speeches of the Day*, 22–23 May 1973, 562–65; "Improving Productivity Growth," Box 3, Folder: Economic Policy Board Collection, GRFL, Arthur Quern Papers; "The News about Productivity Is Better Than You Think," *Fortune*, February 1972, 98–101, 182–90; and Letter from Alan Greenspan to George Kuper, 17 June 1975, Box 12, Folder: National Productivity Commission, GRFL, Alan Greenspan Files.

14 Aronowitz, *False Promises*, 406.

15 See Yankelovich, *New Morality*; and Yankelovich, "Turbulence in the Working World: Angry Workers, Happy Grads," *Psychology Today*, December 1974, 81–87.

16 On the centrality of the steel industry to postwar economic growth, see Stein, *Running Steel, Running America*, 7–36; on the automobile industry, see Edsforth, *Class Conflict and Cultural Consensus*, 13–69.

17 On the increase in white-collar occupations from 1900 to 1979, see Blumberg, *Inequality in an Age of Decline*, 38.

18 Milkman, *Farewell to the Factory*, 25–26.

19 On the relationship between absenteeism and productivity lag, see "Absent Workers—A Spreading Worry," *U.S. News and World Report*, 27 November 1972, 48–49. For Reuther's characterization of the new worker, see "Blue Collar Blues on the Assembly Line," *Fortune*, July 1970, 69–71, 112–17.

20 "The Spreading Lordstown Syndrome," *Business Week*, 4 March 1972, 69.

21 For a history of debates about narcissism during this period, see chapter 5.

22 Transcript of speech given by Dutch Landen, CWA & AT&T Joint Resource Seminar, Chicago, Illinois, 29–30 July 1981, Folder: QWL: General Correspondence, 1981, What Is Quality of Work Life? CWAC.

23 "Is the Work Ethic Going Out of Style?" *Time*, 30 October 1972, 96–97.

24 This description is from John Tabor, a thirty-one-year-old plumber pipe fitter who worked for Ford in Detroit. Interviewed in "Blue Collar Blues on the Assembly Line," 112–17.

25 Ibid., 113.

26 Levitan and Johnston, *Work Is Here to Stay, Alas*, 66.

27 "Blue Collar Blues on the Assembly Line," 69–71, 112–17; Terkel, *Working*, 163.

28 On antiauthoritarianism among the new breed, see Sheppard and Herrick, *Where Have All the Robots Gone?* xi–xxiv; and "It Pays to Wake Up the Blue Collar Worker," *Fortune*, September 1970, 133–68. On family permissiveness and its adverse effects on workers, see Walton, "How to Counter Alienation in the Plant." On the connection between higher levels of education and workplace insubordination, see Yankelovich, "Work, Values, and the New Breed," 3–26.

29 Levitan and Johnston, *Work Is Here to Stay, Alas*, 66. See also E. G. Nicholson, "A Mountain Not Meant for Running: The American Business Scene," *Vital Speeches*, 15 November 1972, 69–73.

30 "General Motors and the UAW," Folder: QWL Meeting, Harvard, January 1982, What Is Quality of Work Life? CWAC. For the argument that prosperity was eroding productivity, see "The New Inefficiency," 45; "The News about Productivity Is Better Than You Think," 182–90; Memorandum from Ken Cole to William Seidman, 14 October 1974, "A Direct Approach to U.S. Productivity," Box 174, Folder: Kenneth Cole, GRFL, L. William Seidman Collection; and "How Bosses Get People to Work Harder," *U.S. News and World Report*, 29 January 1979, 63–64.

31 O'Toole, *Making America Work*, 26.

32 "Blue Collar Blues on the Assembly Line," 117.

33 "The News about Productivity Is Better Than You Think," 98–101, 182–90; "When Boss Isn't Doing His Job —," *U.S. News and World Report*, 13 February 1978, 75–76; "New Breed of Workers," *U.S. News and World Report*, 3 September 1979, 35–38.

34 Yankelovich, "Work, Values, and the New Breed," 12.

35 Ibid.

36 O'Toole, *Making America Work*, 34.

37 Terkel, *Working*, 174–77.

38 Ibid., 168–73.

39 O'Toole, *Making America Work*, 34–35.

40 "The New Face of the Labor Force: An Essential Seminar for the Executive Today," 26 June 1969, Folder: BFS Psychological Associates, Reports, Studies & Arbitration, CWAC.

41 Yankelovich, *New Morality*, 3–5.

42 Aronowitz, *False Promises*, 21–50.

43 See "The Bullet Biters," *Newsweek*, 7 February 1972, 65; and "Sabotage at Lordstown?" 76. For corporate managers' perspectives, see "General Motors and the UAW," Folder: QWL Meeting, Harvard, January 1982, What Is Quality of Work Life? CWAC.

44 Avildsen, director, *Joe*, 1970.

45 On Nixon's "forgotten man" campaign strategy, see Matusow, *Nixon's Economy*, 28, 35.

46 Terkel, *Working*, xlvi.

47 For media discussions of the blue-collar blues and the 1970 report, see "The Blue Collar Blues," *Newsweek*, 13 July 1970, 34–35; "Black and Blue," *New Republic*, 18 July 1970, 9; "Why They Listen to George Wallace—Those Blue Collar Worker Blues," *New Republic*, 23 September 1972, 16–21; and "Life on the Assembly Line—Why Auto Workers Complain," *U.S. News and World Report*, 8 May 1972, 82–84. See also *Work in America: Report of a Special Task Force to the Secretary of Health, Education, and Welfare*, 29–38; Sheppard and Herrick, *Where Have All the Robots Gone?* 17–39; and Strauss, "Is There a Blue-Collar Revolt against Work?" 40–70.

48 On the famous May 1970 clash between hard hats and peace protesters in New York City, see Freeman, "Hardhats."

49 Labor leaders publicly condemned the war, prominent unions adopted platforms calling for the withdrawal of U.S. troops, and workers launched their own antiwar organizations. On the changing position of the labor movement vis-à-vis the Vietnam War, see Jeffrey-Jones, *Peace Now*, 178–221.

50 Quotes from Terkel, *Working*, 189.

51 Ibid., xxxi–viii.

52 Hamper, *Rivethead*, 5.

53 Ibid., 98.

54 "General Motors and the UAW," Folder: QWL Meeting, Harvard, January 1982, What Is Quality of Work Life? CWAC.

55 Reich, *Greening of America*, 260.

56 On the challenges confronting big business during this period, see Vogel, *Fluctuating Fortunes*, 59–92, 113–47. For the mobilization of big business in the face of these new challenges, see ibid., 148–92; and Himmelstein, *To the Right*, 129–64.

57 Here I do not attempt to assess the merits of quality of work life (QWL) programs, although secondary literature suggests that the successes of such programs have been limited at best. For an overview of early QWL programs, see Katzell, Bienstock, and Faerstein, *A Guide to Worker Productivity Experiments*. For a critique of QWL programs in the automobile industry, see Parker, "Industrial Myths and Shop-Floor Reality." For a slightly less skeptical account of QWL programs in the auto industry that nonetheless concludes that they have failed to live up to their rhetoric, see Milkman, *Farewell to the Factory*.

58 On industrial workplace reforms in the 1920s, see L. Cohen, *Making a New Deal*, 161–73.

59 On Elton Mayo, see Lichtenstein, *State of the Union*, 242.

60 On the history of this counteroffensive in the 1970s, see Vogel, *Fluctuating Fortunes*, 193–239. On the formation of the Business Roundtable specifically, see ibid., 154; and Useem, *Inner Circle*, 160–63.

61 Box 9, File 8: Bethlehem Steel Corporation (appeared in *Time*, 6 May 1974), CAC 1974, JWTA.

62 On producerism and the figure of the artisan, see Lears, *No Place of Grace*, 60–96.

63 "General Motors and the UAW," Folder: QWL Meeting, Harvard, January 1982, What Is Quality of Work Life? CWAC.

64 *Work in America: Report of a Special Task Force to the Secretary of Health, Education, and Welfare*, 12. On self-realization, see Maslow, *Toward a Psychology of Being*. For references to Maslow's hierarchy of needs in QWL literature, see "The New Industrial Relations," *Business Week*, 11 May 1981, 85–91; Davis, Cherns, and Associates, *Quality of Working Life*, vol. 1, 101, 125, 138, 306; Davis, Cherns, and Associates, *Quality of Working Life*, vol. 2, 316; and O'Toole, *Work and the Quality of Life*, 63. On the impact of humanistic psychology and Maslow on changing conceptions of masculinity, see Ehrenreich, *Hearts of Men*, 88–98.

65 *Work in America: Report of a Special Task Force to the Secretary of Health, Education, and Welfare*, 51.

66 For the adoption of this slogan, see Mitchell Fein, "Improshare: An Alternative to Traditional Managing," Box 56, Folder 2, UAWRDC, Part II.

67 Report from Don Edward Beck, Folder: QWL General Correspondence 1981, What Is Quality of Work Life? CWAC.

68 Kerr and Rosow, *Work in America*, 181–83.

69 On quality circles, see Davis and Trist, "Improving the Quality of Work Life: Sociotechnical Case Studies," in James O'Toole, ed., *Work and the Quality of Life* (Cambridge: MIT Press, 1974), 246–80.

70 "The Heresy of Worker Participation," *Psychology Today*, February 1977, 111.

71 Box 9, File 16: U.S. Steel Corporation (published in *Business Week*, 12 January 1974), CAC 1974, JWTA.

72 Statement by Daniel C. Burnham, director-officer of Westinghouse Electric Corporation, Hearings before the House Banking, Currency, and Housing Committee, Economic Stabilization Subcommittee, 25 April 1975, Box 85, Folder: National Commission on Productivity and Work Quality, 12/74–10/75, GRFL, L. William Seidman Collection.

73 Northwestern Bell—CWA Statement on Principles, Folder: General Correspondence 1981, What Is Quality of Work Life? CWAC.

74 My italics. "General Motors and the UAW," Folder: QWL Meeting, Harvard, January 1982, What Is Quality of Work Life? CWAC.

75 Ibid., 3.

76 Irving Bluestone, the UAW's director of the GM department, had first proposed the idea of a union-management committee on job enrichment in 1970, but GM rejected the proposal. During that year, negotiations between the UAW and GM had broken down, which led to a strike that lasted for over two months, and many within both the company and the union still viewed the notion of a collaborative program with suspicion.

77 "Japan's Drive to Outstrip U.S.," *U.S. News and World Report*, 6 April 1970, 26–28.

78 "What Foreign Firms Are Doing to Fight Blue Collar Blues," *U.S. News and World Report*, 23 July 1973, 76–78.

79 "Japanese Labor's Silken Tranquility," *Newsweek*, 5 October 1970, 81–82.

80 "Made in Japan," *Reader's Digest*, February 1968, 163–66.

81 "Pioneering a Non-Western Psychology," *Science News*, 11 March 1978, 154–58.

82 "Japanese Labor's Silken Tranquility."

83 On producerism and the figure of the artisan, see Lears, *No Place of Grace*, 60–96.

84 Box 23, File 7: GM Corporation, CAC 1973, JWTA. The fact that the advertisement features an African American worker is also significant in that it affirms GM's commitment to affirmative action programs and to the inclusion of African Americans in the skilled trades, from which they were historically excluded. On this exclusion, see Sugrue, *Origins of the Urban Crisis*, 91–123.

85 For public responses to the term "productivity," see "Developmental Research—Advertising Council 'Productivity' Project Consumer Workshop Sessions," 14 September 1972, Box 7, File: Productivity Project, 1972–73, ACC, HC; "Public Attitudes toward Productivity," Box 1, File: Leonard Woodcock, National Commission on Productivity, UAWRDC, Part II; and "Worker Attitudes Relating to Productivity," Box 31, File: General Correspondence 1975, GRFL, Alan Greenspan Files.

86 Strategy paper by McCann Erickson Advertising Agency for the National Commission on Productivity, 4 January 1973, Washington Office Subject File, Series 13/2/305, Box 24, File: Productivity Campaign, ACC, UIUC.

87 Ibid., 4.

88 Ibid., 8.

89 Ibid., 7.

90 Ibid., 9.

91 Ibid.

92 Ibid.

93 On economic nationalism and "buy American" campaigns in the 1970s and 1980s, see D. Frank, *Buy American*, 131–86.

94 "General Motors and the UAW," Folder: QWL Meeting, Harvard, January 1982, What Is Quality of Work Life? CWAC.

95 Ibid., 6.

96 Ibid., 8.

97 Ibid., 14.

98 O'Toole, *Work and the Quality of Life*, 276.

99 Box 1, Folder: "See Here," October 1971, Wayne State University Archives of Labor and Urban Affairs, Detroit, UAW Local 1112 Collection.

100 "See Here," December 1971, Box 1, File: "See Here" 1971, Wayne State University Archives of Labor and Urban Affairs, Detroit, UAW Local 1112 Collection.

101 For a similar argument about the strategies adopted by blue-collar workers at the Singer Factory in Elizabeth, New Jersey, in the late 1970s and 1980s, see Newman, *Falling from Grace*, 174–201.

102 See Marchand, *Creating the Corporate Soul*.

103 Terkel, *Working*, xxxii.

104 Ibid.

105 Ibid., xxxviii.

106 On deindustrialization, see Bluestone and Harrison, *Deindustrialization of America*. On the auto industry, see Rothschild, *Paradise Lost*. On the decline of the steel industry, see Stein, *Running Steel, Running America*, 229–307; Bensam and Lynch, *Rusted Dreams*; and Hoerr, *And the Wolf Finally Came*.

107 Solicitation Letter from Karen De Crow, president of NOW, undated, Box 13, File 2, "Now 1970–75," Wayne State University Archives of Labor and Urban Affairs, Detroit, U.S. Women's Department: Dorothy Haener Collection.

108 See, for example, Kamarovsky, *The Unemployed Man and His Family*.

109 "Unemployment Hurts More Than Just the Pocketbook," *Today's Health*, March 1976, 23–26.

110 Ibid., 25.

111 See "Unemployment Becomes an Explosive Issue," *Business Week*, 9 November 1974, 154–60; "Falling Apart," *Progressive*, February 1976, 38–40; "The Hidden Psychological Costs of Unemployment," *Intellect*, April 1978, 389–90; Remarks of UAW Vice President Mark Stepp, "Public Hearing on Plant Closings," Philadelphia, 16 February 1980, Box 34, Folder: Plant Closings 1975–80, UAWRDC, Part II; "Overview of Plant Closings and Industrial Migration Issues in the United States," Box 34, Folder: Plant Closings, 1975–80, UAWRDC, Part II; and Memo to UAW International Executive Board on the Consequences of Job Loss, Box 49, Folder: Plant Closings, 1979, UAWRDC, Part II.

112 See "The Hidden Psychological Costs of Unemployment," *Intellect*, April 1978, 389–90.

113 On the perils of using the concept of "crisis" in gender history, see Bederman, *Manliness and Civilization*, 1–44.

114 *UAW Solidarity Newsletter*, 15 August 1980, cover.

115 "Worker Unrest: Not Dead, but Playing Possum," *Business Week*, 10 May 1976, 133.

116 Ibid. For the revival of the work ethic after mid-decade, see also "What's Happening to Social Values?" Box 39, File: Sonia Yuspeh, 1975–77, Writings and Speeches Collection, JWTA.

Chapter Four

1 Moynihan, "The American Experiment," 7.

2 A. Herman, *Idea of Decline in Western History*, 13.

3 Gerstle, *American Crucible*, 9–10.

4 Ibid., 341.

5 ARBA, *Bicentennial of the United States of America: Final Report*, vol. 1, 4. Also quoted in Bodnar, *Remaking America*, 228.

6 On the impact of these social movements on traditional approaches to American history, see Wallace, *Mickey Mouse History*, vii–32. Wallace argues that the late 1960s and the 1970s saw the explosion of grassroots museums and a renewed interest in local history.

7 On black and Chicano nationalisms, see, for example, Student Nonviolent Coordinating Committee, "The Basis of Black Power"; Neal, "Black Art and Black

Liberation"; and First Chicano Nationalism Conference, "El Plan de Aztlán." For a useful discussion of the centrality of history to the Chicano movement in particular, see Alarcón, "The Aztec Palimpsest."

8 Indeed, the 1970s has been described as the decade of white ethnic revivalism. For what has been described as the definitive statement from this revival, see Novak, *Rise of the Unmeltable Ethnics*. On the impact of the new ethnicity on race and class politics, see Steinberg, *Ethnic Myth*. On the motivations and psychology of the revival, see Stein and Hill, *Ethnic Imperative*; and Waters, *Ethnic Options*. For the role of the revival in the larger history of whiteness, see Jacobson, *Whiteness of a Different Color*, 274–80. For its role in the history of race in the United States in the twentieth century, see Gerstle, *American Crucible*, 311–42. On the relationship between white ethnicity and the rise of identity politics, see di Leonardo, "White Ethnicities, Identity Politics, and Baby Bear's Chairs."

9 President Ford received numerous letters from white ethnic leaders demanding Bicentennial recognition for revolutionary heroes. See, for example, Letter from Countess Kovats to Hedley Donovan, 16 July 1976, Box 3, File: Hungarian Ethnic Groups, GRFL, Myron Kuropas Files; Letter from Samuel Rezneck to Milton Mitler, 26 September 1975, Box 20, File: Haym Solomon Recognition, GRFL, Milt Mitler Files; Letter from Harry Sussman to President Ford, 6 September 1975, Box 20, File: Haym Solomon Recognition, GRFL, Milt Mitler Files; and Ukranian National Bicentennial Committee, "Ukrainians in America," Box 6, File: Ukrainian Ethnic Groups, GRFL, Myron Kuropas Files.

10 On the troubled history of the ARBC, see Anthony E. Neville, "Bicentennial Blues," *Harper's Weekly*, July 1972, 32–37. For charges of commercialism, see Jesse Lemisch, "Bicentennial Schlock," *New Republic*, 6 November 1976, 21–23; William Randel, "The Fife and Drum of Big Business," *Nation*, 22 January 1973, 108–10; "Bucks from the Bicentennial," *Time*, 29 September 1975; "The Buycentennial," *Newsweek*, 22 April 1974, 119; and Russell Slocum, "Buycentennial," *New York Times Magazine*, 4 January 1976, 55.

11 My discussion of nationalism here takes its cues from Benedict Anderson's classic *Imagined Communities*. Anderson argues that the nation is "always conceived as a deep, horizontal comradeship" (7) and as "a community moving steadily down (or up) history" (26). The discussion that follows argues that planners seized on the Bicentennial to reaffirm precisely those ties and affiliations that modern nationalism had sought to undermine if not displace.

12 See, for example, Philip Slomovitz, "Nation's Big Birthday Party Emphasizes 'Pluralistic Society,' Rejects Wasp Inference," 29 December 1972, RG 452, Festival, Box 340, Proposal: Folk General, NARA II; "The Bicentennial Theme: Unity with Diversity," RG 452, Series 93, Box 312, Folder: Unity with Diversity (Heritage Theme), NARA II; Memo from Jim Cannon on Bicentennial Themes, June 1976, Box 5, Folder: Bicentennial, 1–16 June 1976, GRFL, James M. Cannon Papers; and Memo from Robert Goldwin on Bicentennial themes, 22 July 1975, Box 65, File: Bicentennial General 6/75–8/75, GRFL, John O. Marsh Files.

13 On the decentralization of the Bicentennial, see Kammen, *Mystic Chords of Memory*, 572; and Bodnar, *Remaking America*, 232–33. See also Capozzola, "It Makes You Want to Believe in the Country."

14 On the Philadelphia plan, see "Spirit of '76," *Newsweek*, 29 September 1969, 79; and "Great Scott, It's Philadelphia!," *Newsweek*, 3 August 1970, 22–23.

15 On the New York World's Fair, see Rydell, Fielding, and Pell, *Fair America*, 105–12.

16 For the position of the People's Bicentennial Commission, see People's Bicentennial Commission, *Voices of the American Revolution*; and People's Bicentennial Commission, *Common Sense II*. Because it was targeting ARBA for the prominent corporate role played throughout the Bicentennial, the commission received scathing criticism in the business press. See, for example, "A Destructive Spirit toward '76," *Nation's Business*, July 1974, 65–68. For an illuminating interview with Jeremy Rifkin, see "Growing Controversy over the Bicentennial: Two Views," *U.S. News and World Report*, 24 March 1975, 35–37.

17 This marked the official beginning of Bicentennial activities, and the demonstration made an impression on federal planners. ARBA's final report later recalled how the protesters had shouted "down with King Richard" and dumped empty oil barrels into Boston Harbor. See ARBA, *Bicentennial of the United States of America: Final Report*, 106–7.

18 Rydell, Fielding, and Pell, *Fair America*, 105–12.

19 ARBA, *Bicentennial of the United States of America: Final Report*, 88. Instead of spending substantial amounts of federal money on a major exposition, each state would be given a flat grant of $40,000 by ARBA, and any additional federal money would need to be matched by state, local, and private sources.

20 These characterizations became very common in news coverage of the Bicentennial after 1974. They also appear in ARBA, *Bicentennial of the United States of America: Final Report*, 9, 23, 34.

21 "A Gala Bicentennial Despite Washington Snafus," *U.S. News and World Report*, 21 October 1974, 52–53.

22 Ibid., 1.

23 "As More Cities Catch the Bicentennial Spirit," *U.S. News and World Report*, 17 December 1973, 60–63.

24 "A Constructive Spirit toward '76," *Nation's Business*, July 1974, 61–63.

25 The term "cultural pluralism" was first coined by Horace Kallen in the 1920s. See Kallen, *Culture and Democracy in the United States*. For some useful discussions of both Kallen and the concept of cultural pluralism, see Walzer, "What Does It Mean to Be an 'American'?"; and Hollinger, *Postethnic America*, 79–104. This chapter proceeds from the premise that cultural pluralism is a precursor to what would later come to be called multiculturalism.

26 See Hollinger, *Postethnic America*, 98–99.

27 See Letter from Richard Kern to Ohio representative Charles Brown, 15 December 1974, RG 452, Native American Programs, Box 289, Folder: Congressional Inquiries Regarding Indian Participation, NARA II.

28 Quote from "Indians Divided on the Bicentennial," *New York Times*, 8 Decem-

ber 1975, no page number, Box 36, Folder: Bicentennial-General (7), GRFL, Stephen G. McConahey Files.

29　ARBA, *Bicentennial of the United States of America: Final Report*, 130.

30　Letter from Charles Cohn, vice president, Northeast Philadelphia Branch, NAACP, to John Warner, 20 January 1976, RG 452, Ethnic Racial Programming, Box 266, Folder: General Correspondence, 1976, NARA II.

31　For the debate over black participation in the Bicentennial, see "What Can Blacks Celebrate during the Bicentennial Year?" *Negro History Bulletin*, January 1976, 500–501; "The Bicentennial and the Black Revolution," *Negro History Bulletin*, January 1976, 495–99; "Should Blacks Celebrate the Bicentennial?" *Ebony*, August 1975, 35–42; Address by Vernon E. Jordan, executive director of National Urban League, at National Conference on Social Welfare, 14 June 1976, Washington, D.C., RG 452, Ethnic Racial Programming, Box 266, Folder: General Correspondence, 1976, NARA II; and "Congressional Black Caucus Statement in Review of American Revolution Bicentennial Commission," 22 August 1972, RG 452, Entry 2, Box 35, Folder: Minority Groups, NARA II.

32　Memo from program officer Samuel H. Johnson to R. Lynn Carroll, deputy executive director of Awareness Program for Black Opinion Makers, May 1971, RG 452, Entry 2, Box 35, Folder: Minority Groups, NARA II.

33　See "Ethnic/Racial Recognition a Bicentennial Hallmark," *Bicentennial Times*, vol. 3, July 1976, 14, Box 64, File: ARBA Bicentennial Times, GRFL, John O. Marsh Files.

34　See BERC Conference Report, June 1974, 1, RG 452, Entries 74–80, Box 270, Folder: Ethnic-Racial Coalition Meeting, 27–28 June 1974, NARA II.

35　ARBA, *Bicentennial of the United States of America: Final Report*, 131.

36　These discussions were ubiquitous throughout planners' writings. See, for example, ARBA, *Bicentennial of the United States of America: Final Report*, 128–31; and Marzio, *A Nation of Nations*, xiii, xv.

37　As the report from the June 1974 BERC gathering explained, the term "minority" was no longer relevant since "ethnic and racial groups taken together make up a majority of the American population." See BERC Conference Report, June 1974, 10, RG 452, Entries 74–80, Box 270, Folder: Ethnic-Racial Coalition Meeting, 27–28 June 1974, NARA II. See p. 28 of the minutes of the second meeting of ARBA Advisory Council, 7 April 1975, Tucson, Arizona, Box 4, File: ARBA Advisory Council, GRFL, Milt Mitler Files.

38　See p. 22 of the minutes of the second meeting of the ARBA Council, 7 April 1975, Tucson, Arizona, Box 4, File: ARBA Advisory Council, GRFL, Milt Mitler Files. For more on Baroni's politics, see Wenk, Tomasi, and Baroni, *Pieces of a Dream*.

39　See "Innovation and Diversity in American Culture," RG 452, Series 7480, Box 276, Folder: Walker A. Williams and Company, NARA II; National Education Association, *NEA Bicentennial Handbook: A Source for Helping Teachers Participate in the Celebration of Our Nation's 200th Anniversary*, Box 2, Folder: Bicentennial—Federal Departments (2), GRFL, John Stiles and Merrill Mueller Files.

40 "The Bicentennial Blues," *Ebony*, June 1976, 152–53.

41 Smith, *Civic Ideals*, 490.

42 See "Your Own American Experience," News from the Office of Public Affairs, Smithsonian Institution, Box 7, File: Kin and Communities 6/14–16/76, GRFL, Myron Kuropas Files. See also Margaret Mead, "Celebrating the Bicentennial—Family Style," *Redbook*, April 1975, 31–37.

43 Examples of these letters from individuals to ARBA can be found in RG 452, Heritage Project, Box 320, Folder: Genealogical Studies, NARA II.

44 See April Fehr and Carolyn Sadler, Draft Information Release, June 1977, "Kin and Communities: The Peopling of America," prepared for the Office of Smithsonian Symposia and Seminars, National Museum of History and Technology, Department of Cultural History, Box 9, Folder: Kin and Community, 1974–77, SIA.

45 See p. 2 of Memorandum from Wilton S. Dillon to Charles Blitzer, 15 April 1974, Program Planning and Reviewing, Office of Smithsonian Symposia and Seminars File, RU 496, Box 1, Folder: Kinship and Communities Book, SIA.

46 "Climbing Family Trees," *Newsweek*, 13 September 1976, 84–85.

47 "White Roots: Looking for Great Grandpa," *Time*, 28 March 1977, 43–44.

48 Haley, *Roots*. On the connection between the renewed interest in family genealogy in the 1970s and its connection to the *Roots* phenomenon, see Kammen, *Mystic Chords of Memory*, 642.

49 See, for example, Alex Haley, "My Furthest Back Person—'The African,'" *New York Times Magazine*, 16 July 1972, 13–16; and "One Man's Family," *Newsweek*, 21 June 1976, 73. To get a sense of the impact of *Roots* on planners at the Smithsonian Institution, see Office of Smithsonian Symposia and Seminars File, RU 500, Box 8, File: Alex Haley, SIA.

50 "What Roots Means to Me," *Reader's Digest*, May 1977, 74.

51 "Haley's Prescription: Talk, Write, Reunite," *Time*, 14 February 1977, 72.

52 On the centrality of reenactments throughout the Bicentennial celebration, see Lowenthal, *The Past Is a Foreign Country*, 295–301. Lowenthal writes: "Scarcely a skirmish of the Revolution went unrepeated during the 1976 Bicentennial celebrations," 295.

53 On women's roles in nonimportation campaigns, see Kerber, *Women of the Republic*, 35–67; and Kerber, *Toward an Intellectual History of Women*, 63–99.

54 See, for example, Topper, *Bicentennial Cookbook*.

55 "The New Jersey Heritage Cookbook," produced for the Bicentennial by Public Service Electric and Gas Company, Box, 1970s-1, File: 1970s Utility Company, Nicole Di Bona Peterson Collection of Advertising Cookbooks, HC. It advised: "Every time you conveniently preheat your oven to 375 degrees and later remove a uniformly golden brown loaf of bread, remember the women who day in and day out tended brick ovens bigger than they were!"

56 Whether or not the colonial period constituted a "golden age" for women has been a long-standing debate within the field of women's history. For some early statements that support this hypothesis, see Lerner, "The Lady and the Mill Girl," 5–15; Ryan, *Womanhood in America*; and E. Zaretsky, *Capitalism, the*

Family, and Personal Life. For challenges to this "golden age" thesis, see Norton, "The Myth of the Golden Age"; Norton, *Liberty's Daughters*; and Ulrich, *Good Wives*.

57 See Kelly, "Did Women Have a Renaissance?"

58 See "Mrs. Ford Helps 'Remember the Ladies' of the Revolutionary Era," *New York Times*, 30 June 1976, page numbers unavailable. Clipping from Box 2, Folder: Ribbon Cutting, "Remember the Ladies" Exhibit, Plymouth, Mass., 29 June 1976, GRFL, Frances Pullen Files.

59 The butter-churning suggestion comes from Lund and Foster, *Illinois Teacher's Bicentennial Resource Guide*, 14; "colonial night" is from NEA, *NEA Bicentennial Handbook*, Box 2, Folder: Bicentennial—Federal Departments (2), GRFL, John Stiles and Merrill Mueller Files.

60 For an overview of this history of dependency, see Fraser and Gordon, "A Genealogy of 'Dependency.'"

61 Central Upper Peninsula Finnish American Bicentennial, "Do You Remember When," Box 2, File: Finnish Ethnic Groups, GRFL, Myron Kuropas Files.

62 Gambino, *Blood of My Blood*, 14.

63 Novak, *Rise of the Unmeltable Ethnics*, 280.

64 I make this claim not only because of the size and ambition of the exhibit, but because the design firm commissioned for it, Chermayeff and Geismar Associates, had worked on the U.S. pavilions of the 1967 Montreal Expo and the 1970 Osaka Expo. The "exposition-like" quality of "A Nation of Nations" was something that was noted (not always favorably) by curators at the Smithsonian Institution at the time.

65 See "A Nation of Nations," 1359–79, Box 22, Folder: A Nation of Nations, Preliminary Outline, SIA, C. Malcolm Watkins Papers.

66 See p. 16 of memorandum from Peter C. Marzio to All Authors of the Nation of Nations Book, 25 September 1974, A Nation of Nations, 1973–78, Box 21, Folder: A Nation of Nations Book Notes, Outlines and Memos, SIA, C. Malcolm Watkins Papers.

67 Marzio, *A Nation of Nations*, 479, 493, 497.

68 In addition, at the most elemental level, the re-creation of this domestic scene in "A Nation of Nations" demonstrated the growing influence of social history and "the history of everyday life" on museum programming during this period. As one Smithsonian curator argued, "The commemorative exhibit reflected the Institution's larger shift away from military and technological history and toward social and cultural history in the early 1970s." See Hughes, "The Unstifled Muse."

69 Gordon Wood, "The Losable Past," *New Republic*, 7 November 1994, 48–49. Wood's formulation is discussed in Gerstle, *American Crucible*, 349.

70 See p. 8 of the proposal "Nation of Nations: An Exhibition of the American People at the Smithsonian Institution," National Museum of History and Technology for the American Bicentennial Year, prepared by Nathan Glazer with Chermayeff and Geismar Associates, January 1973, Box 22, Folder: "A Nation of Nations-Preliminary Outline," SIA, C. Malcolm Watkins Papers.

71 See p. 5 of Letter from C. Malcolm Watkins to Mr. Skramstad, "Comments on Nation of Nations," 5 February 1973, National Museum of History and Technology, Department of Cultural History, Records 1954–79, Box 7, File: Exhibits: Nation of Nations, Bicentennial, 1969–73, SIA.

72 Ibid.

73 Ibid., 7.

74 See p. 1 of Summary (Preliminary Script) for Part II of First Unit, "A Nation of Nations," National Museum of History and Technology, Subject File, Box 7, Folder: Exhibits, A Nation of Nations, Bicentennial, 1974–78, SIA. On the relationship between domesticity and the museum, see West, *Domesticating History*.

75 Novak, *Rise of the Unmeltable Ethnics*, 209–10.

76 On this process of appropriation, see Gerstle, *American Crucible*, 311–42; and di Leonardo, "White Ethnicities, Identity Politics, and Baby Bear's Chairs."

77 Gerstle, *American Crucible*, 330.

78 See pp. 76 and 77 of "President Ford Meets with Italian American Leadership," 5 August 1976, Box 4, File: Italian Ethnic Groups No. 1, GRFL, Myron Kuropas Files.

79 This was part of a parallel interest in social, cultural, and local history during the same period. In 1966, the Smithsonian Institution held its first folk festival and it became an annual event. In the early 1970s, the Library of Congress developed plans for an American Folklife Center that opened in 1976. On Smithsonian efforts to incorporate folk culture into its permanent programs, see Letter from Richard E. Ahlborn to Jewell Dulaney, "Permanent Programs in Folk Culture Studies," 12 April 1976, National Museum of History and Technology, Department of Cultural History, Records 1954–79 and Undated, Box 6, Folder: Committees, Folk Art Committee, 1969–78, SIA. On the broadening interest in folklife during this period, see Kammen, *Mystic Chords of Memory*, 616–17.

80 See p. I-1 of a report of a feasibility study prepared by the ARBC, an American Folklore Performing Company, Smithsonian, Washington, D.C., Division of Performing Arts, RG 452, Festival, Box 339, Folder: Working Contract: Multiethnic, NARA II.

81 ARBA, *Bicentennial of the United States of America: Final Report*, 146.

82 On the corporate sponsorship of folklife celebrations, see Bodnar, *Remaking America*, 233.

83 See p. 11 of "An American Multi-Ethnic Folklore Company: A Feasibility Study for the ARBC," RG 452, Festival, Box 339, Folder: Working Contract Multiethnic, NARA II.

84 See p. II-5 of a report of a feasibility study prepared by the ARBC, an American Folklore Performing Company, Smithsonian, Washington, D.C., Division of Performing Arts, RG 452, Festival, Box 339, Folder: Working Contract: Multiethnic, NARA II.

85 Ibid., I-1.

86 See p. 1 of "The Festival Experience," from Ruth Jordan to Bill Butler, 29 May 1975, RG 452, Festival, Box 347, File: Smithsonian Institution, NARA II.

87 Wexler, *Tender Violence*, 21.

88 Celebrations of folk culture throughout the Bicentennial did not focus exclusively on race, since folk traditions were defined along many other axes of identity, including ethnicity, region, religion, nation, and work. Nor were commemorative tributes to African Americans and Native Americans confined to the folk festival, since diversity programming was reflected in all three of ARBA's thematic areas. But the Bicentennial did establish an affinity between race and folk.

89 This was the definition of folk culture provided by folklorist Alan Lomax at the closing concert of the Festival of American Folklife, in 1968, and was quoted throughout Bicentennial literature. See p. II-4 of a report of a feasibility study prepared by the ARBC, an American Folklore Performing Company, Smithsonian, Washington, D.C., Division of Performing Arts, RG 452, Festival, Box 339, Folder: Working Contract: Multiethnic, NARA II. The description of the living museum comes from p. 2 of "The Festival Experience," from Ruth Jordan to Bill Butler, 29 May 1975, RG 452, Festival, Box 347, File: Smithsonian Institution, NARA II.

90 In this sense, the Bicentennial, regardless of its decentralized form and the altered political landscape in which it took place, was part of a long history of world's fairs and international expositions that, as many scholars have shown, located racial "others" in a premodern idealized past. See Rydell, *All the World's a Fair*; and Gilroy, *Black Atlantic*.

91 "Indian Village," 1976, ARBA, RG 452, Motion Picture, Sound, and Video Recordings, NARA II.

92 See "Festival of American Folklife: Bicentennial Contributions," RG 452, Festival, Box 339, Folder: Festival of American Folklife, NARA II.

93 See "The Big Birthday Party," *U.S. News and World Report*, 5 July 1976, 31–32; and "It Was Quite a Birthday Party," *U.S. News and World Report*, 12 July 1976, 12.

94 See Sanders, *Peddlers of Crisis*; and Yergin, "The Arms Zealots."

95 "Introduction to 'A Third Century,'" *Foreign Policy* (Fall 1975): 97.

96 Kissinger, *White House Years*, 55–56.

97 Warnke and Gelb, "Security or Confrontation?"

98 Holbrooke, "A Sense of Drift, a Time for Calm," 107–8.

99 Ibid., 173–75.

100 "Kissinger on Oil, Food and Trade," *Business Week*, 13 January 1975, 69.

101 "The Real Paul Warnke," *New Republic*, 26 March 1977, 22.

102 The term "enlightened self-interest" comes from Peschek, *Policy-Planning Organizations*, 120.

103 Ibid., 95.

104 Ibid., 87.

105 On the early careers of Donald Rumsfeld and Richard Cheney and their roles in the movement against détente, see Mann, *Rise of the Vulcans*.

106 Podhoretz, *Present Danger*, 30.

107 "America Now: A Failure of Nerve?" *Commentary*, July 1975, 29.

108 "Peace with Freedom: A Discussion by the Committee on the Present Danger before the Foreign Policy Association," 14 March 1978. Transcript reprinted in Tyroler, *Alerting America*, 29.

109 For these descriptions of appeasement, see Walter Laqueur, "The Psychology of Appeasement," *Commentary*, October 1978, 44–50; and Podhoretz, *Present Danger*, 77. The term "moral flaccidity" comes from Theodore Draper, "Appeasement and Détente," *Commentary*, February 1976, 35.

110 Quoted in Sanders, *Peddlers of Crisis*, 162.

111 "'Common Sense and the Common Danger': Policy Statement of the Committee on the Present Danger," reprinted in Tyroler, *Alerting America*, 3–5. On the history of the Committee on the Present Danger, see Sanders, *Peddlers of Crisis*.

112 "America Now? A Failure of Nerve," *Commentary*, July 1975, 16.

113 Podhoretz, *Present Danger*, 49.

114 Robert Tucker, "Oil: The Issue of American Intervention," *Commentary*, January 1975, 27.

115 Eugene Rostow, "America, Europe, and the Middle East," *Commentary*, February 1974, 41.

116 Norman Podhoretz, "The Culture of Appeasement," *Harper's*, October 1977, 31.

117 Ibid.

Chapter Five

1 Sidney Lumet, director, *Network*, 1976.

2 See Engel, "Femininity as Tragedy." Engel argues that Freud's concept of narcissism was premised on a distinctly masculine model of healthy psychosexual development. In fact, according to *Diagnostic and Statistical Manual of Mental Disorders*, the diagnosis of narcissism is typically higher among male patients. See pp. 658–61.

3 Freud, "On Narcissism." For useful secondary interpretations of Freud's essay, see Engel, "Femininity as Tragedy"; and Buhle, *Feminism and Its Discontents*, 63–65.

4 On this postwar shift in symptomatology, see Lasch, *Culture of Narcissism*, 41–42; and Hendin, *Age of Sensation*. Both books are discussed below.

5 See Kernberg, *Borderline Conditions and Pathological Narcissism*, 234.

6 See *Diagnostic and Statistical Manual of Mental Disorders*, 658–61; and Kernberg, *Borderline Conditions and Pathological Narcissism*, 228, 233.

7 E. Zaretsky, "Charisma or Rationalization?"

8 See Love and Feldman, "The Disguised Cry for Help."

9 See Wylie, *Generation of Vipers*, 184–205. For the centrality of Wylie to postwar discourses of white maternal failure, see Buhle, *Feminism and Its Discontents*, 125–64; and Feldstein, *Motherhood in Black and White*, 40–61.

10 On the difference between primary and secondary narcissism, see Freud, "On Narcissism"; and Levin, "Clinical Stories: A Modern Self in the Fury of Being."

11 Kernberg, *Borderline Conditions and Pathological Narcissism*, 235, 276.

12 Hendin, *Age of Sensation*, xiv, 6, 11.

13 Ibid., 44–49, 98, 108–9, 310–16.

14 Ibid., 316.

15 This resonated with earlier efforts to use organic metaphors to describe national health and affliction. The most obvious example is degeneration, which was linked to national and physical health at the end of the nineteenth century. On degeneration, see Chamberlin and Gilman, *Degeneration*; and Pick, *Faces of Degeneration*.

16 On the impact of psychology on American political culture in the twentieth century, see E. Herman, *Romance of American Psychology*.

17 The claim that the 1970s were typified by a sense of political retreat and a turn to purely "personal" preoccupations runs throughout the historical treatments of the period. See, for example, Frum, *How We Got Here*; and Schulman, *The Seventies*.

18 On New Journalism and Wolfe's central role within this movement, see Watson, *Modern Mind*, 598.

19 Tom Wolfe, "The 'Me' Decade and the Third Great Awakening," *New York Magazine*, 23 August 1976, 36.

20 Ibid., 40.

21 See, for example, the definition of narcissism provided in *Diagnostic and Statistical Manual of Mental Disorders*.

22 Lasch argued against this fallacious equating of individualism and narcissism. For Lasch, narcissism is about the breakdown of individualism. See Lasch, *Culture of Narcissism*; and Lasch, *Minimal Self*.

23 Schur, *Awareness Trap*, 7, 43, 77, 94, 122, 159, 172, 183, 193. For an illuminating review of Schur that anticipates some of Lasch's later arguments, see Christopher Lasch, "The Narcissistic Society," *New York Review of Books*, 30 September 1976, 5–13.

24 Schur, *Awareness Trap*, 43. See Jacoby, *Social Amnesia*. As we saw in chapter 3, the concept of self-actualization is most often associated with the work of humanist psychologist Abraham H. Maslow. See Maslow, *Toward a Psychology of Being*.

25 Peter Marin, "The New Narcissism," *Harper's Magazine*, October 1975, 45–56.

26 Here I am playing on the infamous notion of "race suicide" put forth by Theodore Roosevelt at the turn of the twentieth century. On the ways in which anxieties about declining birthrates and feminism spurred fears of "race suicide" among the white upper-middle class during the 1890s and early 1900s, see Mintz and Kellogg, *Domestic Revolutions*, 108.

27 See, for example, Rich, *Of Woman Born*. On debates about motherhood within feminism, see Umansky, *Motherhood Reconceived*.

28 Jacoby, "The Politics of Narcissism."

29 Ibid.

30 Ibid., 191.

31 See "The Way We Live Now," *New York Times Book Review*, 14 January 1979, 1.

32 See p. 5 of Draft of "Salmagundi Response to Critics," Box 19, Folder 4, CLP. For Lasch's critique of Gail Sheehy's *Passages*, see Christopher Lasch, "Planned Obsolescence," *New York Review of Books*, 28 October 1976, 7, 10. Throughout his personal correspondence, Lasch routinely poked fun at what he called the standard "neo-feminist writers" and the explosion of "pop sociology" and "pop-psychology" reflected in works such as *Future Shock*. See, for example, Letter from Lasch to Jerry Graff, 19 May 1975, Box 4, Folder 1, CLP.

33 Letter from Lasch to Otto Kernberg, 30 October 1980, Box 16, Folder 43, CLP. For more on Lasch's biography, see Blake and Phelps, "History as Social Criticism"; Lasch, *True and Only Heaven*, 21–39; and Buhle, *Feminism and Its Discontents*, 280–317.

34 On Lasch's growing sense of alienation from the New Left see Lasch, *True and Only Heaven*, 25; and Letter from Lasch to Otto Kernberg, 30 October 1980, Box 16, Folder 43, CLP. On the role of theatricality and spectacle within the New Left, see Lasch, *Culture of Narcissism*, 86–87.

35 Letter from Lasch to Dante Germino, 9 June 1973, Box 3, File 12, CLP.

36 Letter from Lasch to Ashbel Green, 19 March 1975, Box 4, File 1, CLP.

37 Lasch, *Haven in a Heartless World*, 18.

38 Ibid., 36, 74, 146, 147, 156.

39 For feminist critiques of the ways in which Lasch's theory of narcissism was premised on a distinctly masculine model of psychosexual development, again see Engel, "Femininity as Tragedy"; and Buhle, *Feminism and Its Discontents*, 280–317.

40 See Letter from Lasch to Russell Jacoby, 8 January 1975, Box 4, Folder 1, CLP.

41 On Mitscherlich's influence on Lasch's thinking, see Letter from Lasch to David Davis, 15 February 1977, Box 4, File 11, CLP. On the concept of a "fatherless society," see Mitscherlich, *Society without the Father*. For an example of the Frankfurt School's later position on authoritarianism in the family (and the position that came to inform Lasch's own thinking on the subject), see Horkheimer, "Authoritarianism and the Family Today."

42 For an example of this argument, see Rogow, *Dying of the Light*, 47–79. Echoing Wylie, Rogow argues that the father's emotional absence in the family has led to the cultural decline of the superego.

43 Lasch, *Culture of Narcissism*, 178.

44 Lasch, *Haven in a Heartless World*, 123–24.

45 Lasch, *Culture of Narcissism*, 170–76.

46 Ibid., 33, 38.

47 Lasch, *Minimal Self*, 25.

48 Lasch, *Culture of Narcissism*, 198.

49 On the connection between narcissism and ahistoricism, see ibid., xvii, xviii, 5. Letter from Lasch to Jerry Graff, 14 October 1976, Box 4, File 6, CLP.

50 See Lasch, *Culture of Narcissism*, 49–50, 212–13. On Sheehy, see Christopher Lasch, "Planned Obsolescence," *New York Review of Books*, 28 October 1976, 7, 10.

51 For his analysis of the Moynihan Report, see Lasch, *Haven in a Heartless World*,

164–65; and Lasch, *Culture of Narcissism*, 67–68. On the relationship between the concepts of Momism and black matriarchy, see Feldstein, *Motherhood in Black and White*.

52 Letter from Lasch to Jeanette Hopkins, 26 February 1978, Box 18, File 31, CLP.

53 Lasch, *Culture of Narcissism*, 187–89.

54 Ibid., 187–88, 193–98.

55 Letter from Lasch to John Updike, 6 November 1972, Box 3, File 10, CLP.

56 Lasch, *Culture of Narcissism*, 211.

57 See, for example, Letter from Lasch to Cheryl Gould, 19 December 1977, Box 4, File 12, CLP.

58 See Blake and Phelps, "History as Social Criticism."

59 For reviews and discussions that characterize the book in this way, see "Narcissism in the 'Me' Decade," *New York Times*, 30 November 1977, C1, C5; "Bourgeois Values, No Bourgeoisie?" *Dissent*, Summer 1979, 308–14; "The Way We Live Now," *New York Times Book Review*, 14 January 1979, 1, 26–27; and "Gratification Now Is the Slogan of the 70s, Laments a Historian," *People*, 9 July 1979, 34–36. For Lasch's own response to this characterization, see his draft of "Salmagundi Response to Critics," Box 19, Folder 4, CLP.

60 Draft of "Salmagundi Response to Critics," Box 19, Folder 4, CLP.

61 See Letter from Lasch to Edward and Cheryl Gould, 3 August 1979, Box 5, File 5, CLP.

62 Letter from Lasch to Wini Breines, 4 August 1979, Box 5, File 3, CLP.

63 Draft of "Salmagundi Response to Critics," Box 19, Folder 4, CLP.

64 For feminist criticisms of Lasch, see Barrett and McIntosh, "Narcissism and the Family"; Breines, Cerullo, and Stacey, "Social Biology, Family Studies, and Antifeminist Backlash"; Engel, "Femininity as Tragedy"; and Vivian Gornick, "One Man's Narcissism . . . May Be a Woman's Self-Emergence," *Savvy*, February 1980, 76–78.

65 Letter from Lasch to Jim Holloway, 20 February 1979, Box 5, File 2, CLP.

66 Letter from Lasch to Edward and Cheryl Gould, 3 August 1979, Box 5, File 5, CLP.

67 Letter from Lasch to Edward and Cheryl Gould, 19 December 1977, Box 4, File 12, CLP.

68 Letter from Judith March Goldrich to Lasch, 17 March 1979, Box 5, File 5, CLP; Letter from John Parker to Lasch, undated, Box 19, File 24, CLP; Letter from Deanna Clark to Lasch, 5 August 1979, Box 19, Folder 23, CLP.

69 Letter from Billy Harman to Lasch, 6 January 1979, Box 19, File 23, CLP; and Letter from Marco Ermacora to Lasch, 16 July 1979, Box 19, File 23, CLP.

70 See, for example, Lasch's *True and Only Heaven*.

71 Letter from Lasch to Peter Staple, 10 October 1976, Box 4, File 10, CLP; Letter from Lasch to Johnny Holdren, 29 January 1979, Box 5, File 6, CLP; Letter from Lasch to Jon Marcum, 7 December 1983, Box 19, Folder 24, CLP.

72 The story of President Jimmy Carter's appropriation of Lasch's ideas as he tried to salvage his presidency has received some attention from historians. See,

for example, Lears, "Reconsidering Abundance: A Plea for Ambiguity." Lears mentions that Lasch consorted openly with Carter in the weeks leading up to his "Crisis of Confidence" speech, but he doesn't explore the connection further. See also Horowitz, *Anxieties of Affluence*, 225–44.

73 This is the description offered by Daniel Bell. See Bell, Transcript of the White House Dinner, Box 20, Folder 6, CLP.

74 "Part I: Of Crisis and Opportunity," Patrick H. Caddell, 23 April 1979, Cambridge Survey Research, 3–13, Box 40, Folder: Memoranda: President Carter 1/10/79–4/23/79, Jody Powell, Press Office File, JCPL.

75 Ibid., 1, 16, 27, 36.

76 Ibid., 25.

77 On Caddell's role in the Carter White House, see Elizabeth Drew, "In Search of a Definition," *New Yorker*, 27 August 1979, 45–73. The exact date of the dinner was confirmed to me in a personal communication with Mary Ann McSweeney, an archivist at the Carter Library, dated 15 March 2001. The most exhaustive description of the dinner that I have been able to locate is the unpublished description written by Daniel Bell.

78 The reporters in attendance were Charles Peters (editor of *Washington Monthly*) and Haynes Johnson (a national affairs writer for *Washington Post*). The description of the dinner comes from the Daniel Bell transcript and a letter from Lasch to Mr. Nahmias, 2 February 1985, Box 20, Folder 6, CLP.

79 Patrick Caddell, Speech Outline, Draft 7/11/79, 2, Box 50, Folder 2, Crisis of Confidence Speech, Speechwriters Chronological File, JCPL.

80 See, for example, "Carter Speech Scores in a Midwest TV Poll," *New York Times*, 16 July 1979, 11. According to one account, Carter's speech initially improved his approval rating by as much as 11 percent. See Torricelli and Carroll, *In Our Own Words*, 337–38.

81 Office of the White House Press Secretary, "The White House: Remarks of the President in His Address to the Nation," 15 July 1979, Box 50, File 4, Crisis of Confidence Speech, Speechwriters Chronological File, JCPL.

82 See "Draft of the Foreword to the Trade Paperback Edition of *The Culture of Narcissism*," Box 19, File 1, CLP; Letter from Lasch to Doug Lowell, 29 August 1979, Box 5, File 8, CLP; and Letter from Lasch to Mr. Nahmias, 2 February 1985, Box 20, File 6, CLP.

83 See Lasch's eight-hundred-word statement to *Newsweek* magazine, unpublished, Box 20, File 20, CLP; and Letter from Lasch to Mr. Nahmias, 2 February 1985, Box 20, File 6, CLP.

Conclusion

1 See, for example, Gerstle, *American Crucible*.

2 See Lieven, *America Right or Wrong*.

3 Harvey, *Condition of Postmodernity*; Hobsbawm, *Age of Extremes*.

4 Smith, *Civic Ideals*.

5 McCormick, *America's Half Century*, 187.

6 Ibid.

7 Ibid. See also McAlister, *Epic Encounters*, 198–234.

8 On the hostage crisis, see Farber, *Taken Hostage*; and McAlister, *Epic Encounters*, 198–234.

9 "Carter's Foreign Policy: Paralysis at the Top," *Los Angeles Times*, 30 March 1980, 4:1.

10 "Carter Faces Iran with a Little Stick," *Los Angeles Times*, 5 April 1980, 1.

11 Farber, *Taken Hostage*, 171–76; Mann, *Rise of the Vulcans*, 89; McAlister, *Epic Encounters*, 212.

12 Even before the doomed attempt, polls showed that Americans who had rallied behind the president in the immediate wake of the embassy seizure were losing their patience with him. "Most Back Use of Force, Poll Says," *Los Angeles Times*, 20 April 1980, 16; "Thinking the Unthinkable," *Los Angeles Times*, 24 April 1980, 2:6.

13 "Presidential Fight Shaped by Iran Crisis," *Los Angeles Times*, 19 January 1980, 1.

14 "Carter Dillydallies on Hostage Crisis, Reagan Charges," *Los Angeles Times*, 28 March 1980, 20; "Campaign Shuns Foreign Issues," *Los Angeles Times*, 17 May 1980, 1.

15 "'Won't Stand, Do Nothing' on Iran—Reagan," *Los Angeles Times*, 21 October 1980, 1.

16 Robert Novak, "Reagan's New Coalition," *National Review*, 22 August 1980, 1023–26.

17 On unemployment in Detroit in 1980, see Sugrue, *Origins of the Urban Crisis*, 262; and "Depressed, Desperate, and Poor: A Letter from Detroit," *Los Angeles Times*, 13 July 1980, 5:1.

18 On Reagan's early ambivalence about Detroit as the convention host, see "Script All Set for Reagan to Steal Scene at Detroit," *Los Angeles Times*, 13 July 1980, 1.

19 Earlier voting patterns in Detroit's predominantly white working-class precincts anticipated Reagan's strategy, since Nixon had swept those precincts in both 1968 and 1972. On these voting patterns, see Sugrue, *Origins of the Urban Crisis*, 265.

20 "Script All Set for Reagan to Steal Scene at Detroit," 1.

21 "GOP Platform Panel Votes to Exclude Pro-ERA Plank," *Los Angeles Times*, 9 July 1980, 1; "Solidly Conservative GOP Platform Woos Democrats," *Los Angeles Times*, 12 July 1980, 1.

22 "Percy Assails Plank on Judges' Abortion Stand," *Los Angeles Times*, 15 July 1980, 1.

23 "Symbol of ERA Protest Evokes Memories of '68," *Los Angeles Times*, 15 July 1980, 6; "Plank by Plank, Women Build Protest at GOP Site," *Los Angeles Times*, 14 July 1980, 1.

24 "Anti-Abortion Leaders, ERA Foes Jubilant over Republican Victory," *Los Angeles Times*, 6 November 1980, 12; "Women's Movement in the Wake of Reagan Win," *Los Angeles Times*, 6 November 1980, 5:1.

25 Saloma, *Ominous Politics*, xviii.

26 "The Pro-Family Movement," *Conservative Digest*, May/June 1980, 14–15.

27 "Reagan Views Issues at Home and Abroad," *Los Angeles Times*, 6 March 1980, 1.

28 Saloma, *Ominous Politics*, 23.

29 Greg Sangillo, "Culture Wars and Silent Majorities," *National Journal*, 2 September 2004, 18–19.

30 "Time to Recapture Our Destiny," 17 July 1980, Detroit, Michigan, <http://www.reaganfoundation.org/Reagan/speeches/time_to.asp>, 10 September 2004.

31 Ibid. On the phrase "national stomach" and a description of the drafting of the speech, see Hannaford, *The Reagans*, 264–84.

32 "Time to Recapture Our Destiny."

33 "Reagan Preaches 'New Economics' Gospel," *Washington Post*, 9 April 1980, 3.

34 "Time to Recapture Our Destiny."

35 "TV Reshapes Coverage of Candidates," *Los Angeles Times*, 1 November 1980, 1.

36 "Reagan's Plan: Sidestep Unions, Woo Workers," *Business Week*, 15 September 1980, 148. See also "The Man of the Hour Wears a Blue Collar," *New York Times*, 12 October 1980, 27.

37 "Reagan Preaches 'New Economics' Gospel," *Washington Post*, 9 April 1980, 3.

38 See, for example, "Reagan Steps Up Criticism of Carter," *Los Angeles Times*, 9 January 1980.

39 The list comes from the nomination speech itself, but lists like this were ubiquitous in critiques of Carter's foreign policy. See, for example, "The Disastrous Foreign Policy of Jimmy Carter," *American Opinion*, May 1980, 33–42, 77–82.

40 "Time to Recapture Our Destiny."

41 Ibid.

42 Ibid.

43 "Hostage's Sister Attacks Pattern of Terror by Iran," *Los Angeles Times*, 21 November 1979, 6; "Our People in Teheran," *Newsweek*, 31 December 1979, 22; "Three Children Appeal to Khomeini: Return Our Dad," *Los Angeles Times*, 22 October 1980.

44 McAlister, *Epic Encounters*, 198–234.

45 "When the Hostages Come Home, Their Problems Will Hardly Be Over, A Psychologist Warns," *People*, 24 March 1980, 74–76; "Hostages Families Suffer Most," *Los Angeles Times*, 6 March 1980.

46 "Reagan to VFW: Viet War Was a 'Noble Cause,'" *Los Angeles Times*, 19 August 1980, 1.

47 On the symbolic significance of yellow ribbons throughout the hostage crisis, see McAlister, *Epic Encounters*, 198. On the new nationalism, see Podhoretz, *Present Danger*, 86–89.

48 See T. Frank, *What's the Matter with Kansas?*; and Nicholas Kristof, "Living Poor, Voting Rich," *New York Times*, 3 November 2004.

49 Felix G. Rohatyn, "Time for a Change," *New York Review of Books*, 18 August 1983, 46–49.

50 "Will the U.S. Find the Resolve to Meet Japanese Challenge?" *Wall Street Journal*, 2 July 1990, 1.

51 Huntington, "The U.S.—Decline or Renewal?"

52 On the clock, see Associated Press, "National Debt Clock Stops, Despite Tril-

lions of Dollars of Red Ink," 7 September 2000, <http://archives.cnn.com/2000/ US/09/07/debt.clock>, 2 February 2005.

53 On growing class inequality, see Levy, *Dollars and Dreams*; Phillips, *Politics of Rich and Poor*; Davis, *Prisoners of the American Dream*; Robert Heilbroner, "Lifting the Silent Depression," *New York Review of Books*, 24 October 1991, 6–8; and Nicholas Lemann, "Mysteries of the Middle Class," *New York Review of Books*, 3 February 1994, 9–13. On the heightened vulnerability of the middle class in the 1980s, see Ehrenreich, *Fear of Falling*. On changing conceptions of money and wealth in the 1980s, see Mills, *Culture in an Age of Money*.

54 Hunter, *Culture Wars*, 177 (his italics).

55 Ibid.

56 On the increased visibility of alternative families in the public sphere, see Weston, *Families We Choose*; Carrington, *No Place Like Home*; Melosh, *Strangers and Kin*; Chauncey, *Why Marriage?*; and Stacey, *Brave New Families*.

57 On the ways in which Reagan sought to avoid another Vietnam, see Lieven, *America Right or Wrong*, 58. On Reagan's foreign policy agenda, see McCormick, *America's Half Century*, 216–36.

58 Daniel Patrick Moynihan, "The Peace Dividend," *New York Review of Books*, 28 June 1990, 3–4.

59 Letter to the Editor from Wassily Leontief, *New York Times*, 4 February 1990.

60 Mann, *Rise of the Vulcans*, 201–3.

61 Kennedy, *Rise and Fall of the Great Powers*. Quoted in Mann, *Rise of the Vulcans*, 160.

62 See McCormick, *America's Half Century*, 247–58; and Mann, *Rise of the Vulcans*, 203.

63 On the militarism of the Clinton administration, see Bacevich, *American Empire*.

64 See Mann, *Rise of the Vulcans*.

65 For example, Mann's chapter on 9/11 is entitled "History Starts Today."

66 Hodgson, *More Equal Than Others*, 253.

Archival Sources
Baylor University Editorial Cartoon Collection, Waco, Texas
    Editorial Cartoons—Energy Crisis
Duke University, Special Collections, Durham, North Carolina
    Louis H. Roddis Papers
Gerald R. Ford Library, Ann Arbor, Michigan
    James M. Cannon Papers
    Gerald R. Ford Vice Presidential Papers
    Alan Greenspan Files
    Edward R. Hutchinson Papers
    Myron Kuropas Files
    Theodore C. Marrs Files
    John O. Marsh Files
    Stephen G. McConahey Files
    Milt Mitler Files
    Frances Pullen Files
    Arthur Quern Papers
    L. William Seidman Collection
    John Stiles and Merrill Mueller Files
J. Walter Thompson Company Archives, John W. Hartman Center for Sales,
    Advertising, and Marketing History, Duke University Rare Book,
    Manuscript, and Special Collections Library, Durham, North Carolina
    Company Publications
    Competitive Advertisements Collection
    Domestic Advertising Collection
    Newsletter Collection
    Review Board Records
    Writings and Speeches Collection
Jimmy Carter Presidential Library, Atlanta, Georgia
    Jody Powell, Press Office File
    Speechwriters Chronological File
John W. Hartman Center for Sales, Advertising, and Marketing History,
    Duke University Rare Book, Manuscript, and Special Collections
    Library, Durham, North Carolina
    Advertising Council Collection
    Nicole Di Bona Peterson Collection of Advertising Cookbooks
National Archives and Records Administration II, College Park, Maryland
    Motion Picture, Sound, and Video Holdings
    Records of the American Revolution Bicentennial Administration

Robert F. Wagner Labor Archives, New York University, New York, New York
Communications Workers of America Collection
Reports, Studies & Arbitration
What Is Quality of Work Life?
Smithsonian Institution Archives, Washington, D.C.
National Museum of History and Technology
Department of Cultural History
Subject File
Office of Smithsonian Symposia and Seminars File
C. Malcolm Watkins Papers
University Archives, University of Illinois, Urbana-Champaign
Advertising Council Collection
University of Rochester, Special Collections, Rochester, New York
Christopher Lasch Papers
Vanderbilt Television News Archive, Vanderbilt University, Nashville, Tennessee
Wayne State University Archives of Labor and Urban Affairs, Detroit, Michigan
United Autoworkers Local 1112 Collection
United Autoworkers Research Department Collection, Parts I and II
U.S. Women's Department: Dorothy Haener Collection

Government Documents

American Revolution Bicentennial Administration. *The Bicentennial of the United States of America: A Final Report to the People*. Vol. 1. Washington: Government Printing Office, 1977.

McCubbin, Hamilton, Barbara B. Dahl, Philip J. Metres Jr., Edna J. Hunter, and John A. Plag, eds. *Family Separation and Reunion: Families of Prisoners of War and Servicemen Missing in Action*. Washington: Government Printing Office, 1974.

McCubbin, Hamilton, Edna J. Hunter, and Philip J. Metres Jr. "Adaptation of the Family to the PW/MIA Experience: An Overview." In *Family Separation and Reunion: Families of Prisoners of War and Servicemen Missing in Action*, edited by Hamilton McCubbin, Barbara B. Dahl, Philip J. Metres Jr., Edna J. Hunter, and John A. Plag, 21–48. Washington: Government Printing Office, 1974.

——. "Children in Limbo." In *Family Separation and Reunion: Families of Prisoners of War and Servicemen Missing in Action*, edited by Hamilton McCubbin, Barbara B. Dahl, Philip J. Metres Jr., Edna J. Hunter, and John A. Plag, 65–76. Washington: Government Printing Office, 1974.

Office of the Federal Register. *Public Papers of the Presidents of the United States: Richard Nixon, 1973*. Washington: Government Printing Office, 1975.

Powers, Iris S. "The National League of Families and the Development of Family Services." In *Family Separation and Reunion: Families of Prisoners of War and Servicemen Missing in Action*, edited by Hamilton McCubbin, Barbara B. Dahl, Philip J. Metres Jr., Edna J. Hunter, and John A. Plag, 1–10. Washington: Government Printing Office, 1974.

Spolyar, Ludwig. "The Grieving Process in MIA Wives." In *Family Separation and Reunion: Families of Prisoners of War and Servicemen Missing in Action*, edited by Hamilton McCubbin, Barbara B. Dahl, Philip J. Metres Jr., Edna J. Hunter, and John A. Plag, 77–85. Washington: Government Printing Office, 1974.

U.S. Congress. House of Representatives. *Treatment of American Prisoners by the North Vietnamese*. 91st Cong., 1st sess., 17 September 1969. Washington: Government Printing Office, 1970.

U.S. Congress. House of Representatives. Committee on Armed Services. *Hearing on Problems of Prisoners of War and Their Families*. 91st Cong., 2nd sess., 6 March 1970. Washington: Government Printing Office, 1970.

U.S. Congress. Senate. Subcommittee on Children and Youth of the Committee on Labor and Public Welfare. *Hearings before the Subcommittee on Children and Youth. American Families: Trends and Pressures, 1973*. 93rd Cong., 2nd sess., 24–26 September 1973. Washington: Government Printing Office, 1974.

U.S. Congress. Senate. Senate Select Committee on Nutrition and Human Needs. *Energy Crisis Impact on Low-Income and Elderly*. 93rd Cong., 2nd sess., 22–23 January 1974. Washington: Government Printing Office, 1974.

U.S. Congress. Senate. Senate Subcommittee on Labor of the Committee on Labor and Public Welfare. *Hearing on the Effects of the Energy Crisis on Employment Dislocation*. 93rd Cong., 2nd sess., 12 February 1974. Washington: Government Printing Office, 1974.

U.S. Congress. Senate. Senate Committee on Labor and Human Resources. *Hearing on Unemployment and the Energy Crisis*. 93rd Cong., 2nd sess., 14 February 1974. Washington: Government Printing Office, 1974.

U.S. Congress. House of Representatives. House Select Committee on Missing Persons in Southeast Asia. *Hearings before the House Select Committee on Missing Persons in Southeast Asia*. 94th Cong., 1st sess., 23 September 1975. Washington: Government Printing Office, 1975.

U.S. Congress. Senate. *Hearings before the Select Committee on POW/MIA Affairs*. 102nd Cong., 2nd sess., 1–4 December 1992. Washington: Government Printing Office, 1993.

Periodicals

America	*Fortune*
American Home	*Good Housekeeping*
American Opinion	*Harper's Magazine*
Armed Forces Journal	*House & Garden*
Better Homes and Gardens	*House Beautiful*
Business Week	*Intellect*
Christianity Today	*Ladies Home Journal*
Commentary	*Life*
Conservative Digest	*Look*
Dissent	*Los Angeles Times*
Ebony Magazine	*McCall's*

Military Medicine
Military Review
Nation
National Journal
National Review
Nation's Business
Natural History
Negro History Bulletin
New Republic
Newsweek
New York Daily News
New Yorker
New York Magazine
New York Review of Books
New York Times
Parents
People
Progressive
Psychiatry

Psychology Today
Reader's Digest
Redbook Magazine
San Diego Union
Saturday Evening Post
Savvy Magazine
Science Digest
Science News
Senior Scholastic
Sunset
Time
Today's Health
UAW Solidarity Newsletter
U.S. News and World Report
Vital Speeches of the Day
Vogue
Wall Street Journal
Washington Post

Published Sources

Abbott, Pamela. *The Family and the New Right*. Concord, Mass.: Pluto Press, 1992.

Abramowitz, Mimi. *Regulating the Lives of Women: Social Welfare Policy from Colonial Times to the Present*. Boston: South End Press, 1996.

Adelman, M. A. "Is the Oil Shortage Real? Oil Companies as OPEC Tax-Collectors." *Foreign Policy* 9 (Winter 1972–73): 69–107.

Akins, James E. "The Oil Crisis: This Time the Wolf Is Here." *Foreign Affairs* 51, no. 3 (1973): 462–90.

Alarcón, Daniel. "The Aztec Palimpsest: Toward a New Understanding of Aztlán, Cultural Identity and History." *Aztlán: A Journal of Chicano Studies* 19, no. 2 (1992): 33–68.

Alvarez, Everett, Jr., and Anthony S. Pitch. *Chained Eagle*. New York: Donald I. Fine, 1989.

——, with Samuel A. Schreiner. *Code of Conduct*. New York: Donald I. Fine, 1991.

Amuzegar, Jahangir. "The Oil Story: Facts, Fiction, and Fair Play." *Foreign Affairs* (July 1973): 677–89.

Andersen, Robert S. "Operation Homecoming: Psychological Observations of Repatriated Vietnam Prisoners of War." *Psychiatry* (February 1975): 65–74.

Anderson, Benedict. *Imagined Communities: Reflections on the Origins and Spread of Nationalism*. London: Verso, 1991.

Aronowitz, Stanley. *False Promises: The Shaping of American Working Class Consciousness*. New York: McGraw Hill, 1973.

Avildsen, John G., director. *Joe*. 1970.

Bacevich, Andrew. *American Empire: The Realities and Consequences of U.S. Diplomacy*. Cambridge: Harvard University Press, 2002.

Bane, Mary Jo. *Here to Stay: American Families in the Twentieth Century*. New York: Basic Books, 1976.

Barnet, Richard. *Global Reach: The Power of the Multinational Corporations*. London: Jonathan Cape, 1975.

Barrett, Michele, and Mary McIntosh. "Narcissism and the Family: A Critique of Lasch." *New Left Review* (July–August 1982): 35–48.

Bederman, Gail. *Manliness and Civilization: A Cultural History of Gender and Race in the United States, 1880–1917*. Chicago: University of Chicago Press, 1995.

Bell, Daniel. *The Coming of Post-Industrial Society: A Venture in Social Forecasting*. New York: Basic Books, 1976.

Bensam, David, and Roberta Lynch. *Rusted Dreams: Hard Times in a Steel Community*. New York: McGraw Hill, 1987.

Blake, Casey, and Christopher Phelps. "History as Social Criticism: Conversations with Christopher Lasch." *Journal of American History* (March 1994): 1310–32.

Bloom, Alexander, and Wini Breines, eds. *"Takin' It to the Streets": A Sixties Reader*. New York: Oxford University Press, 1995.

Bluestone, Barry, and Bennett Harrison. *The Deindustrialization of America: Plant Closings, Community Abandonment, and the Dismantling of Basic Industry*. New York: Basic Books, 1982.

Blumberg, Paul. *Inequality in an Age of Decline*. New York: Oxford University Press, 1980.

Bodnar, John. *Remaking America: Public Memory, Commemoration, and Patriotism in the Twentieth Century*. Princeton: Princeton University Press, 1992.

Breines, Wini, Margaret Cerullo, and Judith Stacey. "Social Biology, Family Studies, and Antifeminist Backlash." *Feminist Studies* 4 (February 1978): 43–67.

Brick, Howard. *The Age of Contradiction: American Thought and Culture in the 1960s*. New York: Twayne Publishers, 1998.

Buhle, Mari Jo. *Feminism and Its Discontents: A Century of Struggle with Psychoanalysis*. Cambridge: Harvard University Press, 1998.

Burnham, Michelle. *Captivity and Sentiment: Cultural Exchange in American Literature, 1682–1861*. Hanover, N.H.: University Press of New England, 1997.

Capozzola, Christopher. "'It Makes You Want to Believe in the Country': Celebrating the American Bicentennial in an Age of Limits." In *America in the Seventies*, edited by Beth Bailey and David Farber, 29–49. Lawrence: University Press of Kansas, 2004.

Carrington, Christopher. *No Place Like Home: Relationships and Family Life among Lesbians and Gay Men*. Chicago: University of Chicago Press, 2002.

Carroll, Peter. *It Seemed Like Nothing Happened: America in the 1970s*. New Brunswick: Rutgers University Press, 1990.

Castiglia, Christopher. *Bound and Determined: Captivity, Culture Crossing, and White Womanhood from Mary Rowlandson to Patty Hearst*. Chicago: University of Chicago Press, 1996.

Chafe, William. *The Unfinished Journey: America since World War II*. New York: Oxford University Press, 1991.

Chamberlin, Edward J., and Sander Gilman, eds. *Degeneration: The Dark Side of Progress*. New York: Columbia University Press, 1985.

Chateau, Bertrand, and Bruno Lapillone. "Energy Consumption in the Residential Sector since 1973." In *Consumer Behavior and Energy Policy: An International Perspective*, edited by Eric Monnier, George Gaskell, Peter Ester, Bernward Joerges, Bruno LaPillonne, Cees Midden, and Louis Puiseux, 79–116. New York: Praeger, 1984.

Chauncey, George. *Why Marriage? The History Shaping Today's Debate over Gay Equality*. New York: Basic Books, 2004.

Chesley, Larry. *Seven Years in Hanoi: A POW Tells His Story*. Salt Lake City: Bookcraft, 1973.

Cohen, Deborah. *The War Come Home: Disabled Veterans in Britain and Germany, 1914–1939*. Berkeley: University of California Press, 2001.

Cohen, Lizabeth. *Making a New Deal: Industrial Workers in Chicago, 1919–1939*. Cambridge: Cambridge University Press, 1990.

Collins, Robert. *More: The Politics of Economic Growth in Postwar America*. New York: Oxford University Press, 1999.

Coontz, Stephanie. *The Social Origins of Private Life: A History of American Families, 1600–1900*. London: Verso, 1988.

——. *The Way We Never Were: American Families and the Nostalgia Trap*. New York: Basic Books, 1992.

Cowan, Ruth Schwartz. *More Work for Mother: The Ironies of Household Technology from the Open Hearth to the Microwave*. New York: Basic Books, 1983.

Crawford, Alan. *Thunder on the Right: The "New Right" and the Politics of Resentment*. New York: Pantheon Books, 1980.

Davis, Louis E., Albert B. Cherns, and Associates, eds. *The Quality of Working Life: Problems, Prospects and the State of the Art*. Vol. 1. New York: Macmillan, 1975.

——. *The Quality of Working Life: Cases and Commentary*. Vol. 2. New York: Macmillan, 1975.

Davis, Mike. *Prisoners of the American Dream: Politics and Economy in the History of the U.S. Working Class*. London: Verso, 1986.

Denton, Jeremiah A., Jr. *When Hell Was in Session*. New York: Reader's Digest Press, 1976.

Diagnostic and Statistical Manual of Mental Disorders. 4th ed. Washington: American Psychiatric Association, 1994.

Diamond, Sara. *Roads to Dominion: Right Wing Movements and Political Power in the United States*. New York: Guilford Press, 1995.

di Leonardo, Micaela. "White Ethnicities, Identity Politics, and Baby Bear's Chairs." *Social Text* 41 (Winter 1994): 165–89.

Duberman, Martin. *Stonewall*. New York: E. P. Dutton, 1993.

Echols, Alice. *Daring to Be Bad: Radical Feminism in America, 1967–75.* Minneapolis: University of Minnesota Press, 1990.

Edsforth, Ronald. *Class Conflict and Cultural Consensus: The Making of a Mass Consumer Society in Flint, Michigan*. New Brunswick: Rutgers University Press, 1987.

Ehrenreich, Barbara. *Fear of Falling: The Inner Life of the Middle Class.* New York: Pantheon Books, 1989.

——. *The Hearts of Men: American Dreams and the Flight from Commitment.* New York: Doubleday, 1983.

Elshtain, Jean Bethke. *Women and War*. New York: Basic Books, 1987.

Engel, Stephanie. "Femininity as Tragedy: Re-examining the 'New Narcissism.'" *Socialist Review* 10 (September–October 1980): 77–104.

Erikson, Erik H. *Childhood and Society*. New York: W. W. Norton, 1950.

Evans, Sara. *Personal Politics: The Roots of Women's Liberation in the Civil Rights Movement and the New Left*. New York: Random House, 1979.

Farber, David. *Taken Hostage: The Iran Hostage Crisis and America's First Encounter with Radical Islam*. Princeton: Princeton University Press, 2005.

Feldstein, Ruth. *Motherhood in Black and White: Race and Sex in American Liberalism, 1930–1965*. Ithaca: Cornell University Press, 2000.

First Chicano Nationalism Conference. "El Plan de Aztlán." In *Takin' It to the Streets: A Sixties Reader*, edited by Alexander Bloom and Wini Breines, 181–84. New York: Oxford University Press, 1995.

Fitzpatrick, Tara. "The Figure of Captivity: The Cultural Work of the Puritan Captivity Narrative." *American Literary History* 3, no. 1 (Spring 1991): 1–26.

Ford Foundation. *A Time to Choose: America's Energy Future*. Cambridge: Ballinger Publishing, 1974.

Frank, Dana. *Buy American: The Untold Story of Economic Nationalism*. Boston: Beacon Press, 1999.

Frank, Thomas. *What's the Matter with Kansas? How Conservatives Won the Heart of America*. New York: Metropolitan Books, 2004.

Franklin, H. Bruce. *M.I.A. or Mythmaking in America*. New York: Lawrence Hill Books, 1992.

Fraser, Nancy, and Linda Gordon. "'A Genealogy of Dependency': Tracing a Keyword of the U.S. Welfare State." Reprinted in Nancy Fraser, *Justice Interruptus: Critical Reflections on the "Postsocialist" Condition*, 121–50. New York: Routledge, 1997.

Freeman, Joshua. "Hardhats: Construction Workers, Manliness, and the 1970 Pro-War Demonstrations." *Journal of Social History* (Summer 1993): 725–39.

Freud, Sigmund. "On Narcissism: An Introduction." In *The Standard Edition of the Complete Psychological Works of Sigmund Freud: Volume XIV (1914–1916)*, edited by James Strachey. New York: Norton, 1976.

Friedan, Betty. *The Feminine Mystique*. New York: Norton, 1963.

Frum, David. *How We Got Here: The 70s, the Decade That Brought You Modern Life (for Better or Worse)*. New York: Basic Books, 2000.

294   Galbraith, John Kenneth. *The Affluent Society*. Boston: Houghton Mifflin, 1958.

Gallup Opinion Index, 1974.

Gambino, Richard. *Blood of My Blood: The Dilemma of the Italian Americans*. Garden City: Doubleday, 1974.

Georgakas, Dan. *Detroit, I Do Mind Dying: A Study in Urban Revolution*. New York: St. Martin's, 1975.

Gerstle, Gary. *American Crucible: Race and Nation in the Twentieth Century*. Princeton: Princeton University Press, 2001.

Gilroy, Paul. *The Black Atlantic: Modernity and Double Consciousness*. Cambridge: Harvard University Press, 1993.

Glickman, Lawrence, ed. *Consumer Society in American History: A Reader*. Ithaca: Cornell University Press, 1999.

Gordon, Linda. *Pitied but Not Entitled: Single Mothers and the History of Welfare, 1890–1935*. New York: Free Press, 1994.

——. *Women, the State, and Welfare*. Madison: University of Wisconsin Press, 1990.

Gordon, Linda, and Allen Hunter. "Sex, Family, and the New Right: Anti-feminism as a Political Force." *Radical America* (1977–1978): 9–25.

Gordon, Michael, ed. *The American Family in Social-Historical Perspective*. New York: St. Martin's, 1973.

Gruner, Elliott. *Prisoners of Culture: Representing the Vietnam POW*. New Brunswick: Rutgers University Press, 1993.

Guarino, Larry. *A P.O.W.'s Story: 2801 Days in Hanoi*. New York: Ivy Books, 1990.

Haley, Alex. *Roots*. Garden City, N.Y.: Doubleday, 1976.

Hall, Richard C. W., and Patrick Malone. "Psychiatric Effects of Prolonged Asian Captivity: A Two Year Follow Up." *American Journal of Psychiatry* (July 1976): 788.

Hall, Richard, and William Simmons. "The POW Wife: A Psychiatric Appraisal." *Archive of General Psychiatry* (November 1973): 692.

Hamper, Ben. *Rivethead: Tales from the Assembly Line*. New York: Warner Books, 1986.

Hannaford, Peter. *The Reagans, a Political Portrait*. New York: Coward-McCann, 1983.

Harrison, Bennett, and Barry Bluestone. *The Great U-Turn: Corporate Restructuring and the Polarizing of America*. New York: Basic Books, 1988.

Harvey, David. *The Condition of Postmodernity*. Cambridge: Blackwell, 1990.

Hendin, Herbert. *The Age of Sensation*. New York: W. W. Norton, 1975.

Herman, Arthur. *The Idea of Decline in Western History*. New York: Free Press, 1997.

Herman, Ellen. *The Romance of American Psychology: Political Culture in the Age of Experts*. Berkeley: University of California Press, 1995.

Herring, George. *America's Longest War: The United States and Vietnam, 1950–1975*. New York: Knopf, 1986.

Higonnet, Margaret Randolph, Jane Jenson, Sonya Michel, and Margaret Collins Weitz, eds. *Behind the Lines: Gender and the Two World Wars*. New Haven: Yale University Press, 1987.

Himmelstein, Jerome. *To The Right: The Transformation of American Conservatism.* Berkeley: University of California Press, 1990.

Hobsbawm, Eric. *The Age of Extremes: A History of the World, 1914–1991.* New York: Vintage, 1994.

Hodgson, Godfrey. *More Equal Than Others: America from Nixon to the New Century.* Princeton: Princeton University Press, 2004.

Hoerr, John P. *And the Wolf Finally Came: The Decline of the American Steel Industry.* Pittsburgh: University of Pittsburgh Press, 1988.

Holbrooke, Richard. "A Sense of Drift, a Time for Calm." *Foreign Policy* (Summer 1976): 107–8.

Hollinger, David A. *Postethnic America: Beyond Multiculturalism.* New York: Basic Books, 1995.

Hooks, Bell. *Ain't I a Woman?: Black Women and Feminism.* Boston: South End Press, 1992.

Horkheimer, Max. "Authoritarianism and the Family Today." In *The Family: Its Function and Destiny,* edited by Ruth Nanda Ashen, 359–74. New York: Harper and Brothers, 1949.

Horowitz, Daniel. *The Anxieties of Affluence: Critiques of American Consumer Culture, 1939–1979.* Amherst: University of Massachusetts Press, 2004.

Hubbell, John G. *P.O.W.: A Definitive History of the American Prisoner-of-War Experience, 1964–1973.* New York: Reader's Digest Press, 1976.

Hughes, Ellen Roney. "The Unstifled Muse: The 'All in the Family' Exhibit and Popular Culture at the National Museum of American History." In *Exhibiting Dilemmas: Issues of Representation at the Smithsonian,* edited by Amy Henderson and Adrienne L. Kaepple, 156–75. Washington: Smithsonian Institution Press, 1997.

Hunter, Edna J. "Combat Casualties Who Remain at Home." *Military Review,* January 1980, 29–36.

Hunter, James Davison. *Culture Wars: The Struggle to Define America.* New York: Basic Books, 1992.

Huntington, Samuel. "The U.S. — Decline or Renewal?" *Foreign Affairs* (Winter 1988): 76–96.

Jacobson, Matthew. *Whiteness of a Different Color: European Immigrants and the Alchemy of Race.* Cambridge: Harvard University Press, 1998.

Jacoby, Russell. "The Politics of Narcissism." In *The Problem of Authority in America,* edited by John P. Diggins and Mark E. Kann, 185–94. Philadelphia: Temple University Press, 1981.

——— . *Social Amnesia: A Critique of Conformist Psychology from Adler to Laing.* Boston: Beacon Press, 1975.

Jameson, Fredric. *Postmodernism, Or, the Cultural Logic of Late Capitalism.* Durham: Duke University Press, 1991.

Jeffords, Susan. *The Remasculinization of America: Gender and the Vietnam War.* Bloomington: Indiana University Press, 1989.

Jeffreys-Jones, Rhodri. *Peace Now! American Society and the Ending of the Vietnam War.* New Haven: Yale University Press, 1999.

Jensen-Stevenson, Monika, and William Stevenson. *Kiss the Boys Goodbye: How the United States Betrayed Its Own POWs in Vietnam.* New York: Penguin Books, 1990.

Jespersen, T. Christopher. "The Bitter End and the Lost Chance in Vietnam: Congress, the Ford Administration and the Battle Over Vietnam, 1975–1976." *Diplomatic History* 24, no. 2 (Spring 2000): 265–93.

———. "The Politics and Culture of Nonrecognition: The Carter Administration and Vietnam." *Journal of American–East Asian Relations* 4, no. 4 (Winter 1995): 397–413.

Kallen, Horace M. *Culture and Democracy in the United States.* New York: Boni and Liveright, 1924.

Kamarovsky, Mirra. *The Unemployed Man and His Family—The Effect of Unemployment upon the Status of the Man in Fifty-Nine Families.* New York: Social Studies Association, 1940.

Kammen, Michael. *Mystic Chords of Memory: The Transformation of Tradition in American Culture.* New York: Alfred A. Knopf, 1991.

Katzell, Raymond A., Penney Bienstock, and Paul H. Faerstein. *A Guide to Worker Productivity Experiments in the United States, 1971–5.* New York: New York University Press, 1977.

Kelly, Joan. "Did Women Have a Renaissance?" In Joan Kelly, *Women, History, and Theory: The Essays of Joan Kelly,* 19–50. Chicago: University of Chicago Press, 1986.

Keniston, Kenneth. *All Our Children: The American Family under Pressure.* New York: Harcourt Brace Jovanovich, 1977.

Kennedy, Paul. *The Rise and Fall of the Great Powers.* New York: Vintage, 1989.

Kent, Susan Kingsley. *Making Peace: The Reconstruction of Gender in Interwar Britain.* Princeton: Princeton University Press, 1993.

Kerber, Linda. *Toward an Intellectual History of Women.* Chapel Hill: University of North Carolina Press, 1997.

———. *Women of the Republic: Intellect and Ideology in Revolutionary America.* Chapel Hill: University of North Carolina Press, 1980.

Kernberg, Otto. *Borderline Conditions and Pathological Narcissism.* New York: James Aronson, 1975.

Kerr, Clark, and Jerome M. Rosow, eds. *Work in America: The Decade Ahead.* New York: Van Nostrand Reinhold, 1979.

Kingston, Maxine Hong. *The Woman Warrior: Memoirs of a Girlhood among Ghosts.* New York: Knopf, 1976.

Kissinger, Henry. *Diplomacy.* New York: Simon and Schuster, 1994.

———. *The White House Years.* Boston: Little, Brown, 1979.

———. *Years of Renewal.* New York: Simon and Schuster, 1999.

———. *Years of Upheaval.* Boston: Little, Brown, 1982.

Kozol, Wendy. *Life's America: Family and Nation in Postwar Photojournalism.* Philadelphia: Temple University Press, 1994.

Lasch, Christopher. "The Culture of Consumption." In *Encyclopedia of American*

Social History II, edited by Mary Kupiec Cayton, Elliot J. Gorn, and Peter W. Williams, 1381. New York: Scribner, 1993.

——. *The Culture of Narcissism: American Life in an Age of Diminishing Expectations*. New York: W. W. Norton, 1978.

——. "The Flight from Feeling: Sociopsychology of Sexual Conflict." *Marxist Perspectives* (Spring 1978): 74–94.

——. *Haven in a Heartless World: The Family Besieged*. New York: Basic Books, 1977.

——. *The Minimal Self: Psychic Survival in Troubled Times*. New York: W. W. Norton, 1984.

——. *The True and Only Heaven: Progress and Its Critics*. New York: W. W. Norton, 1991.

Lears, T. J. Jackson. *No Place of Grace: Antimodernism and the Transformation of American Culture, 1880–1920*. Chicago: University of Chicago Press, 1981.

——. "Reconsidering Abundance: A Plea for Ambiguity." In *Getting and Spending: European and American Consumer Societies in the Twentieth Century*, edited by Susan Strasser, Charles McGovern, and Matthias Judt, 449–66. New York: Cambridge University Press, 1998.

——. "From Salvation to Self-Realization: Advertising and the Therapeutic Roots of the Consumer Culture." In *The Culture of Consumption: Critical Essays in American History, 1880–1980*, edited by Richard Wightman Fox and T. J. Jackson Lears, 3–38. New York: Pantheon Books, 1983.

Lee, Robert. *Orientals: Asian Americans in Popular Culture*. Philadelphia: Temple University Press, 1999.

Lekachman, Robert. *Visions and Nightmares: America after Reagan*. New York: Collier Books, 1987.

Lembke, Jerry. *The Spitting Image: Myth, Memory, and the Legacy of Vietnam*. New York: New York University Press, 1998.

Lenzcowski, George. *American Presidents and the Middle East*. Durham: Duke University Press, 1990.

Lerner, Gerda. "The Lady and the Mill Girl: Changes in the Status of Women in the Age of Jackson." *Midcontinent American Studies Journal* 10 (Spring 1969): 5–15.

Levenstein, Harvey. *Paradox of Plenty: A Social History of Eating in Modern America*. New York: Oxford, 1993.

——. *Revolution at the Table: The Transformation of the American Diet*. New York: Oxford, 1988.

Levin, David Michael. "Clinical Stories: A Modern Self in the Fury of Being." In *Pathologies of the Modern Self: Postmodern Studies on Narcissism, Schizophrenia, and Depression*, edited by David Michael Levin, 479–537. New York: New York University Press, 1987.

Levitan, Sar A., and William B. Johnston. *Work Is Here to Stay, Alas*. Salt Lake City: Olympus Publishing Company, 1973.

Levy, Frank. *Dollars and Dreams: The Changing American Income Distribution*. New York: Russell Sage Foundation, 1987.

Lichtenstein, Nelson. *The State of the Union: A Century of American Labor.* Princeton: Princeton University Press, 2002.

Lieven, Anatol. *America Right or Wrong: An Anatomy of American Nationalism.* Oxford: Oxford University Press, 2004.

Lister, Ruth. "Women, Economic Dependency and Citizenship." *Journal of Social Policy* 19, no. 4:445–67.

Little, Douglas. *American Orientalism: The United States and the Middle East since 1945.* Chapel Hill: University of North Carolina Press, 2002.

Love, Sidney, and Yonata Feldman. "The Disguised Cry for Help: Narcissistic Mothers and Their Children." *Psychoanalysis and the Psychoanalytic Review* 48, no. 2 (Summer 1961): 52–67.

Lowenthal, David. *The Past Is a Foreign Country.* Cambridge: Cambridge University Press, 1985.

Luce, Henry. "The American Century." *Life,* 17 February 1941, 61–65.

Lumet, Sidney, director. *Network.* 1976.

Lund, Wilma, and Olive Foster, eds. *Illinois Teacher's Bicentennial Resource Guide.* Chicago: Illinois Bicentennial Commission, 1975.

Mann, James. *Rise of the Vulcans: The History of Bush's War Cabinet.* New York: Viking, 2004.

Marchand, Roland. *Advertising the American Dream: Making Way for Modernity, 1920–1940.* Berkeley: University of California Press, 1985.

———. *Creating the Corporate Soul: The Rise of Public Relations and Corporate Imagery in American Big Business.* Berkeley: University of California Press, 1998.

Marshall, Paule. *The Chosen Place, the Timeless People.* New York: Harcourt, Brace and World, 1969.

Marzio, Peter, ed. *A Nation of Nations: The People Who Came to America as Seen Through Objects, Prints, and Photographs at the Smithsonian Institution.* New York: Harper and Row, 1976.

Maslow, Abraham H. *Toward a Psychology of Being.* New York: Van Nostrand, 1968.

Matusow, Allen J. *Nixon's Economy: Booms, Busts, Dollars, and Votes.* Lawrence: University Press of Kansas, 1998.

May, Elaine Tyler. *Homeward Bound: American Families in the Cold War Era.* New York: Basic Books, 1988.

McAlister, Melani. *Epic Encounters: Culture, Media, and U.S. Interests in the Middle East, 1945–2000.* Berkeley: University of California Press, 2001.

McCain, John, with Mark Salter. *Faith of My Fathers.* New York: Random House, 1999.

McCormick, Thomas. *America's Half Century: United States Foreign Policy in the Cold War and After.* Baltimore: Johns Hopkins University Press, 1995.

McCubbin, Hamilton I., Barbara B. Dahl, Gary R. Lester, and Beverly A. Ross. "The Returned Prisoner of War: Factors in Family Reintegration." *Journal of Marriage and the Family* (August 1975): 471–78.

McCubbin, Hamilton I., Edna J. Hunter, and Barbara B. Dahl. "Residuals of

War: Families of Prisoners of War and Servicemen Missing in Action." *Journal of Social Issues* 31, no. 4 (1975): 95–107.

McDaniel, Dorothy. *After the Hero's Welcome: The POW Wife's Story of a Battle against a New Enemy*. Chicago: Bonus Books, 1991.

McGirr, Lisa. *Suburban Warriors: The Origins of the New American Right*. Princeton: Princeton University Press, 2001.

McIntosh, Elaine N. *American Food Habits in Historical Perspective*. Westport, Conn.: Praeger, 1995.

Melosh, Barbara. *Strangers and Kin: The American Way of Adoption*. Cambridge: Harvard University Press, 2003.

Miles, Michael. *The Odyssey of the American Right*. New York: Oxford University Press, 1980.

Milkman, Ruth. *Farewell to the Factory: Auto Workers in the Late Twentieth Century*. Berkeley: University of California Press, 1997.

Miller, James. *Democracy Is in the Streets: From Port Huron to the Siege of Chicago*. New York: Simon and Schuster, 1987.

Mills, Nicolaus, ed. *Culture in an Age of Money: The Legacy of the 1980s in America*. Chicago: I. R. Dee, 1990.

Mink, Gwendolyn. *Welfare's End*. Ithaca: Cornell University Press, 1998.

Mintz, Steven, and Susan Kellogg. *Domestic Revolutions: A Social History of American Family Life*. New York: Free Press, 1988.

Mitscherlich, Alexander. *Society without the Father: A Contribution to Social Psychology*. New York: Harcourt, Brace, and World, 1963.

Moody, Ann. *Coming of Age in Mississippi*. New York: Dell, 1970.

Moynihan, Daniel. "The American Experiment." *Public Interest* (Fall 1975): 7.

———. "The Negro Family: The Case for National Action." In *The Moynihan Report and the Politics of Controversy*, edited by Lee Rainwater and William L. Yancey, 39–99. Cambridge: MIT Press, 1967.

———. *The Politics of a Guaranteed Income: The Nixon Administration and the Family Assistance Plan*. New York: Random House, 1973.

Neal, Larry. "Black Art and Black Liberation." In *Takin' It to the Streets: A Sixties Reader*, edited by Alexander Bloom and Wini Breines, 159–63. New York: Oxford University Press, 1995.

Nelson, Barbara J. "Women's Poverty and Women's Citizenship: Some Political Consequences of Economic Marginality." *Journal of Women in Culture and Society* 10, no. 2 (1984): 209–31.

Newman, Katherine. *Falling from Grace: The Experience of Downward Mobility in the American Middle Class*. New York: Free Press, 1988.

Norton, Mary Beth. *Liberty's Daughters: The Revolutionary Experience of American Women, 1750–1800*. Boston: Little, Brown, 1980.

———. "The Myth of the Golden Age." In *Women of America: A History*, edited by Carol R. Berkin and Mary Beth Norton, 37–46. Boston: Houghton Mifflin, 1979.

Novak, Michael. *The Rise of the Unmeltable Ethnics: Politics and Culture in the Seventies*. New York: Macmillan, 1971.

Novick, Peter. *The Holocaust in American Life*. Boston: Houghton Mifflin, 1999.

Nye, David. *Consuming Power: A Social History of American Energies*. Cambridge: MIT Press, 1998.

O'Connor, Alice. "The False Dawn of Poor Law Reform: Nixon, Carter and the Quest for a Guaranteed Income." *Journal of Policy History* 10, no. 1 (1998): 99–129.

Odell, Peter. *Oil and World Power*. Harmondsworth, Middlesex: Penguin, 1986.

O'Toole, James. *Making America Work: Productivity and Responsibility*. New York: Continuum Press, 1981.

———, ed. *Work and the Quality of Life*. Cambridge: MIT Press, 1974.

Painter, David S. *Oil and the American Century: The Political Economy of U.S. Foreign Oil Policy, 1941–1954*. Baltimore: Johns Hopkins University Press, 1986.

Parker, Mike. "Industrial Myths and Shop-Floor Reality: The Team Concept in the Auto Industry." In *Industrial Democracy in America: The Ambiguous Promise*, edited by Nelson Lichtenstein and Howell John Harris, 249–74. Cambridge: Cambridge University Press, 1996.

Parks, Hay, John Thornton, Paul Galanti, Richard Stratton, and James Stockdale. *The Code of Conduct*. Annapolis, Md.: U.S. Naval Institute, 1987.

Patterson, James T. *Grand Expectations: The United States, 1945–1974*. New York: Oxford University Press, 1996.

Pearce, Roy Harvey. "The Significances of the Captivity Narrative." *American Literature* 19, no. 1 (March 1947): 1–20.

People's Bicentennial Commission. *Common Sense II*. New York: Bantam Books, 1975.

———. *Voices of the American Revolution*. New York: Bantam Books, 1974.

Perlman, Robert, and Roland L. Warren. *Families in the Energy Crisis: Impacts and Implications for Theory and Practice*. Cambridge: Ballinger, 1977.

Peschek, Joseph. *Policy-Planning Organizations: Elite Agendas and America's Rightward Turn*. Philadelphia: Temple University Press, 1987.

Phillips, Kevin. *The Politics of Rich and Poor: Wealth and the American Electorate in the Reagan Aftermath*. New York: Random House, 1990.

Philpott, Tom, and John McCain. *Glory Denied: The Saga of Jim Thompson, America's Longest Held Prisoner of War*. New York: Norton, 2001.

Pick, Daniel. *Faces of Degeneration: A European Disorder, c. 1845–1918*. New York: Cambridge University Press, 1989.

Podhoretz, Norman. *The Present Danger: Do We Have the Will to Reverse the Decline of American Power?* New York: Simon and Schuster, 1980.

Quandt, William. *Decade of Decisions: American Policy toward the Arab-Israeli Conflict, 1967–1976*. Berkeley: University of California Press, 1977.

Rainwater, Lee, and William L. Yancey. *The Moynihan Report and the Politics of Controversy*. Cambridge: MIT Press, 1967.

Rand, Christopher T. *Making Democracy Safe for Oil: Oilmen and the Islamic East*. Boston: Little, Brown, 1975.

Reich, Charles. *The Greening of America*. New York: Random House, 1970.

Rich, Adrienne. *Of Woman Born: Motherhood as Experience and Institution.* New York: Norton, 1976.

Riesman, David. *The Lonely Crowd: A Study of the Changing American Character.* Garden City, N.Y.: Doubleday, 1953.

Risner, Robinson. *Passing of the Night: My Seven Years as a Prisoner of the North Vietnamese.* New York: Random House, 1973.

Robinson, Jeffrey. *Yamani: The Inside Story.* New York: Atlantic Monthly Press, 1988.

Rochester, Stuart I., and Frederick Kiley. *Honor Bound: American Prisoners of War in Southeast Asia, 1961–1973.* Annapolis, Md.: 1999.

Rogow, Arnold A. *The Dying of the Light: A Searching Look at America Today.* New York: G. P. Putnam's Sons, 1975.

Rosen, Ruth. *The World Split Open: How the Modern Women's Movement Changed America.* New York: Penguin, 2001.

Rothschild, Emma. *Paradise Lost: The Decline of the Auto-Industrial Age.* New York: Random House, 1973.

Ryan, Mary P. *Womanhood in America: From Colonial Times to the Present.* New York: New Viewpoints, 1975.

Rydell, Robert. *All the World's a Fair: Visions of Empire at International Expositions, 1876–1916.* Chicago: University of Chicago Press, 1987.

Rydell, Robert, John Fielding, and Kimberly Pell. *Fair America: World's Fairs in the United States.* Washington: Smithsonian, 2000.

Said, Edward. *Orientalism.* New York: Vintage, 1979.

Saloma, John. *Ominous Politics: The New Conservative Labyrinth.* New York: Harper Collins, 1984.

Sanchez, George. *Becoming Mexican American: Ethnicity, Culture, and Identity in Chicano Los Angeles, 1900–1945.* New York: Oxford University Press, 1995.

Sanders, Jerry. *Peddlers of Crisis: The Committee on the Present Danger and the Politics of Containment.* Boston: South End Press, 1983.

Schlesinger, Arthur, Jr. *The Vital Center: The Politics of Freedom.* Boston: Houghton Mifflin, 1949.

Schulman, Bruce J. *The Seventies: The Great Shift in American Culture, Society, and Politics.* New York: Free Press, 2001.

Schur, Edwin. *The Awareness Trap: Self-Absorption Instead of Social Change.* New York: New York Times Book Company, 1976.

Segal, Julius. "Therapeutic Considerations in Planning the Return of American POWs to Continental United States." *Military Medicine* (February 1973): 73–77.

Sennett, Richard. *The Fall of Public Man.* New York: Alfred A. Knopf, 1976.

Sheppard, Harold L., and Neal Q. Herrick. *Where Have All the Robots Gone? Worker Dissatisfaction in the 1970s.* New York: Free Press, 1972.

Shorter, Edward. *The Making of the Modern Family.* New York: Basic Books, 1977.

Sieminski, Greg. "The Puritan Captivity Narrative and the Politics of the American Revolution." *American Quarterly* 42, no. 1 (March 1990): 35–56.

Slotkin, Richard. *Regeneration through Violence: The Mythology of the American Frontier, 1600–1860*. Middletown, Conn.: Wesleyan University Press, 1973.

Smith, Rogers M. *Civic Ideals: Conflicting Visions of Citizenship in U.S. History*. New Haven: Yale University Press, 1999.

Sollors, Werner. *Beyond Ethnicity: Consent and Descent in American Culture*. New York: Oxford University Press, 1986.

Stacey, Judith. *Brave New Families: Stories of Domestic Upheaval in Late Twentieth-Century America*. New York: Basic Books, 1991.

———. "Der Feminismus als Geburts-Helferin des Postindustrialismus." *Leviathan Zeitschrift für Sozial Wissenschaft* 15, no. 2 (January 1987): 230–41.

Stein, Howard F., and Robert F. Hill. *The Ethnic Imperative: Examining the New White Ethnic Movement*. University Park: Pennsylvania State University Press, 1977.

Stein, Judith. *Running Steel, Running America: Race, Economic Policy and the Decline of Liberalism*. Chapel Hill: University of North Carolina Press, 1998.

Steinberg, Stephen. *The Ethnic Myth: Race, Ethnicity, and Class in America*. New York: Atheneum, 1981.

Stobaugh, Robert, and Daniel Yergin, eds. *Energy Future: Report of the Energy Project of the Harvard Business School*. New York: Random House, 1979.

Stockdale, Jim, and Sybil Stockdale. *In Love and War: The Story of a Family's Ordeal and Sacrifice during the Vietnam War*. New York: Harper and Row, 1984.

Strasser, Susan. *Never Done: A History of American Housework*. New York: Pantheon Books, 1982.

Student Nonviolent Coordinating Committee. "The Basis of Black Power." In *Takin' It to the Streets: A Sixties Reader*, edited by Alexander Bloom and Wini Breines, 152–59. New York: Oxford University Press, 1995.

Sugrue, Thomas. *The Origins of the Urban Crisis: Race and Inequality in Postwar Detroit*. Princeton: Princeton University Press, 1996.

Tavoulareas, William. *A Debate on A Time to Choose*. Cambridge, Mass.: Ballinger, 1977.

Terkel, Studs. *Working: People Talk about What They Do All Day and How They Feel about What They Do*. New York: Random House, 1972.

Thompson, Heather Ann. "Autoworkers, Dissent and the UAW: Detroit and Lordstown." In *Autowork*, edited by Robert Asher and Ronald Edsforth, 181–208. Albany: SUNY Press, 1995.

Tilly, Louise A., and Joan W. Scott. *Women, Work, and Family*. New York: Routledge, 1989.

Topper, Suzanne. *The Bicentennial Cookbook: 200 Years of Traditional American Recipes*. New York: Belmont Tower Books, 1975.

Torricelli, Robert, and Andrew Carroll, eds. *In Our Own Words: Extraordinary Speeches of the American Century*. New York: Washington Square Press, 1999.

Tyroler, Charles, ed. *Alerting America: The Papers of the Committee on the Present Danger*. Washington: Pergamon-Brassey's International Defense Publishers, 1984.

Ulrich, Laurel. *Good Wives: Image and Reality in the Lives of Women in Northern New England, 1650–1750.* New York: Knopf, 1982.

Umansky, Lauri. *Motherhood Reconceived: Feminism and the Legacies of the Sixties.* New York: New York University Press, 1996.

Useem, Michael. *The Inner Circle: Large Corporations and the Rise of Business Political Activity in the U.S. and U.K.* New York: Oxford University Press, 1986.

Veith, George J. *Code-Name Bright Light: The Untold Story of U.S. POW Rescue Efforts during the Vietnam War.* New York: Free Press, 1998.

Vietor, Richard H. K. *Energy Policy in America since 1945.* Cambridge: Cambridge University Press, 1984.

Vogel, David. *Fluctuating Fortunes: The Political Power of Business in America.* New York: Basic Books, 1988.

Wallace, Mike. *Mickey Mouse History and Other Essays on American Memory.* Philadelphia: Temple University Press, 1996.

Walton, Richard E. "How to Counter Alienation in the Plant." *Harvard Business Review* (November–December 1972): 70–81.

Walzer, Michael. "What Does It Mean to Be an 'American'?" *Social Research* 57, no. 3 (Fall 1990): 591–614.

Warnke, Paul, and Leslie Gelb. "Security or Confrontation? The Case for a Defense Policy." *Foreign Policy* (Winter 1970–71): 6–30.

Waters, Mary C. *Ethnic Options: Choosing Identities in America.* Berkeley: University of California Press, 1990.

Watson, Peter. *The Modern Mind: An Intellectual History of the 20th Century.* New York: Harper Collins, 2001.

Wenk, Michael, S. M. Tomasi, and Geno Baroni, eds. *Pieces of a Dream: The Ethnic Worker's Crisis in America.* New York: Center for Migration Studies, 1972.

West, Patricia. *Domesticating History: The Political Origins of America's House Museums.* Washington: Smithsonian Institution Press, 1999.

Weston, Kath. *Families We Choose: Lesbians, Gays, Kinship.* New York: Columbia University Press, 1997.

Wexler, Laura. *Tender Violence: Domestic Visions in an Age of U.S. Imperialism.* Chapel Hill: University of North Carolina Press, 2000.

Williamson, Judith. *Decoding Advertisements: Ideology and Meaning in Advertising.* New York: Marion Boyars, 1987.

Wills, Gary. *Reagan's America.* New York: Penguin Books, 2000.

Wilson, Sloan. *The Man in the Gray Flannel Suit.* New York: Simon and Schuster, 1955.

Work in America: Report of a Special Task Force to the Secretary of Health, Education, and Welfare. Cambridge: MIT Press, 1971.

Wylie, Philip. *Generation of Vipers.* New York: Pocket Books, 1955.

Yankelovich, Daniel. *The New Morality: A Profile of American Youth in the 1970s.* New York: McGraw Hill, 1974.

———. "Work, Values, and the New Breed." In *Work in America: The Decade*

304   *Ahead*, edited by Clark Kerr and Jerome M. Rosow. New York: Van Nostrand Reinhold, 1979.

Yergin, Daniel. "The Arms Zealots." *Harpers Monthly* (June 1977): 64–76.

——. *The Prize: The Epic Quest for Oil, Money, and Power.* New York: Simon and Schuster, 1991.

Young, Marilyn. *The Vietnam Wars, 1945–1990.* New York: Harper Collins, 1991.

Zaretsky, Eli. *Capitalism, the Family, and Personal Life.* New York: Harper and Row, 1976.

——. "Charisma or Rationalization? Domesticity and Psychoanalysis in the United States in the 1950s." *Critical Inquiry* (Winter 2000): 328–54.

Zaretsky, Natasha. "Private Suffering and Public Strife: Delia Alvarez's War with the Nixon Administration's POW Publicity Campaign, 1968–1973." In *Race, Nation, and Empire in American History*, edited by James T. Campbell, Matthew Pratt Guterl, and Robert G. Lee. Chapel Hill: University of North Carolina Press, forthcoming.

I have incurred many debts in the years that I have worked on this book, and it gives me pleasure to acknowledge them here. Thanks first to the many archivists who offered me invaluable assistance along the way. Archivists at the J. Walter Thompson Company Archives, the Gerald R. Ford Library, the Robert F. Wagner Labor Archives, and the Wayne State University Archives of Labor and Urban Affairs were particularly helpful, patiently guiding me through vast collections and often pointing the way to rich sources that I would have otherwise overlooked. The J. Walter Thompson Company Archives and the Gerald R. Ford Library also provided generous travel grants that enabled me to pursue my research. Chris Prom at the University of Illinois and Greg Wendt at Southern Illinois University–Carbondale kindly helped me with illustrations.

When I was a graduate student in the Department of American Civilization at Brown University, both the graduate school and the department supported my doctoral work with fellowships and teaching assistantships, including a Bernstein Dissertation Fellowship. The department's nurturance of its graduate students and its cultivation of a noncompetitive ethos gave me the confidence to pursue my ideas. Special thanks to Kathleen Franz, Jane Gerhard, Kirsten Lentz, Kirsten Ostherr, and Mari Yoshihara for their example and their friendship. Thanks also to Susan Smulyan, who helped me to become a scholar and teacher without losing my sense of humor.

At Brown, I was blessed with a wonderful dissertation committee who believed in this project from its inception. Robert Lee's commitment to placing race and ethnicity at the center of American history has been an inspiration. The late John L. Thomas paved the way for this topic by suggesting early on that I study the recurring theme of decline in American social and intellectual thought. Mari Jo Buhle pushed me to become a more rigorous historian and a more nuanced thinker, while never expressing any doubt that I could tackle a topic that at times seemed overly ambitious in scope. Like so many other scholars who have come before me, I am profoundly indebted to her.

I am also grateful to my colleagues in the History Department at Southern Illinois University–Carbondale who gave me support as I made the transition from student to professor. Both Marji Morgan and Michael Batinski helped me to balance the rigorous demands of teaching, research, and writing, and Holly Hurlburt reminded me to have fun. Marc Torney and Michael Tow provided valuable research assistance, and Jonathan Bean helped me track down photographs. Finally, a very special thanks to Robbie Lieberman and Rachel Stocking, who invited me into their offices and homes and made me feel so welcome from the start. At the endgame, both Andrew Bynom and Rachel Stocking read the manuscript and of-

306 fered feedback that not only made the book better but also helped me bring things to a close.

A few individuals moved the project forward in various ways. My gratitude goes out to Chuck Grench for supporting this book, as well as to Peter Carroll and Judith Smith for their insightful comments on earlier versions of the manuscript. I am also grateful to the University of North Carolina Press staff for its assistance. John Judis helped me make contact with the late Jude Wanniski and Peter Hannaford, who generously shared with me their memories of the 1980 Republican National Convention. Sandra Beth Levy and Kathy Neely provided me with much-needed support and love throughout this process. My childhood friends Cate Corcoran and Bernadine Mellis have been cheering me on from the sidelines for so long now that it is impossible to imagine how I would have gotten this far without them. Finally, I must thank Kimberly Pluskota, Crista Hönig, Michelle Beard, and all of the childcare providers at the Child Development Laboratories at Southern Illinois University–Carbondale and the Free University of Berlin Kita for giving my child so much loving attention during the many hours that I was writing this book.

Lucky for me, I was born into a family where I learned that political and intellectual commitment had everything to do with love. I thank my stepmother, Nancy Fraser, for being such an inspiring role model over the years (as well as for helping me come up with this book's title!). My mother, Linda Zaretsky, has been championing the underdog for decades now, all the while maintaining the humor and warmth that have made her such a beloved member of her community. My father, Eli Zaretsky, brought his capacious talents as both a historian and an editor to bear on this project. But more important, his confidence in me and his excitement about this book have meant more to me than he knows. I also must thank my mother-in-law, Ellen Wiesen, for k'velling so loudly when she read my writing and traveling thousands of miles to share in my achievements. This book is dedicated to the memory of her sister, Judi C. Friedman, who was taken from us so suddenly on a wet New England morning in May 2003. I will always be grateful that for a time we were family, and I wish everyone shared her inclusive understanding of the word. Although my son, Daniel, is still too young to understand what it means that his mother has written a book, he helped move the process along with his robustness and his thousand-watt smile. He is my most welcome and joyful distraction. Finally, my deepest thanks to my husband, the lovely Jonathan Wiesen, who read every chapter again and again, patched my confidence when I felt discouraged, and stole me away to Germany for a year so I could work on the manuscript in peace. But in the end, it is the life we have created together outside of the book that made it possible.

The Endocannabinoid System and Cannabis

A Perfect Partnership for Self-Regulation and Healing

Dr. Scott A. Johnson

The endocannabinoid system and cannabis: A perfect partnership for self-regulation and healing/Scott A. Johnson

Cover design: Scott A. Johnson
Cover Copyright: © Scott A. Johnson 2019

Discover more books by Scott A. Johnson at authorscott.com.

Published by Scott A. Johnson Professional Writing Services, LLC: Orem, Utah

DEDICATION

This book is dedicated to those silent sufferers. Whether from mental, emotional, physical, or spiritual suffering, your affliction is acknowledged and your struggles deserve compassion and support. You are strong. You are heroic. You are loved. You are deserving. You are valued. You are wanted. Hold on and don't ever give up.

Contents

Introduction to the Endocannabinoid System and Cannabis

Many people know cannabis as one of the most frequently used recreational drugs—the psychedelic drug of hippies and stoners that gained popularity in the 1960s for its ability to produce a high. Yet it's not widely known that the cannabis plant is one of the world's oldest medicinal remedies. Reports of its therapeutic use date back to around 2700 BC as recorded in a classical medicine book by the Chinese emperor Shen-Nung.[1] It was also used in Western medicine—mostly by British doctors—during the nineteenth century as an appetite stimulant, muscle relaxant, anticonvulsant, analgesic, and hypnotic. Its medicinal use was even documented in the 1854 United States Dispensary. However, its medicinal use fell out of favor in the early 1900s because of the inconsistent potency of extracts, unreliable effects of oral ingestion—cannabis is an exceedingly complex plant with its effects dependent on the plant variety and composition of phytochemicals—increasing nonmedical use, and the introduction of new synthetic drugs. This falling out of favor was unfortunate given how widely cannabinoids found in cannabis influence human health.

Another reason it fell out of favor is the Marihuana Tax Act of 1937, which essentially banned its use and sale. Paradoxically, the American Medical Association (AMA) opposed the act because it imposed taxes on physicians and pharmacists prescribing and dispensing cannabis. This action was largely to protect profits

associated with cannabis dispensing. Today, that same organization opposes legalization of medical cannabis because it believes "cannabis is a dangerous drug and as such is a public health concern."[2] This blanket statement is not only harmful but also inaccurate, failing to differentiate different cannabis extracts (CBD versus THC) and ignoring escalating research that cannabis is a safe and effective solution for many conditions that drugs do little to address. It appears that the actions of the AMA more than eighty years ago and today may be more financially driven rather than health related.

Beginning in the 1960s, research on the cannabis (*Cannabis sativa* L.) plant led to the discovery of a previously unidentified signaling system, now known as the endocannabinoid system (ECS). We now understand that the ECS is found in both vertebrates and invertebrates and has diverse and significant roles in their health. This groundbreaking discovery and the subsequent research that followed is poised to change the landscape of medicine—both natural and pharmaceutical.

Today, recreational and medicinal use of cannabis is rapidly increasing, and the legislative landscape is continually adapting to this widespread use. With consumer demand for access to medicinal cannabis increasing, legislative bodies are softening past stances against cannabis use. Recently, experts at the World Health Organization (WHO) recommended that whole-plant marijuana and cannabis resin be removed from Schedule IV (the most restrictive category of the 1961 Single Convention on Narcotic Drugs signed by multiple countries around the globe). In addition, they recommended THC be removed from a separate 1971 drug treaty (Convention on Psychotropic Substances) and instead added to Schedule I of the 1961 convention. Furthermore, cannabis extracts and tinctures should be deleted from Schedule I and cannabidiol products with less than 0.2% THC not be scheduled within drug control conventions. CBD preparations were not previously scheduled, but the new letter makes this even more clear. If these recommendations are adopted by the WHO it would be a stark

8

admission by the world's governing bodies that they have been wrong about cannabis and an admission that it has therapeutic value.

Strong scientific evidence suggests that cannabis has a place in the management of glaucoma, chronic pain, chemotherapy-induced nausea, and more, with rapidly emerging evidence that it is useful for insomnia, epilepsy, and other severely debilitating conditions. People with conditions and disorders not easily treatable with pharmaceutical options are turning to this one plant for relief, and scientists and health professionals are seeking to better understand the ECS and the molecules that unlock its therapeutic benefits. Indeed, it is now known that the ECS is critical for the regulation of the optimum function of multiple body processes and systems.

The Cannabis Plant

First off, hemp is not marijuana, and marijuana is not hemp. To make things even more confusing, hemp seed oil (cold-pressed vegetable from the seeds of the plant) is not the same as CBD or marijuana. It is important that we separate the medicinal value of the plant—particularly non-psychoactive CBD—from the recreational or abuse of the plant. Many people are opposed to the medical use

9

of cannabis just because they associate it with recreational use and abuse and the "high" that marijuana produces.

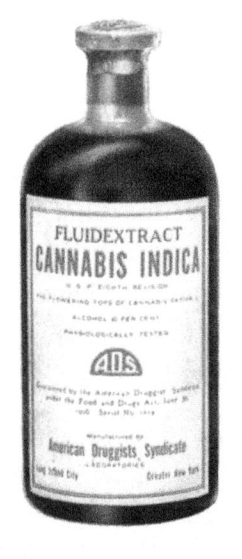

Cannabis plants originated in Central Asia or the foothills of the Himalayas. For millennia, the plant has been valued for food, clothing, rope, medicinal, recreational, and spiritual purposes. Despite a long history of use in Asia, cannabis is a more recent introduction to Western society. There is no trace of them in the Western Hemisphere until the sixteenth century. Cannabis was cultivated in the early 1600s in Jamestown for fiber. It appeared in the U.S. Pharmacopeia in the 1850s for the treatment of neuralgia, tetanus, typhus, cholera, rabies, excessive menstrual bleeding, and more, where it remained until 1942. Indeed, it was widely used as a patent medicine during both the nineteenth and twentieth centuries. Its removal was driven by social reform and propaganda campaigns to demonize the plant.

Not all botanists agree, but generally two species of cannabis plant are recognized—*Cannabis sativa* and *C. indica*. Others argue that cannabis is a single species, while others describe four "strains": *C. sativa, C. indica, C. ruderalis, and C. afghanica*.[3,4] Today, selective breeding of plants has produced several varieties of the plant, most of which are geared toward higher THC potency. The emphasis on producing THC-dominant plants fundamentally ignores the safer and arguably more therapeutic CBD-dominant and balanced plants. This may be due to the amount of people who are seeking a high from cannabis rather than healing from the plant.

The family of cannabis plants produces both brother plants (male) and sister plants (female). The brother and sister plants, and the hemp and marijuana plants, share certain similarities but have several distinct characteristics. Visually, the hemp plant features skinny leaves that concentrate toward the top of the plant, and the

hemp plant is taller and thinner than marijuana. In contrast, the marijuana plant features broad leaves and dense, THC-rich buds, and the marijuana plant has a shorter, bushier appearance. Another major distinction is that hemp plants produce higher levels of CBD with very low concentrations of THC (often 0.3% or less), while marijuana plants concentrate THC (usually between 5% and 40%) with lower levels of CBD. As with all plants, the growing conditions and environment can significant influence the cannabinoids present and some cultivars produce near equal THC and CBD.

C. indica, formerly called *C. sativa* var. *indica*, is a short, bushy plant with broad leaves native to India. The plant is typically described as faster growing than *sativa* varieties, with a higher yield of cannabinoids, and suitable for colder climates with shorter growing seasons. However, the degree of interbreeding and hybridization has made it very difficult to distinguish the two plants—*C. sativa* and *C. indica*—without a biochemical analysis. Like *sativa* strains, *indica* strains can produce many different chemotypes of plants based on the CBD to THC ratios (e.g. THC-dominant, CBD-dominant, and balanced THC/CBD). These are the three most common chemotypes, but selective breeding has also produced chemotypes with high levels of THCV, cannabidivarin, cannabichromene, and even plants with almost exclusively cannabigerol. Because of the disparity among botanists and scientists, it may be better to abandon the *sativa* and *indica* nomenclature in the scientific community and public in favor of distinguishing plants by cannabinoid content.

Cannabis Plant Breeding

Genetics and the environment are the two most important factors that influence any given cannabis plant. Breeding cannabis plants is an intricate art and science with some colorful names (e.g. Sour Diesel, Blue Dream, Durban Poison, etc.). Like humans, the cannabis plant has a diploid (a cell or nucleus with two copies of genetic material, or a complete set of chromosomes, paired with chromosomes carrying the same information from the other parent)

genome, but it has only twenty chromosomes (instead of 22 pairs like humans) and a pair of sex chromosomes (X and Y).

Differences in growing techniques, environment, soil quality, and more play a significant role in how plants turn out. However, given the same genetics, skilled growers are able to produce consistent results. Some cannabis breeders have spent years breeding and crossing plants to create a seed-based strain with specific characteristics. Truly great strains earn a regional, national, and even international reputation among both growers and consumers.

What many cannabis breeders are really trying to accomplish is to create a stable genetic line, called a hybrid. The plant's genetic makeup (genotype) acts as the blueprints for its growth, traits, and characteristics. Whether these characteristics occur (express) is up to the environment. The physical expression (color, shape, smell, etc.) of a cannabis plant—called a phenotype—is determined by what genes the environment triggers in the plant.

The earliest cannabis species is believed to originate from the Hindu Kush region of Pakistan. These varieties were called landrace strains (e.g. Hindu Kush and China Yunnan), and are considered to possess superior genetics. Because they have been growing in this location for centuries they have developed stable, robust genetics that produce consistent offspring. Over thousands of years, the cannabis plant adapted to express the ideal traits for the growing conditions and environment inherent to a specific geographical location. These diverse habitats and environments produced a wide variety of cannabis plants, each with unique characteristics.

Inevitably, cultivation lead to hybridization—intermixing of global localized varieties—of strains. When two strains with different genotypes breed, they produce a first generation hybrid, or F1. When this hybrid is bred together with another F1 sister or brother

from the same batch, an F2 hybrid is created. Repeating this process creates an F3, then F4, then F5. After an F5, the plant can be considered an inbred line (IBL). In other words, after several generations of breeding almost identical genotypes, the strains morph into a different family of strains. White Widow and Northern Lights are well-known IBLs.

You can also produce poly-hybrids by mixing completely different hybrids together. For example, breeding a Hindu Kush with Durban Poison produces an offspring called F1(A); if that F1(A) is breed with the offspring of a Sour Diesel and Blue Dream, called F1(B), it is a poly-hybrid. This means it contains the genetics of multiple hybrid varieties.

Backcrossing refers to breeding a hybrid strain with its original parent plant. It is commonly used to correct certain traits. It is done by crossing the offspring (F1, F2, etc.) with one of the original parents that possesses the desired trait. The result is a BX1, which can be further crossed with the original parent to create a BX2. This process can be repeated to create BX3, BX4, and so forth.

Lastly, mother plants can be crossed with themselves, called an S1. This "selfing" is achieved by reversing the sex of a female plant causing it to produce male flowers and pollen—through chemicals that cause the plant to be stressed—to pollenate itself with. Some examples of S1 include Trainwreck and Tropimango.

Breeding is about time and patience. It is bound to produce non-uniform offspring and some less than desirable plants or plant characteristics. With perseverance, the desired strain is produced and the work of the breeder rewarded.

The Endocannabinoid System

The ECS comprises the following:

- Enzymes that are responsible for the creation and destruction of cannabinoids.

- Receptor sites on cells that receive signals from cannabinoids.
- Molecules known as endocannabinoids that are naturally produced by the body from lipids.

Receptors send vital information obtained outside the cell to within cells, organs, and organ systems that are critical to maintaining optimal health. Binding of molecules to receptor sites initiates physiological responses that alter cellular function. The ECS is believed to have more cellular receptor sites than any other receptor system in the human body. Cannabinoid receptors are so ubiquitous in the human body that the ECS has been called the "universal" or "master" regulator of the human body. The ECS does an admirable job helping maintain homeostasis by utilizing a negative feedback loop that activates neurons and the release of endocannabinoids, despite a continual onslaught of chemicals, poor food, complex cell signals, and genetic mutations.[5] A negative feedback loop involves a reaction that decreases the output of a system so the feedback stabilizes the system, a state often called *homeostasis*. Altogether, the goal of the ECS is to maintain health equilibrium and optimum health and protect against disease progression.

The best way to view these receptor molecule interactions is to compare them to locks and keys. Receptors are locks on cells, and when the right key in the form of a molecule attaches to the receptor, it sends signals inside the cell that unlock certain functions. The widespread distribution of cannabinoid receptors emphasizes how profoundly it can influence overall body function. In fact, deficient endocannabinoid activity may be associated with conditions such as fibromyalgia, irritable bowel syndrome, migraines, cystic fibrosis, infantile colic, bipolar disorder, multiple sclerosis, post-traumatic stress disorder (PTSD), irregular or painful menstruation, and much more.[6,7,8,9,10] Conversely, optimization of the ECS could reverse these difficult to treat conditions that have few real solutions from pharmaceuticals.

Cannabinoid and Receptor Interactions

Canabinoids are known to fit like lock and key into a network of receptors ("locks") found on cell surfaces throughought the body. The endocannabinoid system exists to receive "keys" naturally produced by the body called cannabinoids (e.g. anandamide). Two major receptors exist: CB1 receptors concentrated in the brain and central nervous system and CB2 receptors concentrated in the immune system and peripheral organs. Plant-based cannabinoids, called phytocannabinoids, also interact with these receptors to restore balance and stimulate protective and self-healing mechanisms.

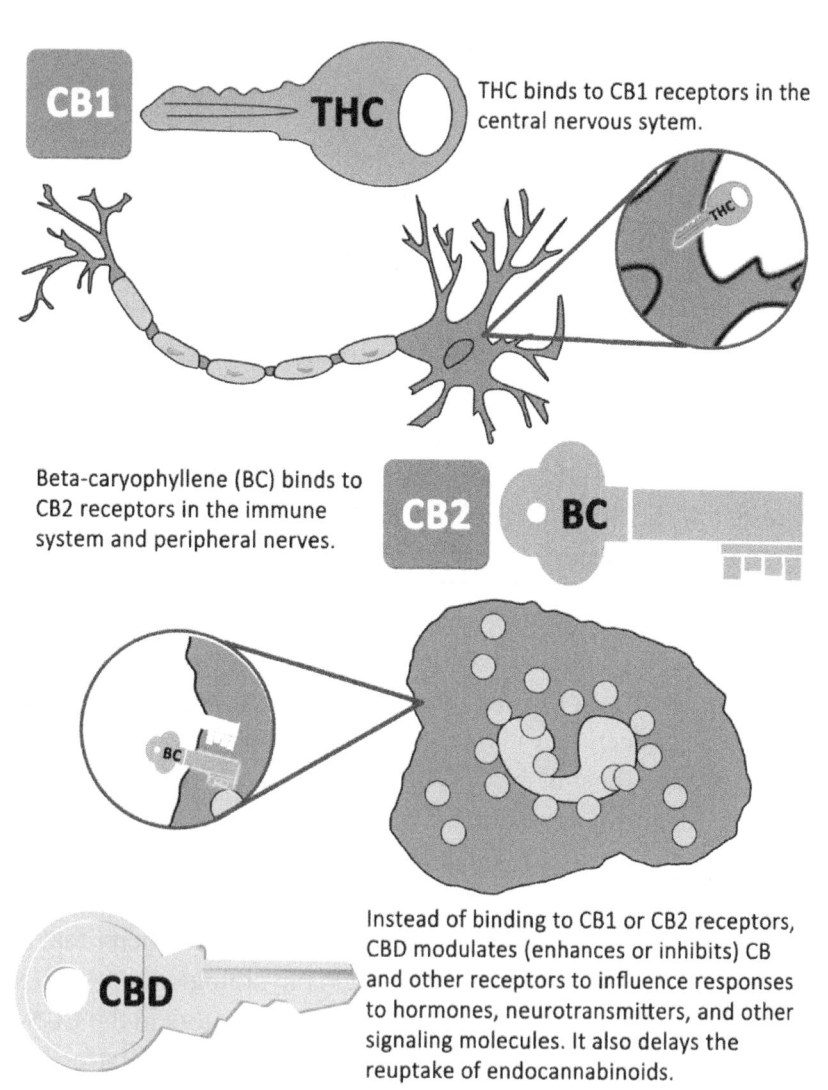

THC binds to CB1 receptors in the central nervous sytem.

Beta-caryophyllene (BC) binds to CB2 receptors in the immune system and peripheral nerves.

Instead of binding to CB1 or CB2 receptors, CBD modulates (enhances or inhibits) CB and other receptors to influence responses to hormones, neurotransmitters, and other signaling molecules. It also delays the reuptake of endocannabinoids.

The Discovery of the Endocannabinoid System, Cannabinoids, and Cannabinoid Receptors

The recreational use of cannabis became pervasive in the 1960s in Western countries. This recreational use and the elucidation and synthesis of Δ-9-tetrahydrocannabinol (THC) sparked a focused study on the psychoactive properties of cannabis. The United States funded research during this time to find and expose the harmful effects of cannabis on the human body, while there was very little interest in its therapeutic potential.[11] Ironically, rather than discrediting cannabis, the research led by the National Institute on Drug Abuse inadvertently assisted in a series of major discoveries about the human brain.

What the research revealed was a new physiological system and exciting discoveries into brain chemistry, as well as a great deal about the pharmacology, biochemistry, and clinical effects of a plant that has been around for thousands of years. The identification and synthesis of THC revealed that it was primarily responsible for the psychotropic effects of cannabis, including elevated mood, reduced anxiety and paranoia, impaired perception of time, impaired memory, altered hearing and eyesight, and drowsiness. However, the research did little to explain the mechanisms by which these effects were produced.

In the mid-1980s, pioneering research conducted in Allyn Howlett's laboratory at St. Louis University discovered conclusive evidence of cannabinoid receptors in rat brains.[12] Since their discovery, a great deal has been learned about cannabinoid receptors and their roles in human health.[13,14,15] With the discovery of cannabinoid receptors, scientists were at the verge of a breakthrough in revealing a major mechanism to regulate human health. The creation of a potent synthetic cannabinoid (CP55940) further enabled researchers to map cannabinoid receptor locations throughout the body that are responsible for multiple mental and physiological processes. Scientists found that there were two primary receptors in the ECS— Cannabinoid Receptor 1 (CB1, or CB1R) and Cannabinoid Receptor

2 (CB2, or CB2R)—that share similar structures and amino acid sequences.

CB1 and CB2 are membrane-bound G-proteins (also called *G protein-coupled receptors*; receptors with membrane-spanning structures that convert stimuli from outside a cell into cellular signals inside the cell). Several cannabinoids can attach to and influence these receptors. They include endogenous cannabinoids, phytocannabinoids, and synthetic cannabinoids. Once attached, they produce neurobehavioral effects and play important signaling roles in the central nervous system that regulate pain perception, inflammation, anxiety, fear, body temperature, muscle control, stress response, ocular pressure, and appetite, to name a few. In essence, these receptors play a primary role in cell-to-cell communication to ensure specific cells in a specific area of the body or brain coordinate their efforts to emphasize overall well-being.

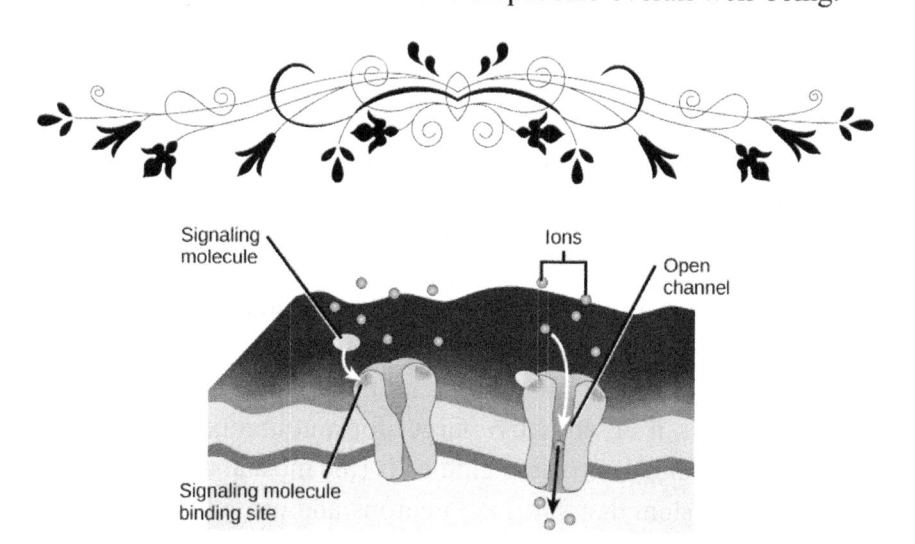

Membrane receptors fall into one of three major classes:

1. G-protein-coupled receptors
2. Ion-channel receptors
3. Enzyme-linked receptors

They receive their names based on the way they transform external signals into internal signals—by protein action, ion-channel

opening, or enzyme activation. Because membrane receptors interact with both signals from outside the cell and molecules within the cell, they provide a means for signaling molecules to influence cell function without actually entering the cell. This gives membrane receptors a distinct advantage in influencing cellular activity because most signaling molecules are too big or too charged to cross the cell's membrane.

CB1 is primarily expressed in the central nervous system, particularly the hippocampus, cerebral cortex, cerebellum, basal ganglia, hypothalamus, and amygdala.[16] It can also be found in the heart, uterus, testis, skin, and small intestine. Certain molecules can bind to this receptor and activate it. When active, the CB1 receptor reduces neurotransmission (the process in which signaling molecules, called neurotransmitters, are released by a neuron and bind to and interact with receptors on another neuron).[17] Consequently, short- or long-term changes in neuron communication change cellular behavior.

The CB2 receptor is primarily expressed in the immune system and other cells associated with immune functions such as the spleen, gastrointestinal system, and skin.[18] Its modulation of the immune response makes it an attractive target for autoimmune conditions. CB2 is also found in activated glial cells (the most abundant cells in the nervous system that surround neurons and provide support and insulation) in the brain.[19] When a molecule binds to this receptor, it becomes active and influences multiple physiological processes, including immune activity (promoting immune equilibrium), apoptosis (programmed cell death), immune-cell migration (movement of cells to tissue in response to infection, injury, or for tissue maintenance), inflammatory responses (reduces), and pain perception (decreases T cell receptor signaling).

Cannabinoid Receptor Expression in the Human Body

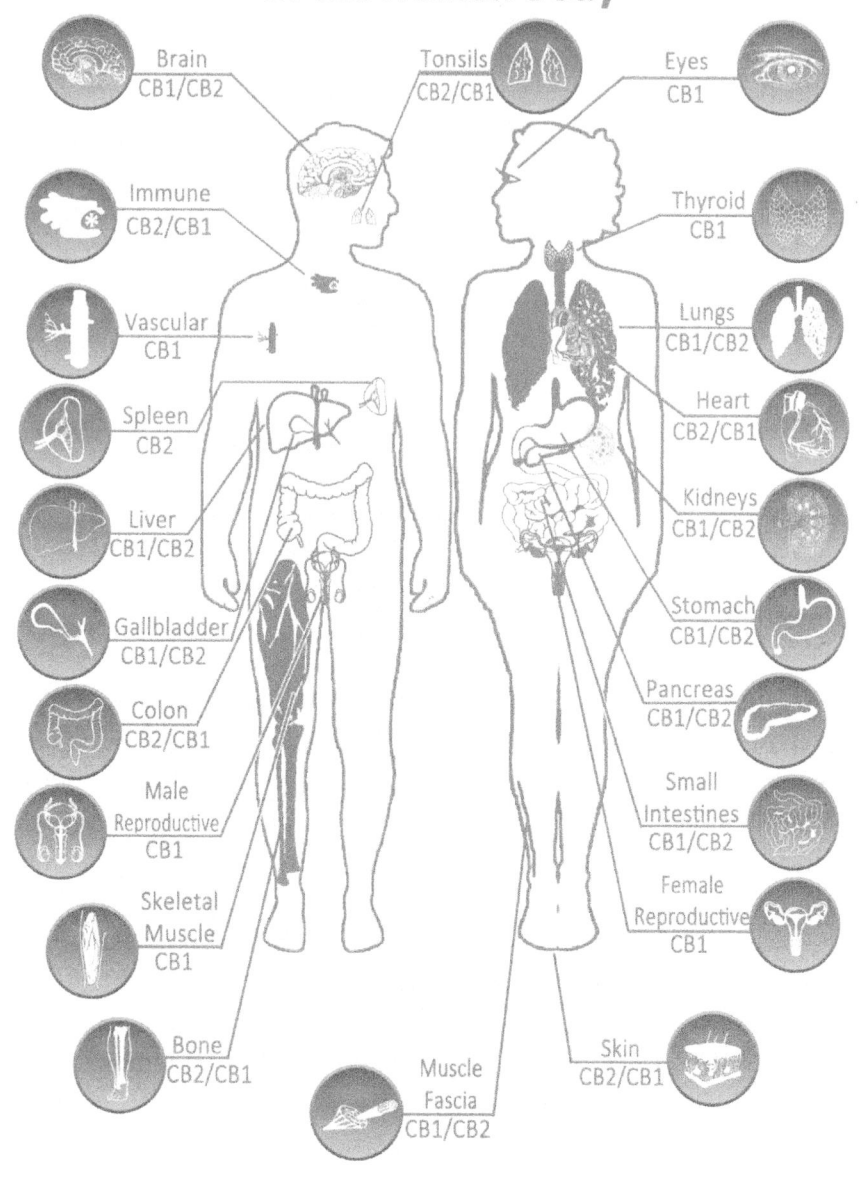

Organ	Receptor
Brain	CB1/CB2
Tonsils	CB2/CB1
Eyes	CB1
Immune	CB2/CB1
Thyroid	CB1
Vascular	CB1
Lungs	CB1/CB2
Spleen	CB2
Heart	CB2/CB1
Liver	CB1/CB2
Kidneys	CB1/CB2
Gallbladder	CB1/CB2
Stomach	CB1/CB2
Colon	CB2/CB1
Pancreas	CB1/CB2
Male Reproductive	CB1
Small Intestines	CB1/CB2
Skeletal Muscle	CB1
Female Reproductive	CB1
Bone	CB2/CB1
Muscle Fascia	CB1/CB2
Skin	CB2/CB1

If both CB1 and CB2 are listed for the same system/organ the first receptor listed is the dominantly expressed receptor.

Emerging evidence suggests there is a third cannabinoid receptor, GPR55, that is distinctly different from CB1 and CB2 receptors, but there is disagreement among scientists.[20,21] Discovered in 1999,[22] this receptor is highly expressed in the brain and spinal cord (dorsal root ganglion) and can be activated by THC, anandamide, and other molecules.[23] It may be responsible for some of the effects produced by anandamide that are not mediated through CB1/CB2 receptors. Scientists are still studying the function of this receptor, but some evidence suggests its activation promotes cancer-cell proliferation, and higher GPR55 expression in cancer cells is associated with more aggressive tumors.[24] Based on this, scientists believe inhibiting the overexpression of GPR55 could be a potential target for cancer therapy.

Other research suggests that this receptor reduces anxiety and stress, relieves pain (both neuropathic and inflammatory pain), and plays a role in bone metabolism.[25,26,27] More research will clarify GPR55's role in the ECS and whether it should be considered a third endocannabinoid receptor or just a receptor that is involved in facilitating overall ECS function.

An argument could also be made that proliferator-activated receptors (PPAR) and transient receptor potential (TRP) receptors are integral parts of the ECS based on their ability to facilitate some endocannabinoid actions. A superfamily of ion channels, TRPs are activated by a diversity of mechanisms. They play crucial roles in responses to external stimuli (touch, light, sound, temperature, and chemicals) and give individual cells the ability to detect changes in the local environment. TRP channels, especially TRPV1, are activated by anandamide under certain conditions.[28] For example, anandamide triggers vasodilation (relaxation and widening of the blood vessels) by activating TRPV1 receptors on sensory nerves in the blood vessels. The TRPs are particularly important and are utilized by the ECS to affect pain signaling and pain perception.[29] The role of TRPs enlarges the complexity of the ECS and how widely it can influence human health.

Anandamide also activates PPAR channels PPARalpha and PPARgamma. Since PPARs play a vital role in the regulation of gene expression—PPARalpha regulates expression of genes related to fatty acid oxidation and energy metabolism; PPARgamma regulates gene expression related to adipocyte (fat-storing cells) differentiation—the ECS may produce some of its effects on cholesterol levels, reproduction, blood sugar control, inflammation, cancer, pain, and obesity through this channel.[30] The complex interactions between the ECS and these additional receptors dramatically influence cellular physiology, gene expression, organ function, and overall human health.

The ECS is present in early human development, is critical for nervous system development, and continues in the brain throughout life. Children's brains undergo significant changes as they grow. By age six, their brains are about 90%–95% of adult size but require significant remodeling before they reach the functionality of the adult brain. Intensive brain remodeling—organization of connections in the thinking and processing part of the brain that are "pruned" away, or the strengthening of other connections—occurs during adolescence, which continues into the midtwenties. This adolescent remodeling makes brain function more efficient. Coinciding with this brain remodeling, the ECS also undergoes significant alterations—fluctuations in CB receptors levels and their locations and levels of endogenous cannabinoids—during adolescence. More evidence that the ECS is critical to human health, particularly in relation to brain connections and function. Scientists propose that changes to the ECS occur during aging as well, meaning more mature adults may respond differently to cannabis.

Not surprisingly, the ECS is different in males and females. Women are more likely to be affected by cannabinoids than men, especially negatively during adolescence. Males have a higher CB1 receptor density when compared to women, which may partly explain why they require more cannabinoids to get the same results.[31] Differences among males and females in cannabinoid metabolism have also been reported. Preclinical research observed that females

21

metabolize THC to 11-hydroxy-THC (the main active metabolite of THC) more readily, whereas males metabolize THC to at least three other less active metabolites.[32] This is a possible clue as to why women are more susceptible to cannabis abuse, dependence, and relapse, and experience more severe withdrawal symptoms. Scientists hypothesize that differences in hormone production are the cause of these ECS differences among men and women, with estradiol being the most influential hormone.[33] What this evidence tells us is that dosing may require adjusting based on sex and women should be more cautious in their use of THC.

The Endocannabinoid System and Disease

The hypothesis that deficient ECS function (called *clinical endocannabinoid deficiency*) is a precursor to many diseases was first proposed in 2001.[34] The theory was based on the fact that many brain disorders are associated with low levels of neurotransmitters— acetylcholine in Alzheimer's disease, dopamine in Parkinson's disease, GABA (gamma-aminobutyric acid) in amyotrophic lateral sclerosis (ALS), and norepinephrine in depression.[35,36,37] Humans possess what is called endocannabinoid tone that reflects the balance between the creation and destruction of endocannabinoids (endocannabinoid levels) and the activity of ECS receptors found throughout the body.

Indeed, the ECS tends to go into overdrive (upregulate) in many disorders including inflammation, pain, neurodegenerative, gastrointestinal, cardiovascular, metabolic, and cancer. It is believed that the increased activity of the ECS in these disease states serves as an innate protective mechanism to diminish disease progression or symptoms. Inadequate levels of endocannabinoids (caused by genetic anomalies, birth defects, disease, or injury) result in disorders of the gut, mood, sleep, and pain system to name a few. Lower levels of endocannabinoids have been documented in people who suffer from migraines, and low ECS function is noted in people with PTSD.[38] Emerging evidence indicates that the ECS could be a clinical target for many modern health disorders.

Endogenous Cannabinoids

Endogenous (produced naturally by the body; also called endocannabinoids or natural cannabinoids) cannabinoids include N-arachidonoylethanolamine, or anandamide (AEA), 2-arachidonoylglycerol (2-AG), and N-arachidonoyl dopamine. They are trace abundant molecules found in human cells, tissues, and body fluids with important biological properties produced (synthesized) from local fatty acids as needed to activate the ECS. Their production and levels depend on diet and are regulated by neuropeptides and hormones (leptin: reduces; ghrelin: increases) involved in energy balance.[39] Since their discovery, scientists have been investigating their role in multiple biochemical processes.

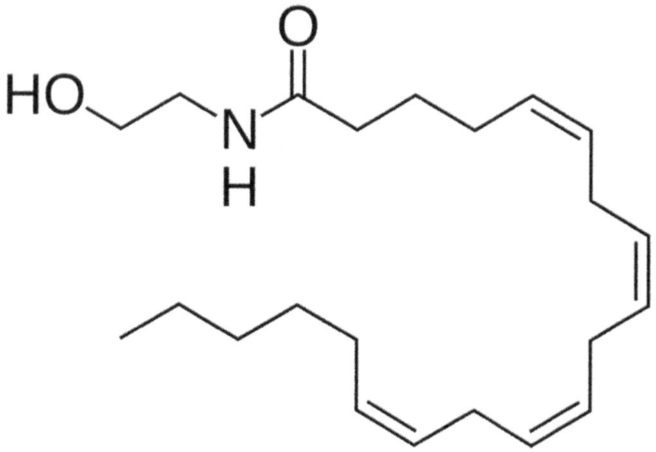

Anandamide structure

Anandamide was first discovered in 1992 and found to influence cognition and mood state.[40] Its name comes from Sanskrit where *ananda* means "inner bliss or tranquility." Because of this it carries the nickname the "bliss molecule." AEA is derived from the nonoxidative metabolism of arachidonic acid (an omega-6 essential fatty acid) via an enzymatic process. Enzymes play a pivotal role in the creation and destruction of endogenous cannabinoids. Fatty acid amide hydrolase (FAAH) degrades anandamide into ethanolamine and arachidonic acid to control how many endocannabinoids are

23

present in the body. In other words, it returns AEA to the original form it was taken from. AEA is highly lipophilic (having an affinity for or tending to combine with or dissolve in fats and lipids) and has a tendency to remain in membranes, where it interacts with enzymes and receptors. It possesses anti-inflammatory, anticancer, cardiovascular (decreases blood pressure and heart rate), and metabolism-regulating properties.[41,42,43,44,45,46,47]

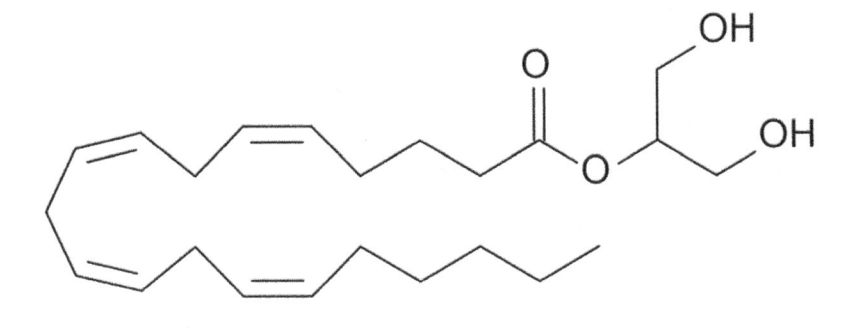

2-arachidonoylglycerol structure

The second endogenous cannabinoid, discovered in 1995, was 2-AG. It's the most abundant endocannabinoid in the human body.[48] It is concentrated in the central nervous system, with levels significantly higher than anandamide. Like anandamide, it is synthesized on demand from phospholipid precursors (fatty acids) in cell membranes probably in response to increased calcium levels inside cells through an enzymatic process involving diacylglycerol lipase α (DGLα).[49] Some evidence suggests that 2-AG is more influential to both CB1 and CB2 receptor activity because it acts as a full agonist (a molecule or substance that triggers a physiological response when combined with a cell receptor) of both receptors, whereas AEA is only a partial agonist (a molecule or substance that binds to a receptor but only partially triggers a physiological response).[50]

The endogenous cannabinoid 2-AG is believed to regulate the transmission of signals across synapses (a gap between two neurons) in the brain,[51] and 2-AG is involved in energy metabolism and food

intake, modulates brain, immune-related, and systemic inflammatory responses, regulates pain perception, reduces cancer progression, and moderates anxiety, depression, and addiction.[52,53,54,55,56,57,58,59] Its abundance in the body and influence on so many key physiological processes make it clear that 2-AG is an important naturally produced molecule for the regulation of health and vitality.

N-arachidonoyl dopamine structure

A natural amide of dopamine and arachidonic acid, N-arachidonoyl dopamine (NADA) is naturally found in the central nervous system, and a known agonist of the CB1 receptor. How it is created and then destroyed is not fully understood, but evidence suggests that it plays an important role in inflammation and pain perception in both the central and peripheral nervous systems.[60] It is protective of the brain (microglial cells, cortical neurons, and hippocampal cells) despite being present in very low concentrations in the brain (striatum, hippocampus, cerebellum, thalamus, midbrain, and dorsal root ganglia).[61,62] Indeed, significantly elevated levels of 2-AG following brain injury suggests that the endocannabinoid system is a vital part of the natural repair system of the brain.[63] In addition, NADA aids cardiovascular function by relaxing blood vessels.[64] Natural creation of NADA in the brain acts as a "self-curing" process to protect and improve brain health.

Primary Phytocannabinoids

Phytocannabinoids are naturally occurring plant molecules that interact with cannabinoid receptors. The cannabis plant reigns supreme as far as the number of cannabinoids present in a single plant. Of more than 450 compounds present in both hemp and marijuana plants, at least sixty have been identified as cannabinoids, and it's estimated there are more than 110 cannabinoids.[65] The greatest emphasis in cannabinoid research has been on THC and CBD, which are significantly active constituents of the cannabis plant. However, the enhancement or suppression of the activity of one cannabinoid by another is well-documented. Both THC and CBD individually have extensive therapeutic properties. They can also be used together in some cases to produce a more balanced therapeutic activity.

Although THC and CBD are the most studied cannabinoids, research is still underway to learn more about the other cannabinoids. There are eight major phytocannabinoid acids found in cannabis—CBGA (cannabigerolic acid), THCA (Δ9-tetrahydrocannabinolic acid), CBDA (cannabidiolic acid), CBCA (cannabichromenic acid), CBGVA (cannabigerovarinic acid), THCVA (tetrahydrocannabivarin acid), CBDVA (cannabidivarinic acid), and CBCVA (cannabichromevarinic acid). These acids must be decarboxylated (elimination of an extra carboxyl ring or group, carboxylic acid) to yield the phytocannabinoids that most people are familiar with, including cannabidiol (CBD), cannabigerovarin (CBGV), cannabigerol (CBG), cannabinol (CBN), cannabichromene (CBC), cannabivarin (CBV), cannabidivarin (CBDV), cannabichromevarin (CBCV), tetrahydrocannabivarin (THCV), and Δ-9-tetrahydrocannabinol (THC). Beta-caryophyllene (BCP) is an irregular cannabinoid and terpene naturally produced via terpenoid precursors and pathways.

Biosynthesis is the term used for the process whereby a living organism synthesizes (creates) a chemical compound on its own. These chemical reactions are completed through a host of systems

and involve a large amount of energy expenditure. Cannabinoid biosynthesis primarily occurs in glandular trichomes that develop on female flowers and, to a lesser extent, the leaves.

Interestingly, cannabinoid biosynthesis and terpenoid biosynthesis share the same precursors and pathways. Cannabinoids are terpenophenolics—compounds that are part terpenes and part phenols—that possess important biological activities important for human health. Isopentenyl diphosphate (IPP) and dimethylallyl diphosphate (DMAPP) are the precursors for the production of terpenoids. Through an enzymatic reaction (catalyzing their addition into geranyl diphosphate (GDP)), terpenoids are pushed into the cannabinoid pathway. Although still being investigated, cannabinoid biosynthesis is believed to start with hexanoate (a short-chain fatty acid anion). Hexanoyl-coenzyme A synthetase present in the trichomes of female flowers triggers the conversion of hexanoate into hexanoyl-coenzyme A. Two enzymes (tetraketide synthase/olivetol synthase) and olivetolic acid cyclase facilitate a chemical reaction that converts hexanoyl-coenzyme A to olivetolic acid. GDP and olivetolic acid are combined to form CBGA. CBGA is modified by various methods to form CBCA, THCA, and CBDA. These acids are further converted to yield the phytocannabinoids that are used medicinally.

THC and CBD are usually the most abundant cannabinoids in cannabis plants, although some strains with high amounts of the minor cannabinoids have been recorded. The minor cannabinoids are present at much lower levels, very often trace amounts. Each of these ligands (molecules that bind to other—usually larger—molecules, causing the receptor to shift to its active form) can be found in the cannabis plant; however, beta-caryophyllene is a sesquiterpene widely distributed in many plants and found in several essential oils, especially copaiba (*Copaifera* species), black pepper (*Piper nigrum*), and guava leaf (*Psidium guajava*). We are still learning about many of the minor cannabinoids and their function in the ECS but what we do know of the most common phytocannabinoids will be explored below.

Biosynthesis of Cannabinoids

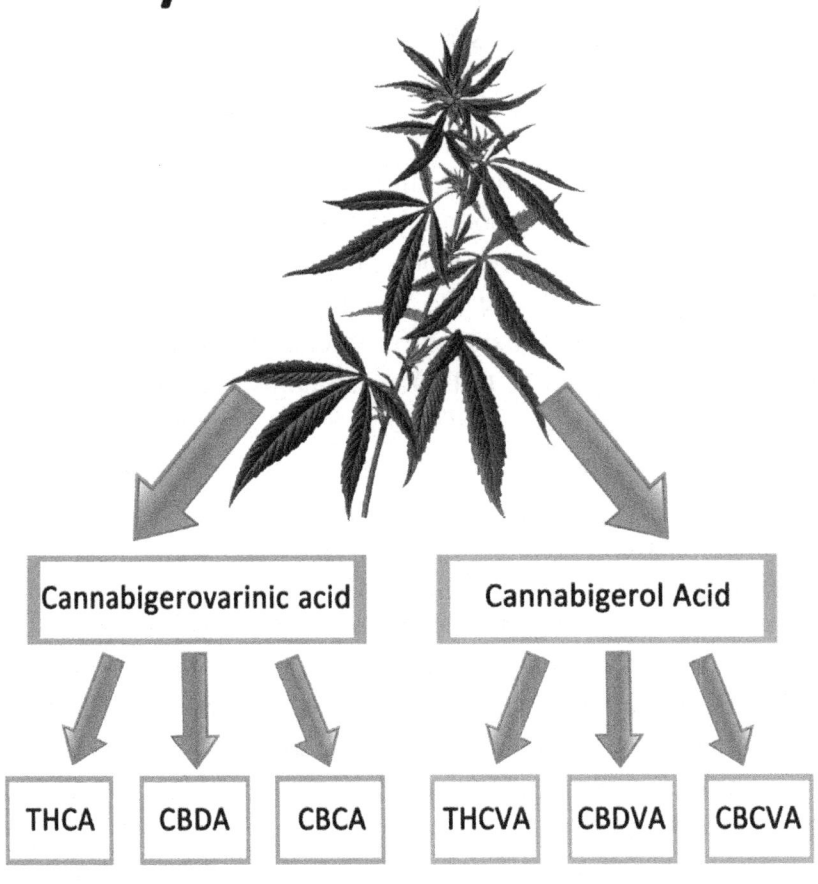

Cannabigerovarinic acid			Cannabigerol Acid		
THCA	CBDA	CBCA	THCVA	CBDVA	CBCVA

Decarboxylation of these acids, usually by
heat, yields a phytocannabinoid, such as THC.

THCA

THC

Δ-9-Tetrahydrocannabinol

As the psychoactive compound in cannabis, Δ-9-tetrahydrocannabinol (THC) has had a great deal of research on its activities, both good and bad. THC is extracted from the resinous flowers (buds) of female cannabis plants. THC attaches to CB1 receptors throughout the central nervous system and body and rapidly overwhelms the ECS. This diminishes the ability of anandamide to fine-tune communication between brain cells. Ultimately, THC's interaction with these receptors produces mental (impaired reaction time, memory, and judgment and triggers a "high" that makes you feel good) and physical (red and dry eyes, reduced intraocular pressure, dry mouth, muscle relaxation, accelerated heart rate, menstrual changes, and changes in feet and hand temperature perception) effects.[66,67] It is no wonder that street cannabis is typically concentrated for THC (to produce a high) and contains very little CBD (0.1 to 0.5%; hashish 8.8%).[68]

THC structure

STRAIN	THC %	CBD %
Kosher Kush	20%–33%	1%–7%
Original Glue	20%–32%	< 1.0%
Bruce Banner	20%–30%	0.1%–1%
Girl Scout Cookies	17%–28%	0.1%–0.3%
Ghost Train Haze	16%–28%	0.1%–1%
OG Kush	20%–27%	2%–15%
Purple Kush	17%–27%	0.1%–1%
Afghan Kush	16%–26%	0.5%–6%
Thai	14%–24%	< 0.5%
Hindu Kush	15%–23%	< 1.0%
Destroyer	15%–22%	< 1.0%
Kilimanjaro	16%–20%	0.1%–1.5%
Sour Diesel	15%–20%	< 1.0%
Trainwreck	14%–20%	< 0.5%
Wappa	15%–19%	0.1%–1.5%

THC only partially activates the CB1 receptor. Consider this like a dimmer switch: while fully activating the receptor turns on the light to full power, partial activation only turns the light on at partial power. Full activation of the CB1 receptor, like some synthetic cannabinoids do, is not desirable because of a significantly increased risk of side effects.

It should be noted that an isomer of THC, Δ-8-tetrahydrocannabinol (Δ-8-THC) is also present in trace amounts in cannabis. They share the same molecular structure, but the atoms are arranged slightly differently. THC oxidizes to Δ-8-THC as the plant ages, so higher levels can be a sign of aged plants or poor storage. Δ-8-THC is also a partial agonist of both CB1 and CB2 receptors.[69,70] Δ-8-THC is considered to possess similar therapeutic properties to THC but is not as psychoactive (about 50% less than THC) and is generally less potent.[71] Both CBD and Δ-8-THC diminish the psychoactivity of

THC, suggesting that combining the three may be an effective medicine while minimizing the negative mental effects of THC.

THC is an analgesic (pain reliever) for multiple types of pain but doesn't work like opioid drugs (a positive thing since opioids are so addictive because of their effects on the nervous system).[72] Opioids bind to receptors in the brain and then send signals called the "opioid effect" that block pain, slow breathing, improve mood, and have a general calming effect. Instead of blocking pain, THC reduces the perception of pain by modulating pain pathways. To retain the pain-relieving effects of THC, it should be combined with CBD, which also reduces tolerance and dependence risk.

Glutamate and the receptors it binds to plays an important role in pain signaling. Inhibition of glutamate (an excitatory neurotransmitter), or glutamate receptors, in the spinal cord and extremities relieves acute and chronic pain, such as migraine, neuropathy, and fibromyalgia. One of the ways that THC reduces pain is by inhibiting glutamate.[73] It also interacts with various other neurotransmitter systems (serotonin and dopamine) that contribute to its analgesic benefits. Its activity is complemented by other phytocannabinoids found in cannabis such as cannabidiol. Truly, some research suggests that the presence of other naturally occurring phytocannabinoids and terpenes is essential to the pain-relieving effects of THC—something some drug companies have ignored.[74] Interestingly, THC enhances the pain-relieving effects of opioids, suggesting they may be able to be combined to reduce the dosage of opioids required to control pain.[75] The current body of evidence suggests that THC should be combined with other molecules (phytocannabinoids or pharmaceuticals) to maximize its analgesic effects and reduce side effects.[76]

Chemotherapy-induced nausea and vomiting (CINV) is a common and distressing side effect. Its occurrence depends on the type of drug used, the dose and frequency of use, and how the drug is administered. Cannabis, and THC, are emerging as options to relieve these side effects. Cannabinoid receptors are present in areas

31

of the brain associated with control of nausea and vomiting. THC likely helps reduce CINV by activating CB1 receptors in the central nervous system. Research suggests that THC only modestly decreases CINV, but people prefer using it over synthetic drugs.[77] People who took THC in a capsule experienced up to 88% relief of CINV. One small study in children found that Δ-8-THC may be more effective than THC for reducing CINV.[78] This is noteworthy considering Δ-8-THC can be given at much higher doses than THC with a lack of major side effects. Western medicine currently uses cannabinoids (smoked or ingested) as an adjunctive therapy after other antiemetic drugs have failed.

Chronic airway inflammation is a feature of many respiratory diseases, such as asthma, cystic fibrosis, and chronic obstructive pulmonary disease. Chronic inflammation causes structural changes (remodeling) to the airways that reduces their function. Cannabis has demonstrated the ability to open the airways and reduce inflammation in the respiratory system. At least if it is taken orally and not smoked. In efforts to determine the cannabinoid(s) responsible for this effect, scientists evaluated the effects of THC, CBD, CBG, CBC, THCV, and cannabidiolic acid in isolated guinea pig trachea. THC was the only cannabinoid that reduced inflammation, bronchial constriction (vagal-induced), and cough responses.[79] THC's effects on the respiratory system indicate it has a role in reducing asthma, cough, COPD, and other airway diseases.

Appetite is a complex interaction between the brain and gut and various hormones, peptides, and neurotransmitters. Circuits in the hypothalamus and brainstem detect changes in energy stores and trigger metabolic and behavioral responses to maintain energy balance. The ability of cannabis to stimulate appetite has been known for centuries.[80] The ECS helps regulate appetite and energy metabolism and may have value for anorexia nervosa. The expression of CB1 and increased anandamide levels have been observed in people with eating disorders.[81] In addition, an increase in the hunger hormone ghrelin has been observed in animals exposed to cannabis.[82] Cannabis triggers brain pathways that

stimulate hunger and modify brain cell activities to ghrelin. Preliminary research in animals was conflicting, but a small clinical study found that oral administration of 2.5 mg (three times daily) to a maximum of 10 mg (three times daily) of THC, ninety minutes before meals, for two weeks increased weight gain in females with anorexia.[83,84,85] It is interesting that THC seems to especially increase desires for sweet and palatable food. Ultimately, the ECS may be a therapeutic target to manage eating disorders and even a therapy for obesity.

Sleep is absolutely essential for human mental, emotional, and physical health, yet restful sleep alludes many teens and adults. New information learned during the day is committed to memory during sleep. People who don't get enough sleep can be moody, irritable, impatient, lack concentration, and make more mistakes. Lack of sleep can alter hormones related to metabolism and appetite, leading to weight gain. Poor sleep even alters immune function making us more prone to illness. Yet it is estimated that around 30% of the adult population experiences symptoms of insomnia—difficulty initiating sleep, difficulty maintaining sleep, waking up too early, and nonrestorative or poor quality of sleep.[86] A renewed interest in cannabis as a sleep aid has emerged as the number of people reporting poor sleep has risen and because of the adverse effects of drugs used as sleep aids (irritability, dependence, complex sleep-related behaviors, and withdrawal).

The improved sleep quality of cannabis is mainly attributed to THC—although many people report improved sleep quality with CBD as well. The limited research available reports that THC reduces time to fall asleep.[87] This makes sense since THC causes sedation. Another potential use of THC surrounding sleep is research showing that it reduces REM sleep time.[88] Reduced REM sleep time means reduced dreaming, which could mean reduced nightmares for people with PTSD, anxiety, and perhaps children with night terrors. Further, controlled trials are necessary to determine if THC is a good option for sleep as initial reports suggest it may impair sleep quality if used long-term.[89]

Post-traumatic stress disorder (PTSD) is a mental health condition triggered by a frightening event (either experiencing it or witnessing it) that involves abnormal memory processing and impaired ability to adapt to changing environmental conditions. While most everyone will experience a terrifying event at some point in their lifetime, those with PTSD have symptoms that get worse or last for months or years. People with PTSD experience severe anxiety, uncontrollable thoughts, nightmares, and flashbacks of the event that interfere with day-to-day life activities and often disturb sleep.

Increasing evidence demonstrates an important role for the ECS in PTSD. The ECS influences brain structures involved in learning, memory, emotional status, cognitive processing, and fear.[90] It facilitates innate coping mechanisms during and after exposure to stress that permit brain adaptations to reduce conditioned fear responses. Impaired CB1 receptor function and lower levels of endocannabinoids (primarily 2-AG) reduces our natural coping abilities, allowing stress, anxiety and fear to accelerate unchecked.

The involvement of the CB1 receptor in, and the fact that people with PTSD have lower levels of circulating endocannabinoids, has led scientists to propose THC as a remedy for PTSD. A small pilot study found that oral administration of THC in people with chronic PTSD and on stable medication reported that THC improved overall symptom severity, sleep quality, frequency of nightmares, and periods of hyperarousal (when the body suddenly goes into high alert including increased alertness and anxiety after thinking of a traumatic event).[91] The study participants took 2.5 mg of THC in olive oil under the tongue, twice daily, one hour after waking up and two hours before retiring for bed. The maximum daily dose used was 5 mg, twice daily. Remarkably, 20% of the participants experienced complete resolution of nightmares by week three. Although the study findings are promising, the small sample size makes further research necessary. In addition, higher doses, and perhaps chronic use, of THC may increase anxiety symptoms.

Glaucoma is one of the leading causes of irreversible blindness for people over age sixty. This group of eye conditions damages the optic nerve usually due to abnormally high eye pressure. Cannabinoid receptors are present in ocular tissues, and studies have found low levels of endocannabinoids in eye tissues of people with glaucoma.[92] THC rapidly and temporarily reduces intraocular pressure (IOP). A controlled pilot study observed decreases in IOP two hours after administration of 5 mg of THC under the tongue (sublingual).[93] Interestingly, the same researchers found that a single sublingual dose of CBD (20 mg) had no effect, while a 40 mg dose of CBD temporarily increased IOP four hours after administration. Another noncontrolled study (orally, 2.5 or 5 mg THC, twice daily, up to a maximum dose of 20 mg/day) demonstrates moderate improvement in IOP in people with end-stage, open-angle glaucoma.[94] A tolerance to the IOP-lowering effects of THC has been reported in some individuals, meaning long-term use may diminish the benefits. The existing research suggests that THC is more beneficial than CBD for glaucoma but may only provide relief for a short period of time as people build up a tolerance to its benefits.

Although the primary benefits of THC are reported above, this is not a completely comprehensive list of therapeutic properties. In reality, THC very likely has many other benefits that have yet to be discovered. While THC has medicinal value, its primary drawback is that it may impair a person's ability to work and drive, limiting its therapeutic use. The possibility of a "high" and dependence are also worrisome. In addition, common adverse effects of THC (dry mouth, headache, sleepiness, and dizziness) may cause some to stop using it. Isolated THC extracts are likely to have the greatest side effects as other cannabinoids, like CBD, buffer some of the negative effects of THC.

Major Molecular Targets of THC[95]	
Target	*Function/Benefit*
CB1 (partial agonist) CB2 (partial agonist)	• Characteristic effects of THC

5-HT3A (antagonist)	• Reduces nausea and vomiting
TRPA1 (agonist) TRPV1 (unknown) TRPV2,3,4 (agonist) TRPM8 (antagonist)	• Reduces pain and inflammation
GlyRα1 (positive allosteric modulator) GlyRα2 (unknown) GlyRα3 (positive allosteric modulator)	• Preserves brain and memory function
δ-OPR (allosteric modulator) μ–OPR (allosteric modulator)	• Involved in neuronal homeostasis • Cardiovascular protection • Relieves pain
GPR55 (agonist) GPR18 (agonist)	• Reduces anxiety and stress • Relieves pain (both neuropathic and inflammatory) • Plays a role in bone metabolism • Influences cellular migration
PPARγ (agonist)	• Modulates gene expression related to cholesterol levels, reproduction, blood sugar control, inflammation, cancer, pain, and obesity

Agonist: Binds to and activates a receptor.

Antagonist: Diminishes the effect of an agonist.

Positive allosteric modulator: Alters the shape of a receptor, which alters the affinity of the receptor to the endogenous ligand, amplifying the effect of an endogenous agonist.

Negative allosteric modulator: Alters the shape of a receptor, which alters the affinity of the receptor to the endogenous ligand, deactivating (inhibiting) the function of an endogenous ligand.

Cannabidiol

Providing many of the same benefits as THC without the "high," cannabidiol (CBD) is considered by many a safer cannabinoid to use. At least, extracts with a higher CBD to THC ratio or enough CBD to reduce the adverse effects of THC. CBD can be extracted from the flowers, leaves, stems, and stalks of the cannabis plant. Both male and female cannabis plants contain CBD, so CBD could be obtained from special marijuana plants (like AC/DC or Charlotte's Web) or industrial hemp plants. CBD shows tremendous promise for improving overall health because of its wide impact on the ECS.

CBD structure

CBD and THC have the same molecular structure (twenty-one carbon atoms, thirty hydrogen atoms, two oxygen atoms) with only

slight differences in how the atoms are arranged. CBD oil is created by extracting CBD from the cannabis plant and then mixing it with a carrier oil (coconut, olive, hemp, etc.). Full spectrum CBD oil— the preferred form—contains trace levels of other major cannabinoids as well. CBD also comes in a water-soluble form (which helps to overcome some of the absorption challenges when used topically) or may be mycelized (transfer of hydrocarbon chains from water into the oil-like interior). CBD use is gaining momentum in the health space as more people experience the benefits and scientists uncover its medicinal properties.

CBD-RICH STRAINS

STRAIN	CBD %	THC %
Sour Tsunami	10%–30%	0.7%–10%
Cherry Wine	15%–25%	0.0%–0.3%
Harle-Tsu	15%–25%	0.1%–1%
Valentine X	15%–25%	0.1%–1%
Corazón	15%–25%	1%–4%
AC/DC	15%–25%	0.5%–6%
Charlotte's Web	15%–24%	0.1%–2.5%
Blue Dragon	14%–24%	0.5%–24%
Ringo's Gift	12%–24%	0.5%–12%
Dancehall	10%–20%	0.1%–10%
Suzy Q	12%–20%	0.1%–1%
Stephen Hawking Kush	5%–20%	0.5%–12%
Remedy	12%–18%	0.1%–1.0%
Danceworld	8%–15%	5%–14%
Hawaiian Dream	6%–15%	4%–8%
Harlequin	6%–15%	4%–10%
Nordle	6%–13%	5%–11%

CBD demonstrates clear therapeutic benefit and good safety for drug-resistant (refractory) seizures.[96] With promising results from preclinical research, scientists were compelled to take the next step and investigate CBD clinically. An open-label trial gave people with treatment-resistant epilepsy—20% Dravet syndrome, 19% Lennox-Gastaut syndrome, 61% intractable epilepsies—2–5 mg/kg per day,

up-titrated (titrated means to continuously adjust the dose of a substance until an effective dose is maintained) to a maximum dose of 25 or 50 mg/kg/day for twelve weeks. What the study found was that CBD reduced seizure frequency by 36.5%.[97] Considering these are seizure disorders that drugs fail to control well or don't respond well to drugs, this is impressive. Adverse events reported in more than 10% of those taking CBD in a safety arm of the trial included sleepiness (25%), decreased appetite (19%), diarrhea (19%), fatigue (13%), and convulsion (11%). A smaller number (6%) experienced status epilepticus (a dangerous condition where epileptic seizures follow one another without recovery of consciousness between them) that may have been related to CBD. The research concluded that CBD warrants randomized, controlled trials to further evaluate the safety and efficacy of CBD for highly treatment-resistant epilepsy.

Reports from the 1970s and 1980s regarding the effects of CBD in healthy individuals, insomniacs, and people with epilepsy from a single laboratory showed efficacy and a good safety profile.[98] Insomniacs who received 160 mg of CBD slept significantly more than people receiving a placebo with less dream recall. As noted in the THC section, less dream recall could benefit people who experience recurring nightmares. The same researchers tested CBD in people with treatment-resistant secondary generalized epilepsy. The participants took 200 to 300 mg CBD daily for up to 4.5 months. What the researchers found was that CBD improved the disease state in seven of the eight participants.

A double-blind, placebo-controlled trial conducted at thirty clinical centers investigated the benefits of CBD in people with Lennox-Gastaut syndrome (LGS; a rare and severe form of epileptic encephalopathy—a brain disease that alters brain function or structure) who experience two or more drop seizures per week. Both a 10 and 20 mg/kg body weight dose of oral CBD significantly reduced seizure frequency (10 mg: 37.2%; 20 mg: 41.9%) when compared to placebo.[99] No serious adverse effects were reported in the CBD group. Common minor adverse effects of decreased

appetite, diarrhea, and sleepiness were reported in the CBD groups—occurring more frequently in the higher dose group. Uncommonly, changes in liver enzymes (elevated aminotransferase concentrations) were observed, suggesting monitoring of liver function with a health care professional is prudent when taking high doses of CBD. Participants in the study were aged two to fifty-five years, showing that CBD can be safely used in children.

Another phase 3 clinical trial (randomized, double-blind, placebo-controlled) administered 20 mg/kg of oral CBD for fourteen weeks in individuals with LGS. A 43.8% median decrease in seizure frequency was noted in the CBD group.[100] The CBD was well-tolerated and effective. Adverse events (sleepiness, diarrhea, decreased appetite, vomiting, and elevated body temperature) were reported in 86% of the CBD group and 69% of those taking placebo. Again, the adverse events suggest high dose CBD is likely to cause some minor adverse events. Partnering with an integrative practitioner is ideal to monitor liver function and work through any adverse experiences.

Dravet syndrome (DS), previously called severe myoclonic epilepsy of infancy, is a rare and severe form of epilepsy that generally presents during the first fifteen months of life as frequent fever-related (febrile) seizures. They can be triggered by temperature changes like getting out of a bath. Most cases of DS are caused by a mutated gene called SCN1A. A family history of seizures is present in up to 35% of cases.[101] Cognitive and intellectual decline generally occurs around age two. As children with DS get older, the intellectual decline stabilizes but many teens and adults with DS require care form others and are unable to live independently. Currently available medicines can't fully control DS seizures and two or more drugs are often prescribed.

In a double-blind, placebo-controlled trial, 120 children and young adults with DS were randomly assigned to receive CBD (20 mg/kg body weight orally per day) or placebo in addition to standard drug therapy for fourteen weeks. On average, the frequency of seizures

declined from 12.4 per month to 5.9 per month in the CBD group; whereas, the placebo group only declined from 14.9 to 14.1.[102] Of those receiving CBD, 43% of them reduced their seizure frequency by at least 50% and 5% were seizure free. Like other CBD-seizure studies, the most frequently reported adverse effects were diarrhea, vomiting, fatigue, elevated body temperature, sleepiness, and abnormal results on liver-function tests. More to come on this, but it would be interesting to see if co-administration of beta-caryophyllene (BCP) could alleviate the abnormal liver-function results—and possibly enhance the antiseizure benefits—since it is strongly liver protective.

COMMON CBD EXTRACTION METHODS

The goal of CBD extraction is to produce an end product rich in CBD and very low in THC. In order to maximize CBD yield one must begin with CBD-rich plant material.

Carbon Dioxide (CO2) Extraction. The most preferred method to extract CBD is with carbon dioxide. CO2 acts like a solvent at specific pressures and temperatures without leaving solvent residue in the end product. It is highly selective and adjustable to extract specific constituents and does not denature or damage the target constituents. It requires sophisticated and expensive equipment that changes CO2 gas into a liquid state. Most commonly, pressure is pushed to supercritical stages (when the CO2 adopts properties between a gas and a liquid simultaneously) and then passed through plant material. The resulting solution is passed through a separator and the various parts of the oil sent to collection containers. In the meantime, the CO2 passes through a condenser and is turned back into a liquid for reuse. The result is a pure and potent CBD oil with trace terpenes and minor cannabinoids.

Solvent Extraction. Food-grade alcohol is the safest solvent used in this method, but more harmful solvents like butane and hexane may also be used. Butane and hexane are not desirable due to adverse health effects and toxicity of trace solvents left in the end product. Food-grade alcohol, or another solvent, is added to plant material to release the cannabinoids and terpenes from the plant material. The resulting liquid is heated and the cannabinoids are separated to evaporate it down to the CBD base oil. This extraction method produces a CBD product with cannabinoids, terpenes, and possibly chlorophyll that is safe for consumption.

Olive Oil Extraction. In this method, olive oil or another fatty vegetable oil, is used to extract the CBD. The plant material is first heated to activate the plant's chemicals (decarboxylate). Then the plant material is added to the oil and heated to 212 degrees Fahrenheit for up to two hours. While you do obtain CBD from this method, the resulting product is highly perishable.

A stroke occurs when blood supply to the brain is restricted and deprives the brain of vital oxygen and nutrients. Frequently after a stroke, damage to the brain interrupts signals between muscles and the brain, causing spasticity (muscle cramps or spasms). This condition makes daily activities such as brushing teeth, eating, and dressing more difficult. Strokes cause a complex series of events to occur, including a massive release of the excitatory transmitter glutamate and proinflammatory cytokines, which plays a major role in brain cell death. Oxidative stress—more free radicals than antioxidants to neutralize them—is evident within seconds to minutes after this type of injury. Scientists revealed that CBD has a potent and long-lasting protective effect on neurons when given before or after stroke, helping to reduce oxidative stress.[103] Interestingly, the protection occurred independent of CB1 receptor

modulation. This identifies a protective and reparative action of CBD during and after brain injury.

With today's fast-paced world and enormous pressure to perform at home, work, school, and life in general, it is not surprising that stress is a factor in most health disorders (including the six leading causes of death in the United States).[104] Anxiety is the most prevalent mental health disorder affecting over 30% of US adults during their lifetime.[105] Anxiety seems to be taking a large toll on adolescents (ages 13 to 18) with almost one-third suffering with an anxiety disorder (38.0% females, 26.1% males; average of 31.9%).[106] A significant portion of the population deals with depression as well— 8.1% of US adults aged twenty and over.[107] This book is not intended to explore all the factors contributing to the increased decline in mental health being seen, but it certainly affects more people than most think and significantly impacts quality of life. As was stated earlier, the ECS is a major regulator of mental and emotional state, suggesting a significant portion of the population could benefit from the use of cannabinoids.

CBD oil has shown promise in the management of stress, anxiety, and depression. Disruption of the ECS in animals triggers a fight-or-flight response by the hypothalamic-pituitary-adrenal axis (HPAA) that increases anxiety, depression, and fear, and impairs cognitive flexibility and normal behavior.[108] These hallmarks of mood disorders may be related to reduced levels of anandamide noted in stressed animals. Endocannabinoids increase our ability to cope with stress by regulating the HPAA and enhancing our ability to overcome emotionally unpleasant memories. Similarly, disruption of the ECS in humans results in increased sensitivity to stress and anxiety, and a reduced ability to feel pleasure.[109,110] Chronic stress also diminishes the ability of the ECS to shield against stress and predisposes one to anxiety and depression.[111] Collectively, the overwhelming evidence indicates that the ECS is critical to maintaining homeostasis, buffering stress, and regulating the HPAA during and after stressful situations.

CBD appears to be the main active cannabinoid responsible for the antianxiety effects of cannabinoids. Low doses of THC can reduce anxiety, but high doses are either ineffective or aggravate anxiety.[112] This effect may be a result of the length of cannabis use. First time users of cannabis with high THC levels can experience significant anxiety and even panic attacks, whereas long-time users report increased relaxation and relief of anxiety. On the other hand, CBD seems to improve our ability to cope with stressful situations that produce anxiety.

Single-photon emission computed tomography (SPECT) brain imaging uncovered one of the reasons CBD may be more effective than THC. CBD decreased blood flow in areas of the brain (limbic and paralimbic cortical areas) associated with anxiety even when challenged by an anxiety-causing situation.[113,114] On the contrary, THC affects different areas of the brain (frontal and parietal areas) than those affected by CBD when it triggers anxiety. Researchers have also discovered that CBD modifies activity in limbic (emotional center) and paralimbic (emotion processing, self-control, goal setting, and motivation) areas of the brain.[115] People with anxiety disorders are in an almost constant state of fight-or-flight causing the body and mind to tense up and feel uncertain, disorganized, and alert. Imagine feeling those stomach "butterflies" and your heart racing consistently and this is what a person with anxiety endures on a regular basis. People with anxiety who use CBD for the first time often report feeling "normal" and not constantly wound up for the first time. CBD calms the areas of the brain linked to anxiety, whereas, THC may increase activity of areas that trigger anxiety attacks.

Involving a fear of social and performance situations, social anxiety disorder (SAD) can be very limiting to quality of life. Generalized SAD involves fears about most social and performance situations, from simple conversations with authority figures to giving speeches. It even prevents people from attending normally pleasing events with friends or family. Ingestion of a single dose of 600 mg of CBD oil by people with generalized SAD prior to a simulation of public

speaking significantly reduced anxiety, cognitive impairment, and discomfort in speech performance compared to a placebo.[116] CBD appears to be promoting adaptations to stress, anxiety, and fear by regulating the HPAA without producing declines in thinking.

Like THC, the benefits of CBD have been investigated in people with PTSD. A randomized, double-blind, placebo-controlled study had people inhale 32 mg (considered a dose below the threshold to reduce anxiety) and found that it reduced fear related to the initial terrifying event.[117] The use of a dose too low to reduce anxiety suggests that the observed effects were mediated by a mechanism other than reducing anxiety. Perhaps balanced HPAA and autonomic nervous system activity is the mechanism by which CBD diminishes PTSD symptoms.

Even children experiencing PTSD may receive benefits from CBD use. A case study reports that a ten-year-old girl suffering with PTSD (anxiety, insomnia, outbursts at school, suicidal ideation, and self-destructive behaviors) related to neglect and sexual abuse improved her anxiety and sleep issues from the use of CBD.[118] She took 25 mg orally at bedtime and sprayed 6 to 12 mg sublingually during the day as needed for anxiety. On the contrary, pharmaceutical medications only provided partial short-term relief and their use was accompanied by major side effects. The CBD oil gradually improved the girl's PTSD symptoms without any side effects. CBD may have a role in reversing emotional and mental disorders related to abuse and neglect in children.

The existing preclinical and clinical evidence strongly supports the use of CBD for generalized anxiety disorder, panic disorder, social anxiety disorder, obsessive–compulsive disorder, and post-traumatic stress disorder when used short-term.[119] Nevertheless, long-term studies are needed to confirm sustained benefits and determine more precise dosing.

When it comes to depression, CBD may exert its antidepressant effects outside of the ECS. Animal research shows that CB1 and CB2 receptors are not activated by CBD.[120] Instead, CBD interacts

with 5-HT (5-HT1A) receptors involved with serotonin (a mood hormone).[121] Activating the 5-HT1A receptor allows for rapid antidepressant effects. This does not mean that the ECS doesn't have an effect on mood and depression. Far from it. Dysfunction of the ECS likely precedes the onset of depression by causing overactivity of the body's stress-response mechanism.

There are two interconnected systems that modulate our response to stressful events—the sympathetic adreno-medullary (SAM) system and hypothalamic-pituitary-adrenal axis (HPAA). The SAM system activates in response to a stressor and the cerebral cortex marks this stimulus as a stressor. A signal is sent to the hypothalamus and the protective fight-or-flight response is initiated. Together, the two systems elevate arousal, increase blood pressure, increase heart rate, etc. and trigger a cascade of hormonal responses (hypothalamus secretes corticotrophin-releasing hormone > hypothalamus releases adrenocorticotropic hormone > adrenal cortex secretes glucocorticosteroids (e.g., cortisol)). Chronic HPAA activation due to prolonged stress disrupts normal HPAA activity and its ability to reset. Unable to properly maintain homeostasis, the ECS can be overwhelmed and we lose a major regulator of the stress response that cascades to depression and anxiety.

Clinical evidence is lacking for the use of CBD in depression, but preclinical research suggests that clinical trials are warranted. Most of the reported antidepressant benefits we see in humans are anecdotal and self-reported by users. The top three medical conditions CBD is used for are pain, anxiety, and depression demonstrating a large market potential if clinical trials are conducted.[122] Unfortunately, mental health is often overlooked at the expense of emphasizing physical health. The reality is that a profound and multilayered connection exists between the mind, body, emotions, and spirit and you can't influence one without influencing the other. Mental and emotional health deserve the same attention that we place on physical health in research.

Autism spectrum disorder (ASD), or autism for short, is a developmental disorder that alters behavior and communication. Signs or symptoms (difficulty communication and interacting with others, repetitive behaviors, restricted interests) usually develop during the first two years of life. It is known as a spectrum disorder because there is great variation in the type and severity of symptoms people experience. Modern medicine has largely failed to address autism and reduce its symptoms.

Knowing the currently limited options (combining essential oils like melissa, ylang ylang, frankincense, lavender, vetiver, and German chamomile show promise) to address ASD, Israeli scientists investigated the benefits of CBD-rich cannabis for ASD. Sixty children, with an average age of twelve, who did not respond to conventional drug therapy received oral cannabis (20:1 ratio of CBD to THC). The maximum dose was titrated up to 10 mg/kg body weight daily. The CBD-rich cannabis reduced behavioral outbreaks in 61%, anxiety in 39%, communication problems in 47%, and disruptive behaviors in 29% of participants.[123] Parents also reported less stress caring for their children. Only mild adverse effects (11% sleep disturbances, 9% irritability, and 9% reduced appetite) were reported. These preliminary findings are very promising and suggest CBD has the ability to improve the lives of people with ASD and their caregivers.

Schizophrenia is a severe and chronic mental disorder that adversely affects how a person thinks, feels, and behaves. It is believed that an imbalance in brain neurotransmitters (dopamine, glutamate, and others) cause people with schizophrenia to lose touch with reality. It is characterized by positive (suspiciousness, paranoia, delusions, perceptual alterations, etc.), negative (emotional withdrawal, psychomotor—movement during conscious mental activity— retardation, etc.), and cognitive (impaired memory, learning, decision-making, attention, etc.) symptoms. Symptoms usually start between the ages of sixteen and thirty. The condition is very disabling and Western treatment largely focuses on symptoms rather than the root cause of the disease.

Evidence is increasing that ECS dysfunction plays a pivotal role in mental health disorders like schizophrenia and psychosis.[124,125,126,127] With the ECS acting as a major control mechanism of emotions and mental health, it is emerging as a major target for mental and emotional therapies. Anandamide signaling seems to be particularly important in the onset of schizophrenia. People with early schizophrenia tend to have higher levels of anandamide.[128] These elevated levels are undoubtedly a desperate attempt by the ECS to balance mood and emotions and stabilize mental health. Elevated anandamide levels in cerebral spinal fluid and the blood of people with active schizophrenia, the fact that antipsychotic drugs target dopamine D2 receptors that decrease anandamide levels to normal, and elevated CB1 receptor expression in areas of the brain (dorsolateral prefrontal cortex, anterior cingulate cortex, and posterior cingulate cortex) associated with schizophrenia further support the major function of the ECS in schizophrenia.[129,130,131] Our mood, anxiety, fear, ability to cope with stress, and happiness, all areas that are disrupted in schizophrenia, are all controlled by the ECS.

Interestingly, use of THC-predominant cannabis at an early age is linked to the development of psychosis among people who are vulnerable to schizophrenia—particularly children who have been abused or have a family history of schizophrenia.[132,133,134] However, this increased risk of schizophrenia is largely caused by THC in cannabis and counteracted by CBD.[135] Early THC use may be overwhelming the ECS and the ability of endocannabinoids to maintain control of mood and emotions.

Adolescent use of THC-rich cannabis and increased risk of schizophrenia makes sense since adolescence is a period of time when the brain's ECS undergoes dynamic changes including increased expression of the CB1 receptors and steady increases in anandamide.[136] Therefore, introduction of THC during this time may impair the delicate balance of endogenous endocannabinoids and initiate dysfunction of the CB1 receptor. Adults do not appear to be as susceptible to an increased risk of schizophrenia with THC

use because this period of ECS alteration and fine-tuning has already occurred.

Preclinical evidence suggests that use of CBD prior to puberty may protect against alerted expression of CB1 receptors and reduce the risk of schizophrenia. Rats administered CBD prior to puberty reversed these negative alterations in the ECS and prevented the appearance of schizophrenia-like deficits.[137] It is possible that CBD could be used in children at greater risk of schizophrenia prior to puberty to reduce the risk of mental illness.

Analysis of 140 individuals who exhibited only THC in their hair was correlated with increased positive symptoms (hallucinations and delusions) of schizophrenia, whereas those with THC and CBD in their hair experienced fewer symptoms.[138,139] An internet-based, cross-sectional study of 1,877 people with a history of long-term cannabis use found that people using a high-potency THC cannabis experienced more psychotic episodes when compared to individuals using cannabis with a higher CBD to THC ratio.[140] Another case-cohort study of 410 people with a first episode of psychosis concluded that daily use of high THC cannabis was associated with a five-fold increase in the risk of first-episode psychosis.[141] Again, this provides further evidence that CBD improves our ability to stabilize mood, anxiety, fear, and our stress response.

Consistent with the preliminary findings, early clinical studies demonstrate the benefits of CBD oil for schizophrenia and psychosis. A 1974 study compared the use of THC, CBD, and CBD/THC combined. Administration of 30 mg of THC dramatically increased psychological reactions (primarily anxiety that approached a state of panic) and significantly impaired cognitive performance.[142] Both the 2:1 ratio (60 mg CBD and 30 mg THC) and CBD alone (30 or 60 mg) countered these negative effects caused by THC or did not produce the same negative effects. Another small study in fifteen healthy individuals found that simultaneous inhalation of CBD (150 mcg/kg body weight) and THC (25 mcg/kg) reduced the euphoric effects of THC and

49

decreased impairments in psychomotor activity caused by THC.[143] Inhaling the same dose of CBD thirty minutes prior to inhaling THC did not produce the same reduction in THC's negative effects suggesting that CBD must be taken at the same time as THC to neutralize some of its effects. A double-blind, placebo-controlled study found that oral administration of CBD reduced the psychoactive effects of THC.[144] THC (0.5 mg/kg) alone caused depersonalization (feelings of being detached from one's thoughts, feelings, and body), disconnected thoughts, paranoia, and anxiety, which was blocked when CBD (1 mg/kg) was taken at the same time. Each of these studies provides strong evidence that THC may aggravate schizophrenia when used alone and CBD can counteract this aggravation when it is taken at the same time.

Clinical studies and case reports also suggest a role for CBD in the management of schizophrenia. One study evaluated the effects of a single dose of CBD (300 or 600 mg orally) in people with schizophrenia. The 300 mg dose significantly improved attention but had no effect on psychosis.[145] Interestingly, the 600 mg dose decreased attention, perhaps due to a sedative effect. A four-week controlled and randomized study compared 200 mg of CBD four times daily to amisulpride (a dopamine D2/D3 antagonist drug used in the treatment of schizophrenia). Both CBD and amisulpride significantly improved symptoms (CBD was equal to the drug), but CBD was better tolerated with fewer adverse effects when compared to the drug.[146] CBD produced an increase in blood levels of anandamide that was not observed in the drug group. Even more important, CBD did not harm the liver (amisulpride is associated with liver injury). Another study found that 600 mg orally per day for four weeks reduced psychosis in people with Parkinson's disease.[147] Lastly, a case report of a nineteen-year-old female with schizophrenia who received haloperidol and oral CBD (1,500 mg daily for twenty-six days) experienced improvement in psychotic symptoms with CBD but not haloperidol. Administration of CBD may be improving physiological responses to endogenous

cannabinoids and improving ECS tone, thus improving overall mental and emotional health.

Taken together, the preclinical and clinical studies suggest CBD may be an effective remedy to manage schizophrenia and psychotic symptoms. It also demonstrates that CBD protects against the psychoactive effects of THC. What needs to be determined is dosing and whether small amounts of THC provide additional benefits or CBD alone is a better option.

Pain is the most common reason people report using cannabis products. Much of this has to do with the significant side effects of drugs used for pain and the very addictive nature of opioid drugs. It is rather odd that some healthcare practitioners express grave concern over the use of medicinal cannabis when they indiscriminately write prescriptions for highly addictive and dangerous opioids. Over 120 people die every day from opioid overdoses in the United States alone.[148] Frankly, opioids were dubiously approved by the FDA based on reassurance from pharmaceutical companies that they were not addicting, but the reality is that between 8%–12% of people who use them develop an opioid-use disorder.[149,150,151] This false reassurance led to the widespread dispensing and misuses of highly addictive opioids. Cannabis is a far less addictive and harmful option for those who suffer with chronic pain and really should be prioritized above dangerous opioids.[152] At the very least, robust evidence suggests that cannabis can reduce the requirement for opioids by enhancing their pain-relieving effects.[153] Combining cannabis with lower doses of opioids is another option for difficult to manage pain that is not responding to standard treatment.

The role of the ECS in pain is well established. Endogenous cannabinoids (anandamide, 2-AG) activate CB receptors and other channels (like TRPV1, a pain receptor channel found on sensory neurons that detects noxious heat and various chemicals involved in pain perception) that modify pain pathways. In addition, higher levels of anandamide and 2-AG are associated with reduced acute

and chronic pain in animals.[154,155,156,157] Lastly, anandamide and 2-AG are susceptible to metabolism by inflammatory enzymes like cyclooxygenase (COX) and lipoxygenase (LOX) that produce molecules that simultaneously increase the production of pain and inflammatory molecules that increase pain perception.[158,159] A perfect storm is created when proinflammatory enzymes are elevated reducing endogenous cannabinoids to reduce pain and increasing molecules that heighten pain. This is akin to firefighters experiencing clogged water hoses at the same time gasoline is being poured on the active fire. The situation worsens and quickly gets out of control. Our current understanding of the ECS and endogenous cannabinoids show how vital regulation of the ECS is in managing pain and inflammation.

One of the keys to the ECS's ability to regulate pain related to various conditions is the location of endocannabinoid receptors at neuronal synapses involved in pain processing (supraspinal, spinal, and peripheral levels).[160,161] Moderate to high levels of CB1 receptors are found in structures that transmit and process pain signals like nociceptors (sensory receptors that detect painful stimuli), the dorsal horn of the spinal cord, thalamus, periaqueductal gray matter, amygdala, and rostroventromedial medulla.[162] CB1 receptors act as a gate that opens and transmits noxious stimuli (pain signals) detected by the peripheral nervous system (nociceptor sensory nerves) to the central nervous system.[163] In the central nervous system, CB1 receptors either enhance or reduce the transmission of pain signals to the brain.[164,165] CB1 receptors act as a processing hub that permit pain signals to be sent to the brain and have the ability to slow or increase the speed at which the pain signals are transmitted. Almost like a Wi-Fi router that is determining which signals can proceed to a peripheral device (like a computer or phone) and what speed the device receives these signals. Higher processing centers of the brain—periaqueductal gray matter and the rostroventromedial medulla—are also influenced by the ECS. CB1 receptors can trigger pathways that inhibit or block the transmission of pain signals to the spinal cord's nociceptive

circuitry.[166,167] The hub either slows or completely prevents pain signaling in this case.

Emotions are intimately connected to sensory centers in the brain. Pain, whether from a broken finger or arthritis, is processed in the brain right alongside areas of the brain focused on emotional regulation. This overlap and connection between brain responses to pain and emotions provides a pathway for people to control pain. Indeed, the development of this ability may partly be responsible for the difference in pain tolerance where some people can handle extreme pain and others are highly disturbed with minor pain. Our emotional response to pain can dramatically influence how much pain we feel. CB1 receptors are highly expressed in areas of the brain (frontal lobe and limbic areas) vital to our emotional response to pain.[168] Awareness of this emotional link to pain can greatly improve both chronic and acute pain.

In addition, CB2 receptors play an important role in pain signaling, particularly chronic pain. Their location in the immune system and expression on a variety of immune cells (macrophages, lymphocytes, and mast cells) and central nervous system cells (astrocytes, microglia) permit wide regulation of inflammatory and pain signaling processes. CB2's primary role is in blocking the release of proinflammatory (increase inflammation) and pro-nociceptive (trigger pain) mediators.[169] By doing so, CB2 receptors reduce inflammation and excessive pain responses. Taken as a whole, it is easy to see how the ECS widely influences multiple mechanisms that cause pain.

Much of the clinical research surrounding pain relief and the ECS utilizes the synthetic cannabinoids making it difficult to directly correlate the effects with CBD. Many synthetic cannabinoid-based drugs are analogies of natural cannabinoids and highly processed for a specific THC to CBD ratio. Increasing the difficulty in determining the benefits of natural CBD alone, some pain research uses smoked cannabis with varying amounts of THC and CBD.

Regulation of neuronal circuits involved in pain signaling by cannabinoids can reduce acute pain perception according to preclinical research.[170] CBD's pain-relieving effects have also been observed transdermally (topically) in a preclinical model of arthritis.[171] Clinical use shows that cannabinoids are more effective for chronic pain (like the arthritis) than acute pain (broken leg, sprained wrist, etc.). A review of cannabinoids (synthetic and phytocannabinoids) concluded that they were not very effective for post-operative (acute) pain, adding further evidence that chronic pain is where cannabinoids excel.[172] Based on this, it may be better to consider other natural options—like essential oils—for acute pain situations.

While the ECS may only mildly influence acute pain, clinical research indicates that it is effective for chronic pain.[173,174,175] Chronic pain generally originates from poorly managed acute pain and is a more complex process (psychophysiological) that involves changes in neurotransmission and sustained plasticity (adaptability to experiences that form new neural connections) changes in both the peripheral and central nervous system.

A small clinical study observed the pain-relieving effects of CBD in people with chronic pain after a kidney transplant. What the researchers found was that oral use of 100 mg per day of CBD completely resolved chronic pain in 28.6% of participants, partially resolved pain in 57.2% of participants, and was ineffective in 14.2%.[176] Common adverse effects included nausea, dry mouth, dizziness, drowsiness, and occasional hot-flash feelings. A decrease to 50 mg per day was required in two of the seven participants because of persistent nausea. Of great importance is the fact that the scientists did not observe any serious adverse effects (liver or kidney function decline, liver toxicity, blood count abnormalities) of CBD in the participants. Much more needs to be determined (dose, CBD:THC ratios, methods) before we can conclusively state CBD is a leading option for pain management, but it certainly warrants further investigation and experimentation.

One cautionary note is that long-term use of significant amounts (10 mg/kg body weight; about 700 mg in the average adult) of CBD may reduce the pain-relieving effects of THC.[177] CBD does act as a buffer for THC's psychoactive effects and may reduce its adverse effects, but a better understanding of how it complements or counteracts the therapeutic action of THC is necessary.

A bump, blow, or violent jolt to the head or body can result in a traumatic brain injury (TBI), which includes a concussion. Research with professional football players has taught us that even repeated non-concussive blows to the head can cause brain injury. Approximately 2.8 million TBI-related emergency department visits, hospitalizations, and deaths (nearly 50,000) occurred in the United States in 2013.[178] A TBI disrupts normal brain function, which can be profound and long-term depending on the severity of the TBI. Brain cells are damaged and destroyed following TBI largely due to glutamate excitotoxicity—excessive stimulation of the brain cell by the neurotransmitter glutamate—and the flood of free radicals that is generated. When brain cells are damaged by a TBI it interferes with their ability to send signals normally. Depending on the parts of the brain that are damaged most, a TBI changes a person's behavior and abilities.

Mounting evidence shows that the ECS plays a fundamental role in the protection and repair of the brain following injury. CBD, in particular, appears to enhance brain protection by reducing brain inflammation and degeneration. Animal research indicates that use of CBD following a TBI reduces short-term brain damage, possibly by increasing anandamide levels after the injury.[179] CBD also protects against cell death caused by free radicals produced after TBI (CBD has demonstrated antioxidant properties) and counteracts glutamate excitotoxicity.[180] While human research on the benefits of CBD following TBI is in its infancy, multiple personal accounts suggest CBD is very helpful in managing chronic traumatic encephalopathy (CTE; a particularly severe form of TBI) symptoms, such as headache, nausea, insomnia, dizziness, agitation, substance abuse, and psychotic symptoms.[181] In addition, a three-year

retrospective review concluded that individuals who tested positive for THC experienced better outcomes (decreased mortality) after a TBI. Given the high number of American football players, other athletes, and soldiers who experience concussions and brain injuries, it may be wise for them to use CBD as a preventive measure. Current evidence suggest use of a CBD-dominant cannabis extract (perhaps with small amounts of THC) may be helpful for people who suffer a TBI and improve their survival odds and quality of life.

There were nearly 47 million people living with dementia in 2015, with this number expected to dramatically increase until it reaches over 131 million by 2030.[182] Alzheimer's disease (AD) accounts for the majority of dementia cases. Abnormal accumulations of neurofibrillary tangles, called tau proteins, and the presence of beta-amyloid plaques are associated with the development of AD.

Healthy neurons receive nutrients and molecules through structures that are stabilized by tau. In AD, tau detaches from the microtubules and clumps together with other tau molecules that form tangles inside neurons. These tangles block the neuron's transportation system and disrupt neuron-to-neuron communication. Think of this like a car accident on the freeway. A car veers out of its lane and crashes into another car, causing a multi-car pileup across all lanes. Traffic comes to a complete standstill until this pileup is cleared. Similarly, communication is halted when tau proteins tangle together.

Beta-amyloid is a naturally occurring protein found between neurons. It normally plays an important role in neural growth and repair. In AD, abnormal levels of beta-amyloid collect between neurons, which disrupts cell function and destroys neurons. Eventually, enough neurons are destroyed that memory and thought function is negatively affected. The leading theory of AD is that a complex interaction with tau and beta-amyloid—along with other factors like the production of proinflammatory cytokines—causes brain changes that lead to AD.

Evolving evidence suggests that the ECS has an important role in neurodegenerative diseases.[183,184] This comes as no surprise given the wide distribution of CB1 receptors and the moderate presence of CB2 receptors in the central nervous system. Molecules that act on the CB2 receptor are of particular promise for neurological disorders because of their nonpsychoactive effects and dual roles in the immune and nervous systems.

CB2 has become the emphasis of research related to the ECS and dementia/AD. Microglia are phagocytic cells—cells that ingest material; think of it like a vacuum, to clean up debris—of the central nervous system. They play a major role in the clearance of proteins and help prune excess, inactive, or dysfunctional synapses (kind of like pruning a fruit tree to ensure the best health of the tree and its fruit). CB2 is abundantly expressed in microglia in the brain of people with AD, particularly where plaques are densest.[185,186] This evidence suggests that the ECS, especially the CB2 receptor system, is activated during the development of AD and plays a vital role in the inflammation associated with AD. Specifically, elevated CB2 expression may be a desperate attempt by the ECS to reduce cytokine production, brain inflammation, and immune-related neuron toxicity and death.

An animal model of AD lends credence to this theory. CB2 receptor activation helped prevent the activation of microglia and the related cognitive impairment caused by beta-amyloid.[187] Other research found that activation of CB2 receptors promoted the clearance of beta-amyloid plaques by phagocytosis and reduced the formation of abnormal tau proteins.[188,189] From the available evidence, it appears that cannabinoids may play a role in the prevention and management of dementia/AD. There have been very few clinical studies on the role of phytocannabinoids—most research used synthetic cannabinoids—in the management of dementia/AD. More animal research is likely to come before human trials are conducted.

Parkinson's disease (PD) is characterized by the progressive degeneration of neurons in the substantia nigra area of the brain that

are responsible for the creation of dopamine. Oral administration of 300 mg per day of oral CBD improved quality of life measures in individuals with PD without psychiatric conditions or dementia.[190] Because the study was small and produced only moderate results, more research is necessary to determine if CBD has a place in the management of PD.

Drug addiction is a chronic condition characterized by compulsive, or difficult to control, use of drugs despite the negative consequences. Dopamine is a neurotransmitter responsible for transmitting signals between neurons in the brain. It plays an important role in multiple brain functions and is a central driver of much of your brain's work. Some of its most important functions involve pleasure, motivation, voluntary movement, memory function, attention, pain processing, and motivation. While the first time a person uses a drug it is a choice, repeated use can alter brain function and activity to make it more difficult to resist urges for the drug. Some illicit drugs (like cocaine) prevent reuptake of dopamine by neurons, which leaves more of it available in the synapse. A synapse is a gap between two neurons, where one is releasing a specific neurotransmitter and the other is receiving it. In order to recycle the neurotransmitter, the releasing neuron absorbs (reuptake) the neurotransmitter so it is available for future use. The prevention of this natural process leads to excessive dopamine levels and a heightened sense of pleasure, as well as a greater desire for the drug. Reactions can be physical (your body physically reacts— moodiness, bowel changes, pain, sickness, shaking, etc.—to not having the drug), mental (emotional and mental), or both.

Several animal and a few human studies have examined the benefits of CBD for addictive behaviors. A systemic review of these studies concluded that the available evidence indicates that CBD may be valuable for addictions to opioids, cocaine, tobacco, cannabis, and psychostimulants.[191] What the review revealed was that CBD appears to reduce intoxication (where the user pushes doses to higher levels to maintain the "high" because of a tolerance buildup) and relapse (the return to use of a substance after becoming sober)

phases of opioid addiction but not the rewarding effects (produces euphoria and a "high") of cocaine and amphetamine.

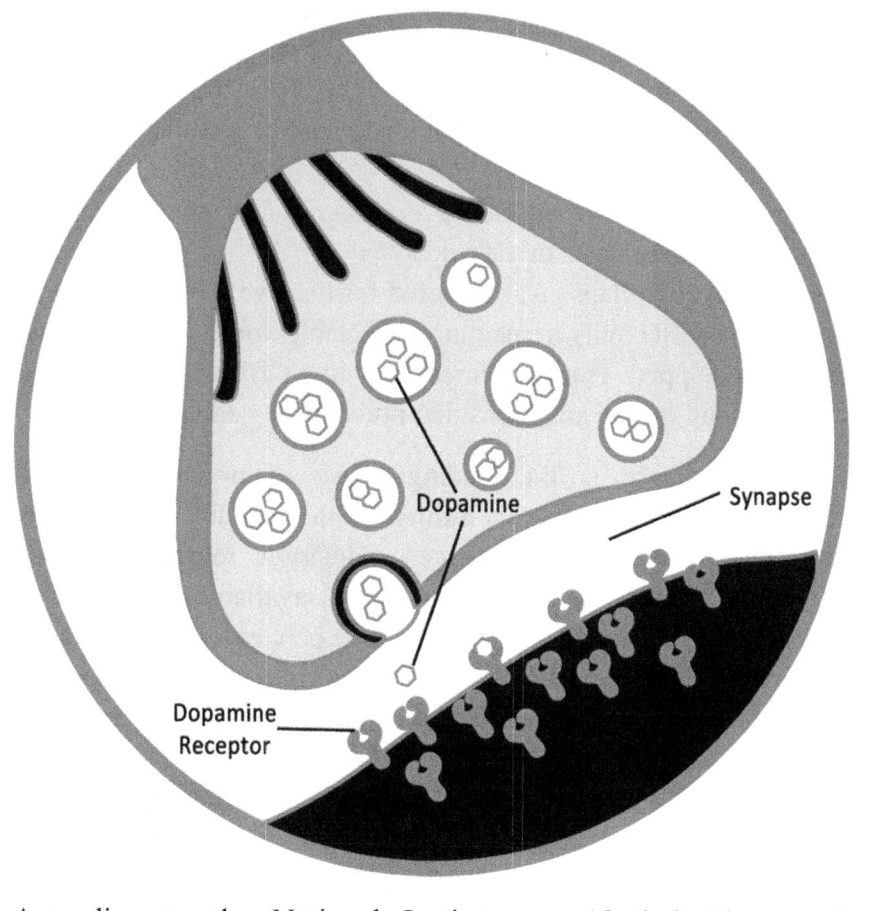

According to the National Institute on Alcohol Abuse and Alcoholism (NIAAA), over eighty thousand alcohol-related deaths occur each year in the United States. Excessive alcohol consumption leads to neurological changes and behavioral and cognitive impairments that may contribute to alcoholism. Signaling in the ECS influences motivation for rewards (palatable food, sexual activity, etc.) and modifies the rewarding effects of addictive drugs. The ECS controls these responses by producing widespread effects of brain-signaling pathways that involve multiple neurotransmitters (GABA, acetylcholine, dopamine, etc.).

Knowing this connection between the ECS and reward circuits, scientists investigated the effects of CBD on addictions. A transdermal CBD gel provided similar protection against brain changes associated with addiction in rats when compared to intravenous administration of CBD.[192] The results demonstrate that CBD can be delivered transdermally and may be a viable option for the reversal of neurological changes associated with alcoholism. Transdermal delivery of CBD (every twenty-four hours for seven days) reduced relapse in rats addicted to alcohol or cocaine.[193] Remarkably, no relapse was reported for the five months of follow up despite CBD only remaining detectable for three days after treatment stopped. These findings show that CBD may cause long-term nervous system adaptions that prevent drug addiction relapse.

Smoking tobacco is the leading cause of preventable death worldwide, causing nearly six million deaths annually.[194] Electronic cigarettes have given the tobacco industry a regrettable boost, especially among teens. Their wide availability, appealing advertisements, variety of flavors, and the perception that they are a safer option has made them the most used form of tobacco among youth.[195] Whether from traditional cigarettes, cigars, or e-cigarettes, nicotine is highly addictive. Furthermore, tobacco use increases the risk of heart disease, stroke, almost all types of cancer, infertility, broken bones, rheumatoid arthritis, poor oral health, cataracts, and type 2 diabetes.[196]

Given the devastating effects of tobacco on human health, even among those who are forced to passively inhale it, a highly successful solution to reduce addiction and use is paramount. CBD could be an integral part of a tobacco-cessation program according to emerging research. Inhalation of CBD (40 mcg) as needed helped reduce the desire for cigarettes in tobacco smokers seeking treatment for nicotine addiction.[197] Interestingly, CBD can also counteract cannabis addiction. A case study reported that oral administration of 300 to 600 mg per day of CBD for eleven days rapidly decreased cannabis withdrawal symptoms.[198] Larger

controlled clinical trials are necessary to determine the benefits of CBD for addiction behaviors, but the initial research is promising.

As was mentioned earlier, the ECS is deeply involved in energy balance. Indeed, it is involved in the regulation of almost every aspect of energy metabolism.[199,200] ECS receptors are expressed in multiple structures—hypothalamus, cortico-limbic, brainstem, digestive organs—involved in energy balance and metabolism. A complex interaction between hormones and peptides (leptin, insulin, ghrelin, cortisol) that regulate energy balance and the ECS controls energy balance.[201] The ECS regulates neurotransmitter and neuropeptide release (serotonin, GABA, etc.) that also play a role in energy balance. Thus, it appears the ECS plays a role in the balance between calories consumed and expended in both the central nervous system and peripheral organs (pancreas, liver, small intestine, adipose tissue). The ECS enhances energy storage into adipose tissue and reduces energy expenditure by influencing both glucose (blood sugar) and lipid (fats) metabolism. Understanding this, it may be possible to manage metabolic disorders like obesity, high cholesterol, and type 2 diabetes by inhibiting the CB1 receptor.

The CB2 receptor also influences energy metabolism, acting almost as a balancer of the CB1 receptor. Activation or suppression of the CB2 receptor improves insulin sensitivity, reduces fat storage in the abdominal region, prevents diet-induced high blood pressure, and reduces proinflammatory immune responses related to poor diet.[202,203,204] The results of preclinical research demonstrate that the CB2 receptor plays a multifaceted role in energy metabolism and weight gain that requires further research.

Elevated insulin and glucose levels increase CB1 signaling, eventually triggering a cascade of events that directly or indirectly leads to diabetic complications. Conversely, evidence suggests that CBD can be used to reduce damage to the insulin-producing pancreas beta cells and reduce the risk of diabetes in non-obese mice.[205,206,207] Moreover, it reduces complications (cardiovascular dysfunction, retinopathy, neuropathy) associated with

diabetes.[208,209,210] Based on this understanding scientists have begun to explore the use of CBD in metabolism disorders.

A randomized, double-blind, placebo-controlled, parallel group pilot study investigated both the efficacy and safety of cannabinoids in people with type 2 diabetes. Sixty-two non-insulin-treated diabetic participants received CBD (100 mg, twice daily), THCV (5 mg, twice daily), CBD and THCV (5 mg of each, twice daily), a 20:1 ratio of CBD to THCV (100 mg and 5 mg, twice daily), or placebo for thirteen weeks. At the end of the study both the CBD and THCV groups experienced positive results, whereas, the combination treatment groups experienced no significant results.[211] The study authors observed that the CBD group experienced reduced resistin (a hormone involved in insulin resistance that is associated with obesity and inflammation) and increased glucose-dependent insulinotropic peptide (a hormone produced by the small intestine after eating that encourages the release of insulin to control blood sugar levels). THCV significantly reduced fasting blood-glucose levels, and improved the function of pancreatic beta cells, adiponectin (a protein hormone involved in glucose regulation) levels, and apolipoprotein A (a protein carried in HDL cholesterol involved in lipid metabolism and associated with a decreased risk of cardiovascular disease) levels. It is possible CBD or THCV could be used to control blood sugar.

Type 1 diabetes is a chronic condition where the pancreas beta cells are damaged causing them to produce little or no insulin. Destruction of the beta cells by invading immune cells causes inflammation of the pancreas. Because CBD reduces the incidence of diabetes in nondiabetic animals in an animal model of type 1 diabetes, researchers investigated the benefits of CBD on early pancreatic inflammation in mice. The mice received 5 mg/kg body weight five times weekly for ten weeks. CBD significantly reduced markers for inflammation in the pancreas.[212] With a benefit to insulin release, glucose control, and protection against pancreas inflammation, CBD warrants further evaluation in diabetes.

Considering all of the preclinical and clinical evidence, larger randomized trials are necessary to determine CBD's role in diabetes, obesity, and metabolic syndrome. Because activation and suppression of both CB1 and CB2 can produce varying positive and negative effects, we need to learn more about how the ECS and cannabinoids affect energy balance.

One of the major obstacles of successful allogeneic hematopoietic cell transplantation (the infusion of progenitor stem cells to establish bone marrow and immune function in people with a variety of disorders) is graft-versus-host disease (GVHD). GVHD is a potentially serious complication where donor immune cells (T cells) attack the host's (recipient of the transplant) healthy tissues and organs. To prevent GVHD, the host typically receives cyclosporine and a short course of methotrexate (together called GVHD prophylaxis). Oral CBD (300 mg daily starting seven days before transplantation and continuing until day thirty) along with standard GVHD prophylaxis significantly reduced the incidence of developing GVHD.[213] The authors concluded that CBD represents a "safe and promising strategy to reduce the incidence of acute GVHD" and that a randomized, double-blind study was warranted.

CBD is emerging as the better option than THC to improve sleep quality. In lower doses, CBD stimulates alertness during the day, which promotes the development of quality sleep patterns at night. This improves consistency of the sleep-wake cycle and your body's internal clock, called the circadian rhythm. Ultimately, better sleep patterns improve mood, concentration, memory, and vital restorative activities that occur while sleeping. At the same time, improved sleep patterns diminish headaches, irritability, and daytime drowsiness.

CBD appears to increase total sleep time, regulate REM sleep (high doses increase time to REM sleep, while midrange doses decrease time to REM sleep), reduce anxiety-related interruption of REM sleep, and decrease insomnia in people with PTSD.[214] However, dosing and the co-administration of CBD plays a huge role in the benefits of THC for sleep. Low doses of THC (15 mg) act as a sedative, and CBD (15 mg) tends to counter these effects when co-administered, promoting greater alertness and increasing awake activity during sleep.[215] Perhaps THC with a low dose of CBD would be a better solution if using THC for sleep. But there is no doubt that CBD improves sleep quality based on the number of people who report more restful sleep and awaking feeling more refreshed after regular use of CBD.

Topical, or transdermal, application of CBD is emerging as an option to overcome poor oral bioavailability and reduce adverse effects of large doses. Orally, CBD is exposed to stomach acid and first pass metabolism by the liver and thereby significantly lowers its bioavailability. Transdermal delivery bypasses the stomach and liver, lowering the stress on the liver and potentially increasing bioavailability. Transdermal delivery may be the preferred method for children because they are more susceptible to liver stress by potent medicinal herbs. Creams, gels, and lotions may only act for a short time because they are rubbed or washed off throughout the day, making deliver with a CBD-infused patch more compelling. Indeed, transdermal patches may be the only way to penetrate the

skin and deliver cannabinoids into the bloodstream because creams, gels, and lotion preparations tend to stay in localized tissue.

Cannabinoid patches come in two types:

- Matrix patches, which are infused with CBD (most commonly in the adhesive layer) and/or THC.
- Reservoir patches contain a small reservoir of CBD (often combined with a gel solution) and/or THC for a more controlled released of cannabinoids.

Transdermal delivery with a patch also allows for the controlled and sustained delivery of CBD for an extended period. Unpublished data suggests that delivery of CBD peaks at about four to six hours.[216] Interestingly, the same data showed a secondary spike of CBD delivery between day four and day five that dramatically increased CBD levels in the blood. Perhaps the CBD was stored in the adipose (fat) tissue located beneath the skin at the site of application and released into the bloodstream at a later date. The factors that trigger cannabinoid release from fat stores are still unknown, but we do know that fat metabolism, exercise, and body temperature may be factors. Preclinical research shows that lipolysis (the breakdown of fats to release fatty acids for energy during periods of fasting or exercise) enhances the release of stored cannabinoids from fat cells.[217] In addition, exercise tends to increase release of cannabinoids from fat cells into the bloodstream, probably by increased lipolysis that occurs during exercise.[218,219] Lastly, exercise increases body temperature and sweating, which is known to influence the delivery of active substances across the skin.[220] More study of this phenomenon is necessary to better understand what factors trigger cannabinoid release outside of those mentioned above and how this influences blood levels and therapeutic activity.

Low doses (less than or equal to 10 mg/day) are also ideal via transdermal delivery. This is because greater blood levels can be achieved through transdermal patch delivery than oral delivery and the delivery is more sustained. In addition, a patch provides an impervious barrier that keeps the CBD in contact with the skin for

enhanced absorption. At the very least, transdermal patches result in a more prolonged delivery of cannabinoids, while minimizing the adverse effects of higher peak concentrations of cannabinoids (such as with intravenous use).

Epidermolysis bullosa (EB) is a group of rare conditions that cause easy blistering of the skin and mucous membranes. Even minor friction or trauma can cause injury and pain. The condition usually shows up in infancy or early childhood and has no cure. One study describes three case reports where CBD was used transdermally in children with EB.[221]

A 6-month-old boy with EB received standard treatment of ointments for wound care, antibiotics to prevent infection, an antihistamine, and morphine for pain. Because of persistent blistering and inadequate pain control by morphine his parents began using a CBD tincture that was misted over the affected areas two to three times daily. Blisters were significantly reduced, chronic wounds healed faster, and the infant no longer required morphine for pain.

The second case involved a 3-year-old girl whose wounds were cared for with petroleum jelly, coconut oil, allantoin, and zinc oxide, In addition, diluted bleach baths and topical bacitracin were used to minimize skin infections. Based on success reported by other mothers of children with EB, her mother began applying CBD and emu oil to the affected areas at least twice daily. The girl experienced reduced pain and quicker healing, allowing her to walk longer distances.

The last case reports the experience of a 10-year old boy with EB managed with topical creams and over-the-counter antibiotics. He had painful keratoderma (thickening of the skin on the palms of the hands and soles of the feet) that required a wheelchair and pain-relievers (naproxen and gabapentin) to control. His parents applied a CBD cream and noticed significant improvements in blistering and reduced painful keratoderma, which allowed him to use his wheelchair less. He also was able to discontinue his pain medication

use. These three stories highlight the benefits of transdermal CBD and its potential for a variety of chronic pain and skin conditions.

The bottom line is that both CBD and THC have massive potential to benefit human health as they become more widely available through legislative actions. CBD may be a more universal option, from children to the elderly, because it is not psychoactive and causes fewer adverse effects. Research, with an emphasis on clinical studies, should accelerate to determine which—and how: dose and method—of these two most abundant phytocannabinoids should be used for the management of multiple disorders.

Major Molecular Targets of CBD[222]	
Target	*Function/Benefit*
CB1 (antagonist; negative allosteric modulator) CB2 (partial antagonist)	• Weight management • Reduces obesity-related cardiovascular dysfunction • Tempers the effects of THC • Reduces drug addiction • Modulates immune activity (autoimmune disorders) • Reduces inflammation • Protects the brain during traumatic injury
5-HT1A (agonist) 5-HT2A (antagonist) 5-HT3A (partial agonist) A1A (agonist)	• Influences autonomic nervous system responses • Improves emotions and behaviors • Enhances cardiovascular function
GABAa (positive allosteric modulator)	• Promotes relaxation and feelings of calm • Reduces anxiety
TRPA1 (agonist) TRPV1,2,3 (agonist) TRPM8 (antagonist)	• Reduces pain and inflammation

GlyRα1 (positive allosteric modulator) GlyRα3 (positive allosteric modulator)	• Preserves brain and memory function
δ-OPR (allosteric modulator) μ–OPR (allosteric modulator)	• Involved in neuronal homeostasis • Cardiovascular protection • Relieves pain
GPR55 (antagonist) GPR18 (antagonist)	• Influences pain, metabolism, vascular function, bone physiology, motor coordination, and cancer progression
PPARγ (agonist)	• Modulates gene expression related to cholesterol levels, reproduction, blood sugar control, inflammation, cancer, pain, and obesity

Agonist: Binds to and activates a receptor.

Antagonist: Diminishes the effect of an agonist.

Positive allosteric modulator: Alters the shape of a receptor, which alters the affinity of the receptor to the endogenous ligand, amplifying the effect of an endogenous agonist.

Negative allosteric modulator: Alters the shape of a receptor, which alters the affinity of the receptor to the endogenous ligand, deactivating (inhibiting) the function of an endogenous ligand.

The "Other" Cannabinoids

THC and CBD get the most attention when it comes to the phytocannabinoids in the cannabis plant because they are the most abundant, well-researched, and understood cannabinoids. However, overlooking the other minor cannabinoids present in the plant would be a mistake. Plant biochemistry is complicated, and the mixture of molecules in each plant is innately designed to fine-tune, synergize, and buffer the entire combination of active and inactive compounds. Some of the most valued drugs were developed by studying plants used in traditional medicine. This fact alone may increase cannabinoid research funding to synthesize a molecule similar to active cannabinoids. From a more natural perspective, cannabinoids represent the next breakthrough in holistic medicine.

Beta-caryophyllene

Beta-caryophyllene structure

Beta-caryophyllene (BCP) is a sesquiterpene alkene produced in high quantities in cannabis. Because it naturally occurs in so many

herbs, spices, and essential oils, its therapeutic properties have been researched more than the other minor cannabinoids. It is sometimes classified as an atypical cannabinoid because its structure is fundamentally different from other cannabinoids. Unlike other terpenes present in essential oils and cannabis (limonene, myrcene, alpha-pinene, linalool, etc.), BCP shares properties similar to cannabinoids, allowing it to trigger similar physiological responses in the ECS. BCP modulates the ECS in a beneficial way that may decrease the incidence and severity of a number of lifestyle diseases.

The therapeutic activity of BCP can be partially attributed to its activity as a full CB2 agonist (activates CB2 receptors). Although isolated in the 1960s, its activity in the ECS was first reported in 2008. Specifically, scientists found that it selectively activated CB2 receptors—a therapeutic target for inflammation, pain, atherosclerosis, and osteoporosis—without activating CB1 receptors.[223] This allows a therapeutic effect without the psychoactive effects. It also potently suppresses homomeric nicotinic acetylcholine receptors ($\alpha 7$-nAChRs; receptors critical to learning, memory, and psychosis), allowing it to influence neuromuscular function.[224]

BCP is considered nontoxic with a wide safety margin.[225] Even high doses are free of adverse effects. One caution for BCP is that it has a lower boiling point than other cannabinoids, so smoking or vaping may degrade or change its chemical properties. Instead, it is best used orally and topically.

Its ability to influence CB2 and other receptors involved in pain perception make it an attractive dietary molecule for chronic pain (both inflammatory and neuropathic).[226] BCP exerts potent anti-inflammatory effects when taken orally, which may be explained by

its ability to inhibit pathways (toll-like receptor complex CD14/TLR4/MD2) that increase the production of proinflammatory cytokines (IL-1β, IL-6; IL-8 and TNFalpha), simultaneously reduce immune-related inflammation, and synergize the μ-opioid receptor pathways (pathways that opioid drugs target to reduce pain).[227,228] The ECS does work in a cooperative manner with opioid receptors to coordinate related pharmacological responses. In total, BCP influences numerous molecular targets to positively influence gene expression and signaling pathways that lead to its considerable therapeutic properties (alleviates neuropathic pain, relieves metabolic diseases, brain protective, heart protective, liver protective, gastrointestinal tract protective, kidney protective, antioxidant, anti-inflammatory, antimicrobial, and immune-modulator).

Much of the research surrounding BCP focuses on its pain-relieving and anti-inflammatory properties. Preclinical models demonstrate that it can reduce inflammation in a variety of inflammatory conditions, including neuropathy, bacterial-caused, eosinophil-related, and more.[229] It can also enhance the effects of other pain medications like morphine.[230] In this way, it modulates pain signaling pathways to enhance the benefits of other pain- or inflammation-relieving solutions. BCP may be part of an synergistic effect with CBD or THC for pain management. Combined with its pain-relieving properties,[231] BCP is a potent option for chronic pain.

Because BCP has similar therapeutic properties to both CBD and THC, it has the potential to enhance their benefits when used simultaneously. Scientists call this synergistic action between phytocannabinoids, terpenes, and other cannabis compounds the *cannabis entourage effect*.[232] The cannabis plant was created with this diversity of therapeutic compounds for a reason, and further study is warranted to determine optimal combinations and ratios of each phytocompound to target specific diseases and symptoms. Indeed, the possibility that BCP may produce phytocannabinoid-terpenoid synergy is an exciting prospect.

Beta-caryophyllene is one of the most powerful anticancer molecules discovered to date. It modulates multiple pathways involved in cancer development (mitogen-activated protein kinase [MAPK], PI3K/AKT/mTOR/S6K1, and STAT3), activates cytotoxic pathways against tumors, potentiates pathways that hinder cancer spread (metastasis), reduces the expression of cancer-causing genes and proteins, and simultaneously increases genes and proteins that destroy cancer cells.[233,234,235,236] It even acts as a cancer preventive.[237,238] Laboratory research shows that BCP kills kidney, lung, colorectal, liver, oral, melanoma, leukemia, lymphoma, and neuroblastoma cancer cells, and protects against obesity-induced progression and invasion by cancer.[239] BCP warrants further research to discover its anticancer potential in humans, particularly given that cancer is now overtaking heart disease as the number one killer of Americans.[240]

We all want to preserve brain and memory function throughout life. Anyone who has witnessed the cognitive decline of a loved one knows just how devastating it is on that individual and the entire family. BCP has demonstrated a neuroprotective role against brain inflammation, stroke, brain degeneration (Alzheimer's disease, Parkinson's disease), and brain cell death due to oxidative stress.[241,242,243] It is clear that BCP protects the brain by multiple mechanisms making it a potential dietary cannabinoid to manage or prevent neurodegenerative diseases.

Cholesterol is a waxy substance found in lipids (fats) in your blood. While it has received a bad rap and is considered by many to be a negative substance, it does serve important functions in the body. Cholesterol is used to build healthy cells (membranes and structures), produce hormones (cortisol, testosterone, progesterone, and estrogen), is an important component of the myelin sheath that insulates and protects nerve fibers, can be converted to vitamin D in the presence of sunlight, and is used to create bile. An unhealthy lifestyle—inactivity and too many unhealthy foods—makes your body to produce excess low-density lipoprotein (LDL) cholesterol

and less high-density lipoprotein (HDL) cholesterol. This imbalance in LDL to HDL cholesterol is a risk factor for heart disease.

In 2008, about 39% of adults aged twenty-five and older had elevated cholesterol levels worldwide.[244] High cholesterol has become such an epidemic that statin (drugs used to treat high cholesterol) use is dramatically increasing.[245] This despite the fact that statins are known to cause serious side effects. HMG-CoA reductase is a major enzyme that regulates cholesterol balance. Increased reactive oxygen species (ROS) and inflammation increase the expression of this enzyme and promote cholesterol imbalance. Preliminary research demonstrates that ingestion of BCP decreases total and LDL cholesterol and increases HDL due to its anti-inflammatory activity, inhibition of HMG-CoA reductase activity, and reduction of ROS.[246] In addition, BCP protected against liver injury caused by high cholesterol levels. The cholesterol-lowering benefits of BCP have the potential to improve cholesterol balance in hundreds of millions of adults and save many lives.

BCP may even contribute to the anticonvulsive and antiseizure properties of cannabis. Mice administered BCP orally (100 mg/kg body weight) experienced reduced seizures caused by pentylenetetrazole (PTZ, a former drug used as a circulatory and respiratory stimulant now frequently used to cause seizures in preclinical models).[247] In a separate set of experiments reported in the same research, the same scientists reported that BCP improved recognition memory. With no adverse effects observed and the proven anticonvulsive activity, the scientists concluded that BCP "should be further evaluated in future development of new anticonvulsant drugs."

Later research discovered the mechanism that BCP provides these antiseizure benefits. Researchers have emphasized CB1 receptors as the target receptors for the anticonvulsant effects of cannabis. However, few have considered the role of the CB2 receptor on seizure susceptibility and epilepsy. That changed with the publishing of a 2018 study. What the researchers found was that

BCP reversed seizures and cognitive impairment in mice, and they attributed this to activation of CB2 receptors.[248] Considering the significant safety of BCP, finding a human dose to reduce seizures should be a priority.

Endometriosis is a debilitating condition characterized by the development of uterine-lining tissue outside of the uterus. Symptoms can include intense to no pain (little to no pain may be experienced in advanced endometriosis), heavy menstruation, and infertility. A preclinical model of endometriosis found that BCP (10 mg/kg body weight orally per day for twenty-one days) suppressed the growth of uterine tissue outside the uterus by 52.5%.[249] It also reduced cysts without negatively affecting fertility. Oral administration of 5 mg/kg body weight daily has also been shown to aid the endocrine system's production of sex hormones (increased estradiol and testosterone).[250] Increases in sex hormones suggests that BCP affects the hypothalamic-pituitary-gonadal axis (HPG axis) or other endocrine sites. Low testosterone is frequently observed in women with endometriosis and may be a preliminary step in the development of premature ovarian insufficiency (loss of normal ovarian function before age forty characterized by insufficient production of estrogen or irregular release of eggs).[251] BCP's promotion of hormonal balance may also benefit women with endometriosis. In addition, since testosterone is decreased in people with pain this may be another mechanism by which BCP relieves pain. Certainly, more research is necessary to see if these results correlate with benefits in humans, but BCP does present as a promising nontoxic remedy for the management of endometriosis.

The modern lifestyle of inactivity and unhealthy foods has produced an epidemic of obesity and diabetes (one in three Americans could have diabetes by 2050 if trends continue).[252] The sugar glucose is the primary source of energy for muscle cells and other tissues. Normally, when we eat food our bodies convert carbohydrates to glucose. The presence of glucose in the bloodstream triggers the secretion of insulin, which helps cells absorb this glucose. In type 2 diabetes, this process doesn't work well and high levels of glucose

build up in the bloodstream. In response, the pancreas beta cells release more insulin in an attempt to control these high glucose levels. Eventually, the function of these cells becomes impaired and they no longer produce enough insulin to control blood sugar levels.

Diabetes is associated with a host of complications and increases the risk of several serious health problems. People with diabetes experience endothelial dysfunction—abnormal function of the inner lining of small arteries and a risk factor for cardiovascular disease (CVD)—when compared to healthy individuals.[253] This abnormal endothelial function increases blood pressure and the risk of stroke and reduces blood circulation to the extremities. Diabetes also accelerates nerve damage (present in about half of people with diabetes), which causes diabetic neuropathy. High blood-glucose levels cause the kidneys to filter too much blood, stressing kidney filters (tiny capillaries with minute holes that act as filters) and potentially damaging the kidneys. In addition, diabetes increases the risk of eye disorders (glaucoma, cataracts), skin disorders (blisters, itching, infections), gastrointestinal complications (gastroparesis: delayed stomach emptying), and ketoacidosis (a serious complication that occurs when excess ketones are produced). Controlling blood sugar levels should be a major emphasis of anyone who wants to be healthy—diabetic or not.

Early research indicates that BCP plays a role in carbohydrate metabolism and may be useful for the management of diabetes. The glucose tolerance test measures how quickly glucose is cleared from the blood. Oral administration of 200 and 400 mg/kg body weight of BCP improved glucose levels, with the 200 mg dose producing a greater insulin-release response in diabetic rats.[254] Even more impressive, the scientists observed significantly improved HbA1c (a test that measures long-term blood sugar control) levels. BCP's effects were comparable to the diabetic drug glibenclamide. In addition, the rats who received BCP experienced significant decreases in food intake, improved body weight (near normal and comparable to glibenclamide), restored activity of enzymes involved in glucose uptake to near normal, and reversal of elevated

gluconeogenic (enzymes that are elevated in diabetics; inhibition of these enzymes improves glucose balance) activity. Lastly, diabetic rats experience elevated glycogen phosphorylase (GP) and diminished glycogen synthase (GS) activity, which caused a reduction in glycogen—a substance that stores glucose in tissues for future use as an energy source—levels. BCP restored glycogen levels and normalized the activity of both GP and GS. The above findings reveal that BCP significantly influences glucose and insulin balance and may be a promising candidate for human studies to manage high blood-glucose levels.

Oxidative stress plays a pivotal role in the development of diabetic complications. An overproduction of superoxide (a reactive free radical) damages the endothelium and heart-muscle tissue (myocardium) and activates pathways and enzymes that increase inflammation and the risk of cardiovascular complications. Diabetic rats given BCP (200 mg/kg of body weight) for forty-five days significantly decreased glucose and insulin levels.[255] BCP improved insulin release by beta cells and protected these cells against oxidative/inflammatory stress. Furthermore, BCP reduced overall inflammation and restored antioxidant activity. Taken as a whole, BCP appears to protect against diabetes progression and some of its complications.

The nonsteroidal anti-inflammatory drug (NSAID) ketoprofen is used to treat pain and inflammation associated with many disorders, including arthritis. However, it is harmful to the liver, especially if too much is taken. Preclinical research shows that BCP improves enzyme activity, signaling pathways, gene/protein expression, and inflammation to protect the liver against damage caused by various agents, including ketoprofen.[256,257,258,259] Given the liver-protective role of BCP and its considerable involvement in pain and inflammation, it makes sense to explore this safe compound, alone or in combination with CBD or THC, to manage inflammatory and painful conditions.

Nonalcoholic fatty liver disease (NAFLD) is the most common liver disease worldwide. It is characterized by the buildup of fat (lipids) in liver cells. Excess fat in the liver can cause fatigue, pain in the upper right abdomen, and an enlarged liver. Research with clove, a spice that contains BCP, found that BCP is the principal component in clove that suppresses fat accumulation in the liver.[260] The researchers further found that BCP does this by activating the CB2 receptor in liver cells, which leads to alteration of signaling associated with fat accumulation. The results suggest that BCP may prevent or reverse NAFLD and its associated metabolic disorders.

In addition to all of the above-mentioned benefits of BCP, it also demonstrates antiviral, antibacterial, antifungal, antioxidant, and insect-control properties, and may even expand lifespan.[261] It appears that we should take greater note of the potential role that BCP has in the observed benefits of cannabis use. This molecule warrants a place right next to CBD and THC because of its myriad benefits to human health.

Cannabichromene

Cannabichromene structure

An analogue of THC, cannabichromene (CBC) is the second most abundant cannabinoid in marijuana (THC-rich) plants. It is a nonpsychoactive cannabinoid that activates both CB1 and CB2 receptors—although its affinity is stronger for CB2—and prevents the inactivation of the ECS.[262,263] It also binds to receptors associated with pain perception (TRPV3: agonist; TRPM8: antagonist; TRPA1: agonist) signifying a role in the pain-relieving effects of cannabis.[264,265,266] Binding to these receptors also

increases levels of endogenous cannabinoids. CBC also inhibits the reuptake (the reabsorption of neurotransmitters by the neuron that released them) of anandamide, making more of it available for neurotransmission.[267] While CBC has its own therapeutic value, scientists hypothesize that CBC is one of the molecules that work synergistically with other cannabinoids, enhancing their effects.

Not surprisingly, CBC exhibits anti-inflammatory and pain-relieving activity.[268] Preclinical research found that CBC reduced inflammation better than the NSAID phenylbutazone.[269] Importantly, CBC is less toxic than phenylbutazone, allowing for larger doses to be used for an improved therapeutic effect.[270] The rostral ventromedial medulla (RVM) plays an important role in pain perception, specifically, pathways that diminish pain. CBC reduced neuron activity in the RVM and reduced pain in rats.[271] In addition, it significantly elevated endocannabinoid levels in an area of the brain that suppress pain (the ventrolateral periaqueductal gray: the primary regulator of pain-reducing pathways that contain encephalin-producing cells that suppress pain). CBC also potentiates the pain-relieving action of THC.[272] CBC reduces pain and inflammation through multiple mechanisms, making it an attractive molecule for painful and inflammatory conditions.

One preclinical study examined the effects of CBC in inflammatory bowel disease (e.g., colitis). Mice given CBC experienced a significant reduction in intestinal damage and excess intestinal permeability as well as diminished myeloperoxidase activity (an enzyme marker for colitis).[273] The intestines must be permeable to allow nutrients to escape from the digestive tract to the bloodstream. However, increased permeability allows larger molecules (allergenic proteins, pathogens, and toxins) to enter the bloodstream. Increased intestinal permeability increases inflammation in the body and is associated with diseases of the gastrointestinal system, such as inflammatory bowel diseases, celiac disease, food allergy, irritable bowel syndrome, obesity, and metabolic syndrome.[274] Another study found that CBC slows accelerated intestinal transit caused by inflammation.[275] This action means it could potentially

reduce diarrhea, particularly Crohn's disease where diarrhea is primarily caused by inflammation. The role of CBC in the digestive tract deserves further research and study.

CBC has also been investigated against human cancers. While CBD was the most potent anticancer cannabinoid of the five tested (CBD, CBG, CBC, cannabidiol acid, THC acid) in one study, CBC also inhibited the growth of breast cancer cells.[276] CBC may be part of an entourage effect in the management of cancer, or it may have benefits alone. Further research is necessary to determine its role in the prevention and treatment of cancer.

Preliminary research suggests that CBC plays a role in preserving brain and memory function. Neural stem progenitor cells (NSPCs) are vital to learning and brain function and health. NSPCs are found in the nervous system and differentiate into neurons as well as astroglial cells (astrocytes)—the most important cells for maintaining brain homeostasis. Astroglial cells are absolutely essential for directing neurotransmitter traffic and a major defense against brain cell death caused by oxidative stress, inflammation, and toxicity.[277] CBC positively affects the viability of NSPCs by influencing multiple mechanism and pathways.[278] Knowing that dysfunction of NSPCs plays a role in neurological conditions like stroke, multiple sclerosis, and Parkinson's disease, it is exciting to know a possible solution may lie in CBC.

Acne is a common and embarrassing skin condition characterized by excess production of sebum and inflammation of the sebaceous glands. Certain bacteria (*Cutibacterium acnes, Corynebacterium granulosum*) are also associated with its development. CBC powerfully reduces acne by reducing inflammation, suppressing excess sebum production, and reducing arachidonic acid (a major dietary omega-6 fatty acid that increases inflammation).[279] It is possible one day that CBC, perhaps combined with CBD, may be a useful remedy for acne.

The involvement of ECS in mood balance is well-known. CBC exhibited a significant antidepressant action in mice, and thus may contribute to the overall mood-enhancing benefits of cannabis.[280] CBC has very low binding affinity to the CB1 receptor, which means that it exerts antidepressant activity by multiple mechanisms.

Studies show that CBC often tempers the negative effects of THC, making it an important molecule for the safety of cannabis extracts. More research is required to determine the full therapeutic activity and potential of this cannabinoid outside an entourage effect.

Cannabichromevarin

Cannabichromevarin structure

Little is known about cannabichromevarin (CBCV), and not much research has been conducted on it since its discovery in 1975. It is related to CBC but has as shorter chemical structure—CBCV has a propyl chain rather than a pentyl chain. Because of its similarities to CBC, it is believed CBCV shares similar therapeutic properties. Based on research with other cannabinoids with propyl chains (CBDV and THCV), it is possible that CBCV has a balancing or adaptogenic effect. THCV enhances or lessens the effects of THC, which may be the same thing CBCV does for CBC. Until this molecule receives more attention and emphasis in research, we won't know its therapeutic value.

Cannabidivarin

Cannabidivarin structure

Like CBCV, cannabidivarin (CBDV; also known as cannabidivarol) is a propyl-chain cannabinoid and not psychoactive. It is more commonly found in *C. indica* strains and low-THC *C. sativa* strains. Similar to many other cannabinoids, CBDC interacts with receptors associated with pain perception (TRPV1,2,3 agonist, TRPA1 agonist).[281,282] It suppresses GPR55, making it a possible remedy for intestinal inflammation, cancer, endothelial dysfunction, and other conditions.[283,284] CBDV research demonstrates that it has the potential to manage rare diseases that currently lack effective medications and treatments.

Despite the approval of numerous drugs for epilepsy, almost one-third of people with epilepsy have epilepsy resistant to available drugs (refractory). Cannabinoids are leading molecules being investigated for the creation of drugs to treat epilepsy. Preclinical research confirms the anticonvulsant activity of CBDV in a variety of epilepsy models by a mechanism independent of CB1-receptor modulation, largely by regulating the expression of genes related to epilepsy.[285,286,287,288] By regulating genes related to epilepsy, CBDV may protect against brain alterations that make a person more susceptible to epilepsy.

Research is progressing with CBDV, making it more likely that it could be used clinically to manage seizures, especially cases unresponsive to drugs.[289,290] Unfortunately, it is likely to be

introduced as a synthetic analogue of CBDV that is patentable rather than using the natural form. Another possibility to make this cannabinoid more available is through breeding of a unique chemotype (plants characterized by their chemical content) with high levels of CBDV. Many who suffer from seizure disorders eagerly await clinical trials.

Duchenne muscular dystrophy (DMD) is a rare genetic disorder that causes chronic inflammation and progressive muscle degeneration and weakness. It is caused by the absence of dystrophin (a protein that protects the integrity of muscle cells). Emerging research suggests that impaired myoblast differentiation and formation of myotubes—a muscle fiber formed by fusion of myoblasts that are essential for healthy muscle development—also plays a role.[291] Impaired autophagy (a cellular-waste-cleanup process) significantly contributes to muscle damage as well. Symptoms usually appear between the ages of three and five, primarily affecting boys. There is no cure for DMD, but treatment consists of steroid injections to moderately slow its progression.

Researchers investigated the effects of CBDV, CBD, and THCV in mice cells and human cells from healthy and people diagnosed with DMD. Both CBDV and CBD promoted differentiation of myoblasts cells into myotubes.[292] CBDV, CBD, and THCV each promoted myotube formation in healthy and DMD human cells. Lastly, the researchers reported that CBDV and CBD restored autophagy, reduced inflammation, and prevented muscle damage. This early research shows that cannabinoids promote normal muscle cell development and other processes that are deficient in people with DMD. Promising preliminary research that could potentially benefit young children afflicted with DMD.

Rett syndrome (RS) is a neurodevelopmental disorder characterized by normal early growth followed by impaired development, loss of hand use, problems walking, seizures, slowed brain and head growth, and intellectual disability. It almost exclusively affects girls, with symptoms beginning after the first six to eighteen months of

development. A genetic cause (mutation of the MECP2 gene) is identified in about 95% of cases. A recent discovery revealed that the GPR55 receptor—animals with RS have increased levels of GPR55 in the hippocampus—plays a role in RS development.[293] RS has no cure, and research has done little to discover effective therapies to slow progression. Instead, treatment emphasizes improving movement and communication, reducing seizures, and providing care and support.

The ECS regulates multiple behavioral and physiological processes that are impaired in RS. Moreover, ECS dysfunction is associated with other disorders that share common symptoms with RS. Scientists evaluated the therapeutic potential of CBDV in a validated animal model of RS. CBDV corrected abnormal brain and behavioral functions, possibly by suppressing GPR55 activity.[294] Remarkably, the scientists also observed that CBDV reversed the compromised general health and reduced brain size, and partially restored motor coordination (the ability to use muscles, joints, and nerves in a coordinated effort to perform a particular task). Highlighted from this research is the emerging therapeutic potential of CBDV that should be investigated in clinical research.

Nausea can be caused by a variety of substances, conditions, and situations, such as motion, pregnancy, medication, gallbladder disease, overeating, concussions, fear, bowel obstruction, and disagreeable odors. The ECS plays a primary role in nausea because of the presence of CB receptors in areas of the brain associated with nausea. Preclinical research found that both CBDV and THCV have therapeutic potential in relieving nausea.[295]

While research into the therapeutic properties of CBDV has increased, we still have much to learn about it. It obviously has medicinal qualities of its own and likely works with other cannabinoids to produce therapeutic benefits.

Cannabigerovarin

Cannabigerovarin structure

Cannabigerovarin (CBGV), also written cannabigevarin, is another cannabinoid with a propyl chain and homologue (similar compounds differing from each other by a repeating unit) of CBG. It potently inhibits GPR55 receptor signaling[296] and desensitizes the TRPV3 channel (a channel involved in temperature sensation and vascular regulation).[297] Additionally, it is a potent inhibitor of L-alpha-lysophosphatidylinositol (see THCV to learn more), which is an endogenous ligand that activates GPR55.[298] Its ability to inhibit GPR55 in more than one way make it an attractive molecule for further investigation regarding cancer development and progression. Indeed, laboratory research showed that CBGV inhibits leukemia cells.[299] Outside of this, we don't know much about this minor cannabinoid yet.

Cannabigerol

Cannabigerol structure

Cannabigerol (CBG) is among the lesser-known cannabinoids and not present in large quantities in most strains; yet it still is worth learning about. It is not psychoactive and has a greater binding affinity for CB2 than CB1. We know that it is a partial agonist of both CB1 and CB2 receptors and inhibits the reuptake of anandamide.[300,301,302,303] In addition, like other cannabinoids, it influences the TRP channels (TRPV1,2: agonist; TRPM8: antagonist; TRPA1: agonist).[304,305] Other receptors targets of CBG include alpha(2)-adrenoceptors (potent activator) and 5HT1A (moderately potent suppressor).[306] Some research has already discovered the therapeutic value of CBG. Much of the research has reported that CBG possesses similar therapeutic properties as THC without the adverse effects or psychoactivity.

The neuroprotective role of other cannabinoids has been well established. They largely protect against neurodegeneration by reducing inflammation and oxidative stress. Pretreatment of motor neurons with CBG protected them against toxicity and death caused by lipopolysaccharide (an endotoxin that promotes the secretion of proinflammatory molecules).[307] The researchers found that CBG reduced both inflammation (IL-1beta, TNF-alpha, IFN-gamma, and PPAR-gamma) and oxidative stress. This preliminary research indicates that CBG may have potential in the management of neuroinflammatory diseases involving oxidative stress (e.g., Alzheimer's disease, Parkinson's disease).

Scientists also studied the effects of CBG in two separate models of Huntington's disease. They found that it was extremely protective of neurons, reduced neuroinflammation, enhanced antioxidant defenses, improved brain gene expression, and diminished motor deficits.[308] Although a very minor constituent (usually less than 1% in most cannabis plants), it may be enhancing the neuroprotective properties of other cannabinoids like CBD.

The search for agents that selectively kill cancer cells is a priority for human health. Current chemotherapy drugs indiscriminately kill cancer and healthy human cells—especially blood cells and immune

cells. By doing so, the individual receiving chemotherapy is more prone to infections, low blood counts, mouth sores, nausea, diarrhea, and hair loss. Cannabinoids have been investigated against various cancer cells. Of five agents tested (geraniol, olivetol, two cannabinoids, and 5-fluorouracil), CBG was the most effective against oral cancer (human oral epithelioid carcinoma).[309] This is remarkable, considering it was more effective than a chemotherapy drug used to treat oral cancers.

Colitis is a condition characterized by irritation and inflammation of the large intestine (colon). Eventually, it leads to ulcers in the lining of the colon. Myeloperoxidase (MPO) activity is a biomarker for colitis, used to detect inflammation level and disease activity. A systemic review of cannabinoids concluded that CBG had the greatest effect in reducing MPO.[310] Another study found that CBG modulates CB2 receptors to reduce inflammation caused by colitis.[311] Based on these studies, it may be possible to reduce intestinal inflammation with CBG.

Other research supports the use of CBG for colon cancer because of its ability to interact with targets involved in cancer. CBG blocks TRPM8, activates TRPA1, TRPV1, and TRPV2 channels, blocks 5-hydroxytryptamine receptor 1A (5-HT1A) receptors, and inhibits the reuptake of endocannabinoids. CBG promoted apoptosis (cell death) in cultured colon cancer cells and inhibited the growth of colon tumors in animals.[312] It is evident that CBG is protective of the colon and promotes healthy function.

Overactive bladder is a condition characterized by bladder contractions that force urine from the bladder and cause leakage. Acetylcholine released from nerves is the main stimulus that causes contraction of bladder muscles. Laboratory research found that CBG significantly reduces mouse bladder contractions caused by acetylcholine.[313] Its ability to reduce bladder contractions was stronger than CBD and CBDV, and equal to THCV. The findings were also confirmed in human cells, where CBG reduced human

bladder contraction triggered by acetylcholine. CBG may have potential to manage overactive bladder.

Like THC, CBG may have a role in the management of glaucoma. Research suggests that it modestly reduces intraocular pressure when acutely administered.[314,315] Even more importantly CBG did not cause the rapid eye movement, sleepiness, ocular toxicity, or neurotoxicity associated with THC. If dosing can be dialed in, CBG may be a better option for glaucoma because of reduced adverse effects and the tolerance that is associated with THC.

Preliminary research suggests that CBG is an appetite stimulant.[316,317] Although THC also increases appetite, it comes with psychoactive properties, which make CBG more attractive. Based on this, it may warrant further investigation for eating disorders and loss of appetite caused by certain medications or treatments.

Signaling by the ECS has a role in the control of skin physiology. In fact, research suggests that a functional ECS is found in the skin, which regulates skin cell health, inflammation, hormone production, and hair follicle and sebaceous gland health.[318] Compartments—epidermis, sebaceous glands, hair follicles—in the skin produce the endocannabinoids anandamide and 2-AG that bind to CB receptors that reduce pain and itching and help maintain skin health. The primary function of the cutaneous ECS is to control proper and balanced skin cell function, disruption of which can result in the development of skin diseases like acne, psoriasis, systemic sclerosis, cancer, and dermatitis.

Preliminary research demonstrates that CBG has potential to relieve skin conditions. A layer of lipids produced by sebaceous glands and keratinocytes covers the surface of the skin. The composition of these lipids influences skin health, function, and the development of certain skin conditions. Emerging research suggests that CBG increases the production of sebaceous lipids and may have potential to restore dry skin.[319] Another study found that CBG significantly reduced the expression of skin differentiation genes (keratins 1 and 10, involucrin and transglutaminase 5, as well as on DNA

methylation of keratin 10) indicating that it may be therapeutic for skin diseases.[320] The identification of a cutaneous ECS is fascinating and may lead to the development of cannabis-derived solutions for a variety of skin conditions.

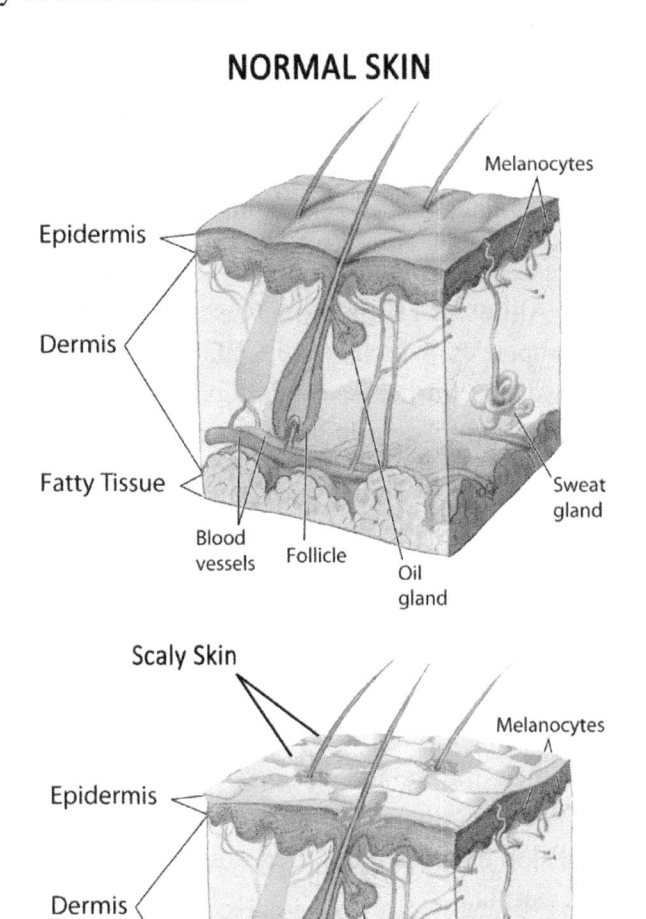

Psoriasis is an inflammatory skin condition caused by the excessive proliferation of keratinocytes and abnormal differentiation of skin cells. The cutaneous ECS helps control the differentiation and proliferation of skin cells. CBG inhibited the proliferation of keratinocytes, supporting a role for CBG in the management of psoriasis.[321] Altogether, the early studies are promising for CBG in skin health and skin diseases.

Several cannabinoids have demonstrated anti-nausea properties, and there may be synergy among multiple cannabinoids to relieve nausea and vomiting. However, CBG appears to reverse the anti-nausea effects of at least CBD. Pretreatment with CBG in rats and shrews reduced the anti-nausea and antiemetic effects of CBD.[322] The scientists hypothesized that CBD and CBG may oppose each other at 5-HT(1A) receptors triggering this effect.

CBG is a nontoxic and nonpsychoactive cannabinoid with emerging therapeutic benefits relevant to human health. Some plants may produce high levels of CBG making it an attractive option for future clinical use.[323]

Cannabinol

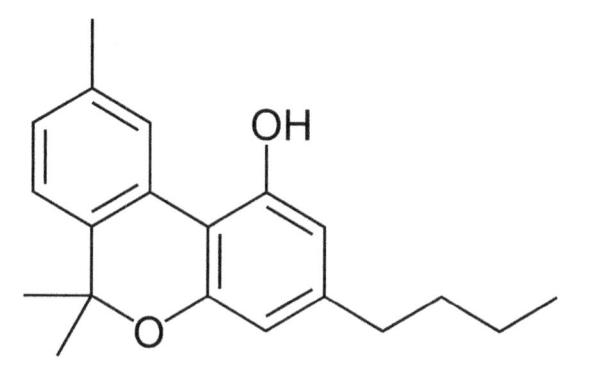

Cannabinol structure

Cannabinol (CBN) is produced when THC is exposed to heat or oxygen causing an oxidative conversion from THC to CBN. Because of this, CBN is present in higher amounts in aged or improperly stored cannabis plants. Its total content rarely eclipses

1% in healthy plants. It shares similar properties and activity to THC when tested in animals.[324] An unexplained phenomenon with CBN is its higher binding affinity for CB1 and CB2 receptors (when compared to THC) but absence of psychoactive properties. It is an agonist (activator) of CB1 and an agonist/inverse agonist of CB2 receptors.[325,326] Inverse agonists deactivate receptors by suppressing their spontaneous activity. It also affects TRP channels (TRPA1: agonist; TRPM8: antagonist), indicating a role in pain perception.[327] As a unique cannabinoid, it may possess untold therapeutic value to human health

One of the most exciting preliminary findings of CBN is its possibility to relieve symptoms of amyotrophic lateral sclerosis (ALS). ALS is a group of progressive rare neurological disorders that affect the neurons responsible for voluntary muscle movement. Early signs (muscle twitching, muscle cramps, muscle weakness affecting one leg, arm, the neck, or diaphragm, slurred speech, difficulty chewing or swallowing, and muscle stiffness) of ALS may be overlooked or brushed off. The symptoms become more apparent as the disease progresses to other parts of the body and worsen. Currently, there is no cure or effective treatment that halts or reverses disease progression. CBN reduced symptom/disease onset in a preclinical model of ALS and improved animal survival rate.[328] It's possible that other cannabinoids may be helpful for ALS. Given the lack of any effective treatment, the investigation of cannabinoids for ALS should be accelerated.

As stated above, psoriasis involves excess skin cell proliferation, which causes the skin to regenerate three to four times faster than normal. CBN inhibited the proliferation of keratinocytes, supporting a role for CBN in the management of psoriasis.[329] It would be interesting to determine if topical or oral administration of CBN, and possibly other cannabinoids, would be an effective way to manage psoriasis.

Like THC, CBN may have potential to prevent or treat glaucoma due to its effects on eye pressure. CBN moderately decreases

intraocular pressure according to preclinical research.[330] They may have a synergistic effect if used together, but this needs to be further evaluated.

Preclinical research noted that CBN increases appetite behaviors in animals.[331] Not being psychoactive, it may be a better option for appetite and eating disorders than THC.

It is recognized that the ECS plays a major role in pain perception. Scientists investigated the effects of cannabinoids on nociceptive primary afferents (neurons involved in pain signaling and local responses to tissue injury). Interestingly, the scientists observed that both THC and CBN reduced pain independent of activation of CB1 and CB2 receptors. What the researchers found was that they influenced capsaicin-sensitive perivascular sensory nerves instead and that the therapeutic effect was not mediated by TRP, glutamate receptors, protein kinases A and C, or voltage-regulated calcium channels.[332] Based on the results the authors hypothesized that there may be a yet undiscovered cannabinoid receptor or ion channel in the pain pathway.

CBN may suppress immune activity by influencing CB2 receptors. It is involved in the regulation of multiple pathways that control immune responses, particularly signaling pathways in activated T cells.[333,334,335,336] T cell activation is critical for the initiation and regulation of immune responses. Their activation increases antibody responses, and allows them to hunt down and destroy cells infected with germs or that have become cancerous. However, an imbalance of T cells is associated with autoimmune diseases. Regulatory T cells initiate pathways and mechanisms that suppress inflammation and hyper-immune responses that lead to autoimmune conditions. The balancing effect of CBN on immune responses and T cells may help prevent or manage autoimmune conditions.

Bone remodeling is a lifelong process of removing old bone tissue and laying down fresh bone matrix. Bone strength is dependent on the balance of these two activities. CBN also plays a role in bone tissue growth. CBN stimulates bone nodule formation and collagen

91

production, suggesting a role in bone strength and a possible role in the management of bone diseases (like osteoporosis).[337,338]

A property not often considered in cannabinoids is their antimicrobial benefits. One study found that CBN, CBG, CBD, THC, and CBC all exhibit potent antibacterial activity against methicillin-resistant *Staphylococcus aureus* (MRSA).[339] We are losing the war waged on MRSA because we are focused on antibiotics rather than natural solutions. Cannabinoids may be another tool to fight bacterial resistance that threatens healthcare as we know it. The antimicrobial activity of cannabinoids deserves further exploration given the widespread resistance of bacteria to first-line antibiotics.

CBN may also reduce morphine withdrawal symptoms. Both THC and CBN reduced morphine withdrawal symptoms in rats, although CBN required an eight-fold higher dose to produce effects.[340]

Like other minor cannabinoids, CBN requires more attention and research. At the very least, it acts as part of the entourage effect but has merit as a medicinal cannabinoid alone as well.

Cannabivarin

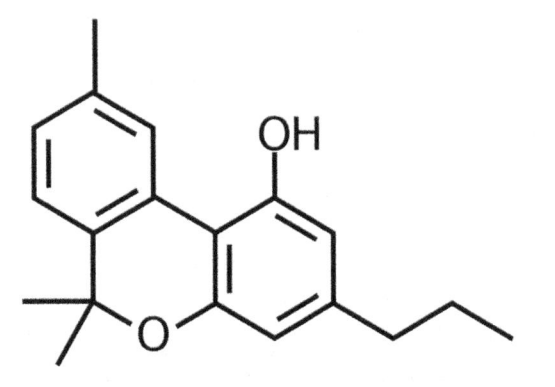

Cannabivarin structure

Cannabivarin (CBV), also known as cannabivarol, is a nonpsychoactive cannabinoid and analogue of cannabinol found in minor amounts in the cannabis plant. It was first identified in 1971

along with THCV.[341,342] It is present in only trace amounts in fresh plants because it is an oxidation product of THCV, meaning it will be found in higher amounts in older plants or those not stored properly. It is a potent inhibitor of L-alpha-lysophosphatidylinositol (see THCV to learn more).[343] We don't currently know much about the benefits of CBV because of scant research, almost all of which currently focuses on its identification and structure.

Δ-9-Tetrahydrocannabivarin

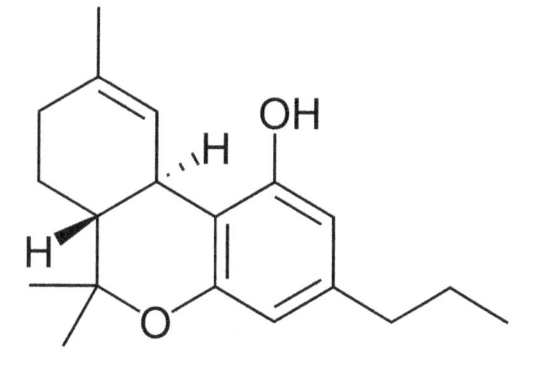

Δ-9-Tetrahydrocannabivarin structure

A homologue of THC, Δ-9-tetrahydrocannabivarin (THCV), is a propyl (3-carbon) chain cannabinoid—instead of the typical pentyl (5-carbon) chains of most other cannabinoids. Despite a similar structure to THC, it is only psychoactive in high doses. THCV is frequently found in higher amounts in landrace strains of *C. sativa* plants grown in Africa. It is a CB1 antagonist, partial agonist of CB2 (with high binding affinity), and a partial agonist of GPR55 and L-alpha-lysophosphatidylinositol (LPI) inhibitor (suggesting a role in cancer).[344,345,346,347,348,349,350,351,352] Certain endocannabinoids can modulate GPR55, but recent studies show that LPI, which activates GPR55 but not CB1 or CB2 receptors, could be the ligand naturally produced by the body to interact with this receptor.[353,354,355,356] Significantly, elevated LPI is present when cancer cells are highly proliferating, and it is a biomarker for poor prognosis (the seriousness of the cancer and the person's chances of survival) in cancer.[357] GPR55 is highly expressed in certain cancer cells, and LPI

causes these cells to aggressively invade, proliferate, and migrate to other tissues within the body.[358,359,360] Inhibition of LPI may be a novel target for the treatment of cancer, particularly against metastasis (growth of a second cancer at a site distant from the primary site of cancer). In addition, THCV inhibits TRPV5 (a channel that helps maintain skeletal homeostasis, specifically bone resorption; inhibiting this channel may reduce osteoporosis) and TRPV6 (a calcium entry channel linked to cancers of epithelial origin—prostate, breast, and others).[361,362,363] As the evidence grows, it demonstrates that THCV plays an important role in many aspects of human health.

Like THC, THCV has a Δ-8-THCV isomer that may possess similar properties. It does appear to activate CB2 receptors to decrease tissue injury and inflammation caused by stroke.[364] Similar to THCV, Δ-8-THCV appears to antagonize some of the effects of THC.[365] Outside of this, research is limited on this isomer of THCV.

THCV may enhance or decrease some of the cognitive, psychological, and physiological effects of THC. This evidence further confirms the entourage effect in cannabis that produces synergistic and buffering effects of the total collection of cannabinoids. To determine the interactions between THC and THCV, ten healthy individuals received 10 mg per day of THCV followed by an intravenous injection of 1 mg of THC. THCV prevented the psychotic symptoms (paranoia), delayed verbal recall, and increased heart rate, and decreased the overall intensity of THC.[366] However, the combination amplified short-term memory impairments.

Obesity and being overweight has become the "norm" of modern society as we eat a plethora of empty calories and become more inactive both in occupations and lifestyle. Disruptions in functional connectivity (connections formed in the brain that allow for the continual sharing of information between brain regions) within specific brain regions related to emotions, cognitive control, and reward-related control is associated with obesity.[367,368] These disrupted brain connections enhance reward sensitivity (a

personality trait involving the dopamine reward system that is linked to risk for addiction) and reduce cognitive control, increasing desire for highly appetizing foods.[369] Preventing or restoring disrupted brain connections and signaling may be a noninvasive way to manage overweight and obesity.

Early human research suggests cannabinoids are worth investigating as an obesity solution. A single dose of 10 mg of THCV improved functional connectivity in the brain that is known to be disrupted in people with obesity.[370] Another study reported that 10 mg of THCV improved neural responses to rewarding and aversive stimuli, suggesting a therapeutic activity in obesity and possibly depression.[371] Both findings suggest THCV promotes adaptations in brain connectivity to reduce food intake driven by pleasure and reward. Finally, THCV causes a temporary increase in energy expenditure, which could improve energy balance.[372] Given that obesity is far more than a calories-in-versus-calories-out problem, THCV may be a novel solution to reduce cravings for high-calorie foods by improving functional brain connections.

Other research suggests that THCV can alleviate fatty liver (hepatosteatosis) caused by obesity and a high-calorie diet as well as metabolic syndrome. Once people surpass a specific threshold of overweight and are inactive, the pancreas can't produce enough insulin to keep glucose and cholesterol levels under control. Eventually, the liver (which helps process and regulate sugar and fat in the blood) gets overwhelmed and begins to store excess fat in liver cells. Nonalcoholic fatty liver disease in obesity has been linked to worsening metabolic syndrome, insulin resistance, and cardiovascular disease. When cannabinoids were tested against fatty liver, the researchers found that both THCV and CBD reduced the accumulation of fat in a hepatosteatosis model by modifying multiple proteins involved in lipid metabolism.[373] Both THCV and CBD may be used as therapeutic agents against obesity and obesity-related conditions.

Obesity causes the reduced expression of various insulin-signaling molecules in skeletal muscle, which can reduce insulin sensitivity.

Resistance to insulin results in elevated blood glucose (sugar). Scientists investigated the effects of THCV in obese—both diet-induced and genetically caused—mice. THCV did not alter food intake or body weight, but temporarily increased energy (calorie) expenditure, restored insulin signaling in insulin resistant muscle cells, and improved glucose tolerance in diet-induced obese mice.[374] THCV also possesses antioxidant and anti-inflammatory properties relevant to diabetes and diabetic complications.[375] These findings suggest THCV may be a potential way to manage obesity-associated glucose intolerance and other diabetic complications.

Diabetes is an epidemic and high priority must be placed on better educating people on the risks of this devastating disease in relation to what they eat and how active they are. In addition, scientists are feverishly searching for new molecules to manage type 2 diabetes. A randomized, double-blind, placebo-controlled study of sixty-two individuals with type 2 diabetes that did not require insulin evaluated the ability of THCV (5 mg, twice daily) to control glucose and lipid levels. THCV significantly decreased fasting glucose levels and improved the function of pancreatic beta cells (cells that produce insulin) and apolipoprotein A (a protein carried in HDL cholesterol involved in lipid metabolism and associated with a decreased risk of cardiovascular disease).[376] No effect on HDL cholesterol was observed. Interestingly, its effects on glucose homeostasis were greater than CBD.

Like other cannabinoids, THCV possesses anti-inflammatory properties. One study found that both a THCV-rich (64.8%) whole cannabis extract and isolated THCV inhibited the production of nitric oxide by LPS (lipopolysaccharide)-stimulated macrophages.[377] Nitric oxide synthase is an enzyme that when induced plays a role in inflammatory and autoimmune diseases. THCV down regulated the overexpression of proinflammatory enzymes (inducible nitric oxide synthase [iNOS], cyclooxygenase-2 [COX-2]) and proteins (interleukin 1β [IL-1β]). Furthermore, it diminished the upregulation (increase in cellular receptors) of CB1—without affecting CB2—caused by the inflammatory

process. The authors concluded that its anti-inflammatory activity was produced via activation of the CB2 receptor. Other research shows that activation of both the CB1 and CB2 receptors by THCV decreases inflammation and pain in mice.[378] THCV has a place in the management of painful and inflammatory conditions.

As was reported with CBG, cannabinoids warrant further testing for overactive bladder. Laboratory research found that THCV significantly reduced mouse bladder contractions caused by acetylcholine.[379] Its ability to reduce bladder contractions caused by acetylcholine—the main stimulus that contracts the bladder—suggests a potential for THCV to be used to manage overactive bladder.

Early research demonstrates the potential of THCV to reduce nausea. Administration of 10 mg/kg reduced nausea in rats.[380] THCV could also be acting as part of an entourage effect for nausea in other cannabis extracts.

Tremors are a hallmark symptom of Parkinson's disease (PD). Acute administration of THCV relieved motor impairments, whereas chronic administration protected against neuron loss through its antioxidant effects.[381] Based on this, THCV may help reduce tremors in PD.

Acne is a common and embarrassing skin condition characterized by excess production of sebum and inflammation of the sebaceous glands. THCV powerfully reduces acne by reducing inflammation, suppressing excess sebum production, and reducing arachidonic acid (a major dietary omega-6 fatty acid that increases inflammation).[382] It is possible one day that THCV may be a useful remedy for acne.

Not surprisingly, THCV has shown anticonvulsant properties in a few animal studies, although its actions are less well understood.[383,384] THCV reduced severity and frequency of seizures in adult rats, demonstrating antiepilepsy and anticonvulsant properties.[385] Because THCV is generally only a minor compound in cannabis plants, it is difficult to determine its value as a naturally occurring molecule. It may enhance the effects of CBD and THC in relation to anticonvulsive activity, or it may be effective alone.

Despite being a homologue of THC, interestingly, THCV does not produce the same psychotic effects. Actually, research suggests it does the opposite. THCV enhanced 5HT1A receptor activation to reduced psychotic behavior and normalized social behavior and cognitive behavior in rats.[386] The study findings indicate a possible therapeutic potential for THCV in reducing symptoms of schizophrenia.

Continued research of THCV and its therapeutic potential may reveal additional clinical uses.

Binding Affinities (K_i)[387,388,389,390,391,392]

Endogenous Cannabinoids		
Molecule	*CB1*	*CB2*
2-AG	3423.6nm±3288.24	1193.8nm±327.71
AEA	239.2nm±61.77	439.5nm±95.89
Phytocannabinoids		
Molecule	*CB1*	*CB2*
THCA	23.51±3.5	56.13±8.2
THC	25.1nm±5.54 to 35.64nm±12.4	8.54nm±6.0 to 35.2nm±5.86
CBD	1458.5nm±158.5	372.37nm±57.5 to 2860nm
CBG	896.8nm±158.5	153.39nm±42.5
CBN	12.7nm±8.5 to 523.5±308.1	16.43nm±11.8 to 168.2±32.16
CBV	Unknown	Unknown
CBGV	Unknown	Unknown
CBDV	14711nm±5733.8	574.2nm±146.1
CBC	713.7nm±318.3	256.52nm±94.1
THCV	46.6nm to 75.4nm	62.8nm
BCP	—	155nm±4
Synthetic Cannabinoids		
Molecule	*CB1*	*CB2*
CP55940	0.58nm	0.68nm
JWH015	383nm	13.8nm
Lower numbers equal greater binding affinity (the ability of ligands to form bonds with a receptor).		

Synthetic and Pharmaceutical Cannabinoids

Synthetic cannabinoids—chemically manufactured and not naturally occurring—have helped further research into the ECS due to their very high affinity for CB1 and CB2 receptors. Studies on synthetic cannabinoids (CP55940, JWH015, HU-210, WIN 55,212, ACEA, SR141716A, and SR144528) have revealed important insights into the functional action of cannabinoids within the ECS. They have also provided a means to identify specific binding sites in the central and peripheral nervous system, which are now recognized as CB receptors.

Pharmaceutical companies have also exploited the exploding research into the benefits of the ECS and developed synthetically created and patented cannabinoid drugs. These are modified analogues of naturally occurring cannabinoids or highly processed extracts with specific cannabinoid ratios in order to obtain a patent. Some of the most common cannabinoid drugs include Marinol, Cesamet, Sativex, ajulemic acid, and the latest newcomer approved by the US Food and Drug Administration (FDA), Epidolex. Each will be briefly discussed below.

Marinol

Marinol (dronabinol; Abbott Products) is a prescription capsule medicine used in adults to treat the loss of appetite and weight loss associated with AIDS (acquired immune deficiency syndrome). In

addition, it is used for nausea/vomiting caused by cancer therapy not controlled by standard antiemetics. The active ingredient is a synthetic form of THC called (6aR,10aR)-6a,7,8,10a-Tetrahydro-6,6,9trimethyl-3-pentyl-6H-dibenzo[b,d]-pyran-1-ol. Warnings for Marinol include worsening of psychiatric symptoms (mania, schizophrenia, depression), impaired thinking, changes in blood pressure, seizures, drug abuse, nausea, vomiting, and stomachache.[393] The recommended adult dose is 2.5 mg, twice daily, preferably later in the day to reduce the frequency of central nervous system adverse reactions. Marinol may also reduce the ability to drive and operate machinery.

Cesamet

A synthetic oral cannabinoid, Cesamet (nabilone; originally developed by Eli Lilly and Company, rights currently with Valeant Pharmaceuticals) is a drug that mimics THC and is indicated for nausea and vomiting associated with cancer therapy in people who fail to respond to standard antiemetic drugs. Its active chemical is called (±)-trans-3-(1,1-dimethylheptyl)-6,6a,7,8,10,10a-hexahydro-1-hydroxy-6-6-dimethyl-9H-dibenzo[b,d]pyran-9-one. Each capsule contains 1 mg of nabilone. Warnings include elevated heart rate, postural hypotension, worsening of psychiatric disorders, potential substance abuse, and cautions in women who are pregnant or nursing. Like other synthetic THC derivatives, you should not drive or operate machinery when using the drug.

Sativex

Sativex (GW Pharmaceuticals) is an oromucosal spray that contains the active ingredient nabiximols (a 1.08:1 ratio of THC and CBD, and other specific minor cannabinoids, terpenoids, and flavonoids). Each single 100 mcL spray contains 2.7 mg THC and 2.5 mg of CBD. GW Pharma has been researching cannabinoids since 1998 and seeks to be the global leader in prescription cannabinoid medicines. Sativex is absorbed in the lining of the mouth, either under the tongue or inside the cheek. It is used in adults with spasticity (muscle spasms/stiffness) due to multiple sclerosis. It is

an approved drug in the United Kingdom and twenty-two other countries (not including the United States). A titration period is required to reach optimal dosing. Warnings for its use include hypersensitivity to cannabinoids or excipients, family history of schizophrenia or psychotic illness, and not for use during pregnancy and while breastfeeding.[394] People shouldn't drive or operate machinery if they experience significant central nervous system effects (e.g. sedation, dizziness) while taking Sativex.

Ajulemic Acid

Another synthetic cannabinoid derivative, the THC metabolite 11-nor-9-carboxy-THC, ajulemic acid (Anabasum, Lenabasum, Resunab; Corbus Pharmaceuticals) is currently being investigated for the treatment of inflammatory and fibrotic conditions (systemic sclerosis, cystic fibrosis, etc.).[395] It preferentially binds to CB2 receptors and is not psychoactive. Researchers are evaluating its safety and efficacy in clinical trials for systemic sclerosis, chronic inflammation, and dermatomyositis.

Epidolex

Epidolex (GW Pharmaceuticals) is a twice-daily oral solution and FDA-approved for use in people age two and older for two specific forms of epilepsy (Dravet syndrome and Lennox-Gastaut syndrome). The starting dose is 2.5 mg/kg of body weight, twice daily, increasing to 5 mg/kg after one week of use (maintenance dose). If further seizure reduction is necessary, the dosage can be increased to a maximum maintenance dose of 10 mg/kg, twice daily. It is a highly purified (at least 98% CBD, up to 1% CBDV, and not more than 0.15% THC) form of CBD and the United States patent states "alternatively, the CBD may be a synthetically produced CBD."[396] Warnings for its use include possible elevations in liver enzymes, an indicator of possible liver damage, sleepiness, suicidal thoughts, hypersensitivity reactions, and possible withdrawal symptoms upon discontinuation.[397]

Concocted in a lab, synthetic and pharmaceutical cannabinoids are out of balance from what Mother Nature intended. Since the majority of lab-produced cannabinoids are missing the rest of their entourage (minor cannabinoids and terpenes), they are likely to be more prone to side effects, dependence, and withdrawal. Each also requires a prescription, limiting availability.

Non-cannabinoids That Activate CB Receptors

The human body is innately designed and continually orchestrates complex interactions between cells, molecules, organs, and more to maintain harmony and balance. At the heart of this is cell signaling. Cell signaling allows cells to receive and process signals from their external environment and then formulate an action plan in response. Cells have proteins called receptors that signaling molecules bind to and initiate physiological responses. Specific molecules bind to specific receptors—insulin-to-insulin receptors, serotonin-to-serotonin (5HT) receptors, and so forth. Think of it as a house key. Your house key won't open your neighbor's door, and neither will your neighbor's house key open your door. Only a specific molecule (key) can unlock the receptors (door) in cells. Once a molecule binds to the receptor outside the cell, it transmits the signal inside the cell through a series of internal signaling pathways. Science has revealed that several non-cannabinoid molecules can bind to or interact with cannabinoid receptors to affect cell function.

Fatty Acid Derivatives

First reported in humans in 1989, the naturally occurring primary fatty acid amide oleamide (cis-9,10-Octadecenamide) is the signaling molecule responsible for inducing sleep.[398] It accumulates in the brain and cerebrospinal fluid during sleep deprivation. It is formed in brain microsomes and significantly influences nervous

system function and activity by interacting with multiple neurotransmitter systems, such as serotonin, dopamine, acetylcholine, vanilloid, and GABA (gamma-aminobutyric acid) receptors.[399,400] Oleamide is structurally similar to anandamide and is a full agonist of the CB1 receptor.[401] In addition to its effects on sleep, oleamide regulates memory processes, reduces depression, stimulates calcium release from cells, influences body temperature, modulates emotional responses to food, and influences pain perception.[402,403,404,405]

N-oleoyl glycine is a fatty acid derivative believed to be an intermediate in the synthesis of oleamide. It is produced from oleic acid and markedly increases the expression of the CB1 receptor.[406] Research suggests that N-oleoyl glycine enhances insulin sensitivity—by activating CB1 and Akt signaling pathways in adipocytes (fat-storing cells)—making it a potential option to reduce obesity and diabetes.[407] Other research suggests that N-oleoyl glycine reduces nicotine withdrawal symptoms.[408] The study of this molecule is currently in its infancy and more may be revealed as scientists continue its investigation.

Botanicals

In the last decade, several non-cannabinoid plant constituents have been discovered that bind to and functionally interact with CB receptors, or target proteins in the ECS that regulate endocannabinoid levels. Until recently, phytocannabinoids were thought to be isolated to the cannabis plant. However, new discoveries have identified other naturally occurring plant molecules that are capable of directly interacting with CB receptors or share chemical similarity with cannabinoids or both. These plant molecules can be classified as direct ligands (molecules with high binding affinity for CB receptors that exert direct functional effects on the ECS) or indirect ligands (molecules that target key proteins within the ECS to regulate endocannabinoid levels or allosteric sites in the CB1 receptor). We now know that several natural molecules from medicinal plants interact with the ECS.

As was mentioned earlier, beta-caryophyllene is a sesquiterpene found in abundance in multiple essential oils. Since the discovery of the ECS and the phytocannabinoids that interact with its receptors, other plant compounds have been identified that can be considered phytocannabinoids (direct or indirect ligands).

Cannabimimetics are a class of plant compounds that bind to CB receptors and produce similar pharmacological effects as cannabis. Loosely, this group of plant compounds could include any compound that has similar pharmacological effects as cannabis. The most well-known include the following:

- o Black truffles (*Tuber melanosporum*) contain the major metabolic enzymes that control endocannabinoid levels in the ECS and produce the endocannabinoid anandamide. Interestingly, these truffles do not have receptors to for endocannabinoids despite producing one. Instead, the production of anandamide is believed to attract animals that will eat them and spread their spores.[409] Animals (pigs, dogs) that sniff out these truffles and eat them experience a euphoric state because of anandamide intoxication. At the same time, the animals spread spores widely throughout the environment, thereby improving the propagation of the truffles.
- o Cocoa and chocolate from the *Theobroma cacao* plant also contain isolated small quantities of anandamide cannabimimetics that activate receptors to increase anandamide levels.[410,411] Chocolate is also believed to enhance the effects of marijuana, therefore reducing the costs and risks of marijuana use. Maybe this is a reason chocolate makes people happy and promotes a craving.
- o Echinacea (*Echinacea* spp.) contains cannabimimetic N-acylethanolamines (NAEs) and N-alkylamides (NAAs) compounds, which interact with EC receptors (without binding to them) to facilitate cell signaling.[412] These NAAs specifically interact with CB1 and CB2 receptors (widely expressed in the immune system and inflammatory-related

105

cells) to promote balanced immune activity and a normal inflammatory response, but their activity is not exclusively mediated through CB receptors.[413]

o A cannabinoid-like compound found in Flax (*Linum usitatissimum*) fiber, comparable to CBD, affects the expression of genes related to inflammation and connective tissue production likely through activation of the CB2 receptor.[414] The fact that linen cloth is made from flax fibers and knowing that it's cannabinoid-like compound has anti-inflammatory and analgesic activity, it may be a good option for wound dressings.

o A member of the daisy family, *Helichrysum umbraculigerum* produces compounds similar to CBG and CBGA called stilbenoids.[415,416] These cannabinoid-like compounds appear to have low binding affinity for the CB receptors and more research is necessary to determine their value in human health.

o Both Japanese (*Radula perrottetii*) and New Zealand liverwort (*Radula marginata*) produce cannabinoids (Japanese: perrottetinene; NZ: perrottetinenic acid). Japanese liverwort yields an analogue of THC (although less psychoactive) that binds to the CB1 receptor as an agonist and possesses both analgesic and anti-inflammatory activity.[417] NZ liverwort contains perrottetinenic acid that is chemically similar to THC.[418]

o Known for its calming effects, kava (*Piper methysticum*) contains kavalactones, one of which (yangonin) significantly binds to the CB1 receptor (KI=0.72 μM), which may be partly responsible for its antianxiety effects.[419] Whether it is a CB1 agonist or antagonist still needs to be determined.

o Peruvian maca root (*Heliopsis helianthoides*) also contains NAAs that modulate ECS activity by inhibiting the enzyme (HAAH) that destroys anandamide as well as anandamide reuptake.[420] Maca (*Lepidium meyenii*) also contains N-benzyl-(9Z,12Z)-octadecadienamide, which selectively

binds to CB1 and potently prevents the reuptake of anandamide making more of it available in the brain.[421]

- o Rhododendron (*Rhododendron anthopogonoides*) contains cannabinoid-like chromane and chromene derivatives (anthopogocyclolic acid and anthopogochromenic acid) and five additional cannabinoid analogues that inhibit histamine release, suggesting a role in relieving allergies.[422]

- o The primary active molecule in Sage of the diviners (*Salvia divinorum*), salvinorin A, which very weakly binds to CB1 and CB2 but activates kappa-opioid receptors that interact with the ECS to trigger overlapping pharmacological responses.[423]

- o Wild carrot (*Daucus carota*) contains falcarinol that binds to CB1 and acts as an inverse antagonist that may trigger dermatitis in skin.[424]

Two medicinal polyphenols, trans-resveratrol (found in the skin of grapes) and curcumin (found in turmeric) are widely used dietary supplements with vast therapeutic benefits. Trans-resveratrol is the active form of resveratrol and used to support normal cholesterol levels, reduce the risk of cardiovascular disease, to improve glucose control, for cancer prevention, and to relieve rheumatoid arthritis. Curcumin is an anti-inflammatory molecule used to manage pain, inflammatory conditions, depression, anxiety, high blood pressure, oxidative stress, high cholesterol, and reduce the risk of cancer. Initial research reported that both of these highly medicinal botanical extracts bind to CB1 receptors with high affinity (trans-resveratrol: 5.9 nm; curcumin 45 nm), exerting therapeutic activity.[425] However, further research using the synthetic cannabinoid CP55940 found that neither molecule actually had a high binding affinity for the CB1 receptor.[426] The influence of curcumin and trans-resveratrol on ECS activity requires additional research and exploration.

The green tea catechin-derivatives epigallocatechin 3-gallate (EGCG) and epigallocatechin also bind to CB1 receptors (33.6 nm and 35.7 nm respectively), but methodological flaws were identified

in their determination of binding affinities, bringing into question the validity of these molecules' influence on ECS activity.[427,428,429]

A coumarin derivative from *Ruta graveolens*, rutamarin, binds weakly to the CB2 receptor.[430] 3,3'-diindolylmethane is a metabolite produced after ingestion of indole-3-carbinol (found in cruciferous vegetables like broccoli, cabbage, kale, etc.) and is a weak partial CB2 receptor agonist.[431] These interactions indicate potential to use them therapeutically for a variety of conditions.

A fascinating but hardly explored topic is the possible synergistic interaction between cannabinoids and other botanicals that share similar properties. For example, moringin from *Moringa oleifera* seems to amplify the anti-inflammatory and antioxidant benefits,[432] copaiba (rich in beta-caryophyllene) with CBD for enhanced ECS activity, chamomile with CBD to reduce anxiety, and more. Essential oils provide additional terpenes already present in cannabis (e.g. lavender and linalool, chamomile and alpha-bisabolol, and ylang ylang and farnesol). Could combining these and other essential oils with cannabis extracts enhance the therapeutic benefit? Possibly. Further exploration and experimentation will tell. Medicinal plants combined with CBD open a whole new realm of therapies that could provide answers to some of the most difficult to manage health conditions afflicting man.

Dosage and Use (Transdermal, Sublingual, Oral, Inhalation, Rectal)

Dosing of cannabis extracts can be challenging given the individual responses to cannabinoids witnessed clinically and in research. Cannabinoids—despite consistency in dose, delivery method, and cannabinoid—do not affect each person in the same way, and what makes this difference is still being investigated. Some emerging information includes personality traits, sex, age, genetic expression, ECS tone, expression of CB receptors, current state of health, and family history of certain conditions.[433,434] Compounding this is the fact that many cannabinoids produces a biphasic effect (low and high doses can produce opposite effects).[435] The most effective dose for each individual is likely identified through experimentation and adjustment. Dosing should be gradually adjusted and fine-tuned until the most effective dose is achieved for each individual.

Cannabinoids can be administered via inhalation (smoking or vaporizing), intranasally (inside the nose), orally (liquids, capsules, sprays), sublingually, as an oromucosal delivery, rectally (suppositories), transdermally (cream, gel, lotion, patch), or intravenously. The metabolism of cannabinoids produces metabolites that can be detected in the hair, saliva, sweat, and blood (depending on the cannabinoid).

Smoking

Smoking cannabis results in rapid but shorter effects and high blood levels.[436] THC delivery varies widely in cannabis cigarettes based on plant material and composition of the cigarette—typically a maximum of 25% to 27% THC is absorbed in to the bloodstream and between 2 to 22 mg of THC enters the brain.[437,438,439] Smoking cannabis appears to provide the best THC delivery (151 ng/mL max THC) method when compared to vaporization (85 ng/mL) and oral administration (15 ng/mL).[440] Bioavailability via smoking is between 2% and 56% depending on smoking technique (puff duration, holding breath, etc.).[441,442] One study reported that smoking cannabis had a long half-life (the time required for the CBD to be reduced to half in plasma) of thirty-two hours.[443] Smoking may be a good option for immediate relief and rapid results but the result will likely be of short duration.

Smoking also has higher risks including lung diseases, airway inflammation, symptoms of chronic bronchitis, potentially increased risk of lung infections, and possibly lung cancer.[444,445,446,447] It is also noteworthy that smoking marijuana cigarettes leads to four times the buildup of tar in the lungs when compared to nicotine cigarettes because of the way it is typically smoked (deeper inhale, held for longer).[448] Knowing these risk factors, experts have debated the value of smoking and vaporizing cannabis because the dose required to achieve a therapeutic effect while avoiding adverse effects is difficult to estimate.

Vaporization

Vaporization of cannabis is often used as an alternative to smoking because it may form fewer toxic byproducts. This is debatable, but people who vape cannabis do report breathing easier and experience less respiratory distress. Delivery of THC is believed to be comparable to smoking, but is largely affected by proper use of the vaporizer, temperature, type of cannabis used, duration of use, and balloon volume.[449,450] However, one study reported that vaporized THC produced greater effects and higher THC concentrations in the

blood than equal doses of smoked cannabis.[451] This suggests that vaporization may be the most efficient method of cannabinoid delivery and possibly most beneficial. However, vaporized cannabinoids are quickly eliminated, providing only short-term benefits.

Inhalation of liquid aerosol CBD or THC is quickly absorbed and eliminated, showing a half-life of no longer than seven and eleven minutes (THC and CBD respectively), with total elimination occurring in twenty to forty minutes.[452] Peak THC concentrations are achieved in only three minutes.[453] Vaporization may provide quick results, but the results will not likely be sustained with its rapid elimination.

Intranasal

Intranasal administration is uncommon, but it has been investigated as a delivery method in preclinical studies. Intranasal administration of 1 mg/kg of body weight in rabbits achieved a peak concentration of THC (20 ng/mL) and CBD (31 ng/mL) at twenty and forty-five minutes respectively.[454] Peak concentrations were observed at twenty and thirty minutes in rats.[455] Similar to smoking and vaping cannabis, intranasal administration appears to rapidly deliver cannabinoids but provide temporary benefits.

Oral, Sublingual, and Oromucosal

Oral administration is the most common way to take CBD and a common route of administration for drug cannabinoids. Oral use produces more gradual onset of action (usually takes hours for benefits), results in lower blood levels of cannabinoids, and generally has longer effects than smoking or vaping cannabis.[456,457] The "high" effects of THC also occurs much more slowly when THC is used orally. Cannabis benefits are slower and more erratic with oral use.

Natural CBD undergoes extensive first-pass metabolism when taken orally, which reduces its bioavailability to as little as 6%.[458] Only 10% to 20% of drug cannabinoids are typically absorbed, reaching

111

peak plasma concentrations of THC around two hours.[459] Sublingual and oromucosal (across the mucosa of the oral cavity, like in the cheek) delivery bypasses first-pass metabolism in the liver, which increases bioavailability and produces faster results when compared to oral use. A phase I open label trial observed a bioavailability of 93.9% of cannabinoids with oromucosal delivery and 87.2% sublingually.[460] Oromucosal delivery results in mean peak plasma concentrations of both THC and CBD between two and four hours.[461] The half-life in humans is reported to be between 1.4 and 10.9 hours after oromucosal spray and two to five days after long-term administration.[462] One drawback of oromucosal and sublingual use is the bitter, earthy, and floral taste of cannabis. This may be overcome by flavoring the product. A great deal of cannabinoids are excreted when used orally making sublingual and oromucosal delivery a better option.

One possibly way to improve oral bioavailability is to combine them with fats. Cannabinoids are lipophilic and research demonstrates that combining them with dietary fats (coconut oil, olive oil, hemp seed oil) may improve absorption.[463,464] Another drawback to oral administration is that studies show that CBD is converted to THC and hexahydrocannabinols when exposed to simulated gastric fluid.[465,466] It is possible that some of the CBD is converted to THC when ingested, which could be positive or negative depending on the purpose of its use.

Rectal

Rectal administration is typically reserved for the pro-drug Δ9-THC-hemisuccinate (THC-HS) because THC is not absorbed via the rectum. THC-HS is rapidly absorbed in the rectum and quickly hydrolyzes to THC in the plasma.[467] It results in higher THC bioavailability because it bypasses first-pass metabolism by the liver.[468] Peak plasma concentrations are achieved within two to eight hours.[469] Rectal administration results in quick results. Rectal delivery is a good delivery method when a person is unable to swallow well, is experiencing nausea, or has a digestive tract

problem, such as a bowel obstruction. Rectal delivery is commonly used with people in long-term and palliative care settings.

Transdermal

Cannabinoids are highly hydrophobic (repelled by or failing to mix with water), which makes penetrating the aqueous layer of the skin the limiting factor in absorption when applied topically (transdermal). The creation of a water-soluble form of CBD (oil or powder) helps to overcome this issue and improves the transport of cannabinoids through the aqueous layer of the skin. Some cannabinoids may permeate the skin better than others. CBD and CBN were found to permeate the skin ten times better than THC.[470] Transdermal delivery has several advantages including no flavor worries, ease of use, long-term delivery, and less liver stress.

Steady-state plasma concentrations (intake and elimination are near equal; about four to five times half-life) of CBD was reached at 15.5 hours in guinea pigs who had a transdermal CBD gel applied to their skin.[471] A patch with 8 mg of THC was used in a guinea pig model and achieved peak plasma concentration within 1.4 hours. Remarkably, this concentration was maintained for at least forty-eight hours, suggesting that occlusion (an air- and water-tight covering or dressing) by a patch may provide a more sustained delivery of cannabinoids.[472] Another study with a 1% CBD cream found that peak plasma concentration was reached at thirty-eight hours.[473] The sustained delivery makes this an attractive method to maintain therapeutic benefits.

Another aspect of transdermal delivery is the interaction of cannabinoids with the cutaneous ECS. Compartments within the skin have CB receptors that help regulate the life cycle of skin cells and the overall health of the skin. It is possible that transdermal delivery not only helps to relieve pain, promote better sleep, increase calm feelings, and improve mood, but simultaneously support skin health and reduce the risk of adverse skin conditions—at least in the localized area of the application. Altogether, transdermal

application may be the most effective administration method for chronic pain due to a sustained and long-lasting delivery.

Intravenous

Intravenous (IV) administration has the most reliable pharmacokinetics (the movement of substances into, through, and out of the body; dealing with its absorption timetable, bioavailability, distribution, metabolism, and excretion), but requires assistance by a medical professional.[474] IV administration of THC is characterized by a steep increase in plasma concentration followed by a rapid decline. Plasma concentrations are raised dramatically through IV administration. Administration of 5 mg of THC resulted in 288 to 302 ng/ML of THC in the blood after only three minutes.[475] Another study found IV administration of 2.5 mg of THC produced a mean plasma level of 68.0 ng/mL at five minutes.[476] The IV half-life is reported to be twenty-four hours.[477] It is a relatively consistent finding that plasma levels are two to three times that of inhalation after IV administration. While a very reliable method, IV administration is more expensive and invasive, may cause reactions at the administration site, and is distressing to some people, particularly children.

Typical Doses from Anecdotal Use and Clinical Studies

The following dosing information is a collection of recommended doses based on anecdotal use, traditional use, and clinical research. It is provided for informational purposes only. Consult your qualified health professional before using cannabis products to determine if you are a good candidate to use cannabis and for individualized dosing based on your age, weight, health history, current state of health, family health history, personality traits, other medications, and more. In addition, many jurisdictions require medical cards to use cannabis extracts or restrict the use of THC-containing cannabis products.

General guidelines:

Oral: Start with 2.5 mg of THC, CBD, or a ratio of both, every eight hours as needed. Maintain this baseline dosage for seven days. If you are not getting the benefits you desire at the 2.5 mg dose, increase the dosage by 1 to 2 mg every three days, up to 5 mg. If the lower doses have been well-tolerated and additional cannabinoids are needed, slowly increase to 10 mg per dose. Do not exceed 30 mg of THC in a twenty-four hour period. Greater amounts of CBD-rich oil (very low THC) can be used, such as working up to 20 mg, three times daily. It is important to note that most CBD products are mixed with a fatty oil (olive, coconut, hemp seed) and so the dose listed on the bottle (e.g. 20 drops, or 1 mL) includes the fatty oil. Read the label carefully to determine how much actual CBD is provided in the total dose (e.g. 5 mg in 1 mL). As with any remedy, natural or drug, children require less than adults. Some experts recommend starting at 0.25 mg per pound, in three divided doses per day and slowly working up to 0.5 mg per pound (three divided doses per day) as a guideline for CBD use in children.

Transdermal: Dosing is less of a concern with transdermal methods. If using a cream, start at the lower end of the suggested use range and gradually increase as necessary, following the package instructions. Use patches as instructed on the product label, and increase the amount used as necessary following label instructions. Do not use other THC products for six hours after using a transdermal product that is rich in THC.

Sublingual: Drop the oil under your tongue and hold it there for thirty to sixty seconds before swallowing. Sublingual doses can be taken as several smaller doses per day or two to three doses per day. Start with 1 to 2 mg of CBD, every eight hours as needed. Increase this as needed and tolerated up to 10 mg per dose.

Condition	Daily Dosing (May Be Divided)
Addiction, Cannabis	Oral: 300–600 mg CBD
Addiction, Nicotine	Inhalation: 40 mcg as needed
Anorexia	Oral: 2.5 mg THC, three times daily, ninety minutes before meals
Anxiety, Social	Oral: 400–600 mg CBD (single dose)
Appetite Loss, Cancer Therapy	Oral: 2.5 mg THC, with or without 1 mg of CBD
Autism	Oral: CBD-rich cannabis (20:1 ratio of CBD to THC) titrated to a maximum dose of 10 mg/kg
Childhood-Onset Epilepsy	Oral: CBD titrated to a maximum of 25 mg/kg, twice daily
Chronic Pain	Oral: 2.5–20 mg CBD, up to three times daily Vaporized: 900 mg cannabis providing 3.56% THC, three times daily
Crohn's Disease	Smoked: 500 mg cannabis cigarette standardized to 115 mg THC, smoked twice daily
Dravet Syndrome	Oral: 2.5 mg/kg, twice daily for one week, then 5 mg/kg twice daily thereafter CBD; or 20 mg/kg CBD
Diabetes	Oral: 100 mg CBD, twice daily Oral: 5 mg THCV, twice daily Oral: 5 mg, twice daily
Dystonia	Oral: 100–600 mg CBD
Epilepsy	Oral: 200–300 mg CBD
General Health	Oral: 2.5–15 mg CBD; generally titrated from the lower dose every two days
Glaucoma	Sublingual: 2.5–5 mg THC, twice daily; do not exceed 20 mg/day Oral/Sublingual: 20 mg CBD Smoked: 900 mg cannabis cigarette standardized to 2% THC as s single dose

Graft-versus-Host Disease (GVHD)	Oral: 300 mg CBD seven days prior to transplantation and continuing until day thirty
Huntington's Disease	Oral: 10 mg/kg body weight CBD
Insomnia	See Sleep Disorders
Lennox-Gastaut Syndrome	Oral: 2.5 mg/kg CBD, twice daily for one week; then 5 mg/kg twice daily thereafter; or 20 mg/kg CBD
Multiple Sclerosis	Sublingual: 2.5 mg CBD as needed up to a maximum of 120 mg per twenty-four hours Oral: One to five capsules cannabis extract with 2.5 mg THC and 0.8–1.8 mg CBN, twice daily Smoked: 800 mg cannabis cigarette providing 4% THC
Nausea, Chemo-induced	Smoked: Cannabis cigarette providing 2.11% THC, 0.3% CBN, and 0.05% CBD Oral (Children 3+): 18 mg/m2 delta-8-THC
Neuropathy	Vaporized: Cannabis providing 1.6–96 mg THC, up to three times daily Smoked: 800 mg cannabis cigarette providing 3.5%–7% THC, smoked in bouts over a three-hour period Vaporized: 800 mg cannabis providing either 1.29% or 10.3 mg THC to 3.53% or 28.2 mg THC
Obesity	Oral: 10 mg THCV (single dose)
Pain, General	Oral: 4.5–45 mg CBD (weight dependent)
Pain (After Kidney Transplant)	Oral: 100 mg CBD
Parkinson's Disease	Oral: 150 mg CBD with weekly dose escalation of 150 mg as needed; or 300 mg CBD Smoked: 500 mg cannabis cigarette

Post-Traumatic Stress Disorder (PTSD)	Sublingual: 2.5 mg THC in olive oil, twice daily, one dose one hour after waking and the other two hours before bed Inhalation: 32 mg CBD Oral/Sublingual: 25 mg CBD at bedtime and 6–12 mg sublingually as needed during the day
Schizophrenia	40 Oral: 300 mg, 600 mg, 1,280 mg, or 1,500 mg CBD; or 200–400 mg CBD, four times daily
Sleep Disorders	Oral: 40–160 mg CBD thirty minutes before bed
Smoking Cessation	Vaporized: 400 mcg as needed CBD
Sturge-Weber Syndrome	Oral: CBD titrated to 10 mg/kg, twice daily
Weight Loss Associated with HIV/AIDS	Smoked: 800 mg cannabis cigarette providing 1.8%–3.9% THC, up to four times daily

As with most remedies, body weight significantly influences the amount of CBD required to produce desirable results. When taking CBD orally, some prefer to take an amount based on weight. Here is a general guide for estimating the amount of CBD to take based on body weight per dose, as three divided doses.

Weight	Severity of Condition		
	Mild	Moderate	Severe
< 25 lbs	2 mg	4 mg	6 mg
26–45 lbs	4 mg	8 mg	11 mg
46–85 lbs	7 mg	12 mg	15 mg
86–150 lbs	10 mg	15 mg	18 mg
151–225 lbs	15 mg	20 mg	25 mg
> 225 lbs	20 mg	30 mg	40 mg

Safety and Cautions

Warnings/Cautions

If you are pregnant, nursing, taking medication, or have a medical condition (mental, emotional, or physical), consult your health care professional before using cannabis extracts.

■ Although preclinical studies show the ECS and endocannabinoid tone play crucial roles in fertility and fetal/placental development,[478,479,480] there is a risk that maternal exposure to cannabis extracts may adversely affect conception and maintenance of pregnancy. Two reviews published in 2016 came to conflicting conclusions. One review found that cannabis extracts increased the risk of anemia in the mother and low birth weight and increased need for placement in the neonatal intensive care unit (NICU) in the baby.[481] The other review attributed adverse outcomes during pregnancy to confounding factors like concurrent use of tobacco.[482] Other research suggests an increased risk of long-term developmental problems in children exposed to cannabis in the womb.[483,484] These findings may be only related to THC but there is currently insufficient reliable information to determine the safety of CBD during pregnancy and lactation, so it is safest to avoid use. THC readily crosses the placenta[485] and given its harmful effects in children and adolescents it makes sense that THC is likely harmful to developing babies. It reduces offspring viability in mice and impairs offspring male reproductive structure and function at maturity.[486] Cannabinoids are excreted in breast milk and may be

absorbed by nursing infants.[487,488] It is best to avoid cannabis, particularly THC-rich cannabis, use during pregnancy and while lactating until more conclusive evidence comes forth.

■ Men intending on starting a family should avoid cannabis extracts with THC due to the risk of reduced male fertility.[489] THC may also increase the risk of testicular cancer.[490,491]

■ Avoid the use of THC and THC-rich cannabis extracts in children under age eighteen (possibly up to age nineteen when adolescence ends) due to an increased risk of schizophrenia and neurodevelopmental delays, unless advised to use them by a qualified health professional.[492,493] CBD has been safely used in children aged one and older in clinical research,[494] but many experts suggest two and older as an appropriate age for use when its medicinal use is warranted. Consult a qualified health practitioner to determine risks versus benefits of CBD use in children.

■ Chronic use of THC could potentially lead to ovarian dysfunction based on THC's inhibition of follicle-stimulating hormone (FSH).[495] Avoid the use of THC in women with a family history of premature ovarian failure or who have undergone ovarian surgery, such as surgery for endometriosis.

■ Avoid THC in anyone with psychosis (schizophrenia, bipolar disorder, etc.) or a family history of psychosis due to an increased risk of triggering a psychotic reaction.[496,497,498]

■ Use cautiously in people with cardiovascular disease. Marijuana may temporarily increase heart rate and blood pressure and increase the risk of heart attack.[499,500] It may also increase the risk of second stroke in people who use marijuana again after a first stroke.[501]

■ Avoid cannabis use (THC-containing cannabis) in people with suicidal thoughts or tendencies. Research suggests that heavy cannabis use is associated with an increased incidence of suicide, especially if started early in life and heavily used.[502,503,504]

■ CBD may worsen the symptoms of Parkinson's disease (resting tremor, hypokinesia—partial or complete loss of muscle movement) in some individuals with PD, use cautiously.[505] CBD helps some with PD, suggesting an individual response occurs.

■ Tolerance and addiction may occur with cannabis extracts that contain sufficient THC.[506,507,508] CBD does not cause dependence and is actually used to reverse cannabis dependence.[509]

■ Do not drive or operate heavy machinery when using THC due to impaired alertness and physical coordination.[510,511]

■ Discontinue use of marijuana one to two weeks prior to surgery to avoid interference with anesthesia drugs and an increased risk of bleeding.[512] The antiplatelet effects of other cannabinoids and possibility to interfere with sedation drugs warrant discontinuation of all cannabinoids at least one week prior to surgery.

■ To avoid overdose, do not smoke/vaporize cannabis and consume oral cannabinoids simultaneously.[513,514]

Potential Drug Interactions

Intravenous, inhalation, oral, sublingual, oromucosal, and rectal use of cannabinoids have the greatest risk of interaction with drugs, particularly if the cannabinoid product is used at the same time as the drug. Transdermal administration has the lowest risk, but should not be ignored as cannabinoids buildup in the fat cells. Cannabinoid use at least one to two hours after medication may minimize risk of interactions. Although every effort was made to identify known drug interactions, this should not be considered a conclusive list. Consult your health care professional for more information regarding interactions with the medications you currently take.

■ Avoid THC use with other CNS depressant drugs (like barbiturates) and alcohol due to an increased sedating effect.[515,516,517,518,519,520] CBN may also interfere with sedatives due to its amplification of CNS depressant effects in mice.[521] High doses of CBD (200 mg or more daily) could potentially increase the sedating properties of drugs as well.[522] CBD and THC may enhance the impairments to motor and psychomotor performances and intoxicating effects of alcohol.[523]

■ Avoid THC use with sympathomimetic drugs (stimulants) like amphetamines due to the potential to increase the adverse side effects of these drugs (abnormally rapid heartbeat and heart toxicity).[524]

121

■ THC may interact with opioid drugs (e.g., fentanyl, oxycodone) and antipsychotic medications (e.g., clozapine) and increase their adverse effects or efficacy.[525,526,527,528]

■ THC and CBD inhibit antipyrine (an NSAID) metabolism and may increase serum levels of the drug.[529]

■ Avoid THC use with tricyclic antidepressants (amitriptyline, amoxapine, and desipramine) due to adverse effects like high blood pressure, abnormally rapid heartbeat, and drowsiness.[530] THC may also promote hypomania in people taking the SSRI fluoxetine (Prozac).[531] It is safest to suppose that other antidepressants may also interact with THC.

■ THC may interfere with cholinergic/anticholinergic medications (e.g., atropine, antihistamines, scopolamine) and significantly increase the adverse (rapid heartbeat and drowsiness) side effects of these drugs.[532]

■ Higher doses of the anesthetic drug propofol may be required to achieve loss of consciousness in chronic marijuana users.[533]

■ Cannabinoids (THC and CBD) may interfere with platelet aggregation (low risk) and increase the risk of bleeding among people with bleeding disorders when taking aspirin, antiplatelet, or anticoagulant drugs.[534,535,536] One case report also suggests that smoking marijuana decreases warfarin metabolism or the binding of warfarin to plasma proteins, therefore increasing warfarin effects and an abnormal international normalized ratio (INR).[537]

■ Smoking marijuana may increase the metabolism of theophylline (a drug used to treat asthma and other lung problems, such as emphysema and chronic bronchitis) and reduce its effectiveness.[538]

■ CBD, THC, and CBN may interfere with drugs (analgesics, antipyretics, anti-inflammatories, chemotherapy agents, antivirals, anesthesia drugs, hormone replacement therapy, etc.)[539] metabolized by CYP1A1, CYP1A2, CYP1B1, CYP2D6, and CYP2C19 enzymes.[540,541,542,543] Substances that inhibit CYP2C9, CYP2C19, and CYP3A4 (certain antidepressants (e.g., fluoxetine, fluvoxamine, moclobemide, and nefazodone), proton pump inhibitors (e.g., cimetidine and omeprazole), macrolides (e.g., azithromycin, erythromycin, telithromycin, troleandomycin),

antimycotics (e.g., itraconazole, fluconazole, ketoconazole, miconazole, voriconazole, posaconazole), calcium antagonists (e.g., diltiazem, verapamil), HIV protease inhibitors (e.g., ritonavir, indinavir, nelfinavir, saquinavir, telaprevir, atazanavir, boceprevir, lopinavir), amiodarone, conivaptan, sulfaphenazole, azamulin, ticlopidine, nootkatone, grapefruit juice, mibefradil, and isoniazid) should not be used with cannabis extracts because they could potentially increase THC bioavailability and the risk of adverse effects associated with THC.[544,545,546,547] These same substances may interfere with the absorption and effectiveness of CBD.[548] Substances that accelerate CYP2C9 and CYP3A4 enzymes (e.g., rifampicin, carbamazepine, phenobarbital, phenytoin, primidone, rifabutin, troglitazone, avasimibe, and Saint John's wort) may reduce bioavailability of THC and CBD and reduce their effectiveness.[549,550]

■ Avoid CBD use with the antiseizure drug valproic acid, because of potential liver toxicity and low blood platelet counts (thrombocytopenia).[551,552,553]

■ There is a high risk that CBD will increase serum levels of N-desmethylclobazam, the primary active ingredient of clobazam (an antiseizure drug)—up to 60%—and increase sleepiness and possible other adverse effects.[554,555] CBD also moderately increases serum levels of other antiseizure drugs (e.g., eslicarbazepine, rufinamide, topiramate, zonisamide).[556]

■ CBD may enhance the anticonvulsant activity of phenytoin.[557,558]

■ CBD may interact with anesthetic drugs (like ketamine) and augment their activity.[559]

■ People with a compromised immune system (chronic skin conditions, autoimmune disorders, allergies) or sensitive skin may be more susceptible to skin irritation when cannabinoids are applied topically. THC and CBN were found to be very sensitizing, CBD, Δ-8-THC, and CBC moderate sensitizers, and CBG and CBN were not sensitizing when applied to guinea pigs.[560]

■ THC may interact with drugs used to treat alcoholism (e.g., disulfiram) and trigger hypomania.[561]

Potential Adverse Reactions

Cannabinoid	Common Adverse Effects	Less Common Adverse Effects
Marijuana *THC*	▶ Headache ▶ Dizziness ▶ Drowsiness ▶ Fatigue ▶ Dry mouth ▶ Paranoid thinking ▶ Nausea ▶ Disconnection from thoughts, feelings, and body	▶ Increased appetite ▶ Cough or other respiratory symptoms (smoking) ▶ Impaired motor coordination, visual perception, and reaction time, (higher doses) ▶ Hallucinations ▶ Emotional disturbances ▶ Impaired memory ▶ High blood pressure, heart palpitations ▶ Allergic reactions
CBD	▶ Dry mouth ▶ Diarrhea ▶ Decreased appetite ▶ Weight loss ▶ Drowsiness or fatigue (high doses)	▶ Elevated liver enzymes (high doses) ▶ Low blood pressure ▶ Changes in body temperature ▶ Vomiting

Cannabis and Drug Tests

With the rise in cannabis use, more people are concerned about failing a drug test, particularly those subject to regular, random drug tests at work. Marijuana use, medicinal or recreational, will almost certainly result in a positive drug test depending on the complexity of the test and the length of use. Regrettably, CBD may also produce a positive drug test result under certain circumstances. Prominent cases of athletes, top-level executives, and employees terminated

from their employment after purportedly only using CBD products are emerging.

Drug tests are designed to detect metabolites of THC, specifically 11-nor-9-Carboxy-THC (THC-COOH), and generally not other cannabinoids like CBD. Nevertheless, CBD can contain trace amounts (less than 0.3%) THC and CBD may be converted to THC in stomach acid, making it possible to detect this metabolite in the blood after CBD use. Whether it is detected largely depends on the type, sensitivity, and complexity of the testing method utilized (e.g. hair follicle, urine, saliva, or blood) and how long and how much CBD a person has used. A significant amount of CBD—estimated to be 1,000 to 2,000 mg per day—would likely need to be consumed over a long period of time to trigger a positive drug test, but it still is a risk that should be considered.

An adulterated or mislabeled product is also a concern. A 2017 study found that almost 70% of CBD products tested had higher or lower CBD amounts than those listed on the label.[562] THC was detected in 21% of samples, some of which had sufficient levels to potentially produce intoxication or impairment. The high THC content observed in commercial samples certainly could affect a drug test and is particularly concerning for children who are more prone to intoxication and impairment.

ROUTES OF ADMINISTRATION: ABSORPTION AND DISTRIBUTION[563]

SMOKING	
	• Rapid and efficient absorption of THC
	• Number, duration, hold time, inhalation volume, and hold time of puffs greatly influences delivery
	• Delivery from the lungs to the brain (greater abuse potential)
	• Plasma concentrations decrease rapidly due to rapid tissue distribution and liver metabolism

ORAL	• Slower absorption of cannabinoids, with lower, more-delayed peak THC concentrations • Significant first-pass metabolism in the liver to active 11-OH-THC • Significant amount of cannabinoids are excreted in the urine
TRANSDERMAL	• Avoids first-pass metabolism in the liver, which improves bioavailability • Slower, more sustained delivery of cannabinoids to tissues

After cannabis use—marijuana or CBD—your liver begins processing the cannabinoids into a variety of metabolites in order to eliminate them from the body. THC and its metabolites (THC-COOH and 11-hydroxytetrahydrocannabinol', also called 11-OH-THC) bind to proteins in the blood and are carried throughout the body for absorption into tissues. THC is initially absorbed by tissues like the lungs, heart, brain, and liver. Any remaining THC not absorbed into tissues is transformed (metabolized) into water-soluble metabolites like THC-COOH for excretion in the urine. THC-COOH has a long half-life and can remain in the body for more than seven days after a single use. THC-COOH builds up in fat (adipose) tissues after long-term use and can remain for up to sixty days. The presence of THC-COOH in the blood at >15 ng/mL is a strong indicator that a person has used marijuana; >100 ng/mL indicates relatively recent use, probably within the past 7 days; and >500 ng/mL suggest chronic and recent use. Virtually any cannabis-based product has the potential to trigger a positive drug test for marijuana. Although the risk of a positive test after using CBD is low, any individual subject to drug testing should seek qualified, medical counsel from his or her personal health care professional before using CBD or marijuana medicinally or recreationally.

Conclusion

The ECS has emerged as a very important regulator of multiple physiological functions key to optimum health. It is quite amazing that one single plant contains such a wide array of medicinal molecules that so widely influence human homeostasis—the innate drive within all cells that promotes healing and optimal function of organs and organ systems. With some regulatory obstacles removed, scientists can more freely research the influence of cannabinoids on the ECS and how that affects overall human health. Clinical studies can further explain how cannabis can be incorporated into mainstream medicine for the prevention and management of a variety of disorders.

Full spectrum CBD, as opposed to isolated CBD, is emerging as the leading cannabinoid for medicinal use because of its high therapeutic value and minimal risks. Similarly, beta-caryophyllene provides high reward with low risk. The reality is that this one single plant is endowed with more than its fair share of medicinal molecules each of which has potential to improve human health. This is particularly true for rare and difficult to treat conditions that have no real pharmaceutical solutions. Cannabis research, with an emphasis on clinical research to determine safe and effective doses and administration methods should be prioritized and fast-tracked. Relief from chronic and debilitating conditions may be discovered if it is.

It is an exciting time for those interested in realizing optimum health naturally. Trailblazing research is redefining how we look at health and disease in relation to the ECS, and ways to enhance its activity are slowly being revealed. Modulating CB receptors and endogenous cannabinoids represent new approaches for the management of a variety of functional disorders.

In essence, the ECS could be called the body's self-healing and self-regulatory mechanism—a system intelligently designed to maintain a general state of well-being and restore health when something goes awry. To date, the ECS has not received the attention it deserves in the modern medical system, nor among research funding. If a shift occurs to place greater emphasis on new discoveries in the system in relation to human health and disease, the public health would be greatly elevated. Here's to the next few decades of cannabis research that could unlock the secrets to preventing and reversing multiple conditions plaguing man.

REFERENCES

[1] Gumbiner J. History of Cannabis in Ancient China. Available at: https://www.psychologytoday.com/us/blog/the-teenage-mind/201105/history-cannabis-in-ancient-china.

[2] American Medical Association. Clinical implications and policy considerations of cannabis use. Available at: https://assets.ama-assn.org/sub/meeting/documents/i16-resolution-907.pdf.

[3] Clarke RC, Merlin MD. Cannabis: evolution and ethnobotany. University of California Press: Berkeley, CA, 2013.

[4] Small E. Evolution and classification of Cannabis sativa (marijuana, hemp) in relation to human utilization. *Bot Rev.* 2015;81:189–294.

[5] Alger B. Getting High on the endocannabinoid system. Cerebrum: The Dana Forum on Brain Science, 14. 2013.

[6] Russo EB. Clinical Endocannabinoid Deficiency Reconsidered: Current Research Supports the Theory in Migraine, Fibromyalgia, Irritable Bowel, and Other Treatment-Resistant Syndromes. *Cannabis Cannabinoid Res.* 2016;1(1):154–165.

[7] Fride E. Cannabinoids and cystic fibrosis: a novel approach. *J Cannabis Ther.* 2002;2:59–71.

[8] Järvinen T, Pate DW, Laine K. Cannabinoids in the treatment of glaucoma. Pharmacol Ther. 2002 Aug; 95(2):203-20.

[9] Russo E. Cannabis treatments in obstetrics and gynecology: a historical review. *J Cannabis Ther.* 2002;2:5–35.

[10] Ashton CH, Moore PB, Gallagher P, et al. Cannabinoids in bipolar affective disorder: a review and discussion of their therapeutic potential. *J Psychopharmacol.* 2005 May; 19(3):293-300.

[11] Paton WDM, Pertwee RG. 1973. The actions of cannabis in man Marijuanaed. Mechoulam, R. pp. 287–333. New York: Academic Press.

[12] Devane WA, Dysarz FA 3rd, Johnson MR, et al. Determination and characterization of a cannabinoid receptor in rat brain. *Mol Pharmacol.* 1988 Nov;34(5):605-13.

[13] Howlett AC, Barth F, Bonner TI, et al. International Union of Pharmacology. XXVII. Classification of cannabinoid receptors. *Pharmacol Rev.* 2002 Jun;54(2):161-202.

[14] Pertwee RG. Pharmacological actions of cannabinoids. *Handb Exp Pharmacol.* 2005;(168):1-51.

[15] Steiner H, Bonner TI, Zimmer AM, et al. Altered gene expression in striatal projection neurons in CB1 cannabinoid receptor knockout mice. *Proc Natl Acad Sci U S A.* 1999 May 11;96(10):5786–5790.

[16] Kano M, Ohno-Shosaku T, Hashimotodani Y, et al. Endocannabinoid-mediated control of synaptic transmission. *Physiol Rev.* 2009 Jan;89(1):309-80.

[17] Kano M, Ohno-Shosaku T, Hashimotodani Y, et al. Endocannabinoid-mediated control of synaptic transmission. *Physiol Rev.* 2009 Jan;89(1):309-80.

[18] Lee MA. The discovery of the endocannabinoid system. The Prop 215 Era. Available at: https://www.beyondthc.com/wp-content/uploads/2012/07/eCBSystemLee.pdf.

[19] Scheller A, Kichhoff F. Endocannabinoids and Heterogeneity of Glial Cells in Brain Function. *Front Integr Neurosci*. 2016; 10: 24.

[20] Shi QZ, Yang LK, Shi WL, et al. The novel cannabinoid receptor GPR55 mediates anxiolytic-like effects in the medial orbital cortex of mice with acute stress. *Molecular Brain*. 2017;10:38.

[21] Shore DM, Reggio PH. The therapeutic potential of orphan GPCRs, GPR35 and GPR55. *Front Pharmacol*. 2015; 6: 69.

[22] Sawzdargo M, Nguyen T, Lee DK, et al. Identification and cloning of three novel human G protein coupled receptor genes GPR52, PsiGPR53 and GPR55: GPR55 is extensively expressed in human brain. *Brain Res Mol Brain Res*. 1999;64:193–198.

[23] Lauckner JE, Jensen JB, Chen HY, et al. GPR55 is a cannabinoid receptor that increases intracellular calcium and inhibits M current. *Proc Natl Acad Sci U S A*. 2008 Feb 19; 105(7): 2699–2704.

[24] Hu G, Ren G, Shi Y. The putative cannabinoid receptor GPR55 promotes cancer cell proliferation. *Oncogene*. 2011 Jan 13;30:139-41.

[25] Shi QX, Yang LK, Shi WL, et al. The novel cannabinoid receptor GPR55 mediates anxiolytic-like effects in the medial orbital cortex of mice with acute stress. *Molecular Brain*. 2017;10:38

[26] Staton PC, Hat her JP, Walker DJ, et al. The putative cannabinoid receptor GPR55 plays a role in mechanical hyperalgesia associated with inflammatory and neuropathic pain. *Pain*. 2008 Sep;139(1):225-36.

[27] Whyte LS, Ryberg E, Sims NA, et al. The putative cannabinoid receptor GPR55 affects osteoclast function in vitro and bone mass in vivo. *Proc Natl Acad Sci U S A*. 2009;106:16511–16516

[28] Zygmunt PM, Petersson J, Andersson DA, et al. Vanilloid receptors on sensory nerves mediate the vasodilator action of anandamide. *Nature*. 1999 Jul 29;400:452-7.

[29] Storozhuk MV, Zholos AV. TRP Channels as Novel Targets for Endogenous Ligands: Focus on Endocannabinoids and Nociceptive Signalling. *Curr Neuropharmacol*. 2018 Jan 30;16(2):137-150.

[30] O'Sullivan SE. An update on PPAR activation by cannabinoids. *Br J Pharmacol*. 2016 Jun;173(12):1899–1910.

[31] Rubino T, Parolaro D. Sexually dimorphic effects of cannabinoid compounds on emotion and cognition. *Front Behav Neurosci*. 2011 Sep 28;5:64.

[32] Narimatsu S, Watanabe K, Yamamoto I, et al. Sex difference in the oxidative metabolism of delta 9-tetrahydrocannabinol in the rat. *Biochem Pharmacol*. 1991 Apr 15;41(8):1187-94.

[33] Craft RM, Marusich JA, Wiley JL. Sex differences in cannabinoid pharmacology: a reflection of differences in the endocannabinoid system? *Life Sci*. 2013 Mar 19;92(8-9):476-81.

[34] Russo EB. Hemp for headache: an in-depth historical and scientific review of cannabis in migraine treatment. *J Cannabis Ther*. 2001;1:21–92

[35] Francis PT. The interplay of neurotransmitters in Alzheimer's disease. *CNS Spectr*. 2005 Nov;10(11 Suppl 18):6-9.

[36] Warren N, O'Gorman C, Lehn A, et al. Dopamine dysregulation syndrome in Parkinson's disease: a systematic review of published cases. *J Neurol Neurosurg Psychiatry*. 2017 Dec;88(12):1060-1064.

[37] Moret C, Briley M. The importance of norepinephrine in depression. *Neuropsychiatr Dis Treat*. 2011;7(Suppl 1):9–13.

[38] Russo EB. Clinical Endocannabinoid Deficiency Reconsidered: Current Research Supports the Theory in Migraine, Fibromyalgia, Irritable Bowel, and Other Treatment-Resistant Syndromes. *Cannabis Cannabinoid Res*. 2016;1(1):154–165.

[39] Matias I, Bisogno T, Di Marzo V. Endogenous cannabinoids in the brain and peripheral tissues: regulation of their levels and control of food intake. *Int J Obes (Lond)*. 2006 Apr;30 Suppl 1:S7-S12.

[40] Hanus LO. Discovery and Isolation of Anandamide and Other Endocannabinoids. *Chem Biodivers*. 2007;4:1828-41.

[41] Rettori E, De Laurentiis A, Zorrilla Zubilete M, et al. Anti-inflammatory effect of the endocannabinoid anandamide in experimental periodontitis and stress in the rat. *Neuroimmunomodulation*. 2012;19(5):293-303.

[42] Park SW, Kim JE, Oh SM, et al. Anticancer effects of anandamide on head and neck squamous cell carcinoma cells via the production of receptor-independent reactive oxygen species. *Head Neck*. 2015 Aug;37(8):1187-92.

[43] De Petrocellis L, Melck D, Palmisano A, et al. The endogenous cannabinoid anandamide inhibits human breast cancer cell proliferation. *Proc Natl Acad Sci U S A*. 1998 Jul 7;95(14):8375–8380.

[44] Adinolfi B, Romanini A, Vanni A, et al. Anticancer activity of anandamide in human cutaneous melanoma cells. *Eur J Pharmacol*. 2013 Oct 15;718(1-3):154-9.

[45] Engeli S, Blüher M, Jumpertz R, et al. Circulating anandamide and blood pressure in patients with obstructive sleep apnea. *J Hypertens*. 2012 Dec;30(12):2345-51.

[46] Martin Ginenez VM, Noriega SE, Kassuha DE, et al. Anandamide and endocannabinoid system: an attractive therapeutic approach for cardiovascular disease. *Ther Adv Cardiovasc Dis*. 2018 Jul;12(7):177–190.

[47] Karlsson C, Hjorth S, Karpefors M, et al. Baseline Anandamide Levels and Body Weight Impact the Weight Loss Effect of CB1 Receptor Antagonism in Male Rats. *Endocrinology*. 2015 Apr;156(4):1237–1241.

[48] Mechoulam R, Ben-Shabat S, Hanus L, et al. Identification of an endogenous 2-monoglyceride, present in canine gut, that binds to cannabinoid receptors. *Biochem Pharmacol*. 1995 Jun 29;50(1):83-90.

[49] Shonesy BC, Winder DG, Patel S, et al. The initiation of synaptic 2-AG mobilization requires both an increased supply of diacylglycerol precursor and increased postsynaptic calcium. *Neuropharmacology*. 2015 Apr; 0: 57–62.

[50] Gonsiorek W, Lunn C, Fan X, et al. Endocannabinoid 2-arachidonyl glycerol is a full agonist through human type 2 cannabinoid receptor: antagonism by anandamide. *Mol Pharmacol*. 2000 May;57(5):1045-50.

[51] Castillo PE, Younts TJ, Chavez AE, et al. Endocannabinoid signaling and synaptic function. *Neuron.* 2012 Oct 4;76(1):70-81.

[52] Jung KM, Clapper JR, Fu J, et al. 2-arachidonoylglycerol signaling in forebrain regulates systemic energy metabolism. *Cell Metab.* 2012 Mar 7;15(3):299-310.

[53] Jesudason D, Wittert G. Endocannabinoid system in food intake and metabolic regulation. *Curr Opin Lipidol.* 2008 Aug;19(4):344-8.

[54] Zhang J, Chen C. Endocannabinoid 2-Arachidonoylglycerol Protects Neurons by Limiting COX-2 Elevation. *J Biol Chem.* 2008 Aug 15;283(33):22601-11.

[55] Alhouayek M, Lambert DM, Delzenne NM, et al. Increasing endogenous 2-arachidonoylglycerol levels counteracts colitis and related systemic inflammation. *FASEB J.* 2011 Aug;25(8):2711-21.

[56] Guindon J, Hohmann AG. The Endocannabinoid System and Pain. *CNS Neurol Disord Drug Targets.* 2009 Dec; 8(6): 403–421.

[57] Tegeder I. Endocannabinoids as Guardians of Metastasis. *Int J Mol Sci.* 2016 Feb; 17(2): 230.

[58] Hill MN, Patel S. Translational evidence for the involvement of the endocannabinoid system in stress-related psychiatric illnesses. *Biol Mood Anxiety Disord.* 2013; 3: 19.

[59] Melis M, Perra S, Muntoni AL, et al. Prefrontal cortex stimulation induces 2-arachidonoyl-glycerol-mediated suppression of excitation in dopamine neurons. *J Neurosci.* 2004 Nov 24;24(47):10707-15.

[60] Lawton SK, Xu F, Tran A, et al. N-Arachidonoyl Dopamine Modulates Acute Systemic Inflammation via Nonhematopoietic TRPV1. *J Immunol.* 2017 Aug 15;199(4):1465-1475.

[61] Grabiec U, Dehghani F. N-Arachidonoyl Dopamine: A Novel Endocannabinoid and Endovanilloid with Widespread Physiological and Pharmacological Activities. *Cannabis Cannabinoid Res.* 2017;2(1):183–196.

[62] Huang SM, Bisogno T, Trevisani M, et al. An endogenous capsaicin-like substance with high potency at recombinant and native vanilloid VR1 receptors. *Proc Natl Acad Sci U S A.* 2002 Jun 11;99(12):8400-5.

[63] Shohami E, Cohen-Yeshuruh A, Magid L, et al. Endocannabinoids and traumatic brain injury. *Br J Pharmacol.* 2011 Aug; 163(7): 1402–1410.

[64] O'Sullivan SE, Kendall DA, Randall MD. Characterisation of the vasorelaxant properties of the novel endocannabinoid N-arachidonoyl-dopamine (NADA). *Br J Pharmacol.* 2004;141:803–812

[65] Aizpurua-Olaizola O, Soydaner U, Öztürk E, et al. Evolution of the Cannabinoid and Terpene Content during the Growth of Cannabis sativa Plants from Different Chemotypes. *J Nat Prod.* 2016 Feb 26;79(2):324-31.

[66] Shrivastava A, Johnston M, Tsuang M. Cannabis use and cognitive dysfunction. *Indian J Psychiatry.* 2011 Jul-Sep; 53(3): 187–191.

[67] Thomas G, Kloner RA, Rezkalla S. Adverse cardiovascular, cerebrovascular, and peripheral vascular effects of marijuana inhalation: what cardiologists need to know. *Am J Cardiol.* 2014;113(1):187-190.

[68] Schubart CD, Sommer IE, van Gastel WA, et al. Cannabis with high cannabidiol content is associated with fewer psychotic experiences. *Schizophr Res.* 2011 05/16;130(1573-2509; 1-3):216-21.

[69] Qin N, Neeper MP, Liu Y, et al. TRPV2 is activated by cannabidiol and mediates CGRP release in cultured rat dorsal root ganglion neurons. *J Neurosci.* 2008;28:6231.

[70] De Petrocellis L, Ligresti A, Moriello AS, et al. Effects of cannabinoids and cannabinoid-enriched Cannabis extracts on TRP channels and endocannabinoid metabolic enzymes. *Br J Pharmacol.* 2011;163:1479.

[71] US Patent. Concersoin of cbd to delta8-thc and delta9-thc. Available at: https://patents.google.com/patent/US20040143126A1/en.

[72] Elikottil J, Gupta P, Gupta K. The Analgesic Potential of Cannabinoids. *J Opioid Manag.* 2009 Nov-Dec; 5(6): 341–357.

[73] Russo EB. Cannabinoids in the management of difficult to treat pain. *Ther Clin Risk Manag.* 2008 Feb; 4(1): 245–259.

[74] Naef M, Curatolo M, Petersen-Felix S, et al. The analgesic effect of oral delta-9-tetrahydrocannabinol (THC), morphine, and a THC-morphine combination in healthy subjects under experimental pain conditions. *Pain.* 2003 Sep;105(1-2):79-88.

[75] Cichewicz DL. Synergistic interactions between cannabinoid and opioid analgesics. *Life Sci.* 2004 Jan 30;74(11):1317-24.

[76] Musty R, Rossi R. Effects of smoked cannabis and oral delta-9-tetrahydrocannabinol on nausea and emesis after cancer chemotherapy: A review of state clinical trials. *J Cannabis Therapeutics* 2001;1(1):29-42.

[77] Health Canada. Information for Health Care Professionals: Cannabis (marihuana, marijuana) and the cannabinoids. Available at: https://www.canada.ca/en/health-canada/services/drugs-medication/cannabis/information-medical-practitioners/information-health-care-professionals-cannabis-cannabinoids.html#a4.3.

[78] Abrahamov A, Abrahamov A, Mechoulam R. An efficient new cannabinoid antiemetic in pediatric oncology. *Life Sci* 1995;56:2097-102.

[79] Makwana R, Venkatasamy R, Spina D, et al. The effect of phytocannabinoids on airway hyper-responsiveness, airway inflammation, and cough. *J Pharmacol Exp Ther.* 2015 Apr;353(1):169-80.

[80] Cota D, Marsicano G, Lutz B, et al. Endogenous cannabinoid system as a modulator of food intake. Int J Obes Relat Metab Disord. *Int J Obes Relat Metab Disord.* 2003 Mar;27(3):289-301.

[81] Monteleone P, Maj M. Dysfunctions of leptin, ghrelin, BDNF and endocannabinoids in eating disorders: Beyond the homeostatic control of food intake. *Psychoneuroendocrinology.* 2013 Mar;38(3):312-30.

[82] Davis JF, Choi PQ, Kunze J, et al. Investigating the Neuroendocrine and Behavioral Controls of Cannabis-Induced Feeding Behavior. Presented July 2018, Society for the Study of Ingestive Behavior, Bonita Springs, FL.

[83] Lewis DY, Brett RR. Activity-based anorexia in C57/BL6 mice: Effects of the phytocannabinoid, Delta9-tetrahydrocannabinol (THC) and the anandamide analogue, OMDM-2. *Eur Neuropsychopharmacol.* 2010 09;20:622-31.

[84] Verty AN, Evetts MJ, Crouch GJ, et al. The cannabinoid receptor agonist THC attenuates weight loss in a rodent model of activity-based anorexia. *Neuropsychopharmacology*. 2011 06;36:1349-58.

[85] Gross H, Ebert MH, Faden VB, et al. A double-blind trial of delta 9-tetrahydrocannabinol in primary anorexia nervosa. *J Clin Psychopharmacol*. 1983 06;3(0271-0749; 3):165-71.

[86] Ancoli-Israel S, Roth T. Characteristics of insomnia in the United States: results of the 1991 National Sleep Foundation Survey. I. *Sleep*. 1999 May 1; 22 Suppl 2():S347-53.

[87] Tringale R, Jensen C. Cannabis and Insomnia. *O'Shaughnessy's*. 2011 Autumn. Available at: http://files7.webydo.com/92/9209805/UploadedFiles/5E9EC245-448E-17B2-C7CA-21C6BDC6852D.pdf.

[88] Schierenbeck T, Riemann D, Berger M, et al. Effect of illicit recreational drugs upon sleep: cocaine, ecstasy and marijuana. *Sleep Med Rev*. 2008 Oct;12(5):381-9.

[89] Gorelick DA, Goodwin RS, Schwilke E, et al. Tolerance to effects of high-dose oral delta9-tetrahydrocannabinol and plasma cannabinoid concentrations in male daily cannabis smokers. *J Anal Toxicol*. 2013;37(1):11–6.

[90] Lutz B. The endocannabinoid system and extinction learning. *Mol Neurobiol*. 2007 08;36:92-101.

[91] Roitman P, Mechoulam R, Cooper-Kazaz R, et al. Preliminary, open-label, pilot study of add-on oral Delta9-tetrahydrocannabinol in chronic post-traumatic stress disorder. *Clin Drug Investig*. 2014 Aug;34(8):587-91.

[92] Chen J, Matias I, Dinh T, et al. Finding of endocannabinoids in human eye tissues: Implications for glaucoma. *Biochem Biophys Res Commun*. 2005 May;330:1062-7.

[93] Tomida I, Azuara-Blanco A, et al. Effect of sublingual application of cannabinoids on intraocular pressure: A pilot study. *J Glaucoma*. 2006 10;15:349-53.

[94] Flach AJ. Delta-9-tetrahydrocannabinol (THC) in the treatment of end-stage open-angle glaucoma. *Trans Am Ophthalmol Soc*. 2002;100:215-22.

[95] Morales P, Hurst DP, Reggio PH. Molecular Targets of the Phytocannabinoids-A Complex Picture. *Prog Chem Org Nat Prod*. 2017;103:103–131.

[96] Ružić Zečević D, Folić M, Tantoush Z, et al. Investigational cannabinoids in seizure disorders, what have we learned thus far? *Expert Opin Investig Drugs*. 2018 Jun;27(6):535-541.

[97] Devinsky O, Marsh E, Friedman D, et al. Cannabidiol in patients with treatment-resistant epilepsy: an open-label interventional trial. *Lancet Neurol*. 2016 Mar;15(3):270-8.

[98] Carlini EA, Cunha JM. Hypnotic and antiepileptic effects of cannabidiol. *J Clin Pharmacol*. 1981 Aug-Sep;21(S1):417S-427S.

[99] Devinsky O, Patel AD, Cross JH, et al. Effect of Cannabidiol on Drop Seizures in the Lennox-Gastaut Syndrome. *N Engl J Med*. 2018 May 17;378(20):1888-1897.

[100] Thiele EA, Marsh ED, French JA, et al. Cannabidiol in patients with seizures associated with Lennox-Gastaut syndrome (GWPCARE4): a randomised, double-blind, placebo-controlled phase 3 trial. *Lancet*. 2018 Mar 17;391(10125):1085-1096.

[101] Epilepsy Foundation. Infants and Epilepsy. 2012. Available at: http://www.epilepsyfoundation.org/aboutepilepsy/syndromes/rareepilepsysyndromes/severe-myoclonic-epilepsy-of-infancy.cfm.

[102] Devinsky O, Cross JH, Laux L, et al. Trial of Cannabidiol for Drug-Resistant Seizures in the Dravet Syndrome. *N Engl J Med*. 2017 May 25;376(21):2011-2020.

[103] Hayakawa K, Mishima K, Fujiwara M, et al. Therapeutic Potential of Non-Psychotropic Cannabidiol in Ischemic Stroke. *Pharmaceuticals (Basel)*. 2010 Jul 8;3(7):2197-2212.

[104] Salleh MR. Life Event, Stress and Illness. *Malays J Med Sci*. 2008 Oct; 15(4): 9–18.

[105] National Institute of Mental Health. Any Anxiety Disorder. Available at: https://www.nimh.nih.gov/health/statistics/any-anxiety-disorder.shtml.

[106] National Institute of Mental Health. Any Anxiety Disorder. Available at: https://www.nimh.nih.gov/health/statistics/any-anxiety-disorder.shtml.

[107] Brody DJ, Pratt LA, Hughes JP. Prevalence of Depression Among Adults Aged 20 and Over: United States, 2013–2016. NCHS Data Brief No. 303, February 2018.

[108] Morena M, Patel S, Bains JS, et al. Neurobiological interactions between stress and the endocannabinoid system. *Neuropsychopharmacology*. 2016 Jan;41(1):80-102.

[109] Morena M, Patel S, Bains JS, et al. Neurobiological interactions between stress and the endocannabinoid system. *Neuropsychopharmacology*. 2016 Jan;41(1):80-102.

[110] Hillard CJ. Stress regulates endocannabinoid-CB1 receptor signaling. *Semin Immunol*. 2014 Oct;26(5):380-8.

[111] Hill MN, Patel S. Translational evidence for the involvement of the endocannabinoid system in stress-related psychiatric illnesses. *Biol Mood Anxiety Disord*. 2013 Oct 22;3(1):19.

[112] Rubino T, Zamberletti E, Parolaro D. Endocannabinoids and mental disorders. *Handb Exp Pharmacol*. 2015;231:261-83.

[113] Crippa JA, Zuardi AW, Garrido GE, et al. Effects of cannabidiol (CBD) on regional cerebral blood flow. *Neuropsychopharmacology*. 2004 02;29:417-26.

[114] Fusar-Poli P, Crippa JA, Bhattacharyya S, et al. Distinct effects of {delta}9-tetrahydrocannabinol and cannabidiol on neural activation during emotional processing. *Arch Gen Psychiatry*. 2009 01;66:95-105.

[115] Crippa JA, Derenusson GN, Ferrari TB, et al. Neural basis of anxiolytic effects of cannabidiol (CBD) in generalized social anxiety disorder: a preliminary report. *J Psychopharmacol*. 2011 Jan;25(1):121-30.

[116] Bergamaschi MM, Costa Queiroz RH, Nisihara Chagas MH, et al. Cannabidiol Reduces the Anxiety Induced by Simulated Public Speaking in Treatment-Naïve Social Phobia Patients. *Neuropsychopharmacology*. 2011 May; 36(6): 1219–1226.

[117] Das RK, Kamboj SK, Ramadas M, et al. Cannabidiol enhances consolidation of explicit fear extinction in humans. *Psychopharmacology (Berl)*. 2013 Apr;226(4):781-92.

[118] Shannon S. Effectiveness of Cannabidiol Oil for Pediatric Anxiety and Insomnia as Part of Posttraumatic Stress Disorder: A Case Report. *Perm J*. 2016 Fall;20(4):108–111.

[119] Blessing EM, Steenkamp MM, Manzanares J, et al. Cannabidiol as a potential treatment for anxiety disorders. *Neurotherapeutics*. 2015 Oct;12(4):825-36.

[120] de Mello Schier AR, de Oliveira Ribeiro NP, Coutinho DS, et al. Antidepressant-like and anxiolytic-like effects of cannabidiol: a chemical compound of Cannabis sativa. *CNS Neurol Disord Drug Targets*. 2014;13(6):953-60.

[121] Linge R, Jiménez-Sánchez L, Campa L, et al. Cannabidiol induces rapid-acting antidepressant-like effects and enhances cortical 5-HT/glutamate neurotransmission: role of 5-HT1A receptors. *Neuropharmacology*. 2016 Apr;103:16-26.

[122] Corroon J, Phillips HA. A Cross-Sectional Study of Cannabidiol Users. *Cannabis Cannabinoid Res*. 2018 Jul 1;3(1):152-161.

[123] Aran A, Cassuto H, Lubotzky A. Cannabidiol Based Medical Cannabis in Children with Autism- a Retrospective Feasibility Study (P3.318). *Neurology*. 2018 Apr;90(15 Supplement):318.

[124] Rubino T, Zamberletti E, Parolaro D. Endocannabinoids and mental disorders. *Handb Exp Pharmacol*. 2015;231:261-83.

[125] Radhakrishnan R, Wilkinson ST, D'Souza DC. Gone to pot - A review of the association between cannabis and psychosis. *Front Psychiatry*. 2014 May 22;5:54.

[126] Fernandez-Espejo E, Viveros MP, Nunez L, et al. Role of cannabis and endocannabinoids in the genesis of schizophrenia. *Psychopharmacology (Berl)*. 2009 11;206(1432-2072; 0033-3158; 4):531-49.

[127] Ibarra-Lecue I, Pilar-Cuéllar F, Muguruza C, et al. The endocannabinoid system in mental disorders: Evidence from human brain studies. *Biochem Pharmacol*. 2018 Nov;157:97-107.

[128] Parolaro D, Realini N, Vigano D, et al. The endocannabinoid system and psychiatric disorders. *Exp Neurol*. 2010 Jul;224(1):3-14.

[129] Dean B, Sundram S, Bradbury R, et al. Studies on [3H]CP-55940 binding in the human central nervous system: Regional specific changes in density of cannabinoid-1 receptors associated with schizophrenia and cannabis use. *Neuroscience*. 2001;103(1):9-15.

[130] Dalton VS, Long LE, Weickert CS, et al. Paranoid schizophrenia is characterized by increased CB1 receptor binding in the dorsolateral prefrontal cortex. *Neuropsychopharmacology*. 2011 Jul;36(8):1620-30.

[131] Newell KA, Deng C, Huang XF. Increased cannabinoid receptor density in the posterior cingulate cortex in schizophrenia. *Exp Brain Res*. 2006 Jul;172(4):556-60.

[132] Manaseau MW, Goff DC. Cannabinoids and Schizophrenia: Risks and Therapeutic Potential. *Neurotherapeutics.* 2015 Oct;12(4):816–824.

[133] Chadwick B, Miller ML, Hurd YL. Cannabis use during adolescent development: Susceptibility to psychiatric illness. *Front Psychiatry.* 2013 Oct 14;4:129.

[134] French L, Gray C, Leonard G, et al. Early cannabis use, polygenic risk score for schizophrenia and brain maturation in adolescence. *JAMA Psychiatry.* 2015 Oct 1;72(10):1002-11.

[135] Iseger TA, Bossong MG. A systematic review of the antipsychotic properties of cannabidiol in humans. *Schizophr Res.* 2015 Mar;162(1-3):153-61.

[136] Chadwick B, Miller ML, Hurd YL. Cannabis use during adolescent development: Susceptibility to psychiatric illness. *Front Psychiatry.* 2013 Oct 14;4:129.

[137] Stark T, Ruda-Kucerova J, Iannotti FA, et al. Peripubertal cannabidiol treatment rescues behavioral and neurochemical abnormalities in the MAM model of schizophrenia. *Neuropharmacology.* 2018 Nov 26;146:212-221.

[138] Morgan CJ, Curran HV. Effects of cannabidiol on schizophrenia-like symptoms in people who use cannabis. *Br J Psychiatry.* 2008 Apr;192(4):306-7.

[139] Morgan CJ, Gardener C, Schafer G, et al. Sub-chronic impact of cannabinoids in street cannabis on cognition, psychotic-like symptoms and psychological well-being. *Psychol Med.* 2012 Feb;42(2):391-400.

[140] Schubart CD, Sommer IE, van Gastel WA, et al. Cannabis with high cannabidiol content is associated with fewer psychotic experiences. *Schizophr Res.* 2011 05/16;130(1573-2509; 1-3):216-21.

[141] Di Forti M, Marconi A, Carra E, et al. Proportion of patients in south london with first-episode psychosis attributable to use of high potency cannabis: A case-control study. *Lancet Psychiatry.* 2015 Mar;2(3):233-8.

[142] Karniol IG, Shirakawa I, Kasinski N, et al. Cannabidiol interferes with the effects of delta 9 - tetrahydrocannabinol in man. *Eur J Pharmacol.* 1974 09;28:172-7.

[143] Dalton WS, Martz R, Lemberger L, et al. Influence of cannabidiol on delta-9-tetrahydrocannabinol effects. *Clin Pharmacol Ther.* 1976 Mar;19(3):300-9.

[144] Radhakrishnan R, Wilkinson ST, D'Souza DC. Gone to pot - A review of the association between cannabis and psychosis. *Front Psychiatry.* 2014 May 22;5:54.

[145] Hallak JE, Machado-de-Sousa JP, Crippa JA, et al. Performance of schizophrenic patients in the stroop color word test and electrodermal responsiveness after acute administration of cannabidiol (CBD). *Rev Bras Psiquiatr.* 2010 Mar;32(1):56-61.

[146] Leweke FM, Piomelli D, Pahlisch F, et al. Cannabidiol enhances anandamide signaling and alleviates psychotic symptoms of schizophrenia. *Transl Psychiatry.* 2012 Mar 20;2:e94.

[147] Leweke FM, Piomelli D, Pahlisch F, et al. Cannabidiol enhances anandamide signaling and alleviates psychotic symptoms of schizophrenia. *Transl Psychiatry.* 2012 Mar 20;2:e94.

[148] CDC/NCHS, National Vital Statistics System, Mortality. CDC WONDER, Atlanta, GA: US Department of Health and Human Services, CDC; 2018. https://wonder.cdc.gov.

[149] Muhuri PK, Gfroerer JC, Davies MC. Associations of Nonmedical Pain Reliever Use and Initiation of Heroin Use in the United States. *CBHSQ Data Rev.* August 2013.

[150] Cicero TJ, Ellis MS, Surratt HL, et al. The Changing Face of Heroin Use in the United States: A Retrospective Analysis of the Past 50 Years. *JAMA Psychiatry.* 2014;71(7):821-826.

[151] Carlson RG, Nahhas RW, Martins SS, et al. Predictors of transition to heroin use among initially non-opioid dependent illicit pharmaceutical opioid users: A natural history study. *Drug Alcohol Depend.* 2016;160:127-134.

[152] Reiman A, Welty M, Solomon P. Cannabis as a Substitute for Opioid-Based Pain Medication: Patient Self-Report. *Cannabis Cannabinoid Res.* 2017; 2(1): 160–166.

[153] Nielsen S, Sabioni P, Trigo JM, et al. Opioid-Sparing Effect of Cannabinoids: A Systematic Review and Meta-Analysis. *Neuropsychopharmacology.* 2017 Aug;42(9):1752-1765.

[154] Jayamanne A, Greenwood R, Mitchell VA, et al. Actions of the FAAH inhibitor URB597 in neuropathic and inflammatory chronic pain models. *Br J Pharmacol.* 2006 Feb;147(3):281-8.

[155] Desroches J, Charron S, Bouchard JF, et al. Endocannabinoids decrease neuropathic pain-related behavior in mice through the activation of one or both peripheral CB(1) and CB(2) receptors. *Neuropharmacology.* 2014 Feb;77:441-52.

[156] Kinsey SG, Long JZ, O'Neal ST, et al. Blockade of endocannabinoid-degrading enzymes attenuates neuropathic pain. *J Pharmacol Exp Ther.* 2009 Sep;330(3):902-10.

[157] Chang L, Luo L, Palmer JA, et al. Inhibition of fatty acid amide hydrolase produces analgesia by multiple mechanisms. *Br J Pharmacol.* 2006 May;148(1):102-13.

[158] Turcotte C, Chouinard F, Lefebvre JS, et al. Regulation of inflammation by cannabinoids, the endocannabinoids 2-arachidonoyl-glycerol and arachidonoyl-ethanolamide, and their metabolites. *J Leukoc Biol.* 2015 Jun;97(6):1049-70.

[159] Rani Sagar D, Burston JJ, Woodhams SG, et al. Dynamic changes to the endocannabinoid system in models of chronic pain. *Philos Trans R Soc Lond B Biol Sci.* 2012 Dec 5;367(1607):3300-11.

[160] Kraft B. Is there any clinically relevant cannabinoid-induced analgesia? *Pharmacology.* 2012;89(1423-0313; 0031-7012; 5-6):237-46.

[161] Woodhams SG, Sagar DR, Burston JJ, et al. The role of the endocannabinoid system in pain. *Handb Exp Pharmacol.* 2015;227:119-43.

[162] Rani Sagar D, Burston JJ, Woodhams SG, et al. Dynamic changes to the endocannabinoid system in models of chronic pain. *Philos Trans R Soc Lond B Biol Sci.* 2012 Dec 5;367(1607):3300-11.

[163] Woodhams SG, Sagar DR, Burston JJ, et al. The role of the endocannabinoid system in pain. *Handb Exp Pharmacol.* 2015;227:119-43.

[164] Sagar DR, Jhaveri MD, Richardson D, et al. Endocannabinoid regulation of spinal nociceptive processing in a model of neuropathic pain. *Eur J Neurosci.* 2010 04;31(1460-9568; 0953-816; 8):1414-22.

[165] Pernia-Andrade AJ, Kato A, Witschi R, et al. Spinal endocannabinoids and CB1 receptors mediate C-fiber-induced heterosynaptic pain sensitization. *Science.* 2009 Aug 7;325(5941):760-4.

[166] Burns HD, Van Laere K, Sanabria-Bohorquez S, et al. 18F]MK-9470, a positron emission tomography (PET) tracer for in vivo human PET brain imaging of the cannabinoid-1 receptor. *Proc Natl Acad Sci U S A.* 2007 Jun 5;104(23):9800-5.

[167] Nadal X, La Porta C, Andreea Bura S, et al. Involvement of the opioid and cannabinoid systems in pain control: New insights from knockout studies. *Eur J Pharmacol.* 2013 Sep 15;716(1-3):142-57.

[168] Lee MC, Ploner M, Wiech K, et al. Amygdala activity contributes to the dissociative effect of cannabis on pain perception. *Pain.* 2013 Jan;154(1):124-34.

[169] Burston JJ, Woodhams SG. Endocannabinoid system and pain: An introduction. *Proc Nutr Soc.* 2014 Feb;73(1):106-17.

[170] Azad SC, Monory K, Marsicano G, et al. Circuitry for associative plasticity in the amygdala involves endocannabinoid signaling. *J Neurosci.* 2004 11/03;24:9953-61.

[171] Hammel DC, Zhang LP, Ma F, et al. Transdermal cannabidiol reduces inflammation and pain-related behaviours in a rat model of arthritis. *Eur J Pain.* 2016 Jul;20(6):936–948.

[172] Stevens AJ, Higgins MD. A systematic review of the analgesic efficacy of cannabinoid medications in the management of acute pain. *Acta Anaesthesiol Scand.* 2017 Mar;61(3):268-80.

[173] Christie MJ, Mallet C. Endocannabinoids can open the pain gate. *Sci Signal.* 2009;2:pe57.

[174] Ostenfeld T, Price J, Albanese M, et al. A randomized, controlled study to investigate the analgesic efficacy of single doses of the cannabinoid receptor-2 agonist GW842166, ibuprofen or placebo in patients with acute pain following third molar tooth extraction. *Clin J Pain.* 2011 05/02;27:668-76.

[175] Manzanares J, Julian M, Carrascosa A. Role of the cannabinoid system in pain control and therapeutic implications for the management of acute and chronic pain episodes. *Curr Neuropharmacol.* 2006 07;4:239-57.

[176] Cuñetti L, Manzo L, Peyraube R, et al. Chronic Pain Treatment With Cannabidiol in Kidney Transplant Patients in Uruguay. *Transplant Proc.* 2018 Mar;50(2):461-464.

[177] Greene NZ, Wiley JL, Yu Z, et al. Cannabidiol modulation of antinociceptive tolerance to Δ9-tetrahydrocannabinol. *Psychopharmacology (Berl).* 2018 Nov;235(11):3289-3302.

[178] Taylor CA, Bell JM, Breiding MJ, et al. Traumatic Brain Injury–Related Emergency Department Visits, Hospitalizations, and Deaths — United States, 2007 and 2013. *MMWR Surveill Summ.* 2017;66(No. SS-9):1–16.

[179] Shohami E, Cohen-Yeshurun A, Magid L, et al. Endocannabinoids and traumatic brain injury. *Br J Pharmacol.* 2011 Aug;163(7):1402-10.

[180] Hampson AJ, Grimaldi M, Axelrod J, et al. Cannabidiol and (-)Delta9-tetrahydrocannabinol are neuroprotective antioxidants. *Proc Natl Acad Sci U S A.* 1998 Jul 7;95(14):8268-73.

[181] Russo EB. Cannabis Therapeutics and the Future of Neurology. *Front Integr Neurosci.* 2018;12:51.

[182] Alzheimer's Disease International. Dementia statistics. Number of people with dementia. Available at: https://www.alz.co.uk/research/statistics.

[183] Benito C, Nunez E, Pazos MR, et al. The endocannabinoid system and alzheimer's disease. *Mol Neurobiol.* 2007 08;36:75-81.

[184] Koppel J, Davies P. Targeting the endocannabinoid system in alzheimer's disease. *J Alzheimer's Dis.* 2008 11;15:495-504.

[185] Benito C, Núñez E, Tolón RM, et al. Cannabinoid CB2 receptors and fatty acid amide hydrolase are selectively overexpressed in neuritic plaque-associated glia in Alzheimer's disease brains. *J Neurosci.* 2003 Dec 3; 23(35):11136-41.

[186] Ramírez BG, Blázquez C, Gómez del Pulgar T, et al. Prevention of Alzheimer's disease pathology by cannabinoids: neuroprotection mediated by blockade of microglial activation. *J Neurosci.* 2005 Feb 23; 25(8):1904-13.

[187] Ramírez BG, Blázquez C, Gómez del Pulgar T, et al. Prevention of Alzheimer's disease pathology by cannabinoids: neuroprotection mediated by blockade of microglial activation. *J Neurosci.* 2005 Feb 23; 25(8):1904-13.

[188] Ehrhart J, Obregon D, Mori T, et al. Stimulation of cannabinoid receptor 2 (CB2) suppresses microglial activation.
J Neuroinflammation. 2005 Dec 12; 2():29.

[189] Esposito G, De Filippis D, Carnuccio R, et al. The marijuana component cannabidiol inhibits beta-amyloid-induced tau protein hyperphosphorylation through Wnt/beta-catenin pathway rescue in PC12 cells. *J Mol Med (Berl).* 2006 Mar; 84(3):253-8.

[190] Chagas MH, Zuardi AW, Tumas V, et al. Effects of cannabidiol in the treatment of patients with Parkinson's disease: an exploratory double-blind trial. *J Psychopharmacol.* 2014 Nov;28(11):1088-98.

[191] Prud'homme M, Cata R, Jutras-Aswad D. Cannabidiol as an intervention for addictive behaviors: A systematic review of the evidence. *Subst Abuse.* 2015 May 21;9:33-8.

[192] Liput DJ, Hammell DC, Stinchcomb AL, et al. Transdermal delivery of cannabidiol attenuates binge alcohol-induced neurodegeneration in a rodent model of an alcohol use disorder. *Pharmacol Biochem Behav.* 2013 Oct;111:120-7.

[193] Gonzalez-Cuevas G, Martin-Fardon R, Kerr TM, et al. Unique treatment potential of cannabidiol for the prevention of relapse to drug use: preclinical proof of principle. *Neuropyschopharmacology.* 2018 Mar;43:2036-45.

[194] Centers for Disease Control and Prevention. Smoking & Tobacco Use. Fast Facts. Available at:
https://www.cdc.gov/tobacco/data_statistics/fact_sheets/fast_facts/index.htm.

[195] National Institute of Drug Abuse. Electronic cigarettes (E-cigarettes). Available at: https://www.drugabuse.gov/publications/drugfacts/electronic-cigarettes-e-cigarettes.

[196] Centers for Disease Control and Prevention. Health Effects of Cigarette Smoking. Available at: https://www.cdc.gov/tobacco/data_statistics/fact_sheets/health_effects/effects_cig_smoking/index.htm

[197] Morgan CJ, Das RK, Joye A, et al. Cannabidiol reduces cigarette consumption in tobacco smokers: Preliminary findings. *Addict Behav.* 2013 Sep;38(9):2433-6.

[198] Crippa JA, Hallak JE, Machado-de-Sousa JP, et al. Cannabidiol for the treatment of cannabis withdrawal syndrome: A case report. *J Clin Pharm Ther.* 2013 Apr;38(2):162-4.

[199] Mazier W, Saucisse N, Gatta-Cherifi B, et al. The endocannabinoid system: Pivotal orchestrator of obesity and metabolic disease. *Trends Endocrinol Metab.* 2015 Oct;26(10):524-37.

[200] Gatta-Cherifi B, Cota D. Endocannabinoids and metabolic disorders. *Handb Exp Pharmacol.* 2015;231:367-91.

[201] Di Marzo V, Piscitelli F, Mechoulam R. Cannabinoids and endocannabinoids in metabolic disorders with focus on diabetes. *Handb Exp Pharmacol.* 2011:75-104.

[202] Deveaux V, Cadoudal T, Ichigotani Y, et al. Cannabinoid CB2 receptor potentiates obesity-associated inflammation, insulin resistance and hepatic steatosis. *PLoS One.* 2009;4:e5844.

[203] Agudo J, Martin M, Roca C, et al. Deficiency of CB2 cannabinoid receptor in mice improves insulin sensitivity but increases food intake and obesity with age. *Diabetologia.* 2010 12;53:2629-40.

[204] Schmitz K, Mangels N, Haussler A, et al. Pro-inflammatory obesity in aged cannabinoid-2 receptor-deficient mice. *Int J Obes (Lond).* 2016 Feb;40(2):366-79.

[205] Weiss L, Zeira M, Reich S, et al. Cannabidiol arrests onset of autoimmune diabetes in NOD mice. *Neuropharmacology.* 2008 Jan; 54(1):244-9.

[206] Lehmann C, Fisher NB, Tugwell B, et al. Experimental cannabidiol treatment reduces early pancreatic inflammation in type 1 diabetes. *Clin Hemorheol Microcirc.* 2016;64(4):655-662.

[207] Weiss L, Zeira M, Reich S, et al. Cannabidiol lowers incidence of diabetes in non-obese diabetic mice. *Autoimmunity.* 2006;39:143–151.

[208] Rajesh M, Mukhopadhyay P, Bátkai S, et al. Cannabidiol attenuates cardiac dysfunction, oxidative stress, fibrosis, and inflammatory and cell death signaling pathways in diabetic cardiomyopathy. *J Am Coll Cardiol.* 2010 Dec 14;56(25):2115-25.

[209] Horváth B, Mukhopadhyay P, Haskó G, et al. The endocannabinoid system and plant-derived cannabinoids in diabetes and diabetic complications. *Am J Pathol.* 2012;180:432–442.

[210] Gruden G, Barutta F, Kunos G, et al. Role of the endocannabinoid system in diabetes and diabetic complications. *Br J Pharmacol*. 2016 Apr; 173(7): 1116–1127.

[211] Jadoon KA, Ratcliffe SH, Barrett DA, et al. Efficacy and safety of cannabidiol and tetrahydrocannabivarin on glycemic and lipid parameters in patients with type 2 diabetes: A randomized, double-blind, placebo-controlled, parallel group pilot study. *Diabetes Care*. 2016 Oct;39(10):1777-86.

[212] Lehmann C, Fisher NB5, Tugwell B, et al. Experimental cannabidiol treatment reduces early pancreatic inflammation in type 1 diabetes. *Clin Hemorheol Microcirc*. 2016;64(4):655-662.

[213] Yeshurun M, Shpilberg O, Herscovici C, et al. Cannabidiol for the Prevention of Graft-versus-Host-Disease after Allogeneic Hematopoietic Cell Transplantation: Results of a Phase II Study. *Biol Blood Marrow Transplant*. 2015 Oct;21(10):1770-5.

[214] Babson KA, Sottile J, Morabito D. Cannabis, Cannabinoids, and Sleep: a Review of the Literature. *Curr Psychiatry Rep*. 2017;19:23.

[215] Nicholson AN, Turner C, Stone BM, et al. Effect of Delta-9-tetrahydrocannabinol and cannabidiol on nocturnal sleep and early-morning behavior in young adults. *J Clin Psychopharmacol*. 2004 Jun;24(3):305-13.

[216] Zija International. Internal research report. Pharmacokinetic study of CBD administered by tail vein injection, orally, and skin patch in rats.

[217] Gunasekaran N, Long LE, Dawson BL, et al. Reintoxication: the release of fat-stored Δ9-tetrahydrocannabinol (THC) into blood is enhanced by food deprivation or ACTH exposure. *Br J Pharmacol*. 2009 Nov; 158(5): 1330–1337.

[218] Wong A, Montebello ME, Norberg MM, et al. Exercise increases plasma THC concentrations in regular cannabis users. *Drug Alcohol Depend*. 2013 Dec 1;133(2):763-7.

[219] Wong A, Keats K, Rooney K, et al. Fasting and exercise increase plasma cannabinoid levels in THC pre-treated rats: an examination of behavioural consequences. *Psychopharmacology (Berl)*. 2014 Oct;231(20):3987-96.

[220] Hao J, Ghosh P, Li SK, et al. Heat effects on drug delivery across human skin. *Expert Opin Drug Deliv*. 2016 May; 13(5): 755–768.

[221] Chelliah MP, Zinn Z, Khuu P, et al. Self-initiated use of topical cannabidiol oil for epidermolysis bullosa. *Pediatric Dermatol*. 2018:1-4.

[222] Morales P, Hurst DP, Reggio PH. Molecular Targets of the Phytocannabinoids-A Complex Picture. *Prog Chem Org Nat Prod*. 2017;103:103–131.

[223] Gertsch J, Leonti M, Raduner S, et al. Beta-caryophyllene is a dietary cannabinoid. *Proc Natl Acad Sci U S A*. 2008 Jul 1; 105(26): 9099–9104.

[224] Sharma C, Al Kaabi JM, Nurulain SM, et al. Polypharmacological Properties and Therapeutic Potential of β-Caryophyllene: A Dietary Phytocannabinoid of Pharmaceutical Promise. *Curr Pharm Des*. 2016;22(21):3237-64.

[225] Gertsch J. Anti-inflammatory cannabinoids in diet: Towards a better understanding of CB2 receptor action? *Commun Integr Biol*. 2008 Jul-Sep; 1(1): 26–28.

[226] Klauke AL, Racz I, Pradier B, et al. The cannabinoid CB2 receptor-selective phytocannabinoid beta-caryophyllene exerts analgesic effects in mouse models of inflammatory and neuropathic pain. *European Neuropsychopharmacology.* 2014 Apr;24(4):608-20.

[227] Gertsch J. Anti-inflammatory cannabinoids in diet: Towards a better understanding of CB2 receptor action? *Commun Integr Biol.* 2008 Jul-Sep; 1(1): 26–28.

[228] Paula-Freire L, Andersen M, Gama V, et al. The oral administration of trans-caryophyllene attenuates acute and chronic pain in mice. *Phytomedicine.* 2014;21:356–362.

[229] Johnson SA. Supercritical Essential Oils. A Companion Resource to Medicinal Essential Oils. 2017. Scott A Johnson Professional Writing Services, LLC: Orem, Utah.

[230] Katsuyama S, Mizoguchi H, Kuwahata H, et al. Involvement of peripheral cannabinoid and opioid receptors in β-caryophyllene-induced antinociception. *Eur J Pain.* 2013 May;17(5):664-75.

[231] Johnson SA. Supercritical Essential Oils. A Companion Resource to Medicinal Essential Oils. 2017. Scott A Johnson Professional Writing Services, LLC: Orem, Utah.

[232] Ben-Shabat S, Fride E, Sheskin T, et al. An entourage effect: inactive endogenous fatty acid glycerol esters enhance 2-arachidonoyl-glycerol cannabinoid activity. *Eur J Pharmacol.* 1998 Jul 17; 353(1):23-31.

[233] Fidyty K, Fiedorowicz A, Strzadala L, et al. β-caryophyllene and β-caryophyllene oxide—natural compounds of anticancer and analgesic properties. *Cancer Med.* 2016 Oct;5(10):3007–3017.

[234] Kim C, Cho SK, Kim KD, et al. β-Caryophyllene oxide potentiates TNFα-induced apoptosis and inhibits invasion through down-modulation of NF-κB-regulated gene products. *Apoptosis.* 2014 Apr;19(4):708-18.

[235] Di Sotto A, Mazzanti G, Carbone F, et al. Inhibition by beta-caryophyllene of ethyl methanesulfonate-induced clastogenicity in cultured human lymphocytes. *Mutat Res.* 2010 Jun 17;699(1-2):23-8.

[236] Zheng GQ, Kenney PM, Lam LK. Sesquiterpenes from clove (Eugenia caryophyllata) as potential anticarcinogenic agents. *J Nat Prod.* 1992 Jul;55(7):999-1003.

[237] Di Giacomo S, Mazzanti G, Di Sotto A. Mutagenicity of cigarette butt waste in the bacterial reverse mutation assay: The protective effects of β-caryophyllene and β-caryophyllene oxide. *Environ Toxicol.* 2016 Nov;31(11):1319-1328.

[238] Di Sotto A, Evandri MG, Mazzanti G. Antimutagenic and mutagenic activities of some terpenes in the bacterial reverse mutation assay. *Mutat Res.* 2008 May 31;653(1-2):130-3.

[239] Johnson SA. Supercritical Essential Oils. A Companion Resource to Medicinal Essential Oils. 2017. Scott A Johnson Professional Writing Services, LLC: Orem, Utah.

[240] Harding MC, Sloan CD, Merrill RM, et al. Transitions From Heart Disease to Cancer as the Leading Cause of Death in US States, 1999–2016. *Prev Chron Dis.* 2018;15:180151.

[241] Machado KDC, Islam MT, Ali ES, et al. A systematic review on the neuroprotective perspectives of beta-caryophyllene. *Phytother Res.* 2018 Dec;32(12):2376-2388.

[242] Johnson SA. Supercritical Essential Oils. A Companion Resource to Medicinal Essential Oils. 2017. Scott A Johnson Professional Writing Services, LLC: Orem, Utah.

[243] Askari VR, Shafiee-Nick R. The protective effects of β-caryophyllene on LPS-induced primary microglia M1/M2 imbalance: A mechanistic evaluation. Life Sci. 2019 Jan 5. [Epub ahead of print]

[244] World Health Organization. Global Health Observatory (GHO) data. Cholesterol. Available at: https://www.who.int/gho/ncd/risk_factors/cholesterol_prevalence/en/.

[245] Salami JA, Warraich H, Valero-Elizondo J, et al. National Trends in Statin Use and Expenditures in the US Adult Population From 2002 to 2013: Insights From the Medical Expenditure Panel Survey. *JAMA Cardiol.* 2017;2(1):56-65.

[246] Baldissera MD, Souza CF, Grando TH, et al. Hypolipidemic effect of β-caryophyllene to treat hyperlipidemic rats. *Naunyn Schmiedebergs Arch Pharmacol.* 2016 Dec 2.

[247] de Oliveira CC, de Oliveira CV, Grigoletto J, et al. Anticonvulsant activity of β-caryophyllene against pentylenetetrazol-induced seizures. *Epilepsy Behav.* 2016 Mar;56:26-31.

[248] Tchekalarova J, da Conceição Machado K2, Gomes Júnior AL, et al. Pharmacological characterization of the cannabinoid receptor 2 agonist, β-caryophyllene on seizure models in mice. *Seizure.* 2018 Apr;57:22-26.

[249] Abbas MA, Taha MO, Zihlif MA, et al. β-Caryophyllene causes regression of endometrial implants in a rat model of endometriosis without affecting fertility. *Eur J Pharmacol.* 2013 Feb 28;702(1-3):12-9.

[250] Fiorenzani P, Lamponi S, Magnani A, et al. In vitro and in vivo characterization of the new analgesic combination Beta-caryophyllene and docosahexaenoic Acid. *Evid Based Complement Alternat Med.* 2014;2014:596312.

[251] Ono Y, Tanabe A, Nakamura Y, et al. A Low-Testosterone State Associated with Endometrioma Leads to the Apoptosis of Granulosa Cells. *PLoS One.* 2014; 9(12): e115618.

[252] US Centers for Disease Control and Prevention. Number of Americans with Diabetes Projected to Double or Triple by 2050. Available at: https://www.cdc.gov/media/pressrel/2010/r101022.html.

[253] Tooke JE, Goh KL. Vascular function in type 2 diabetes mellitus and pre-diabetes: the case for intrinsic endotheiopathy. *Diabet Med.* 1999;16:710–715.

[254] Basha RH, Sankaranarayanan C. β-Caryophyllene, a natural sesquiterpene, modulates carbohydrate metabolism in streptozotocin-induced diabetic rats. *Acta Histochem.* 2014 Oct;116(8):1469-79.

[255] Basha RH, Sankaranarayanan C. β-Caryophyllene, a natural sesquiterpene lactone attenuates hyperglycemia mediated oxidative and inflammatory stress in experimental diabetic rats. *Chem Biol Interact.* 2016 Feb 5;245:50-8.

[256] Cho HI, Hong JM, Choi JW, et al. β-Caryophyllene alleviates D-galactosamine and lipopolysaccharide-induced hepatic injury through suppression of the TLR4 and RAGE signaling pathways. *Eur J Pharmacol.* 2015 Oct 5;764:613-21.

[257] Mahmoud MF, Swefy SE, Hasan RA, et al. Role of cannabinoid receptors in hepatic fibrosis and apoptosis associated with bile duct ligation in rats. *Eur J Pharmacol.* 2014 Nov 5;742:118-24.

[258] Calleja MA, Vieites JM, Montero-Meléndez T, et al. The antioxidant effect of β-caryophyllene protects rat liver from carbon tetrachlorideinduced fibrosis by inhibiting hepatic stellate cell activation. *Br J Nutr.* 2013 Feb 14;109(3):394-401.

[259] Kelany ME, Abdallah MA, et al. Protective effects of combined β-caryophyllene and silymarin against ketoprofen-induced hepatotoxicity in rats. *Can J Physiol Pharmacol.* 2016 Jul;94(7):739-44.

[260] Kamikubo R, Kai K, Tsuji-Naito K, et al. β-Caryophyllene attenuates palmitate-induced lipid accumulation through AMPK signaling by activating CB2 receptor in human HepG2 hepatocytes. *Mol Nutr Food Res.* 2016 Oct;60(10):2228-2242.

[261] Johnson SA. Supercritical Essential Oils. A Companion Resource to Medicinal Essential Oils. 2017. Scott A Johnson Professional Writing Services, LLC: Orem, Utah.

[262] Esposito G, Scuderi C, Valenza M, et al. Cannabidiol reduces Aβ-induced neuroinflammation and promotes hippocampal neurogenesis through PPARγ involvement. *PLoS One.* 2011;6:e28668.

[263] Romano B1, Borrelli F, Fasolino I, et al. The cannabinoid TRPA1 agonist cannabichromene inhibits nitric oxide production in macrophages and ameliorates murine colitis. *Br J Pharmacol.* 2013 May;169(1):213-29.

[264] Kathmann M, Flau K, Redmer A, et al. Cannabidiol is an allosteric modulator at mu- and delta-opioid receptors. *Naunyn Schmiedebergs Arch Pharmacol.* 2006;372:354.

[265] O'Sullivan SEO, Kendall Da, Randall MD. Further Characterization of the Time-Dependent Vascular Effects of D9 -Tetrahydrocannabinol. *J Pharmacol Exp Ther.* 2006;317:428.

[266] Iannotti FA, Hill CL, Leo A, et al. Nonpsychotropic plant cannabinoids, cannabidivarin (CBDV) and cannabidiol (CBD), activate and desensitize transient receptor potential vanilloid 1 (TRPV1) channels in vitro: potential for the treatment of neuronal hyperexcitability. *ACS Chem Neurosci.* 2014 Nov 19;5(11):1131-41.

[267] O'Sullivan SEO, Kendall Da, Randall MD. Further Characterization of the Time-Dependent Vascular Effects of D9 -Tetrahydrocannabinol. *J Pharmacol Exp Ther.* 2006;317:428.

[268] DeLong GT, Wolf CE, Poklis A, et al. Pharmacological evaluation of the natural constituent of Cannabis sativa, cannabichromene and its modulation by Δ(9)-tetrahydrocannabinol. *Drug Alcohol Depend.* 2010 Nov 1;112(1-2):126-33.

[269] Turner CE, Elsohly MA. Biological activity of cannabichromene, its homologs and isomers. *J Clin Pharmacol.* 1981 Aug-Sep;21(S1):283S-291S.

[270] Wirth PW, Watson ES, ElSohly M, et al. Anti-inflammatory properties of cannabichromene. *Life Sci.* 1980 Jun;26(23):1991-5.

[271] Maione S, Piscitelli F, Gatta L, et al. Non-psychoactive cannabinoids modulate the descending pathway of antinociception in anaesthetized rats through several mechanisms of action. *Br J Pharmacol.* 2011 Feb;162(3):584-96.

[272] Davis WM, Hatoum NS. Neurobehavioral actions of cannabichromene and interactions with delta 9-tetrahydrocannabinol. *Gen Pharmacol.* 1983;14(2):247-52.

[273] Romano B, Borrelli F, Fasolino I, et al. The cannabinoid TRPA1 agonist cannabichromene inhibits nitric oxide production in macrophages and ameliorates murine colitis. *Br J Pharmacol.* 2013 May;169(1):213-29.

[274] Bischoff SC, Barbara G, Buurman W, et al. Intestinal permeability – a new target for disease prevention and therapy. *BMC Gastroenterol.* 2014;14:189.

[275] Izzo AA, Capasso R, Aviello G, et al. Inhibitory effect of cannabichromene, a major non-psychotropic cannabinoid extracted from Cannabis sativa, on inflammation-induced hypermotility in mice. *Br J Pharmacol.* 2012 Jun;166(4):1444-60.

[276] Ligresti A, Moriello AS, Starowicz K, et al. Antitumor Activity of Plant Cannabinoids with Emphasis on the Effect of Cannabidiol on Human Breast Carcinoma. *J Pharmn Exp Ther.* 2006 sep;318(3):1375-87.

[277] Belanger M. The role of astroglia in neuroprotection. *Dialogues Clin Neurosci.* 2009 Sep;11(3):281–295.

[278] Shinjyo N, Di Marzo V. The effect of cannabichromene on adult neural stem/progenitor cells. *Neurochem Int.* 2013 Nov;63(5):432-7.

[279] Oláh A, Markovics A, Szabó-Papp J, et al. Differential effectiveness of selected non-psychotropic phytocannabinoids on human sebocyte functions implicates their introduction in dry/seborrhoeic skin and acne treatment. *Exp Dermatol.* 2016 Sep;25(9):701-7.

[280] El-Alfy AT, Ivey K, Robinson K, et al. Antidepressant-like effect of delta9-tetrahydrocannabinol and other cannabinoids isolated from Cannabis sativa L. *Pharmacol Biochem Behav.* 2010 Jun;95(4):434-42.

[281] Kathmann M, Flau K, Redmer A, et al. Cannabidiol is an allosteric modulator at mu- and delta-opioid receptors. *Naunyn Schmiedebergs Arch Pharmacol.* 2006;372:354.

[282] O'Sullivan SEO, Kendall Da, Randall MD. Further Characterization of the Time-Dependent Vascular Effects of D9 -Tetrahydrocannabinol. *J Pharmacol Exp Ther.* 2006;317:428.

[283] Vigli D, Cosentino L, Raggi C, et al. Chronic treatment with the phytocannabinoid Cannabidivarin (CBDV) rescues behavioural alterations and brain atrophy in a mouse model of Rett syndrome. *Neuropharmacology.* 2018 Sep 15;140:121-129.

[284] Anavi-Goffer S, Baillie G, Irving AJ, et al. Modulation of L-α-lysophosphatidylinositol/GPR55 mitogen-activated protein kinase (MAPK) signaling by cannabinoids. *J Biol Chem.* 2012 Jan 2;287(1):91-104.

146

285 Ružić Zečević D, Folić M, Tantoush Z, et al. Investigational cannabinoids in seizure disorders, what have we learned thus far? *Expert Opin Investig Drugs.* 2018 Jun;27(6):535-541.

286 Amada N, Yamasaki Y, Williams CM, et al. Cannabidivarin (CBDV) suppresses pentylenetetrazole (PTZ)-induced increases in epilepsy-related gene expression. *PeerJ.* 2013 Nov 21;1:e214.

287 Hill TD, Cascio MG, Romano B, et al. Cannabidivarin-rich cannabis extracts are anticonvulsant in mouse and rat via a CB1 receptor-independent mechanism. *Br J Pharmacol.* 2013 Oct;170(3):679-92.

288 Hill AJ, Mercier MS, Hill TD, et al. Cannabidivarin is anticonvulsant in mouse and rat. *Br J Pharmacol.* 2012 Dec;167(8):1629-42.

289 Bialer M, Johannessen SI, Koepp MJ, et al. Progress report on new antiepileptic drugs: A summary of the Fourteenth Eilat Conference on New Antiepileptic Drugs and Devices (EILAT XIV). II. Drugs in more advanced clinical development. *Epilepsia.* 2018 Oct;59(10):1842-1866.

290 Greco M, Varriale G, Coppola G, et al. Investigational small molecules in phase II clinical trials for the treatment of epilepsy. *Expert Opin Investig Drugs.* 2018 Dec;27(12):971-979.

291 Nesmith AP, Wagner MA, Pasqualini FS, et al. A human in vitro model of Duchenne muscular dystrophy muscle formation and contractility. *J Cell Biol.* 2016;215(1):47.

292 Iannotti FA, Pagano E, Moriello AS, et al. Effects of non-euphoric plant cannabinoids on muscle quality and performance of dystrophic mdx mice. *Br J Pharmacol.* 2018 Aug 3. [Epub ahead of print]

293 Vigli D, Cosentino L, Raggi C, et al. Chronic treatment with the phytocannabinoid Cannabidivarin (CBDV) rescues behavioural alterations and brain atrophy in a mouse model of Rett syndrome. *Neuropharmacology.* 2018 Sep 15;140:121-129.

294 Vigli D, Cosentino L, Raggi C, et al. Chronic treatment with the phytocannabinoid Cannabidivarin (CBDV) rescues behavioural alterations and brain atrophy in a mouse model of Rett syndrome. *Neuropharmacology.* 2018 Sep 15;140:121-129.

295 Rock EM, Sticht MA, Duncan M, et al. Evaluation of the potential of the phytocannabinoids, cannabidivarin (CBDV) and Δ(9) -tetrahydrocannabivarin (THCV), to produce CB1 receptor inverse agonism symptoms of nausea in rats. *Br J Pharmacol.* 2013 Oct;170(3):671-8.

296 Anavi-Goffer S, Baillie G, Irving AJ, et al. Modulation of L-α-lysophosphatidylinositol/GPR55 mitogen-activated protein kinase (MAPK) signaling by cannabinoids. *J Biol Chem.* 2012 Jan 2;287(1):91-104.

297 De Petrocellis L, Orlando P, Moriello AS, et al. Cannabinoid actions at TRPV channels: effects on TRPV3 and TRPV4 and their potential relevance to gastrointestinal inflammation. *Acta Physiol (Oxf).* 2012 Feb;204(2):255-66.

298 Anavi-Goffer S, Baillie G, Irving AJ, et al. Modulation of L-α-Lysophosphatidylinositol/GPR55 Mitogen-activated Protein Kinase (MAPK) Signaling by Cannabinoids. *J Biol Chem.* 2012 Jan;287:91-104.

[299] Scott KA, Shah S, Dalgleish AG, et al. Enhancing the activity of cannabidiol and other cannabinoids in vitro through modifications to drug combinations and treatment schedules. *Anticancer Res.* 2013 Oct;33(10):4373-80.

[300] Esposito G, Scuderi C, Valenza M, et al. Cannabidiol reduces Aβ-induced neuroinflammation and promotes hippocampal neurogenesis through PPARγ involvement. *PLoS One.* 2011;6:e28668.

[301] Scuderi C, Steardo L, Esposito G. Cannabidiol promotes amyloid precursor protein ubiquitination and reduction of beta amyloid expression in SHSY5YAPP+ cells through PPARg involvement. *Phyther Res.* 2014;28:1007.

[302] Ahrens J, Demir R, Leuwer M, et al. The nonpsychotropic cannabinoid cannabidiol modulates and directly activates alpha-1 and alpha-1-beta glycine receptor function. *Pharmacology.* 2009;83:217.

[303] Kathmann M, Flau K, Redmer A, et al. Cannabidiol is an allosteric modulator at mu- and delta-opioid receptors. *Naunyn Schmiedebergs Arch Pharmacol.* 2006;372:354.

[304] Kathmann M, Flau K, Redmer A, et al. Cannabidiol is an allosteric modulator at mu- and delta-opioid receptors. *Naunyn Schmiedebergs Arch Pharmacol.* 2006;372:354.

[305] Vara D, Morell C, Rodríguez-Henche N, et al. Involvement of PPARγ in the antitumoral action of cannabinoids on hepatocellular carcinoma. *Cell Death Dis.* 2013;4:e618.

[306] Cascio MG, Gauson LA, Stevenson LA, et al. Evidence that the plant cannabinoid cannabigerol is a highly potent alpha2-adrenoceptor agonist and moderately potent 5HT1A receptor antagonist. *Br J Pharmacol.* 2010 Jan;159(1):129-41.

[307] Gugliandolo A, Pollastro F, Grassi G, et al. In Vitro Model of Neuroinflammation: Efficacy of Cannabigerol, a Non-Psychoactive Cannabinoid. *Int J Mol Sci.* 2018 Jul 8;19(7).

[308] Valdeolivas S, Navarrete C, Cantarero I, et al. Neuroprotective properties of cannabigerol in Huntington's disease: studies in R6/2 mice and 3-nitropropionate-lesioned mice. *Neurotherapeutics.* 2015 Jan;12(1):185-99.

[309] Baek SH, Kim YO, Kwag JS, et al. Boron trifluoride etherate on silica-A modified Lewis acid reagent (VII). Antitumor activity of cannabigerol against human oral epitheloid carcinoma cells. *Arch Pharm Res.* 1998 Jun;21(3):353-6.

[310] Couch DG, Maudslay H, Doleman B, et al. The Use of Cannabinoids in Colitis: A Systematic Review and Meta-Analysis. *Inflamm Bowel Dis.* 2018 Mar 19;24(4):680-697.

[311] Borrelli F, Fasolino I, Romano B, et al. Beneficial effect of the non-psychotropic plant cannabinoid cannabigerol on experimental inflammatory bowel disease. *Biochem Pharmacol.* 2013 May 1;85(9):1306-16.

[312] Borrelli F, Pagano E, Romano B, et al. Colon carcinogenesis is inhibited by the TRPM8 antagonist cannabigerol, a Cannabis-derived non-psychotropic cannabinoid. *Carcinogenesis.* 2014 Dec;35(12):2787-97.

[313] Pagano E, Montanaro V, Di Girolamo A, et al. Effect of Non-psychotropic Plant-derived Cannabinoids on Bladder Contractility: Focus on Cannabigerol. *Nat Prod Commun.* 2015 Jun;10(6):1009-12.

[314] Colasanti BK. A comparison of the ocular and central effects of delta 9-tetrahydrocannabinol and cannabigerol. *J Ocul Pharmacol.* 1990 Winter;6(4):259-69.

[315] Colasanti BK, Craig CR, Allara RD. Intraocular pressure, ocular toxicity and neurotoxicity after administration of cannabinol or cannabigerol. *Exp Eye Res.* 1984 Sep;39(3):251-9.

[316] Brierley DI, Samuels J, Duncan M, et al. A cannabigerol-rich Cannabis sativa extract, devoid of [INCREMENT]9-tetrahydrocannabinol, elicits hyperphagia in rats. *Behav Pharmacol.* 2017 Jun;28(4):280-284.

[317] Brierley DI, Samuels J, Duncan M, et al. Cannabigerol is a novel, well-tolerated appetite stimulant in pre-satiated rats. *Psychopharmacology (Berl).* 2016 Oct;233(19-20):3603-13.

[318] Biro T, Toth BI, Hasko G, et al. The endocannabinoid system of the skin in health and disease: novel perspectives and therapeutic opportunities. *Trends Pharmacol Sci.* 2009 Aug;30(8):411–420.

[319] Oláh A, Markovics A, Szabó-Papp J, et al. Differential effectiveness of selected non-psychotropic phytocannabinoids on human sebocyte functions implicates their introduction in dry/seborrhoeic skin and acne treatment. *Exp Dermatol.* 2016 Sep;25(9):701-7.

[320] Pucci M, Rapino C, Di Francesco A, et al. Epigenetic control of skin differentiation genes by phytocannabinoids. *Br J Pharmacol.* 2013 Oct;170(3):581-91.

[321] Wilkinson JD, Williamson EM. Cannabinoids inhibit human keratinocyte proliferation through a non-CB1/CB2 mechanism and have a potential therapeutic value in the treatment of psoriasis. *J Dermatol Sci.* 2007 Feb;45(2):87-92.

[322] Rock EM, Goodwin JM, Limebeer CL, et al. Interaction between non-psychotropic cannabinoids in marihuana: effect of cannabigerol (CBG) on the anti-nausea or anti-emetic effects of cannabidiol (CBD) in rats and shrews. *Psychopharmacology (Berl).* 2011 Jun;215(3):505-12.

[323] Fournier G, Richez-Dumanois C, Duvezin J, et al. Identification of a new chemotype in Cannabis sativa: cannabigerol-dominant plants, biogenetic and agronomic prospects. *Planta Med.* 1987 Jun;53(3):277-80.

[324] Järbe TU, Hiltunen AJ. Cannabimimetic activity of cannabinol in rats and pigeons. *Neuropharmacology.* 1987 Feb-Mar;26(2-3):219-28.

[325] Huffman JW, Liddle J, Yu S, et al. 3-(1',1'-Dimethylbutyl)-1-deoxy-Δ8-THC and related compounds: Synthesis of selective ligands for the CB2 receptor. *Bioorganic Med Chem.* 1999;7:2905.

[326] Razdan RK, Dalzell HC, Herlihy P, et al. Hashish. Unsaturated side-chain analogues of delta8-tetrahydrocannabinol with potent biological activity. *J Med Chem.* 1976;19:1328. [PubMed]

[327] Kathmann M, Flau K, Redmer A, et al. Cannabidiol is an allosteric modulator at mu- and delta-opioid receptors. *Naunyn Schmiedebergs Arch Pharmacol.* 2006;372:354.

[328] Weydt P, Hong S, Witting A, et al. Cannabinol delays symptom onset in SOD1 (G93A) transgenic mice without affecting survival. *Amyotroph Lateral Scler Other Motor Neuron Disord*. 2005 Sep;6(3):182-4.

[329] Wilkinson JD, Williamson EM. Cannabinoids inhibit human keratinocyte proliferation through a non-CB1/CB2 mechanism and have a potential therapeutic value in the treatment of psoriasis. *J Dermatol Sci*. 2007 Feb;45(2):87-92.

[330] Green K, Symonds CM, Oliver NW, et al. Intraocular pressure following systemic administration of cannabinoids. *Curr Eye Res*. 1982-1983;2(4):247-53.

[331] Farrimond JA, Whalley BJ, Williams CM. Cannabinol and cannabidiol exert opposing effects on rat feeding patterns. *Psychopharmacology (Berl)*. 2012 Sep;223(1):117-29.

[332] Zygmunt PM, Andersson DA, Hogestatt ED. Delta 9-tetrahydrocannabinol and cannabinol activate capsaicin-sensitive sensory nerves via a CB1 and CB2 cannabinoid receptor-independent mechanism. *J Neurosci*. 2002 Jun 1;22(11):4720-7.

[333] Herring AC, Kaminski NE. Cannabinol-mediated inhibition of nuclear factor-kappaB, cAMP response element-binding protein, and interleukin-2 secretion by activated thymocytes. *J Pharmacol Exp Ther*. 1999 Dec;291(3):1156-63.

[334] Herring AC, Faubert Kaplan BL, Kaminski NE. Modulation of CREB and NF-kappaB signal transduction by cannabinol in activated thymocytes. *Cell Signal*. 2001 Apr;13(4):241-50.

[335] Yea SS, Yang KH, Kaminski NE. Role of nuclear factor of activated T-cells and activator protein-1 in the inhibition of interleukin-2 gene transcription by cannabinol in EL4 T-cells. *J Pharmacol Exp Ther*. 2000 Feb;292(2):597-605.

[336] Herring AC, Koh WS, Kaminski NE. Inhibition of the cyclic AMP signaling cascade and nuclear factor binding to CRE and kappaB elements by cannabinol, a minimally CNS-active cannabinoid. *Biochem Pharmacol*. 1998 Apr 1;55(7):1013-23.

[337] Idris AI, Ralston SH. Role of cannabinoids in the regulation of bone remodeling. *Front Endocrinol (Lausanne)*. 2012;3:136.

[338] Scutt A, Williamson EM. Cannabinoids stimulate fibroblastic colony formation by bone marrow cells indirectly via CB2 receptors. *Calcif Tissue Int*. 2007 Jan; 80(1):50-9.

[339] Appendino G, Gibbons S, Giana A, et al. Antibacterial cannabinoids from Cannabis sativa: a structure-activity study. *J Nat Prod*. 2008 Aug;71(8):1427-30.

[340] Chesher GB, Jackson DM. The quasi-morphine withdrawal syndrome: effect of cannabinol, cannabidiol and tetrahydrocannabinol. *Pharmacol Biochem Behav*. 1985 Jul;23(1):13-5.

[341] Merkus FWHM. Cannabivarin and Tetrahydrocannabivarin, Two New Constituents of Hashish. *Nature*. 1971 Aug;232:579-80.

[342] Merkus FWHM. [Cannabivarin, a new constituent of hashish]. *Pharm Weekbl*. 1971 Feb 26;106(9):69-71.

[343] Anavi-Goffer S, Baillie G, Irving AJ, et al. Modulation of L-α-Lysophosphatidylinositol/GPR55 Mitogen-activated Protein Kinase (MAPK) Signaling by Cannabinoids. *J Biol Chem.* 2012 Jan;287:91-104.

[344] Bakas T, Devenish S, Van Nieuwenhuizen P, et al. The actions of cannabidiol and 2-arachidonyl glicerol on GABA-A receptors. 26th Annu. Symp. Cannabinoids, Int. Cannabinoid Res. Soc; Bukovina, Poland. 2016. p. 28.

[345] Rosenthaler S, Pöhn B, Kolmanz C, et al. Differences in receptor binding affinity of several phytocannabinoids do not explain their effects on neural cell cultures. *Neurotoxicol Teratol.* 2014;46:49.

[346] Izzo A, Borrelli F, Capasso R, et al. Non-psychotropic plant cannabinoids: new therapeutic opportunities from an ancient herb. *Trends Pharmacol Sci.* 2009;30:515.

[347] Ma YL, Weston SE, Whalley BJ, et al. The phytocannabinoid Delta(9)-tetrahydrocannabivarin modulates inhibitory neurotransmission in the cerebellum. *Br J Pharmacol.* 2008 May;154(1):204-15.

[348] Dennis I, Whalley BJ, Stephens GJ. Effects of Delta9-tetrahydrocannabivarin on [35S]GTPgammaS binding in mouse brain cerebellum and piriform cortex membranes. *Br J Pharmacol.* 2008 Jul;154(6):1349-58.

[349] McPartland JM, Duncan M, Di Marzo V, et al. Are cannabidiol and Δ(9) - tetrahydrocannabivarin negative modulators of the endocannabinoid system? A systematic review. *Br J Pharmacol.* 2015 Feb;172(3):737-53.

[350] Cascio MG, Gauson LA, Stevenson LA, et al. Evidence that the plant cannabinoid cannabigerol is a highly potent α 2-adrenoceptor agonist and moderately potent 5HT 1A receptor antagonist. *Br J Pharmacol.* 2010;159:129.

[351] Thomas A, Stevenson LA, Wease KN, et al. Evidence that the plant cannabinoid Delta9-tetrahydrocannabivarin is a cannabinoid CB1 and CB2 receptor antagonist. *Br J Pharmacol.* 2005;146:917.

[352] Lauckner JE, Jensen JB, Chen H-Y, et al. GPR55 is a cannabinoid receptor that increases intracellular calcium and inhibits M current. *Proc Natl Acad Sci U S A.* 2008;105:269.

[353] Ryberg E, N Larsson, S Sjögren, et al. The orphan receptor GPR55 is a novel cannabinoid receptor. *Br J Pharmacol.* 2007;152(7):1092–1101.

[354] Johns DG, Behm DJ, Walker DJ, et al. The novel endocannabinoid receptor GPR55 is activated by atypical cannabinoids but does not mediate their vasodilator effects. *Br J Pharmacol.* 2007;152(5):825–831.

[355] Oka S, Nakajima K, Yamashita A, et al. Identification of GPR55 as a lysophosphatidylinositol receptor. *Biochem Biophys Res Commun.* 2007;362(4):928–934.

[356] Henstridge CM, Balenga NA, Ford LA, et al. The GPR55 ligand L-alpha-lysophosphatidylinositol promotes RhoA-dependent Ca2+ signaling and NFAT activation. *FASEB J.* 2009;23(1):183–193.

[357] Ross RA. L-α-Lysophosphatidylinositol meets GPR55: a deadly relationship. *Opinion.* 2011 May;32(5):265-9.

[358] Piñeiro R, Maffucci T, Falasca M. The putative cannabinoid receptor GPR55 defines a novel autocrine loop in cancer cell proliferation. *Oncogene.* 2011 Jan 13;30(2):142-52.

[359] Andradas C, Caffarel MM, Pérez-Gómez E, et al. The orphan G protein-coupled receptor GPR55 promotes cancer cell proliferation via ERK. *Oncogene.* 2011 Jan 13;30(2):245-52.

[360] Ford LA, Roelofs AJ, Anavi-Goffer S, et al. A role for L-alpha-lysophosphatidylinositol and GPR55 in the modulation of migration, orientation and polarization of human breast cancer cells. *Br J Pharmacol.* 2010 Jun;160(3):762-71.

[361] Janssens A, Silvestri C, Martella A, et al. Δ9-tetrahydrocannabivarin impairs epithelial calcium transport through inhibition of TRPV5 and TRPV6. *Pharmacol Res.* 2018 Oct;136:83-89.

[362] Wei Y, Zheng D, Guo X, et al. Transient Receptor Potential Channel, Vanilloid 5, Induces Chondrocyte Apoptosis in a Rat Osteoarthritis Model Through the Mediation of Ca2+ Influx. *Cell Physiol Biochem.* 2018;46(2):687-698.

[363] Landowski CP, Bolanz KA, Suzuki Y, et al. Chemical inhibitors of the calcium entry channel TRPV6. *Pharm Res.* 2011 Feb;28(2):322-30.

[364] Bátkai S, Mukhopadhyay P, Horváth B, et al. Δ8-Tetrahydrocannabivarin prevents hepatic ischaemia/reperfusion injury by decreasing oxidative stress and inflammatory responses through cannabinoid CB2 receptors. *Br J Pharmacol.* 2012 Apr;165(8):2450-61.

[365] Pertwee RG, Thomas A, Stevenson LA, et al. The psychoactive plant cannabinoid, Delta9-tetrahydrocannabinol, is antagonized by Delta8- and Delta9-tetrahydrocannabivarin in mice in vivo. *Br J Pharmacol.* 2007 Mar;150(5):586-94.

[366] Englund A, Atakan Z, Kralj A, et al. The effect of five-day dosing with THCV on THC-induced cognitive, psychological and physiological effects in healthy male human volunteers: A placebo-controlled, double-blind, crossover pilot trial. *J Psychopharmacol.* 2016 Feb;30(2):140-51.

[367] Berthoud HR. Metabolic and hedonic drives in the neural control of appetite: who is the boss? *Curr Opin Neurobiol.* 2011;21:888–896.

[368] Jensen CD, Kirwan CB. Functional brain response to food images in successful adolescent weight losers compared with normal-weight and overweight controls. *Obesity.* 2015;23:630–636.

[369] Moreno-Lopez L, Contreras-Rodriguez O, Soriano-Mas C, et al. Disrupted functional connectivity in adolescent obesity. *Neuroimage Clin.* 2016;12:262–268.

[370] Rzepa E, Tudge L, McCabe C, et al. The CB1 Neutral Antagonist Tetrahydrocannabivarin Reduces Default Mode Network and Increases Executive Control Network Resting State Functional Connectivity in Healthy Volunteers. *Int J Neuropsychopharmacol.* 2015 Sep 10;19(2).

[371] Tudge L, Williams C, Cowen PJ, et al. Neural effects of cannabinoid CB1 neutral antagonist tetrahydrocannabivarin on food reward and aversion in healthy volunteers. *Int J Neuropsychopharmacol.* 2014 Dec 25;18(6).

[372] Wargent ET, Zaibi MS, Silvestri C, et al. The cannabinoid Δ(9)-tetrahydrocannabivarin (THCV) ameliorates insulin sensitivity in two mouse models of obesity. *Nutr Diabetes.* 2013 May 27;3:e68.

[373] Silvestri C, Paris D, Martella A, et al. Two non-psychoactive cannabinoids reduce intracellular lipid levels and inhibit hepatosteatosis. *J Hepatol.* 2015 Jun;62(6):1382-90.

[374] Wargent ET, Zaibi MS, Silvestri C, et al. The cannabinoid Δ(9)-tetrahydrocannabivarin (THCV) ameliorates insulin sensitivity in two mouse models of obesity. *Nutr Diabetes.* 2013 May 27;3:e68.

[375] Horváth B, Mukhopadhyay P, Haskó G, et al. The endocannabinoid system and plant-derived cannabinoids in diabetes and diabetic complications. *Am J Pathol.* 2012 Feb;180(2):432-42.

[376] Jadoon KA, Ratcliffe SH, Barrett DA, et al. Efficacy and safety of cannabidiol and tetrahydrocannabivarin on glycemic and lipid parameters in patients with type 2 diabetes: A randomized, double-blind, placebo-controlled, parallel group pilot study. *Diabetes Care.* 2016 Oct;39(10):1777-86.

[377] Romano B, Pagano E2, Orlando P, et al. Pure Δ9-tetrahydrocannabivarin and a Cannabis sativa extract with high content in Δ9-tetrahydrocannabivarin inhibit nitrite production in murine peritoneal macrophages. *Pharmacol Res.* 2016 Nov;113(Pt A):199-208.

[378] Bolognini D, Costa B, Maione S, et al. The plant cannabinoid Delta9-tetrahydrocannabivarin can decrease signs of inflammation and inflammatory pain in mice. *Br J Pharmacol.* 2010 Jun;160(3):677-87.

[379] Pagano E, Montanaro V, Di Girolamo A, et al. Effect of Non-psychotropic Plant-derived Cannabinoids on Bladder Contractility: Focus on Cannabigerol. *Nat Prod Commun.* 2015 Jun;10(6):1009-12.

[380] Rock EM, Sticht MA, Buncan M, et al. Evaluation of the potential of the phytocannabinoids, cannabidivarin (CBDV) and Δ9-tetrahydrocannabivarin (THCV), to produce CB1 receptor inverse agonism symptoms of nausea in rats. *Br J Pharmacol.* 2013 Oct;170(3):671–678.

[381] Garcia C, Palomo-Garo C, Garcia-Arencibia M, et al. Symptom-relieving and neuroprotective effects of the phytocannabinoid Δ9-THCV in animal models of Parkinson's disease. *Br J Pharmacol.* 2011 Aug;163(7):1495–1506.

[382] Oláh A, Markovics A, Szabó-Papp J, et al. Differential effectiveness of selected non-psychotropic phytocannabinoids on human sebocyte functions implicates their introduction in dry/seborrhoeic skin and acne treatment. *Exp Dermatol.* 2016 Sep;25(9):701-7.

[383] Hill AJ, Hill TDM, Whalley BJ. The development of cannabinoid based therapies for epilepsy. In: Murillo-Rodríguez E, Onaivi ES, Darmani NA, et al. Endocannabinoids: molecular, pharmacological, behavioral and clinical features. Sharjah, United Arab Emirates: Bentham Science, 2013:164-204.

[384] Gaston TE, Friedman D. Pharmacology of cannabinoids in the treatment of epilepsy. *Epilepsy Behav.* 2017 May;70(Pt B):313-318.

[385] Hill AJ, Weston SE, Jones NA, et al. Δ9-Tetrahydrocannabivarin suppresses in vitro epileptiform and in vivo seizure activity in adult rats. *Epilepsia.* 2010 Aug;51(8):1522-32.

[386] Cascio MG, Zamberletti E, Marini P, et al. The phytocannabinoid, Δ9-tetrahydrocannabivarin, can act through 5-HT₁A receptors to produce antipsychotic effects. *Br J Pharmacol.* 2015 Mar;172(5):1305-18.

153

[387] McPartland JM. Meta-analysis of cannabinoid ligand binding affinity and receptor distribution: interspecies differences. *Br J Pharmacol.* 2007;152:583–593.

[388] Rosenthaler S, Pohn B, Kolmanz C, et al. Differences in receptor binding affinity of several phytocannabinoids do not explain their effects on neural cell cultures. *Neurotoxicol Teratol.* 2014;46:49–56.

[389] Zuardi AW, Crippa JA, Hallak JE, et al. Cannabidiol for the treatment of psychosis in parkinson's disease. *J Psychopharmacol.* 2009 Nov;23(8):979-83.

[390] Aung MM, Griffin G, Huffman JW, et al. Influence of the N-1 alkyl chain length of cannabimimetic indoles upon CB1 and CB2 receptor binding. *Drug Alcohol Depend.* 2000 Aug;60(2):133–40.

[391] Gertsch J, Leonti M, Raduner S, et al. Beta-caryophyllene is a dietary cannabinoid. *Proc Natl Acad Sci U S A.* 2008 Jul 1; 105(26): 9099–9104.

[392] Pertwee RG. The diverse CB1 and CB2 receptor pharmacology of three plant cannabinoids: Δ9-tetrahydrocannabinol, cannabidiol and Δ9-tetrahydrocannabivarin. *Br J Pharmacol.* 2008 Jan; 153(2): 199–215.

[393] Marinol (dronabinol) capsules. Available at: http://marinol.com/.

[394] EMC. Sativex Oromucosal Spray. Available at: https://www.medicines.org.uk/emc/product/602/smpc#PREGNANCY.

[395] Burstein SH. Ajulemic acid: potential treatment for chronic inflammation. *Pharmacol Res Perspect.* 2018 Apr;6(2):e00394.

[396] USPTO Patent No. 9,205,063. Available at: http://patft.uspto.gov/netacgi/nph-Parser?Sect1=PTO2&Sect2=HITOFF&p=1&u=%2Fnetahtml%2FPTO%2Fsearch-bool.html&r=1&f=G&l=50&co1=AND&d=PTXT&s1=%22GW+Pharma%22&OS=%22GW+Pharma%22&RS=%22GW+Pharma%22.

[397] FDA. Prescribing Information. Epidolex. Available at: https://www.accessdata.fda.gov/drugsatfda_docs/label/2018/210365lbl.pdf.

[398] Cravatt BF, Lerner RA, Boger DL. Structure Determination of an Endogenous Sleep-Inducing Lipid, cis-9-Octadecenamide (Oleamide): A Synthetic Approach to the Chemical Analysis of Trace Quantities of a Natural Product. *J American Chem Soc.* 1996;118(3):580-90.

[399] Mendelson WB, Basile AS. The Hypnotic Actions of the Fatty Acid Amide, Oleamide. *Neuropsychopharmacology.* 2001 Nov;25(5 Suppl):S36-9.

[400] Akanmu MA, Adeosun SO, Ilesanmi OR. Neuropharmacological effects of oleamide in male and female mice. *Behav Brain Res.* 2007 Aug 22;182(1):88-94.

[401] US Library of Medicine. National Center for Biotechnology Information. Oleamide. Available at: https://pubchem.ncbi.nlm.nih.gov/compound/Oleamide#section=Top.

[402] Murillo-Rodríguez E, Giordano M, Cabeza R, et al. Oleamide modulates memory in rats. *Neurosci Lett.* 2001 Nov 2;313(1-2):61-4.

[403] Akanmu MA, Adeosun SO, Ilesanmi OR. Neuropharmacological effects of oleamide in male and female mice. *Behav Brain Res.* 2007 Aug 22;182(1):88-94.

[404] Méndez-Díaz M, Rueda-Orozco PE, Ruiz-Contreras AE, et al. The endocannabinoid system modulates the valence of the emotion associated to food ingestion. *Addict Biol.* 2012 Jul;17(4):725-35.

[405] Mueller GP, Driscoll WJ. Biosynthesis of oleamide. *Vitam Horm.* 2009;81:55-78.

[406] Wang S, Xu Q, Shu G, et al. N-Oleoyl glycine, a lipoamino acid, stimulates adipogenesis associated with activation of CB1 receptor and Akt signaling pathway in 3T3-L1 adipocyte. *Biochem Biophys Res Commun.* 2015 Oct 23;466(3):438-43.

[407] Wang S, Xu Q, Shu G, et al. N-Oleoyl glycine, a lipoamino acid, stimulates adipogenesis associated with activation of CB1 receptor and Akt signaling pathway in 3T3-L1 adipocyte. *Biochem Biophys Res Commun.* 2015 Oct 23;466(3):438-43.

[408] Donvito G, Piscitelli F, Muldoon P, et al. N-Oleoyl-glycine reduces nicotine reward and withdrawal in mice. Neuropharmacology. 2018 Mar 19. [Epub ahead of print]

[409] Pacioni G, Rapino C2, Zarivi O, et al. Truffles contain endocannabinoid metabolic enzymes and anandamide. *Phytochemistry.* 2015 Feb;110:104-10.

[410] James JS. Marijuana and chocolate. *AIDS Treat News.* 1996 Oct 18;(No 257):3-4.

[411] Zurer P. Chocolate may mimic marijuana in brain. Chem Eng News. 1996;74(36):31–32.

[412] Blancaflor EB, Kilaru A, Keereetaweep J, et al. N-Acylethanolamines: lipid metabolites with functions in
plant growth and development. *The Plant Journal.* 2014;79:568-83.

[413] Raduner S, Majewska A, Chen JZ, et al. Alkylamides from Echinacea Are a New Class of Cannabinomimetics. CANNABINOID TYPE 2 RECEPTOR-DEPENDENT AND -INDEPENDENT IMMUNOMODULATORY EFFECTS. *J Biological Chem.* 2006 May;281:14192-206.

[414] Styrczewska M, Kulma A, Ratajczak K, et al. Cannabinoid-like anti-inflammatory compounds from flax fiber. *Cell Mol Biol Letters.* 2012 Sep;17(3):479-99.

[415] Bohlmann F, Hoffmann E. Cannabigerol-ähnliche verbindungen aus Helichrysum umbraculigerum. *Phytochem.* 1979;18(8):1371-4.

[416] Pollastro F, De Petrocellis L, Schiano-Moriello A, et al. Amorfrutin-type phytocannabinoids from Helichrysum umbraculigerum. *Fitoterapia.* 2017 Nov;123:13-17.

[417] Chicca A, Schafroth MA, Reynoso-Moreno I, et al. Uncovering the psychoactivity of a cannabinoid from liverworts associated with a legal high. *Sci Adv.* 2018;4(10):eaat2166.

[418] Toyota M, Shimamura T, Ishii H, et al. New bibenzyl cannabinoid from the New Zealand liverwort Radula marginata. *Chem Pharm Bull (Tokyo).* 2002 Oct;50(10):1390-2.

[419] Ligresti A, Villano R, Allarà M, et al. Kavalactones and the endocannabinoid system: The plant-derived yangonin is a novel CB1 receptor ligand. *Pharm Res.* 2012;66(2):163–9.

[420] Hajdu Z, Nicolussi S, Rau M, et al. Identification of endocannabinoid system-modulating N-alkylamides from Heliopsis helianthoides var. scabra and Lepidium meyenii. *J Nat Prod.* 2014 Jul 25;77(7):1663-9.

[421] Hajdu Z, Nicolussi S, Rau M, et al. Identification of endocannabinoid system-modulating N-alkylamides from Heliopsis helianthoides var. scabra and Lepidium meyenii. *J Nat Prod.* 2014 Jul 25;77(7):1663-9.

[422] Iwata N, Kitanaka S. New cannabinoid-like chromane and chromene derivatives from Rhododendron anthopogonoides. *Chem Pharm Bull (Tokyo).* 2011;59(11):1409-12.

[423] Capasso R, Borrelli F, Cascio MG, et al. Inhibitory effect of salvinorin A, from Salvia divinorum, on ileitis-induced hypermotility: cross-talk between kappa-opioid and cannabinoid CB(1) receptors. *Br J Pharmacol.* 2008 Nov;155(5):681-9.

[424] Leonti M, Casu L, Raduner S, et al. Falcarinol is a covalent cannabinoid CB1 receptor antagonist and induces pro-allergic effects in skin. *Biochem Pharmacol.* 2010 Jun 15;79(12):1815-26.

[425] Seely KA, Levi MS, Prather PL. The dietary polyphenols transresveratrol and curcumin selectively bind human CB1 cannabinoid receptors with nanomolar affinities and function as antagonists/inverse agonists. *J Pharmacol Exp Ther.* 2009;330:S31–S39.

[426] Prather PL, Seely KA, Levi MS. Notice of retraction. *J Pharmacol Exp Ther.* 2009;331:1147.

[427] Korte G, Dreiseitel A, Schreier P et al. An examination of anthocyanins' and anthocyanidins' affinity for cannabinoid receptors. *J Med Food.* 2009;12:S1407–S1410.

[428] Korte G, Dreiseitel A, Schreier P, et al. Tea catechins' affinity for human cannabinoid receptors. *Phytomedicine.* 2010;17:S19–S22.

[429] Gertsch J, Pertwee RG, Marzo VD. Phytocannabinoids beyond the Cannabis plant – do they exist? *Br J Pharmacol.* 2010;160:523-9.

[430] Rollinger JM, Schuster D, Danzl B, et al. In silico fishing for rationalized ligand discovery exemplified on constituents of Ruta graveolens. *Planta Med.* 2009;75:S195–S204.

[431] Yin H, Chu A, Li W, et al. Lipid G protein-coupled receptor ligand identification using beta-arrestin PathHunter assay. *J Biol Chem.* 2009;284:S12328–S12338.

[432] Rajan TS, Giacoppo S, Iori R, et al. Anti-inflammatory and antioxidant effects of a combination of cannabidiol and moringin in LPS-stimulated macrophages. *Fitoterapia.* 2016 Jul;112:104-15.

[433] Atakan Z. Cannabis, a complex plant: different compounds and different effects on individuals. *Ther Adv Psychopharmacol.* 2012 Dec;2(6):241-54.

[434] Fattore L, Fratta W. How important are sex differences in cannabinoid action? *Br J Pharmacol.* 2010 Jun; 160(3): 544–548.

[435] Rey AA, Purrio M, Viveros MP, et al. Biphasic Effects of Cannabinoids in Anxiety Responses: CB1 and GABAB Receptors in the Balance of GABAergic and Glutamatergic Neurotransmission. *Neuropsychopharmacology.* 2012 Nov;37(12):2624-34.

[436] Huestis MA. Human cannabinoid pharmacokinetics. *Chem Biodivers.* 2007 08;4:1770-804.

[437] Zuurman L, Ippel AE, Moin E, et al. Biomarkers for the effects of cannabis and THC in healthy volunteers. *Br J Clin Pharmacol.* 2009 01;67:5-21.

[438] Carter GT, Weydt P, Kyashna-Tocha M, et al. Medicinal cannabis: Rational guidelines for dosing. *IDrugs.* 2004 05;7:464-70.

[439] Adams IB, Martin BR. Cannabis: Pharmacology and toxicology in animals and humans. *Addiction.* 1996 Nov;91(11):1585-614.

[440] Newmeyer MN, Swortwood MJ, Barnes AJ, et al. Free and glucuronide whole blood cannabinoids' pharmacokinetics after controlled smoked, vaporized, and oral cannabis administration in frequent and occasional cannabis users: Identification of recent cannabis intake. *Clinical Chemistry.* 2016;62(12):1579-92.

[441] Grotenhermen F. Pharmacokinetics and pharmacodynamics of cannabinoids. *Clin Pharmacokinet.* 2003;42(4):327-60.

[442] Huestis MA. Pharmacokinetics and metabolism of the plant cannabinoids, delta9-tetrahydrocannabinol, cannabidiol and cannabinol. *Handb Exp Pharmacol.* 2005:657-90.

[443] Millar SA. Stone NL, Yates AS, et al. A Systematic Review on the Pharmacokinetics of Cannabidiol in Humans. *Pharmacol.* 2018 Nov 26;9:1365.

[444] Tashkin DP. Effects of marijuana smoking on the lung. *Ann Am Thorac Soc.* 2013;10(3):239-247.

[445] Owen KP, Sutter ME, Albertson TE. Marijuana: respiratory tract effects. *Clin Rev Allergy Immunol.* 2014;46(1):65-81.

[446] Polen MR, Sidney S, Tekawa IS, Sadler M, et al. Health care use by frequent marijuana smokers who do not smoke tobacco. *West J Med.* 1993;158(6):596-601.

[447] Hashibe M, Morgenstern H, Cui Y, et al. Marijuana use and the risk of lung and upper aerodigestive tract cancers: results of a population-based case-control study. *Cancer Epidemiol Biomark Prev Publ Am Assoc Cancer Res Cosponsored Am Soc Prev Oncol.* 2006;15(10):1829-1834.

[448] Hancox RJ, Poulton R, Ely M, et al. Effects of cannabis on lung function: a population-based cohort study. *Eur Respir J.* 2010;35(1):42-47.

[449] Abrams DI, Vizoso HP, Shade SB, et al. Vaporization as a smokeless cannabis delivery system: A pilot study. *Clin Pharmacol Ther.* 2007 04/11;82:572-8.

[450] Hazekamp A, Ruhaak R, Zuurman L, et al. Evaluation of a vaporizing device (volcano) for the pulmonary administration of tetrahydrocannabinol. *J Pharm Sci.* 2006 06;95:1308-17.

[451] Spindle TR, Cone EJ, Schlienz NJ, et al. Acute Effects of Smoked and Vaporized Cannabis in Healthy Adults Who Infrequently Use Cannabis: A Crossover Trial. *JAMA Netw Open.* 2018;1(7):e184841.

[452] Meyer P, Langos M, Brenneisen R. Human Pharmacokinetics and Adverse Effects of Pulmonary and Intravenous THC-CBD Formulations. *Med Cannabis Cannabinoids.* 2018 Jun;1(1):36-43

[453] Abrams DI, Couey P, Shade SB, et al. Cannabinoid-opioid interaction in chronic pain. *Clin Pharmacol Ther*. 2011 12;90:844-51.

[454] Al-Ghananeem AM, Malkawi AH, Crooks PA. Bioavailability of delta(9)-tetrahydrocannabinol following intranasal administration of a mucoadhesive gel spray delivery system in conscious rabbits. *Drug Dev Ind Pharm*. 2011 Mar;37(3):329-34.

[455] Paudel KS, Hammell DC, Agu RU, et al. Cannabidiol bioavailability after nasal and transdermal application: Effect of permeation enhancers. *Drug Dev Ind Pharm*. 2010 Sep;36(9):1088-97.

[456] Cone EJ, Johnson RE, Paul BD, et al. Marijuana-laced brownies: Behavioral effects, physiologic effects, and urinalysis in humans following ingestion. *J Anal Toxicol*. 1988 Aug;12:169-75.

[457] Huestis MA. Human cannabinoid pharmacokinetics. *Chem Biodivers*. 2007 08;4:1770-804.

[458] Welty T, Luebke A, Gidal BE. Cannabidiol: Promise and Pitfalls. *Epilepsy Curr*. 2014 Sep-Oct; 14(5): 250–252.

[459] Abbott Products Inc. Marinol product monograph. 2010.

[460] Guy GW, Robson P. A phase I, open label, four-way crossover study to compare the pharmacokinetic profiles of a single dose of 20 mg of a cannabis based medicine extract (CBME) administered on 3 difference areas of the buccal mucosa and to investigate the pharmacokinetics of CBME per oral in healthy male and female volunteers. *J Cannabis Ther*. 2003;3:79–120.

[461] Pharmaceuticals G. Sativex product monograph. 2010.

[462] Millar SA. Stone NL, Yates AS, et al. A Systematic Review on the Pharmacokinetics of Cannabidiol in Humans. *Pharmacol*. 2018 Nov 26;9:1365.

[463] Zgair A, Wong JCM, Lee JB, et al. Dietary fats and pharmaceutical lipid excipients increase systemic exposure to orally administered cannabis and cannabis-based medicines. *Am J Transl Res*. 2016; 8(8): 3448–3459.

[464] Xgair A, Bong Lee J, Wong JCM, et al. Oral administration of cannabis with lipids leads to high levels of cannabinoids in the intestinal lymphatic system and prominent immunomodulation. *Sci Rep*. 2017; 7: 14542.

[465] Merrick J, Lane B, Sebree T, et al. Identification of psychoactive degradants of cannabidiol in simulated gastric and physiological fluid. *Cannabis Cannabinoid Res*. 2016;1(1):102-12.

[466] Watanabe K, Itokawa Y, Yamaori S, et al. Conversion of cannabidiol to Δ9-tetrahydrocannabinol and related cannabinoids in artificial gastric juice, and their pharmacological effects in mice. *J Forensic Toxicol*. 2007;25(1):16-21.

[467] ElSohly MA, Gul W, Walker LA. Pharmacokinetics and Tolerability of Δ9-THC-Hemisuccinate in a Suppository Formulation as an Alternative to Capsules for the Systemic Delivery of Δ9-THC. *Med Cannabis Cannabinoids*. 2018;1:44-53.

[468] ElSohly MA, Little TL Jr, Hikal A, et al. Rectal bioavailability of delta-9-tetrahydrocannabinol from various esters. *Pharmacol Biochem Behav*. 1991; 40: 497–502.

[469] Paudel KS, Hammell DC, Agu RU, et al. Cannabidiol bioavailability after nasal and transdermal application: Effect of permeation enhancers. *Drug Dev Ind Pharm*. 2010 Sep;36(9):1088-97.

[470] Stinchcomb AL, Valiveti S, Hammell DC, et al. Human skin permeation of Delta8-tetrahydrocannabinol, cannabidiol and cannabinol. *J Pharm Pharmacol*. 2004 03;56.:291-7.

[471] Paudel KS, Hammell DC, Agu RU, et al. Cannabidiol bioavailability after nasal and transdermal application: effect of permeation enhancers. *Drug Dev Ind Pharm*. 2010 Sep;36(9):1088-97.

[472] Valiveti S, Hammell DC, Earles DC, et al. Transdermal delivery of the synthetic cannabinoid WIN 55,212-2: In vitro/in vivo correlation. *Pharm Res*. 2004 07;21:1137-45.

[473] Giacoppo S, Galuppo M, Pollastro F, et al. A new formulation of cannabidiol in cream shows therapeutic effects in a mouse model of experimental autoimmune encephalomyelitis. *Daru*. 2015 Oct 21;23:48,015-0131-8.

[474] Englund A, Stone JM, Morrison PD. Cannabis in the arm: what can we learn from intravenous cannabinoid studies? *Curr Pharm Des*. 2012;18(32):4906-14.

[475] Lindgren JE, Ohlsson A, Agurell S, et al. Clinical effects and plasma levels of delta 9-tetrahydrocannabinol (delta-9-THC) in a heavy and light users of cannabis. *Psychopharmacology (Berl)*. 1981;74(3):208-12.

[476] D-Souza DC, Perry E, MacDougall L, et al. The psychotomimetic effects of intravenous delta-9-tetrahydrocannabinol in healthy individuals: Implications for psychosis. *Neuropsychopharmacology*. 2004;29(8):1558-72.

[477] Millar SA. Stone NL, Yates AS, et al. A Systematic Review on the Pharmacokinetics of Cannabidiol in Humans. *Pharmacol*. 2018 Nov 26;9:1365.

[478] Maccarrone M. Endocannabinoid signaling in female reproductive events: A potential therapeutic target? *Expert Opin Ther Targets*. 2015;19(11):1423-7.

[479] Battista N, Pasquariello N, Di TM, et al. Interplay between endocannabinoids, steroids and cytokines in the control of human reproduction. *J Neuroendocrinol*. 2008 05;20 Suppl 1(1365-2826; 0953-8194):82-9.

[480] Correa F, Wolfson ML, Valchi P, et al. Endocannabinoid system and pregnancy. *Reproduction*. 2016 Dec;152(6):R191-200.

[481] Gunn JK, Rosales CB, Center KE, et al. Prenatal exposure to cannabis and maternal and child health outcomes: A systematic review and meta-analysis. *BMJ Open*. 2016 Apr 5;6(4):e009986.

[482] Conner SN, Bedell V, Lipsey K, et al. Maternal marijuana use and adverse neonatal outcomes: A systematic review and meta-analysis. *Obstet Gynecol*. 2016 Oct;128(4):713-23.

[483] Calvigioni D, Hurd YL, Harkany T, et al. Neuronal substrates and functional consequences of prenatal cannabis exposure. *Eur Child Adolesc Psychiatry*. 2014 Oct;23(10):931-41.

[484] Richardson GA, Ryan C, Willford J, et al. Prenatal alcohol and marijuana exposure: Effects on neuropsychological outcomes at 10 years. *Neurotoxicol Teratol*. 2002 May-Jun;24(3):309-20.

[485] Grant KS, Petroff R, Isoherranen N, et al. Cannabis use during pregnancy: Pharmacokinetics and effects on child development. *Pharmacol Ther.* 2017 Aug 25.

[486] Hatoum NS, Davis WM, Elsohly MA, et al. Perinatal exposure to cannabichromene and delta 9-tetrahydrocannabinol: separate and combined effects on viability of pups and on male reproductive system at maturity. *Toxicol Lett.* 1981 May;8(3):141-6.

[487] Perez-Reyes M, Wall ME. Presence of delta9-tetrahydrocannabinol in human milk. *N Engl J Med.* 1982 09/23;307(0028-4793; 13):819-20.

[488] Garry A, Rigourd V, Amirouche A, et al. Cannabis and breastfeeding. *J Toxicol.* 2009;2009:596149.

[489] Gundersen TD, Jorgensen N, Andersson AM, et al. Association between use of marijuana and male reproductive hormones and semen quality: A study among 1,215 healthy young men. *Am J Epidemiol.* 2015 Sep 15;182(6):473-81.

[490] Lacson JCA, Carroll JD, Tuazon E, et al. Population-based case-control study of recreational drug use and testis cancer risk confirms an association between marijuana use and nonseminoma risk. *Cancer.* 2012;118(21):5374-5383.

[491] Daling JR, Doody DR, Sun X, et al. Association of marijuana use and the incidence of testicular germ cell tumors. *Cancer.* 2009;115(6):1215-1223.

[492] Borgelt LM, Franson KL, Nussbaum AM, et al. The pharmacologic and clinical effects of medical cannabis. *Pharmacotherapy.* 2013; 33(2): 195– 209.

[493] Meier MH, Caspi A, Ambler A, et al. Persistent cannabis users show neuropsychological decline from childhood to midlife. *Proc Natl Acad Sci U S A.* 2012;109(40):E2657–E2664.

[494] Gaston TE, Bebin EM, Cutter GR, et al. Interactions between cannabidiol and commonly used antiepileptic drugs. *Epilepsia.* 2017 Sep;58(9):1586-1592.

[495] Adashi EY, Jones PB, Hsueh AJ. Direct antigonadal activity of cannabinoids: suppression of rat granulosa cell functions. *Am J Physiol.* 1983 Feb;244(2):E177-85.

[496] Schoeler T, Petros N, Di Forti M, et al. Effects of continuation, frequency, and type of cannabis use on relapse in the first 2 years after onset of psychosis: An observational study. *Lancet Psychiatry.* 2016 Oct;3(10):947-53.

[497] Di Forti M, Marconi A, Carra E, et al. Proportion of patients in south london with first-episode psychosis attributable to use of high potency cannabis: A case-control study. *Lancet Psychiatry.* 2015 Mar;2(3):233-8.

[498] Marconi A, Di Forti M, Lewis CM, et al. Meta-analysis of the association between the level of cannabis use and risk of psychosis. *Schizophr Bull.* 2016 Sep;42(5):1262-9.

[499] Cappelli F, Lazzeri C, Gensini GF, et al. Cannabis: a trigger for acute myocardial infarction? A case report. *J Cardiovasc Med (Hagerstown).* 2008;9(7):725-728.

[500] Nawrot TS, Perez L, Kunzli N, et al. Public health importance of triggers of myocardial infarction: a comparative risk assessment. *Lancet.* 2-26-2011;377(9767):732-740.

[501] Hackam DG. Cannabis and stroke: systematic appraisal of case reports. *Stroke.* 2015;46(3):852-6.

[502] Shalit N, Shoval G, Shlosberg D, et al. The association between cannabis use and suicidality among men and women: A population-based longitudinal study. *J Affect Disord*. 2016 Nov 15;205:216-224.

[503] Carvalho AF, Stubbs B, Vancampfort D, et al. Cannabis use and suicide attempts among 86,254 adolescents aged 12-15 years from 21 low- and middle-income countries. *Eur Psychiatry*. 2018 Nov 14;56:8-13.

[504] Borges G, Bagge CL, Orozco R. A literature review and meta-analyses of cannabis use and suicidality. *J Affect Disord*. 2016 May;195:63-74.

[505] Consroe P, Sandyk R, Snider SR. Open label evaluation of cannabidiol in dystonic movement disorders. *Int J Neurosci*. 1986;30(4):277-82.

[506] Desrosiers NA, Himes SK, Scheidweiler KB, et al. Phase I and II cannabinoid disposition in blood and plasma of occasional and frequent smokers following controlled smoked cannabis. *Clin Chem*. 2014 Apr;60(4):631-43.

[507] Budney AJ, Roffman R, Stephens RS, et al. Marijuana Dependence and Its Treatment. *Addict Sci Clin Pract*. 2007 Dec;4(1):4–16.

[508] Volkow ND, Baler RD, Compton WM, et al. Adverse health effects of marijuana use. *N Engl J Med*. 2014 Jun 5;370(23):2219-27.

[509] Prud'homme M, Cata R, Jutras-Aswad D. Cannabidiol as an intervention for addictive behaviors: A systematic review of the evidence. *Subst Abuse*. 2015 May 21;9:33-8.

[510] Ramaekers JG, Moeller MR, van RP, et al. Cognition and motor control as a function of Delta9-THC concentration in serum and oral fluid: Limits of impairment. *Drug Alcohol Depend*. 2006 11/08;85:114-22.

[511] O'Kane CJ, Tutt DC, Bauer LA. Cannabis and driving: A new perspective. *Emerg Med (Fremantle)*. 2002 09;14:296-303.

[512] Hollister, L. E. Interactions of cannabis with other drugs in man. *NIDA Res Monogr*. 1986;68:110-116.

[513] Abbott Products Inc. Marinol product monograph. 2010.

[514] Pharmaceuticals G. Sativex product monograph. 2010.

[515] Bramness JG, Khiabani HZ, Morland J. Impairment due to cannabis and ethanol: Clinical signs and additive effects. *Addiction*. 2010 06;105:1080-7.

[516] Ronen A, Chassidim HS, Gershon P, et al. The effect of alcohol, THC and their combination on perceived effects, willingness to drive and performance of driving and non-driving tasks. *Accid Anal Prev*. 2010 11;42(1879-2057; 0001-4575; 6):1855-65.

[517] Sewell RA, Poling J, Sofuoglu M. The effect of cannabis compared with alcohol on driving. *Am J Addict*. 2009 05;18:185-93.

[518] Ashton CH. Adverse effects of cannabis and cannabinoids. *Br J Anaesth*. 1999 10;83:637-49.

[519] Chait LD, Perry JL. Acute and residual effects of alcohol and marijuana, alone and in combination, on mood and performance. *Psychopharmacology (Berl)*. 1994 07;115:340-9.

[520] Lukas SE, Orozco S. Ethanol increases plasma delta(9)-tetrahydrocannabinol (THC) levels and subjective effects after marihuana smoking in human volunteers. *Drug Alcohol Depend*. 2001 10/01;64:143-9.

161

[521] Hatoum NS, Davis WM, Waters IW, et al. Synergism of cannabichromene and CNS depressants in mice. *Gen Pharmacol.* 1981;12(5):351-6.

[522] Carlini EA, Cunha JM. Hypnotic and antiepileptic effects of cannabidiol. *J Clin Pharmacol.* 1981;21(8-9 Suppl):417S-27S.

[523] Consroe P, Carlini EA, Zwicker AP, et al. Interaction of cannabidiol and alcohol in humans. *Psychopharmacology (Berl).* 1979;66(1):45-50.

[524] Abbott Products Inc. Marinol product monograph. 2010.

[525] Kosel BW, Aweeka FT, Benowitz NL, Shade SB, Hilton JF, Lizak PS, Abrams DI. The effects of cannabinoids on the pharmacokinetics of indinavir and nelfinavir. *AIDS.* 2002 03/08;16:543-50.

[526] Berman JS, Symonds C, Birch R. Efficacy of two cannabis based medicinal extracts for relief of central neuropathic pain from brachial plexus avulsion: Results of a randomised controlled trial. *Pain.* 2004 12;112:299-306.

[527] Zullino DF, Delessert D, Eap CB, et al. Tobacco and cannabis smoking cessation can lead to intoxication with clozapine or olanzapine. *Int Clin Psychopharmacol.* 2002 05;17(0268-1315; 3):141-3.

[528] Abrams DI, Couey P, Shade SB, et al. Cannabinoid-opioid interaction in chronic pain. *Clin Pharmacol Ther.* 2011 12;90:844-51.

[529] Benowitz NL, Jones RT. Cardiovascular and metabolic considerations in prolonged cannabinoid administration in man. *J Clin Pharmacol.* 1981;21(8-9 Suppl):214S-223S.

[530] Abbott Products Inc. Marinol product monograph. 2010.

[531] Marinol Prescribing Information. Solvay Pharmaceuticals. Available at: http://www.solvaypharmaceuticals-us.com/static/wma/pdf/1/3/2/5/0/004InsertText500012RevMar2008.pdf.

[532] Abbott Products Inc. Marinol product monograph. 2010.

[533] Goyal H, Awad HH, Ghali JK. Role of cannabis in cardiovascular disorders. *J Thorac Dis.* 2017;9(7):2079-2092.

[534] Formukong EA, Evans AT, Evans FJ. The inhibitory effects of cannabinoids, the active constituents of Cannabis sativa L. on human and rabbit platelet aggregation. *J Pharm Pharmacol.* 1989 Oct;41(10):705-9.

[535] Levy R, Schurr A, Nathan I, et al. Impairment of ADP-induced platelet aggregation by hashish components. *Thromb Haemost.* 1976 Dec;36(3):634-640.

[536] Shere A, Goyal H. Cannabis can augment thrombolytic properties of rtPA: Intracranial hemorrhage in a heavy cannabis user. *Am J Emerg Med.* 2017;35(12):1988.e1-1988.e2.

[537] Yamreudeewong W, Wong HK, Brausch LM, et al. Probable interaction between warfarin and marijuana smoking. *Ann Pharmacother.* 2009;43:1347-53.

[538] Marinol Prescribing Information. Solvay Pharmaceuticals. Available at: http://www.solvaypharmaceuticals-us.com/static/wma/pdf/1/3/2/5/0/004InsertText500012RevMar2008.pdf.

[539] Rendic S. Summary of information on human CYp enzymes: Human P450 metabolism data. *Drug Metab Rev.* 2002;34(1&2):83-448.

[540] Yamaori S, Okushima Y, Yamamoto I, et al. Characterization of the structural determinants required for potent mechanism-based inhibition of

human cytochrome P450 1A1 by cannabidiol. *Chem Biol Interact.* 2014 May 25;215:62-8.

[541] Yamaori S, Okushima Y, Masuda K, et al. Structural requirements for potent direct inhibition of human cytochrome P450 1A1 by cannabidiol: role of pentylresorcinol moiety. *Biol Pharm Bull.* 2013;36(7):1197-203.

[542] Yamaori S, Okamoto Y, Yamamoto I, et al. Cannabidiol, a major phytocannabinoid, as a potent atypical inhibitor for CYP2D6. *Drug Metab Dispos.* 2011 Nov;39(11):2049-56.

[543] Yamaori S, Kushihara M, Yamamoto I, et al. Characterization of major phytocannabinoids, cannabidiol and cannabinol, as isoform-selective and potent inhibitors of human CYP1 enzymes. *Biochem Pharmacol.* 2010 Jun 1;79(11):1691-8.

[544] Office of Medicinal Cannabis,The Netherlands Ministry of Health,Welfare and Sports. Medicinal cannabis, information for health care professionals. 2008.

[545] Spina E, Santoro V, D'Arrigo C. Clinically relevant pharmacokinetic drug interactions with second-generation antidepressants: An update. *Clin Ther.* 2008 07;30:1206-27.

[546] Stout SM, Cimino NM. Exogenous cannabinoids as substrates, inhibitors, and inducers of human drug metabolizing enzymes: A systematic review. *Drug Metab Rev.* 2014 Feb;46(1):86-95.

[547] Stott C, White L, Wright S, et al. A phase I, open-label, randomized, crossover study in three parallel groups to evaluate the effect of rifampicin, ketoconazole, and omeprazole on the pharmacokinetics of THC/CBD oromucosal spray in healthy volunteers. *Springerplus.* 2013 May 24;2(1):236.

[548] Stout SM, Cimino NM. Exogenous cannabinoids as substrates, inhibitors, and inducers of human drug metabolizing enzymes: A systematic review. *Drug Metab Rev.* 2014 Feb;46(1):86-95.

[549] Spina E, Santoro V, D'Arrigo C. Clinically relevant pharmacokinetic drug interactions with second-generation antidepressants: An update. *Clin Ther.* 2008 07;30:1206-27.

[550] Stott C, White L, Wright S, et al. A phase I, open-label, randomized, crossover study in three parallel groups to evaluate the effect of rifampicin, ketoconazole, and omeprazole on the pharmacokinetics of THC/CBD oromucosal spray in healthy volunteers. *Springerplus.* 2013 May 24;2(1):236.

[551] Devinsky O, Cross JH, Laux L, et al. Trial of cannabidiol for drug-resistant seizures in the Dravet Syndrome. *N Engl J Med.* 2017 May 25;376(21):2011-2020.

[552] Thiele EA, Marsh ED, French JA, et al. Cannabidiol in patients with seizures associated with Lennox-Gastaut syndrome (GWPCARE4): a randomised, double-blind, placebo-controlled phase 3 trial. *Lancet.* 2018 Mar 17;391(10125):1085-1096.

[553] Gaston TE, Bebin EM, Cutter GR, et al. Interactions between cannabidiol and commonly used antiepileptic drugs. *Epilepsia.* 2017 Sep;58(9):1586-92.

[554] Gaston TE, Bebin EM, Cutter GR, et al. Interactions between cannabidiol and commonly used antiepileptic drugs. *Epilepsia.* 2017 Sep;58(9):1586-92.

555 Geffrey AL, Pollack SF, Bruno PL, et al. Drug-drug interaction between clobazam and cannabidiol in children with refractory epilepsy. *Epilepsia.* 2015 Aug;56(8):1246-51.

556 Gaston TE, Bebin EM, Cutter GR, et al. Interactions between cannabidiol and commonly used antiepileptic drugs. *Epilepsia.* 2017 Sep;58(9):1586-92.

557 Tamir I, Mechoulam R, Meyer AY. Cannabidiol and phenytoin: A structural comparison. *J Med Chem.* 1980 Feb;23(2):220-3.

558 Consroe P, Wolkin A. Cannabidiol--antiepileptic drug comparisons and interactions in experimentally induced seizures in rats. *J Pharmacol Exp Ther.* 1977 Apr;201(1):26-32.

559 Hallak JE, Dursun SM, Bosi DC, et al. The interplay of cannabinoid and NMDA glutamate receptor systems in humans: preliminary evidence of interactive effects of cannabidiol and ketamine in healthy human subjects. *Prog Neuropsychopharmacol Biol Psychiatry.* 2011 Jan 15;35(1):198-202.

560 Watson ES, Murphy JC, Turner CE. Allergenic properties of naturally occurring cannabinoids. *J Pharm Sci.* 1983 Aug;72(8):954-5.

561 Abbott Products Inc. Marinol product monograph. 2010.

562 Bonn-Miller MO, Loflin MJE, Thomas BF. Labeling Accuracy of Cannabidiol Extracts Sold Online. *Jama.* 2017;318(17):1708-9.

563 Huestis MA. Human Cannabinoid Pharmacokinetics. *Chem Biodivers.* 2007 Aug;4(8):1770-1804.

Caution or Drug	Cannabinoid
Addiction/Substance Abuse	THC
Alcohol	CBD, THC
Alcoholism Drugs	THC
Amphetamines	THC
Anesthetics	CBD
Anticholinergic Drugs	THC
Anticoagulant Drugs	CBD, THC, and possibly other cannabinoids (low risk)
Antidepressants (Tricyclic, SSRIs)	THC
Antiplatelet Drugs	CBD, THC, and possibly other cannabinoids (low risk)
Antipsychotic Drugs	THC
Antiseizure Drugs (eslicarbazepine, rufinamide, topiramate, zonisamide)	CBD
Aspirin	CBD, THC, CBN, possibly other cannabinoids (low risk)
Barbiturates	THC, CBN, CBD (high doses)
Bipolar Disorder	THC (including family history)
Bleeding Disorders	CBD, THC, and possibly other cannabinoids (low risk)
Blood Pressure Meds	CBD, THC
Blood Thinners	CBD, THC, CBN, possibly other cannabinoids (low risk)
Cardiovascular Disease	THC
Children	THC
Cholinergic Drugs	THC
Clobazam	CBD
CNS Depressant Dugs	THC, CBN, CBD (high doses)
Compromised Immune System (Topical use; Skin irritation)	THC, CBN
Compromised Immune System	THC (may decrease immune activity)
Cross-Allergenicity	THC (food pollens, peach, tomato, mugwort, banana, citrus)

Depression	THC
Diabetic Meds	CBD (anecdotal reports)
Drugs metabolized by CYP450 Enzymes (CYP1A1, CYP1A1, CYP1A2, CYP1B1, CYP2D6, CYP2C19, CYP3A4)	CBD, THC, CBN
Driving	THC
Fertility, Female	THC
Fertility, Male	THC
Gabapentin	CBD, THC
Multiple Sclerosis	THC
NSAIDS (Antipyrine)	THC, CBD
Operating Heavy Machinery	THC
Opioids	THC
Overdose (Cannabis)	Simultaneous use of oral and inhaled or smoked cannabis
Parkinson's Disease	CBD (some people with PD; large oral doses)
Phenytoin	CBD (enhances activity)
Pregnancy/Lactation	All cannabinoids, with THC being the greatest risk
Propofol	THC
Psychosis (including family history)	THC
Respiratory Diseases	THC & CBD (smoking or vaping)
Schizophrenia (including family history)	THC
Sedatives	THC, CBN, CBD (high doses)
Sensitive Skin	CBD, THC (Topical)
Stimulant Drugs	THC
Stroke	THC
Suicidal Thoughts	THC
Surgery	THC (two weeks prior); All cannabinoids (one week prior)
Theophylline	THC (smoking)
Valproic Acid	CBD
Warfarin	THC (smoking), CBD (oral)

Potential Botanical & Supplement Interactions Quick Reference

Botanical	Potential Interaction
Botanicals and supplements with sedative properties (5-HTP, ashwagandha, berberine, kava, St. John's wort, hops, skullcap, calamus, poppy, catnip, Jamaican dogwood, valerian, chamomile, etc.)	THC, CBD (High doses); Possible potentiation of sedating effects with high doses of CBD
Botanicals and supplements that affect platelet aggregation (ginger, garlic, ginkgo biloba, clove, angelica, Panax ginseng, American ginseng, black cumin seed, feverfew, green tea, glucosamine, bromelain, chondroitin, senna, turmeric, etc.)	CBD, THC; May increase the risk of bleeding in some people